D1238398

SUMMERHAYS'
ENCYCLOPAEDIA
FOR HORSEMEN

Summerhays'

Compiled by

Revised by

WITH 32 HALF-TONE PLATES AND

FREDERICK

012791

ENCYCLOPAEDIA FOR HORSEMEN

R. S. SUMMERHAYS

Stella A. Walker

OVER 80 LINE ILLUSTRATIONS

WARNE

Published by

FREDERICK WARNE & CO LTD: LONDON

FREDERICK WARNE & CO INC: NEW YORK

First published 1952

Sixth edition revised and reset
© Frederick Warne & Co Ltd 1975

LIBRARY OF CONGRESS CATALOG NO 74–80621

ISBN 0 7232 1763 7

Printed in Great Britain by
William Clowes & Sons, Limited
London, Beccles and Colchester
419.475

CONTENTS

PREFACE   vii

ACKNOWLEDGEMENTS   viii

LIST OF PLATES   ix

MAIN ARTICLES

The Arabian Horse   *Lady Anne Lytton*   11
The Horse in Australia   *R. M. Williams*   17
Breeding   *Henry Wynmalen*   38
Bridles, Saddles and Leather   *E. Hartley Edwards*   44
The Horse in Canada   *Dorinda Fuller*   57
Coaching   *Marylian Watney*   72
Dressage   *Jean Froissard*, Ecuyer-professeur F.F.S.E.   95
Driving   *Marylian Watney*   99
Breeds of Horses in Europe   *Daphne Machin-Goodall*   108
The Evolution of the Horse   *Stella A. Walker*   110
Farriery   *C. Richardson*, F.W.C.F.   115
Feeding   *M. A. P. Simons*, M.R.C.V.S.   120
Foxhunting in Britain Today   *Dorian Williams*, M.F.H.   130
Horse Trials   *Sheila Willcox*   164
Care of the Mare and Foal   *I. M. Yeomans*   201
The Mountain and Moorland Ponies of the British Isles   *Glenda Spooner*   214
The Racehorse and Racing in Great Britain   *Bill Curling*   261
The Principles of Riding   *Cherrie Hatton-Hall*, F.B.H.S.   269
International Show Jumping   *Dorian Williams*, M.F.H.   293
Horses and Riders in South Africa   *Jean Edmunds*   303
Horses in South America   *M. Popp*   307
Stable Management   *Mary Rose*, F.B.H.S.   314
The English Thoroughbred   *Bill Curling*   333
The Horse World in the United States of America   *Francis McIlhenny
Stifler*   346
Veterinary Science and the Veterinary Profession   *R. H. Smythe*, M.R.C.V.S.   354

RESULTS OF LEADING EVENTS

Dressage Championships   378
Driving Championships   378
Harness Championships   379

Horse Trials (Three-Day Events)   380
Polo Results   382
Racing Results   384
Show Jumping Results   403

LIST OF HUNTS

Foxhounds—England and Wales   408
Foxhounds—Scotland   411
Foxhounds—Ireland   411
Staghounds—England   412
Staghounds—Ireland   412
Harriers—England and Wales   412
Harriers—Ireland   413
Draghounds—England, Wales and Channel Islands   413
Recognized and Registered Foxhound Hunts of Canada and the U.S.A. 413
Hunts in Australia, South Africa and New Zealand   415

BRITISH HORSE SOCIETY'S LIST OF HORSE AND
    PONY ORGANISATIONS   417

POLO CLUBS AND ASSOCIATIONS   417

GLOSSARY OF FOREIGN TERMS   418

PREFACE TO THE SIXTH EDITION

This encyclopaedia was first published nearly a quarter of a century ago; in the ensuing years, in spite of the advent of the atomic age, the popularity of the horse and equestrian activities have grown at an incredible speed. Today, in the United Kingdom alone, more than 400,000 horses provide recreation for 1.8 million people. But in addition the horse has become an international figure: today we have not only British and European Championships but World Championships. Therefore, though this sixth edition of the Encyclopaedia is basically the mixture as before (with approximately 400 additional entries), articles on the horse and its activities in other continents have been introduced.

Racing and dressage have received more space, but many obsolete words and customs have still been included to save them from possible ultimate oblivion. Posterity may be grateful.

The policy of including no living personalities, either human or equine, is still followed, with two important exceptions—His Grace, the Duke of Beaufort as the current Master of the Horse and Sir Gordon Richards as the first jockey to receive a knighthood.

ACKNOWLEDGEMENTS

R. S. Summerhays and Stella A. Walker would like to thank the following people for their kind assistance in the revision of this sixth edition of the Encyclopaedia: H.M. The Queen for her gracious permission to reproduce the painting 'William Anderson and Two Saddle Horses' by George Stubbs (copyright reserved) on the jacket of this book; the contributors of the main articles, whose names appear on the contents page, and especially to Jean Froissard, F.F.S.E. and Bill Curling respectively for advice on dressage and racing entries; J. A. Allen & Co Ltd whose publication *Baily's Hunting Directory* has been of great assistance in compiling the list of hunts in the British Isles, Australia, South Africa and New Zealand; Jennifer Baker and Judith Payne for their careful checking of the proofs; Christine Bousfield for the new drawings appearing in this edition; Lily Powell Froissard for compiling the glossary of foreign terms; the Master of Foxhounds Association of America for supplying the material on which the list of Canadian and U.S.A. hunts is based; and to the Oxford University Press, New York, for their kind permission to reproduce the Gaits Table from *Horses* by George Gaylord Simpson. Thanks must also be given to the following photographers and owners of horses for allowing us to reproduce their photographs: American Quarter Horse Association Ltd for Pl. 5 *below*; Anglo-Austrian Society for Pl. 31 *above*; Australian News and Information Bureau for Pls 4 *centre* and 24 *centre*; British Tourist Authority for Pl. 26 *above*; Canadian Government Travel Bureau for Pl. 7 *above*; Fiona Forbes for Pl. 30 *below*; Leslie Lane for Pls 8, 9, 10 *above*, 11 *centre and below*, 14 *above*, 15, 17 *above*, 22, 23 *below*, 25 *below*, 26 *below*, 28 *below*, and 31 *below*; *Light Horse* for Pl. 5 above © P. Sweetman; Frank H. Meads for Pls 13 *below* and 19 *above*; Monty for Pls 18 *above* and 28 *above*; D. J. Murphy (Publishers) Ltd for Pl. 24 *below*; Les Nelson and Mr and Mrs Cebern L. Lee for Pl. 30 *above*; John Nestle for Pl. 3 *below*; Photonews for Pls 1 *above*, 11 *above* and 32 *above*; *Pony/Light Horse* for Pl. 24 *above*; Press Association Ltd for Pls 10 *below* and 13 *above and centre*; Royal Agricultural Winter Fair, Canada, for Pl. 7 *below*; Sally Anne Thompson, Animal Photography Ltd, for Pls 1 *below*, 2 *above*, 4 *above*, 14 *below*, 16, 17 *below*, 23 *above* and 25 *above*; and the Zoological Society of London for Pl. 32 *below*. Gratitude must also be given to the many people too numerous to mention who have supplied valuable advice and information.

LIST OF PLATES

Plate 1   Anglo-Arab
Akhal Teké

Plate 2   Andalusian
American Saddlebred

Plate 3   Appaloosa
Arab

Plate 4   Budyonovsky
Waler
Anglo-Argentino

Plate 5   The Normandy Bank at Badminton
Barrel-racing

Plate 6   Bits and Bridles

Plate 7   Calgary Stampede
The Royal Canadian Mounted Police

Plate 8   Clydesdale
Cleveland Bay

Plate 9   Cob
Connemara

Plate 10   Windsor Greys leaving Royal Mews
Coronation Coach

Plate 11   Dartmoor Pony
Dales Pony
Exmoor Pony

Plate 12   Feet and Shoes

Plate 13   The Grand National
The Derby at Tattenham Corner
A Point-to-point

Plate 14   Fell Pony
Fjord Pony

Plate 15   Hackney Pony
Hack
Hackney Horse

Plate 16   Haflinger
            Hanoverian

Plate 17   Highland Pony
            Holstein

Plate 18   Hunter
            Morgan

Plate 19   Hunting: going to draw
            Show Jumping

Plate 20   Show Jumps

Plate 21   Markings

Plate 22   New Forest Pony
            Welsh Cob

Plate 23   Orlov Trotter
            Palomino

Plate 24   Polo
            Polocrosse
            American Trotting Championship

Plate 25   Percheron
            Shetland Pony

Plate 26   Pony Trekking
            Private Drag

Plate 27   Saddles

Plate 28   Shire
            Show Pony

Plate 29   Stable Equipment

Plate 30   Tennessee Walking Horse
            English Thoroughbred

Plate 31   Riders of the Spanish Riding School of Vienna
            Small Hacks at the Royal Windsor Horse Show

Plate 32   Welsh Mountain Pony
            Wild Horse and Foal

POINTS OF THE HORSE

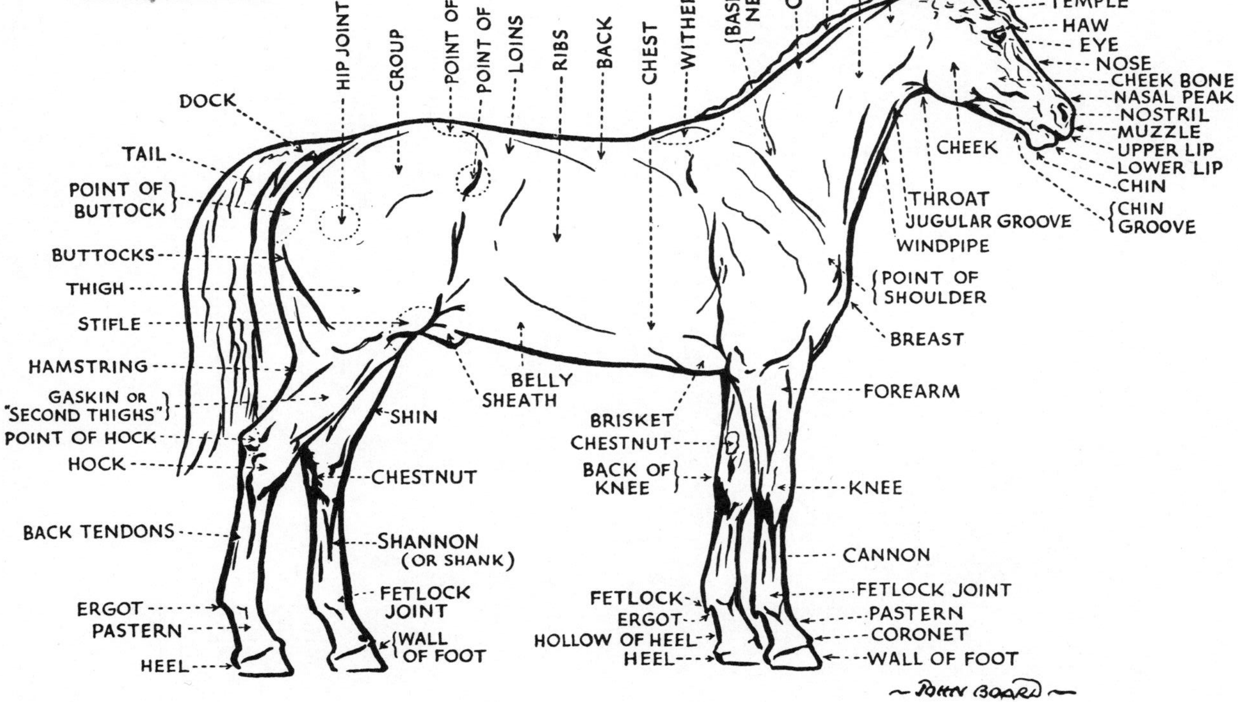

EAR
FORELOCK
TEMPLE
HAW
EYE
NOSE
CHEEK BONE
NASAL PEAK
NOSTRIL
MUZZLE
UPPER LIP
LOWER LIP
CHIN
{CHIN GROOVE

ATLAS
AXIS
NECK
MANE
CREST
{BASE OF NECK
WITHERS
CHEST
BACK
RIBS
LOINS
POINT OF HIP
POINT OF CROUP
CROUP
HIP JOINT
DOCK
TAIL
POINT OF BUTTOCK}
BUTTOCKS
THIGH
STIFLE
HAMSTRING
GASKIN or "SECOND THIGHS"}
POINT OF HOCK
HOCK
BACK TENDONS
ERGOT
PASTERN
HEEL

CHEEK
THROAT
JUGULAR GROOVE
WINDPIPE
{POINT OF SHOULDER
BREAST
FOREARM
KNEE
CANNON
FETLOCK JOINT
PASTERN
CORONET
WALL OF FOOT

BRISKET
CHESTNUT
BACK OF KNEE}
FETLOCK
ERGOT
HOLLOW OF HEEL
HEEL

BELLY
SHEATH
SHIN
CHESTNUT
SHANNON (OR SHANK)
FETLOCK JOINT
{WALL OF FOOT

~ PETER BIEGEL ~

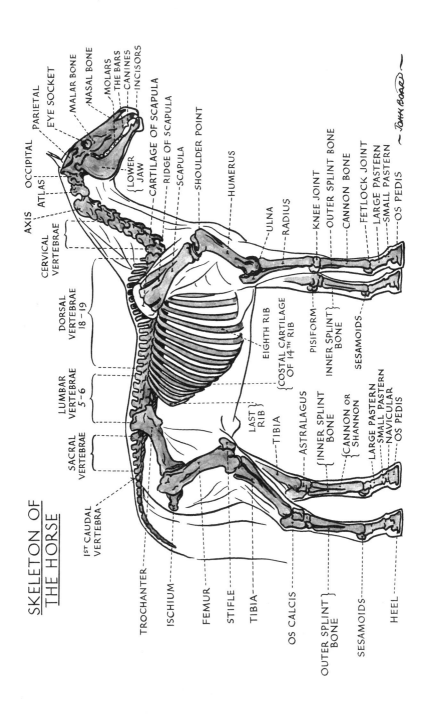

SKELETON OF THE HORSE

~ TOM BOND ~

OCCIPITAL
PARIETAL
EYE SOCKET
MALAR BONE
NASAL BONE
MOLARS
THE BARS
CANINES
INCISORS
LOWER JAW
CARTILAGE OF SCAPULA
RIDGE OF SCAPULA
SCAPULA
SHOULDER POINT
HUMERUS
ULNA
RADIUS
KNEE JOINT
OUTER SPLINT BONE
CANNON BONE
FETLOCK JOINT
LARGE PASTERN
SMALL PASTERN
OS PEDIS

AXIS
ATLAS
CERVICAL VERTEBRAE
DORSAL VERTEBRAE 18-19
LUMBAR VERTEBRAE 5-6
SACRAL VERTEBRAE
1ST CAUDAL VERTEBRA

EIGHTH RIB
COSTAL CARTILAGE OF 14TH RIB
LAST RIB
TIBIA
ASTRALAGUS
INNER SPLINT BONE
CANNON OR SHANNON
LARGE PASTERN
SMALL PASTERN
NAVICULAR
OS PEDIS

PISIFORM
INNER SPLINT BONE
SESAMOIDS

TROCHANTER
ISCHIUM
FEMUR
STIFLE
TIBIA
OS CALCIS
OUTER SPLINT BONE
SESAMOIDS
HEEL

MUSCULAR SYSTEM OF THE HORSE

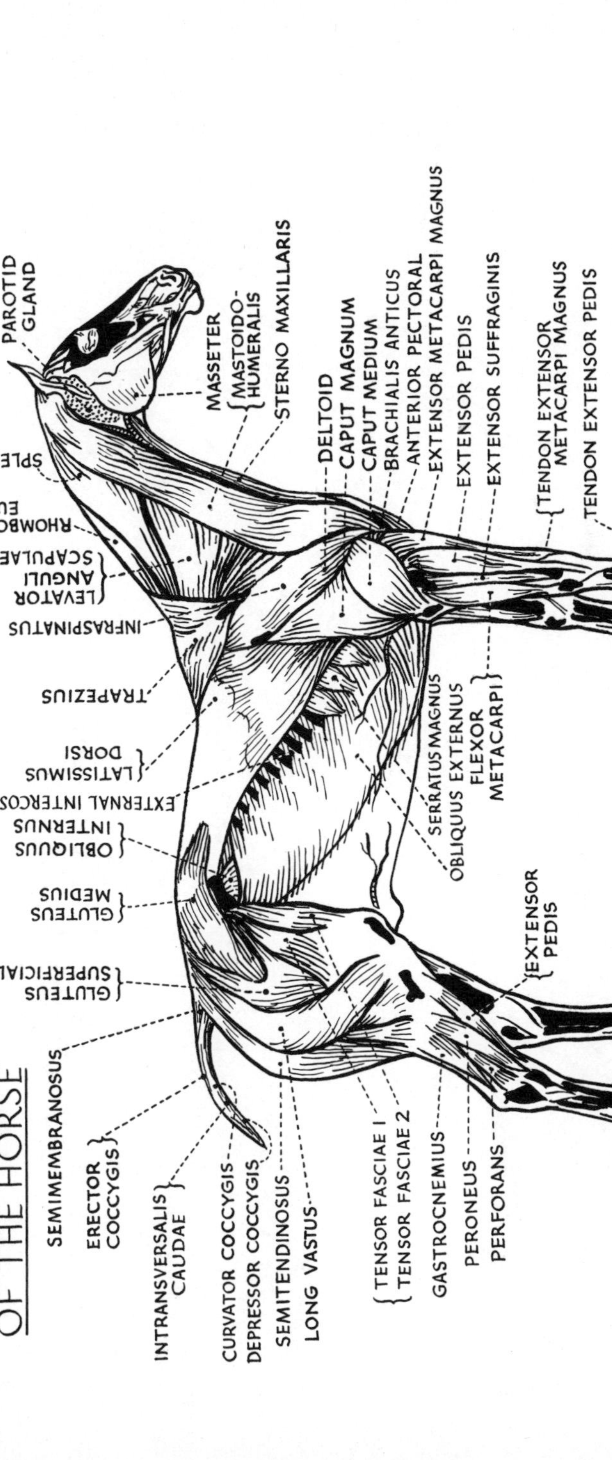

PAROTID GLAND
SPLENIUS
RHOMBOID-EUS
LEVATOR ANGULI SCAPULAE
INFRASPINATUS
TRAPEZIUS
LATISSIMUS DORSI
EXTERNAL INTERCOSTAL
OBLIQUUS INTERNUS
GLUTEUS MEDIUS
GLUTEUS SUPERFICIALIS
SEMIMEMBRANOSUS
ERECTOR COCCYGIS
INTRANSVERSALIS CAUDAE
CURVATOR COCCYGIS
DEPRESSOR COCCYGIS
SEMITENDINOSUS
LONG VASTUS
TENSOR FASCIAE 1
TENSOR FASCIAE 2
GASTROCNEMIUS
PERONEUS
PERFORANS
EXTENSOR PEDIS
SUSPENSORY LIGAMENT
SERRATUS MAGNUS
OBLIQUUS EXTERNUS
FLEXOR METACARPI
MASSETER
MASTOIDO-HUMERALIS
STERNO MAXILLARIS
DELTOID
CAPUT MAGNUM
CAPUT MEDIUM
BRACHIALIS ANTICUS
ANTERIOR PECTORAL
EXTENSOR METACARPI MAGNUS
EXTENSOR PEDIS
EXTENSOR SUFFRAGINIS
TENDON EXTENSOR METACARPI MAGNUS
TENDON EXTENSOR PEDIS
JOHN BOAR

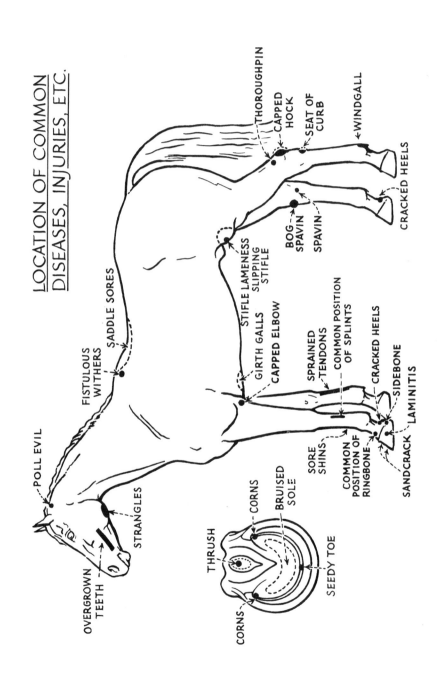

LOCATION OF COMMON DISEASES, INJURIES, ETC.

THOROUGHPIN

CAPPED HOCK

SEAT OF CURB

WINDGALL

CRACKED HEELS

BOG SPAVIN

SPAVIN

STIFLE LAMENESS SLIPPING STIFLE

SADDLE SORES

GIRTH GALLS

CAPPED ELBOW

COMMON POSITION OF SPLINTS

SPRAINED TENDONS

CRACKED HEELS

SIDEBONE

LAMINITIS

FISTULOUS WITHERS

POLL EVIL

SORE SHINS

COMMON POSITION OF RINGBONE

SANDCRACK

STRANGLES

OVERGROWN TEETH

THRUSH

CORNS

BRUISED SOLE

SEEDY TOE

CORNS

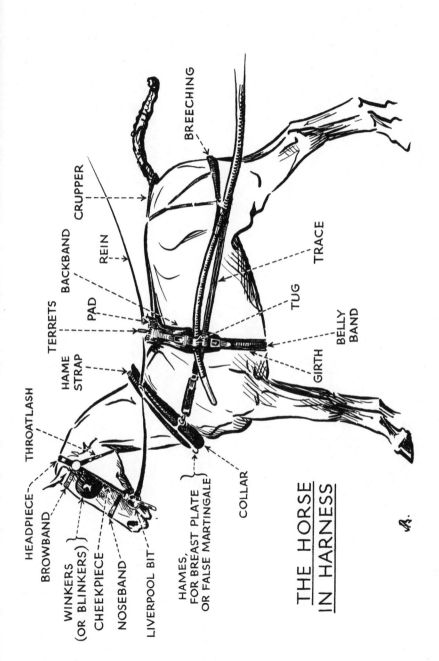

THE HORSE
IN HARNESS

BREECHING

CRUPPER

BACKBAND

REIN

TERRETS

PAD

TUG

TRACE

HAME
STRAP

BELLY
BAND

GIRTH

THROATLASH

HEADPIECE

BROWBAND

WINKERS
(OR BLINKERS)

CHEEKPIECE

NOSEBAND

LIVERPOOL BIT

HAMES,
FOR BREAST PLATE
OR FALSE MARTINGALE

COLLAR

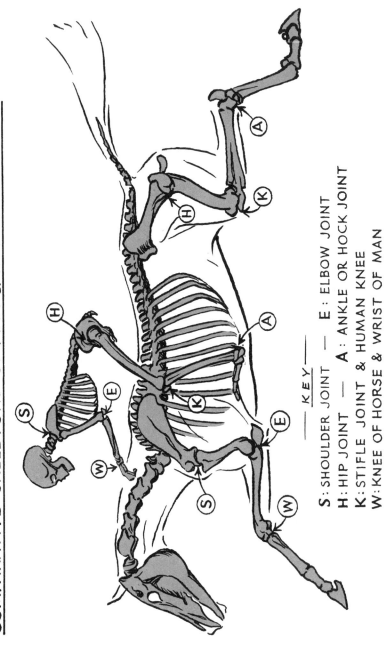

COMPARATIVE SKELETONS OF MAN & HORSE IN ACTION

—— K E Y ——

S: SHOULDER JOINT   —   **E** : ELBOW JOINT

H: HIP JOINT   —   **A** : ANKLE OR HOCK JOINT

K: STIFLE JOINT & HUMAN KNEE

W: KNEE OF HORSE & WRIST OF MAN

* A *

A.A.S.B. Anglo-Arab Stud Book.

A.B.R.S. Association of British Riding Schools.

A.H.S. Arab Horse Society.

A.H.S.A. American Horse Shows Association.

A.H.S.B. Arab Horse Stud Book.

Above the Bit The horse is above the bit when its head is raised and stretched forward with the mouth above the rider's hand. It is a serious fault entailing poor control of the horse, and eventually spoils its paces.

'Above the Ground' Airs above the ground are those movements sometimes called the 'school jumps', which are performed with either the fore-legs suspended off the ground or all four feet off the ground. They consist of the Levade (q.v.), the Courbette (q.v.), the Capriole (q.v.), the Ballotade (q.v.) and the Croupade (q.v.). The Ballotade and the Croupade are not often shown in displays.

Abscess May be acute or chronic and be caused by bacteria infection, thorns, splinters, etc., or through some disease. *Treatment:* apply hot fomentations or antiphlogistine (q.v.) to bring it to a head. If it will not burst a veterinary surgeon must be consulted. Many abscesses can be prevented by the administration of antibiotics and this applies especially to those arising during the disease known as strangles (q.v.). In solitary superficial abscess foreign bodies must always be suspected.

Acceptance Entries for all races are made some time before the race takes place. There may be one or more acceptance stages according to the conditions of the race. Four days before the race, horses have to be declared to run. Their names can be withdrawn or cancelled without additional cost up to 11 a.m. on the day before running.

Acceptances and Declarations to Run have to be made at the Racing Calendar Office or the Overnight Declarations Office of the Jockey Club at Weatherbys, Wellingborough, Northants.

Account for The number of foxes killed during a season.

Accumulator A bet in which two or more horses are backed collectively, and all have to win.

Accumulator Competition (Show Jumping) Course consists of from 5–7 obstacles of progressive difficulty, with points scored mounting accordingly.

'Acey-deucey' American racing term for riding in flat-races with one stirrup-leather longer than the other.

Acland, Sir Thomas Founder of the famous Acland breed of Exmoor ponies (q.v.). In or about 1818 a Mr Knight purchased the Crown lands of Exmoor Forest. Acland, being outbid, retained the best 20 of the 400 ponies said to be then running on the Moor, to form the nucleus of a new herd. From these are descended only true Exmoors. An anchor on the near quarter is the official brand.

Acne A skin eruption usually associated with a staphylococcus infection, more frequently present beneath the saddle or where the harness rubs, also on the face and withers. Usually treated by the veterinary surgeon with sulfa drugs, antibiotics and local applications.

Action Good action when on a hard road at a walk, produces a regular succession of 1–2–3–4 beats, and should appear as follows. Feet flat on ground, toes reaching ground a fraction before heels; fore-feet, toe and heel in line with body, turned neither in nor out, with straight and full extension of fore limbs, and free shoulder action; hind quarters free and loose, with feet carried far under the body by perfect flexion of the hocks, which should have a slight inward tendency with toes turned slightly outwards; the distance between fore legs and hocks neither narrow nor wide. The whole should be free, easy, smooth and slightly languorous. At the trot the legs of each diagonal biped (*q.v.*) must be raised and set down simultaneously, producing a regular succession of two-time. Daisy-cutters (*q.v.*) are prone to stumble, while exceedingly high action saps unnecessary energies. The good horse trots from the shoulders, not the knee, legs moving on a straight line, toeing neither in nor out, hindlegs engaging themselves freely and with suppleness. At the canter the stride must be ample, smooth and regular, covering maximum ground with minimum effort, without becoming disunited, and sounding three distinct beats: 1–2–3 (*see* WALK, TROT, CANTER, GALLOP *and* GAITS TABLE, *page* 136).

Added Money Money actually contributed towards the stakes by the racecourse or from other sources as distinct from money contributed by the owners of horses engaged.

Advance Flag Where starting stalls are not in use this flag is raised by an assistant stationed in advance of the starting line about 1 furlong's distance (220 yd; 201 m) down the course. In the event of a false start the horses are returned.

African Horse Sickness This disease, to which the horse is the only fully susceptible animal, is of considerable antiquity and is most prevalent in warm and moist climates. It is caused by a small virus spread by a night-flying, biting insect. It was formerly confined to Africa and some Middle East countries, but in more recent years it has spread further afield to places including Cyprus, India and Afghanistan and also in southern Spain in 1966. Horses may carry the virus for three months and in its mild form the illness may consist only of fever and malaise. In the acute form the heart is affected, breathing is laboured, swellings appear on the head and neck, there is nasal discharge and the horse may show signs of severe distress. The onset is very rapid and death may occur within a few hours.

'Against the Clock' A show-jumping term indicating that the result will be decided in favour of the competitor completing the course with the least number of faults in the fastest time.

Aga Khan Trophy Competed for by International teams in the Prix des Nations Show Jumping event at the Dublin Horse Show (*q.v.*).

Age The length of life of a horse varies according to usage, care and attention. Light and regular work and good food have a large bearing on age. The greatest recorded age is that of 'Old Billy', who originally worked as a farm horse and was later purchased by the Manchester and Irwell Navigation Co., as a barge horse and died aged 62.

Age, to Tell the The horse has six incisor teeth above and six below. In the lower set, for example, the following applies (calling the middle pair 'centrals', the next on either side 'laterals', and the two outer teeth 'corners'): centrals—cut at 2½, fully up (level) at 3 years; laterals—cut at 3½, fully up (level) at 4 years; corners—cut at 4½, fully up (level) at 5 years. At 2 years a horse has six incisors in each jaw—milk teeth with necks—and five cheek teeth on either side of each jaw. At 5 years it has six permanent incisors and six cheek teeth. A notch appears on the hinder edge of each corner tooth at 7 years, wears down and reappears at 11 years (*see also* GALVAYNE MARK). At 6 years the upper and lower incisors meet at a right angle. As the years pass they become longer and are inclined in a forward direction until at 20 and over they are almost parallel. In the male tushes appear at about 4 years. By

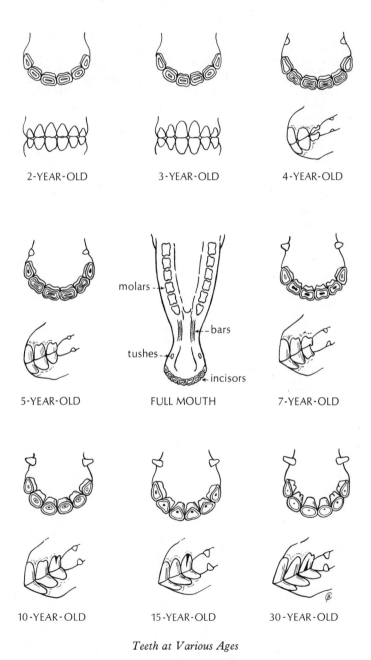

2-YEAR-OLD   3-YEAR-OLD   4-YEAR-OLD

5-YEAR-OLD   FULL MOUTH   7-YEAR-OLD

molars -
- bars
tushes -
- incisors

10-YEAR-OLD   15-YEAR-OLD   30-YEAR-OLD

Teeth at Various Ages

8 years the grooves in the tables of the incisor teeth have worn away and from then on the tables begin to become triangular rather than oval.

'Aged'   Describes a horse when it reaches the age of 7 or over.

Ageing   The process of telling the age of a horse by its teeth—'to age a horse' (*see* diagram on page 3).

Age of Horses   The age of an ordinary horse or pony is reckoned from May 1 of the year in which it was foaled. The age of a Thoroughbred race-horse (i.e. one entered in the General Stud Book) dates from January 1 of the year in which it was foaled. South of the Equator the age of a Thoroughbred race-horse dates from August 1.

Agist   To take in horses or cattle to graze.

Agisters (or Marksmen)   Persons employed by the Verderers (*q.v.*) in the New Forest to collect marking fees in respect of all commonable ponies and other animals turned out in the Forest.

Agripin   Trade name for rubber treads inserted into stirrup irons to assist the rider in maintaining his foot position.

Aids   Signals through which the rider directs and conveys instructions to his horse. The hands, through the reins, direct and control the forehand; the lower part of the legs and the heels collect, control and impel the hindquarters through application behind the girth. The voice is an additional aid; whips and spurs are artificial ones (*see* DIAGONAL AIDS and LATERAL AIDS).

Aintree   The historic racecourse on the edge of Liverpool, where the Grand National (*q.v.*) has been run since 1837. Present distance 4 miles 856 yd (7.219 km). Races on the flat and over hurdles are also run at Aintree. Liverpool-born Mr William Davies bought Aintree in the autumn of 1973 from Mrs Mirabel Topham allegedly for £3 million and gave an undertaking to run the

Grand National for a minimum of a further five years.

Aintree Breast Girth   A simple web breast girth used to prevent a saddle slipping back. Also made in elastic.

Air   The correct bearing of a horse in its different movements and paces, being also the correct rhythm to each of these.

Airer Saddle   A wooden stand to hold a saddle so that the panel will dry more readily. A more sophisticated type is now made of fibre glass, into which electrical heating elements are incorporated. This type can also be used to air and dry clothing.

'Airing'   A term applied to horses which run in a race but are not intended to show their best form.

Airing Clothing   It is desirable that clothing be properly aired from time to time, either in front of a fire or in the sun, particularly if there is the slightest suspicion of dampness.

Airs, Artificial   These consist of paces, other than the normal gaits of walk, trot and canter, and which can only be obtained from the horse at the will of the rider, by careful schooling in the classical manner. Examples are Passage and Piaffe (*see* HIGH SCHOOL).

Akhal-Teké   A breed of saddle horse found in Southern Turkmenia and one of the first Russian horses to have its own stud book. Beautiful horses, with good bone and carriage. Bay, grey and a characteristic golden shade with black points are the usual colours. Height 14.2–15 h.h. (144–152 cm) (*see Plate* I).

Albert Headcollar   The best-known English pattern of headcollar. It is made with either brass or galvanized ('tin') mountings and the cheeks are stitched either two or three rows.

Albino   A congential deficiency of colouring pigment in the skin and hair, resulting, in the horse, in white hair, pink skin and blue eyes (sometimes brown).

Albino Horse The White or Albino Horse has since 1937 been fostered and developed in America under an organization known as The American Albino Horse Club. The foundation horse is said to be 'Old King' foaled in 1906, but its breeding is unknown, though believed to be Arabian-Morgan horse. The Club develops a riding horse of pure white. The Albino is not a breed but a colour type (*see* ALBINO).

Al Borak The mythological winged horse of Mahomet. It was supposedly white in colour with a human head, and of dazzling splendour and incredible speed.

Alcock Arabian All grey Thoroughbreds are descended in direct (though not exclusively) male line from the grey Alcock Arabian (*see* BREEDING, page 39).

Aldin, Cecil Charles Windsor (1870–1935) A prolific sporting artist, one time Master of the South Berkshire Hunt. His pictures of hunting countries and famous English inns brought him great popularity. He illustrated his own books including *Ratcatcher to Scarlet* (1926), *Dogs of Character* (1927) and *Scarlet to M.F.H.* (1913).

Alfalfa A leguminous plant known and cultivated for more than two thousand years, having a red and purple flower standing on a strong stalk; more generally known in England as Lucerne. Whether in a green state or as hay, it is a very valuable crop, and can be mown four times a season; it survives any drought, as its roots, many feet long, find water at a great depth.

Alken, Henry Thomas, Senr. (1785–1851) The most talented of the famous Alken family of sporting artists. Born in Soho, London, a pupil of John Thomas Barber, he first became a miniaturist to the Duke of Kent. He visited Leicestershire and hunted from Melton Mowbray where he obtained first-hand experience of the sporting scene. He also wrote sporting articles under the pseudonym of 'Ben Tallyho'. His pictures in both oils and watercolours are full of incident, specializing in hunting, racing and some coaching scenes. Illustrator of several books including *National Sports of Great Britain*, *Jorrocks' Jaunts and Jollities* and *Memoirs of the Life of the late John Mytton*.

Alken, Samuel, Senr. (1756–1815) Senior member of the Alken family of sporting artists, and uncle of Henry Alken, Senr. His subjects covered many sports, including hunting; he was an admirable horse artist and also an engraver in aquatint.

Alken, Samuel Henry Miscalled Henry Alken Junior (1810–1894). Son of Henry Alken Senior, born at Ipswich, he depicted similar sporting subjects to those of his father, though of inferior talent. Confusion is caused by his deliberate use of the same signatures 'H. Alken' or 'H.A.'.

'All On' Hunting term used by the whipper-in to indicate that every hound in the pack is present.

'All Right, The' When the jockeys have weighed in after a race to the satisfaction of the Clerk of the Scales, the Stewards authorize a signal (blue flag) to be hoisted over the number board. All bets can then be settled. This flag shall not be hoisted until the five minutes allowed for an objection has lapsed.

'All-round My Hat' Cast *see* SMITH, TOM.

All-weather Rug *see* RUG, NEW ZEA-LAND.

Aloes By tradition the horse's purgative but now superseded by safer and less drastic drugs.

Also Ran Any horse which started in a race but finished unplaced.

Altér A Portuguese saddle horse with some Andalusian origins.

Alter, to To castrate or geld a horse or colt.

Alteratives Medicines which improve a horse's general condition without purging.

Amateur The F.E.I. (*q.v.*) rules that any person aged 18 and over not attempting to make a profit through competition and not engaging in activities of the Professional (*q.v.*), ranks as an Amateur. He may not sell more than three International Competition Horses in one year unless authorized by his national federation.

Amateur Rider He is a person who holds a permit from the Jockey Club to ride as an amateur. This may be limited to either flat races or steeplechases and hurdle races. Any person who has ever held a professional jockey's licence or has been paid for riding in a race or has within the period of the last three years been paid as a stable employee in a licensed stable or as a groom or a Hunt servant, is considered to have 'ridden for hire' and is not eligible to ride as an amateur.

Amble An irregular trot produced by the alternate play of the right and left limbs—the limbs on the right are raised and lowered simultaneously, the left limbs alternating with them, the body thus always being out of equilibrium. Great rapidity is gained by the amble, the smooth and gliding motion of which is very pleasant though tiring for the horse—nevertheless, overworked and fatigued horses will sometimes amble. From ambling developed what is called 'pacing' in trotting circles.

Amble, Broken Essentially an American term applied to the gait of four beats as displayed by the five-gaited saddle horse. Each beat of the foot operates separately. It is also termed the single-foot (*q.v.*).

Ambury *see* ANBURY.

American Headcollar This pattern differs from the English one in the employment of looped squares on the cheeks, and by having an adjustable rear strap running through a central leading ring set into the back-stay. It is always three-row sewn, and brass fittings are used.

American Horse Council A national trade organization representing over a million American horsemen. It advises on government legislation on equestrian affairs.

American Horse Shows Association, The The controlling body in the U.S.A. of all recognized shows. It also evaluates and lists judges as Registered (Senior) or Recorded (Junior), publishes annually a Rule Book of correct conduct of all concerned with horse shows and also records the addresses of all breed organizations.

American Quarter Horse *see* QUARTER HORSE, AMERICAN *and* THE HORSE WORLD IN THE UNITED STATES OF AMERICA, *page* 350.

American Runabout A strongly built, but light, 4-wheeled, seated utility carriage which enjoyed great popularity in its time.

American Runabout

American Saddlebred A recognized type of American riding horse. The English Thoroughbred 'Denmark', imported in 1839, was the official founder of the present type, although the parent of the present breed, the

Kentucky Saddle Horse, was an established product before that time. 'Denmark' was put to a mare known as the Stevenson mare and as a result 'Gaines Denmark' was foaled; through him most animals in the American Saddle Horse Registry trace in one or more lines. Now bred almost exclusively for the show ring the horse exhibits brilliance, high proud head and tail carriage. This is the standard 3- or 5-gaited (*q.v.*) horse. The characteristic tail carriage is obtained by nicking the muscles of the dock and setting in position with a crupper. Average height 15–15.3 h.h. (152–155 cm); prevailing colours bay, brown and chestnut, but rarely black or grey (*see* THE HORSE WORLD IN THE UNITED STATES, *page 350 and Plate 2*).

American Saddlehorse *see* AMERICAN SADDLEBRED.

American Standardbred *see* STANDARDBRED.

American Trotter *see* STANDARDBRED.

American Trotting Championship, The *see* TROTTING CHAMPIONSHIP, THE AMERICAN.

Americas, Pony of the *see* PONIES OF THE AMERICAS, and THE HORSE WORLD IN THE UNITED STATES OF AMERICA.

Amnion The innermost membrane enclosing the foetus before birth.

Amulets Brass ornaments said to have been used on camels in the desert and found on cart-horse harness; they are occasionally of nickel plate or other metal. Their origin is found in superstition, a token to ward off 'evil eye'— the chances and dangers of the road. A great number of different designs exist, many being based on the moon, sun and stars. Formerly metal 'cast', more recently they were mostly stamped from sheet metal (commonly known as Horse Brasses).

Anaemia A condition arising from lack of haemoglobin, the colouring matter of the blood, and associated with a scarcity of red blood corpuscles. It is often associated with parasitism; lack of minerals, particularly iron; and it accompanies certain diseases and some types of poisoning. It is a serious cause, or accompaniment, of debility. The horse loses strength, breathes more rapidly when exerted, and shows paleness of the visible mucous membranes. Oedematous swellings may appear beneath the abdomen and in extreme cases the head and lower limbs swell. Diarrhoea sometimes occurs but this may be the result of parasitism. *Treatment*: The veterinary surgeon will seek the cause and treat accordingly.

Anbury A soft tumour or spongy wart on horse or oxen. Also known as Ambury.

Andadura *see* THE HORSE WORLD IN THE UNITED STATES OF AMERICA.

Andalusian The Iberian (Spanish) horses were light, clever and surefooted. Crossed with the Barb, they became known as the Andalusian, taking the name of the province in the south of Spain where they were bred. There were two types, the light Jennet and the heavier Villanos, but the latter was chiefly bred in Castile. Up to the present time the Andalusian horse has been further crossed with French and English blood, but is said to have retained the Barb head. The Andalusian is a strong, deep bodied horse, normally having a good front and high strong quarters. Its temperament is excellent, and it can be a good and attractive ride (*see Plate 2*).

Angleberry *see* WARTS.

Angle Pelham A Pelham Bit with a straight bar mouth, with right-angle bends at each end; the best known is 'The Scamperdale' perfected by Sam Marsh (*see* SCAMPERDALE PELHAM BIT).

Anglo-Arab The Arab Horse Society of England rules that an Anglo-Arab is the cross from a Thoroughbred stallion and an Arab mare, or *vice versa*, with their subsequent re-crossing: that is to say they have no strains of blood other than Thoroughbred and Arabian in their pedigrees. Australia, Canada and Sweden follow this designation, but in other parts of the world a certain minimum percentage of Arabian blood is demanded; in the U.S.A. not less than 25 per cent of Arabian nor more than 75 per cent Thoroughbred; in France, South Africa and U.S.S.R. a minimum of 25 per cent Arabian; in Poland 12½ per cent Arabian.

The Anglo-Arab is a horse of outstanding quality, possessing all the best attributes of the Thoroughbred and with the more classic head, vivid tail carriage and intelligence of the Arab. It is successful as hunter, hack, in dressage, three-day events and show jumping. *Breed Society:* in England, The Arab Horse Society (*see Plate* 1).

Anglo - Argentino Horse or polo pony; a cross between a Thoroughbred stallion and Criolla mare. Is an excellent stock horse and outstanding polo pony, and the bigger type make good jumpers (*see* HORSES IN SOUTH AMERICA, *page* 308 *and Plate* 4).

Anglo-Donetz *see* DON

Anglo-Kabardin Russian horse bred and developed in the Stavropol Region and the Kabardin Republic (North Caucasus), as the result of crossing English Thoroughbred stallions with Kabardin mares. Average height 15.2 h.h. (154 cm). *See also* KABARDIN.

Anglo-Kozakh A Russian agricultural horse. A type developed at one time by crossing Mongolian mares with English Thoroughbreds.

Anglo-Norman The foundation of this French breed originated with the strong, powerful Norman horse which deteriorated through crossing with Danish and Mecklenburg cart-horses. Since 1775 the infusion of Arab and English Thoroughbred blood and, nearly a century later, Norfolk Trotter blood resulted in the production of light carriage horses and racing trotters. Today there are two types of Anglo-Norman: a draught horse (with addition of Percheron (*q.v.*) and Boulonnais (*q.v.*) blood) of 15.2–17 h.h. (154–173 cm) bred largely in the Mortagne region, and also a good type of saddle horse used for the Army and sport, being bred in the district round Caen and now known universally in France as the Cheval de Selle Français.

Animalintex A type of veterinary poultice used in conjunction with oilskin.

Ankle The fetlock joint (*q.v.*).

Ankle Boots A loose term embracing a number of protective boots made from kersey (*q.v.*), boxcloth or light leather. A true ankle or fetlock boot is designed to prevent brushing and is made with one, two, three or four straps. Brushing boots for the hind legs are made with five straps. The straps are occasionally set on elastic, and clips, instead of buckles, are also used.

Ankle Boot

Ankylosis (or Anchylosis) Loss of joint movement caused by the deposition of lime salts, usually associated with an arthritis. It is in reality a terminal healing process and a horse may travel comfortably in many cases after ankylosis has become complete in a joint. For example a lame horse, while developing a spavin, may travel almost free from pain after the affected bones have become fused together, although there will be some loss of hock flexion.

Anne, Queen (1665–1714) Established the Royal Buckhounds Kennels at Ascot and hunted enthusiastically, driving herself in a chaise with a fast horse. At her command in 1711 the race-course on Ascot Heath was laid out.

Anodynes Medicines which relieve and soothe pain.

Ante-Post Betting *see* BETTING.

Anthrax A notifiable disease caused by a bacillus, the spores of which remain viable for a great many years outside the body. While until recently it has been a disease with a high mortality rate it now responds in most cases to large doses of penicillin repeated frequently. In the horse it often attacks the throat, with high temperature, and interference with breathing. Untreated cases usually die within a few days or death may occur suddenly.

Anti-Cast Roller A stable roller in which the pads are connected by an iron hoop or arch. It is claimed that the hoop prevents a horse from becoming cast in the box. More importantly it ensures that the spine is not subjected to any pressure. The best type is where the plates, on to which the pads are attached, are hinged on to the hoop, so making the roller adjustable to any shape of back. Also known as an Arch Roller.

Anti-Lug Bit A jointed snaffle bit in which one side of the mouthpiece is shorter than the other, and in which the curve is greatly accentuated. It is used mainly on race horses which hang to one side. The short side is fitted on the

opposite side from that to which the horse hangs.

Antiphlogistine An American proprietary name given to Denver clay, and similar to all kaolin poultices widely used for sprains.

Anti-Rearing Bit A circular bit which, if correctly adjusted, is believed to correct rearing. Known by racing men as a 'Chifney', its use is confined to led animals who may be difficult to control.

Anti-Sweat Sheet A mesh cotton sheet which, when used under an outer covering, creates insulating air pockets next to the body and prevents 'breaking out' (*q.v.*).

Anvil A base or bed for shaping a horse's shoe. Made of wrought iron or steel with a hardened steel top, its main features consist of hanging end, punching hole, tool hole, face, step, table, bick and throat.

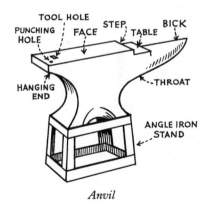

Anvil

'Any to Come' Bet *see* 'IF CASH'.

Apocalypse, Four Horsemen of the Described by St John, in Revelations, chapter 6, as riding a white, red, black and a pale horse, symbolizing conquest, war, famine and death.

Appaloosa Horse The name appears to derive from a breed developed by the

Nez Percé Indians in the Palouse country of Idaho, U.S.A., and a similar type of horse is the Colorado Ranger. Characteristic of the Appaloosa is the pink skin and the silky white coat with a large number of superimposed spots of varying sizes, more profuse on the quarters and which can be felt. The first mention of 'leopard-marked' horses refers to them as originating from the coasts of Arabia, afterwards spreading to India, where the colour still exists. Not all spotted horses can be called Appaloosas, for there are other definite breeds in which spots are either characteristic or are likely to occur, such as the Danish Knabstrup (*q.v.*) and the Austrian Pinzgauer (*q.v.*). Spotted horses have been known at all times through the ages in many parts of the world and shown in Chinese painting of 3000 years ago. *Breed Society:* in England, The British Spotted Horse Society, which classifies three types of marking: Leopard, Blanket and Snowflake (*qq.v.*) (*see Plate* 3).

Apperley, Charles James (1778–1843) Most important sporting journalist of his day. He worked for *The Sporting Magazine* (*q.v.*) and *Sporting Review* under the *nom de plume* of Nimrod. Author of several sporting reminiscences including *Post and Paddock, Scott and Sebright, Memoirs of the Life of John Mytton.*

Appetite *see* FEEDING, *page* 120.

Appointment Card The hunting programme of forthcoming meets, showing dates and places.

Appointments A term generally referring to the harness and saddlery which a horse wears when at work. The award of a percentage of marks for the care of appointments in turn-out, harness and other classes is a recognition of this. In the U.S.A. the term applies to the garb of rider as well as of the horse. These may count for 15 per cent in such classes as Corinthian (*q.v.*) Appointments.

'Apprentice, The' Colloquial name for severe whip, formerly used by drivers of heavy coaches (*see* SHORT TOMMY).

Apprentices Allowances All lads who are formally apprenticed to a licensed flat-racing trainer for a term of not less than three years are permitted during their apprenticeship to claim the following allowances: 7 lb (3.17 kg) until they have won 10 flat races, thereafter 5 lb (2.26 kg) until they have won 50 flat races, thereafter 3 lb (1.36 kg) until they have won 75 flat races — apprentice races being excepted in all the above cases. These allowances cannot be claimed in races confined to apprentices, nor in certain of the more valuable races as set out in the Rules of Racing.

Approaching a Horse This should be done quietly, deliberately, and, as far as possible, from the front, but let it take a good look at you first. Allay the horse's natural suspicions, and always allow your hand to be smelt—closed for choice, against possible bites.

Appuyer French word for half-pass (*q.v.*).

Apron, Astride Riding Usually made in double-texture mackintosh. The material is cut and shaped as an apron, intended to fall about 8 in (20 cm) below the level of the knees. It is cut away between the legs to allow for the astride position. It fastens on the right side by a belt at the waist. Leg straps are also fitted to keep the apron in a secure position whilst riding.

Apron (Driving) Of light weight for summer driving, and of heavy boxcloth for winter use, this is worn over the knees of the coachman or coach passengers.

Apron (Farriers) A divided apron reaching below the knees, usually fitted with a pouch and made from tough horse hide.

Arab Arabian horses are those in whose pedigrees there is none other than Arabian blood. The purest and most beautiful of the equine race and of the greatest antiquity, the Arab has had more influence on other breeds than any other. The breed is known to the Arabs as 'Kehailan', an Arabic word meaning pure-bred, and purity of blood has been guarded fanatically for centuries. The breed is divided into numbers of strains, and is possessed of great soundness of wind and limb, freedom from leg troubles, extreme endurance and the power to thrive on a frugal existence. Because of this nearly every breed and cross breed has had an infusion of Arab blood, and every registered English Thoroughbred has Arab blood in its pedigree. Its prepotency is most vivid and persistent. In recent years the popularity of the breed has increased dramatically all over the world and many countries have their own breed society. Amongst the most important are: World Arabian Horse Organization (q.v.); in the United Kingdom, the Arab Horse Society (q.v.); and in the United States of America, the Arabian Horse Registry of America Inc. and the International Arabian Horse Association (see THE ARABIAN HORSE, *Plate* 3).

Arab, Half-bred see ARAB, PART-BRED.

Arab Horse Families There are several principal families: amongst those usually mentioned are Kehailan, Saglawi, 'Ubayan, Hamdani, Managhi and Hadban.

Arab Horse Society Founded in England in 1918 to promote the breeding and importation of pure bred Arabs and to encourage the reintroduction of Arab blood into English light horse breeding. The Society holds an annual breed show, performance shows, horse trials and instructional seminars, and publishes twice yearly the Arab Horse Society News and from time to time three stud books for Arabs, Anglo-Arabs and part-bred Arabs.

Arab, Part-bred Horses other than an Anglo-Arab (q.v.), being those in the British Isles possessing a minimum of 12½ per cent Arabian blood in their pedigrees, the other ingredient being from any breed other than Thoroughbred. From January 1, 1974 the Arab Horse Society (U.K.) ruled that requirements for registration of Partbreds foaled after that date must be a minimum of 25 per cent Arab blood. Definitions vary widely in the Continental countries. In the United States of America and in Canada the Part-bred is known as the Half-bred Arabian and the sire or dam must be pure-Arabian, thus giving a minimum of 50 per cent Arabian blood. Australia also demands this percentage, with the sire or dam being either pure Arabian, a registered Anglo-Arabian with at least 50 per cent Arab blood or of registered Part-bred Arabian parentage.

Arab (Show-ridden) Stallions, mares or geldings of any age, entered or accepted for entry in the Arab Stud Book of the Arab Horse Society. They are ridden astride or side-saddle, and are ridden and judged as riding horses.

The Arabian Horse * Lady Anne Lytton

In his description of the Arabian Horse published by the *Standard Cyclopedia of Modern Agriculture* 1908, Wilfrid Scawen Blunt states that the balance of scientific opinion in our day seems to be that the Kehailan or Arabian Thoroughbred represents, in reality as by tradition, a primitive wild horse stock indigenous to the Arabian peninsular; and that, like the Barb, his fellow progenitor of the

English racehorse, the Kehailan would seem to have acquired his special characteristics of speed, sobriety and endurance, with his fineness of coat and limb, from the long isolation of his kind among desert surroundings, which have imparted the like qualities of beauty and what we call high breeding to the hare, the fox and the gazelle, indeed to all desert mammals, and goes on to say that these qualities can hardly have been acquired under domestication and must therefore represent peculiarities inherited from the wild state. The Arabian is probably an offshoot of the Asiatic, and the Barb of the European wild stock, and are distinguished from each other by marked differences of conformation, the Barb being 'ram-headed' or having a convex profile, and the Arabian having the upturned nostrils and slightly concave profile of the gazelle. He also has a high wither which makes him essentially a saddlehorse, and above all his tail, instead of being set low and carried meanly between his hocks (the Barb characteristic), springs from the highest level of the quarters and is carried high. These are points of bone structure which are important in the Arabian as indications of pure breeding. I think it would be true to say that all quality seen in other breeds stems from the Arabian Horse. According to Wilfrid Blunt the systematic introduction of pure Kehailan into Europe dates from the eighteenth century only. During the previous century racing had come greatly into fashion in England and much Eastern blood had been imported, principally Spanish and Barb, but now for the first time stallions of authentic blood were procured from Aleppo and other towns on the desert edge, with an immediate effect on the quality and speed of the English racehorse. The most famous of these sires and the best authenticated was the Darley Arabian of the Managhi strain, *one of the best breeds of the Anazeh Arabs.* This last statement is important in view of the fact that the Managhis have been denigrated by modern writers on the Arabian horse, and described as coarse headed and possibly even not pure. He makes also this important statement—'It is impossible to enter into any nice calculation, but it may be affirmed generally that at least three-fourths of the blood of the modern English Thoroughbred is derived from Arabia and that to the Kehailan he owes the initial quality of speed.'

Not until 1878 were more Arabian horses imported to England in any numbers. I refer to those brought here by Wilfrid Scawen and his wife Lady Anne Blunt when they made a journey in the spring of that year to Aleppo, Baghdad and Damascus, when they visited all the great horse-breeding tribes of the northern deserts and purchased from them mares and stallions of their best breeds. These visits were repeated in 1879 during a journey to Nejd, the central province of Arabia, and again with the object of procuring horses in 1881, to the Hamad or great desert south of Palmyra. Twenty-five broodmares were thus got together and imported to England. New stallions, likewise of the purest and most authentic strains of blood, have been obtained from the same sources at intervals since. The only considerable importation of mares since 1890 was the purchase by Mr Blunt in 1896 of the remainder of the once celebrated stud of the Viceroy of Egypt, Abbas I. This consisted of six first-class mares and four stallions. It was known as the stud of Ali Pasha Sherif and was the last of the great studs of pure-bred Arabs once so numerous on the Arab borderlands. The decline of Arab horses in the East and the fact that the Arabs were selling their best colts and reserving for their own use the stallions less good, thus producing degeneration among the tribes, was the main reason for the founding in England of the Crabbet Stud, to preserve the best of the breed and to save it from extinction.

However, another very valuable horse was added to Crabbet by the Blunts' only daughter, Lady Wentworth, in 1920. This was the Polish pure-bred Arab, 'Skowronek', imported to this country by Mr Walter Winans and owned for some years by Mr H. V. Musgrave Clark, and eventually acquired by Lady Wentworth, thus forming, as she said, a new dynasty at the Crabbet Stud, which was then greatly in need of fresh blood. 'Skowronek' was bred by Count Potocki and became as he aged a beautiful pure white of true type. He proved to be highly prepotent and a prolific stockgetter, and is no doubt the most famous sire of modern times as he also had a very great influence in America mainly through his in-bred son Raffles. For many years the Crabbet Stud was the chief supplier of Arabs to the U.S.A., also to Australia, South Africa, Spain and Holland.

At the end of the 1950s another infusion of Polish Arab blood commenced through some horses imported to this country by Miss Patricia Lindsay. America has also turned to Poland for fresh blood, and more recently to Egypt, which had retained some good blood from the old studs and from Lady Blunt's Sheykh Obeyd stud, and even reintroduced Arabs from Crabbet, partly through stock which had been imported by Mr Trouncer in order to race them, after his death in the early 1950s. Russia also imported stock from Crabbet as well as from Poland.

The Arabian horse, though outstripped by the Thoroughbred Racehorse for speed, has always retained his own reputation as a tough horse, capable of great endurance; and some Crabbet stock sold to America took part in several long-distance races of 300 miles (483 km) in which they distinguished themselves. But the main purpose in the early days was to keep the breed pure, and apart from sales overseas to all parts of the globe the Arab was too busy increasing and multiplying to lead a more active life. The horse is no longer needed for transport and harness, and while formerly an excellent Polo pony,

as well as a racer in his own right, the Arab is now no longer required for these purposes, so that other things must be thought of to bring out his fine qualities.

In America the Arab horse is used in many activities—harness, all types of riding, Arab races, cutting cattle and, probably most important of all, for long-distance treks of 100 miles (161 km) over difficult country. Fortunately the 300-mile (483 km) tests have long been discontinued and this modern version is well supervised so that unfit horses are withdrawn. The treks are open to all breeds; the pure-bred Arabs almost invariably win, and those that finish are usually part-bred Arabs, sometimes with pony mixtures.

There is a strong move in the United Kingdom to run riding events for the Arab. Being a small horse, the pure-bred has so far been unable to compete over the very big jumps of the Cross Country courses of the Badminton and Burghley Horse Trials, but Badminton has twice been won by a half-Arab, and Burghley once. There are now a great number of breeders in this country and they are very much aware of the importance of keeping the beautiful type of the best Arabian while remembering that good conformation is extremely important.

It should not be forgotten that his trotting action is one at which he most excels and this should be like 'a deer trotting through fern', with the hocks well flexed and moving as though floating with extreme grace, and the whole picture one of great beauty and refinement.

Height Wilfrid Blunt says: 'The best height for an Arab stallion is from 14.2 to 15 h.h. [144–152 cm] rather less than more, 14.2½ [145 cm] being perhaps perfection.' This he wrote more than sixty years ago. Today the average seems to have increased, and now a large number are 15 h.h. (152 cm) or a bit over, which formerly was a rare occurrence. This is very noticeable among mares. Nearly all the great champions have been rather below than above 15 h.h., with some exceptions.

Colour 'There can be little doubt that bay or chestnut was the original wild colour and there is a clear tendency to reversion to them. The Bedouins themselves prefer bay, which they think the hardest; chestnut with three white feet is perhaps still more preferred and it is usually in this combination that the handsomest types of Kehailan are seen. White and fleabitten greys are favourite with the townspeople. Brown is an uncommon colour and black an extremely rare one.' Wilfrid Blunt adds this important comment, which point of view was held by Lady Wentworth: 'It is generally admitted by breeders that the type is more perfectly produced with a chestnut sire than with any other. It is also believed that chestnut is the original, as it is the most consistent Kehailan colour.'

POINTS OF AN ARABIAN

Head small and tapering, very broad in the forehead, with very large widely opened dark eyes set low in the skull (about half-way between the ear and nostril); very small, sharply cut ears set wide apart, but carried much pricked and very delicately modelled in what should be a most exquisite curve; nostrils very large and widely opened, thin-edged and mobile; chin also sharply cut; jowl deep and circular and very clearly defined, and throat set into it in a distinctly arched curve; this is most important; neck must not be angular at the throat, but arched, especially in stallions, where it should be accentuated by the arched crest.

Profile concave, like a gazelle's, and generally more pronounced in mares than in stallions, which may have an extra broad forehead with a very subtle curve tapering to the muzzle. When the forehead is very prominent, this prominence, viewed in profile, must continue to just below the eyes—some concave heads are all wrong because the bulge is too high up, and after dipping it rises again in a long arch over the nose. Because of the dipped curve these are often mistakenly thought to be typical Arabian heads, whereas such a curve gives a common look. The head is much more important in Arabians than in other breeds. It betrays coarseness sooner than any other point except the tail, where a slack trailing carriage generally accompanies a straight head and small eyes.

Shoulder should be long and sloping, with well-defined withers, which, however, are not generally as high in vertebrae as in Thoroughbreds, but a loaded 'pudding' shoulder should be taboo.

Back short, level, carried on by a level croup, strong loins which should never cave inwards in front of the hips, and a tail set on a level with the back and carried high in a perfect arch when in motion.

Hocks strong and straight, quarters very broad and thighs big and muscular.

Chest broad and deep—it cannot be too broad. Plenty of heart room, ribs well rounded and body deep and roomy, never tucked up and shallow.

Legs hard as iron, back tendons like steel bars, feet large and round, never small, contracted or mule-like. The feet of an Arabian are seldom defective. When they are so, it is a far more fatal defect than in other breeds, because of the fundamental general excellence, durability and hardness of their hooves. Weakness shows degeneracy due either to hereditary defect or to excessive in-breeding.

Action should be brilliant, walking fast and swinging, with much over-stepping of the hind feet over the front hoof marks. Trotting action should be very smart, exceedingly free at the shoulder, foot well thrown out and stifles swinging right forward with hocks well lifted, the whole appearance giving a floating, dancing movement, as if on air and springs. The horse should trot slightly wide when seen from behind; contracted close action is bad.

Galloping action is astonishingly free and fast, with powerful hind quarter drive and an absolutely unique capacity for 'turning on a sixpence'.

Cross breeding For crossing with other breeds the Arabian has one great advantage over the Thoroughbred racehorse —an admirable temper which he usually transmits to his offspring, and for crossing with ponies for children this is quite essential; also he never spoils the pony type by giving a horse's head. But perhaps the most interesting riding type to breed is the Anglo-Arab (*q.v.*), which is merely reintroducing Arab blood back into the registered Thoroughbred (*q.v.*). This can produce a magnificent horse both in looks and conformation and in size (*see* BREEDING, *page* 39, *and* THE ENGLISH THOROUGHBRED, *page* 333 *and Plate* 3).

* * *

Archer, Frederick (1857–1886) Born at Cheltenham, Fred Archer became champion English jockey for 13 seasons. From the age of thirteen in 1870 until his death, he rode 8084 races and won 2748. His will was proved at £66,662. Nicknamed 'The Tinman', he was a great believer in the persuasive powers of whalebone and steel (*see* RICHARDS, SIR GORDON).

Arch Pelham A bit with an arch mouth, giving maximum tongue room.

Arch-roller *see* ANTI-CAST ROLLER

Ardennais This may be considered as a French or Belgian horse, according to the exact locality of the mountains from which it originally came. A very hardy old breed, it is most resistant to all unfavourable conditions of climate and feeding. During the seventeenth century the breed was used for cavalry, and again during the First World War as artillery wheelers, as the type had changed. Today, in the mountains, there exist 14.2–15 h.h. (144–152 cm) ponies, nearest to the old type, while others are on heavy draught lines. A very popular breed in France, Belgium, Sweden and Poland.

Argentine Horse *see* THE HORSE IN SOUTH AMERICA, *and Plate* 4.

'Arkle' Champion and very popular steeplechaser by 'Archive' out of 'Bright Cherry'. Foaled in 1957, he stood 16.2½ h.h. (165 cm) and was bought by Anne, Duchess of Westminster, and trained in Ireland by Tom Dreaper. In a brilliant career, which included winning three Cheltenham Gold Cups, he won 27 of his 35 races.

Arkwright Bit A curb bit with the curb rein ring hanging directly from the cheek, without a neck. Also known as the Lowther Bit.

Armlets The programme number of each racehorse paraded in the paddock must be worn on the arm of the lad in charge.

Armour, George Denholm, O.B.E. (1864–1949) A well-known sporting artist and author whose drawings, mostly in pen and ink, appeared in leading periodicals of the day.

'Arterxerxes' 'A stiff bay with white legs and a bang tail', the second horse of John Jorrocks, M.F.H. So called because he came 'arter Xerxes' when driven tandem (*see* JORROCKS, XERXES).

Articulation Where two or more bones meet, forming a joint.

Artzel Obsolete term for a horse with a white mark on its forehead.

Arve A call to a horse to turn left; 'Gee' is the call to turn right. Both used chiefly with agricultural horses. Other terms are used in different districts.

Ascot, Ascot Heath Ascot Races

were started by Queen Anne (*q.v.*) in 1711 and have been consistently supported by the Royal Family ever since. The four-day Royal meeting in June is known as Royal Ascot, at which the Queen drives in procession down the course before racing. The other Ascot meetings are sometimes known as Ascot Heath meetings.

Ascot Gold Cup The principal long-distance race of the English flat-racing season. Founded in 1807 it is run over $2\frac{1}{2}$ miles (4 km) at the Royal Ascot meeting in June. From 1845 to 1853 it was known as the Emperor's Plate. For results *see page* 384.

'As Hounds Ran' The distance covered by hounds in a run, measuring each turn from field to field as opposed to 'as the crow flies', which is a straight line from start to finish.

Asinus isabellinus The Isabella Quagga. A wild ass of a pale yellow colour, which existed in large herds in South Africa over one hundred years ago but is now extinct (*see* QUAGGA).

'Asking the Question' When a horse has been well tested in a gallop or in a race. When it has been pushed to the limit.

Asl (or Asil) An Arabic word implying a horse of illustrious race—a horse of noble lineage.

Ass There are more than half a dozen races of wild ass living in the world today, falling into two distinct groups, the African and the Asiatic (*see* KIANG and ONAGAR). All breeds of domestic ass (*Equus asinus*) are believed to be descended from the wild ass of Nubia and other parts of North Africa between the Nile and the Red Sea. Though Egyptians used them before horses, they were long in reaching Europe.

The dorsal band and shoulder stripe are rarely apart in the grey, but in others they show considerable variation. Great numbers of asses are now bred in Eire, where the 'ass-cart' is a familiar sight. As distinct from the ergots (*q.v.*) on horses, which tend to be pointed, those of the ass resemble pads. The Ass varies in height according to the strain, but is generally fleet, docile, intelligent and very long lived. The male is known as the jackass and the female as the she-ass.

Assateague   *see* CHINCOTEAGUE.

Asthma A chronic condition rarely found in horses. The breathing becomes irregular and very distressed. Damp all feeds.

Astley, Philip (1742–1814) Creator of the modern circus. An ex-Sergeant-Major turned trick rider. He left the Army when aged 24 with the gift of a fine white horse, 'Gibralter', which formed the nucleus of his first circus in a field near the present Waterloo Station. Astley's Amphitheatre eventually became the scene of one of London's most popular diversions where spectacular equestrian dramas and daring feats of horsemanship were staged. Astley appeared before the French Court and toured Europe as far east as Belgrade.

Atherstone Girth A baghide girth shaped at the elbows to prevent galling. Similar to the 'Balding' girth (*q.v.*).

Atlas The first vertebra of the neck which unites with bones at the back of the head to allow this to move up and down.

Auction When contemplating a purchase at an auction of horses, the purchaser should acquaint himself with the warranties applying (*see* WARRANTY).

The Horse in Australia   *   R. M. Williams

Numbers and Types Official statistics concerning the horse in Australia are based on returns from farmers and station owners, racehorse organizations and official stud organizations, but these figures do not take into account the horses of the metropolitan areas or the pleasure horses which today could be greater by far than those listed through statistical channels. Government statistics place the figures as somewhere less than a million horses in Australia, but the actual numbers probably exceed this figure considerably.

The types of horses being used or kept for pleasure fall into strict categories except for the nameless legion of stock horses, or Walers as some like to call them. These are the horses without specific breed and which comprise the largest single group of horses in the country, to be dealt with later under the heading of THE AUSTRALIAN STOCK HORSE (*see page* 19).

The numbers of Thoroughbreds registered every year are known, as also are the number of Arabians and Quarter Horses registered with their breed societies. Stud ponies also are a known quantity but the number of unregistered ponies which comprise the bulk of the pony club horses and the children's ponies cannot be assessed correctly nor even estimated.

The Thoroughbred Most important in terms of value, usefulness and importance to the horse industry is the Thoroughbred. The racing business which promotes the breeding and training of Thoroughbreds is in itself almost a billion dollar industry, this figure being supplied by the 1972 All Breeds Congress of Australia and quoted by Sir Clive Uhr, president of the Thoroughbred Breeders Association.

Most of the Australian Thoroughbred blood comes from England, Ireland and France, regular importations having been made for over a century and are still being made. The quality now is such that America has taken considerable numbers of top racing stock, and continues to purchase outstanding horses, many of which have become famous stud names in America.

The stud book is kept by the racing industry itself and is controlled by the Thoroughbred Breeders Association and the Australian Jockey Club which dominates racing. Horses other than stud stock may be raced by registering them with the Australian Jockey Club but their progeny may not be entered in the stud book which is a closed book.

All racecourses and racing stock are controlled by the A.J.C. and no racing which does not have the official approval is recognized; in fact, such meetings are discouraged. Race distances and riding weights were officially converted to the metric system in Australia in 1972.

All breeding of stud stock is in private hands and there is no government-owned or controlled stud in Australia except for two small State-owned Arabian studs at Hawksbury and Gatton Agricultural colleges. Each year in the capital cities a yearling sale of stud stock is held, also of pure-bred unregistered stock, the largest sale being at Sydney, New South Wales, where 1500 yearlings are sold annually, with 600 to 1000 being sold at Brisbane, Melbourne, Adelaide and Perth.

The Thoroughbred has traditionally been the base stock used for station sires and almost all the working stock horses of Australia have been from the progeny of Thoroughbreds. Both stock horse and Quarter Horse breeders still look to the Thoroughbred for the upgrading of their working or racing stock.

The Trotter The trotting horse, although not an exclusive Australian breed, has been developed and promoted in Australia to the point where it is quite a distinctive type, and the stud book of the Australian Trotting Association, now a closed book, lists the pedigrees for many generations of Australian-born horses.

In number the trotter in Australia is not as great as some other types, but in monetary value of turnover in betting and from sales the trotter must take second place in importance. Besides night trotting at well-established tracks in every large city and country town, there are trots at most large provincial shows.

The Arabian The number of Arabians in Australia is perhaps not as great as some other breeds of horses, but it is one of the oldest established breeds in Australia and has had considerable influence on the working horses throughout the last century and for most of the period of Australia's development.

Until 1960 all those wishing to register their horses used the English stud book, and a few still double register their horses in both the Australian stud book and the English stud book, but now that the Australian book is well established there are few using the English book.

Practically all the Arabians in Australia came from English stock, but now there are a few Polish, American and Egyptian blood lines and the quality of stock is steadily rising, a few even being exported.

The Arab Horse Society of Australia, with headquarters in New South Wales, is growing rapidly and within the past few years has doubled its numbers. There are several thousand registered horses now in the Australian stud book kept by the Arab Horse Society of Australia, fourth largest in the world. Arab breeders are being encouraged to compete in open company with their horses, and there is a growing number of useful working and competitive horses among the registered Arabians.

The Pony Ponies for children belonging to pony clubs form a major group of the horse population of Australia, which has the largest pony club organization in the world, with a club operating in almost every important town in the country and with scores of clubs in some major cities. The ponies range from Shetlands to 14 h.h. (142 cm) mixed breed small horses, the basis of this breeding having come from England and America. The Welsh Mountain played a big part in establishing the breed but today the Australian pony is for the most part in a class by itself, being lighter than the Welsh and considered much more active than most of the English breeds.

The pony club instructors ask for considerable action in the gatherings which constitute the rallies or meetings, and although instruction plays some part, still the action is the holding or uniting factor and children are asked to jump and run in flag races, so altogether the slow pony is not suitable. Therefore the children after learning to ride quickly graduate to an active and taller animal. The figures for pony population are not possible to gauge accurately, but there are at least 20,000 known registrations. This figure of course is taken from pony club activities and does not include the stud pony registry of pure-breds. Registered office of the stud pony organization is with the various State Agricultural societies, the head office being the Royal Agricultural Society office, Sydney.

The Quarter Horse The Quarter Horse (*q.v.*) has very lately come to Australia, having been imported in large numbers during the years 1970–72 from the U.S.A. The registered pure-breds now number 700 with 4000 first cross and 2000 second cross. Pure-breds may be graded up from second cross. The Quarter Horse is still the plaything of the wealthy, because of the high cost involved in owning a pure-bred, and even the first cross still costs more than pony club members or working stockmen can afford.

Very good blood lines have been selected and there are now two distinct strains of Quarter Horses in the country.

One is a working stock horse which is the heavier type and the other is the lighter racing strain which is the original Quarter Horse crossed with the American racing horses or registered Thoroughbreds.

With the introduction of the Quarter Horse and its influential backers many new American types of competitions have made their appearance in the Australian show ring and rodeo arena—cutting, trail riding competitions, Western riding—and for the most part the American influence has been confined to those particular types of competition suited to the Quarter Horse. Campdrafting does not suit the Quarter Horse particularly and jumping is another area where the Quarter Horse does not do well. Nor does the Quarter Horse excel at long-distance races such as the 100-mile Quilty Race over the Blue Mountains near Sydney. But the Quarter Horse, as its name implies, is a quarter-mile racer, and this distance is becoming quite a new and exciting type of race and the Quarter Horse Association is pushing this distance at special races for any comers, knowing that the Quarter Horse does excel at this distance.

Cutting is another competition where the Quarter Horse excels and this sport is taking on fast in Australia. The Quarter Horse certainly has a place in Australia and is increasing quickly; there are now over a thousand members belonging to the Quarter Horse Association. Headquarters are in Sydney.

The Draught Horse The heavy horse almost became extinct in Australia with just a few pockets of heavy horses doing service in the cane fields of Queensland and a few stud masters breeding Percherons and Clydesdales. But the tide seems to have turned and there are increasing numbers of breeders finding use for their product in various fields; the Percherons as sires for heavy working saddle horses and the Clydesdales as sires for crossing with Thoroughbreds for jumping horses, although this cross is again losing favour and the Clydesdales are crossed for a few specialists who like to use delivery horses in such vehicles as brewery waggons. There are a few, very few, Suffolks still in Australia. Carriage horses are almost extinct. Cob types are not seen any more, so that the heavy horse has little place in the Australian scene.

The Palomino The Palomino (*q.v.*) has found a niche in the show ring and among those who like the colour and the glamour of the golden horse. Palomino breeding associations exist in every state and although not strong they are growing with the popularity of the show and saddle horses generally, and the numbers of Palominos, although not great, are increasing.

The Appaloosa The Appaloosa (*q.v.*) has come to Australia very recently. The colour has not become as popular as expected and there will probably be a lapse of time before the breed becomes well known and in demand. Prices are high and numbers increasing.

The Australian Stock Horse The name is new but the breed is old, the name having been coined recently for the Waler or original cross-bred horse of outback Australia, the horse which served Australia so well in the First World War and which has for generations been the backbone of the Australian cattle industry.

The Waler (Australian Stock Horse) is the end product of many crossings, mainly Thoroughbred but including every known type: Pony, Percheron, Arabian, Coach horse. All have a place in the history of the Stock Horse, the result being a useful Thoroughbred-looking animal with lots of endurance and lots of ability (*see Plate* 4).

The introduction of the Quarter Horse with its publicity boost made the Australian bushman angry and the people of the eastern seaboard united to form the Australian Stock Horse Society. The society has as its standard chiefly camp-drafting and likes to believe that this is the essence of the Stock Horse's ability, but its horizon will have to be widened to include endurance riding, jumping and the various abilities which have characterized the Stock Horse of the past. Also there is a tendency for the classifiers to include running or racing ability as one of the main qualities of the Stock Horse. This, of course, is desirable, but was never the strong point of the Stock Horse of the past. Racing is the province of the Thoroughbred.

The society is young and its ambitions will clarify with time, and no doubt the Australian Stock Horse will become the chief breed of the future if only because of its general acceptance and its national character. The breed will tend towards the Thoroughbred but will for many generations be a mixture because of the acceptance by the society of almost all fair types and the need for the society to get established.

The Horse Industry   The horse industry in Australia has been described by its leaders as a billion dollar business, and at the 1972 All Breeds Horseman's Congress this point was explained in detail by economic experts who had researched the subject.

This makes the horse industry the second largest business in Australia, as it is in America. The industry includes Breeding, Racing, Training, Feeding, Hardware, Saddlery, Stud Property, Race Tracks, Gambling, Shoeing, Medication. When a million pleasure horses are serviced with all the care and luxury of special attention, then the costs are high.

Race tracks are booming; the horse-care industry has caused shops specializing in medicated feeds and medication to open up in every centre; schools are being run for blacksmiths. The pleasure side of riding has created new demands for new types of clothing and literature, all with growing and expanding avenues of sales. The breed societies are growing at a particularly high rate as shown by the Arabian's claim that the Arab Horse Society of Australia has doubled in numbers in the past 5 years.

*   *   *

Australian Cheeker   *see* AUSTRALIAN NOSEBAND.

Australian Loose Ring Snaffle   A cheek snaffle fitted with a broad, jointed mouthpiece and loose, i.e. traversing, rings. This bit is now better known as the Fulmer snaffle due to the extensive use made of it by Robert Hail of Fulmer, who virtually reintroduced it to Britain (*see Plate* 6).

Australian Noseband   A rubber device slipped over the bit rings on either side of the mouth, joining on the nose and running up the face to a fastening on the headpiece. It keeps the bit up in the mouth, preventing the horse getting his tongue over the bit, and exerts slight restraining pressure on the nose at the same time as pressure on the mouth. Also known as an Australian Cheeker.

Australian Stock Horse   *see* THE HORSE IN AUSTRALIA, *page* 19, *and Plate* 4.

Australian Noseband

Austria, Elizabeth, Empress of
(1837–1897) An accomplished horse-woman, she studied equitation seriously and had lessons in the Spanish Riding School of Vienna. Hunted with great enthusiasm in England and Ireland between 1876–1882, when her skill, courage and elegance created a minor sensation. She is remembered for her remark to her pilot, Captain 'Bay' Middleton, 'I don't mind the falls, but, remember, I will not scratch my face.'

Autorisation Spéciale (Show Jumping) A pink card which riders must obtain from their national federation before competing at an International Horse Show.

Autumn Double The coupling of the winners of the Cambridgeshire and the Cesarewitch (*see* DOUBLE).

Avelignese A draught horse bred in northern and central Italy. Very strong and muscular. Chestnut with light mane and tail. About 14.2 h.h. (144 cm).

'Away from You' A ditch on the far side of a fence is 'away from you'; on the near side it is 'to you'.

Azoturia Nowadays more often termed *Haemoglobinuria*. Occurs in horses kept too long in the stable, well-fed without exercise. Symptoms: pain, sweating, lameness acute and rapidly increasing. The horse has a tendency to go down and be unable to rise. Hard swelling in groups of muscles, usually over quarters. Urine stained red. May terminate in death, but mild cases recover sometimes if horse is pulled up and rested immediately symptoms are shown on the road. Horses that recover may suffer afterwards from atrophy of affected muscles.

* B *

b. bay

Bbv (Racing) Broke blood vessel.

B.D.S. British Driving Society.

B.E.F. British Equestrian Federation.

B.F.S.S. British Field Sports Society.

B.H.S. British Horse Society.

B.H.S.A.I. British Horse Society Assistant Instructor.

B.H.S.I. British Horse Society Instructor.

Bl. Black.

B.M.P.S. Brood Mare Premium Scheme.

B.P.S. British Palomino Society.

br. brown.

B.S.H.C.A. British Show Hack and Cob Association.

B.S.J.A. British Show Jumping Association.

B.S.P.S. British Show Pony Society.

B.V.A. British Veterinary Association.

Babbler A hound which throws its tongue too much, either when it is not sure of the scent or when it is very far behind the leading hound.

Babieca The white horse of Diaz de Bivar (d. 1099), the Spanish Cid. Famous in verse and legend.

Back, to (Racing) To make a bet on a horse.

Back, to A term commonly used when an unbroken horse is first mounted.

Back, to To make a horse move backwards.

Back, Hollow When the natural concave line of the back is exaggerated and unnatural.

Back-at-the-Knee *see* CALF-KNEE.

Backband A strap going over or through the pad and carrying the weight of shafts or traces.

Back Blood or Back-breeding A term applied to a hereditary trait in any particular family of horses which is liable to influence constitution and conformation of succeeding generations.

Backgammon Board Seat on the roof at the rear of a coach.

Backing Stage in breaking and training when trainer essays, and ultimately succeeds in, sitting on horse's back.

Back Strap *see* TUGS. The term is sometimes used outside the saddlery trade to denote the Backband.

Back Straps Strips of leather from top of counter and running up back seams of boot legs to cover and protect them.

'Back Up' *see* COLD BACK.

Badger-pied A lightly marked cream or lemon hound with back and ears shaded into fawn and black.

Badikins An arrangement for harnessing a horse to the plough, a crossbar to which the traces are fixed, also known as suppletrees, swiveltrees and whippletrees.

'Badminton' (Badminton House, Gloucestershire, ancestral home of the Dukes of Beaufort). The name is synonymous with the very soul of fox-hunting. In 1949 it was here the first Three-Day Event in this country took place (other than the Olympic Competition in Great Britain the previous year). It is now held annually and attracts numerous competitors and thousands of spectators (*see Plate* 5).

Badminton Horse Trials The Great Badminton Championship Event. For results *see page* 380. See *also* HORSE TRIALS *and Plate* 5.

Bag-fox A fox kept temporariiy in captivity and turned down for the purpose of being hunted on a given day in a given locality. Generally deemed a disreputable practice. Colloquially known as Bagmen, there was a considerable demand for them in the nineteenth century by poachers who sold them again to the hunts. A recognized source was Leadenhall Market in the City of London, hence another name for a bag-fox—a 'Leadenhaller'.

Baghide Name given to the cowhide which has an imprint or pattern on it and which covers any imperfections of the hide. Used for well-known 3 folded (baghide) girth.

'Bahram' Unbeaten winner of ten races and won £43,000 in stakes for the Aga Khan. Won the 2000 Guineas, Derby and St Leger in 1935, and thus became the 14th winner of the Triple Crown (*q.v.*) in English racing history.

Baiga *see* BUZKASHI.

Baily's Hunting Directory The annual directory of the hunts of the British Isles, overseas Dominions, Europe and the U.S.A. Published by J. A. Allen & Co. (London).

Bait When a horse is stood in a stable for any brief period, and provided with food, it is said to be 'at bait'.

Balance When a horse carries its own weight and the weight of the rider in such a way that it can use and control itself to best advantage at all paces and in all circumstances.

Balassiren A method of controlling horses by mesmerism.

Bald Face A horse with an entirely white face.

'Bald Headed' (to go at it bald headed) Lieutenant-General the Marquis of Granby on July 31st, 1760 at the Battle of Warburg, when leading the 6th Inniskilling Dragoons in a cavalry charge, lost his wig and so originated 'Going at it bald headed'.

Balding Gag Bridle A large ring gag snaffle; size and weight of rings prevent gag effect coming into play till considerable pressure is used. Perfected by the late William Balding of Rugby (well-known Polo Player).

Balding Girth A cleverly constituted, non-gall girth. The girth is split into three and plaited, thus giving maximum room for horse's arms. Perfected by the late William Balding of Rugby.

Balding Girth

Balearic An ancient and very distinctive type of horse found on the Island of Majorca in the Balearic group, and most abundant in Palma district. Differs from all other breeds in its slender limbs, free graceful carriage, short, thick, arched neck, delicate head, Roman nose, ears directed backwards, and thick, upright mane. Believed to be survivor of those horses depicted on ancient vases and Greek coins.

Bales Very stout, oblong lengths of timber hanging from stable roof to convert any space (possibly a loose box or barn) into stalls.

'Balios' *see* 'XANTHUS'.

Balking (or Baulking) When a horse refuses a jump or refuses to move at all (*see also* JIBBING).

Balling A hard 'caking' of an ice-like lump of snow found within the confines of the shoe when a horse is ridden in snow. *Prevention*: grease soles of feet thoroughly before the horse leaves the stable.

Balling   Administering physic in the form of a ball (*see* MEDICINE BALL).

Balling Gun   A tubular device enabling a physic ball to be given with ease and safety. There are various types, of brass, wood and leather. Also called balling iron.

Balloon Bit   A hack bit with fancy cheek, in shape of balloon; similar to well-known Globe cheek bit (*q.v.*).

Ballotade   High school air above the ground where the horse is almost parallel to the ground when at the summit of its leap. The forelegs are bent at the knees, hindlegs showing their shoes, as happens in a kick, except that the legs are not stretched as they would be in kicking.

Ball's Bridge, Dublin, Eire   Headquarters of the Royal Dublin Agricultural Society and show ground of the Dublin Horse Show.

Bampton Fair (Devonshire)   One-day annual fair held in October and dating from 1258. Noted for the sale of Exmoor ponies. Officially supported by the Exmoor Pony Society.

Banbury Bit   Revolving and sliding mouthpiece, found in both curb and Pelham bits. Encourages the horse to 'mouth' the bit and prevents his 'catching hold' of it.

Bandages   These are used on the tail for protection and to keep the hair in place (tail bandages); on the legs of sick or lame horses for warmth, to reduce heat or inflammation and as a protection against sprains (stable bandages); during fast work (exercise bandages). Various materials are used for the different purposes, e.g. flannel, cotton, stockinette. Bandages should never be put on tightly. For steeplechasing, etc., they should be placed over a thick layer of cotton wool to prevent cuts and overreaches, and sewn on in preference to attaching them by strings (*see Plate* 29).

Bang-tail   A tail with hair squared off close to dock or solid part of tail. Those connected with heavy horses refer to banging up the tail in the sense of tying it up.

Bank and Ditch   Dimensions are those in use at the Dublin Horse Show and recognized by the British Show Jumping Association: ditch (take-off side), 3 ft wide; bank, 5 ft 7 in high; platform (top of bank), 6 ft; drop, 4 ft 2 in. The bank is 45 ft in breadth.

Bank (Double) and Ditches   Dimensions are those in use at the Dublin Horse Show and recognized by the British Show Jumping Association: ditch (take-off side), 3 ft 6 in (106 cm); bank, 6 ft 4 in (193 cm) high; platform (top of bank), 7 ft (213 cm); drop, 6 ft 10 in (208 cm); ditch (landing side), 4 ft (122 cm). The bank is 45 ft (18 m) in breadth.

Double Bank and Ditches

Barb   Originated in Morocco and Algeria. Stands 14–15 h.h. (142–152 cm) and has flat shoulders, rounded chest, relatively long head, and tail set lower than an Arab, with hair of mane and tail very profuse. The breed is hardy in constitution and docile in temperament, though less spirited than the Arab and of far less refinement and quality. Owing to cross-breeding, the pure-bred Barb is hard to find.

Bard or Bardel   Covering of armour for the breast and flanks of a warhorse. Also a term occasionally used for an ornamental covering for a horse, and for a stuffed pack saddle for an ass or mule.

Bardot French term denoting off-spring of pony or horse sire and female ass (*see* HINNY, GENET).

Bardy A type more than a breed, now extinct but known at one time in the Eastern Counties (*see* LINCOLNSHIRE TROTTER, FEN TROTTER, SUFFOLK COB).

Bare-back Riding Riding without use of saddle or blanket.

Barême French term for the three tables of show-jumping faults set by the Fédération Equestre Internationale (*q.v.*). Under Table A a knockdown equals 4 faults, first refusal 3 faults and the second 6. Under Table B a knock-down equals 10 seconds. Under Table C penalties vary from 3–17 seconds according to length of the course.

Barley Normally too expensive to feed and must be fed with great care, as it is liable to cause derangement of digestion with irritation of bowels and skin. Advantageous to feed boiled and is useful for horses in bad condition.

Barlow, Francis (*c.* 1626–1702) Considered the earliest artist of the British Sporting School. He worked in London as an etcher as well as a painter of English country sports. Some of his finest pictures can be seen at Clandon Park, near Guildford.

Bar Mouth Name describing any straight mouthpiece. It can be found in either the snaffle, Pelham or curb bit but the name usually refers to a stallion bit.

Bar Muzzle Two bars laid over the open end of the muzzle allow the horse to drink but make bed-eating, crib-biting, rug-tearing, etc., impossible.

Barnum A schooling device named after the American circus owner, it is similar to a bridle used by the horse trainer, Jesse Beary. It consists of a leather head strap sewn to the offside

ring of a rubber snaffle and a cord so arranged as to pull the bit upwards and tighten on the head should the horse resist or attempt to break away from the trainer. It can also be used as a form of twitch.

'Bar One' (or any number) A racing expression indicating a wager offered or accepted on any runner except the selected one or more.

Barnet Fair (Hertfordshire) Annual fair for horses, ponies and cattle held by Charter granted in 1199 by King John to the Abbot of St. Albans. Well-known market for small tradesmen's and costermongers' horses and ponies.

Barouche Large open carriage of family capacity with a high box-seat. Used from Regency to early Victorian times with four horses or a pair.

Barouche-Sociable *see* VIS-À-VIS.

Barra Pony The Highland breed of pony indigenous to the Outer Hebrides islands.

Barrage *see* JUMP-OFF.

Barraud, Henry (1811–1874) **and William** (1810–1850) Two brothers who painted individually and also collaborated in sporting pictures. Well-known work is splendid portrait of 'Charles Davis, Huntsman to Queen Victoria's Buckhounds on his Grey Hunter, Hermit'.

Barrel Body of the horse, extending from behind forearms to loins.

Barrel-racing A form of horse-racing which is practised in Australia and the U.S.A. where competitors pass between and around barrels. Both countries have their own associations which issue governing rules and conditions of entry (*see* Plate 5).

Barrenness Incapacity to conceive and produce a foal. Sometimes develops after a pregnancy with tearing of the perineum resulting in an intake of air into the vagina. This is repaired by

Caslick's operation, usually with success. A number of bacterial organisms may be involved in outbreaks of barrenness in studs and these require identification by the laboratory examination of swabs. Some of these can be transmitted by service. Stallions may stock certain mares, in the absence of disease, and prove infertile with others.

Bars   To which the leaders' traces are attached; the main bar is hung on the pole hook and two swing bars hang from the main one. The pole hook is called the 'swan-neck' and is also known as Stradstick, Swingletrees, Whippletrees and Badikins.

Bar-shoe   Suitable for a diseased hoof. Made as an ordinary flat shoe with somewhat longer piece of iron. The ends of the branches are bent inward, bevelled, laid one over the other and welded together to form the bar. The design is valuable because it protects from pressure weak heels affected with corns, which are relieved of weight-carrying by the bar transferring weight to the frog. Mostly used on draught horses and often with hunters (*see Plate* 12).

Bar Shoe, Three-quarter   Suitable for bad corn inside heel. Bar on frog with inside branch of shoe terminating at quarter.

Bars of Bits   The cheek-pieces on arms of all forms of curb-bits.

Bars of Foot   Partial outer surround to frog. Inflection or turning in of wall at heels.

Bars of Mouth   Space between tushes and molar teeth on which the bit lies in the mouth. That portion of the lower jaw where the gums are devoid of teeth.

Bars of a Saddle   Metal strips under the skirts of a saddle to which stirrup leathers are attached.

Bascule   The act of a horse clearing the summit of an obstacle by dropping his head and neck, which acts as a balance, and folding his front legs up. Derived from the French *basculer*, to see-saw.

Bashkirsky   Russian horse of two types—mountain and steppe—bred in southern foothills of Urals, used for riding. The mares are famous for their milk used in making koumiss (*q.v.*).

Basket Saddle   A saddle for a very small child which is fitted with a basket, attached to a pad, in which the child can be carried in safety.

Bass Brooms   Stable brooms; made of South African Bahia.

Basse-école   The phase preparatory to haute-école (*q.v.*), during which the horse is exercised on one and two tracks with a view to developing its natural paces which must attain perfect regularity.

Bastard Strangles   A condition which arises should the swollen glands typical of strangles (*q.v.*) burst and the infection penetrate and be carried into the blood stream, when abscesses may eventually form in the lungs, liver, spleen, kidneys or brain, in which case death may follow.

Basterna   A Roman horse litter with poles attached to a horse in front and behind, as in a form of sedan chair.

Basuto   Famous and hardy breed of South African pony, though not indigenous to the country, being descended from four Arab and Barb horses imported from Java to the Cape by the Dutch East London Co. in 1653. Became founders of Cape horse, direct ancestor of Basuto pony. Importation of Arabs, Barbs and Persians continued until 1811, when English Thoroughbreds were introduced of the very best lines. The pony was much bred and respected up to time of Boer War, since when it has declined in number and deteriorated, owing to lack of interest. Possessed of great powers of endurance and can carry

13–14 stone (182–196 lb; 83–89 kg) for 60–80 miles (95–130 km) a day.

Bat   Familiar name for stick carried for riding.

Batak (or Deli)   Pony bred in Batak Hills of Sumatra and exported from Singapore in large numbers. Handsome, high-bred looking heads and high crested necks. Differ strongly from Mongolian and Yarkandi ponies which are ewe-necked, this difference being due to a heavy infusion of Arab blood. Average height about 11.3 h.h. (115 cm) or slightly larger, brown the predominating colour. A stouter built pony (Gayoe) with shorter, thicker legs and heavier hind quarters is found in Gayoe Hills at northern end of island.

Bath and West and Southern Counties Society (Founded 1777)   Holds annual four-day show, with many classes for horses, carries out and subsidizes much agricultural research. Permanent show ground now at Shepton Mallet, Somerset.

Batys   A word used by Irish tinkers (gypsies) when referring to piebalds or skewbalds.

Baucher, François (1796–1873)   Famous French horseman and instructor. Author of *Principles of Equitation*. Has had great influence on modern riding.

Baucher's Snaffle   see FILLIS BRIDOON.

Baulking   see BALKING.

Bausonned   (Archaic Northern and Scottish term of French derivation.) Having any large white marking not amounting to piebald or skewbald. Stockings (*q.v.*) but not socks (*q.v.*), a white face, or a big blaze (*q.v.*) and snip (*q.v.*), not just a star (*q.v.*).

Bay   Essentially angry or baffled cry of hound.

Bay   see BROW, BAY AND TRAY.

Bay (to be or stand at)   Where a hunted stag or boar turns and faces and challenges hounds.

Bayard   The battle charger of Renaud, eldest of the four famous sons of Aymon, Duke of Dordon, who lived in France in the time of the Emperor Charlemagne (A.D. 742–814). The horse was of phenomenal strength and extraordinary intelligence and figured in many mediaeval songs and stories. Another Bayard belonged to Fitzjames in Sir Walter Scott's *The Lady of the Lake*.

Bay-brown Colour   Where predominating colour is brown with bay muzzle, black limbs, mane and tail.

Bay Colour   Bay varies considerably in shade from dull red approaching brown, to a yellowish colour approaching chestnut, but can be distinguished from the chestnut by the fact that the bay has a black mane and tail and almost invariably has black on the limbs.

Bayo   Criollo (*q.v.*) term to describe cream colour in horses.

Beagles   Small hounds used for hunting hares on foot.

Beam   Dimension of main antler of stag, i.e. heavy beam or light beam.

Beaning   Coper's trick. When an animal was lame on one front foot, a small piece of metal or sharp stone was placed in between shoe and wall of sound hoof in order to cause temporary pain, so that, being tender in both front feet, the horse appeared to go sound.

Beans   Heating food, but excellent for animals in hard work, as they contain much nutritive and stimulant matter. Should be at least one year old, hard, full and sweet and fed cracked. Daily allowance in addition to other forage should not exceed 4 lb (1.8 kg). To counteract over-heating use equal parts with maize.

Beans   The black centres of incisor teeth.

Bearing   The surface of the shoe in contact with the foot.

Bearing Rein   Rein from pad to bridle, used when necessary to stop horse lowering the head beyond a certain point. Much used at one time to induce and retain high head carriage in harness horse.

Bearing Rein (Full)   Gag-like rein for supporting head of harness horse. Unlike bearing rein (simple), it runs from billet stitched to 'head' and is then passed through swivel on bridoon bit, from which it is taken through another swivel to terret (q.v.).

Bearskin-cape   A cape worn by coachmen of the best class private 'town' vehicles in cold weather.

Beast   Name applied to horse by some people, but not by horsemen except to an animal justifying the opprobrious term.

Beaufort, Henry Hugh Arthur Fitzroy Somerset, 10th Duke of (born 1900)   Master of the Horse to King George VI and Queen Elizabeth II. The Beaufort Hunt is a family pack which has never been out of the possession of a member of the family since its foundation and the present Duke is the Master.

Beaulieu Road Sales   Near Lyndhurst, New Forest, where periodical sales of New Forest Ponies take place under the auspices of The New Forest Pony and Cattle Breeding Society.

Beberbeck Stud   Originated from region of same name in N.W. Germany, famed for excellent natural conditions for breeding horses. Stud of that name existed for 100 years before First World War, but was subsequently bought by Polish Government. Local mares were crossed with Arabs and later Thoroughbred horses were used. Somewhat like a heavier type of Thoroughbred they proved very useful cavalry horses. Of good conformation,

deep girth and with much bone, they stand over 16 h.h. (162 cm), and make good light cart horses.

Becher, Captain Martin William (1797–1864)   Served abroad for three years with the army of occupation after the Napoleonic Wars. Made his first appearance in cap and jacket in 1823 and was one of the greatest steeplechase riders of his day. In the third Grand National at Aintree in 1839, Becher rode 'Conrad'. At the fence with double rails and large ditch dammed on the far side, the horse hit the rails and the captain went over its head. The brook is called 'Becher's' to this day.

Beckford, Peter (1740–1811)   Eminent sportsman and Master of Foxhounds. Described minutely and accurately the whole system of the sport of hunting, in scholarly style in *Thoughts on Hunting*, published in 1781. 'Never', wrote Sir Egerton Brydges, 'had fox, nor hare the honour of being chased to death by so accomplished a hunter, nor a huntsmen's dinner graced by such urbanity and wit. He would bag a fox in Greek, find a hare in Latin, inspect his kennels in Italian and direct the economy of his stables in exquisite French.' His writings on hunting are recognized today as classics for all time.

'Bedded Down'   Implies that the horse's bed is 'set' and comfortable for the night.

Bedding   May consist of wheat straw, sawdust, chips, peat-moss litter or dried bracken.

Bedding-eating   A pernicious and to some extent harmful habit acquired by some horses. A vice. The use of a muzzle (q.v.) at non-feeding times is suggested.

Bedford Cord   Very hard-wearing material used for breeches. The rounded cord effect is produced in the weave with sunken lines which run lengthwise. For exceptionally hard wear, cotton thread is introduced into the warp.

Bedford Cords, however, are made in all wool, all worsted and all cotton, or a combination of any of them. Originally made in Bedford. Now being superseded by man-made fibres.

Beetewk   Original breed of heavy Russian horse bred on banks of Beetewk river, where Peter the Great put Dutch stallions to local mares, the progeny being put to Orlov Trotting Stallions (*q.v.*). Have great strength and will pull over three tons. Having good action, high spirits, great obedience and docility, they make valuable agricultural horses.

Behind the Bit   The horse is behind the bit when, refusing to keep the contact with it, it draws the lower head towards the chest and thus evades its action (*see* OVERBENT). It is the consequence of a lack of impulsion and a bad hand.

Bell Boots   Another name for overreach boots (*q.v.*).

Belgian Heavy Draught (also known as Brabançon and Flemish) A horse of great weight and traction power, standing 16–17 h.h. (163–173 cm), originating in low-lying country in Belgium where there is fertile soil and succulent herbage. This heavy horse has a good temperament, a strong constitution and is a willing worker. It has often been exported to England where it is claimed to have had a certain influence on the Shire. It was also bred in the Gorki Province of Russia.

'Belling'   Weird and somewhat terrifying note uttered by stag in mating season.

Bell-Mare   Usually a steady and reliable old mare, who has a bell hung round her neck, thus causing her to act as a signal and guide to other horses in a herd to follow her.

Bellyband (Harness)   In single harness, usually one long piece of double sewn leather forming bellyband and

backband, sliding through pad or saddle. In double harness, is attached to pad.

Belmont Stakes   This is the senior of the three American Classic Races (*q.v.*), having been launched in 1867 at Jerome Park, which is no longer in use. It was run at Morris Park from 1890 until Belmont Park opened in 1905. It has been run at various distances: $1\frac{5}{8}$ miles (2.6 km) from 1867 to 1873; $1\frac{1}{2}$ miles (2.4 km) from 1874 to 1889; $1\frac{1}{4}$ miles (2.01 km) from 1890 to 1892; $1\frac{1}{8}$ miles (1.8 km) from 1893 to 1894; $1\frac{1}{4}$ miles (2.01 km) in 1895; $1\frac{3}{8}$ miles (2.2 km) from 1896 to 1903, $1\frac{1}{4}$ miles (2.01 km) from 1904 to 1905; $1\frac{3}{8}$ miles (2.2 km) from 1906 to 1925; and the present $1\frac{1}{2}$-mile (2.4 km) route was established in 1926. The race was not renewed in 1911 and 1912, when New York racing was closed by anti-gambling legislation. The race is conditioned for three-year-olds—geldings were excluded until 1957—and is held early in June. For results *see page* 386.

Belvoir Tan   Fox-hound of dark rich mahogany and black with no white unless in the form of a collar. Derived from 'Senator', a hound whose head adorns a wall in Belvoir Castle, and is a foxhound colour consisting of rich black-tan with no white above the legs.

Benches   Kennel term for broad wooden shelf or platform on which hounds sleep.

Bending Tackle   Form of breaking tackle specifically used for altering 'carriage' of horse. Best known is called Gooch Set; perfected by the late J. Walker, M.R.C.V.S. Tension is from horse's hind quarters and a device incorporating the use of Jodhpur curb (*q.v.*), is used to raise horse's head to prevent over-bridling. A Wilson bit (*see* WILSON SNAFFLE) in a special bridle is always used with this tackle so that pressure is brought on to the nose and not the mouth.

Benjamin   A coat consisting of as many as six capes, often with big pearl buttons, worn by coachmen. It had a double layer of cloth extending the full length of the outside of the sleeves for extra warmth.

Bennett, Geoffrey D. S. (1884–1953) Best known authority on Hackney Horses and Ponies of his time, having been a lifelong student of the breed; possessed of an expert knowledge of pedigrees, he wrote *Famous Harness Horses* which is regarded as the most important contribution on the subject.

Bentinck Benevolent Fund   Lord George Bentinck was largely instrumental in an objection to 'Running Rein', in the Derby of 1844. In appreciation of his services a public subscription was started and £2100 was collected, but he refused to accept anything. So in 1847 it was decided that the amount subscribed should be applied to form the nucleus of a charitable fund. Beneficiaries are licensed flat-race trainers and jockeys in necessitous circumstances, and their dependants. Administered by Weatherbys (*q.v.*).

Bentinck Bit   A ported curb mouth with additional gated port attached.

Berenger, Richard (d. 1782) Author of *The History and Art of Horsemanship*, London, 1771.

Beresford Trust   Founded in 1902 by Mr William Whitney of New York in memory of Lord William Beresford. To create the fund, Mr Whitney gave investments and securities the equivalent of the Derby Stakes won by his horse 'Volodyovski' in 1901. Beneficiaries are unlicensed stable and stud employees, or their dependants, who are no longer able to work through old age or ill-health. Administered by Weatherbys (*q.v.*).

Berkley Bit   A Pelham with rings attached to existing top ring, similar to Rugby Pelham bit (*q.v.*), usually Mullen mouth (*q.v.*).

Best Trained Horse Class   A competition for highly trained horses, according to requirements laid down by Fédération Equestre Internationale (*q.v.*).

Betting   In connection with horse-racing is of two kinds: 'Post' when wagering does not begin until numbers of runners are hoisted on board; and 'Ante-post', when wagering opens any time before the event.

Betting Shop   Prior to the Betting, Gaming and Lotteries Act of 1963 all off-course cash betting in Britain was illegal. This Act legalized cash betting in licensed betting shops, of which there are about 15,000 in Britain.

Bhutan   A pony bred in parts of Nepal and other Himalayan regions from Punjab to Darjeeling. It has much the same characteristics as the Spiti (*q.v.*) though is slightly bigger, averaging 13.3 h.h. (135 cm). Predominant colours are grey and iron-grey.

Bianconi Car   A public passenger vehicle of large capacity, used in place of stage coaches in Ireland before the advent of railways. Sideways seating provided as in Jaunting car (*q.v.*), but on four wheels and drawn by a team or unicorn. Introduced and popularized by an Italian who gave it his name.

Bib   A stout leather protection strapped beneath the stable headcollar to prevent a horse from biting its clothing.

Bib Martingale   *see* MARTINGALE, BIB.

Bicorne   Two-cornered hat of Napoleonic origin. Now worn by the riders of the Imperial Spanish Riding School of Vienna (*q.v.*).

Bidet   A term used during the 18th century for a small saddle horse hired out for riding.

Biggest Horse   The world record for height is held by a Percheron (*q.v.*) gelding 'Dr. Le Gear', standing 21 h.h.

(213 cm), which died in St. Louis, Missouri, U.S.A. in 1919. The heaviest horse is recorded as 'Brooklyn Supreme', a Belgian stallion weighing 3200 lb (1451 kg), which died in Callendar, Iowa, U.S.A. aged 20 in 1948.

Big Head (Osteoporosis) A swelling of the bones of the face, which increases size of lower part of head. The bones become porous and brittle, general weakness supervenes, and is often accompanied by lameness. Bad pasture is usually believed to be the cause of this disease, which can terminate fatally. *Treatment :* isolate, administer mild dose of opening physic such as linseed oil. Keep on mashes and green food, into which one dram of sulphate of iron has been mixed. Give salt lick.

Bigourdan *see* TARBENIAN.

'Bike' Hunting pronunciation of 'back'—'Tally-ho bike' means 'back'.

Bike (U.S.A.) The two-wheeled, pneumatic-tyred, steel-spoked sulky (*q.v.*) used for trotting and pacing races for Standardbreds or racing ponies, or Roadster Classes at shows.

Bilgoraj *see* KONIK

Billesdon Coplow Run Took place in 1800, when Hugo Meynell hunted the Quorn. Finding in covert from which the run took its name, it lasted 2 hours 15 minutes. Distance 28 miles (45 km).

Billet A term for buckle and strap attachment on a bridle.

Billet The excreta of a fox.

Binder A hunting term given to the top horizontal branch of cut and laid fence (*q.v.*).

Biped The combination of two limbs; there are six bipeds—*fore biped :* the two forelegs; *hind biped :* the two hindlegs; *near lateral biped :* near fore and hind; *off lateral biped :* off fore and hind; *near diagonal biped :* near fore

and off hind; *off diagonal biped :* off fore and near hind.

'Bird-eyed' An expression, now little used, denoting a horse whose manners may in other respects be impeccable, but which shies, usually violently, at imaginary objects in hedges.

Bishoping Filing or otherwise altering the exterior or cups of a horse's teeth to give a false indication of age. Where black marks have disappeared with age, they can be reproduced artificially by burning with a hot iron.

Bit, Action of *see* REIN AIDS.

Bit Connectors *see* BIT-STRAPS.

Bit Covers Tubular rubber which covers and enlarges mouth of any bit.

'Bite' Coaching term for wet whip-thong being caught up.

Biting A horse given to biting humans, clothing and other horses is a source of vexation and danger to its owner. Nothing is so effective as a muzzle.

Bitiug Carthorse *see* VORONEZH HARNESS HORSE.

Bitless Bridle *see* HACKAMORE

Bits The word covers all the varieties used in riding and driving. The snaffle, Pelham (*q.v.*) and Weymouth (*q.v.*) are used on the riding horse. Driving bits are usually of the curb type, such as the Liverpool (*q.v.*), the cheek of which permits placing of the rein in one of three levels. Buxton bits (*q.v.*) are still used in dress vehicles and sometimes in coaching. Snaffles are rarely used except in cases of very light-mouthed horses, when a Wilson ring (*see* WILSON SNAFFLE) is the most common. (*See also* BRIDLES, SADDLES AND LEATHER, *page* 44, *and Plate* 6).

Bit Shields Originally oval leather 'safes', fitted round the mouthpiece of the bit and lying against the face, to prevent chafing of the corners of the lips. Now made as circles of latex rubber which can be stretched over the bit ring. Rubber is softer and more satisfactory.

Bit-straps   Small straps used to connect a bit to the squares of a head collar. Oval spring hooks are also used for this purpose and are known as bit connectors.

Bitted   *see* EARS, IDENTIFICATION MARKS.

Black Colour   Where black pigment is general throughout body, coat, limbs, mane and tail, with no pattern factor present other than white markings.

Black and Tans   Colloquial name for the well-known Irish Scarteen foxhounds, also known locally as 'Kerry Beagles'.

'Black Beauty'   Published in 1877, it was written by Miss Anna Sewell (1820–1875), the daughter of a Quaker grocer in Yarmouth. It is perhaps the best known and best loved work of fiction on the life of a horse.

'Black Bess'   The high-quality mare of Dick Turpin, the highwayman (*q.v.*). The famous ride from London to York on 'Black Bess' is only legendary and made famous by Harrison Ainsworth's vivid account in his novel *Rookwood*.

Black-brown Colour   Where predominating colour is black, with muzzle, and sometimes flanks, brown or tan.

Blacking Liquid and Paste   Only used on leather finished on flesh side. Surface grease must be 'killed' with an acid such as vinegar and a black 'filler' containing ingredients such as carbon and dextrose. Application of bone anneals fibres of leather, removes scratches and gives a surface finish similar to patent leather (*see* BONING).

Black Marks   The term used to describe small areas of black hairs among white or any other colour.

Black Masters   Horse funeral furnishers, who used black sterilized stallions for drawing funeral carriages.

Black Saddlers   *see* SADDLERS, BLACK.

Blacksmith   *see* FARRIER.

Blackwell Breaking Tackle   A dumb jockey made of gutta-percha, with side reins attached to two cross pieces, thus raising the height or tension. Rubberside reins are not desirable as they tend to produce an overbent position.

Blacque-Belair   (Lt-Col   Henri Louis)   (1862–*c.*1920)   Chief Instructor at the Cavalry School, Saumur, France. Author of a number of books on equitation. *Cavalry Horsemanship and Horse Training* was translated into English by J. Swire in 1920.

Blanket   *see* CLOTHING.

Blanket-marking   In which only the rump is spotted on a white or light-coloured background. One of the three group-markings required by The British Spotted Horse Society (*q.v.*) (*see also* LEOPARD-MARKING, SNOWFLAKE MARKING and APPALOOSA HORSE).

Blanket Riding   The horse is ridden with a bridle and a blanket held in position by a surcingle. Safer, more comfortable than, and preferable to, bareback riding.

Blaze   A white marking covering almost whole of forehead between the eyes and extending down front of face, involving whole width of nasal bones, usually down to the muzzle (*see Plate* 21).

'Blazers, The'   Famous fox-hound pack of County Galway, Eire, founded early in nineteenth century.

Bleeder   A horse used for laboratory work in the production of serum.

Blemish   A permanent mark left by an old injury or possibly by a disease. In show ring, probably of little detriment in a Hunter class but important in Hack, all riding and show pony classes; of no importance in any breed classes.

Blind   A hunting term indicating that the fences (hedges) are still in leaf and the ditches ill-defined—the condition existing in autumn.

Blindness Many blind horses are excellent workers in harness provided they are carefully driven. Usually pick up feet well.

'Blind of an Eye' *see* SIGHT.

Blinkers A head-covering with leather eye-shields which allow the horse to see only to his front. Blinkers are made with either full or half cups or occasionally with very large ones known as 'wide-eyes'. Used in racing on 'doggy' horses. Sometimes, probably unfairly, referred to as the 'rogue's badge' (*q.v.*).

Blinkers

Blinkers or Winkers (Harness) A blocked leather covering for eyes to confine the vision of a harness horse.

Blister A counter-irritant producing a severe form of inflammation, the effect being to draw blood to affected area, thus expediting process of repair —commonest form of blister being cantharides ointment (black blister)— 1 part cantharides with 7 parts lard; milder form 1 part biniodide of mercury with 8 parts lard. There are other good proprietary blisters.

Blood The amount of blood a horse's body contains is about one-eighteenth of its total weight, distributed roughly: heart and larger blood vessels one quarter, liver and intestines one quarter, muscles one quarter, other parts one quarter. It is carried by arteries from heart to all parts of body, and returns through veins, the heart acting as a pump. Should it happen to coagulate and form a clot instead of passing through vessels, serious trouble may occur.

Blood, to A term applied when young hounds are given their first taste of blood of their hunted fox.

Blooded A hunt ceremony when young people, on the first occasion of following hounds mounted, are blooded by the huntsman who touches each cheek with blood of the hunted fox. Origin of custom uncertain; now rarely used.

Blood-horse Name universally used to indicate the English Thoroughbred.

Bloodstock Horses bred for racing (*see* THE RACEHORSE AND RACING IN BRITAIN).

Bloodstock Breeders' Review An annual illustrated worldwide survey of the British Thoroughbred, founded by Ernest Coussell and Edward Moorhouse of the British Bloodstock Agency Ltd. of 26 Charing Cross Road, London, W.C.2 in 1912, and edited and published ever since from their London Offices.

Blood Weed Thoroughbred of low standard—often the gassy, shallow, and light-of-bone type—known to old-time dealers as 'Blood Tit'.

Blower *see* HIGH-BLOWING.

Blower, The Telephone service between Bookmakers' offices off course and Tattersalls' enclosure on course.

Blowing Away The huntsman blows hounds away on to the line of a fox which has left the covert.

Blowing Out The huntsman blows hounds out of a covert in which they have drawn blank or in which they have lost their fox.

'Blue Cap' Black-pied Cheshire foxhound, aged four, won the challenge match against Hugo Meynell's 'Richmond' and another over the Beacon Course at Newmarket in 1763, for stake of 500 guineas a side. The partner of 'Blue Cap' was his daughter 'Wanton', but the partner of 'Richmond' was unnamed. Hounds ran a drag.

Blue Eye   see WALL-EYE.

Blue Feet   A dense blue-black colouring exemplified by the feet of the Percheron (*q.v.*).

Blue Grass Country   A horse-breeding area in Kentucky, U.S.A., with Lexington as a rough centre, where is found grass so rich in lime and phosphates as to be ideal for breeding horses.

Blue Riband of the Turf   The Derby Stakes (*q.v.*).

Bluff   A bandage with leather eye sockets, put over heads of bad-tempered or excitable horses to keep them quiet.

Blunt, Wilfrid Scawen (1840–1922) Traveller and man of letters. With his wife, Lady Anne Blunt, he made several visits to the Arabian desert in the late 1870s and 1880s. They brought back to England the finest selected Arabian horses to found the Crabbet Park Arabian Stud, which passed to their daughter, the Rt. Hon. the Lady Wentworth, and which proved a vital influence in the improved breeding all over the world of the Arabian horse (*q.v.*).

Boadicea (d. A.D. 62)   Said to have been the first British Queen to maintain a racing stud. She also bred horses for export to Rome.

Boards (Polo)   In England, U.S.A. and Argentina the side lines are defined by boards. In India and the East generally boards are not used.

Bobbery Pack   An expression, believed to have originated in India, to describe a mixed pack of hounds or dogs for the purpose of hunting any available quarry. (Bobbery—a noisy row.)

Bobby-backed   see SWAY-BACKED.

Bob-tailed   A fox with no brush or only a very short one.

Bocado (South American)   A leather bit made of rawhide, usually passed through the mouth and tied under the chin.

Bodenricks   see CAVALLETTI.

Body-brush   An oval brush, made of short, closely set bristles, used for removing dust, dirt and sweat from body, neck and quarters—the hand is slipped between a band of webbing and the back of the brush when brush is in use (*see Plate* 29).

Boerperd (Farmer's Horse)   A stocky, versatile little horse of South Africa, resembling both the Morgan Horse (*q.v.*) and the Welsh Cob (*q.v.*). There are two types, one rather plain with low action, the other more refined, often Part-Saddler (*see* AMERICAN SADDLEBRED).

'Boiler, The'   The kennelman who makes the puddings and skins and boils the flesh for hounds.

Bokara   see PERSIAN HORSE.

Bolt a Fox   To force a fox out of a drain or earth.

Bolt-hole   The hole to receive the perch bolt on a coach.

Bolting   Galloping out of control. A horse that has once bolted is, for the remainder of its life, a source of danger as it is likely to repeat the offence.

Bolting Food (i.e. greedy feeder) Usually a result of decayed teeth and is the source of indigestion, which leads to other troubles. Attend to teeth and feed the horse on bruised oats and chaff. Place a brick in manger, to prevent bolting of food.

Bolts All bolts and fastenings on doors, especially those on the inside of stable, should be fixed so as not to project beyond woodwork, otherwise they are liable to injure horse and give lasting blemish.

Bona-fide Term used in Point-to-Point races signifying that a particular horse holds a certificate from the appropriate M.H. that it is a genuine hunter.

Bone A measurement of bone immediately beneath the knee or hock. 'Good bone', 'plenty of bone'. The term is applicable also to a hound.

Bone in the Ground A hunting term, describing state of ground during or following immediately after frosty weather—still hard even under a soft surface.

Bonheur, Marie Rosalie (Rosa) (1822–1899). French artist, born in Bordeaux. Her masterpiece, 'The Horse Fair', shown at the Paris Exhibition in 1855, was many times reproduced. Also celebrated for 'The Duel', illustrating the fight between the two stallions 'Hobgoblin' and 'The Godolphin Arabian' for possession of the mare 'Roxana'.

Boning After cleaning and polishing boots or shoes with liquid blacking or paste on Bordeaux calf leather, a bone (preferably shank bone of a deer) is rubbed over the surface and finally brush polished and silk or chamois leather applied, giving patent leather polish. Only used on leather finished on flesh side.

Bonnet A term applied to one who expatiates on the merits of a horse with a view to assisting owner to sell it. Most copers used to employ services of a bonnet, who was sometimes known as a Chaunter.

Book, in The Expression indicating that the horse or mare has been entered or accepted for entry in the General Stud Book (*q.v.*).

'Book, The' A colloquialism for the General Stud Book (*q.v.*).

Bookmaker One who, on or off the racecourse, will accept bets either in cash or on credit, and lay agreed odds against a horse or a greyhound winning a race, or bet on other sports. In Britain there is betting through bookmakers or the Totalisator (Pari-Mutuel), but in the U.S.A., France and the majority of other racing countries legalized betting is through the totalisator only.

Boot (of a vehicle) A built-in receptacle for luggage, etc. A coach has hind boot beneath rear seats and fore boot below box. In Royal Mail coaches hind boot was designed for mail bags.

Boot-Hooks Bone, wood or ivory handle with metal hook, for pulling on top boots.

Boot Jack A wooden contrivance of many designs to assist in removing boots from leg.

Boot Lifts A metal device made to facilitate top of high boot passing over leg of breeches.

Boots, Horse These exist in great variety and are designed either to give protection to a particular part of the leg, and/or to support. The materials used in manufacture are boxcloth, kersey (*q.v.*), leather, felt and elastic.

Boots and Shoes, Re-Soling The sole should always be carried to the length of the foot. Half-soles can catch the stirrup-iron and may prove dangerous if the rider is thrown.

Boot-tops *see* HUNTING BOOTS.

Boot Trees *see* TREES, BOOT.

Bordeaux (Waxed Calf) Vegetable-tanned leather used for all first-grade black riding boots. Only leather on which a bone should be used (*see* BONING).

Boring When a horse in action appears

to carry the full weight of the forehand on the bit. To lean heavily on the bit.

Boring (Racing)   When a horse, to improve its position, pushes another to the extent of interfering with its chances, it is said to be boring. This can be the subject of an objection.

Bosal   A rawhide noseband and rein used in the Americas for breaking purposes.

Bosnian   Native mountain pony bred in the Balkans, resembling the Hucul (*q.v.*). Arab blood has recently been introduced.

Bots   Not true worms but arise from attack by gad fly or bot fly, which lays eggs on legs of horses at grass. Legs are then licked by horse and eggs transferred to stomach where they hatch out. Not injurious except in very large quantities when they cause loss of condition and debility with dry staring coat. Few horses are entirely free. *Treatment :* starve for 24 hours, give drench of 2 tablespoonsful of turpentine and a pint (0.56 l) of linseed oil— and bots may be expelled in dung. Removal of eggs from legs of horses is best effected with blunt blade in safety razor.

Bottom   A hunting term. In the Midlands this generally denotes a fence with a big and deep, though jumpable ditch with it. In other parts it may mean a quite unjumpable ditch or brook running at the bottom of a deep gulley or ravine.

Bottom   A term denoting staying power and endurance in a horse.

Boulnois' Cab   A London hackney cab in use before the hansom. Two-wheeled; door at rear like an omnibus; driver's seat on roof in front.

Boulonnais   A heavy horse bred in Northern France during the Crusades and much improved by Arab and Barb stallions brought from the East by French Crusaders. Submitted to many changes of type and existed in immediate pre-railway days as a very strong horse with good action and stamina and used in coaches for fast transport. Today found as heavy draught, 16–17 h.h. (163–173 cm), quick growing with great bone and muscle and used for farm work at 18 months. Although name is derived from Boulogne, it is bred also in Flanders, Picardy, Artois, and Haute Normandie. Many hold that a dash of Boulonnais blood improves any heavy breed, as Arab or Thoroughbred does to most of the light breeds.

Box   *see* LOOSE BOX.

Box   Coachman's seat; beside this, to left, is the Box Seat, a privileged seat for an honoured passenger on a coach.

Boxcloth   A material similar to Melton (*q.v.*) produced in the West Country. Boxcloth has a smoother face and is suitable for liveries and extensively used for gaiters, leggings and horse boots. In earlier days the material was considered ideal for outdoor wear in the worst of weathers, especially for coach driving.

Boxing   The carriage of a horse from one place to another, by railway in a special truck, by road in a motor horse box or in a trailer drawn by a motor car.

Box-seat   *see* BOX.

Box Spurs   A type which fits into regimental, dress and other boots used for riding. The heel is fitted with a small box to receive spur fitting.

Box Spur

Boxy Foot (known also as club, donkey or mule foot). A foot with a small frog and a high heel.

Brabançon *see* BELGIAN HEAVY DRAUGHT.

Brace, The Footwork is more essential in polo, perhaps, than in any other game. This term denotes the stance from which a stroke is played. The principles of rackets apply equaliy to all polo strokes.

Brace (of foxes) A fox-hunting term indicating two foxes. One fox equals half a brace—e.g. two and a half brace equal 5 foxes.

Bradoon *see* BRIDOON.

Braids Term in the U.S.A. for plaits (*q.v.*).

Brake A large vehicle for team or pair driving. There are several types, the Waggonette Brake being the most frequent survivor; behind a high box it seats a number of people facing each other.

Brake To retard progress of vehicle. A hand lever or a foot pedal causes a block to press on the surface of the tyres on the rear wheels.

Bran Refuse of grain. A safe and useful food; about 2 lb (1 kg) a day mixed with the oat feed assists digestion; it is somewhat constipating if given dry but acts as a mild laxative when fed damp, and is valuable therefore to regulate bowels. Fed dry to a hungry horse, it may cause impaction of the oesophagus and choking. A useful treatment is to tie the horse beside a tank of cold water allowing it to drink and wash out its oesophagus as it wishes.

Branch The surface of the shoe from toe to heel on each side of the foot.

Branding Hot iron branding is the most common means of distinguishing horses belonging to different owners who turn out stock to graze on common land. Owing to the resulting dis-figurement, branding is often done under the saddle. Other methods are on the hoof and tattooing the gums. The former grows out. Recent experiments in the U.S.A. of a new freeze brand system, where hieroglyphics are branded under the mane of the horse, have met with success.

Bran Mash Scald 2 or 3 lb (1–1.3 kg) of bran in a bucket with boiling water. Stir well with stick. Cover the bucket with a sack until the mash is cool enough to feed. Correctly made, the mash should be 'wringing wet' but not sloppy. It may be made more palatable by a small addition of salt. Bran mash has valuable laxative properties.

Break A horse's action is said to break when it changes from one gait to another.

Break When a fox leaves covert it is said to 'break'.

Breaking The education of a horse to the various purposes for which it is required; the breaking of its will to man's so that it knows no other when its education is complete. The term now largely substituted for Breaking is 'Schooling'.

Breaking Cart *see* SKELETON-BREAK.

'Breaking-out' The act of profuse and unnatural sweating despite previous drying. The usual causes are strenuous exercise or unusual and excessive excitement. Horses in a weak state are most susceptible.

Breaking Tackle The complete set consists usually of a cavesson breaking head collar with metal nose part and ring and padded noseband, a bridle for later use, a roller, adjustable each side, and side reins, crupper and driving reins, and lungeing rein.

Break-up When hounds are eating the carcase of their hunted fox they are said to 'break-up' their fox.

Breastbone The sternum. A keel-shaped bone consisting of seven fused segments, each giving attachment to the lower ends of the corresponding ribs. It lies between the forelimbs, and forms the lower boundary of the thorax.

Breast Collar   In some harness, but not coaching, this broad band of leather across the breast takes the place of collar and hames.

Breast Girth   *see* AINTREE BREAST GIRTH.

Breast Piece or Breast Plate   A leather neck strap attached to the D's of the saddle by short straps, and to the girth which passes through a loop, and worn a few inches below the withers to prevent the saddle from slipping back. Useful for inexperienced riders to hold when riding uphill. Lightweight breast plates for racing are made either of very thin leather or web.

Breathing Bridoon   A straight cylindrical snaffle bit having a number of circular holes. This device is thought to be effective with windsuckers (*q.v.*).

Brecon   Agricultural   Society   Founded in 1755. Said to be the oldest Agricultural Society in Great Britain.

Breeches   The accepted form of covering for the lower limbs when riding. Breeches are worn with hunting or riding boots and leggings and high-lows

(*q.v.*); jodhpur breeches are worn with jodhpur boots. Some prefer shoes.

Breeches Ball   A cloth ball (colour according to choice) used in the cleaning of strappings on breeches which should first be scrubbed in warm, slightly soapy water, allowed to dry partially, when the ball is applied. Drying should then be completed and surplus ball brushed off.

Breeching   A broad leather band behind a horse's quarters to take the weight of the vehicle in pulling up, backing, or descending a hill.

Breeching Harness (Long)   More suitable for a four-wheeled vehicle and is adjusted by a 'square'. It is very neat, and acts as a kicking strap if correctly adjusted.

Breeching Harness (Short)   The best-known type is attached to the shaft through the shaft staples.

Breeching Proper   This comprises crupper, crupper dock, hip straps, breeching body, and breeching straps.

Breed Classes   These are always shown in hand at shows, and are open to stallions, mares, colts and fiilies. The entry of geldings is sometimes permitted as a guide to the excellence of their forebears.

Breeding   *   Henry Wynmalen

The basic principle of breeding is the fact that, when breeding from a certain sire and from a certain dam, we are in reality breeding from that dam's and from that sire's ancestry. Also that, when considering the points of any horse from the breeding angle, we will do well to remember that the better such a horse is bred, the more surely are his characteristics likely to be fixed in him, and the more likely he will be to transmit them to his descendants.

The stallion and the mare are both

equally potent in stamping upon the foal their type and make-up, and the foal will therefore be a blend of its parents' qualities and defects. But the equal potency of the parents applies oniy in so far as both are equally well-bred, for if one of the parents is better-bred than the other, then that better-bred one will be markedly prepotent. This is due, of course, to the accumulated influence of a flawless ancestry.

And that is the leading principle whereon all breed-improvement is based and without which no breed improvement would be possible. The influence of any high-class stallion upon the improvement of an inferior breed may be quite enormous, and in that respect the English Thoroughbred is extremely potent. He has been used for that very purpose with immense success the world over. In France that very good breed, *le cheval Anglo-Normand,* has been created by the free admixture of Thoroughbred blood with the original native stock of Normandy horses.

The potency of the Arab in this respect is greater still; his blood permeates that of the Thoroughbred himself, and he is the fountainhead wherefrom the best characteristics of all breeds of warm-blooded horses derive. The Arab carries, compressed as it were in his small body, the greatest possible array of equine qualities, and moreover these qualities, by centuries of pure breeding, have become so firmly fixed that his potency to infuse them into other breeds is almost beyond belief. As an illustration thereof we may refer to the Alcock Arabian, who is, as has already been mentioned on page 5, the ancestor of all grey Thoroughbreds now living, the colour having persisted in unbroken descent for 240 years.

It is well known that the Arab is much less liable to any of the many hereditary unsoundnesses that are so troublesome in other breeds, including diseases of the bone and, of course, wind. The Arab's bone is especially hard, compact and dense and any bony defects are almost unknown; the Arab's wind is always perfect, and whistlers, roarers or broken-winded Arabs are very rare. I have it on the authority of the great State Studs in Hungary, where Arab sires are used constantly for the improvement of native breeds, that one single infusion of Arab blood has often been found sufficient to outbreed prevalent types of native unsoundness of the types I have just mentioned.

But, however beneficial the use of Thoroughbred and Arab blood may be for the improvement of native breeds, and equally for the purpose of breeding individual produce from mares of less refined breeding, there is one limitation that should not be lost sight of. There must be a reasonable affinity between the breeds or types to be crossed.

Do, by all means, put a hunter mare or any type of half-bred mare, a good pony mare, a Hackney mare, a trotting mare or even a Cleveland Bay to a Thoroughbred or an Arab stallion and be confident of the results. Possibly it is not wise to be too confident about the results of crossing the really heavy horse of unknown breeding with the lighter horse, although several very useful jumpers and heavyweight hunters have been bred, and indeed are being bred, from crossing Thoroughbreds and Clydesdales; Arabs and Suffolk Punches cross quite well; Thoroughbreds and Suffolks have produced many good ones with a marked jumping ability. We have also seen many well-known show jumpers who were part heavy horse. The second generation, bred from crossing Thoroughbred with a registered heavy horse and put to a Thoroughbred again, is a splendid animal likely to be of great value to the breeder needing to get something that will carry 16 or more stone (224 lb; 102 kg).

The ancestry of the horses wherefrom we intend to breed is of great importance, therefore, because good ancestry enhances the likelihood of such horses passing on their good points. In well-bred horses good points are no 'flash in the pan', as they are sometimes in less well-bred animals. We may even go further than that, since good breeding will often outweigh minor defects in conformation; the chances are that the animal's ancestry may enable him not to pass on such defects; no such likelihood exists in the case of animals of more common breeding.

However, unless we know what our animal's ancestors have been like and how they have been able to perform, as we will do in the case of high-class racing stock, the knowledge that our animal is a well-bred one is largely a theoretical consideration, though an important one, whereby to back up our judgement.

But that judgement itself, in practical form, can be directly concerned only with the actual animals wherefrom we propose to breed. Now points that are similar in both parents are likely to be confirmed in the foal or even accentuated; so two animals with a good head are almost certain to produce a foal with a good head, and probably one with an exceedingly good one; but similarly two parents with a bad head can be relied upon to produce a bad head, and more than likely a very bad head in the foal. If one parent is poor in one particular point, there is a very reasonable chance of improving upon it in the foal, provided that the same points are particularly good in the other parent.

Now it is most satisfactory, of course, to be able to pair two parents with nothing but good points matching each other, in which case we may be pretty certain of producing a first-class foal. Unfortunately, such a combination of perfections is so rare as to be almost impossible.

The next best thing, and in practice about the only thing that we may hope to achieve, is to match our horses in such a way that the stallion be particularly good in points wherein the mare may be deficient, and vice versa. The worst thing to do is to match two horses that fail to any marked degree in an identical respect.

It follows that in order to be a successful breeder one must be also a judge of a horse, not necessarily in the sense of being able to judge horses in the show ring, but most definitely in the sense of being able to appreciate the relative importance of certain short-comings in our stock, having regard to the purpose whereto their produce will be put. A good many people are quite capable of, and often quick enough in spotting short-comings in other people's horses, whilst they appear genuinely unable to spot the weaknesses in their own animals. And that is about the most serious defect in any breeder's armour.

We must remember that no such thing as a perfect horse exists; every animal, however great his class and quality, is bound to fail to come up to the ideal in some respect or other, however slightly that may be. In fact, the failing may be so slight that it might escape many an experienced eye during a cursory examination; but it should not escape the eye of his owner, who sees his animals every day, under all sorts of conditions, in every kind of attitude, alert and sleepy, fat and thin, polished and rough, at their best and at their worst. It is up to him to study his animals constantly, carefully and above all with an unprejudiced mind; that is, open to recognize and to admit short-comings as well as qualities. It is in fact more important to recognize the former than the latter, for it is only so that we shall be able to make a wise and reasonable breeding selection.

From a breeding point of view all the leading characteristics of the sire and of the dam are hereditary, that is temperament, action, conformation, constitution, and soundness and, as a result thereof, performance.

I place temperament first, because for most purposes even the most perfect horse will be greatly marred if his temperament be unsuitable, whereas actual vice may render him almost or even entirely useless. This applies to all horses, no matter for what purpose they are intended, but it applies particularly to horses intended for some form of personal use. It does not perhaps matter quite so much in the case of racehorses, when speed is the all-predominant requirement, but even racehorses that are too temperamental are seldom reliable.

Naturally, the exact requirements that we are entitled to place upon temperament vary within very wide limits from one breed or type of horse to another. Whereas we want to see courage and grit in all types of horses, we would no doubt condemn the highly strung temperament that is normal in a horse with much blood, such as a Thoroughbred or an Arab, if it were met with in a cart-horse; we would do so because a hot cart-horse would not be very suitable for his job, which requires a placid animal. Likewise, although we cannot have true blood and quality without high, and sometimes even exuberant, courage, we do not want too hot and certainly not too gassy a temperament in a hunter, since horses so endowed are too difficult to manage, and may even be impossible in company. Manners are very important.

But no matter what type of horse we are dealing with, we are entitled to look for kindness and confidence, since these two traits will, under suitable surroundings, go a very long way in making up for excessive courage.

I place action second, because however good he may appear in other respects when standing, a horse that cannot move well and truly is but a poor specimen. If a mare is deficient in this respect she should be sent to a stallion who is himself a brilliant mover. True action is straight action, without dishing; and level, without lameness. Slight defects in straightness of action may be overlooked, provided again that the stallion is irreproachable in this respect. Lameness is of no importance when due to an accident, but is a grave defect if due to constitutional causes, such as debility or rickets, or other causes pre-disposing to unsoundness. All Premium stallions under the Hunters Improvement Society are vetted free of hereditary unsoundness, which is greatly to their advantage.

Conformation is very important, because whatever we breed, we all want good looks, for a number of reasons. Good looks, in the first place, are a pleasure in themselves, and enhance the enjoyment to be derived from our animals and the justifiable pride to be taken in them. Good looks have a very great influence on the value of a horse. Finally, good looks are more often than not the visible expression of excellence.

In judging conformation we shall never go far, in my opinion, if we divide the horse into a catalogue of points and try to assess all those individually; conformation, again in my opinion, can only be judged effectively by looking at the picture that the animal presents, both standing and in movement, and if that picture is a real eyeful of quality and balance, there is probably not a great deal wrong with him or her. I look for quality first, see the animal as he approaches me, or as I approach him, head, front and shoulders, expression and bearing. These characteristics are unmistakable.

If they don't please me, I have no interest in detailing the animal further. But if the first impression is pleasing, I will look him over in more detail and will try to take in all the good points first—breast, depth of body, loins and quarters, tail-setting, and carriage, limbs and feet. No horse is perfect, and it is therefore useless to expect one without short-comings or faults. If we look for faults first we are making a wrong mental approach, and are liable to condemn a good animal, merely because we are fault-conscious, for some short-comings that may be relatively unimportant. For the importance of most short-comings is only relative, inasmuch as it depends primarily on the precise purpose wherefore we are breeding. As an instance, the best quarters should be long, level and broad; sloping quarters in a riding horse are certainly against him as a point of conformation, and would weigh pretty heavily in the show-ring; but provided these sloping quarters are of appropriate length and broad and muscular, they will not affect the horse's performance either as a hunter or as a racehorse; in fact, it is noted that such horses are frequently outstanding jumpers. But sloping quarters that are at the same time short, render a horse unsuitable as a riding horse, although they are no detriment in a cart horse. And if in addition to being short, they are also narrow and therefore weak, they become indeed a serious fault in any type of horse.

Similarly, we all like a straight hind-leg and sickle hocks are certainly no show point; but they are no detriment to speed or performance, and many first-class Thoroughbreds have them; they need be regarded with circumspection only in cases where the hocks are also narrow and weak, as in that case they are liable to lead to trouble.

The same thing applies again to horses standing over at the knees. Though not exactly pretty it is, if the animal is born that way and the disfigurement, if it may be so called, is not due to the effects of work, a sign of strength rather than of weakness. Such horses will very seldom break down. Conversely, standing back at the knee, which is less easy to notice and far more prevalent than standing over at the knee, is a much more serious fault since it is a sign of weakness in the limb.

A horse with pin-toes, that is toes turned inwards, is never liable to strike himself and therefore pin-toes are much less serious, as a defect, than toes turned outwards which are liable to make him do so, and even to bring him down as a result.

These and similar short-comings are relative in the sense explained above, but they are relative also in the sense that most or all of them can be bred out in the foal, or at any rate vastly improved, by the judicious choice of a stallion who makes up in excellence in the very points where the mare shows deficiency.

Now a good brood mare, though bound to have some weak points, since no living creature is without any, will not have very many defects to guard against, and it will be comparatively easy to find a stallion that will compensate for her short-comings. But however excellent stallions may be, they too will be found to have their short-comings. And it follows therefrom that it will

become utterly impossible to find a stallion perfect enough to engender a first-class foal from any mare that is, as some are, a walking exhibition of defects in conformation. In other words, whilst we need not be unduly perturbed if our mare can be crabbed on one or two points, if she is otherwise a good one, yet we had better not attempt breeding from any mare that is full of faulty points.

Flat-ribbed, narrow-breasted, shallow or herring-gutted animals miss the proper room for heart and lungs and those are very serious faults, since they affect constitution as well as conformation. In a mare these faults are quite unpardonable, since they deprive her of the necessary room wherein to carry and to develop her foal. Brood mares must be wide and roomy, which means well ribbed up and broad and muscular over loins and quarters.

Colour, though not really a point of conformation, is yet one that affects a horse's looks, and is therefore not without importance. People are sometimes inclined to very strong preferences for certain colours, mostly on the ground that they are either flashy, such as chestnuts, or distinguishing, such as greys. In certain colours, mostly on the ground emerges that a stallion will get by far his best stock all of one colour. So much effect has this on buyers that colts of the 'wrong' colours will probably sell for far less than the others. On the whole, we may assume that any colour is good, provided it is clear and definite, with some depth to it, and not washy or mealy.

Constitution is the next important factor to take into consideration, since we want strong, healthy and thriving stock. As I have already pointed out, certain defects in conformation, such as narrow chests and flat-sided ribs, imply that the animal's constitution cannot be first-class, since there is insufficient heart and lung room.

Though I have left soundness to the last, it is by no means the least important consideration; in fact it may well be the most important one, because an unsound horse is no good to anyone, and because so many forms of unsoundness, or rather the tendency to contract them, are very hereditary. That does not apply, of course, to unsoundness as the result of an accident.

There are various forms of unsoundness which the prospective brood mare may have contracted after birth, such as roaring, navicular disease, sidebones, curbs, ringbone and spavin. Such forms of unsoundness cannot and will not be transmitted by her to the foal, who will not be born with any of these defects existent at birth. But what the mare quite likely may transmit is a tendency to contract such infirmities, due to weakness or malformation of certain organs or joints.

Since the question as to what unsoundness is, and what is not, hereditary is subject to some controversy, I will not attempt to give a comprehensive list. I will say only, but this with considerable emphasis, that any kind of unsoundness in a studhorse should always be viewed with considerable suspicion, and that applies to the following in particular; any kind of defective wind or eyesight, spavin, curb, or any diseases of the foot, and any bone diseases.

This article has undergone recent revision by Mrs I. M. Yeomans, whose article 'Care of the Mare and the Foal' (page 201) provides further information.

* * *

Breeder's Foaling Table.

Date of Service	Due to Foal	Date of Service	Due to Foal	Date of Service	Due to Foal	Date of Service	Due to Foal
Jan. 1	Dec. 6	Apr. 2	Mar. 7	July 2	June 6	Oct. 1	Sept. 5
8	13	9	14	9	13	8	12
15	20	16	21	16	20	15	19
22	27	23	28	23	27	22	26
29	Jan. 3	30	Apr. 4	30	July 4	29	Oct. 3
Feb. 5	10	May 7	11	Aug. 6	11	Nov. 5	10
12	17	14	18	13	18	12	17
19	24	21	25	20	25	19	24
26	31	28	May 2	27	Aug. 1	26	31
Mar. 5	Feb. 7	June 4	9	Sept. 3	8	Dec. 3	Nov. 7
12	14	11	16	10	15	10	14
19	21	18	23	17	22	17	21
26	28	25	30	24	29	24	28

Breeds of Horses   There are nearly 200 recognized breeds and types of horses and ponies in the world.

Breton   A French horse, bred on the rather poor land of Brittany and exposed to rough winter climate; has an excellent reputation, due to its hardiness and working qualities. There are three types: heavy draught 15.2–16.2 h.h. (154–164 cm), draught post 15–16 h.h. (152–162 cm), and mountain draught up to 14.3 h.h. (145 cm).

Breeze Along, to   A term for galloping in the U.S.A.

Breeze Fly   *see* HORSEFLY.

Brick Paving   The hardest and non-absorbent Stafford Blue makes the best flooring for the stable.

Bridle   A complete snaffle bridle consists of bit, one pair of reins, a pair of cheek pieces, a head piece, in which is incorporated the throatlatch, a browband and a noseband. A Pelham bridle has an additional pair of reins, the curb rein always being ⅛ in (3 mm) narrower than the bridoon. A Weymouth or double bridle in addition to an extra pair of reins has an extra head strap and cheek piece, known as a 'slip head', to which is fastened the bridoon. Bits are attached to the bridle by sewing, studs, buckles, occasionally snap billet hooks, and sometimes by a loop arrangement (*see* BRIDLES, SADDLES AND LEATHER).

Bridle, Bitless   As the name implies any bridle which is used without a bit. There are a number of varieties: Blair's Pattern Hackamore, W. S. Bitless, Scawbrig and the American bosals, etc. (*see* HACKAMORE).

Bridle, Double   A common term for the Weymouth bridle (consisting of curb and bridoon) (*see Plate* 6).

Bridle, Inventor of   *see* PELETHRONIUS.

Bridle Back   A full length of cowhide taken from the top of the back from tail to head. The extra length so obtained is useful for full length reins. Backs of heavier substance are used for body rollers, etc.

Bridle Bracket   A japanned metal or plastic covered stable fitting to carry the bridle and the end of the reins if desired.

Bridle Butt   Best bridle leather is sold in pairs of butts. A butt is cut on either side of the spine from the tail to the beginning of the shoulder. The best leather is that nearest to the spine; the lower part of the flank where the hide is coarser is not part of a butt.

Bridle Hand   The hand in which the reins are carried, generally the left hand.

Bridle Head   That part of the bridle passing over the poll, which incorporates the throatlatch and to which the cheeks are attached.

Bridle Hook   A fixture in the saddle room for cleaning or hanging bridles.

Bridlepath   *see* BRIDLEWAY

Bridles, Saddles and Leather   *   E. Hartley Edwards

The most significant trend in modern saddlery over the past 20 years has been towards a greater simplicity in construction and a notable reduction in the variety of items available. Plain economics have been responsible to a large degree, but the advance in general equestrian knowledge has also played its part. Standard present-day equipment for the young horse, for instance, is the snaffle bridle, used either with or without the drop-noseband. Strange and complicated bitting arrangements, many of them dependent upon combinations of martingales and other extraneous gadgetry that seek to *force* a desirable carriage, are rightly condemned and even the relatively harmless running martingale is not now so frequently in evidence. Safety devices, too, like 'quick-release'

stirrup bars and the once numerous patterns of ingenious safety irons are now virtually museum pieces, the modern rider preferring to put his trust in a pair of heavy, good size, stainless steel stirrup irons and a well-fitting hard hat or crash helmet.

None the less, although the variety of bits obtainable is much decreased the principal groups that assist the rider in the control and positioning of his horse remain in their simpler form. They are the *snaffle, double bridle, pelham, gag* and those bridles which employ no bit in the mouth at all, and are therefore termed *bitless*.

The basic definition of the bit, or hand aid, is that in conjunction with the other aids, i.e. the influences of the legs, back, seat and body weight, it controls the speed and direction and assists in the positioning of the head and neck.

These objectives are achieved by the bit exerting pressure upon one, or more, of seven parts of the horse's head.

The seven parts subjected to pressure are: (1) the lips or corners of the mouth; (2) the bars of the mouth; (3) the tongue; (4) the nose; (5) the curb groove; (6) the poll; (7) the roof of the mouth. This latter, most properly, is rarely used and would, in any case, require the use of a curb bit having a very high central port.

The simplest and most popular form of control is the *Snaffle* which will vary in its action according to the stage reached in the horse's training and the consequent position in which the head is carried. In the case of the young horse, whose balance is more or less on the forehand, the action of the bit is an upward one exerted against the corners of the lips. As the training progresses, however, and the weight is carried more by the quarters, the head will be raised in consequence and the action of the bit will tend to be more across the lower jaw and will include the bars of the mouth to a greater extent.

The principal division in the snaffle group is between the jointed mouthpiece and the mullen, or half-moon, mouth. The former removes pressure from the tongue but because of its 'nutcracker' action the effect upon the corners of the lips and the bars is more severe, an action that increases in intensity if the mouthpiece is twisted instead of being plain. The mullen mouthpiece, particularly when constructed of rubber, or even of nylon or vulcanite, is the mildest of all, but it involves a greater bearing on the tongue and rather less on the parts mentioned.

Of all forms of bridle the *Double,* or *Weymouth,* is the most sophisticated and, in theory, it should be reserved for the trained horse whose schooling allows it to be used to the greatest advantage.

The bridle comprises two bits, a light snaffle, or bridoon, and a curb bit fitted with a curb chain and having a central tongue port in the mouthpiece. The object of the port is to allow room for the tongue, thus ensuring a more direct bearing on the bars, which might otherwise be covered in part by that organ. The action of the curb is to effect a lowering of the head and a retraction of the nose. This is achieved when the cheeks of the curb assume an angle of approximately 45° in response to rein pressure. In this position the bit bears downwards on the bars and, through the eyes of the bit attached to the cheek pieces of the bridle, exerts additional downward pressure on the poll. The curb chain, acting on the curb groove, induces a relaxation of the lower jaw and otherwise assists the downward action. The longer the cheek of the curb, below the mouthpiece, the greater is the possible leverage. The length of cheek above the mouthpiece controls the degree of pressure on the poll in a similar fashion.

The bridoon completes the action of the bridle by allowing an upward pressure in the same way as the snaffle.

The *Pelham,* of all the bridles, is the great compromise. It seeks to achieve with one mouthpiece what the double bridle does with two.

Theoretically and possibly practically, also, this is impossible. Nonetheless it is a bridle in which many horses go very kindly, probably for the very reason that its action is so indefinite. Additionally it is a useful bit for some of the cobby-type animals, the structure of whose jaws, by reason of their short length, prohibits the fitting of a Weymouth. Conversely, the generally longer, narrower, jaw construction of the Thoroughbred, for instance, is entirely unsuited to a Pelham. In these cases if the bit is correctly fitted to cause a slight wrinkle of the lips the curb chain will be placed too high, out of the curb groove and bearing upon the unprotected jaw bones.

In the common forms of Pelham the mouthpiece is usually half-moon shaped and is frequently made of either vulcanite or its modern counterpart nylon. In this form greater pressure is placed on the tongue and less on the bars. Otherwise the bit exerts pressures in the same way as the Weymouth, but only, of course, when one rein predominates almost exclusively.

The *Gag* bridle is an accentuated form of snaffle with the cheek-pieces, running as they do through eyes in the bit rings, allowing a greater upward influence. It is always unwise to ride a horse entirely on the gag rein; an additional rein should be attached to the bit and the gag rein used only as the occasion warrants. Continuous riding on the gag induces resistance and stiffness in the head and neck, and can affect a horse's ability to extend himself.

Bitless bridles have achieved a greater popularity in recent years, particularly in Great Britain, due to increased interest in Western-style riding. There are numerous patterns but all achieve control by pressure exerted on the nose. Apart from Western riding, where a bitless bridle is an integral part of the training, many horses who are difficult to control in a conventional bridle, for reasons of a damaged mouth or otherwise, will go surprisingly well when ridden in a bridle of this type.

Although variations in construction occur, a snaffle bridle will generally consist of a headpiece, which incorporates the throatlatch, a browband, a pair of cheek-pieces, a plain cavesson or a drop-noseband and one pair of reins, which may be one of a number of patterns, i.e. rubber hand-part, laced or plaited, etc. A Pelham will have a plain cavesson noseband and an extra pair of reins, the curb rein usually being $\frac{1}{8}$ in (3 mm) narrower than the bridoon rein. The same applies to the Weymouth, only in this case there is an additional head-strap and cheek, known as a sliphead, to which is attached the bridoon.

The best-quality bridles are made from cow-hide 'butts'. A pair of butts is the portion on either side of the backbone, continuing down the flanks to the point where the leather loses its substance and quality on reaching the belly, and stretches from the tail to the withers. The shoulder is stout, cheaper to buy, but coarser in texture and its use is therefore confined to head collars, flap leather for cheaper saddles and second-grade bridlework. It is estimated that four first-class bridles can be made from that part of the butt on either side of the backbone.

In order to obtain the necessary length for the reins a 'back' of leather is used, the butt being in fact extended to include the neck. Belly leather is useful for odd jobs, etc., but is otherwise too thin for work requiring a substantial leather.

Top-class leather has plenty of 'substance' or thickness, the better to absorb and retain a fat content; the 'flesh' side (the inside) will be smooth in texture without any rough or loose fibres being visible; it will feel slightly greasy and in no way be dry, and will be firm to the touch; finally, when bent in the hand, neither side, either 'grain' (outside) or flesh, should form bubbles on the outer surface.

At the present time Havana or even Warwick shades of leather are preferred; the former being the colour of a good cigar and the latter rather darker. London colour, however, the golden yellow, is still used.

Auxiliaries Auxiliaries can be defined as items used to assist, intensify or to add to the existing action of the bit. Those in most common usage are the *Drop-noseband* and the two simple martingales, the *Running* and the *Standing*.

The drop-noseband assists the action of the snaffle by preventing the evasions of opening the mouth or of sliding the bit to one side. Since it also applies pressure to the nose, it assists in bringing the head down into a position which gives the rider the greatest amount of control. Such pressure allows a degree of flexion which might not always be possible when the snaffle is used with an ordinary noseband.

The running martingale acts on the mouth, because of its position on the rein, to prevent the head being thrown up or to correct an excessively high head carriage resulting in the horse being above the bit. If used with a Weymouth or Pelham bridle (it should not be necessary in the case of the former) the martingale should be fastened to the curb rein to accentuate the lowering action rather than on the bridoon rein, the action of which it would contradict. It is advisable to fit stops on a rein carrying a running martingale to prevent the rings sliding forward and becoming caught on either the rein fastening or over a tooth. The correct fitting of the running martingale is for the rings to be on a level with the withers. A tighter adjustment, causing the rein to form an angle between the bit and the hand, is often seen and is thought to give greater control.

A standing martingale opposes any undue raising of the head but the opposition is against the nose instead of the mouth, the martingale being attached to the rear of an ordinary cavesson noseband. A standing martingale should not be used under any circumstances in conjunction with a drop-noseband.

In national jumping competitions the use of both martingales is permitted, but under FEI rules the standing variety is banned.

The use of the standing martingale is defended on the grounds that if properly adjusted (again, in line with the wither) no restriction of the head and neck occurs, since a horse stretches the head and neck down and out when jumping and does not, or should not, throw the head upwards.

Saddles While the conventional English hunting saddle still survives and is recognizable in the design of the cheaper present-day children's saddles, it has, in general, been superseded by the modern dipped seat saddle built with forward-set supporting rolls on the panel; a design that is so much more suitable for the precision riding that is now demanded.

The advantages of the modern saddle are many. It places the rider, for instance, as nearly as possible over the moving point of balance of his horse and helps him to maintain that position in comfort and without undue physical effort. Furthermore, the rider is afforded a much closer contact with his horse, because of the design of tree and panel, than was ever possible in the older conventional patterns.

Most modern saddles used for jumping and general cross-country purposes, but not all, are built on spring-trees. In contrast to the old rigid tree, which was traditionally made of beech, the modern spring-tree is made of laminated wood bonded under pressure and formed in a mould. Two strips of tempered steel, the springs, are then laid from the head to the cantle to give a resilience to the seat which is more comfortable to both horse and rider and allows the latter closer contact through his seat bones.

Trees are generally made in three fittings, broad, medium and narrow, and providing the tree fits the horse's back the completed saddle should follow suit.

Good-quality British saddles almost always employ pigskin as a covering for the seat, a material which because it is thin and elastic is ideally suited for this purpose. The pigskin is put on the prepared tree in damp condition, enabling it to be stretched tightly, so that on drying a neat, tight seat is produced. In other European countries, however, calf skin is frequently used, but this cannot be regarded as being so durable as pigskin.

The flaps of saddles and the skirts are made invariably from cow-hide embossed with a grain to match the characteristic bristle marks of the pigskin. Because of its light substance, pigskin would be unsuitable for flaps, although for that reason it is ideal for the very light racing saddles weighing from 8 oz to 2½ lb (227–1134 g).

While the spring-tree, forward-cut saddle is used for a wide range of activities it is not suitable for the specialized pursuits of racing, showing or dressage. The British show saddle has a flatter seat, to present an uninterrupted line of the back, and is made almost straight in the cut of the flap in an endeavour to emphasize a horse's front. Dressage saddles are even more highly specialized and, while being almost as straight as a show saddle in front, to allow for the longer length of leather required, have a deep, centrally positioning seat and a panel which gives a degree of support to knee and thigh.

The panels of saddles, that is the cushion between the tree and the horse's back, are traditionally stuffed with wool, being covered with either leather, serge, or serge covered with linen. Leather coverings, however, are now in more general use than the other two, but cheaper saddles often have a serge covering to the panel. In show saddles the panel is often made of shaped felt covered with leather which permits the saddle to lie very close to the back; this type of panel is often referred to as a 'skeleton' panel.

A fairly recent innovation, contributing materially to the light weight of the saddle, is the use of firm plastic foam as a panel filling.

Because of the increased popularity of riding and driving, the number of retail saddlery establishments is probably increasing, although many are a far cry from the old saddler's shop. Not a few shops are, in reality, riding boutiques selling clothes and fancy gifts as well as saddles and bridles. Such shops, and indeed the greater part of the British retail trade, obtain their supplies from the midlands town of Walsall, which for centuries has been a centre for saddlery, harness making, bridle furniture (buckles etc.) and bits. Walsall, as well as supplying the home trade, enjoys a buoyant export market, particularly in America, and continues to uphold Britain's position as the world's leading riding equipment manufacturing town (see Plates 6 and 27).

* * *

Bridle-trail see TRAIL-RIDE.

Bridleway or Bridlepath A highway over which the public have a right of way on foot and on horseback or leading a horse.

Bridle-wise see INDIRECT REIN.

Bridoon The name given to the small snaffle bit used in Double or Weymouth Bridles. *Varieties:* plain, twisted, ring in centre, egg-butt and turn-cheek. Known also as Bradoon.

'Brinekind' Noseband This brings circular pressure around the nose by attaching each end to curb hooks; thus when the curb rein is pulled this sometimes highly desirable pressure is brought into play. A device perfected by the late George Brine. Also known as Jobey noseband.

Brisket The lowest portion of the chest.

British Driving Society, The Founded in 1957 and affiliated to the British Horse Society to encourage and assist those interested in the driving of horses, ponies and donkeys.

British Equestrian Federation Founded in 1972 to bring together the major policy interests of common concern to the British Horse Society (q.v.) and the British Show Jumping Association (q.v.) for the benefit of both bodies. *Headquarters:* National Equestrian Centre, Stoneleigh, Warwickshire.

British Equine Veterinary Association Founded in 1961, being a society of veterinary surgeons formed to promote veterinary and allied sciences for the welfare of the horse, to provide a forum for discussion and the exchange of ideas on the management, health and diseases of the horse, to encourage research into equine problems and to cooperate with other bodies interested in these objects.

British Field Sports Society Founded 1930 to further the interests of all field sports.

British Horse Society, The Founded in 1947 by the amalgamation of the National Horse Association of Great Britain and The Institute of the Horse and Pony Club (*q.q.v.*), and is the authority and parent body of all horse and pony interests in Great Britain. *Headquarters:* National Equestrian Centre, Stoneleigh, Warwickshire.

British Jumping Derby First held annually at Hickstead (*q.v.*) in 1961 and open to international riders. For results *see page* 403.

British Palomino Society, The *see* PALOMINO.

British Racehorse, The This illustrated magazine was first published in 1949. It deals with racing and breeding and contains articles by acknowledged experts. It is produced five times a year, the last four in conjunction with the principal sales of bloodstock. The Spring Issue is largely devoted to pedigrees and pictures of the leading racehorses of the previous season.

British Show Hack and Cob Association Founded 1938 to further the interests of owners and breeders of hacks and cobs.

British Show Jumping Association Officially founded in 1925 to improve the standard of show jumping. The controlling body of show jumping in Great Britain, with over 15,000 members. *Headquarters:* National Equestrian Centre, Stoneleigh, Warwickshire.

British Show Jumping Association National Championship For results *see page* 404.

British Show Pony Society Founded in 1949, it is the controlling body for improving and regulating the showing of children's riding ponies.

British Spotted Horse *see* APPALOOSA HORSE.

British Spotted Horse Society, The Founded 1947 to promote the interests of the British Spotted Horse of riding type (*see* APPALOOSA).

Brittle Hoofs The causes are neglect of the feet, mutilation in shoeing or an hereditary disposition to grow poor horn. *Treatment:* apply red blister (1 part biniodide of mercury with 8 parts of lard mixed cold) to the coronet to stimulate growth of new horn, and dress feet daily with castor oil.

Britzchska A type of travelling carriage like the Dormeuse (*q.v.*) in which passengers could lie flat for sleeping, postillion driven, with a rumble (*q.v.*). Introduced from Germany about 1820.

Brocket A male deer at 2 years. (Also known as knobber or knobbler, terms which are now obsolete.)

Broken Coloured A colloquial term applied generally to donkeys that are piebald (*q.v.*) or skewbald (*q.v.*).

Broken-kneed Description of any horse having knees scarred by some form of injury.

Broken Wind An affection of the lungs (also called 'Heaves'), due to the rupture of air sacs, and exhibited by a short hollow characteristic cough and difficult expiration most marked at the flank; the type of breathing consists of a normal inspiration followed by a double expiratory effort; inspiration, however, is smooth and steady. The horse is fit only for light work. On some occasions benefit is derived from antihistamines and the careful administration of cortisone. Some horses do better out of doors during the summer months; others appear allergic to pollen and must be kept in. Relapses are common, even when treatment brings apparent relief.

Broken Wind, Cough due to   *see* COUGHS.

Broncho (Mustang *q.v.***)**   Western American cow pony. The name, derived from Spanish, rough and rude, originally applied to the wildest, untamable mustangs, but is now a generic term. Often shortened to 'Bronc'.

Broncho-busting   Breaking-in a mustang for riding.

Brood Mare   The name given to a mare used for breeding, and which must have a sound constitution, a good roomy middle, a set of good short legs, and should be entirely free from any hereditary disease.

Brood Mare Premium Scheme   First initiated by the Arab Horse Society in 1948, whereby Premiums at various centres are given annually to suitable mares in foal to registered Arabian or Anglo-Arabian stallions and likely to produce a good foal to the mating. Adopted by other breed societies.

Broomtail   A Western American term meaning a small horse not worth breaking. Sometimes extended to all mustangs.

Brothers and Sisters   Full brothers and sisters or own brothers and sisters: animals having the same sire and dam. Half Brothers and Sisters: animals out of the same dam but by a different sire. Three-quarters: Brothers and Sisters or Three-parts Brothers and Sisters: animals out of the same dam and having as their sires animals who were half-brothers or were by the same sire but out of a different dam.

Brougham   The most popular of closed carriages, for pair or single. The first was built for Lord Brougham about 1839.

Brougham

Brough Hiller Fair   A famous old fair held annually in Westmorland.

Brow, Bay and Tray   The side branches or tines on the antlers of a stag, called 'rights' and differentiated from points 'on top'. There are generally three points 'atop'.

Browband (also known as Front)   A leather strap attached to the bridle through loop-ends forming a semicircular fitting immediately under the horses's ears. It is used to prevent the bridle from slipping back on the neck. In harness it is usually ornamented with brass, and in road coaching with coloured leather to match the coach. For hunting the browband should be of plain leather. For racing and hack classes it is permissible to have the front covered in silk or plastic in the stable colours (*see* FLY FRONT).

Browbands, Buffed   A type of roughed leather 'front' used (and usually whitened) upon stable headcollars when horses are 'set-fair'. Also used for show headcollars.

Brown Colour   Where there is a mixture of black and brown pigment in the coat with black limbs, mane and tail.

Browne, Hablot Knight ('Phiz')   (1815–1882) Illustrator of many Victorian novels, including most of

Dickens's, Ainsworth's, Lever's and some of Surtees', Browne exemplified a talent for drawing horses in some of these books and in many independent drawings of the hunting field. Most, but not all of his sketches were in a humorous vein, and were usually signed 'Phiz'.

'Brown Jack'   Won the Queen Alexandra Stakes at Ascot six years in succession, i.e. 1929–34 (see DONOGHUE, STEVE).

Brown Saddlers   see SADDLERS, BROWN.

Brucellosis   An infection caused by ingestion of *Brucella abortus,* which causes contagious abortion in cattle. May be contracted when grazing with dairy cattle. Foals may catch the disease if fed on unsterilized cow's milk. Symptoms may be vague with slight fever and loss of condition and appetite. Symptoms may reappear after apparent recovery. The organism may become localized in the ligamentum nuchae (*q.v.*) and give rise to fistulous withers or poll evil. It also invades synovial cavities and may set up arthritis. Tendonitis has been ascribed to this infection. Diagnosis is by blood tests carried out by a veterinary surgeon. The disease may be communicated to man.

Bruce Lowe Figure System   This system was originated at the beginning of the twentieth century by an Australian of this name and is the medium of tracing descent through the mares in the General Stud Book, from which some 30 families have been enumerated. These tap-root mares were allotted numbers according to the number of times their descendants had won classic races. All these families trace their origin to one of the three Arab sires—the Byerley Turk (1689), the Darley Arabian (1704), and the Godolphin Arabian (1730) (*qq.v.*) (see THE RACEHORSE AND RACING IN GREAT BRITAIN, *page* 262).

Brumby   An Australian term. In the early days of the first settlers a certain number of their horses wandered off into the wild scrub country and they and their offspring became entirely wild and became known as Brumbies. Though some have proved to be excellent, most are considered to be of very little use—even if broken-in—owing to their wild nature. On Australian racecourses a wild and uncontrollable horse is referred to sometimes as a Brumby.

Brush   The tail of a fox.

Brush-fence   An obstacle, either natural or artificial, composed of brushwood or some other suitable hedging plant.

Brushing   When a horse in motion strikes the fore or hind leg with the opposite one inside the fetlock joints; it is usually the result of faulty conformation or action. Turning the toes out can be responsible for it in front, going too close, behind. Other causes are lack of condition, fatigue, bad riding or driving, youth, old age, rough ground or faulty shoeing.

Brushing Boots   Usually made of boxcloth, kersey (*q.v.*), leather and occasionally felt with a padded protective portion running down the inside of the boot, this being wider at the bottom to protect the joint. There are many patterns.

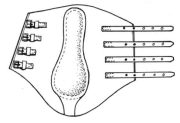

Brushing Boots

Brushing Ring   A hollow rubber ring, cut so that a thin strap can be passed through, and fitted around the leg to prevent injury.

Brush Pricker A circular piece of leather studded with bristles which is fitted round the mouthpiece of the bit, bristles inwards, to discourage a horse from hanging to one side.

Brute Term applied to the horse by some, but not by horsemen, except in the case of an animal justifying such an opprobrious term.

Bucephalus The horse of Alexander the Great; bought for thirteen talents by his father, Philip of Macedon, but no one was able to ride it or break it in except the young Alexander. It carried him through his Asian campaigns, died in India, 326 B.C., and was buried by the Jhelum River.

Buckboard General utility vehicle in U.S.A. countryside.

Bucked Shins (U.S.A.) *see* SORE SHINS.

Buckeroo One who is engaged in the breaking of broncos; the term is applied also to rodeo riders.

Buckets, Stable These are of oak or teak, grained, varnished or painted. A metal rim should be fixed round the inside, at the top of the bucket, to prevent horses chewing the wood. Buckets should never be allowed to dry out otherwise the wood slats will contract. Rubber buckets, which are lighter, less likely to cause damage and possibly more hygienic, are now used in many stables.

Buck Eye A term applied to a prominent eye. At one time the phrase referred to a small-eyed animal.

Buckhounds Hounds used for the pursuit of deer.

Buckhounds, Royal Originally established about 1154 in the reign of Henry II, and reached a peak of popularity under George III when, soon after his accession, Parliament granted

£5000 a year towards their upkeep. Finally disbanded by Queen Victoria.

Buckjumping (Bucking, U.S.A.) The action of a horse in trying to unseat its rider by arching its back like a spring and jumping into the air with all four legs at once, the whole done in one violent movement and repeated with rapidity. Not to be confused with pig-jumping (leaping and kicking). The term is of American origin but the word used there is always bucking. True buckjumpers are generally only found among the ranch horses of America and Australia, but most fresh horses on a cold morning or when over excited or under-worked will occasionally buck.

Buckjumping

Buck Knee Also known as 'Calf-knee' (*q.v.*) or 'Back-at-the-Knee'.

Buckskin An American farmers' term used in the West for the colour a shade darker than cream (*q.v.*). The accepted term in showing is dun.

Budyonovsky Horses of Russian breeding from the Rostov region. They descend from the crossing of Don horses (*q.v.*) with Thoroughbred saddle breeds. They combine speed with great endurance. Average height is about 16.1 h.h. (163 cm) (*see Plate* 4).

Buffalo Bill *see* CODY, WILLIAM FREDERICK.

Buggy In England, a two-wheeled gig-like vehicle; abroad, various four-wheeled traps are called buggies.

Bull A horse which grunts when tested for wind soundness by feinting a blow across the ribs (*see* GRUNTING).

Bulldogging A competition in rodeos in which a cowboy, after chasing a steer, jumps from his horse and throws the steer to the ground by grasping the horns and twisting its head.

Bullfinch (Hunting) A thick high fence which cannot be jumped over, but must be scrambled or pushed through.

Bullfinch (Horse Trials type)

Bulnois Cab A two-wheeled London hackney cab which preceded the Hansom cab (*q.v.*).

Bumper Race An amateur's race.

Bumping A jockey is guilty of bumping in a race when he collides, deliberately or otherwise, with a competitor in such a way as to interfere adversely with the latter's chances in the race.

Bunbury, Sir Charles (1740–1821) Noted racing character of his day and a close friend of the Duke of York. With his horse, 'Diomed', he won the first Derby in 1780. Exercised a great influence on racing (*see* DERBY STAKES).

Bunbury Mile The straight mile on the Newmarket July course, which is used during the summer months at Newmarket, while the Newmarket Rowley Mile course is used in the spring and autumn. The courses are separated by The Ditch. The Bunbury Mile is named after Sir Charles Bunbury, a leading member of the Jockey Club in the 1780s.

Bung Tail A docked tail (*see* DOCKING).

Burford Saddle *see* MOROCCO SADDLE.

Burghley Horse Trials For results *see page* 380.

Burmese (or Shan) Ponies bred by the hill-tribes of the Shan States and believed to be closely related to the Mongolian ponies, though modified by foreign blood. They are strong, though somewhat slow in movement. A still smaller pony, closely allied to the Manipur, is much faster and is used for polo, of which game Manipur is one of the original homes (*see* MANIPUR).

Burnisher A device for cleaning and polishing steel bits, stirrup irons and other articles of steel, and consisting of a small square of close, interlinked steel chains having a background or base of leather. Now seldom used as the items mentioned are made in stainless steel or other non-rust metals.

Burro (Spanish) A donkey.

Bursae Blind sacs, containing fluid and acting as pads. Through irritation, strain, overwork, etc., these are liable to become distended and somewhat solidified. Examples: windgall, capped elbow, capped hock.

Burst The first part of a run when hounds get away close to their fox. Hence: to burst him, i.e. to kill a fox in the burst.

Bush Fence (British Show Jumping Assn.) Made of gorse or birch, with a horizontal rail placed on landing side 9 in (23 cm) below the top and 1 ft (30 cm) away from the centre of the Bush fence on the landing side.

'Butcher' A rider with excessively heavy and rough hands, also termed 'Mutton-fisted'.

Butcher-boots Plain black high boots without tops.

Butterflies Short distance public coaches.

Butterfly Snaffle *see* SPRING MOUTH.

Buttock That part of the horse which lies at the back of the thighs; the point of the buttock projects a few inches below the root of the tail.

Buttress The angle formed by the inflexion of the wall to form the bar of the horse's foot. What is known as 'buttress foot' is caused by the fracturing of the pyramidal process of the pedal bone, which sometimes occurs in a low ringbone.

Buxton Bit This bit is characterized by a long bent cheek. Principally used for driving, there were many variations. There were a few used for riding.

Buzkashi (From *buz*—a goat, *kashidan* —to pull.) A rudimentary form of Rugby football on horseback. Its origin appears to be unknown, but it survives today in Central Asia where it may well have originated; it is to be seen from time to time in the neighbourhood of Kabul, the capital of Afghanistan. It is played by teams, each of which may exceed twenty-five in number, and several teams may play at the same time. The riders carry a whip with a short wooden handle with which they may hit an opponent but not his pony. The ground is unlimited in size, and rocks and precipitous hills are looked upon with favour. Two single goalposts lie about ½ mile (0.8 km) distant from each other; round each is drawn a circle of about 50 yd (46 m) in diameter. The 'ball' is a stuffed goatskin, and the object of the game is to pick it off the ground without dismounting, tuck it under the knee, gallop round the far goal-post and back to the circle. The game starts with the 'ball' thrown into a 'scrum' as in Rugby. Umpires decide which is the winning side. In Turkestan the game is known as Baiga, and is played regularly at Samarkand and generally in High Asia; it is sometimes called 'Dragging the Goat'.

Bye-day An extra hunting day which has not been advertised on the appointment card.

Byerley Turk The first of the three stallions considered as the founders of the Thoroughbred. Imported by Captain Robert Byerley in 1689, having been captured from the Turks at the Siege of Buda, and ridden by him at the Battle of the Boyne. This stallion established the Herod line, one of the most important in the breeding of the Thoroughbred Racehorse (*see* BRUCE LOWE FIGURE SYSTEM, THE ARABIAN HORSE, EVOLUTION OF THE HORSE, THE RACEHORSE AND RACING IN GREAT BRITAIN *and* THE ENGLISH THOROUGHBRED).

C. Colt.

C.A. Concours d'Attelage (*q.v.*).

C.C.I. Concours Complet International.

C.C.I.O. Concours Complet International Officiel.

C.D.I. Concours de Dressage International.

C.D.I.O. Concours de Dressage International Officiel.

ch. Chestnut.

C.H. Concours Hippique (*q.v.*).

C.H.I. Concours Hippique International.

C.H.I.O. Concours Hippique International Officiel.

C.S. Concours de Saut (*q.v.*).

C.S.I. Concours de Sauts d'Obstacles International. Officially replaces C.H.I. (*q.v.*).

C.S.I.O. Concours de Sauts d'Obstacles International Officiel. Officially replaces C.H.I.O. (*q.v.*).

Cab Originally an abbreviation of Cabriolet (*q.v.*) (*see* HACKNEY CARRIAGE).

Caballo (Spanish) A horse.

Cabriolet High, single horse, two-wheeled, hooded vehicle for two, with rear platform for the 'tiger' (midget groom) to stand on. Fashionable in early Victorian era. In 1823 David Davies, Coachbuilder of Albany, put the first licensed cabriolets on the streets.

Cacolets Iron-framed, adjustable chairs used in army transport for carrying sick and wounded. They are carried on either side of the horse.

'Cad' A slang term for conductors of London's early horse buses. They were not noted for good manners. Also the name given in posting days to men working in stable yards which supplied the post-horses. Their work was to look after the horses, wash the post-chaises, call the post-boys at night, light the lamps and when short of a rider, to ride a stage. This name was also given to the footman of a stage-coach whose main job was to apply the brake.

Caddis A worsted ribbon used by carters for binding horses' manes.

Cade A foal brought up by hand.

Cadence Dressage term referring to the rhythm and tempo of a horse's paces, the horse covering equal space of ground in equal space of time.

Cadenettes *see* POITOU ASS.

Cadre Noir Group name of the riding instructors of Saumur whose uniform is black. This group was an integral part of the cavalry school of Saumur until 1968. Since then it has been attached to the Institut National d'Équitation (a semi-civilian, semi-military organization), which in 1972 changed its name to École Nationale d'Équitation. Its purpose is the training of civilian instructors and the advanced training of riders for competition.

Cajol Norwegian dog cart.

Calash or Calèche A light low-wheeled carriage with a folding top and Cee-springs (*q.v.*).

Calcutta Light Horse Challenge Trophy Awarded to the owner of the horse gaining the highest number of points during one season at any officially recognized Three-Day Event or Horse Trials.

Calf Name for both stag and hind in their first year. Red deer only are called calves. Fawns are the young of fallow deer.

Calf, Brown-stained Vegetable tanned leather similar to Polo Brown Calf but with slightly more dressing in it, therefore, more hard-wearing and waterproof.

Calf-knee Fore-legs which, viewed from the side and having imaginary line drawn through them, tend to concavity below the knees. (Also known as Back-at-the-knee and Buck knee.)

Calf-knee

Calgary Stampede see THE HORSE IN CANADA, *page* 58, *and Plate* 7.

Calico Pony see PINTO.

Calkins, Caulkins, Caulks Projections turned down at the extremity of horseshoes either to lift heels off the ground in faulty conformation or as an aid to the harness horse in holding his load. In polo, movable type only is permitted and placed at heel of shoe. Frost nails and studs are not allowed (*see* FARRIERY, *page* 118, *and Plate* 12).

Calling (Polo) Good calling wins matches. Calls come from the captain or member of the team in the best position to see, and must be instantly obeyed. Examples 'Take him out', 'turn back', 'leave it', 'get on', 'back-hander' (or 'back it'), 'mine'. The expression 'all right' is never used.

Call-over Certain bookmakers conduct ante-post betting on the chief races of the year, and there are call-overs at which the odds against the horses engaged in the race in question are called-over and varied according to supply and demand.

Camargue House (Camarguais) The 'wild white horses of the sea' used by the *gardiens* (French cowboys) working the black fighting bulls of the Camargue, the desolate marsh region lying at the mouth of the Rhône in Southern France. Of very ancient origin, this breed may descend from the Solutrean 'ram-headed horse', the prototype of the modern Barb (*q.v.*). They are nearly all grey, exceptionally hardy and seldom exceed 15 h.h. (152 cm).

Camarillo A type of albino horse with pink skin and black eyes. Found in California.

'Cambridge Mouth' Trade name for a ported mouthpiece as used in a curb bit.

Camera Patrol A system to photograph with moving camera the running of races both from head on and from the side so as to enable the stewards to pinpoint incidents in a race. Its advent has put jockeys on their mettle and led to less interference in racing.

Camp, to A horse standing with fore and hind feet spread as far apart as possible to make them immobile when passengers entered or left a carriage. Also known as spreading and stretching.

Campagne (*Equitation de Campagne*) Riding out of doors.

'Campagne' School A term for elementary dressage.

The Horse in Canada * Dorinda Fuller

After the disappearance of *Eohippus* (*q.v.*) from the Western Hemisphere horses eventually returned to North America with the Spanish Conquistadores, and in Canada their descendants still roam the Rocky Mountain valleys as wild herds of mustangs. Many of these have been domesticated and refined into Canada's most popular breed, the Quarter Horse (*q.v.*) who, like his counterpart in the United States, possesses exceptional speed for short distances of one quarter of a mile (hence his name).

Racing From before 1763 racing on the Plains of Abraham gave impetus to the importation of faster horses. In 1843 British regiments in London, Ontario, staged a steeplechase along the forks of the Thames River, and the painting of the London West Steeplechase in that same year by Lady Alexander, wife of the commanding officer, is the first pictorial record of such a sporting event in Canada. Sir Daniel Lysons, on garrison duty at that time, mentioned in his diary that 'the horses which they procured from the farmers thereabouts were remarkable for their ability to jump timber fences'.

Racing has always retained its popularity and Thoroughbreds in recent times have improved in both quality and quantity. Montreal's Blue Bonnets Course has 58 days' racing a year and Ontario's major tracks, Fort Erie, Greenwood and Woodbine, have 197 days. The Western tracks of Winnipeg, Saskatoon, Regina, Edmonton, Calgary, Kamloops and Vancouver are ever popular. The 50-year-old Queen's Plate run at Woodbine Park, Toronto, is the classic for Canadian-bred three-year-olds with 50 guineas, as well as the $100,000 purse, to the winner. There are also 108 major harness racing tracks in operation all winter long for Standard-breds (trotters and pacers). Many of the country's top drivers emanate from the Maritime Province. Today steeplechasing is for the most part held in conjunction with Hunter Trials.

Hunting Since the British garrison days when Toronto was called 'Muddy York', the Toronto North York Hunt formed in 1850 and then the Eglinton Hunt have provided sport. Montreal Hunt, established in 1826, had a French counterpart about 1890 in La Club de Chasse's Courre Canadien and today has an excellent second hunt called Lac de Deux Monts where English and French share their sport with great enthusiasm. Other hunts are the Ottawa Valley, the London, the Frontenac at Kingston, Kitchener-Waterloo, Hamilton-Wentworth, Winnipeg and Frazer River Valley, British Columbia. Canadian hunting is all too short a season with August cubbing, then only September, October, November and, with luck, part of December before cold, snow and ice drive all but the hardiest back to their indoor arenas.

Registered Canadian Hunters After World War I so many horses had been shipped overseas as remounts that there was a shortage of suitable horses to hunt. However, extending across much of Canada is a great stretch of limestone soil, which, in common with Ireland, Virginia and Kentucky, has the rare combination of conditions exceptionally suitable for the production of good-boned substantial horses. Sportsmen such as Sir Clifford Sifton in 1920 imported suitable English Thoroughbred stallions and a notable French Thoroughbred stallion, 'Matelot', to improve the half-bred hunter. Breeding each cross back to the Thoroughbred reproduced too closely to Thoroughbred type, so by selective breeding a hunter breed has evolved with fixed hunter type and characteristics. The Clydesdale and Thoroughbred cross, also the French-coach and Thoroughbred cross proved extremely useful. This programme progressed to become the Canadian Hunter Society, formed in 1926, which controls a list of registered and approved Canadian Hunter stallions, inspects foundation brood mares and issues preliminary foal certificates. Each animal is inspected at 36 months for approval before registration becomes complete.

Polo Interest is such that a Western Canadian team representing the clubs of Calgary, Vancouver and Victoria were invited to Britain's Hurlingham Polo Association to tour some of the British clubs in 1973. Five of Canada's clubs are near Toronto and play regular matches amongst themselves and also with the United States and the West Indies.

Show Jumping Show jumping competitions are generally held indoors to escape the fierce winters and though the Canadians have been at a disadvantage over outdoor courses when horses are required to jump at speed, nevertheless Canadians have been in and out of the international scene since 1909 when Sir Adam Beck of London, Ontario, took a show jumping team to the Royal International Horse Show at Olympia. In 1925 Canada won a Nations Cup in New York, a team was sent to Aachen and Dublin in 1938 and today teams compete regularly on the North American International circuit of Washington, New York, Toronto. Mrs Pamela Carruthers, the British international course designer, has been engaged recently to lay out courses for the outdoor 'Rothman's Grand Prix' competitions from Halifax to Vancouver. Television coverage of this series has increased public interest. Canada won the Olympic team Gold Medal in Mexico in 1968 and another team Gold at La Baule in 1970 in the World Championships.

Three-day Events A team benefited from a training period at Badminton and competed in the Olympic Games at Helsinki in 1952, and at the Olympic Games in Stockholm in 1956 they achieved a bronze medal. Chicago Pan-American Games in 1960 brought a gold medal and a Silver Individual in the Three-Day Pan-American Games at Winnipeg 1967 as well as an individual jumping gold; then all three gold medals for the equestrial team events were won by Canada in Cali, Colombia in 1971.

Dressage Dressage is making headway in Canada with team and individual gold medals at the Pan-American Games, Cali, in 1971. A full team was sent to the Olympics at Munich where one competitor reached the ride-off finals and the team finished in 6th position.

Shows The National Equestrian Federation governs 300 recognized horse shows and approves judges. The Royal Agricultural Winter Fair held in Toronto in November is Canada's show window for agriculture but is, in addition, a great international horse show. The Royal Canadian Mounted Police Musical Ride and international jumping teams highlight nine days and nights before capacity crowds. Classes include Palomino Parade events, Hackneys and Hackney ponies, the country doctors' horses, the Roadsters, the Arabians, three- and five-gaited Saddle horses, four-in-hand driving competitions, Clydesdales, Percherons and Belgians. There are green conformation, open conformation and working hunters all shown over hunting-type obstacles. In-hand breeding classes also take place daily.

Another unique feature of the horse scene is the Calgary Stampede, held each July and considered Canada's top rodeo. The crowds enjoy the drums and dancing of the Indians, the Thoroughbred racing and the stage show, but most especially the Chuck Wagon races which have their origin in groups of lunching cowboys under sudden attack by Indians in the past, when they threw all equipment including the cooking stove into the back of the wagon and, with four horses pulling the wagon and outriders, raced for safety (*see Plate* 7). But the great attraction is the rodeo events. These include bronc riding, bare-back bronc riding, steer wrestling, calf-roping, wild horse racing, wild cow milking, Brahma bull riding, even wild buffalo riding.

A feature of the Calgary Stampede and an integral part of the Canadian scene is the Musical Ride of the Royal Canadian Mounted Police. The proud claim of this famous police force founded in 1873 was, and is, that they 'always get their man'. Fortunately for Canada, prairie settlement was relatively peaceful because the rule of law was first established by the Mounties before the influx of homesteaders. A hundred years ago the Mounties were paid a dollar per man per day to tame the West. Though the Musical Ride is still part of a rookie Mountie's training today, his education is becoming increasingly more sophisticated and technical (*see Plate* 7).

Some Canadian universities are offering courses in horsemanship. Veterinary schools have full enrolment. Stretching from coast to coast are branches of the Pony Club, first established by the late Colonel R. S. Timmis, D.S.O., with the Eglinton Pony Club near Toronto in 1932. With the distances making it expensive to transport horses to interclub rallies, the host pony club frequently provides mounts for visiting clubs. The rally format is the Three-Day Event but of equal importance are the practical phases of Stable Management· and General Knowledge.

Breeds On Canadian farms one sees young riders, riding mostly Western style on Shetland, Welsh, New Forest, Exmoor and Connemara ponies. The numbers of the Quarter Horse increase annually and he is ideal for cattle work with his tremendous muscling of thighs, stifles, gaskins, and with his notably short cannon bones. 'Cutting' is a popular competition in which the horse is guided by his rider to the selected calf, then the rider sits with loose rein while the horse manoeuvres the calf away from the herd. The horse faces the calf with lowered head and pivots to thwart the calf's attempts to rejoin the herd. This cutting is done frequently for exhibition purposes without a bridle to demonstrate how the horse works on his own. Quarter horses excel in this type of competition.

Numbers are on the increase in such breeds and types as Appaloosas, Pintos, Morgans, Standardbreds and Hunters, and every possible àdmixture of them. The fact that there are now over 4000 Arabians in Canada speaks well for this ancient breed's continuing popularity. The original importations were from Lady Wentworth's Crabbet Stud in England and the·influence of this classical breeding is still evident. Since World War II Polish, British, American and Egyptian-bred Arabian horses have been imported. Though the average Arabian has increased in size the classical quality has not been compromised. Arabians are consistently placed in the Canadian Endurance Rides, of which the most important are under Ontario Competitive Trail Rides regulations, i.e. Flesherton, Rockwood, Creemor, Waterloo, and Trent Valley. British Columbia, the West and now Quebec and the Maritimes are also trail riding and there is frequent cross-entering in competitions between U.S.A. and Canada.

* * *

Canadian International Championship An open race for three-year-olds and upwards. In 1938 it was run as the Long Branch Championship for three-year-olds. The distance was $1\frac{1}{16}$ miles (1.71 km) from 1938 to 1952; $1\frac{1}{8}$ miles (1.81 km) in 1953 and 1954; and $1\frac{3}{16}$ (1.91 km) in 1955. Now it is run over $1\frac{5}{8}$ miles (2.61 km) (turf). Canada's richest race. For results *see page* 387.

Canadian Mounted Police, The Royal The 'Mounties'. Famous police force of Canada, founded in 1873 to 'Maintain the Right'. Their proud claim was, and is, that they 'always get their man' (*see Plate* 7).

Canas   An equestrian sport introduced into Spain by the Arabs, in which riders threw their spears at one another simultaneously, warding off their opponents' spears with leather shields.

Canes (Riding)   These are made of Malacca, Whanghee (knobbed), Nilgeri, black thorn, etc. Sometimes leather-covered.

Canker   Softening of the horn on sole of the foot forming a moist cheese-like growth with an objectionable smell. *Cause:* badly drained stables; prevalent in marshy districts. *Symptoms:* starts in frog, extending to sole, and horn becomes sodden, with, sometimes, pain and lameness. Consult a veterinary surgeon.

Cannon Bone (or shin bone)   Bone of foreleg below knee ending at fetlock. Corresponding bone in hind leg below hock termed shank. It should be short for strength, broad and flat when looked at from the side. If there is insufficient circumference measurement immediately below the knee, the horse is said to be 'short of bone', or 'tied in at the knee'. Owing to the unobservable but exceptional density of texture, lightness of bone, within reason, is no great defect in the Arab.

Canteen   A case containing hunting-man's sandwich-case and flask combined which is attached to saddle by D's (*q.v.*).

Canter   A contraction of 'Cantering gallop' which was an easy gallop used by the Pilgrims, on their way to the Shrine at Canterbury, along stretches of the downs.

Canter, Aids for   Depending on the degree of the horse's training and the rider's skill, different aids may be used. The most elementary are the lateral aids (*q.v.*) but the classical diagonal aid, resulting in a strike off from a state

of balance, is preferred. For the left canter, for example, the diagonal aids (*q.v.*), left hand and right leg; the lateral inside aids are left hand and leg.

Canter, Change of Leg at the   *see* FLYING CHANGE.

Canter, Collected   Cantering slowly with much impulsion, head carried high and flexed, quarters low, speed about 250 yd (228 m) per minute, the horse moving in a true pace of three-time (*see* CANTER, RHYTHM OF).

Canter, Counter   *see* COUNTER LEAD.

Canter, Disunited   The sequence of hoof beats when a horse is cantering disunited is off hind, near fore and near hind together, off fore (leading leg); or near hind, off fore and off hind together, near fore (leading leg)—in other words, the horse performs a left canter in front and a right canter behind, or vice versa (*see* CANTER, RHYTHM OF).

Canter, Extended   The strides are longer than the ordinary, without the cadence becoming precipitous. The entire topline lengthens somewhat, without the head changing to a great extent from its vertical position.

Canter, False   The horse is following a curve at the canter on the outside lead; e.g. near lead turning right. This when performed on purpose is called counter canter (*q.v.*).

Canter, Rhythm of   Canter is pace of three-time, in which three hoof beats are heard in following sequence: near hind, near fore and off hind together, off fore (leading leg); or off hind, off fore and near hind together, near fore (leading leg). The canter is faulty if four beats are heard, a consequence of lack of impulsion through faulty collection.

Canter, True   The horse is following a curve at the canter on the inside lead; e.g. near lead turning left.

Cantle Back of saddle.

Canvas Rugs The best variety of night rug, also called Sail Cloth. Durable and practically impossible for horse to bite or destroy, hence its popularity for use with two-year-old race-horses. Not to be confused with Jute rugs.

Cap A hunting term indicating the collection of money from persons who follow hounds but who are not subscribers to the hunt. Subscribers can be capped for special funds, e.g. 'Poultry', 'Wire'. Amount varies with the hunt. In the U.S.A. it is often referred to as Capping Fee.

Cap Jockey's peaked head-piece with owner's registered distinctive colours covering crash-helmet (see SKULL CAPS (RACING)).

Cap Curb see JODHPUR CURB.

Cape-cart Similar in type to the curricle being the only recognized two-wheeled cart drawn by two horses to a single pole and yoke. Much used at one time in South Africa.

Cape Horse Found in Cape Colony when Great Britain took possession in 1806. The original stock consisted of Barbs, Persians or Arabs imported by the East India Company who first colonised the country. At a later date English roadsters, Thoroughbreds and American-bred stallions were imported and in 1807 Spanish horses were captured from a ship en route for Buenos Aires. These latter are said to have been the progenitors of the red roans and odd colours, later renowned for their hardiness and endurance (see HORSES AND RIDERS IN SOUTH AFRICA, page 303).

Capel Thick-set farm horse used in mediaeval times.

Capel Wen-like swelling on the heel of the hock or point of the elbow. Also known as Capulet.

Capped Elbow A circumscribed pendulous tumour in the region of the elbow, soft in the early stages, hard later. Usually caused by the inner heel of shoe bruising the elbow when horse is lying down on insufficient bedding, or on rough uneven floor. *Treatment:* massage with lead lotion or Fuller's earth and vinegar. Shoe with a three-quarter shoe. Sausage boot (*q.v.*) will prevent recurrence, or a straw bind bandaged around the cannon bone at night will prevent further bruising. Also known as shoe-boil.

Capped Hock Caused by kicking in stable, shortage of bedding, or injury sustained during transit. *Symptoms:* swelling on point of hock. *Treatment:* same as for capped elbows (*q.v.*). *Preventive Treatment:* sufficient bedding and a hock boot. Bed with thick sawdust or peat moss. Apply kaolin poultices held in position by stocking material.

Capped Hock

Capping Fee see CAP.

Caprilli, Federico (1868–1907) Italian Cavalry officer, instructor at Cavalry School, Pinerolo (1904). Caprilli is the undoubted inventor of the modern forward style of riding, introduced by him in 1890, and known since 1907 as the Italian or Forward Seat. Published *Principi di Equitazione di Campagna* in 1901.

Capriole High school air 'above the ground': horse makes a half-rear with hocks drawn under and very flexed, jumps forward and up in the air to a considerable height, then kicks hind legs out with great energy, and lands collectedly on four legs. A difficult exercise to perform, making great demands upon firmness and balance of rider.

Capsular Ligament   Embraces all joints where movement takes place. Can be regarded as a continuation of the periosteum in a strengthened, thickened form.

Capulet   see CAPEL.

Carholme, The   Former racecourse at Lincoln, but now only used for point-to-points.

Carlburg Tackle   A simple form of bending tackle operating from the rump but having no means of elevating the head.

Carousel or Carrousel   A musical ride executed by group of riders, performing a number of figures on horseback designed to resemble old-fashioned formal dances such as the Quadrille (q.v.) or the Lancers. Such rides are frequently done in period dress and, if well done, supply a most attractive spectacle.

Carriage, the First   The Romans used carriages with four wheels. The first recorded carriage in England was built in 1555 by William Rippon for the Second Earl of Rutland. Rippon also supplied one to Queen Mary in 1556 and Queen Elizabeth I in 1564.

Carriage Museums   Several carriage museums now exist in the British Isles, notably: The Royal Mews, Buckingham Palace, London; The Tyrwhitt Drake Museum, Maidstone, Kent; Shuttleworth Museum, Biggleswade, Bedfordshire; Dodington Park, Chipping Sodbury, Glos.; Breamore House, Fordingbridge, Hants.; Arlington Court, Barnstaple, Devon; Aysgarth Museum, Richmond, Yorks.; Shibden Hall, Halifax, Yorks.; Transport Museum, Hull, Yorks.; Transport Museum, Glasgow, Scotland; Transport Museum, Belfast, N. Ireland; Carriage Museum, Luggala, Roundwood, Co. Wicklow, Ireland.

Carries the Scent   Said of a hound which actually smells the fox's line when the pack is running.

Carrots   Best of all roots, especially for hunters and others in hard work as well as for unthrifty horses. Slice from end to end to avoid choking, which may result from feeding round cross sections.

Carry   Ploughland is said to 'carry' when it is sticky and is picked up on the feet of hounds or fox.

Carry Both Ends   see WEAR.

'Carrying a Scent'   Said of good scenting country or of a hound which works with its nose when the pack is running.

'Carrying the Bar'   An old coaching term for a horse whose bar is an inch or two before its partner's.

Cart   The general term for any two-wheeled vehicle.

'Carted'   A familiar term indicating a rider whose horse runs away.

Cartilage (Articular)   Is bathed in most joints by synovia (q.v.) which acts as a lubricant. The bodies of the spinal vertebrae, behind the atlas, are united by cartilage without synovia. The cartilage is then known as the intervertebral disc. They are also united by the apposition of their transverse and oblique processes which form joints lined by cartilage and bathed by synovia.

Cartilages (Lateral)   Two plates of cartilage, concave on their inner surfaces, one on each side of the foot, holding between them the plantar cushion. The lateral cartilages spread outwards each time the horse's weight lands on the horny frog. Inflammation of the pedal bone or coronet bone may extend to the lateral cartilage, causing calcification. This hardening of the cartilage is termed side bone (*q.v.*). However, a certain amount of calcification occurs normally in many horses after the 12th–14th year of life without giving rise to lameness.

'Carty' A cold-blood and any heavy draught horse. A 'carty sort' means common-bred.

Cast An effort made by hounds, either on their own initiative or at their huntsman's direction, to recover the scent at a check.

Cast Said of a horse when it is lying in a stall or box unable, either through lack of space or because it is lying too close to an adjacent wall or division, to rise without assistance.

Cast Horse considered inferior or unsuitable.

Casting Coat A horse casts its coat twice a year, in autumn and spring, the exact time depending upon the early approach of cold weather or otherwise, whether it carries a coarse or fine coat, is stabled or at grass, and whether it is an early or late foal.

Casting Horse Throwing horse to ground. Generally resorted to for the purpose of a veterinary operation but used for the clipping or shoeing of a vicious animal. Special hobbles are required, and are fitted to all four pasterns. An unbroken colt is best cast (for castration usually) by the use of rope sidelines.

Cast Metal Bits, stirrup irons, etc., are cast in a mould as opposed to being hand forged. This latter is now an almost dead art.

Castors *see* CHESTNUT.

Castration The operation of emasculation of the male horse, i.e., gelding. Best performed in the spring or autumn to avoid infection of the wound by flies.

Catch To find a mare 'in season' when running out at grass.

Catch-hold A horse is said to catch-hold when he pulls.

Catch-hold A huntsman is said to catch-hold of hounds when he lifts the pack (*see* LIFT).

Catching (or Folding) a Whip The act of lapping the thong of a team or tandem whip round the crop by a skilful turn of the coachman's wrist (*see* DOUBLE THONG).

Catch Pigeons Racing term for sprinters.

Catch-up Bringing in of horses off grass.

Catch-weights Racing term usually applied in a race where two owners have challenged each other to a match where no weights are specified. It follows that the Clerk of the Scales (*q.v.*) is not concerned.

Cat-hairs The long untidy hairs which grow in a horse's coat after the second clipping and which show early in the new year. They should be removed by singeing (*q.v.*).

Cat-hammed Descriptive of a horse with weak hocks that stand back and away from the natural stance.

'Cattle' Slang term for horses.

Cattle Men's Carnivals Australian Rodeos.

Caulkins or Caulks *see* CALKINS.

Cavalcade A procession of persons on horseback.

Cavalier A horseman, especially a horse soldier. A name (originally reproachful) for the supporters of Charles I against the Roundheads.

Cavalletti Low movable wooden jump or series of jumps in appearance a trestle—similar to a table knife rest. Invaluable for schooling young horses. 9-ft (2.7 m) poles or logs are rested on stout X's at either end. 'Arms' are not crossed quite at right angles, and by changing from close to open stance, the height is lowered (in Germany known as 'Bodenricks ').

Cavalletti

Cavalry   Horse soldiers, a troop of horses or horsemen.

Cavalry Twill   Cavalry Twill is a development from a double twill used prior to 1914 for blue uniform breeches, and was first made in khaki in the West of England during the early part of the First World War for Cavalry Regiments.

Cavendish, William   *see* NEWCASTLE, WILLIAM CAVENDISH, DUKE OF.

Cavesson   (From French Caveçon) The word can either refer to Cavesson

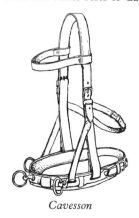

Cavesson

Noseband or a Breaking Cavesson and should be so qualified. A breaking, or lungeing Cavesson is used in the training of the young horse and is a superior form of head collar, having a padded nose-piece on to which is set a metal plate fitted with three swivelling rings, to any of which the lunge rein is fastened (*see Plate* 6).

Cavings   *see* CHAFF.

Cavvy   Bunch of horses on a cattle ranch in North America.

Cayuse   A strong, hardy Indian pony descended from Spanish horse.

Cee-spring   A C-shaped spring to which is attached a leather strap, situated at the back of early horse-drawn vehicles. Used before the invention of the elliptic spring.

Celle Stud   Near Hanover, Germany. Has existed for more than two centuries, and even after Second World War housed over 360 stallions, heavy, medium and light-weight.

Centaur   An ancient race of savage men living in hills of Thessaly who, according to Greek fable, were offspring of Ixion and a cloud. In ancient works of art the Centaur was represented as man from head to loins, with remaining part of body that of a horse. This seems to have arisen from fact that Thessalians were celebrated horsemen. Jason, hero of the Argonauts, was educated by Chiron the Centaur.

Chaff   The residue from corn stack after threshing, hence the saying 'Old birds are not easily caught by chaff'. (Also known as Cavings.)

Chaff Cutters   Machine which cuts hay or straw into short lengths, for mixing with oats, etc.

Chafing   *see* GALL.

Chain, Rack   *see* RACK CHAIN.

Chain, Stallion   A brass or steel chain about 18 in (45.7 cm) long, having a swivel fitting on one end to which is fastened the lead rein and a spring hook on the other. Its use gives more control and prevents the stallion biting through the lead.

Chain Mouth Snaffle   Bit, the mouthpiece of which is a chain rather than solid metal (*see* WELLINGTON SNAFFLE).

Chair, The   An open ditch of 6 ft (1.8 m) followed by a fence of 5 ft 2 in (1.6 m) in the steeplechase course at Aintree. This, the biggest fence in the Grand National course (*q.v.*), is situated in front of the stands and is only jumped once on the first circuit of the race. So called because there was an iron chair placed beside the jump for the use of the distance judge.

Chaise   A pleasure or travelling carriage, especially a light open carriage with a top for one or two persons, originally drawn by one horse.

'Chalk-jockey' (Racing)   One who has not ridden sufficient races to warrant his name being painted on a board for insertion in the frame of the course's number-board (*q.v.*). His name is lettered in chalk on a black-board.

Challenge   A hound which 'opens' is said 'to challenge'.

Chalon, Henry Bernard (1770–1849) Born in London of Dutch parentage, a talented animal painter also noted for his sporting pictures. He painted racehorses and hunting scenes in a style much influenced by Stubbs.

Chamber Horse   An exercise chair for use in the bedroom in Georgian times, which simulated the up and down motion of horse riding.

Chambon   A schooling device, of French origin, consisting of a strap from the girth passing between the forelegs and dividing at the breast into two cord attachments. These pass through rings on a poll pad and are then connected to the bit. The object is to induce a gradual lowering of the

head, a rounding of the back and engagement of the quarters.

Chamfrain   Protective armour for a horse's head in mediaeval times.

Chamois Leather   Name sometimes given to common wash leather the product of a sheepskin. Leather from real Chamois would be a rarity.

Champ, to   To chew and mouth the bit.

Change in the Air   *see* FLYING CHANGE OF LEG.

Change of Leg   *see* FLYING CHANGE OF LEG.

Change of Ponies (Polo)   Ponies are changed after each chukka with an interval of 3 minutes for the purpose. Ponies may be changed at any time during play, but no stoppage is then permitted.

Chaparajos   *see* CHAPS.

Chapman Horses   Name (now in disuse) for Cleveland Bays, because of their popularity with itinerant 'chapmen' (travelling salesmen) of a century ago. Later known as pack-horses.

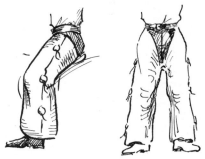

Chaps

Chaps (from the Spanish word *Chaparajos*) Form of riding trouser in fact covering ordinary trousers for the full length of leg and made of calf skin. Used by cowboys primarily for protection against thorns, heat and cold.

Char-à-banc Large, high vehicle for a number of passengers on forward-facing seats. Formerly popular for sight-seeing.

Charger A horse ridden in military action in the eighteenth century.

Chariot Closed carriage for posting or state driving, in the eighteenth century, seating only two inside. Originally a car used in ancient warfare.

'Charley' An affectionate name for a fox.

Charlier Shoe Invented by a Frenchman of that name; the principle is that the shoe is sunk into the wall of the hoof (small nails are used, but no clip), thus allowing the frog to be, in theory, always in contact with the ground. Some skill is required as the foot must be grooved with a special knife to receive the shoe. Used with varying success (known also as 'Periplantar shoeing').

Charolais Half-bred horse of French origin (*see* LIMOUSIN).

Chase Me Charlie A show-jumping event in which competitors 'follow-my-leader'. A knock-down or refusal results in elimination.

'chaser *see* STEEPLECHASER.

Chaugan *see* POLO HISTORY.

Chaunter *see* BONNET.

Check When hounds lose scent of fox temporarily.

Check Rein A rein used for harness horses to correct the carriage of the head. It runs from the bit to the harness pad, or through D's attached to the crownpiece, and so to the pad. It acts, too, as a valuable method of control.

Cheek (of bit) Shank or leg of bit, of varying length. Also refers to cheek of snaffle bit, i.e., Dee cheek, eggbutt cheek.

Cheek Guards Cheek guards for snaffles consist of circular leather or rubber; those for Pelhams are pear-shaped. They prevent chafing.

Cheek-piece Part of bridle to which snaffle and bridoon bits are attached (sewn, billeted or hook-studded), and which in turn is buckled to slip-head or head.

Chef d'Équipe Captain or Director of a competing team of horsemen.

Cheltenham Gag A gag snaffle with eggbutt rings or cheeks as opposed to loose, traversing rings.

Cherries *see* ROLLER MOUTH.

Cheshire Cradle *see* CRADLE.

Cheshire Martingale *see* MARTINGALE, CHESHIRE.

Chesnut Variant form of chestnut (colour) (*q.v.*).

Chest Situated behind forearms. Must be deep for heart and lungs to function properly.

Chester, City of One of the earliest homes of horse-racing in England. Racing started there in about 1540 on the course used today and known as the Roodeye.

Chestnut (or Castor) Small horny prominence found on inside of all four legs (some 3 in (7.5 cm) above knees on inside, and on hind legs on inner and lower part of hock joint). Does not appear on the hocks of a hybrid.

Chestnut Colour This colour consists of yellow hair in different degrees of intensity (golden and liver). A 'true' chestnut has a chestnut mane and tail which may be lighter or darker than the body colour. Chestnuts may have flaxen manes and tails.

Cheval de Selle Français *see* ANGLO-NORMAN.

Chevasse, Pierre A French loriner, associate of Latchford (*q.v.*), who settled in Walsall in the latter part of the last century. His work gave impetus to the local craft.

Chifney, Samuel (1753–1807) Born in Norfolk and entered Foxe's Stables at Newmarket. Won the Derby on 'Skyscraper'. Wrote of himself in 1773 'I can ride horses in a better manner in a race to beat others than any person ever known in my time', and, in 1775, 'I can train horses for running better than any person I knew in my time'. His theory was to ride with a slack rein. First jockey to adopt the method of riding a waiting race, coming to finish with tremendous rush. Inventor of the bit bearing his name (*see* CHIFNEY BIT *and* ANTI-REARING BIT). Later he became involved in scandals and died in poor circumstances. His two sons, William and Samuel, were both successful jockeys.

Chifney Bit A bit with the upper part of the cheek swivelling on the mouthpiece and independent of the lower part. No poll pressure occurs but the curb action is proportionately more severe.

China-eye *see* WALL-EYE.

Chincoteague These and similar Assateague ponies are named after the islands they inhabit off the coast of Virginia and Maryland, U.S.A. In July the ponies are rounded up for an annual auction sale. Many are pinto colours (piebald and skewbald), small in size and rather stubborn in character.

Chine (or backbone) Obsolete term which was used when referring to the spine or top line of the back.

Chin Groove Small declivity found above the lower lip on which the curb chain lies when brought into action.

Chink Back *see* JINKED BACK.

Choking In horses choking is indicated by convulsive swallowing movements accompanied by much arching of the neck and the muzzle turning in towards the sternum. Sometimes semi-fluid material trickles out of the nostrils. The chief danger is pneumonia from inhalation. As the material causing the oesophagus impaction is usually bran (*q.v.*) or chaff, recovery usually occurs after a period varying from a few minutes to a few hours. If it has not done so after an hour, veterinary assistance should be sought. In most cases access to water hastens recovery.

Chop Term generally applied to chopped hay or straw, erroneously described as chaff. Also mixture of corn or roots or both, with bran.

Chop When hounds kill a fox which has had no opportunity to escape and which is suddenly disturbed or half awake.

'Chop, to' Term in horse dealing for exchange of two horses, usually accompanied by payment on one side.

'Chopping' Old coaching term for hitting horse on quarters with whip.

Christian, Dick A celebrated Leicestershire horsebreaker and steeplechase rider in first half of the nineteenth century; rode 'Clinker' (*q.v.*) in the famous match against Squire Osbaldeston (*q.v.*) on 'Clasher'. Christian maintained, 'The gentlemen get the worst falls as they ride on horses which fall like a clod and don't try to get out of a difficulty. I am safer riding twenty young horses than one old one' (*see* DICK CHRISTIAN BRIDOON).

Chrome Calf, Black and Brown Very tough chrome tanned leather, waterproof; used for boots for hard wearing conditions.

'Chronicle of The Horse, The' (U.S.A.) First published in 1937 as *The Middleburg Chronicle*; under the present title it is now a weekly equestrian periodical with the largest circulation in every state of the Union and in Canada. It is concerned with all aspects of horse and hound activities.

Chukker (U.S.A.)   *see* CHUKKA.

Chuck Wagon   Western term for wagon which houses cooking and camping equipment.

Chukka or Chukker   Polo term for periods into which the game is divided. In Argentina, U.S.A. and Great Britain chukkas are now 7 minutes. In Argentina a full game is 8 chukkas, in Great Britain and U.S.A. only 6 (*see* POLO, *page* 246).

Churn Barrel   Roomy, well ribbed-up.

Chute   A stall in which rodeo horses are saddled, bridled and mounted.

Cimarron (South American)   A wild horse.

Cinch   American term for a saddle-girth. The cinch does not buckle on to straps as an English girth but is adjusted with a 'tie' knot on a ring.

Circle Cheek Snaffle   A riding bit having cheeks similar to a Liverpool bit but with a central rein loop. Used to keep a horse running straight.

Circus Horses   There are three categories of Circus Horses. Liberty Horses (*q.v.*) which appear unridden in groups of 6 to 16 or more. Haute École horses which are ridden solo or sometimes in twos or threes, performing complicated movements based on classical High School (*q.v.*) traditions. Costume and saddlery are specially decorative. Rosinbacks (*q.v.*) which take their name from the resin rubbed on to the horse's back to prevent the performer from slipping.

Citation Bridle   Specially designed bridle to prevent a horse putting its tongue over the bit.

Claiming Race   This is a race in which every horse running may be claimed for a certain price as laid down in the conditions of the race.

Clarence   In 1842 a carriage was produced and known by this name. It has been described as 'midway between a brougham (*q.v.*) and a coach (*q.v.*)'. Shortly after the introduction of the brougham a more formalized vehicle was produced, known as a Surrey Clarence, with a hammer-cloth box and rear platform for footmen, and having the appearance of a hybrid chariot-brougham.

'Clasher'   A good-looking 15.3 h.h. (155 cm) brown hunter gelding owned by 'Squire' George Osbaldeston and ridden by him in the famous match in the Quorn Country against Captain Ross's 'Clinker' (*q.v.*) in 1829. The stake was 1500 guineas a side and the riders carried 12 st (168 lb; 76 kg).

Classics   A racing term to denote the five classic races for three-year-olds only: the 2000 Guineas and the 1000 Guineas (fillies only), run at Newmarket over one mile (1.6 km); the Derby and the Oaks (fillies only) run at Epsom over $1\frac{1}{2}$ miles (2.4 km); and the St Leger run at Doncaster over about $1\frac{3}{4}$ miles (2.8 km).

Classics (Racing, U.S.A.)   The Kentucky Derby, $1\frac{1}{4}$ miles (2.01 km), the Preakness Stakes, $1\frac{3}{16}$ miles (1.91 km), the Belmont Stakes, $1\frac{1}{2}$ miles (2.41 km) and the Coaching Club American Oaks, $1\frac{1}{2}$ miles (2.41 km) for fillies only.

Clay Bed   For treatment of laminitis (*q.v.*). Made by thoroughly wetting clay and ramming it until it forms a pudding. Must be re-wetted and rammed daily.

Clean Bred   An animal of any breed whose pedigree is of pure blood.

Clean Ground   Hunting term indicating that land is neither foiled nor stained.

Clean-leg   Breed without hair in any abundance, e.g. Suffolk, Cleveland Bay, as distinct from Shire and Clydesdale.

Clean Leg   One free from blemishes.

Cleaning (Harness and Saddlery) Take to pieces, remove all mud and sweat deposits with slightly damp sponge and soft soap. For harness apply paste when dry, and polish. For saddlery, glycerine soap can be rubbed in and all items should be treated with 'Kocholine' (*q.v.*) or a similar preparation once a week. Bits and stirrup irons, if of rustless metal should be washed in warm water (*see* STABLE MANAGEMENT).

Cleft   An interruption of continuity of the wall of the foot, at right angles to the direction of the horn-tubes. Can be caused by injury to the coronet. The space lying between the branches of the frog (*q.v.*).

Clench, Clinch   Term applied to points of nails when holding the shoe on the hoof. Clenches are formed by the blacksmith hammering sufficient protruding nail shank over and downwards.

Clerk of the Course (Racing)   Sole person responsible to the stewards for the general arrangements of a race meeting. He requires an annual licence from the Jockey Club and is paid by the racecourse executive.

Clerk of the Course (Show Jumping) Official responsible for planning, erecting and maintaining a course.

Clerk of the Scales (Racing)   Official responsible for weighing out and weighing in the jockeys. He must furnish the starter with the list of runners. He is responsible for all signals on the number board, including variations in the weights, apprentice allowances, objections and enquiries, etc. He requires an annual licence from the Jockey Club and is paid by them. He was originally responsible for the draw for places for flat racing, but this is now done the previous day at the Racing Calendar Office.

Clerk of the Scales (Show Jumping) Official responsible to the Judge for seeing that each competitor scales the specified weight.

Cleveland Bay   Breed of great antiquity of uncertain origin but practically indigenous to the county of Yorkshire; a century ago it was probably the nearest to a fixed type as any breed in England. Even then two types existed, for agriculture and coaching. A clean-legged active horse much used for breeding hunters. Average height 16–16.2 h.h. (162–164 cm), with short legs and always of a whole bay colour. Action should be straight and true and of the kind for getting over the ground; high action is not desirable but knees must flex. Very sound hard blue feet essential. *Breed Society:* the Cleveland Bay Horse Society (*see Plate* 8).

Cleveland Bay Horse Society of Great Britain (Founded 1884) *Objects:* to promote the interests of the breed, and of horse breeding generally.

Click   A sound often made by the driver to start or accelerate his horse.

Clicket   Mating call of vixen.

Clicking   *see* FORGING.

Climate   Cold climates generally breed small and hardy horses, the warmer, bigger and less hardy animals. It is an observable fact that the greatest height in horses is found in temperate climates, i.e. in W. Europe and the British Isles. In countries of great extremes of cold, caused either by latitude or altitude, horses remain small.

Clinch   *see* CLENCH.

Clinching   The operation in shoeing of nipping off protruding nail points, leaving sufficient to turn down to form clinch, and smoothing off with a rasp.

'Clinker'   A Thoroughbred 16.1 h.h. (163 cm) bay hunter gelding, up to 14 st (196 lb; 89 kg), owned by Captain Ross and ridden by Dick Christian (*q.v.*) in the famous match against 'Squire' Osbaldeston's horse 'Clasher' (*q.v.*) in 1829.

Clip   That part of the horseshoe which is at the extreme forward point of the toe formed by the metal being drawn up and backwards, giving the shoe a decided grip on the hoof. There is one clip on the front shoes, one or two on each hind, depending on the nature of the work required of the horse.

Clipping   The removal, by hand or machine, of the coat or the mane, the object being to facilitate the drying of the former after excessive work. Clipping is done after the winter coat has grown, and before it is shed. The whole coat can be clipped, or the body and legs down to slightly above the knees and hocks; in a hunter or riding horse the area covered by the saddle should be left unclipped. The first clipping should be done all over, using the coarser blades on the legs, leaving all hair in the heel hollows; the second clipping should leave the saddle mark and legs uncut. For horses working at slow paces (e.g., draught horses), trace-clipping is often adopted when the belly and upper part of all four legs are clipped. Mane clipping or hogging is a matter of personal choice, usually employed to improve an excessively heavy or cresty neck. Electric clippers are virtually in universal use today.

Clipping Machines   These are nearly all electrically operated, this type having superseded the old hand clipper requiring two men to operate it. Blades are either fine, for close clipping, or coarse for use on legs. There are two types of machine, the hand variety and the larger and more powerful one suspended from the roof.

Clog   A form of restraint used on kickers in a yard; it was made of wood and cord and looped round the horse's back legs. When the horse kicked, the clog came down and gave him a sharp

rap across the hocks. It was used in East Anglia.

Close-coupled   Indicating a short, deep, compact body with well-sprung ribs, showing no slackness or weakness in the loins.

Closing   The conditions of every race under Jockey Club rules have to be published in the Racing Calendar (*q.v.*) before it closes for entries. The advertisement in the Racing Calendar before closing must state the dates on which a meeting is to be held, the dates for closing the races to further entries, and other particulars as laid down by rule.

Clothing (Blankets)   Yorkshire woollen blankets, usually striped, are sold in three weights, and are 'teased' and rough. Unshaped and without buckles they are worn under top sheet or night rug.

Clothing (Coolers)   Cooling-off-sheet. Square rug (with tape front) usually 81 in by 108 in (205 cm × 274 cm) and made of camel-hair material or of aertex net type cloth. Thrown over a perspiring horse after a race or chukka of polo.

Clothing (Day Rug)   Rugging of various colours, usually Yorkshire or Oxfordshire wool, bound in contrasting colours, and having sewn-on initials or monograms. Sizes are in 3 in (76 mm) from 4 ft to 6ft 6 in (121–197 cm) measured from centre of brisket to buttocks.

Clothing (Exercise)   Suit consists of quarters sheet 4 ft (121 cm) long, of varying weight, according to climate and season. Used daily for all racehorses, with head cap to match.

Clothing (Head Cap)   Head covering forming part of paddock or exercise suit.

Clothing (Hood)   Head and neck covering.

Clothing (Night) Varying qualities of jute and twilled jute, partly or fully lined with light-weight woollen material. Best is made of sail cloth and similarly lined. Racing stables use two surcingles, front padded.

Clothing (Pad Cloth) Oval-shaped pad to match clothing upon which it is used beneath roller. Now seldom used.

Clothing (Paddock or Racing Suit) Consists of quarter sheet usually 3 ft 10 in (1 m) long, 28 in (71 cm) deep, of good quality material, dyed to owner's requirements, with special cloth binding and crest or monogram. Head cap, narrow roller and breast girth to match.

Clothing (Summer) Day rugs of linen or cotton material, usually in some check pattern.

Clothing (Waterproof) Suit Consists of a waterproof rug with hood and surcingle, which completely envelops the horse for travelling in the rain. The best have perforations for ventilation.

Clothing-tearing Like many other disagreeable habits this is a vice (*q.v.*). The use of a bar muzzle or the impregnation of the rug with one of the proprietary 'chewing inhibitors' is suggested.

Cloud Dark mark on the face of a horse.

Club Feet Feet with small frogs and high heels, known also as mule or boxy feet.

Clucking Encouraging sound made by rider or driver (*see* CLICK).

Clydesdale Native of Lanarkshire, Scotland. It dates to the middle of the eighteenth century when the hardy native breed, by the use of Flemish stallions, was graded up to meet the trade demand for more weight and substance. The Clydesdale combines quality and size without grossness and bulk, possesses exceptionally sound feet and limbs and is an active mover. About 16.2 h.h. (165 cm). *Breed Society :* the Clydesdale Society (*see Plate 8*).

Clydesdale Horse Society of Great Britain and Ireland (Founded 1877) *Objects :* to maintain the purity of the Clydesdale breed, and to collect and preserve their pedigrees. The Society holds an annual Stallion Show, and various Horse Sales.

Coach The coach was introduced into England in the sixteenth century and was named after Kotje, a small town in Hungary where it was first made.

Coach-dog The spotted Dalmatian is trained to run between the wheels of a vehicle, immediately behind the horse's heels. It was originally a gundog in the Balkans and Italy, but about the middle of the seventeenth century it was used in France as a guard against highwaymen. This was probably the origin of its place under the travelling carriage in England where it was introduced in the eighteenth century.

Coach-horn A straight horn, usually of brass or copper, used by coachguards to clear the road and sound calls or simple airs. In pre-railway days they were seldom longer than 36 in (91 cm); longer horns have greater scope, and modern ones usually measure 52 in (1.4 m) or more (*see* 'THREE FEET OF TIN' and 'YARD OF TIN').

Coach Horse Except for the Yorkshire coach horse (*q.v.*), now virtually extinct, there is no particular type of coach horse, Hackneys, Cleveland Bays, and other types of harness horses being in many respects suitable to drive as a team.

Coach-house This should be airy, well-ventilated, but not cold, and should be heated when it is frosty. The sun should not shine directly on the vehicles. The floor should be level, made of cement or any smooth surface; the doors should extend the whole width of the house and should be provided with stops to keep them open when vehicles are being run in and out.

Coaching * Marylian Watney

Travel in England during the early centuries was both slow and uncomfortable, for the first vehicles were huge, cumbersome stage waggons drawn by teams of six to eight heavy horses urged on by a drover on horseback, but these ran only in summer, for the roads were no more than tracks, and extremely rough at that.

The first coach is said to have been introduced into England from the town of Kotje in Hungary, during the reign of Queen Elizabeth I, and this was a large square vehicle, open at the sides. From then on more coaches appeared, and the road surfaces also improved, until in 1784 the first mail coach service was established by John Palmer of Bath—the mails having previously been carried by post-boys on horseback, who were frequently both attacked and robbed. Apart from security, the mail coaches also became popular as a means of conveyance, for not only were they speedy, but they could carry up to nine passengers at a charge of 5d a mile for inside seats, and half that amount for those on top—thus giving rise to the term 'an outsider'.

Then, in 1815, the engineers Teiford and MacAdam perfected the road surfaces, and more coaches, both Stage as well as Mails, were put on the roads. Stage coaches were built very like the Mails, but could carry many more passengers on top—up to twelve—the space at the back of a Mail coach being occupied, for security reasons, solely by the guard in charge of the mail bags, whereas on a Stage this area provided accommodation for eight more seats. Another difference between them was in the painting, for while Mails were always finished in Royal colours: black, with maroon panels on which the Monarch's cypher was inscribed, and scarlet wheels and undercarriage, Stage coaches, which plied solely for trade, were painted in brilliant colours with the names of their stopping places in gold letters. They also developed sporting names like 'Tally

Ho', 'Red Rover', 'Magnet', etc., and it became the fashion for young men about town to drive them. Like the Mails, they also carried a red-coated guard, whose job was to sound the horn, guard the luggage and keep the coachman up to time.

With the arrival of the railways in the 1830s, Mail and Stage coaches gradually went off the roads, but the fashion for four-in-hand driving remained, and gentlemen's coaches, or Private Drags, were developed. These were lighter in construction than Stage coaches, and painted in more sombre colours with the owners' crest or monogram on the boots and door panels, while two grooms in livery sat on the back seat. This century also saw the formation of several driving clubs, and wagers concerning both skill and speed with a four-in-hand.

When Queen Victoria acceded to the Throne the coaching industry was waning, and by 1850 the main coaching routes were hardly used. Later, however, a revival took place when some sportsmen took to putting Stage coaches back on their original roads. This revival was at its zenith during the reign of King Edward VII, and lasted until the outbreak of World War I, when the call-up of both horses as well as men caused it to end.

After the war, however, there were still a few sportsmen about anxious to revive coaching once again, and so, on a limited scale and during the summer only, some of the old Stage coaches were run yet again to their original destinations such as Oxford, Brighton, etc., and this lasted until the outbreak of World War II.

The attraction of coaching and its immense history of early communications, or else the urge to drive a four-in-hand, appears to have been so strongly embedded in some Englishmen that soon after the end of hostilities another generation of sportsmen began to resuscitate coaching. Apart from horse shows, where as many as sixteen coaches have been seen in the ring, long distance runs were also planned, and journeys from London to both Brighton and Southampton, Portsmouth to Scar-borough, and even Edinburgh to London, have been achieved over the years. The Coaching Club is well supported and recently celebrated its centenary year.

* * *

Coaching Club Formed in 1871 under the Presidency of the 8th Duke of Beaufort, and last survivor of various similar driving clubs of earlier date. Members must be able to drive a four-in-hand, and drive *private* (as opposed to road or stage) coaches, which are called 'Drags'. Meets are held at the Royal Windsor Horse Show in May, and at the Magazine, Hyde Park, London, in July.

Coaching Crop Correct term for coaching whip.

Coaching Marathon Marathon for four-horse coaches, first introduced by the Royal International Horse Show of 1909, and since then a popular feature of this and other shows. Brief intervals separate the departures of the coaches from a given point, the drive ending in the show ring. Points are given for horses, turnout and condition of horses on arrival, not for speed, though the journey must be completed within a set time limit and without a change of coachman.

Coachman One who drives one or more horses.

'Coachman's Elbow' In giving or returning a salute, a driver does not raise his hat. The hand holding the whip is raised to face level, with the whip aslant the body, thus raising the elbow. Hence the origin of this expression.

Coat Horse's coat grows towards the end of September in preparation for the winter. There is new growth again in the spring. Underbreds and horses at grass grow the heaviest coats. A dull staring coat is often an indication of ill-health.

Cob Not a breed, but a well-established type. Big-bodied, short-legged, 'stuffy' horse or pony standing no higher than 15.3 h.h. (155 cm), with small 'quality' head set on a neck arched and elegant. The back must be short with great girth and showing strength with the tail carried high and gaily, and the mane hogged. The horse must have balance with bold but kindly presence. The cannon bone must be extremely short. Primarily used as hacks for heavy-weight, elderly riders, and as such, must have immaculate manners. *Breed Society*: The British Show Hack and Cob Association (*see Plate* 9).

Cob (Show) Not exceeding 15.1 h.h. (153 cm), capable of carrying 14 st (196 lb; 89 kg). To be ridden.

Cockade Ornamental rosette as badge of office fastened to the side of top hats worn by liveried servants employed by members of the nobility and armed forces (i.e. those entitled to bear arms). Introduced into England during the reign of George III.

Cock-eyed Stirrup Irons Type with 'eye' $1\frac{1}{4}$ in (31 mm) out of the perpendicular and 'tread' sloped towards the heel, thus encouraging inward slope and lowered heel. Often known as Kournakoff irons after the riding instructor who popularized their use.

Cock Fences (Hunting) Where thorn fences are cut very low.

Cockhorse Extra horse used on very steep hills to assist a stage coach in ascent; it was attached ahead of leaders and was ridden by a Cockhorse-boy. Derivation obscure and it has been suggested that the name was derived from a horse so used, being stabled at

'The Cock Inn' at the foot of a steep hill.

Cocking Cart   Extremely high-hung two-wheeled cart, designed to take fighting game cocks, popular for tandem driving in early nineteenth century. Usually seated two, with additional seat for groom at the rear.

Cocks Eyes, Cockeyes   Metal eyes at the ends of leaders' traces to hook on to the bars.

Cocktail   A horse of racing qualities but not a Thoroughbred.

Cock-tailed   Having tail docked (*see* DOCKING). Term used in the eighteenth century.

Cock Throttled   Term applied where the head is set wrong and the gullet stands out in convex shape as in throat of a cock.

Cody, William Frederick (1846–1917)   Famous American Showman, known as Buffalo Bill. One of the riders in the Pony Express (*q.v.*). Became an army scout and guide, and served in U.S. Cavalry. He killed the Cheyenne Chief, Yellow Hand, in single combat. In 1883 he organized the Wild West Show which first toured Europe in 1887.

Coffee-housing   Familiar expression for objectionable habit of chatting at covert side.

Coffin   A cross-country fence used in horse trials (*q.v.*), comprising post and rails on take-off side, a ditch and another set of post and rails.

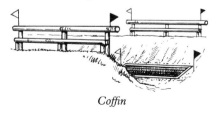

Coffin

Coffin Bone   *see* FARRIERY, *page* 117.

'Coffin' Cab   London hackney cab in use before the hansom. It was two-wheeled, with a coffin-like body for two passengers; the driver's seat was between the body and the off wheel.

Coffin Head   Coarse, ugly face in which jowl lacks prominence.

Coggins Test   Official diagnostic test for equine infectious anaemia which is adopted by the U.S. Department of Agriculture.

Cold Back   Said of a horse when he dislikes the pressure of a cold saddle and 'plays up'. Warming saddle first will often prevent bucking. It is best to saddle up and girth loosely some time before mounting.

Coldblood   *see* WARMBLOOD.

Cold-scenting   Term applied to some hunting countries which irrespective of day-to-day conditions, are liable to carry little scent.

Cold-shoeing   When a shoe is nailed to the foot without having been heated and shaped immediately beforehand.

Colds in Horses   *see* EQUINE INFLUENZA.

Colic   Disease of the digestive organs due to improper food, very cold water, sudden change of diet, and other causes. Also called Gripes. *Symptoms:* Obvious sudden pain, with the horse pawing and kicking at belly, looking round at flanks, lying down and rolling. *Treatment:* If the cause is indigestion, treat with purgative medicines and enemas. With slight attacks, a draught composed of a stimulant with an opiate (nitric ether and tincture of opium) generally effects a cure. Three or four ounces of whisky given in a quart of tepid water will sometimes answer equally well. The patient should be walked about. Whenever signs of colic persist for an hour, a veterinary surgeon should be called in to make a diagnosis.

Collar (Harness) Of heavily padded leather, it carries the hames, and correct fitting is most important.

Collar of a Whip The metal band at the top of the leather hand piece. It should mark the place where the hand grasps the whip.

Collar Work Driving term for work uphill or any calling for strain through the traces to the collar.

Collected Term applied to a horse when ridden well up to its bit with its neck flexed, jaw relaxed and hocks well under it and, having full control over its limbs at all paces, is ready and able to respond to the aids of its rider.

Collecting Ring A ring immediately adjoining the showing or jumping ring where competitors assemble with their horses. A steward is in charge.

Collection A combination of *ramener* (*q.v.*) and *engagement* (*q.v.*) of the hind-legs, it gives the horse's body a general position ensuring maximum mobility in all directions.

Collection Classes Unknown at shows in Great Britain but popular in the U.S.A. and open to 3 or more exhibits from one stable, each stable being judged as one entry.

Collier Type of west Wales pack or draught horse once generally used in mines. Short-legged with feather, and strong quarters. Average height 14–15 h.h. (142–152 cm). Also known as pitter.

Collier's Horse A knocker (*q.v.*).

Collinge's Axles Type of axle now seen on most carriages except coaches; the removable cap facilitates greasing.

Colorado Ranger *see* APPALOOSA HORSE.

Colours, Body The principal colours are black, brown, bay, chestnut and grey, although the latter correctly is not a colour but a failure of pigment to produce colour. Where there is any doubt as to the colour, the muzzle and eyelids should be carefully examined for guidance. The Royal College of Veterinary Surgeons publishes a pamphlet dealing fully with *The Colours and Markings of Horses*.

Colours, Registration of Every owner, or part-owner, in whose name a racehorse runs is required to register his racing colours annually on payment of a fee of £2. Colours so registered cannot be taken by another person.

Colours of The Royal Family The following are the racing colours used by the Royal Family.
H.M. Queen Elizabeth II: Purple, gold braid, scarlet sleeves, black velvet cap with a gold fringe.
H.M. Queen Elizabeth, The Queen Mother: Blue, buff stripes, blue sleeves, black cap with a gold tassel.

Colt Male ungelded horse up to four years old. Usual to denote male sex of foal as 'colt foal'.

Comanche Twitch A variant of the gag twitch, in which the cord is attached to the near-side 'D' of the head collar.

Combination Obstacle (Show Jumping) Combination of two or more jumps. Maximum distance between each must not exceed 39 ft 4 in (12 m).

Combined Competitions Comprise a dressage test and a show jumping round. In 1974 the title was changed to Dressage with Jumping (*see* HORSE TRIALS).

Combined Martingale *see* MARTINGALE, COMBINED.

Combined Training *see* HORSE TRIALS.

Combing Avoid combing mane and tail, as it removes hair and thins them out. If the mane is too thick, it may be combed well from the under side to remove superfluous hair.

Combs These should be of bone or metal; large size for mane and tail, small size for tail trimming. Should be used very sparingly on tails, especially on Thoroughbreds.

'Comes Again' Said of a horse (whether hunting or racing) which, though apparently flagging, will suddenly 'take hold' of the bit and gallop on with renewed zest. In hunting often termed 'second wind'.

Comfrey A special type of this plant is cultivated as horse feed. It is high in both calcium and phosphate content and is sometimes used freely as a substitute for hay in summer.

Commentator (Racing) A running commentary of a race is now given over the racecourse public address system. The names of the commentators are often given on the race card.

Common Riding see HAWICK COMMON RIDING.

Commons, Open Spaces and Footpaths Preservation Society (Founded 1865) *Objects:* to protect commons, and ensure public enjoyment of them for recreation, to promote the extension of open spaces, and to provide for the preservation and proper maintenance of public footpaths, bridleways and other highways.

Concours d'Attelage (C.A.) Refers to events where the competitions are exclusively for driving.

Concours Complet d'Equitation see HORSE TRIALS.

Concours de Saut (C.S.) Refers to events where the competitions are exclusively for jumping.

Concours Hippique (C.H.) Refers to events which include competitions of more than one discipline.

Concrete Often used as flooring for stables, but it is not recommended since, being smooth, it affords poor foothold, and if the surface be made rough, it soon crumbles away. On the other hand, concrete allows water to run off quickly.

Concussion Result of fast work on hard roads, producing heat and tenderness resulting in lameness, and often ending in navicular (*q.v.*). Paring the frog and throwing all the weight on to the walls is a usual cause. *Treatment:* remove shoes, place feet in cold bandages. Administer mild purgative and keep the horse on cooling food. In bad cases the horse may be shod with a strip of sponge or leather, $\frac{1}{2}$ in (12 mm) thick, between the wall of the foot and the shoe to reduce the chances of concussion.

Condition In proper condition a horse should be at its very best in both looks and health, showing plenty of muscle, and should feel hard to the touch when the hand is run along the crest and neck. A hand placed on the sides should show the skin freely movable over the ribs. Good condition is produced by proper attention to details of management, correct feeding, exercise, teeth and grooming.

Condition Race A race that is not a handicap and is governed by some conditions, such as 'for horses that have not won a race value £500'. Sometimes called a 'terms race'.

Confidential A term for a horse suitable for the novice or elderly rider.

Conformation A horse's make and shape.

Connemara A pony of great antiquity, bred in western Eire. It shows signs of Spanish and Arab blood, due perhaps to merchants of Galway trading with Spain. Hardy and tireless, docile, sound and intelligent, it stands 13–14.2 h.h. (132–144 cm) and makes an excellent small hunter. Colour, grey, black, brown, dun with occasional chestnuts and roans, but grey predominates. *Breed Societies:* The Connemara Pony Breeders' Society, Galway, Eire; and the English Connemara Pony Society (*see Plate* 9).

Connemara Pony Breeders' Society, The (Founded in Eire, 1923, offices in Galway). *Objects:* to encourage the breeding of Connemara ponies and their development and maintenance as a pure breed.

Connemara Pony Society, The English (Founded 1946). *Objects:* to encourage the breeding and the utilization of improved types of Connemara Ponies in England.

Conestoga Wagon Primitive covered wagon (canvas over wooden hoops) of the western American plains, used in the nineteenth century. Also known as Prairie Schooner.

Conquistadores The name given to the Spanish Conquerors of Mexico in the sixteenth century. This small troop of cavalry brought the first horses to the Western Hemisphere since their disappearance millions of years before, and the natives thought horse and rider were one being. Panic and terror spread in their ranks and Bernal del Castillo Diaz, the contemporary historian of the invaders, wrote, 'After God we owed the victory to the horses'.

Constipation Recognizable by small hard droppings. *Cause:* faulty feeding and lack of exercise. *Treatment:* soft food, laxative and an enema if necessary. Recurrence can be avoided by laxatives and small doses of salts.

Contact The link through the reins between the mouth of the horse and the hands of the rider. It should be positive yet light, and on a well-schooled horse it may be maintained by the weight of the reins alone.

Continental Martingale *see* MARTINGALE, CONTINENTAL.

Continental Panel A term used to describe a forward-cut saddle panel with knee and thigh rolls.

Contracted Heels When the frog has been pared away too much and has become dry and is not in contact with the ground. Frog pressure is both a prevention and a cure. *Treatment:* the wall should be well rasped down at the heels so that the frog makes contact with the ground, and this will encourage expansion. Contracted heels are a serious defect, being the forerunner of navicular disease (*q.v.*).

Cooked Food With the exception of bran mashes, these are not recommended except in cases of sickness.

Cooling The best way to cool a horse on returning to the stables is to rack him up, loosen belly band or girths, release the tail from the crupper and let the horse stand for a few minutes. Remove the harness or saddle and go lightly over with the wisp. The horse must be kept out of draughts, and after 10–15 minutes clothing should be put on.

Cooper, Abraham, R.A. (1787–1868) Son of a tobacconist. He was a self-taught artist, apart from some instruction from Ben Marshall (*q.v.*). He exhibited 352 pictures over 58 years at the Royal Academy and is known for a variety of animal and sporting subjects, especially racehorses.

'Cope' A hunting cry—'cope-forrard', cheer of whipper-in.

'Copenhagen' The charger of phenomenal stamina which the Duke of Wellington rode at the battle of Waterloo. 'Copenhagen' was by 'Meteor' by the illustrious 'Eclipse' (*q.v.*), and raced in the colours of General Grosvenor as a 3-year-old, but his turf career was not crowned with much success, and he passed into the possession of the Iron Duke. The name of 'Copenhagen' was expunged from the General Stud Book because of a fault in his pedigree. His dam, 'Lady Catherine', carried General Grosvenor at the Siege of Copenhagen (hence the name), and embarked for England in foal.

Coper   Horse-dealer; the modern use of the word is usually opprobrious, implying one who practises sharp or underhand methods to influence the sale of a horse. Also known as Horse-coper.

Cording   The cruel practice of fixing a hard piece of cord round a horse's tongue and attaching the ends to the bit in such a manner that a slight jerk would cause the tongue to be cut. The idea was that the sudden pain would make the horse step higher. The practice is now prohibited.

Cordwainers' Company   (After the Spanish name for leather known as 'cordovan' or 'cordwain' used in boot-making.) The first reference to the Guild was recorded in 1272 and a Charter was granted by Henry VI in 1439. The Guild was then composed almost entirely of shoemakers, and there are still many practical boot-makers among its Liverymen. The Company grants numerous pensions and supports the Cordwainers Technical College.

Corinthian (U.S.A.)   A class for hunters, both conformation and work-ing, in U.S.A. shows, 'to be ridden in full hunting attire by amateurs who are members of (or in cases of a subscrip-tion pack, fully accredited subscribers to) a recognized or registered Hunt'. Judged on performance and soundness, with emphasis on brilliance 85 per cent, appointments 15 per cent. Shown over natural hunting field jumps in the ring. Appointments include those of both horse and rider.

Corinthians   A name applied generally to the 'bloods' of Regency days, who delighted to drive well-horsed coaches, curricles and Highflyer phaetons (*q.v.*).

Corium   The skin-like membraneous covering of the pedal bone and lateral cartilages, on which are spread the sensitive laminae, or to which the sensi-tive laminae are attached.

Corn, Seat of   The terminal portion of the wings of the sole between the bars and the wall at the heel.

Corn Bin   Receptacle for holding corn; it should be made of metal and not be kept in the stable in case a horse breaks loose, finds the bin uncovered and gorges to excess.

Cornish Snaffle   *see* SCORRIER SNAFFLE.

Corns   Caused by undue pressure by the shoe, due to bad shoeing or to the shoes having been left on too long. They are visible as reddish-yellow or bluish-red discolorations of the sole in the heel region. In horses with small frogs or in those which have been unduly pared, the heels may make heavy contact with the ground and produce corns.

Cornucrescine   An ointment for promoting hoof growth.

Coronary Band   This lies at the top of the foot between the perioplic band and the sensitive laminae or fleshy leaves of the hoof. This band, or cushion as it is also called, consists of fibro-fatty tissue, covered by a vascular fleshy covering, which nourishes and from which grows the hoof wall. This lies in the coronary groove around the upper border of wall.

Coronation Coach   Correctly desig-nated the State Coach, was ordered in 1758 but was finished four years later, just too late for the Coronation of George III. The cost complete was £7562, of which £1673 went to the coachmaker, Butler, £2500 to the carver, Wilton, and £933 to the gilder, Pajolas. Cipriani, the painter of the lovely panels, received £315 and the balance was paid to harness-makers, saddlers, drapers and cover-makers, etc. The back wheels of the coach are nearly 6 ft (1.8 m) in diameter and modelled on those of an ancient trium-phal car. The original damask is still retained, but new sponge-rubber cushioning, modern lighting and special rubber tyres were fitted for the Coronation of Queen Elizabeth II (*see Plate* 10).

Coronet The coronary band surrounding the top of the foot at the lower extremity of the growth of hair.

Coronet Bone *see* PASTERN, SHORT.

Coronet Boot A felt boot reinforced with leather worn just above the coronary band to prevent injuries from treading, overreaching, etc.

Coronitis A chronic inflammation of the coronet which may become gangrenous. The condition may lead to an abnormal growth of the coronet which, in its turn, may result in the hoof actually becoming separated from the coronet. The horse becomes lame and develops a shuffling gait. A veterinary surgeon must be consulted. Mules, and horses engaged in fast work, are most prone to this trouble, which is also known as Villitis. Septic coronitis is usually the result of a nail prick or a picked-up nail which introduces infection. Pus finds its way up through the sensitive laminae and usually breaks out at the coronary band.

Corporal of Horse A rank in either of the two regiments of the Household Cavalry and equivalent in rank to a sergeant in other regiments.

Corral A high stout timber-built fenced-in enclosure for containing horses, cattle, etc. (*see* POUND).

Corrugated Iron Being a conductor of heat and cold, this is undesirable for stable roofing. It can, however, be underdrawn with straw thatch, thus disposing of these objections, and it then has the advantage of not sweating.

Cosh Familiar name for a stick carried for riding (also known as a 'bat').

Cottage Windows The windows of a stage coach when they are divided into four small panes.

Coughing off Grass *see* COUGHS.

Coughs Any form of cough is an unsoundness while it lasts. It may not be serious, but it is necessary to find the cause. *Cough due to broken wind:* a chronic condition, recognizable as a distressing, long-drawn-out cough. All food should be fed damp, and every few days linseed oil should be mixed with it. *Coughing off grass:* on being stabled after a period on grass, a horse will often cough because of impure air in the stable or because of indigestion. Leave the stable door wide open to give all possible air, and let the change to hard food be gradual. *Cough due to indigestion:* the trouble arises in the stomach and intestines and its removal is often a matter of considerable time. The digestive organs must return to normal working, and doses of linseed oil should be given. If worms are suspected, treat for them. *Cough due to teething:* this will probably be quite a temporary trouble which will clear up when the teething period is over. Keep the horse warm and generally comfortable, and see that the bowels are kept open. *Note:* in cases of throat or lung trouble, medicines should never be given in the form of a drench, but should be administered in food or water or in the form of a ball. Coughing in the form of an epidemic is usually caused by a virus (*see* EQUINE INFLUENZA).

Counter Canter *see* CANTER FALSE.

Counter Changes of Hand on Two Tracks The half-pass (*q.v.*) executed in a series, alternately from left to right and right to left, with a predetermined number of steps.

Counter Lead Cantering on the right rein with the near fore-leg leading, or on the left rein with off-fore leading (*see* CANTER FALSE).

'Counters' The heel portion of the leg of a boot. Stiffeners are used between these and the leg.

Country   A hunting term indicating the area of a particular country over which any pack may hunt.

County Cup   *see* HURLINGHAM POLO ASSOCIATION MEDIUM CHAMPIONSHIP.

Coupé   A short four-wheeled closed carriage with an inside seat for two and an outside seat for the driver. Also the front or after compartment of a Continental diligence (*q.v.*).

Couple   A term denoting two fox-hounds. The number in a pack is reckoned in couples and couples and a half, e.g. twelve and a half couple. One hound is not described as half a couple but as one hound.

Couples   Hound collars, joined by a metal distance link, carried on the 'D' of a whipper-in's saddle. The term can also refer to the two buckle or snap-hook ends of a lead rein.

Couples Lead   Leading couples of either leather or chain, connecting the bit rings, and having a central ring to which the lead rein is attached.

Coupling Reins   In pair and team they buckle to the insides of the bits at one end and join the draught reins (*q.v.*) at the other. The correct adjustment of their length to suit the horses is very important and not easy to achieve.

Coupling Up   Fastening the coupling reins in pair and team driving.

Courbette   High school air 'above the ground' (*q.v.*) in which the horse assumes the position of almost a full rear, jumps forward off its hocks and lands again with hocks bent, maintaining the position of the rear, and so proceeds in short bounds.

Courier   Seventeenth-century military term for a light horseman acting as a scout or skirmisher.

Course   To course a fox is to run it in view, the opposite of hunting it by scent.

Course (Show Jumping)   The circuit of jumps a competitor must follow to complete a round.

Court   The paved yard attached to hound kennels.

Cover   A stud term (*see* SERVICE).

Cover   The width of the 'web' (*q.v.*) (whole substance of the horseshoe).

Covered School   A building used for riding, with a suitable floor of tan, sand or sawdust. A full-size school measures about 65 yd by 22 yd (59.4 m × 20.1 m).

Covering-boots   For use on hind feet of mares during service. They are made of thick felt, heavily reinforced with leather, and are strapped on.

Covert   (pronounced 'Cover'). A Hunting term indicating any wood other than a very large one (*see* 'WOOD-LAND').

Covert Coat   In earlier days hunting men hacked to covert side in a light top coat of fine Venetian Twill—hence the name—and later the cloth used became known as Covert cloth, which is used mostly for light-weight coats for riders and is usually of thigh length. Covert is made with whipcord weave, the best qualities containing warp threads of worsted twist which impart a flecked appearance. Although not waterproof it is showerproof, because the yarns from which the cloth is made are proofed before weaving. A product of the West of England.

Covert Hack   A horse formerly used to convey a rider to a meet of hounds. Of a good riding type, it possessed well-placed shoulders, short sound legs, and a good back and quarters. It was up to weight, a nice easy mover at the trot and the canter, and also able to jump in case the hunter failed to arrive at the meet.

Cowboy or Cow Puncher   A man employed on the big cattle ranches of N.

Anglo-Arab

Akhal-Teké

(*above*) Andalusian

PLATE 2

(*below*) American Saddlebred

Appaloosa

Arab

PLATE 4

(*left*) Budyonovsky

(*right*) Waler

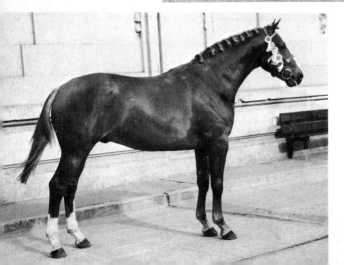

(*left*) Anglo-Argentino

PLATE 5

(*right*) The
Normandy Bank at
Badminton

(*below*) Barrel-racing

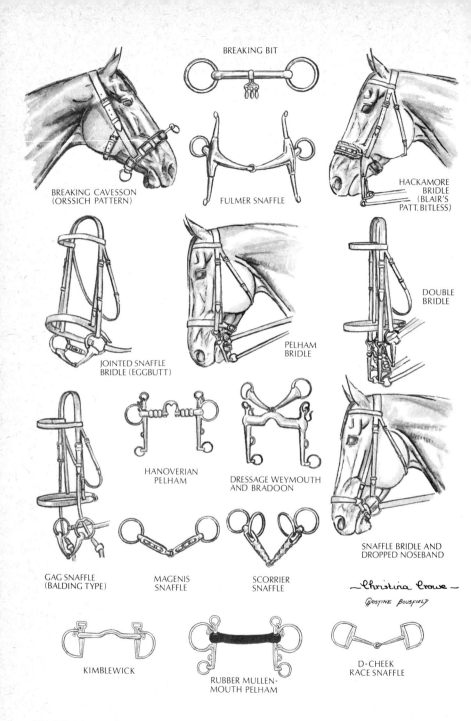

BREAKING BIT

BREAKING CAVESSON
(ORSSICH PATTERN)

FULMER SNAFFLE

HACKAMORE
BRIDLE
(BLAIR'S
PATT. BITLESS)

JOINTED SNAFFLE
BRIDLE (EGGBUTT)

PELHAM
BRIDLE

DOUBLE
BRIDLE

GAG SNAFFLE
(BALDING TYPE)

HANOVERIAN
PELHAM

DRESSAGE WEYMOUTH
AND BRADOON

MAGENIS
SNAFFLE

SCORRIER
SNAFFLE

SNAFFLE BRIDLE AND
DROPPED NOSEBAND

Christina Crowe

CRISTINE BOUSFIELD

KIMBLEWICK

RUBBER MULLEN-
MOUTH PELHAM

D-CHEEK
RACE SNAFFLE

PLATE 6   Bits and Bridles

Calgary Stampede

PLATE 7

The Royal Canadian Mounted Police

(*above*) Clydesdale

PLATE 8

(*below*) Cleveland Bay

(*above*) Cob

PLATE 9

(*below*) Connemara

Windsor Greys leaving Royal Mews

PLATE 10

Coronation Coach

PLATE 11

(*left*) Dartmoor
Pony

(*right*) Dales Pony

(*right*) Exmoor Pony

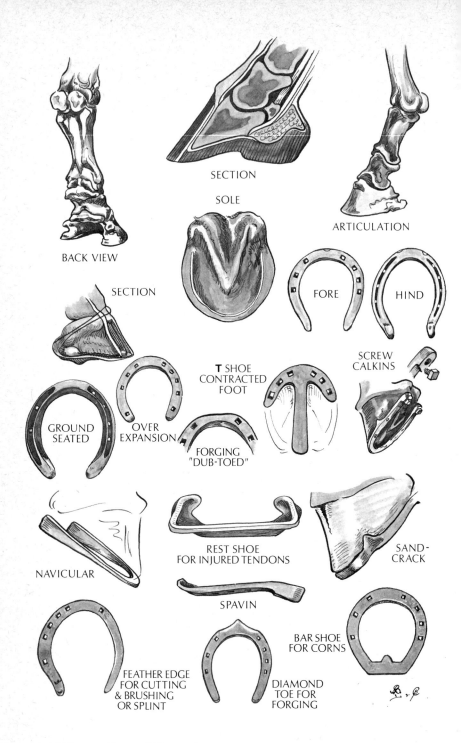

BACK VIEW

SECTION

ARTICULATION

SOLE

SECTION

FORE

HIND

SCREW CALKINS

GROUND SEATED

OVER EXPANSION

T SHOE CONTRACTED FOOT

FORGING "DUB-TOED"

NAVICULAR

REST SHOE FOR INJURED TENDONS

SAND-CRACK

SPAVIN

BAR SHOE FOR CORNS

FEATHER EDGE FOR CUTTING & BRUSHING OR SPLINT

DIAMOND TOE FOR FORGING

PLATE 12   Feet and Shoes

(*right*)
The Grand National

PLATE 13

(*right*) The Derby at
Tattenham Corner

(*right*) A Point-to-
point

(*above*) Fell Pony

PLATE 14

(*below*) Fjord Pony

PLATE 15

(*right*) Hackney
Pony

(*left*) Hack

(*right*) Hackney
Horse

(above) Haflinger

PLATE 16

(below) Hanoverian

America to watch, guard and round up cattle which roam almost wild on the ranges.

Cow-collar A leather strap which circles the neck with ring attachment for lead. Most useful on horses which habitually slip their head collars at grass but unpopular as it wears down the mane.

Cowdray Park Open Gold Cup (Polo) Took the place of the Polo Championship Cup in 1956. For results *see page* 383.

Cow-gulleted Saddle *see* LANE-FOX SADDLE.

Cowhide The leather from which 95 per cent of saddlery is made; its substance (i.e. thickness) varies according to the purpose of its use. Colours are: London — light, Havana — medium, Warwick — dark.

Cow-hocks Hocks which are turned inwards at the points, as in a cow.

Cowhocks

Cow Horn The American hunting horn still used with some American fox-hounds, mostly south of Philadelphia.

Cow-kick Forward kick which some horses give with the hind legs. It could be a serious danger to a rider mounting or standing beside it.

Cow-mouthed Saddle *see* LANE-FOX SADDLE.

Cow Pony The mount of the cowboy or cow puncher usually of great stamina and hardiness, though generally lacking in beauty (*see* ARGENTINE PONY and CRIOLLO).

Cowt North country term for a young male horse. Local pronunciation of colt (*q.v.*).

Crab Unfavourable criticism of a horse, likely to depreciate its value or prevent a sale.

Cracked Heels Dermatitis or inflammation involving the skin and its glands in the hollow of the heel, particularly in the hind legs. *Causes:* insufficient drying of the legs after washing, clipping the hair from the hollows, and standing in dirty stalls or boxes. White legged horses suffer most, probably because their legs are washed more often, especially if soft soap is used. *Symptoms:* the animal is stiff and sore on first leaving the stable, and may move as though afflicted with stringhalt, or walk on the toe for a step or two. The pastern joints become swollen and painful, and the hollow of the heel breaks out with a bloody discharge. *Treatment:* a veterinary surgeon will probably prescribe an ointment containing hydrocortisone and an antibiotic. Kaolin poultices are often useful and the old-fashioned lead liniment, made up from a solution of acetate of lead emulsified with olive or rape oil, is a useful dressing both in early cases and as a preventive.

'Cracking the Nostrils' *see* HIGH BLOWING.

Cracks The foot is subject to various cracks which are distinguished according to location as toe-cracks, side-cracks, quarter-cracks, bar-cracks and sandcracks. The term sandcrack usually covers the whole foot, 'toe', 'quarter', etc., denoting location (*see also* SAND-CRACK).

Cradle   A device consisting of several lengths of rounded wood fastened at intervals by leather straps to form a necklet around the horse's neck from throat to shoulder, and designed to prevent a horse which is suffering from irritation or under treatment from biting the afflicted area. An improved version is known as the Cheshire Cradle. This consists of a padded, curved metal bar encasing the chest and fastened to the roller, with a further bar projecting from the centre fastening to the headcollar. It is more comfortable and does not chafe.

Cradle

Cradle Stirrup Irons   Irons where the tread is rounded to give a circular appearance. Used for racing under both Rules. This shape allows a lighter iron and is more comfortable to a foot encased in a thin boot. Made from steel and also aluminium.

Cramped Action   A term used when a horse fails to move with freedom.

Crash Helmet (Racing)   *see* SKULL CAPS.

Cream Colour   The body coat is of a cream colour, with unpigmented skin. The iris is deficient in pigment and is often devoid of it, giving the eye a pinkish or bluish appearance.

Crib   A rack or manger in a stable.

Crib Biting   A disagreeable and harmful vice, similar to that of the windsucker (*q.v.*). The horse lays hold of the rim of the manger, or any other projection, with its teeth and sucks wind at the same time.

Crib-biting Device   This may be one of many patterns, all of which in some way or another bring pressure upon the horse's gullet in an attempt to prevent both this unpleasant habit and wind sucking.

Crinet   Horse armour for the neck and throat.

Criollo   A descendant of horses brought over by the Spaniards in the Conquest of South America, which were mainly Barbs and Andalusian horses. This hardy breed comes in many colours from dun to roan, brown, black and skewbald (*see* THE HORSE IN SOUTH AMERICA, *page* 309).

Crocker's Bit   *see* ROCKWELL BRIDLE.

Cronet   The hair growing over the top of a horse's hoof. Part of the armour of a horse.

Crop   *see* WHIP, HUNTING.

Cropped Ears   *see* EARS, IDENTIFICATION MARKS.

Cross-breeding   The mating of pure-bred individuals of different breeds.

Crossing Feet   A horse whose fore-legs are faulty, and whose freedom of action is thereby impaired, is liable to cross its feet. (Commonly called 'Plaiting' or 'Lacing'.)

Crossing Traces   The inside trace of one leader fastening to the inside hook of its partner's bar. This levels up two leaders which are working unevenly.

Cross Noseband   A loose term covering the Grakle or Figure 8 nosebands (*qq.v.*), both of which have intersecting straps.

Cross-saddle All riding saddles other than the side-saddle (*q.v.*).

Croup The *upper line* from loins to root of tail which should be *convex* even when a fairly heavy weight is carried.

Croupade High school air above the ground, almost identical with the *ballotade* (*q.v.*), except that the horse is not showing its shoes.

Croupade

Crowned Old term for a horse with 'broken' knees where a certain portion of the hair has become removed.

'Crudwell' Flat racer and steeplechaser who won 50 out of 108 races from 1949–1960, the biggest number of any racehorse in the twentieth century in Britain. Named after Wiltshire village where he was born.

Cruelty Our increased knowledge of the practice of anaesthesia, local and general, makes even minor surgery quite painless. Under recent legislation surgical operations without anaesthetics constitute a punishable offence. Not only is cruelty contemptible in and degrading to those responsible for it, but also it is entirely useless, as it is of absolutely no educational value to the horse—in fact, it is likely to give every encouragement to the development of many vices. Overwork and under-

feeding are indirect forms of cruelty. Undue use of whip and spur must be included.

Crupper, Breaking Constructed as those for riding, etc., but should have fastened buckles on either side of the dock piece to permit fitting and adjustment without upsetting the pupil.

Crupper, Harness A leather loop which is passed under the tail and is attached to the 'D' on the pad of a harness horse to keep it in position. It is best to fill it with linseed, which exudes a certain amount of grease, thus preventing friction.

Crupper, Riding A strap-shaped, padded piece of leather which passes under the tail and is attached to the saddle to steady it. A riding crupper is frequently used on ponies when deficient withers make it hard to keep the saddle in place. As with the harness crupper (*see above*), it should be filled with linseed to avoid chafing.

Crust of Hoof or Wall The hard outside covering of the wall, like the crust of a loaf of bread; the term comprises the *whole* of the crust, not the outside portion only.

Cry A hunting term indicating the sound made by the pack when actually hunting its quarry.

Csikos Hungarian cowboys who tend the herds of horses during their long summer sojourn on the *Puszta* or Hungarian grazing plains.

C-Spring *see* CEE-SPRING.

Cub When applied to foxes the term indicates any young fox up to November 1st. Cubs are usually born in March, though they may arrive any time between Christmas and May; the average number in a litter is five, though as many as thirteen have been known.

Cub-hunting This may begin any time between the end of July and the end of September depending on the gathering of the harvest. The objects are to teach young unentered hounds to hunt, and fox cubs to leave their coverts, as well as to reduce a fox population which is deemed excessive. In this case there is no question of the huntsman showing sport nor, strictly, should followers be there, except on the invitation of the Master. It follows that no cap (*q.v.*) should be taken.

Cubes, Horse   Modern method of concentrated feeding for horses, in the form of cubes. These are claimed to be scientifically balanced and may vary according to manufacturers' prescriptions.

Cumeling   A thirteenth-century name for a horse which, of its own accord, attached itself to, and became the property of the lord of the manor.

Cup (Show Jumping)   Shaped metal holder for fence pole.

Cur-dog   Name applied in hunting to a dog of any breed other than hound. Originally 'Care' dog: a dog which took care of sheep and which was usually responsible for coursing a hunted fox.

Curb   Indicating a curb bit.

Curb   This occurs as a thickening of the tendon or ligament on the back of the hock, about a hand's breadth below the point, and is caused by undue strain. It is not necessarily accompanied by lameness. *Treatment:* Rest the heel with calkins or a wedge-shaped shoe and apply cold water and, if necessary, a blister. Firing generally effects a permanent cure.

Curb-chain   A chain fitted to the eye of the curb or Pelham bit and lying in the groove of the jaw just above the lower lip. Added pressure on the lower rein increases the leverage and tightens the curb-chain. The chain itself consists of approximately 17 flat or semi-flat links, full size, with a ring in the centre through which the leather lip-strap passes. A less severe curb can be constructed from soft leather or doubled elastic.

Curb Hook   Fastened to one side to save losing chain. Made in pairs and varying from $1\frac{1}{4}$ in to $2\frac{1}{2}$ in (32–64 mm).

Curb Hook, Circle   A round flat disc, with the centre part taken away to enable the hook to fit snugly inside. Reputed to be gall proof.

Curb Hook, Liverpool   Single hook, can be used either side.

Curb-reins   These are the reins attached to the lower rings of the bars forming part of the curb bit. The curb-rein is narrower in width by $\frac{1}{8}$ in (3 mm) than the snaffle rein.

'Curby Hocks'   An expression indicating hocks affected by curb trouble, or ones shaped in such a manner that they are liable to be sprained, and so spring a curb. False curbs are present when the head of the inner splint bone (small metatarsal) is larger than normal, causing the appearance of curb.

Curragh, The   Site of the well-known racecourse in County Kildare, Eire, where the Irish Derby is run annually.

Curre-type (pronounced 'Cur')   A type of foxhound predominantly English-bred with one or more strains of Welsh foxhound blood. The breed was originated by the late Sir Edward Curre.

Curricle

Curricle   The only English two-wheeled carriage designed for a pair of horses driven abreast. As applied to harnessing, the term denotes the putting of a pair to a two-wheeled vehicle by means of a curricle bar.

Curricle Bar   A transverse bar over the horses' backs used to put to a pair-driven curricle.

Currier   *see* CURRY, TO.

Curry, to   To rub down or dress a horse with a comb, hence currier, an obsolete term for a groom.

Currycomb   A flat piece of metal having on one side either a handle ('jockey' pattern) or a webbing loop through which the hand is passed, and, on the other side, strips of metal into which blunt teeth are set at right angles. The comb is used for scraping the dust from a body brush, etc. Combs are now made in plastic and rubber and can be used on the body to remove a shedding coat or mud (*see Plate* 29).

Curtal, or **Curtall**   In the sixteenth and seventeenth centuries a horse with its tail cut short (and sometimes ears cropped) of a small size or breed (*see also* EARS, IDENTIFICATION MARKS).

Curvet   A light leap in which the horse raises its forelegs together, followed by the hind legs with a spring, before the forelegs touch the ground again. A leap; a frolic.

Cut   Gelded.

Cut and Laid   A fairly low fence made by cutting thorn branches half way through and binding them in and out among stakes set into the middle of the fence.

Cut and Laid Fence

'Cut a Voluntary'   Hunting slang meaning to fall off a horse as opposed to 'take a fall' which implies that the rider *and* horse both have a fall.

Cutaway (Coat)   *see* SHADBELLY.

Cut-Back Head   Denotes a saddle, the tree of which is cut away at the head to provide clearance for the withers. Trees are made from quarter cut-back to full cut-back. The latter is known as a 'cow-mouth' (*see* LANE-FOX SADDLE).

Cut 'Em Down   Nineteenth-century colloquial hunting term meaning reckless and ruthless riders.

Cutting Horse   Cow pony schooled in 'cutting out' (separating) selected beasts from a herd of cattle.

Cuttop   The protections covering the top of the wheels, which shelter the axle-tree arms from dirt.

D (Racing)   Abbreviation for distance.

D.B.H.S.   Diploma of the British Horse Society.

D.B.S.   Donkey Breed Society.

'D.M.'   Formerly the official Racing Calendar abbreviation for the Ditch Mile (on Newmarket Racecourse). No longer used.

D's   Metal fittings on the saddle, shaped like the letter *D*, and to which can be attached the breast-plate, hound couples, and sundry other items such as raincoats, flasks, etc.

'D' Shape Bit   *see* SNAFFLE BIT.

Daily Double   *see* TOTE DOUBLE.

Daisy-cutting   Descriptive of the action which is at the walk or trot close to the ground and shows little elevation, eg., the Arab.

Dalby, David (1790–1840)   A capable Yorkshire artist with a first-hand acquaintance with sport. He was popular with northern squires; his subjects included hunter and racehorse portraits, hunting and, occasionally, driving scenes.

Dales   A breed of pony native to the eastern part of northern England, similar to but slightly larger than the Fell breed, associated with the western side. In the past they were crossed with Clydesdales for size, presumably to meet demands, but now they rarely exceed 14.1 h.h. (143 cm). They may be black, bay or brown in colour and are exceptionally strong, sure-footed and active. Their tendency to a straight shoulder makes them more suitable to drive than ride. *Breed Society:* The Dales Pony Society (*see Plate* 11).

Dales Pony Improvement Society, The   Founded in 1917 to encourage and improve the standard of the Dales Pony.

Dales Pony Society   Formed in 1964 by the amalgamation of the Northern Dales Pony Society and the Dales Pony Improvement Society.

Dally   An American expression used to denote the rapid passing of a lariat round the saddle horn.

Dam   Female parent of a horse or foal.

Damage Fund   A small cap made by some Hunts, usually at each meet, on all present, including foot followers, to compensate landowners and others for damage (often combined with a Poultry Fund).

Damp Food   The giving of damp food, grain, chaff, etc., is not to be recommended, except in the case of an animal affected in the wind.

Dandy   A horse-drawn railway-carriage used in Cumberland from 1861–1914.

Dandy Brush   A wooden-backed brush with strong bristles, or plastic or nylon tufts, used for removing dried mud. It should not be used on manes or tails, where a water-brush is the correct implement (*see* STABLE MANAGEMENT, *page* 315, *and Plate* 29).

Dandy Cart   Spring cart once used by tradesmen, especially milkmen.

Danebury Mark   An old racing expression given to very light racehorses (often having to wear a breast-girth to keep saddles from slipping forward) which show a deep mark or groove running down the quarters on either side of the tail.

Danish Horse   The horse indigenous to Denmark was small and thick-set, and was crossed at various times with Dutch, Spanish, Turkish and English Thoroughbreds. Thus were created Danish breeds such as the Frederiksborg, named after the town near Copenhagen, where a great stud existed from 1562 to 1862. A useful strong cart horse, resembling the Schleswig, is bred in Jutland, and in some coastal districts a small pony is found belonging to the same group as the Iceland Pony.

Danloux Saddle   A saddle designed by the great French horseman Robert Danloux. Its peculiarity is a squab set under the flap in the bend of the rider's knee and a high forward roll giving support well above the knee. Usually used with a thick felt numnah (*q.v.*).

Dark Horse (Racing)   A horse whose form is unknown outside its stable.

Darley Arabian, The   Imported into England in 1704 by Mr Richard Darley, a Yorkshire squire. The Darley Arabian was of the Managhi strain, one of the best breeds of the Anazeh Arabs, and became the most famous progenitor of the Thoroughbred (*q.v.*). He sired the 'Flying Childers' and was great-great grandsire of 'Eclipse' (*q.v.*) (*see* THE ARABIAN HORSE, *page* 112, EVOLUTION OF THE HORSE, *page* 112 *and* THE ENGLISH THOROUGHBRED, *page* 333).

Dartmoor Pony   A small indigenous pony found in a semi-wild state in the district of that name in the extreme south-west of England. One of the nine mountain and moorland or native breeds of the British Isles (which includes the Connemara), the Dartmoor provides a riding pony of 12 h.h. (122 cm), of great hardiness, some elegance and much charm. Many show hacks and ponies of the highest class have been bred up from Dartmoor ponies. *Breed Society:* The Dartmoor Pony Society (*see Plate* 11).

Dartmoor Pony Society, The   (Founded 1920) *Objects:* To promote and encourage the breeding of pure Dartmoor ponies, which can be entered in the National Pony Society Stud Book.

Dartnall Rein   A specially soft plaited cotton rein shaped to the rider's hands and used for show jumping. Handmade by the Dartnall family of Richmond, Surrey.

Dash Board   The upright protection in front of the coachman's feet in some vehicles; of stiff leather or wood.

Davis, Richard Barrett (1782–1854) A sporting artist born to a sporting atmosphere, being a son of Richard Davis, Huntsman to the Royal Harriers, and brother of Charles Davis, Huntsman to the Royal Buckhounds. Living much at Windsor, he painted many spirited hunting scenes and numerous mounted portraits of Masters and huntsmen (often engraved), including the well-known portrait of his brother Charles on his horse 'Hermit'. Another brother, W. H. Davis, also painted sporting scenes, and horse and cattle portraits.

Day Rug   *see* CLOTHING.

Dead Heat   When two or more horses pass the winning post in a dead line. The dead heat is not run off; when two horses run a dead heat for first place, all prizes to which the first and second horses would have been entitled are divided equally between them. Each horse that divides a prize for first place is deemed a winner for penalties. Stallions siring these are each credited with a winner.

Dead Meat (Racing)   A term used when a stable has no intention that a horse shall win.

Deafness   Often associated with great docility, deaf horses being very easily controlled by the rein.

Deal   A common term in the horse trade when a sale is completed.

Dealer's Rug   A jute rug, usually half-lined, rectangular in shape and fastening by means of a surcingle around the breast.

Dealer's Whip   A steel-lined drop thong whip used by horse-dealers, chiefly at fairs.

Decarpentry, General Albert Edouard Eugène (1878–1956)   Instructor at Saumur; President of the

F.E.I. Panel of Dressage Judges; author of works on dressage and equestrian history and biography. *Piaffe and Passage* and the famous *Academic Equitation* are available in English. During his lifetime he was generally looked upon as the ultimate international authority and today as the greatest equitation master of the twentieth century.

Declaration of Forfeit   All entries of horses in races must be made to the Racing Calendar Office at Weatherby's, Wellingborough, Northants, by the owner of the horse or his authorized agent, which is usually his trainer. The terms of the races vary. Most big races with £4000 or more added money have one or more forfeit stages, when it must be decided whether to pay more to keep the horse in the race or 'Declare forfeit'; i.e. forfeit the entry fee, etc., and take the horse out of the race.

Declaration of Runners   A horse entered in a particular race must be declared a runner in that race to the Overnight Declarations Office of the Jockey Club (Weatherby's, Wellingborough, Northants) normally four days before the race is to be run, Sunday being a *non dies*. Declarations to run can be cancelled normally up to 11 a.m. on the day prior to the running of the race.

Deep (Hunting)   A term indicating that the 'going' (*q.v.*) is soft or heavy (*see* HOLDING).

Deep through the Girth   Descriptive of a horse that is well ribbed up with generous depth of girth behind the elbows (*see* HEART ROOM).

Déjuger, se   French term meaning that the hind feet touch down behind the imprints left by the forefeet (*see* JUGER, SE and MÉJUGER, SE).

Deli   *see* BATAK.

Demi-mail Phaeton (or Semi-mail)   A lighter and more elegant form of Mail Phaeton (*q.v.*). Unlike this it had a wheel arch in the body and was without a perch. It was used in town as well as country.

Demi-Pique   Abbreviated term for the Demi-piqued saddle which was used by heavy cavalry and ordinary travellers in the eighteenth century. It was a saddle with a half horn or low peak half as high as that on the original heavy cavalry saddle of the mid-seventeenth century, and properly termed the 'Great Saddle'.

Demi-sang   A term used in many countries to describe a first Thoroughbred cross.

Dennett   An early form of gig, an improved version of the Whiskey (*q.v.*).

Derby, British Jumping   *see* BRITISH JUMPING DERBY.

Derby, Edward George Villiers, 17th Earl of (1865–1948)   One of the greatest patrons of the turf, and most successful owner and breeder, Lord Derby won twenty classics (1000 Guineas seven times, The St Leger six, The Derby three, and The Oaks and 2000 Guineas twice each), and gained £800,000 in stake money. He was the owner of 'Hyperion', 'Fairway', 'Swynford' and 'Phalaris', among others.

Derby Dinner at Tattersall's   The head of the famous firm, Richard Tattersall, gave an annual 'Derby Dinner' when each guest was required to drink the toast 'John Warde and the Noble Science' in a silver fox's head which held almost a pint of port. No heel-taps were admitted. None stood the ordeal better than Warde himself.

Derby Stakes, The   The Blue Riband of the Turf, run annually over a distance of $1\frac{1}{2}$ miles (2.4 km) on Epsom Downs normally on the first Wednesday in June. The race is for three-year-old colts and fillies. Colts carry 9 st (57.15 kg), fillies 8 st 9 lb (54.88 kg). The race was first run in 1780 under the auspices of the 12th Earl of Derby, who won the privilege of using his name by tossing a coin with Sir Charles Bunbury (*q.v.*), winner of the first Derby with 'Diomed' (*see Plate* 13). For results *see page* 387.

Description of Colour and Markings In 1954 the Royal College of Veterinary Surgeons recommended the following sequence for certification of horses: colour; breed; sex; age; height; marks on head (including eyes); marks on limbs, fore first, then hind, commencing from below; marks on body, including mane and tail; acquired marks, congenital abnormalities, whorls or any other features of note.

Destrier A war-horse (French), from the Latin *dextrarius* (the right side), the side on which the squire led his master's horse.

Destruction of Horse When a horse-slaughterer with a humane killer is not available, and a revolver or shot gun must be used, to find the vital spot draw an imaginary line from the base of the right ear to the top of the left eye and similarly from the left ear to the right eye, and fire at the intersection at close range. If the horse is lying down, making this difficult, aim at the back of the ear towards the brain.

Devon Horse Show and County Fair An eight-day show held in Devon, Pennsylvania, run for the benefit of the Bryn Mawr Hospital. One of the premier horse shows in the U.S.A.

Devonshire Slipper Stirrup

Devonshire Slipper Stirrup This type accommodates the entire foot as in a leather slipper, and revolves on a bar. Benjamin Latchford (*q.v.*) in his treatise of 1883 illustrates a number of similar types. Now almost unobtainable.

Diagonal Aids Right rein used with left leg or, alternatively, left rein with right leg.

Diana A Roman divinity who, amongst other things, was the goddess of hunting.

Diarrhoea *see* PURGING.

Dick Christian Bridoon or Snaffle This pattern has a ring in the centre, which eliminates tongue pressure.

Dickey A seat at the rear of a vehicle for a servant.

'Dictator of the Turf' *see* ROUS, ADMIRAL.

Diligence A carriage used in pre-railway times in parts of Europe for the purpose served by the Stage Coach in England, i.e. carrying passengers travelling long distances by stages. Diligences had various 'classes' at differing rates of fare for inside and outside passengers, and were lumbering vehicles usually drawn by five horses.

Dioropha A two-headed carriage which could be used either open or closed. The two heads were moved by a pulley in the coach-house (*c.* 1851).

Dipped Back Descriptive of a horse when the dip between the withers and the croup is abnormally pronounced. Often noticeable in old age.

Directory of the Turf First published by Stud and Stable Ltd in 1961. New editions bring up to date biographical details of almost all of those professionally engaged in racing in Britain, with separate sections for owners, trainers, jockeys, studs, racecourses and the racing press.

Direct Rein A heading or opening rein, the action of which turns the horse's head towards the direction in which it is required to move. A natural rein action.

Dirt Tracks   Unknown in Britain for either flat or steeplechasing but in general use in many other countries. In the U.S.A. most 'big tracks' are dirt, a mile (1.6 km) oval (or longer) often with a turf course just inside the dirt track.

Diseases of the Horse   *see diagram on page* xiv.

Dish-face   *see* JIBBAH

Dishing   A faulty action. The foot of one or both of the forelegs is thrown outward and forward when moving forwards.

Dismounting   Take all the reins and the riding stick into the left hand and hold on to the horse's neck. Withdraw the feet from the stirrup irons, put the right hand on the front arch of the saddle, lean slightly forward and vault to the ground.

Distance, A   The lengths between horses at the finish of a race, if over twenty, are called 'a distance' (*see next entry*).

Distance, The   The 240 yards (219 m) from the winning post.

Disunited   *see* CANTER, DISUNITED and GALLOPING, DISUNITED.

Dixon, Henry Hall (1822–1870) English author who, under the pen-name of 'The Druid', wrote *Post and Paddock* (1856); *Silk and Scarlet* (1858); *Scott and Sebright* (1862); *Field and Fern* (1865); *Saddle and Sirloin* (1870).

Dock   That part of the tail upon which the hair grows as well as the bare underside.

'Docker, The'   A slang term for the short whip used by poor class drivers.

Docking   The amputation of a portion of the tail. Although the after effects were considered cruel by very many people and the practice was forbidden by law in most countries, it was permitted in England under the Anaesthetics Act and was practised on certain classes of horses. A portion of the tail, varying in length according to the owner's fancy, was clipped of hair and the end removed by a docking knife or scissors, the bleeding being stopped by the application of a hot docking-iron. Great care was required as lock-jaw or blood-poisoning might follow. The practice is now illegal in Britain by the Docking and Nicking Act, 1948. In ancient times this mutilation probably served some ritual purpose and still does in West Africa. Docking was sometimes used in England as early as the Mediaeval and Tudor eras and became widespread for harness horses at the beginning of the eighteenth century.

Dr Bristol Bit   Originally 'trotting man's bit'. Its action is 'non-nut-cracker', as it has an oval plate in the centre of the snaffle mouth; it is bent to ensure the maximum comfort for the tongue.

'Dr Green'   A term used to suggest the benefits of the new spring grass.

Dodman   East Anglian name for a snail. The slowest working horse on the farm was often named Dodman.

Doeskin   Used to cover a saddle where the rider requires assistance in gripping or extra comfort. Foam knee pads covered in doeskin are often inlaid into the flap of modern saddles.

Doer   'Good-doer'—a horse which thrives and keeps its flesh and condition; the converse, a 'bad-doer', one which lacks these in spite of every care.

'Dog'   A sluggish horse which has constantly to be forced into its work; also such racehorses as have failed in public races to reproduce home form.

Dog-cart   A two- or four-wheeled trap for one horse, seating, at full capacity, four people, the two at the rear sitting with their backs to the horse. Subject to many variations.

Dog-cart

Dog Fox   Male fox.

'Doggy' horses   *see* BLINKERS.

DØle Pony   A breed of northern Norway. A powerful pony but not heavy, with a strong arched neck, broad chest and quarters.

Dolls   Portable, lightweight barricades of wood used on racecourses to keep horses to the desired course.

Domador (South American)   A horse-breaker, trainer.

Domestication   *see* EVOLUTION, *page* 110.

Don   Russian Steppe horse, bred in the Don Valley. It is the largest of the native breeds, with a very characteristic ram-like head, about 14 h.h. (142 cm) and, thanks to its qualities as a saddle horse, it has proved an object of interest to the Russian Army which, for improvement, has crossed the breed with English Thoroughbreds, thereby creating the Anglo-Don.

'Done'   Said of a horse that is exhausted. Also used to refer to a horse when its grooming is completed.

Donkey   Term for the ass (*q.v.*). First used colloquially in 1785.

Donkey Breed Society, The   Founded in 1967 to promote the breeding and showing of donkeys and to assist all those who breed, own or are interested in them. (Formerly Donkey Show Society.)

Donkey Foot   An upright, narrow foot with a pinched-in heel and a contracted frog (*see* BOXY FOOT).

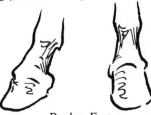

Donkey Foot

Donoghue,   Stephen   (1884–1945) Born in Warrington, Lancs. He was champion jockey in England 1914–1923. Won the Derby six times from 1915 to 1925, had six successive wins in the Queen Alexandra Stakes at Ascot on Sir Harold Wernher's 'Brown Jack' (*q.v.*).

Donsky   Russian breed developed in the Don Steppes for more than 200 years. It descends from crossing the local steppe horses with Karabakh, Turkmen, Persian, and later with the Orlov-Rastopchin   breed   and Thoroughbred saddle horses. Average height 16 h.h. (163 cm).

Doorman   The farrier whose work it is to prepare the feet, nail on the shoes, finish off (clinch up) and help to make new shoes (*see* FIREMAN).

Doped Fox (or 'touched up fox')   A fox which, to ensure a hunt, is caused to tread in some strong smelling liquid placed at the exit of the place where it is known to lie.

Doping   The practice of administering or causing to be administered, for the purpose of affecting the speed of a horse, drugs or stimulants, internally, by hypodermic or other methods. The administration of certain medicines properly prescribed by a veterinary surgeon may be regarded as doping if the horse is raced while such drugs remain within the system and can be detected by analysis.

Dormeuse   A heavy four-wheeled vehicle, invariably drawn by four horses, used in the nineteenth century by those who could afford to travel in their own carriages on the Continent. A description given by the then Duke of Beaufort is 'a travelling chariot with a long boot in front, into which one could, by letting down the front of it, put one's legs, the front fixing under the seat—made a good bed, a rolled-up mattress was kept in the boot, and this formed the cushions the travellers sat on. Imperials, bonnet-boxes, cap-boxes and wells under the seats held the luggage. On the dickey behind was a cabriolet head to keep the servants dry'. The hooded-dickey gave almost the appearance of a separate carriage joined to the greater one.

Dorsal Stripe   A continuous black, brown or dun stripe extending from the line of the neck to the tail, and sometimes continuing down the latter. Typical of Scandinavian and other types of north European and Asiatic breeds; many Highland ponies are so marked. Professor Ewart is of the opinion that all horses were once of a dun colour with a dorsal stripe and zebra markings on the fore-arms.

D'Orsay   A light carriage of the Brougham type, named after Count D'Orsay.

Dos-à-dos   A two- or four-wheeled dog-cart with seats placed back to back.

Dosage System   see VUILLIER DOSAGE SYSTEM.

Double   When a backer couples two horses to win in separate races. If the first horse wins, the amount won on it plus the original stake go on to the second horse. Both horses must win or the bet is lost.

Double (Hunting)   A fence or bank with a ditch on both sides.

Double (Show Jumping)   Two obstacles so spaced that they are judged as one obstacle.

Double Bank   Bank with a ditch on both the take off and the landing sides (see BANK [DOUBLE] AND DITCHES).

Double Bridle   see BRIDLE, DOUBLE, and WEYMOUTH BIT.

Double Harness   Pair harness.

Double the Horn, to   The notes made by the Huntsman, short, sharp and pulsating, indicate that a fox has been roused, has crossed a ride, or has been holloaed away.

Double Oxer (Hunting)   Any fence (hedge) having a protective rail just below the top of either side.

Double Oxer (Show Jumping)   A brush fence with poles on both sides, forming a spread fence (see Plate 20).

Double Thong   When a four-horse whip is 'caught' on the crop (as it is carried in normal use when not wanted for touching up the leaders), enough 'double thong' is left loose to reach the wheelers.

Draft   Hounds selected for the day's hunting or those, for any reason, weeded out from kennels.

Drag   An artificial scent made by trailing something which has been soaked in a strong-smelling liquid. For foxhounds the best drag is made from soiled litter from a tame fox's kennel, or a sack so impregnated. Aniseed is frequently used.

Drag   A slang name for a private or park coach kept for one's own driving as distinct from a stage or road coach (q.v.). They were painted in their owner's colours and with a monogram or crest emblazoned on both doors and on the boot in the rear. Accommodation was provided on the back seat for two grooms dressed in livery to match the paintwork of the coach (see Plate 26).

Park Drag

'Dragging the Goat' *see* BUZKASHI.

Drag-hunt To hunt with a pack of hounds on an artificial scent or drag laid by trailing material suitably impregnated (*see* DRAG).

Drag-Shoe *see* SKID-PAN.

Dragsman A coachman.

Drag Stick or **Drag Prop** A round pole of wooden construction about 3 in (7.5 cm) thick and headed with a sharp iron spike some 4 in (10 cm) long. The stick is fitted to the back axle of a cart about half-way between the centre of the axle and the rear offside wheel. An eye in the axle joins an eye fitted on the end of the drag stick, which is some 3 ft 6 in (1 m) in length. The purpose of the stick is to take the weight off the horse when the van is stationary on an incline, and to prevent the cart 'running back'. When not in use it can be hung up on the rear axle.

Drain In hunting this indicates an underground drain, pipe, culvert, ditch or watercourse, used as a refuge by foxes.

Draught Horse A horse used for drawing any vehicle, but it is a term more usually associated with the heavy breeds.

Draught Reins The main reins in pair and team driving, from the outside of the bits to the coachman's hand. To them are buckled the coupling reins (*q.v.*) that connect to the inside of the bit of the partner horse.

Dravelling Bit A breaking bit with three movable ports of different sizes attached. The choice can be made of which to use as 'port', the remaining two acting as 'keys'.

Draw A term used when hounds seek their fox in a covert or another place where it is accustomed to lie.

Draw The area selected for a day's hunting.

Draw When the huntsman or whipper-in removes a hound from the pack he is said to 'draw' it.

Draw (Show-jumping) To decide the order in which competitors enter to jump.

Draw for Places A draw for flat racing only is made by the Overnight Declarations Office (*q.v.*) to determine the stall or place each jockey shall take at the start, No. 1 being always on the extreme left as the horses face the start.

Drawing-knife A farrier's knife with a handle at each end, used for paring the hoof.

Draw Rein A rein attached to the girth and coming to the hand through the bit rings. Extremely severe means of control.

Draw Rein

Draw Yard The yard or other place in kennels where the hounds are collected before being drawn off by the huntsman to their respective lodging rooms.

Dray A low cart without sides for carrying a heavy load.

Drench Medicine suspended in warm or cold water, thin gruel, warm ale or in linseed or castor oils, and administered as a drink. It is resorted to when the bulk of the medicine makes it impracticable for it to be given as a ball. A special drenching bottle with a tapering neck and without a shoulder is employed for the purpose (*see* DRENCH, TO).

Drench, to Buckle the ends of a narrow leather strap together, forming a loop, and place this in the horse's mouth behind the incisor teeth. Insert the prong of a stable fork in the loop, raise the fork, thus elevating the head, and administer the drench. This should be in a special drenching bottle, the neck of the bottle should be inserted in the off-side of the mouth and the contents should be given slowly and carefully. So many medicines can now be administered by injection that drenching has now almost completely gone out of fashion.

Drenching Bit A bit having a circular perforated, tube mouthpiece, one end sealed, the other having a funnel attached.

Drenching Bottle A leather or metal bottle suitably shaped for administering 'drinks'.

Drenching Bottle

Dress, Correct (For Men) For *Hunting in Great Britain and Ireland* the following dress is correct: (1) Scarlet (pink) coat with skirt, or 'cutaway' with long tails, canary or other coloured vest with flap pockets, white breeches, black hunting boots with mahogany or 'flesh-coloured' tops, white leather garters, silk hat, hunting whip (crop) with thong and lash attached, spurs, white hunting tie (stock) with plain (undecorated) gold safety-pin. (2) Black or very dark grey coat with skirt, canary or other coloured vest with flap pockets, white breeches, black hunting boots with or without mahogany tops, black leather garters (or brown if tops are brown), silk hat, crop, spurs, white stock and gold safety-pin as above. (3) Black or very dark grey coat with skirt, coloured or check vest, fawn or brick-red breeches, black butcher boots, silk hat (or hunting cap if farmer), crop and spurs, white stock and safety-pin as above. (4) Black or tweed hacking coat, fawn or brick-red breeches, black boots with black coat (brown with tweed), white or discreetly coloured stock, safety-pin as before, black bowler (or hunting cap if farmer), crop, blunt spurs fitted to lie above the ankle. *Note :* None of the above is customary before the opening meet. Masters and hunt servants have five buttons on their hunting coats, which are square cut.

Rat-catcher (only worn during cub hunting): Tweed or covert riding coat, tweed or any coloured vest, stock, or collar and tie, fawn or brick-red breeches, bowler, brown boots or high ankle boots and leggings. Spurs and crop optional.

For *Stag Hunting and Harriers* neither scarlet nor formal clothes are worn. Those in (4) or Rat-catcher are suggested.

Hunts customarily have special designs for collars and buttons. The privilege of being invited to wear these rests with the M.F.H. For their own or other hunt balls male subscribers may wear livery of their hunt, whether scarlet or other colour, with collar and lapel facings and hunt buttons as decreed.

In *Hunter Classes at Shows* refs (2), (3) or (4) are correct. At more formal shows and evening performances refs (1), (2) or (3) can be worn. In *Hack Classes* black swallow-tail coat with tight overalls strapped down, 6-in (15.2 cm) black boots, white collar and grey tie, silk hat and showing stick are correct.

(For Ladies) For *Hunting and Formal Shows* the following dress is correct:
Side-saddle Habit may be black, navy or very dark grey with silk hat or bowler and veil, pale primrose-coloured waistcoat, stock with plain gold safety-pin, black boots, crop with thong and lash. When *cub hunting side-saddle*, tweed habit and bowler, discreetly coloured shirt and tie.

Astride Black or navy or very dark grey hunting jacket, light breeches, black bowler or velvet hunting cap, stock with plain gold safety-pin, black boots with black leather garters, spurs and crop. For *cub hunting* as for *Rat-catcher for men;* jodhpur breeches may be worn. Coloured browbands and button-holes are undesirable for hunting or cub hunting.

For *Shows in Hunter and Hack Classes* dress as for hunting is correct; generally a collar and tie is worn instead of a stock. At formal shows and evening performances (and always when a silk hat is worn) a stock is obligatory.

Note: Women now generally wear velvet hunting caps for both hunting and showing, although traditionally only correct in the hunting field for farmers' wives and daughters.

(For Children) At *Shows and Hunting* the following dress is correct:
Leading Rein Classes Tweed or dark jacket with light coloured jodhpurs, black or dark blue velvet hunting cap, collar and tie.

12.2 to 14.2 h.h. (124 to 144 cm) Classes Black or dark blue hunting cap, collar and tie, colour usually to match pony's browband, black, dark blue, brown or tweed jacket, small flower in button-hole if desired, light fawn jodhpurs, black or brown jodhpur boots, white, yellow or string gloves, or brown leather or wash leather, stick, leather bound or cane. Breeches and black hunting boots may be worn by the older child.

Note: Child's hair must be neat and tidy, with net if necessary.

Dressage   *   Jean Froissard, ECUYER-PROFESSEUR, F.F.S.E.

The art of riding, as most others, first flowered in the Italy of the Renaissance. Academies in Naples, Ferrara, Padua and other cities attracted horsemen from all over Europe, the best of whom became great masters in their own right. The heyday of the famed Italian schools was soon over; they were supplanted by a profusion of academies in France and the German countries, culminating in the *Spanische Hofreitschule* in Vienna, the *Ecole de Versailles* and the *Ecole de Saumur*, and somewhat later the *Reitinstitut* of the University of Gœttingen. Gœttingen and Versailles disappeared in the nineteenth century.

The French students had taken home Italian terms (*capriola, volta, passeggiare*), Frenchified them and, as they added technique, added their own. When the French academies took over the international role held till the latter part of the sixteenth century by the Italian ones, their visiting students incorporated the French terms into every European equestrian vocabulary.

Dressage is such a word, meaning the training of a riding (or carriage) horse, as distinct from that of a racehorse, which is called *entrainement*. The corresponding verbs are *dresser* and *entrainer*. The same distinctions were made in

England; Gervase Markham trained a running horse and dressed a riding horse, and so it remained into and throughout the eighteenth century.

Modern English employs the term *dressage* when the sole objective of the exercise is school work and has dropped the expression *to dress* entirely. From this has come the great misconception that dressage means some sort of sophisticated equitation superior to and independent of ordinary training. Actually, at its elementary stage, where the horse is trained physically and mentally to become a pleasant and obedient ride, dressage does not differ from the *systematic training* of any horse intended for use under the saddle.

Changes in *mores* and manners, the tastes of fashion and the needs of the military have inevitably brought about changes in the ends and means of horse training. But the chief and final purpose has remained the same: for ordinary utilitarian purposes a horse obedient and pleasant to ride; for artistic purposes a horse to which higher training has returned the natural grace and nobility of movement it possessed in a state of liberty and has lost on being subjected to the weight of a master. Newcastle summed it up as 'perfecting nature by the subtleties of art', and indeed to arrive at such perfection requires the most subtle and patient care in the exercise of body and mind. To obtain instant obedience to the lightest of aids is difficult enough, but to obtain this from a horse rendered unconditionally submissive without having robbed it of its 'bloom' exceeds mere technique and becomes an art. Once on this loftier plane, the horse is trained to perform the same easy movements, as well as more difficult ones, with so much additional ease and grace that it seems to be acting on its own, and the term dressage is replaced by *haute-école*. Any normally gifted horse should be able to meet the requirements of ordinary school work; few are apt to go beyond it into *haute-école*.

Dressage tests, as their name conveys, are simply and purely tests permitting us to evaluate the level and quality of the horse's education. They are structured on a scale of increasing difficulty in the nature, sequence and execution of their movements. The higher the test level, the more is expected, above all in their execution. On the lower and medium levels they are drawn up by each country's own equestrian federation, the higher and highest by the F.E.I., and only these (*Prix Saint Georges, Reprise Intermédiaire, Grand Prix*) are used in international competition.

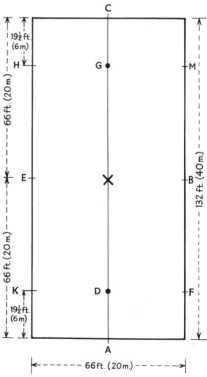

Plan of the small Dressage Arena, 132 × 66 ft (40 × 20 metres). This is used for the Pony Club, Novice and other Tests of Elementary Standards up to and including the Medium Tests if desired

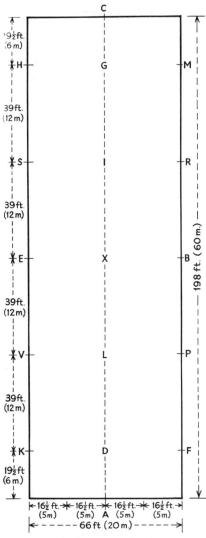

C

$19\frac{1}{2}$ ft.
(6 m)

H   G   M

39 ft.
(12 m)

S   I   R

39 ft.
(12 m)

198 ft. (60 m)

E   X   B

39 ft.
(12 m)

V   L   P

39 ft.
(12 m)

K   D   F

$19\frac{1}{2}$ ft.
(6 m)

←$16\frac{1}{2}$ ft.→ ←$16\frac{1}{2}$ ft.→ ←$16\frac{1}{2}$ ft.→ ←$16\frac{1}{2}$ ft.→
(5 m)   (5 m)   A (5 m)   (5 m)
←- - - - - 66 ft (20 m) - - - - -→

Plan of the large Dressage Arena, 198 × 66 ft (60 × 20 metres). This is used for International Competitions, for Tests from Medium Standards upwards, and including the Grand Prix (Note: when smaller arena is in use the markers R, S, V, P, L, and I are not required)

Essentially, the primary education, called *basse-école*, develops the physical horse and also makes it basically submissive; the progressive gymnastics employed represent 'physical culture'. The higher education, called *haute-école*, provides rather an aesthetic culture where the natural movements are stylized in form and cadence; 'physical culture' is now replaced by 'rhythmic gymnastics'. As happens in training a ballet dancer, at this point aesthetics take precedence over athletics.

Haute-école paces are more cadenced and more amply developed in gesture. Collection, placing the horse in the ideal balance for each movement, gives it overall lightness and grace. When cadence at the trot is allied with extreme impulsion the movement becomes airy, the raised diagonal keeps hovering longer above the ground and the pace takes on the name of *passage*, where the horse advances by much shorter yet loftier strides than at the trot. When the *passage* slows to the point of no advance it takes the name of *piaffe*.

The leaps a horse makes naturally in a state of freedom have been stylized by the *haute-école* under the name of school-leaps or airs artificial (*q.v.*). Not used in dressage tests, they continue, however, to be practised at the Spanish Riding School in Vienna and at the Cadre Noir at Saumur. The *pesade* or *levade* (synonymous, *q.v.*) is the preparation for them all; the horse learns to balance itself by resting solely on its sharply bent hindlegs, forelegs in the air and bent at the knees. From this initial position, common to all leaps, it then performs the *courbette* (*q.v.*), *croupade* (*q.v.*), *ballotade* (*q.v.*) and *capriole* (*q.v.*).

The touchstone of *haute-école*, however, is not any one movement, but the *lightness* with which any and each is executed. The underlying obedience requires a horse that, free of any resistance or contraction, finds itself in the exact balance allowing it to perform the movement with good measure, which in turn is contingent on perfect measure in the rider's aids. Lightness is clearly mirrored in the perfection and ease of performance (the old masters used to say, prettily, that 'the horse is enjoying its airs') and in the mobile jaw and flexible haunches. Such lightness cannot be attained unless the horse is *straight* from head to dock when moving on a straight line and harmoniously bent along the curves it travels. In both cases, the hindlegs follow in the exact tracks of the corresponding forelegs.

Since the most skilful trainer can only improve, not change the natural horse, the *haute-école* horse must be carefully chosen for conformation, paces, character and apparent aptitudes for academic equitation. Once found, it is conditioned physically and morally. In the indoor school it learns in short, and if need be often repeated lessons to understand the rider's 'language' and to obey it; outdoors it is taught to use its body and be accustomed to all the sights and sounds it is bound to encounter in its career. Throughout this period calm and forward movement on the lunge line and under the saddle are emphasized and no attempt is made to slow the paces, but always to extend them, the main concern being their ampleness and regularity. The contact with the bit, capital point, must become permanent at all times, including the halt, and this is achieved not by a hand retreating in search of the horse's mouth but by a horse moving forward seeking the bit. The maxim during this entire phase is 'extension before collection'; is not the steel of a spring tempered and stretched before it can acquire elasticity?

Next comes *the work on the circle*, at the walk and above all at the trot, correcting undesirable natural inflexions and suppling the spine laterally which is longitudinally suppled by *speed-ups* and *slow-downs, changes of pace* and *rein-backs*. Eventually *half pirouettes* (*q.v.*) and *half pirouettes renversées* (*q.v.*) add the finishing touches to such suppling exercises; first the half-pirouette ren-

versée, the rider starting off at a walk, using initially hand and leg on the same side to shift the haunches, but eventually obtaining the rotation by the leg alone, while the hand only keeps the forehand in place. In the half pirouette it is, above all, the hand opposite the direction of the turn made by the forehand which acts, using a neck rein, while the leg on the same side keeps the haunches in place. *The engagement of the hindlegs* has meanwhile been improved at first individually, by *half pirouettes renversées*, then further by *transitions* between paces, the first *pirouettes*, as well as the rein-back where both hindlegs exercise themselves equally.

The half-turns on forehand and haunches have directly prepared the horse for *the work on two tracks* (*q.v.*), begun by the *shoulder-in* (*q.v.*) and continued by the *half-pass* (*q.v.*).

The *shoulder-in* further supplies the spine, lightens the forehand, develops the shoulder movement, increases the engagement and introduces the horse to oblique travel. This exercise, where the horse is evenly bent in its entire length, is a powerful remedy for any unwelcome inflexions. For the left shoulder-in, for example, the horse is set on to a left circle tangent with the track. At the instant of return to the track and starting already into the next circle, forefeet already on an inner track, hindfeet still on that along the wall, the aids are changed and a shift to the right is requested, principally by the left hand moving right, the inflexion carefully maintained unchanged. The smaller the circle, the more pronounced is of course the crossing of the legs. Bending the neck too much and the barrel too little is a common fault in this exercise; only a very slight flexion at the neck should make the horse look away from where it is headed.

The *half-pass* aids, for example to the left, are left opening rein drawing the head slightly left, right neck rein, right leg somewhat retracted to shift shoulders and haunches to the left, left leg slightly advanced to maintain the forward movement.

One of the main difficulties in the entire work on two tracks is maintaining undiminished impulsion. *The work at the canter* goes forward simultaneously with all this. Initiaily it consists only of exercises to give equal ease on both leads to the horse which is subsequently taught to counter-canter, first on wide curves, then on serpentines without a change of lead. The counter-canter straightens the horse and improves its balance. *Departures at the canter* made from the walk with equal ease on either lead and without a single intervening stride of the trot will lead quite naturally to single *flying changes of leg*. During this whole period chief attention has been riveted on improving straightness and forward movement.

Now only begins the *haute-école* proper, where lightness must be ever present, whatever the movement or pace.

The collected paces now take on the loftiness which earns them the names of *school walk, school trot* and *school canter*. Raised at the base now, rounded along the entire crest, the neck in conjunction with a nearly vertical position of the head has lightened the forehand. The lowering of the haunches permits the engagement of the hindlegs under the body, source of an impulsion directed not only forward now but also upward. Thereby the paces have been transformed, are more elastic and airy, and the horse is *truly collected*. The *combination of ramener (q.v.) and engagement (q.v.)* distributes the weight harmoniously, giving the horse a balance enabling it to make swift, effortless changes between extended and collected paces and between different movements.

Once this has been achieved, the horse can gracefully execute the most difficult airs of the *haute-école: passage (q.v.)*, *piaffe (q.v.), flying changes of leg at every stride (q.v.), the pirouette at the canter.*

*   *   *

Dress Chariot   Nobleman's carriage used for civic and state occasions. (*c.* 1837.)

Dressage Championships   For results *see page* 378.

Dressage Classes   Different tests are recognized officially in order of increasing difficulty: Pony Club; P. Preliminary; N. Novice; E. Elementary; M. Medium; A. Advanced; Prix St. Georges—Grand Prix.

Dressage with Jumping   *see* COMBINED COMPETITIONS.

Dressage Weymouth   *see* WEYMOUTH, DRESSAGE.

Drift, The   A West Country term applied to the annual rounding-up of moorland ponies for branding.

Drivers   Those who drive. In an uncomplimentary sense, the term implies those with less art than 'coachmen'.

Driving   *   Marylian Watney

Although driving began entirely as a means of conveyance in the early centuries, it soon began to be the subject of many wagers concerning both the speed of the horse and skill of the driver. It also became apparent that there was a thrill to be experienced in handling a

horse with a responsive mouth, and so driving was elevated to a sport which attracted not only men, but also women, and even children.

Over the centuries there have been many accounts written of the prowess of famous harness horses and their drivers, and equally over the centuries there have been many enthusiasts who drove purely for the pleasure it gave them. It may come as a surprise, therefore, to find that in this highly mechanized age, driving should still be popular with all ages and classes of people, both in this country as well as abroad.

On account of this modern interest in driving, the British Driving Society (*q.v.*) was formed—its purpose being to help all those interested in the sport by bringing together the experts, the novices, the elderly and the young for tuition in the form of lectures and demonstrations, and also the providers of equipment: harness, whips and vehicles. The Society now has well over a thousand members in Britain, as well as several from overseas.

Whereas driving in England has latterly been confined to singles, pairs, tandems and four-in-hands trotting sedately on country roads or in the show ring, on the Continent all types of harness, including teams of up to twelve stallions, have been shown in the different gaits up to the gallop, negotiating hazards such as rough ground, steep hills and water! This has now been recognized as a sport under the F.E.I. (*q.v.*), rules for pairs and four-in-hands have been established, and International competitions have taken place. These competitions are similar to those held for ridden horses, involving dressage, cross-country work at various speeds, and an obstacle course, and are held over two or three days.

With this increasing revival in the art of driving it might be thought that only the experts compete, but this is not so. Apart from meets and rallies held all over the country by the British Driving Society, there are classes in the showring catering for all sizes of horse or pony, as well as several for donkeys—many of whom go extremely well in harness. Apart from providing pleasure for their owners, the spectacle of driving horses also appears to give pleasure to onlookers.

*   *   *

Driving Competitions   In 1969 the F.E.I. (*q.v.*) established rules and tables for International competitions. Tests were set out under three tables: A Presentation and Dressage; B Marathon; C Obstacle Driving.

Driving Reins   Reins (about 21–25 ft; 6.3–7.6 m) of web for long rein driving, buckling to the bit and passing through rings on the breaking roller. Plough lines are also used; these taper at the bit end and put less weight on the mouth.

Driving with a Full Hand   Having the reins passing through the fingers singly. This method is occasionally used in tandem driving, but incorrectly, since the same procedure should be used in tandem driving as in the case of a four-in-hand; the first finger should divide the leaders' reins and the second finger the wheelers'.

Drooping Quarters   A term applied to quarters which, instead of being level, fall away behind the croup, the result being a low set of the tail (*see* GOOSE-RUMPED).

Drop Fence   A fence with the landing side lower than the take-off.

Droppings   The term usually applied to the normal excreta of the horse. When the animal is in perfect health, the droppings should be formed into balls which break on reaching the ground.

Dropping the Shoulder   The action, usually at the canter, of suddenly dropping either shoulder, causing the rider to be unseated. It seems impossible to anticipate this and generally to remain in the saddle.

Droshky   A low four-wheeled carriage much used in Russia.

'Druid, The'　*see* DIXON, HENRY HALL.

Dry Single　A hunting term indicating a bank without a ditch.

Dual Paternity　A term applied to the pedigree of an animal whose dam has been covered by two different stallions during the covering season in which it was conceived.

Dublin Horse Show (Royal Dublin Society, Ball's Bridge, Dublin) Founded in 1731 for many agricultural purposes, but no horse show classes were held for agricultural horses until 1861. The Horse Show proper was first held in 1868 on the site of the present Parliament of Eire, and moved to Ball's Bridge and opened there in 1881, since when over half a million pounds has been spent on the show grounds. The accommodation has been increased from time to time, and now consists of 50 acres (20 ha). Held during the first week of August.

Dude　An inexperienced horseman who takes up ranch life in the western States of America. The term originally meant a 'stranger'.

Dude Ranch　A cattle ranch in the western States of America which offers accommodation and riding facilities to guests. Many such ranches have become largely artificial.

Dülmen　An ancient mixed breed of pony living in semi-wild conditions in the Meerfelder Bruch in Westphalia. Privately owned by the Duke of Cröy who holds an annual sale of stock. Height about 12.3 h.h. (125 cm).

Dumb-jockey　A wooden contrivance fastened on a young horse's back in the position of a saddle, and from which reins are passed to the mouth in such a way that the head is placed in any position desired. This form of training is advocated by many, but is violently opposed by others as being cruel and restricting as opposed to the give and take on the mouth of the experienced horseman in the saddle.

Dumb Jockey

Dumping　Shortening the toe by rasping the front of the wall of the hoof.

Dumpling　An unusually large and comfortable box cushion on some coaches.

Dun (Blue)　A horse whose black colouring, evenly distributed over the body, gives the appearance of blue. It can be with or without a dorsal band (list) or withers stripes, but always has a black skin, mane and tail.

Dun (Yellow)　A horse with a diffuse yellow pigment in the hair. The skin is black, as is the mane and tail, and there may or may not be a dorsal band (list), withers stripes and bars on the legs.

Duncan Gag (sometimes called the Duncombe) A plain or twisted mouth gag with a small cheek upwards with two round holes for a rounded gag rein. Designed for use in conjunction with a curb bit.

Duncombe Gag　*see* DUNCAN GAG.

Dung　*see* DROPPINGS.

Dung-eating　The unnatural and objectionable habit acquired by some horses of eating their droppings. A vice. The use of a muzzle (*q.v.*) at non-feeding times is desirable.

Durban July Handicap　The Major flat race of South Africa which was first run in 1897 over 1 mile (1.6 km), was gradually extended to 1¼ miles

(2 km) by 1916 and in 1970 became 2200 metres. For results *see page* 389.

Dutch Draught Horse, The Claimed to be the most massively built and most heavily muscled of all European heavy horses. Descent traces back to the second half of the last century by means of the Stud Books of the Royal Netherlands Draught Horse Society which includes all Dutch Draught Horse Breeds. The neck is notably short, carrying a not-too-heavy head. The withers are little developed and the shoulders heavily loaded while the legs and quarters are immensely strong. The whole a massive, hard, deep animal.

Dutch Slip A simple form of headcollar, made of leather or tubular web, suitable for foals.

Dwelling Where hounds linger too long on the line of scent.

Dziggetai A species of wild ass, mulelike in appearance, inhabiting the elevated steppes of Tartary.

E.H.P.S. Endurance Horse and Pony Society.

Each Way (Racing) Abbreviation: e.w. To back a horse 'each way' is to back it to win, or to be placed first, second or third.

Ears, Identification Marks From early times ears of animals were cut in various ways as a means of identification. For horses this practice continued until the sixteenth century (and much later in the northern counties and the southwest of England). *Bitted:* a piece 'bitten' from the inner edge of ear. *Cropped:* cut straight across half way down the ear, originally used purely for identification but continued in the eighteenth century as a mode of fashion to achieve a 'smart' effect. *Fold-bitted:* ear folded over and a piece removed from folded edge. *Fork-stowed:* nicked at the top in a fish tail shape. *Ritt:* the top slit lengthwise. *Stowed:* the tip cut straight across. *Under-bitted:* a piece 'bitten' from outer edge.

Ear-stripping Process of stroking or pulling hands over ears from base to tip to induce circulation and bring comfort to a cold or tired horse; it is always appreciated by the horse.

Earth The underground home of a fox.

Earth Stopper A man employed by a hunt to block the entrance to an earth when the fox is out during the night previous to the day's hunt (*see* STOPPING EARTH).

East Dean Run, The At Goodwood there is a quaintly worded vellum manuscript telling of a run beginning at 7.45 a.m. on January 26th, 1739, ending at 5.50 p.m. near the wall of Arundel river with only three followers up.

Eastern Horses The group which is roughly covered by the Arabian, Barb, Turkish and Syrian breeds.

East Prussian Horse *see* TRAKEHNER.

Écart An expression used in the Vuillier Dosage System (*q.v.*), meaning the degree of deviation from the standard number of dosage strains.

'Eclipse' A stallion bred by H.R.H. the Duke of Cumberland in 1764, by 'Marske' out of 'Spiletta', and owned jointly at first by Mr William Wildman and Col. Dennis O'Kelley. His first race was in May 1769, his last in the autumn of 1771. Never beaten; the only horse said to have extended 'Eclipse' in a race was 'Bucephalus', who never recovered from the effort. In racing and as a sire the phrase applied to him was 'Eclipse first, the rest nowhere', for he was immeasurably the greatest racehorse of his century and, if his predominating influence on the breed be taken into consideration, of all time; over 100 of his descendants have won the Derby.

Eclipse Gag A veterinary gag used to keep open the mouth.

Eclipse Stakes First run at Sandown Park (near London) in 1886. It is a race for three-year-olds and upwards over 1¼ miles (2 km) in July. For results *see page 390*.

Écuyer A Master of the Horse. A riding master—instructor.

Eczema An irritation of the skin on any part of the body. Infection may be introduced by rubbing and the condition then becomes purulent—'wet eczema'. It is usually an allergy associated with food or an external irritant such as lime, certain sprays, soft soap, pollen from grass or plants, or embrocations. A horse may exhibit an allergic reaction to its own sweat if the skin is covered with harness and the sweat dries beneath it. It is common also in the mane and tail in horses at grass in the spring, when it may arise from allergy to pollen, fly- or insect-bites, harvest mites (*Leptus autumnalis*) or other grass mites. The mites from poultry will cause skin irritation in horses (*see also* SWEET ITCH). Eczema will be treated by the veterinary surgeon with soothing applications and either antihistamines or corticosteroids.

Edward VII   Keen patron of the Turf both as Prince of Wales and King. Won the Derby three times, with 'Persimmon' (1896), 'Diamond Jubilee' (1900), and 'Minoru' (1909), and the Grand National with 'Ambush' (1900).

Edwards, Lionel Dalhousie Robertson (1878–1966)   A talented sporting artist and painter of equestrian portraits, but also author and press illustrator. Being a keen naturalist and foxhunting man, his pictures exhibit unique perception of the English sporting scene. Equally at home in water-colours as well as oils. Many prints were published after his works. Wrote several books, including *Reminiscences of a Sporting Artist* and *Thy Servant a Horse*.

Eel-stripe   *see* DORSAL STRIPE.

Eggbutt   Term used for the hinge in the mouth of a bit. Construction obviates pinching of the lips. Can be obtained with slots in the ring for cheek attachment so that the bit keeps in the correct position.

Egg Link Pelham   A jointed Pelham with an egg-shaped link in the centre.

Eglentine   Stainless metal of excellent quality and finish, used in the manufacture of stirrup irons, bits and bridles.

Eight Horses, Legend of the   Chinese in origin. The Emperor of the Chou Dynasty (ninth century B.C.) was smitten with a wanderlust. He wanted to travel all over the world. He got together eight horses, called Wah Lau, Luk Yee, Chik Kee, Pak O, Kue Wong, Yu Lung, Du Lee and Sam Chee (for each of these names there is another slightly different version). These horses were able to travel thirty thousand li (Chinese miles) in one day. The Emperor had a good tour. At last he went to the West and climbed the Kun Lun Mountains. There he met the goddess, Si Wong Mu, and made a long stay. The Baron of Chu, profiting by the absence of the Emperor, attempted to seize the throne. Emperor Mu heard of it, and, thanks to the eight horses, was able to rush home in time to suppress the rebel. After that the Emperor made no more expeditions but from time to time the Goddess would send him messages by a blue bird.

Eild   Scottish term for barren mares or ewes (*see* YELD).

Einsiedler   An ancient breed of riding and light draught horse of Switzerland, very popular in the sixteenth century. After the French Revolution the studs were looted and the breed declined. English Hackneys were introduced early this century and breeding since has been based on Anglo-Norman stallions.

Ekka   A one-horse cart used in India which is drawn without traces, the pad being prevented from slipping backwards by a broad strap attached to it which passes across the horse's breast.

Elastic Curb   *see* HUMANE CURB.

Elastics   Elastic bands worn round the wrists by a jockey to keep the cuffs of the racing jacket in position.

Elberfeld Horses   In 1900 William von Osten, of Berlin, to prove his theories on equine intelligence, appeared to train a Russian stallion, Kluge Hans, to calculate by pawing the ground with his hoof. They proceeded to reading, colour differentiation, etc., up to the general standard of knowledge of a 14 year-old-child. Enormous publicity resulted and exhaustive tests by learned committees and societies for evidence of collusion proved negative. In 1904, however, Oskar Pfungst, the German psychologist, demonstrated that the horse answered to unconscious and almost imperceptible signs from his owner. At von Osten's death a wealthy Elberfeld manufacturer inherited Kluge Hans and with two Arab stallions and other horses he worked to prove von Osten's ideas with apparent success; but most experts, though not all of them, remained unconvinced of the animals' mental capabilities. At the outbreak of World War I the group of horses was dispersed.

Elbow The upper joint of the fore-leg.

Eldonian Trade name used by makers of cast stainless steel bits, stirrups, spurs, etc.

Electuary The name given to a medicinal agent in which the drugs are made into a paste with a base of treacle or honey. Excellent for sore throats. Dosage is by smearing the paste on to the tongue, roof of mouth or back teeth with a smooth flat piece of wood twice daily.

Elephant Ear Sponge The popular name for a flat stable sponge.

Elephantiasis Chronic abnormal thickening of connecting tissues beneath the skin on the limbs. The horse may continue with slow work on a farm, feeding and doing well, but the leg, which may grow to an enormous size, will become very unsightly. *Treatment:* apply a cold water hay bandage to the leg every night. Tarring the limb and a good winter's run at grass have very good effects.

Elicampane A herb used in mediaeval times, and later, to revive horses suffering from exhaustion and to renew appetite.

Elijahs Straps worn below the knees by horsemen instead of leggings. East Anglian term.

Elizabeth I (1533–1603) Was known to be an excellent horsewoman and encouraged the breeding of riding hacks and racehorses. The heavy armour of horse and man of the late Plantagenet and early Tudor times had become obsolete and Queen Elizabeth, also, had not inherited the physical amplitude of her father, Henry VIII, so the massive 'great horse' of his reign was replaced by a lighter type of hack.

She loved riding as a form of exercise and relaxation, and hunted with enthusiasm all her life until her seventieth year. On her many journeys across England, often as far afield as Warwickshire, Suffolk and Devon she rarely used a litter but rode with her court on horseback. On some occasions, however, she rode pillion behind her Master of the Horse, and there are records of her travelling from Exeter to London and also attending St Paul's in state in this manner. She maintained a racing establishment called The Barbary Horse Stables at Greenwich where she kept forty Arabs, Barbs and Turks.

Elk Lip A wide and somewhat loose and overhanging upper lip.

Elk Lip

Elliptic Spring Invented by a coachbuilder named Elliot in 1804, this spring revolutionized carriage building, and is composed of laminated steel plates in an elliptical form. It is in general use today.

El Morzillo The black horse belonging to Hernando Cortès, conqueror of

Mexico in the sixteenth century (*see* CONQUISTADORES). This horse died during the expedition to Guatemala in 1524, and was deified by the natives in the form of a huge stone statue which was discovered and destroyed by Spanish Franciscan missionaries in 1697.

Embrocation (General)   Olive oil, 8 tablespoonfuls, Turpentine 3 and strong liquid ammonia 2.

Empty Mare   A mare not in foal.

Emston New Zealand Rug   The original pattern in this country, it is secured without resort to a surcingle which might cause chafing (*see* RUG, NEW ZEALAND).

Endosteum   A very fine vascular membrane, lining the internal or medullary cavities of the long bones, wherein lies the marrow, or medulla.

Endurance Tests   Few have been held in England but in 1920, 1921 and 1922 tests were held by the Arab Horse Society, open to Arab, Anglo-Arab and part-bred Arab stallions, mares and geldings, to carry 13 st (182 lb; 82.5 kg) over a course of 300 miles, with consecutive daily runs of 60 miles (97 km) (*see* TEVIS RIDE and QUILTY RACE).

Enema   An injection of soapy warm water given direct into the rectum for medicinal purposes, by means of a special pump apparatus. Grease or oil the nozzle well before inserting and ensure that the injection is made slowly. Retention is facilitated by holding down the tail after removing the syringe nozzle. An enema is most commonly resorted to for the relief of colic.

Engaged   1 (of a horse) Entered for a race. 2 (of a jockey) Retained by an owner or stable to ride in a race or races.

Engagement   The hindlegs advance further under the body because the haunches have been lowered by the flexion of the principal joints (coxo-femoral, stifle and hock) of the quarters.

'Enlarged'   The act of releasing the carted deer at a stag-hunt.

Enlargements, Bone   These are chiefly found amongst horses raised on marshy ground.

Enter   A young hound is 'entered' from the time he is taught to hunt a fox.

Enteritis   A severe internal complaint usually the result of a bad chill and more often affecting foals. Immediate veterinary attention is required.

Entire   *see* STALLION.

Entry (Hunting)   Young unentered hounds.

Entry (Racing)   Horses have to be entered for racing in Britain through the Racing Calendar Office (*q.v.*) at Weatherbys, Wellingborough, Northants. All entries close at noon on Wednesdays. Later horses have to be 'declared to run' before they can take part in a race.

Eohippus   The generic name given in the theory of the evolution of the horse (*q.v.*) to the first equine ancestor.

Eohippus

Epistaxis   Bleeding from the nose due to haemorrhage in the upper part of the nose. More frequent in racehorses especially at the end of a race, but may be spontaneous.

Epona   A Celtic goddess, patroness of horse breeders, whose cult was widely diffused in north-west Europe in Iron-Age times and was spread still wider under the Roman era.

Equerry   Originally the stable of a royal establishment but now refers to an officer of the household in occasional attendance on the Sovereign.

Equestrian Pertaining to horses or horsemanship. One who rides on horseback. *Fem.* Equestrienne.

Equihose Elasticated socks used to give support to the legs either in the stable or at work.

Equine Pertaining to a horse.

Equine Animals (Importation) Order 1973 All importations of equine animals will be subject to the granting of licences and there will be no statutory list of prohibited countries. This means that applications to import equines from countries previously infected with African horse sickness, but now clear of the disease, will be considered on their individual merits.

Equine Influenza An extremely infectious disease due to a virus. One attack seldom provides prolonged resistance to further infection, or it may be that other virus infections may produce similar symptoms. The virus can be windborne over considerable distances or carried by transport vehicles, mangers, pails, bits and harness—or by grooms or jockeys riding a succession of horses. Sporadic in training stables and wherever large numbers of horses are congregated. Affects all classes of horses. Symptoms are debility, frequent coughing, fever, and in rare cases pneumonia. Convalescence may take several weeks. The intramuscular or subcutaneous injection of polyvalent mixed strains of influenza early in the spring is attended by a certain measure of success, provided the strain causing the infection is one covered by the vaccine, but, as in human influenza, new strains are constantly cropping up. Injections may be made at intervals of one to four weeks. A primary vaccination is not recommended in foals under three months or in pregnant mares, but

mares vaccinated two months before service may receive booster doses.

Equine Research Station Part of the Animal Health Trust at Balaton Lodge, Newmarket, Suffolk. It was established in 1947 through the generosity of Lady Yule and Miss Gladys Yule.

Equinia Glanders (*q.v.*) or farcy.

Equipage A carriage and attendant retinue.

Equirotal Phaeton Consisting of two vehicles—a gig (*q.v.*) in front and a curricle (*q.v.*) or a cabriolet (*q.v.*) behind, which, by adding two couplings between the bodies turned it into a phaeton (*q.v.*). The four wheels being of equal size explained the name Equirotal. Invented by W. Bridges Adams in 1838.

Equus caballus The domesticated horse of Europe.

Equus caballus forma silvatica Wild horses which live in central and north-western Europe, having resemblance to and consanguinity with the ponies of Poland and the Scottish Highlands.

Equus przevalskii gmelini antonius forma silvaticus The wild Tarpan (*q.v.*).

Equus przevalskii przevalskii poljakoff The Asiatic wild horse (*see* WILD HORSE).

Ergot A horny growth at the back of the fetlock joint.

Ermine Marks Small black or brown marks on white, closely resembling ermine fur surrounding the coronet of one or more feet (*see Plate 21*).

Escutcheon The division of hair which begins below the point of the hips and extends downwards on the flanks.

Breeds of Horses in Europe　*　Daphne Machin-Goodall

There are around 114 known and registered breeds of horses and ponies in Europe and this also includes those of the U.S.S.R. Amongst these breeds are numbered the heavy horse and light horse, including both the Arab and Thoroughbred and the various pony breeds.

Great Britain has the largest number of native pony breeds of any country. There are nine and these are generally increasing in number and are exported to Denmark, Holland, France and Germany. These countries have taken Shetland, Welsh and New Forest ponies. It is realized that children learn to ride so much better if they can begin on ponies. There are also four heavy breeds in Great Britain—the Suffolk Punch, Shire, Clydesdale and the Percheron which was originally imported from France. The world-famous Thoroughbred racehorse originated in England around 300 years ago. It is one of the most prolific and valuable breeds of horses known, since it has been exported to studs and racing stables all over the world. The Thoroughbred horse has been used to fix and improve other warm-blood breeds.

The Hackney horse and pony are seen in harness competitions at home and abroad, while Cleveland in Yorkshire produced a first-class carriage horse which when crossed with the Thoroughbred produces show jumpers of considerable talent. In Ireland both the Connemara and the Irish Draught horse are bred, and when the latter is crossed with home-bred mares, hunters, steeplechasers and jumpers are bred in numbers.

It is difficult to assign the western-bred Arab horse to any one country since there are many studs in Great Britain, France (Pompadour), Germany (Weil-Marbach), Hungary (Mesohegyes, Shagya Arabian), Poland (Janow Podlaski) and the U.S.S.R. (the Strelets Arab bred at Tersk).

France The feral grey Camargue pony of the Rhône Delta, used for cow-punching, is an attraction for tourists and is, none the less, a very ancient breed. There are also a number of heavy horse breeds of which the Percheron, exported to the U.S.A., Ardennes and Boulonnais are the best known. The Poitou horse breeds large mules when crossed with the large Poitou jackass, and these too are exported to America and Spain. The Thoroughbred and Anglo-Arab make up France's largest equine population. There are a number of studs in Normandy, while Pompadour, Aurillac and Pau are famous for their Anglo-Arabs which have proved to be very good show jumpers.

The best known warm-blood horses are the Breton, Norman and Anglo-Norman, the latter having helped to found the Noram (Norman-American) trotter.

Spain and Portugal were once one country and still share certain breeds of horses including the wild and feral dun Sorraia (*q.v.*) with dorsal stripe and striped legs, which was long ago a probable ancestor of the Barb horse. The Garranos (*q.v.*) is also an ancient primitive breed, as is the Minho of north Portugal. Both countries breed light saddle and harness horses. Spain specializes in Arabs, the Carthusian and the elegant Andalusian whose near relative is the Portuguese Lusitano and Altér. Most of the above breeds contributed to the creation of the Criollo of South America.

Holland, at one time ruled by Spain, specializes in trotters, and the Métis trotter is a cross between the Orlov (*q.v.*) and the Standardbred (*q.v.*). The Friesian is a very ancient breed always dark brown or black, and has been revived from near extinction. The Gelderland, a useful harness horse possessing some of the old Norfolk Roadster (*q.v.*) blood, is also used as a saddle horse and for jumping. Heavy horses are rarely seen now that the Groningen breed is no longer wanted. Shetland, Welsh and New Forest ponies are bred in Holland.

Germany is best known for the breeding of the refugee East Prussian (Trakehner, *q.v.*) warm-blood horse, and there are private studs at Rantzau, Schmoel and scattered throughout West Germany. In the Solling, East Prussian colts are raised together with those of the Hanoverian breed which has made enormous strides forward during the past two decades. The Hanoverian (*q.v.*) has improved in conformation and is now a medium and heavyweight hunter type with excellent jumping ability. The State Stud is at Celle where over 200 stallions are stabled before leaving for their country stations each season. Annually, in the autumn, these stallions put on two exhibitions at Celle. The chestnut Haflinger (*q.v.*) with flaxen mane and tail is the most important mountain pony—one might almost call it a cob. This pony is generally used in harness and for pack transport and by farmers living in the Alps of southern Germany and Austria, Bavaria and the Tirol. The sturdy Noriker (*q.v.*) is another working breed of south German horses, whilst the Schleswig-Holstein belongs to the north.

Austria has produced the Lipizzaner (*q.v.*) known throughout Europe and America for its splendid exhibitions of High School Airs on and above the ground. For this work usually only grey stallions are used although the Lipizzaner may be any colour. The main stud is at Piber, Graz. Both Yugoslavia and Bulgaria breed Lipizzaners which are used in harness and agriculture.

Switzerland has increased her mounted regiments and her studs. Both the Freiburger (based on Shagya blood) at Avenches and the Einsiedler are native breeds. To these breeds one must add the imported Swiss Holstein and the Swiss Anglo-Norman.

Denmark once led Europe in breeding horses for the courts. The famous Fredericksborg horses from the royal stud of that name were bred with the help of imported Spanish stallions. Today the breed produces very useful harness horses.

Norway has exported her native sturdy dun Fjord mountain pony to many countries, including Canada.

Sweden breeds the Döle-Gudbrandsdal (*q.v.*), used for light farm and forestry work; whilst the Döle trotter, a fairly new innovation, is making trotting races a popular sport. Sweden also breeds the elegant Swedish warm-blood horse. For this purpose Trakehner (*q.v.*) stallions were imported, although for the past twenty-five years no further outside blood has been used. The State Stud is at Flynge. Sweden's Olympic riders have been mounted on home-bred horses for the past three Olympic Games.

Poland has of recent years improved her light horse breeds, particularly the Masurian which is, in fact, descended from East Prussian mares and stallions found abandoned at the end of the war. These horses are bred true to the old tradition and many have been sent to Switzerland. The Posnan horse is a heavy harness type and is used in many provinces in agriculture. Both the Huçul and Konik are primitive pony breeds, improved by Arab blood. Once again the Tarpan roams the great forest on the Sperding lake. The forest Tarpan, *Equus przevalskii gmelini antonius*, once inhabited many forested areas in central and eastern Europe and was decimated to the point of almost extinction about 100 years ago.

On the river Bug, near Brest, lies the famous Janow Podlaski Arabian Stud. It was here that the grey Skowronek was bred and later helped to influence the stamp of breed of Arab horses in Great Britain.

Hungary, for so long historically connected with both Austria and Poland, is since the Magyar and Hun invasions one of the most densely populated equine countries. The Hungarians breed the large and small Nonius, Gidran and Furioso and the Shagya Arabian. The horses are bred on the open plains under the care of a mounted *csikós*, whilst the art of riding and driving is kept very much alive at the studs of Hortobágy and Mesohegyes.

The U.S.S.R. is rich in steppe, mountain and harness breeds of horses. The steppe breeds, with the exception of the Strelets Arab, rightly belong to Asia, but European Russia and the Baltic States have their native Toric, Lithuanian and Latvian heavy draught breeds. The hardy Viatka resembles the Konik (small horse) and the Zemaituka.

The Azerbaijan district produces the Karabakh (*q.v.*)—a strain which might qualify as 'Arabian'. The stallion Zaman was presented to H.M. the Queen. The best known Russian breed is the 17-h.h. (173 cm) Orloff trotter which originated in 1777 and was evolved by Count Alexis Grigorievich Orloff by crossing Arab, Dutch Harddraver, Thoroughbred, Mecklenburg and the Danish Fredericksborg.

In some European countries, including Italy, trotting races are much more popular than races on the flat, and the trotter—the humble cousin of the Thoroughbred—is regarded with great esteem. All the breeds mentioned have their own stud books and all breeding stock is carefully selected; some have to undergo stiff tests for physical fitness and temperament.

*   *   *

European Dressage Championship For results *see page* 378.

European Driving Championship For results *see page* 378.

European Championship Three-Day Event For results *see page* 381.

European Junior Championship (F.E.I. Show Jumping) For results *see page* 404.

European Junior Championship Three-Day Event For results *see page* 381.

European Ladies' Championship (F.E.I. Show Jumping) For results *see page* 404.

European Men's Championship (F.E.I. Show Jumping) For results *see page* 404.

Even Money (Racing) Where the odds are one unit for one unit.

'Event Horse' Descriptive of one likely to prove suitable for the exacting tests required in the Three-day Event or Horse Trials (*q.v.*).

The Evolution of the Horse   *   Stella A. Walker

Most scientists believe that the first animal capable of producing our modern horse was found originally in both the Eastern and the Western hemispheres, but the distribution of fossils seems to show that it became extinct in the Old World and that the first equine ancestor proper (*Eohippus*) lived approximately fifty-five million years ago in North America.

It has been deduced that it was a creature the size of a fox with short hair, thick neck and stumpy tail. Its fore-feet were divided into four toes and the 'splint' of a fifth toe, and the hind feet had three toes with either one or two additional 'splints'.

As swamp was gradually replaced by forest and grassland this pre-historic animal, over a period of many millions of years, appears to have adapted its conformation to the new physical conditions. The legs became longer, the head was raised higher and the toes started to contract on the harder ground. This growth made concealment from its enemies difficult, so speed was developed as a means of escape. Increased movement brought further leg and muscular expansion until a three-toed horse with a good turn of speed, and the size of an Exmoor pony, gradually evolved. It is interesting to note, though, that at six weeks the modern equine embryo of today still has the three-toed foot conformation. The necessity for increased speed may have caused the broadening of the central toe until the lateral toes became mere 'pettitoes' and the final major evolutionary change to a foot of one toe resulted in the *Equus* of the Pleistocene Age. It is this animal which is readily recognizable as the forerunner of the modern horse: and this is the broad theory of the evolution of the horse held by most scientists today. It is borne out by fossils found in many parts of the United States, especially in the asphalt pits of California. As recently as 1953 eight practically perfect skulls of *Eohippus* have been found in a fossil bed in Colorado.

There were many types of this primitive horse in North and South America, its growth varying with geographical conditions from mere pigmy size to the *Equus giganteus* of 20 h.h. (204 cm) which inhabited Texas. Eventually some cause, possibly disease perhaps spread by a primitive tsetse fly or a form of rabies, and the coming of the Glacial Age rendered the horse extinct in the Western hemisphere, and it was not seen there again until the invasion by Cortès in the sixteenth century.

Before the complete disappearance of the horse in the Americas, however, herds must have crossed to the eastern hemisphere by the still existent land bridges between the continents. Here it had escaped extinction by the Glacial Age, as only the more northerly regions of Europe and Asia were affected; but the ultimate subsidence of the land connecting the eastern and western worlds eventually made the horse an inhabitant solely of the Old World.

There were two distinct types of horses. The first was a northern dun species which is still represented today by the wild pony of Western Mongolia known as the Przevalski horse, after the nineteenth-century Russian explorer. It is the only truly wild horse still in existence and is about 12 h.h. (122 cm) high with an ungainly head, short erect mane and no forelock. It is yellowish-dun in colour with a light muzzle and narrow, ass-like feet. Certain characteristics of this northern type of horse are seen today in the ponies of Norway and Iceland.

It seems possible, though scientifically unproved as yet, there may have been a subdivision of this Northern species into a European forest type, heavily built, large boned and hairy legged, which became the primitive ancestor of our Shires and Clydesdales.

The second type was the Southern Horse, living in the Caspian and Mediterranean areas. It was a thinner skinned animal, less heavy, quicker in movement and intelligence and darker in colour. It can be claimed as the prehistoric forerunner of the Arab, Barb and Turk.

These herds of wild horses were very common and were hunted and killed extensively by Palaeolithic man for food. The bones of tens of thousands have been found outside one prehistoric cave settlement near Lyons.

Domestication of the horse did not occur until many hundreds of years later, possibly about 2500 B.C. amongst tribes of the Near East, being tamed probably first for its milk and flesh, then for haulage and much later for riding. Marauding forays into Babylonia and Syria spread this domestication westwards until we have evidence in 1900 B.C. of the horse being driven and ridden by the Egyptians.

Among the isolated and nomadic tribes of Arabia the Southern Horse seems to have possessed even then the qualities unequalled by those in other regions. Some authorities trace the real genesis of the Arabian horse to Libya and Morocco, and others to India. The fact remains that, wherever its origin, it is the Arab type of horse that has always been used down the ages to improve the northern stock. We hear of this Arab strain being imported by the horse-loving Greeks; the Arab blood was used also by the Romans to improve the native ponies in their conquests in Northern Europe, Asia and Africa.

War has always been an incentive to the development of a better type of horse. Saracen invasions brought the Barb to France; Moorish occupation introduced it into Spain. The ever-increasing use of armour in mediaeval warfare made weight and size the supreme aim in horse-breeding, and the Percherons of today are the descendants of those weight-carriers of the Middle Ages. Eventually the arrival of firearms rendered obsolete the huge load of armour on man and beast and the end of the sixteenth century brought a demand for a lighter horse of speed and dexterity. In England racing and hunting became enormously popular under the Stuarts and as a result Barbs, Arabs and Turks were imported in great numbers. Between 1689 and 1730 there arrived the three famous stallions, the Byerley Turk, the Darley Arabian and the Godolphin Arabian, and from these three horses all modern English Thoroughbred stock can trace its descent. This alliance of the sturdiness and vigour of the Northern Horse to the beauty, speed and stamina of the Southern Horse has resulted in the superb English Thoroughbred, an animal unsurpassed by any other horse in the world, and epitomizing the miracle of evolution.

*   *   *

Ewe Neck   Where the crest of the neck (between the poll and the withers) is concave rather than convex. An 'upside-down neck'.

Ewe Neck

Exercise   A horse requires two to three hours a day.

Exhaustion   This is usually the result of over-work, probably when unfit. *Symptoms:* refusing food, excessive thirst, desire to lie down, breaking out into a cold and clammy sweat after drinking. *Treatment:* remove the bit, unbuckle tack, turn the animal's head into the breeze. Bathe its face, head, and poll with cold water. Give small quantities of bran mash, boiled linseed or oatmeal gruel with half a tumbler of rum or whisky in warm water as a tonic. Rug up well and apply flannel bandages loosely all round legs below the knee. Provide a good deep bed, and suspend heavy grooming or other interference until the horse has recovered.

Exmoor Pony   One of the most distinctive of the nine mountain and moorland breeds of the British Isles, the Exmoor pony is very popular on account of its charming character and extreme hardiness, and makes an excellent child's pony. It is found in

Exmoor Forest, which lies in the south-west of England, partly in Devonshire, but mostly in Somerset. The breed is noted for the heavy mane falling to either side of the neck, for its 'mealy' nose, and its very prominent, wide-set eyes with mealy upper and lower lids, called locally 'toad-eyes'. The colour is bay-brown or dun, a typical shade being mousey-brown merging into 'mealy' up the legs, under the belly and inside the forearms and legs. Height: mares not exceeding 12.2 h.h. (124 cm) at any age; stallions and geldings not exceeding 12.3 h.h. (125 cm) at any age. *Breed Society:* The Exmoor Pony Society (*see Plate 11*).

Exmoor Pony Society, The (Founded 1921) *Objects:* to improve and encourage the breeding of Exmoor Ponies of the Moorland Type, to institute shows of breeding stock, and to examine and approve all pony stallions used in the district. Ponies are entered in the National Pony Stud Book. The Society also holds annual sales.

Exostosis A lump of new bone.

Export of Horses Regulations are complicated. The Ministry of Agriculture, Fisheries and Food provides *Notes for the Guidance of Persons Intending to Export Horses and Ponies*. Official numbered mane or tail tags and a certificate of minimum value from a recognized valuer or judge or inspector of a breed society are required, also reservation at approved lairage (*q.v.*) and examination there by a veterinary surgeon.

Exposure Horses withstand cold well, provided they grow a full coat or, alternatively, are well clothed. They are, however, very susceptible to draughts and cold winds, and care should be taken to avoid exposure to these. Wind-screens should be available to horses at grass, and loin cloths provided for working horses when standing.

Extension Stirrup Leathers Stirrup leathers where the mounting side leather is fitted with a metal hook and an extra web length, to enable the rider to mount with a longer leather. It is hooked up to normal when the rider is in the saddle. Also known as 'hook-up' stirrup leathers.

'Extravagant Action' The very high knee and hock action of a Hackney.

Eye Horses have acute powers of vision as their eyes are set in the head neither entirely laterally nor entirely frontally. The horse can see laterally with each eye and is also aware of what goes on behind him. He finds this lateral vision easier than direct forward sight which requires the head to be slightly raised in a straight line with the body for both eyes to focus on an object ahead—a slight deviation may result in monocular vision. The horse's ears prick forward when both eyes simultaneously look ahead, and tend to lop a little or point backwards when lateral vision is being used. When grazing a horse can see in every direction between its legs. Horses are colour-blind.

* F *

f. filly.

f. (Racing) Fell.

F.B.H.S. Fellow of British Horse Society.

FEGENTRI Fédération Internationale des Gentlemen Riders.

F.F.S.E. Fédération Français des Sports Equestres.

F.E.I. Fédération Equestre Internationale (*q.v.*).

F.R.C.V.S. Fellow of the Royal College of Veterinary Surgeons.

F.S. Foundation Stock.

Face-piece Harness decoration consisting of a metal crest or other decoration set in a pear-shaped leather foundation which falls from the bridle headpiece.

Fadge Pace which is neither walk nor trot. Sometimes called Hound Jog or Hound Pace (*q.v.*).

Fairly Hunted To have been fairly hunted a horse must have a certificate to this effect from the master of the hunt with which the horse is supposed to have been hunted. These certificates must be registered at Weatherby's before entries can be made for hunter steeplechases or point-to-points.

Faking Improper tampering in order to conceal some fault or fraudulently to alter the appearance of a horse.

Falabella A miniature horse developed on Recreo de Roca Ranch near Buenos Aires, evolved by crossing small Thoroughbreds and Shetlands. Size does not exceed 30 in (76.2 cm) and they come in any colour. Hardy, good tempered and intelligent. Two or three studs have started to breed Falabellas in England.

Fall A horse is considered to have fallen when the shoulder and quarters on the same side touch the ground or (in show jumping) touch the obstacle and ground. A rider technically fails in show jumping when he is separated from the horse and has to remount, but in ordinary parlance a *rider* does not fall but *comes down* with his horse.

Fallen Horse Should a horse come right down on the road, kneel or sit on its head to prevent it banging against the ground in the effort to rise. Place a rug or piece of sacking near the forefeet to give a foothold. Horses are liable to damage themselves by dislocating their hips while trying to rise.

Falling Horses Term used to describe horses in the film world, specially trained to make spectacular falls. They are first taught to lie down on a sand or sawdust bed; then gradually progress from a walk to a gallop to being able to fall undamaged in a hard run. Few horses have the nerve to accomplish this feat successfully and those with the necessary ability command high fees.

False Nostril An anatomical peculiarity, found as a dead end or cul-de-sac in the top edge of the nostril (*see* HIGH BLOWING).

False Quarter A term used of the hoof when an injury has occurred to the coronary band, affecting the horn's oil secretion, and thus leaving a permanent weakness in the hoof wall. In most cases the injury is attributable to a wound caused by the sharpened heels of the shoe during frosty weather. There must be no pressure by the shoe on the affected part; the gap in a bar shoe will prevent this.

False Ribs Ribs to the rear of the eighth rib (*see* RIBS).

Fan Extension at the rear of military saddles for the attachment of equipment.

Fancy Curb Name for all single rein curb bits with fancifully designed cheeks, e.g. globe, heart, acorn.

Fanning A term used when a cowboy rides a buckjumper waving his hat (Stetson) in the air and slapping his horse with it. This encourages the horse to buck harder and helps the rider to retain his balance.

'Fanning' Old coaching term for the light use of the whip.

Fan Tail The tail of a docked horse which is not squared, but cut shorter at the sides near the root, presenting the appearance of a fan.

Far North country term for the off side (q.v.) of an animal.

Faradism Electrical therapy for limb injuries first used on humans and now extensively on horses.

Farcy see GLANDERS.

Faroe Islands Pony Somewhat similar in type to the Iceland Pony (q.v.).

Farrier From 1356, this name was applied by The Worshipful Company of Farriers to the man who attended a sick horse, and today it is the farrier in the army who, under the supervision and guidance of the veterinary surgeon, attends to sick horses and mules. More generally used today for a man in a shoeing forge, who may be either Fireman or Doorman (qq.v.). The axe is the symbol of the farrier, as carried in ceremonial processions, e.g. Trooping the Colour.

Farriers and Blacksmiths, Amalgamated Society of (Founded 1805) *Objects:* to regulate wages and the relations between employers and employed, and to assist members and their families in cases of unemployment, sickness, accident, disablement and death. It claims to be the oldest Trade Union in existence.

Farrier's Shop see SHOEING FORGE.

Farriers, The Worshipful Company of One of the ancient Livery Companies of London, dating back to the fourteenth century, it received its Charter from King Charles II in 1674. The Guild keeps its association with its craft by granting certificates of proficiency to Shoeing Smiths after a searching practical examination, and also in other ways.

Farriery * C. Richardson, F.W.C.F.

In giving a brief outline of this subject, it will be as well to start with a study of the hoof itself, which can be divided into various parts:
1 The Wall or outer crust, as seen when the horse is in a standing position; 2 The Sole; 3 The Frog; 4 The Bars; 5 The White Line; 6 The Periople; 7 The Horny Laminae; 8 The Coronary Groove or cavity.

The hoof, although continually growing, is dead matter and the hoof is, therefore, the insensitive horny covering of the sensitive structures of the foot.

1 *The Wall* Generally speaking the wall grows from the coronary band or cushion; strictly speaking it does, excepting the laminal sheath, or innermost section, of the wall, which is secreted by the sensitive laminae. This is not quite the hard, solid substance it appears to be, but is really composed of three kinds of horn: (a) a mass of hair-like tubes called 'tubular horn'; all of these very fine tubes are attached to and grow from the papillae (cone-like points) of the coronary band or cushion; (b) an inter-tubular horn, also secreted by the coronary cushion, which is a glutinous horn substance cementing the horn tubes into the solid-looking mass we usually see; (c) the intra-tubular or

cellular horn whose chief function appears to be as a conveyer of moisture. The average thickness of the wall is about $\frac{1}{2}$ in (12.7 mm), thickest at the toe, thinner towards the heels, and should contain about 16 to 24 per cent of moisture. Part of this natural moisture is derived from the blood and part by absorption from the soil, and therefore much depends upon the conditions under which the horse is kept. The varied conditions also affect the rate of growth, but roughly it may be said to take about nine to twelve months for a new wall to grow from coronet to toe (ground surface).

2 and 3 *The Sole and Frog* are composed of similar kinds of horn, but the horn tubes assume a more irregular wavy line than they do in the wall, and the frog is composed more of the glutinous intertubular horn than the tubular. The sole is about $\frac{3}{8}$ in (9.5 mm) thick, and contains about 36 per cent of moisture; it should be arched in shape, or when the foot is picked up, it should be seen to be somewhat hollow or concave; this gives greater strength and great clearance from the ground. It should be remembered that the sole acts as the floor of the foot and is there chiefly for protective purposes.

The frog is that wedge-shaped mass of rubber-like horn situated between the heels, and normally it should contain about 42 per cent of moisture. This high percentage accounts for its softness, and its tough, rubber-like qualities are derived from a supply of wax-like secretions from the fatty frog or plantar cushion situated above and forming the bulbs of the heels. The functions of the frog, when allowed to come into play, are:

(a) To grip the ground and prevent slipping.
(b) To minimize concussion.
(c) To assist in carrying the weight of the horse.
(d) To assist expansion and prevent contraction of the hoof.
(e) To promote (in conjunction with the lateral cartilages) a healthy

and natural supply of blood to the foot.

4 *The Bars* are a continuation of the wall at the heels, where the wall turns inwards on each side of the frog, forming the bars. They continue towards the point of the frog, until about halfway where they become lost in the sole. Their function is to strengthen the heels and prevent contraction.

5 *The White Line* is a soft horn containing about 50 per cent of moisture and forms the connection of the sole with the wall. It denotes the exact thickness of the wall, and can be regarded as a guide to the farrier. Nails can enter the white line, but on *no account* must they penetrate beyond it. In removing overgrowth or, as it is termed, in preparing the foot for the new shoe, the white line should not be seen too clearly, if at all. If it does show too much, the foot can be regarded as over-dressed, or over-lowered, and in that state grave risk is being run of tenderness or even actual lameness.

6 *The Periople* is a thin, varnish-like horn, secreted by the perioplic ring, which is situated around the extreme upper border of the coronary cushion. The periople can be seen very plainly when distended with moisture. Its function is to protect the young horn of the wall and to prevent undue evaporation of moisture from the wall. It also joins the skin with the horn of the wall.

7 *The Horny Laminae* These are thin flat plates of horn standing out at right angles from the anterior or inside surface of the wall and inter-locking with the sensitive laminae (thin fleshy vascular leaves) which cover the pedal bone and the lateral cartilages, forming a secure union of the hoof to the sensitive foot.

8 *The Coronary Groove* or cavity runs around the top of the inner side of the wall, to the depth of about $\frac{1}{2}$ in (12.7 mm) or a little more, and the coronary band or cushion fits into it. Examination with a magnifying glass will reveal in this cavity a very large number of tiny

holes—the commencement of the horn tubes of the wall.

As well as a knowledge of the structure of the hoof itself, every farrier should have some knowledge of the sensitive foot and the bones of the leg to knee and hock, particularly the joints, and how the sensitive structures may be affected by shoeing. The bones we should note in both fore and hind legs are the same in number:

(a) Metacarpal or cannon bone, the main shin or shank bone from knee to fetlock; in hind leg the metatarsal.

(b, c) Two small metacarpal or splint bones.

(d) Long pastern bone.

(e, f) Two sesamoid bones.

(g) Short pastern or coronet bone.

(h) Navicular bone.

(i) Pedal or coffin bone.

The pedal bone, navicular and lower portion of the coronet bone are entirely within the hoof, as also are the sensitive laminae, already mentioned, the sensitive sole and frog, and the sensitive covering of the coronary cushion. These sensitive or fleshy parts are liberally supplied with blood and it is from these that the respective parts of the hoof are secreted. The terminal portions are a flexor (at the back) and an extensor tendon (at the front), the two lateral cartilages which are attached to the wings of the pedal bone, ligaments holding the bones together, blood vessels and nerves, navicular bursa, and a mass of fibro-fatty tissue filling up the space behind the pedal bone and forming the bulbs of the heels, known as the plantar cushion or fatty frog.

The above-named bones comprise the three joints the farrier is mainly concerned with, namely the fetlock, pastern and foot joints. As these joints are true hinge joints (or nearly so), allowing backward and forward movement only, it is essential for the comfort of the horse that when the foot is prepared for the new shoe it should be quite level. When removing overgrowth, care should be taken that the heels are of the same height and the operation carried out level all round, thus avoiding uneven pressure of the bones at the joints, and any uneven strain of the ligaments binding and holding the joints.

A few words must suffice in regard to the composition of ligaments, tendons and bursae. Ligaments bind or hold bones in place. Chiefly these are the tendons originating from muscle above the knee and hock, which pass down the leg to become attached to the bones of the leg and foot and give the horse the power of movement or locomotion. Bursae are little blind sacs, containing a fluid similar to synovia (joint oil). They are placed either in a depression or on a prominent part of a bone, usually to assist the easier working of a tendon over these parts.

One very important ligament, i.e. the suspensory ligament, must have special mention, as this frequently gives trouble with the riding animal. It arises at the back of the knee, occupying the space between the two small metacarpals (splint bones) lying close against the large metacarpal or shin bone, passing down like a strong cord until, at about its lower third, it divides and each branch is firmly inserted into the sesamoid bones situated posteriorly or at the back of the fetlock joint. The fetlock joint can be said to be slung or suspended by this ligament, hence its name 'the suspensory ligament'. Its peculiar and important function renders it very liable to sprain. When severe this is known as a breakdown.

The essential difference between ligaments and tendons is that ligaments are more or less elastic, according to the amount of movement required, while tendons are totally inelastic. For sprains of the suspensory ligament and so-called sprained tendons, which by the way *seldom* become strained or stretched (injury more often affects the connective tissue of the tendon sheath than the actual tendon itself), a Platten shoe may be used until recovery is reached or lameness ceases. This is a shoe with a raised bar across the heels; the bar should be light and rather wide in cover.

It is important for a farrier to avoid mutilation of the hoof, when the foot will take care of itself. In re-shoeing all that is needed is to remove the overgrowth of the wall on the ground surface and remember, for reasons already stated, to do this level, and to lower almost to the level of the sole, which will usually bring the hoof back to normal; a slight blunting of the sharp edge and the foot, with the full thickness of the wall preserved, is ready for the fitting of the shoe. Beyond removal of the loose flakes, no paring and weakening of the sole or frog is permissible and no cutting out the bars or opening the heels.

When fitting the shoe, it is bad practice to cut out a 'V' or half round aperture to receive the clip; the clip is flat, or should be, on the inside surface, so the cut out should be straight to receive the clip, which should be set back somewhat to the same degree of slope as the hoof. The shoe having been satisfactorily fitted, with nail holes well made, it should be an easy matter to nail it on, leaving little or no surplus of horn to rasp off when clenching up.

The less the outside of the wall is rasped the better, for this leaves the periople more or less intact. When excessive rasping is carried out, this exposes the inner section of the wall where the horn tubes are full, round and soft and contain more moisture, and consequently we get undue evaporation of moisture from the wall, causing dry and brittle feet. If the horse be turned out into a wet pasture or a wet period be prevailing, the mutilated wall will absorb more moisture than it should normally contain and we get the opposite—soft, spongy or rotten feet. Some owners are too prone to order the farrier to shorten the toes well back if a horse stumbles, be it serious or not. Far better to roll the toe of the shoe and shorten that way than to 'dump' the toe.

The general types of shoes in use for the hunter and other riding animals are what are known as concave shoes, that is, with the inner edge hollowed or chamfered out. In the fore shoe, it makes for lightness and a better grip of the ground. In the hind shoe for all riding animals, the inner edge around the toe especially should always be concave or hollowed out, as a precaution in case of an over-reach. Even then damage may be done to the bulbs of the heels of the fore-foot, but it is obvious that the injury would be much more serious if the hind shoe were of a flat section with a sharp inner edge around the toe. In addition, the orthodox hunting shoe is always made somewhat square at the toe, with two clips, so that the shoe can be fitted under the wall at the toe, and the overhanging wall left on, blunting the sharp edge only. Opinions differ as to whether calkins on the hind shoes of a hunter are an advantage or not.

Those in favour of calkins forget that they wear down quickly, and for about two-thirds of the life of the shoe are practically flat. Having examined the imprints left in soft ground by the hunter and *always* finding them deepest at the toe, one must conclude that both in taking off and landing over a fence the toe is more depended upon than the heels. For the flat, weak-soled fore-foot, it is best to discard the concave shoe, and use a flat shoe with the inner edge of the foot surface seated or hollowed out, to give clearance to the sole of a foot of that type.

Another thing the farrier has to guard against is the liability to cut, or brush as it is called, the fetlock joint. It may be that the horse is young, tires easily, throws himself about a good deal and hits his joints; even the older horse in good condition may get an extra long day and in his over-tired state do the same; or again the horse may be, as we say, badly put together, and may habitually damage his joints. For each of these cases, there are many different kinds of shoes, one or the other will generally be found to meet the case, and either cut the damage down to a minimum or wipe it out altogether. The young horse should always be watched and precautions taken at once should he show a tendency to cut or hit himself, or permanently enlarged joints may be the result.

In conclusion, *so-called* corns must be mentioned. A corn is in reality a bruise of the sensitive sole. The sole is thin at the point where it terminates towards the heel between the bar and wall, consequently the sensitive sole underneath is easily bruised, and when this happens the escaping blood will stain and permeate the horny sole and, if the injury be serious enough to cause lameness and the foot be searched, we see the stained horn and are satisfied the horse has a corn. If this should be neglected, suppuration or festering may take place. The pus must be allowed to escape by opening the wound, for as such it must now be treated. If treated early enough by hot fomentations and poultices the soreness usually disappears quite soon.

The hunter is often said to be particularly liable to corns. If the heels of the fore shoe are properly prepared and they are fitted with correct bearing to the end of the heels, the hunter need be no more liable to corns than any other class of horse.

Common causes of corns are: shoes too short—shoes kept on too long are in consequence carried forward by growth, becoming too short in this way, and embedding themselves under and into the seat of the corn, causing bruising; pressure by the shoe over the seat of corn (that part of horny sole which fits in between bar and wall); flat feet with low, weak heels and, *per contra*, feet with high contracted heels, both predisposed to corns. Suitable shoes for corns are $\frac{3}{4}$-shoe, $\frac{3}{4}$-bar shoe, bar shoe, shoe with set down heel, all of which are designed to avoid pressure on the affected part. Shoes should never be sprung (bent upwards from the foot) for this purpose. It may be added that it is rare to find hind feet affected with corns (*see Plate 12*).

* * *

Fast Cheek *see* FIXED CHEEK.

Fastest Speed (Racehorse) 41.98 m.p.h. (67.5 km.p.h.) over 5 furlongs (1100 yd; 1 km) by 'Indigenous' at Epsom in 1960. The distance was covered in 53.6 seconds. The fastest mile was run by 'Soueida' in 1 minute 31.8 seconds (39.21 m.p.h.; 63.1 km.p.h.) at Brighton in 1963. This record was equalled by 'Loose Cover' over the same course in 1966.

Fat This often covers a multitude of faults (*see* CONDITION).

Father of Foxhunting, The *see* WARDE, JOHN.

Father of Racing, The *see* FRAMPTON, TREGONWELL.

Fault, At When hounds lose or run out of scent.

'Favouring a Leg' When a horse in movement avoids placing its full weight on one of its limbs. The practice will, of course, vary in extent in proportion to the pain or injury in the favoured limb, and is a clear indication of lameness.

Feather All fetlocks are covered with

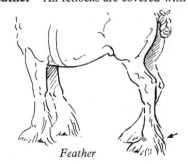

Feather

hair but when this is found abundantly long as in Shires and Clydesdales it is termed feather (see HAIR).

Feather When a hound believes it owns the scent but is uncertain, it will not speak to it, but will 'feather', indicated by waving its stern and by driving along the presumed line with its nose to the ground.

'**Feather Edging**' Driving near to anything.

Fédération Equestre Internationale (F.E.I.) International Equestrian Federation which governs, on an international basis, the sport of riding, and is composed of representatives of the affiliated national bodies of all leading countries.

Fédération International des Gentlemen Riders (FEGENTRI) Formed in 1955.

Feeding   *   M. A. P. Simons, M.R.C.V.S.

The art of feeding horses depends on a knowledge of the natural history and digestive function of the animal.

In the wild the horse is a creature of the plains, ever on the move in search of food. So much bulk is required that most of the day and much of the night is spent in grazing. The horse's lips, incisor teeth, and tongue are adapted for the intake of a wide variety of grasses and herbage. The molar teeth disrupt the structure of the vegetation so that the ferments secreted by the digestive glands of the gut can break down the foodstuffs to simple substances for absorption. Modifications of the intestine provide a place where even cellulose, the resistant skeleton of plant-life, can be broken down by fermentation and used by the horse. The relative capacities of the small and large intestines compared to those of a meat-eating animal are twice and four times as great, respectively.

Like other mammals the horse requires three main groups of nutriment: protein, carbohydrate, fat and a variety of minerals, vitamins and other essential substances. Equine nutrition is a neglected subject and many 'requirements' have been extrapolated from other animals without due regard to the considerable differences in structure, and function, in the horse. However, the basic needs are known but are affected by several variables. Variations in type,

size, age, temperament, environment and the work required of the animal must be taken into account. It is the ability to estimate the relative importance of these factors which constitutes the art of feeding.

The natural food of the horse is grass and herbage, and this is taken selectively, some species of grasses and plants being preferred to others. The intake of food is adequate for body maintenance. In the domesticated state the horse is required to work. The extra food needed is provided by feeding a restricted diet of dry and processed foods, or concentrates. The nutritive value of these depends on the soil on which they have been grown, the climatic conditions and the way in which they have been preserved.

Long experience has proved that oats are the best grain for horses with a good balance of body requirements. Good oats are clean, hard, dry, sweet, heavy, plump and full of flour. In a well-grown sample every oat is nearly the same size. There are few small or imperfect grains. The skin should be thin and the kernel hard. There is no smell and the flour should be almost tasteless but sweet to the palate. A bad sample of oats can be recognized by lack of these qualities: softness, the first effect of damp; mustiness, detected by the smell; mould and sprouting.

As a guide, the ration of oats for a

stabled horse in work can be based on body-weight at the rate of 2 lb (0.9 kg) for the first hundredweight (112 lb; 51 kg), and 1 lb (0.45 kg) for every additional hundredweight. Oats are best fed crushed to break the husk and aid digestion.

Barley can be fed to horses and is valuable for fattening. It should be fed boiled.

Maize is a valuable grain in compounding a ration. A good sample should be dry, hard, of bright colour, with a sweet taste but no smell. Common defects are mustiness or mouldiness. Maize is fed crushed or flaked.

A ration composed of oats, two parts to one part each of bran, barley and maize is well balanced in most essential nutriments.

Bran, a by-product of the milling of wheat for flour, is used to encourage mastication of the food and add bulk. The nutritive value of bran depends on the amount of flour it contains and with efficient milling this is low. Good bran is dry and sweet, flaky, free from lumps and floury. A bad sample is sour and lumpy.

A bran mash is the traditional mild laxative for the horse. The mash is made by scalding about 2 lb (0.9 kg) of bran in a bucket with boiling water, covering and allowing to cool. A little salt should be stirred in before the mash is fed.

Beans and peas are highly nutritious, rich in protein, and on this account may be fed only in small quantities of 1 lb (0.45 kg) or so at a time. Beans and peas should be at least a year old, hard and dry, sweet to the taste and free from weevil and split.

Linseed, the seed of the flax plant, is another fattening food for horses. The seeds should be plump and well filled, bright and free from dirt. The husk is tough and the seed must be boiled. It is customary to soak linseed, bring it to the boil and allow it to simmer all day. From ½–1 lb (0.22–0.45 kg) is fed at a time. Boiling is important, as

soaking alone may release a poisonous substance from the seed, but this is destroyed by heat.

Green food ('green meat') is relished by the stabled horse. Commonly vetches are grown for this purpose, to be cut for use in spring and summer.

Carrots, turnips and mangolds are also useful to supplement dry food. Roots should be free from disease and soil, and sliced lengthwise for feeding, to avoid the mischance of an animal choking on a piece too large to be swallowed.

Sugar-beet pulp can be fed to horses but contains little nourishment, being mainly cellulose with a small amount of sugar. The pulp must be well soaked before adding to the feed, as when dry it absorbs up to four times its own bulk of water and will cause severe indigestion unless this precaution is taken.

Hay consists of grass and other plants cut, dried and matured in a stack. The quality and value of hay depend on the grasses and herbage (plants not grasses) of which it is composed, the soil on which it has been grown, the stage of growth at which the grass has been cut, and the way in which it has been 'saved' or dried and matured.

Hay made from old pasture can be recognized by the large variety of grasses, and the fineness of growth. The presence of water-grasses, sedges and rushes, indicates inferior hay made from a water-meadow. Seed or mixture hay is characterized by the small variety of grasses, the coarseness of their growth and the large proportion of clover present. Useful grasses include the Meadow grasses, the Fescues, Meadow Fox-tail, Timothy and the Rye-grasses. Amongst the inferior grasses are classed Couch-grass, Yorkshire Fog, Field Brome, Slender Fox-tail and Tufted Hair-grass. Hay can also be made from clover, lucerne or sainfoin.

Grass is best cut for hay just before the opening of the flower heads, when digestibility is high, owing to a high proportion of leaf to stem and nutritive value is at a maximum.

'Saving' of hay includes drying, carrying and stacking. Rain washes out of the cut grass many of the nutriments. Prolonged exposure to sunlight also causes damage. In the rick chemical changes take place which improve the digestibility of the final product.

Good hay has a high proportion of well-grown useful grasses in early flower, green or brown in colour, crisp to the feel, sweet to taste and with a pleasant smell. Useless grasses and weeds should be few or absent. Defects in hay are brittleness, dust, must and mould. Excessive fermentation in the stack produces heat and charring: the resulting hay is said to be 'mow-burnt'.

Old hay is between six and eighteen months old, when it is reckoned to be at its best.

Chopped hay or chaff is used to add bulk to the ration and to encourage the horse to chew the feed.

The amount of hay fed depends on the rest of the ration, the more concentrates the less hay. Hay can rarely, if ever, be eliminated from the diet of the stabled horse since it provides the bulk required for efficient digestion.

Horses require salt and other minerals. A lump of rock salt in the manger is an excellent source of supply, but owing to modern methods of salt-mining, rock salt is difficult to obtain. A little kitchen salt may be added to the feed instead. Proprietary mineral licks are also useful.

The concentrate in the ration can be provided by the use of horse nuts or cubes. These are produced by several national feeding-stuff compounders, from a variety of cereal and protein sources such as maize and linseed meal, with the addition of minerals and vitamins. Nuts or cubes are an aid to horse management, but most brands require supplementing with hay, to provide bulk, and none can replace an individual ration devised to meet the special requirements and tastes of an individual horse.

A plentiful supply of clean water is essential to health and efficient digestion in the horse. The horse is the best judge of the amount required and the best course is to give the animal free access to water at all times. It is important to realize that the capacity of the gut of the average horse may approach 50 gal (227 l), and digestion depends upon the greater part of this being occupied.

The principles of feeding the stabled horse are based on an understanding of the structure of the digestive tract and the function of digestion.

The horse's natural habit of grazing little and often has resulted in the evolution of a small stomach. Hence the rule is feed little and often.

The natural diet is confined to grass and herbage. The successful digestion of the plant skeleton, cellulose, requires the intervention of bacteria. Bacteria are also known to synthesize essential food substances which are utilized by the horse. Evolution has resulted in capacious intestines where an extensive bacterial population can function. Bulk is required to keep these organs active. Changes in diet must be gradual to allow the digestive bacteria to adjust to them.

The work done dictates the energy requirements of the horse, and hence the ration required. The ration must be of the best available, clean and wholesome, for the horse is a selective feeder.

Feeding at regular hours and introducing variety into the ration with green-stuff or special concentrates will assist both appetite and digestion. Last, but not least, the horse must be given quiet and time to eat its feed and digest the same.

*   *   *

Feet The feet of a horse need the utmost care. They are recognized to be the most important part of the anatomy, as witness the well-known saying: 'No feet, no horse' (*see* FARRIERY; *Plate* 12).

Fellow, Felloe (pronounced felly) The section of the wheel rim that holds the spokes and carries the tyre.

Fell Pony A pony which was once identical with the original Dales pony, and which is now found on the western side of the Pennine range of hills in northern England. For fifty years or more, it was used as a pannier pony to carry lead from the mines to the sea, travelling 240 miles (386 km) in a week carrying 16 st (224 lb; 102 kg). It is now an excellent ride and drive pony, standing 13.2 h.h. (134 cm), mostly black or dark brown, of a true mountain type, powerfully built, and alert-looking with abundant hair on mane, tail and heels, is very tough, hardy and sure-footed. *Breed Society :* The Fell Pony Society (*see Plate 14*).

Fell Pony Society, the (Founded 1927) *Objects :* to promote the breeding and registration of pure-bred Fell ponies; the animals are entered in the National Pony Stud Book. The Society holds an annual show.

Femur The thigh bone which extends from the hip joint to the stifle.

Fence The general term applicable to all obstacles met in racing or hunting (with the exception of hurdle races). There are many particular names, e.g. open-ditch and water in racing; bull-finch and oxer in hunting.

Fence, to The act of leaping over an obstacle.

Fenners Bit A Pelham type of bit, sometimes called a Parallel Bit, with two mouthpieces. The upper one slides up and down and the one at the lower end slides backwards. The two mouthpieces are joined by a rubber band at the centre of the mouth.

Fenners Pelham A once popular straight bar (Chifney action bit).

Fen Trotter *see* LINCOLNSHIRE TROT-TER, the definition of which is probably applicable in this case.

Ferneley, John, Senr. (1782–1860) A very gifted painter of horses, hunting scenes and personalities, particularly associated with Melton Mowbray. A wheelwright's son, he became a pupil of Ben Marshall and gained great popularity with the hunting aristocracy of the Shires, painting portraits of them and their horses. His horses have great natural dignity, and in scenes depicting movement the atmosphere of the Golden Age of fox-hunting in the Shires is perhaps better conveyed by Ferneley than by any other artist. He painted a few racehorses and some driving subjects. Three of his children inherited some of his talent. Two sons, John Ferneley, Junr. (1815–1862) and Claude Loraine Ferneley (1822–1891), both painted horse portraits and hunting subjects of merit. A daughter, Sarah Ferneley, produced paintings and lithographs.

Ferrule The 'shaft' of a hunting horn.

Fertility This varies with individual horses of either sex in different breeds, but it is claimed of the Arab that its fertility lasts longer than that of the Thoroughbred. In the former case, stallions will propagate till 35, while mares will breed throughout their lives. A general average of years of fertility throughout the breeds must be considered lower than this.

Fetlock, the Tuft of hair behind the fetlock joint (*q.v.*).

Fetlock Boots *see* BRUSHING BOOTS.

Fetlock Joint The joint lying at the lower extremity of the cannon bone and joining it to the pastern (*q.v.*).

Fever *see* TEMPERATURE.

Fever in the Feet *see* LAMINITIS.

Fiadore (Western)   Equivalent of a throatlatch (*q.v.*).

Fibreglass-lined   Whip centres are made from fibreglass as whalebone is no longer available.

Fibre-shoes   *see* ROPE SHOES.

Fibula   The smaller of the two bones, the tibia and the fibula, which extend between the stifle joint and the hock. The tibia goes the whole length, to articulate with the astragalus of the hock joint, but the fibula terminates two-thirds of the way down the tibia.

Fidding, Figging   A discreditable practice to make a mare carry her tail higher, this consists of applying ginger or cayenne pepper to the sex organ. It constitutes an act of cruelty (*see* GINGERING).

Fiddle-head   A large, plain, coarse and ugly-shaped head.

Field   A hunting term indicating all the mounted followers of both sexes assembled and intending to hunt on any particular day.

Field (Racing)   'The Field' in betting implies all the competitors in the race. If a bookmaker offers 'two to one the field' it implies the shortest price offered, that is, on the favourite.

Field (Racing)   'The Field' when applied to a sweepstake, for which tickets can be bought, refers to any 'chance' horse not named in the draw.

Field Boots   In brown and sometimes black leathers, generally of a tougher tannage than polo boots, to withstand campaigning. There are two main styles: laced at the neck, and open leg fastened by buckles and straps with lacing at the neck. Most have toe caps for protection.

Field Master   Master of the Pack, or, if he be hunting his hounds, someone appointed to control the field when hounds are drawing or hunting.

Field Money   Tip given to hunt servant, also a cap (*q.v.*) or capping fee.

Fiennes, Celia (1662–1737)   She made extensive tours on horseback through England, visiting every county and recording her impressions in a diary. In the summer of 1698 she covered 1551 miles 'many of them long miles' from Salisbury to Newcastle and Cornwall.

Fifth Leg   A horse which is clever in recovering from a mistake at a fence is said to have a fifth leg.

'Figure 8' Noseband   Similar to the Grakle noseband (*q.v.*), but of an improved pattern.

Filing Teeth   *see* TOOTH-RASPING.

Filled Legs   Usually caused by over-feeding or lack of exercise. The limbs swell suddenly and become very tender and stiff. Young horses and those run down by over-work are the most prone to this ailment.

Fillet Strap   An ornamental strap which hangs from the back strap in pair horse harness.

Fillet String   The cord attached to the near corners of the sheet (summer rug) to prevent its blowing up. Also called a tail string.

Fillis, James (*circa* 1850–1900)   A well-known equestrian authority and author of *Breaking and Riding* and other instructional works. An Englishman who lived most of his life in France, he was at one time instructor at the Imperial School of Russia. Though he was undoubtedly a great horseman, much of his work belonged more to the circus than to classical riding.

Fillis Bridoon   A bit with a low, wide port, hinged on both sides and having a separate eye for the cheek pieces. Baucher's snaffle is similar. It is suspended in the mouth rather than resting on it.

Filly A female horse under the age of four.

Find (or Unkennel) To dislodge a fox, to get him moving.

'Fine' (Harness Class, U.S.A.) Harness classes in the U.S.A. when saddlebreds are shown to show wagons or traps.

Fino-fino see THE HORSE WORLD IN THE UNITED STATES OF AMERICA, *page* 351.

Fir-tar see TAR.

Fireman The name applied to a farrier whose work is to make and fit the shoes (*see* DOORMAN).

Firing The operation of firing tendons and joints such as the hock in cases of spavin, and the coronets for the relief of pain and lameness resulting from various types of exostosis, has to some extent been frowned upon by the modern generation of veterinary surgeons. In its place they advocate injections of cortisone preparations, various forms of counter-irritation employing, in the place of the old-fashioned blisters, short-wave therapy and electrical machines designed to produce rhythmic muscular contractions. In practice some of these bring about improvement which is often only transient and the treatment needs frequent repetition. Firing, carried out by an experienced operator, appears still to be the least unsatisfactory method of treatment in selected cases, particularly those involving chronic tendon lameness.

Firing Irons see FIRING.

Firr, Tom Famous huntsman to the Quorn, from 1872–1898. He said it was a piece of gross impertinence to interfere with hounds until they had made their own cast.

First-cross The progeny of any two animals of separate breeds registered in the stud books of such breeds.

First Jockey Principal jockey engaged to ride for an owner or stable.

Fistula A tubular ulcer in any part of the body, but found more particularly at the poll or withers. An operation is necessary, and a cure can only be effected by draining the ulcer and removing the diseased tissue.

Fistulous Withers One or more fistulae may originate from a necrotic dorsal vertebra, especially when the summit of a spine is affected. Pus develops and breaks through the overlying or adjoining skin and may burrow downwards and appear in various parts of the shoulder and also in the axilla (armpit). Infection may result from saddle pressure at the withers, a blow or a *Brucella* infection. Operation involves removal of all necrotic bone and drainage. Antibiotics may assist healing after the operation but will have no effect on necrotic bone.

Fitzwilliam Girth A double web and leather girth usually 5 in (127 mm) and 3¼ in (82 mm) respectively. Now little used.

Five-barred Gate Any gate in the hunting field.

Five-gaited Saddlehorse An American term for a horse which has, in addition to the normal gaits (walk, trot and canter), the 'slow gait' (a sort of shuffle between walk and trot) and 'rack' (*q.v.*). A five-gaited horse is always shown with a foretop and full mane and tail.

Fixed Cheek, Fast Cheek A curb bit where the mouth bit is immovable, i.e. does not slide.

Fjord Pony A Norwegian pony whose chief feature is its distinctive colour, between cream and dun with a dark dorsal stripe. The mane is usually clipped to stand up in a fine crest. Docile and hardworking (*see Plate 14*).

Flagging Another term for docking (*q.v.*).

Flags   The floor of hounds' kennel courts.

Flanchard   Protective armour for the flanks of a mediaeval war horse.

Flank   That part of the horse's body behind the ribs and below the loins extending down to the belly.

Flapping Meeting   Any race meeting which is held without the sanction of a recognized turf authority.

'Flash' Noseband   An ordinary cavesson noseband in the centre of which are sewn two diagonally crossing straps which fasten beneath the bit. Used when a standing martingale and drop noseband is required.

Flask (Hunting)   This can be one of several shapes, and is carried, during hunting, in a leather holster or in a sandwich case, either being attached by short leather straps to the 'D's' on the saddle.

Flat, on the   A race without obstacles; a flat race.

Flat-bone   A term of commendation indicating legs or knees of clean, hard and chiselled appearance—the reverse of round bone.

Flat-catcher   A horse having outwardly all the looks and virtues, but whose hidden defects appear on closer acquaintance.

Flat-footed   A horse is said to be flat-footed when, owing to the lowness of the wall of the hoof, he goes on the heels more than on the toes, instead of putting the feet squarely and evenly to the ground. The fault is usually associated with a large soft frog and brittle horn, and horses reared on soft ground are the most subject to it.

Flat Race   see FLAT, ON THE.

Flat Ring   A flattened bit ring as opposed to a round or wire ring. Both are loose rings. The disadvantage of the former is that it requires a larger hole

in the mouthpiece through which to pass, and this factor can cause pinching of the lips.

Flat-sided   A horse is said to be flat-sided when its ribs are not rounded or 'well-sprung'. Also known as slat- or slab-sided.

Flatulence (Wind)   This is generally caused by indigestion. *Treatment*: administer a purge to clear internal obstructions and then give small doses of bicarbonate of soda twice a day for a week. Avoid feeding beans or peas. When pain is associated with flatulence, a veterinary surgeon should be called in immediately.

Flea-bitten   Description of horse with grey coat flecked with hairs of darker tones.

Fleam   A mid-sixteenth-century lancet used for bleeding horses.

Flèche, à la   A circus act in which a rider drives a horse in the lead on long reins.

Flecked   Where small collections of white hairs occur, distributed irregularly in any part of the body, it is described as 'flecked'.

Flemish   see BELGIAN HEAVY DRAUGHT.

Flesh   A kennel term indicating the meat on which hounds are fed.

Flesh Cart   Vehicle for conveying to kennels the carcases of animals on which hounds feed.

Flesh Hovel   A kennel term indicating the room where carcases are skinned and jointed and where the meat is hung.

Flesh Marks   Patches, where the pigment of the skin is absent, are described as 'flesh marks' (*see Plate 21*).

Flesh Side   The inside of a piece of leather. Nourishment in the form of oils, etc., should be applied to the flesh side where the pores are unsealed. The grain side (outside) of the leather is waterproofed and does not absorb oil so readily.

Flexalan   An oil dressing for leather containing lanolin.

Flexing Hocks   Usually applied to Hackney action, as this horse, more than other breeds, bends the hocks and gets the legs further under its belly.

Flexions   A horse flexes when it yields its jaw to the pressure of the bit, with its head bent at the poll.

Flies   For stabled horses a fly-net or a cotton sheet worn by day gives some protection, and the stable should be kept rather dark. Cobwebs should not be removed from stables much subject to presence of flies. For horses at grass, spray their coats with some compound disliked by flies, which, however, usually attack eyes and other sensitive parts which should not be sprayed. An eye-fringe attached to the headstall gives the best protection to eyes, but it is preferable to bring horses in during the day.

Flies   Fences which, when hunting, are not jumped on and off, as with single and double banks in Ireland.

Flight of Hurdles   A row of hurdles (*see* HURDLE RACE).

Float   A country vehicle, low to the ground like a Governess Cart (*q.v.*). It had a forward-facing driving seat. Also a utility flat platform on two wheels with a low surround for retaining goods and for easy loading.

Floating   U.S.A. term for tooth rasping (*q.v.*).

Floorman   A doorman (*q.v.*).

Floorman   A racecourse bookmaker's runner.

Flute Bit   A perforated hollow mouth-piece bit used to prevent wind-sucking.

Fly   A one-horse four-wheeled covered carriage plying for hire.

Fly, to   *see* FLY FENCE.

Fly-caps   A net worn over the ears as a protection against flies.

Fly-caps

Fly Fence   A hunting term indicating any fence which can be cleared (jumped) at a gallop.

Fly Front   A browband laced with hanging lengths of cord or strips of leather to keep flies away from the eyes.

Flying Change of Leg   A change of leading leg at the canter during the fourth or silent time of the movement when the horse has all four legs in the air. For the movement to be correct, fore and hindlegs must change together during the fourth time, though the hindlegs slightly precede the forelegs. These flying changes may be performed singly or in quite close succession and spaced regularly by a given number of strides, at every fourth, third or second stride; or at every stride.

Fly-link   The link on a curb chain through which the lip-strap passes.

Fly-noseband   A noseband laced in the same manner as a fly front (*q.v.*).

Fly Sheet   A sheet or net worn over the back and quarters as a protection against flies.

Fly-terrets (Harness)   A matching brass or other metal terret, with a 'swing' fitting in a circular ring, was sometimes fitted to the slip head in the hope of attracting flies which would otherwise cause discomfort to the horse.

Fly Whisk   A horse-hair switch carried by a rider for removing flies from the horse. Is often dyed in gay colours.

Fly Whisk

Foal   A colt, gelding or filly up to the age of 12 months, described accordingly as colt-foal or filly-foal.

Foal Bit   *see* TATTERSALL BIT.

Foal Headcollar   Made of light leather or tubular web, adjustable at head, throat and nose, and fitted with a hand tag at the rear (*see* DUTCH SLIP).

Foal-heat   Period from the seventh to the fifteenth day after foaling when a mare's first heat may be expected.

Foaling Table   *see page* 43.

Foaling-time   Old horseman's saying, as a guide:

'She bags up her udder a few days before—
She waxes and slackens some hours before—
She sweats and she fidgets some minutes before—
She foals.'

Foal-lap   *see* HIPPOMANES.

Foal Slip   *see* FOAL HEADCOLLAR *and* DUTCH SLIP.

Fodder, Forage   Any feeding stuffs normally fed to horses.

Foil (Hunting)   When sheep or other animals cross the line of a hunted fox, obliterating the scent, they are said to foil the ground.

Foix, Gaston de   Author of *Le Livre de la Chasse* (1387), which became the textbook on hunting in France, and was circulated throughout Europe; the English translation *The Master of Game* is the oldest book on hunting in England, and was made by Edward, Duke of York (1373–1415).

Fold-bitted   *see* EARS, IDENTIFICATION MARKS.

Fold the Whip   By one flick of the whip hand to twist and wrap the thong and lash of any driving whip lightly around the shaft, thus keeping it in control.

Foot Board   On a coach, a board on which the coachman's feet rest.

Foot-stool   *see* SHOEING BLOCK.

Forage   *see* FODDER *and* WEIGHTS (FORAGE).

Fordham, George (1837–1887) Champion jockey nine times. Won the Derby in 1879 on Baron Lionel de Rothschild's 'Sir Bevys'. First big success was in 1852 when he won the Cambridgeshire, riding at only 3 st 12 lb (24.48 kg), at the age of 15. Brilliant jockey, who often contrived to deceive opponents out of a race. The only serious rival of Fred Archer (*q.v.*) in his heyday. An owner presented Fordham with a Bible and a gold-mounted whip inscribed 'Honesty is the best policy', which advice he always followed.

Fore-arm   That part of the front leg which extends from the elbow to the knee; it contains two bones, the radius and the ulna.

Fore Carriage   The front part of the undercarriage of any four-wheeled vehicle which turns to the left or right with the front wheels when a turn is made.

Forecast A betting term denoting the prophecy of the experts on the prices which will be offered against each horse's chance of winning the race. This forecast, which appears in daily papers under the list of probable runners for each race, is based on past form and information, and is therefore apt to be inaccurate.

Forensic Laboratory The Newmarket laboratory where dope testing is carried out.

Forfeit (Racing) see DECLARATION OF FORFEIT.

Forfeit List (Racing) A list of people owing money in entry fees, etc., and the horses on which the arrears are due. The Unpaid Forfeit List is published regularly in the *Racing Calendar*. A winning horse whose owner is in the forfeit list can have an objection laid against him.

Forfeit Stakes see DECLARATION.

Forefooted An American term used when a horse is roped by the front feet.

Forehand The head, neck, shoulders, withers and forelegs of a horse.

Forehead Drop, Forehead Piece An ornament which hangs down the horse's forehead on some harness.

Foreign Terms see GLOSSARY, *page* 418.

Forelock A continuation of the mane which extends between the ears and hangs over the forehead.

Forging The collision of the hind shoe with the fore shoe when the horse is trotting. It can be recognized by the clicking noise as one shoe strikes against the other, and occurs when the horse is young and green, when it is uncollected or fatigued, or when it is being ridden or driven in a slovenly manner. When a horse is liable to forge, the inner borders of the fore shoes should be bevelled off and concaved, and the hind shoes should be made with a bevelled square toe and two clips, and should be let back at the toe wherever possible. A flat hind shoe, thinnest at the heel, is best.

Fork Stable forks are usually 4 ft (121 cm) in length with blunted prongs; they are sometimes made of split wood.

Fork-stowed see EARS, IDENTIFICATION MARKS.

Form A hollow or indentation in the ground in which a hare will lie.

Form (Racing) Record of a horse's achievements by which its chances in a race are assessed.

'Forrard' A huntsman's cheer to hounds: 'Forrard'; 'Forrard-on'; 'Hark forrard to . . .' (a reliable hound).

'Forty Thieves' An old term for the gipsy and hawker fraternity to be found at horse fairs.

Forward Seat A term applied to the seat of a rider; the reverse of one who sits on the back of the saddle and whose feet and legs from the knees downwards are in front of the girth. The forward seat is the *balanced* seat (*see* DRESSAGE, *page* 95, *and* PRINCIPLES OF RIDING, *page* 269).

Fothering-time A corruption of foddering time, i.e. feeding time in hunting and farm stables. It is rarely used in racing establishments, where the equivalent is 'morning' and 'evening' stables. The passage in front of cattle stalls is called the Fother-gang.

Foundation Mares (Racing) see BRUCE LOWE FIGURE SYSTEM.

Founder Another name for Laminitis (*q.v.*).

Four-in-hand A team of four horses, two wheelers and two leaders. The term is sometimes used to describe a coach and four as a complete turn-out. A four-in-hand coach can be either a mail, park, road, or stage coach (*qq.v.*).

Four-time Applied to the definition of a pace; a pace of four-time is so called because it is marked by four hoof-beats at each stride.

Four-wheeled Dog-cart A popular trap with body and seating as in a dog-cart but on four wheels, for a single horse or a pair.

Four-wheeler *see* 'GROWLER'.

Fox A wild animal of the family *Vulpes* notorious for its cunning. Its body colour is red-brown to reddish-grey.

Foxhound A hound bred and kept for hunting the fox. Measuring from 22 to 25 in (55.8–63.5 cm) at the shoulder, it is usually white with black, tan and light markings on the head and body.

Foxhound Kennel Stud Book, The This was first compiled in 1841 by Mr. Vyner, and a subsequent volume in 1866 by Mr. Cornelius Tongue. By a resolution passed at the Annual General Meeting of members of the Masters of Foxhounds' Association held at Tattersall's on May 28th, 1906, these two volumes were re-published, and subsequently, and at frequent intervals, other volumes have been issued. The first volume contained a list of His Majesty's Buckhounds and of forty-six packs of foxhounds.

'Foxhunter' International show jumper of great personality. He was owned by Lt.-Col. H. M. Llewellyn, C.B.E. Foaled in 1940, 'Foxhunter', a bay gelding, 16.3 h.h. (166 cm), was by T. B., sire, 'Erehwemos', out of 'Catcall' who went back to a pure bred Clydesdale mare. He represented Great Britain 35 times and had 78 International wins to his credit. He won the King George V Cup (*q.v.*) three times. Semi-retired in 1953, he made his final farewell to show jumping in 1956 when he won the final Committee Trophy at the Dublin Show. He died in 1959.

Foxhunter Competition (Show Jumping) An adult event for registered horses in Grade C, the property of and to be ridden by members of the B.S.J.A. (*q.v.*). The two highest-placed horses are eligible to compete in one of the regional finals. The two highest-placed horses in each regional final qualify to compete in the Foxhunter Championship at the Horse of the Year Show in October. These competitions are sponsored by the *Daily Express* and named after the famous International Show Jumper, 'Foxhunter' (*q.v.*).

Foxhunting in Britain Today   *   Dorian Williams, M.F.H.

It is not easy accurately to state just when and where foxhunting started in Britain. That there had been hunting carried on all over the British Isles ever since the Conquest, and indeed before, is beyond doubt, yet it was almost certainly not until the eighteenth century that packs were used exclusively to hunt the fox. Up to that time hounds hunted any quarry, in particular the deer.

By the end of the seventeenth century, however, those who hunted—and they were for the most part the great landlords—were beginning to realize that the hunting of the fox provided better sport than any other animal. The reason for this was because the fox had greater stamina than the hare, had not so strong a scent as the deer, was more crafty than either, and so presented a great challenge to a huntsman and his hounds.

Just 300 years ago the great Duke of Buckingham who hunted his vast territories in the north of England is alleged to have exclaimed that he would willingly exchange a flock of his fattest sheep for a similar number of foxes.

By the middle of the eighteenth century, thanks largely to the enthusiasm of such great aristocrats as the Duke of

Buckingham and other members of the Royal family, hunting the fox was the most flourishing sport in England.

A hundred years later and it was far and away the most popular. At this time the great landlords were finding it impossible even for them to maintain the magnificent set-ups employed to hunt the fox over large areas—the Dukes of Berkeley hunted from Bristol to London, the Duke of Beaufort from Bath to Oxford—so thanks to the Industrial Revolution there were many more of the new gentry who could afford to hunt, and subscription packs were started, hunting smaller areas; but because the subscribers felt that they were paying for sport which they were entitled to have, the hunting was much more efficiently organized.

There was, obviously, a certain anomaly here. The Duke, or other noble landlord, owned the hounds and probably most of the country, but other people paid the bills—a fact which His Grace almost certainly resented, as he did the interference of a committee which the subscribers felt entitled to appoint.

The nineteenth century, therefore, is full of stories of rows and arguments and clashes between the landlord and the followers. A situation so fraught with incendiary problems was bound to take a little time to settle down. It could even be said that in some parts of the country it has never entirely settled down!

So often thought to be the hey-day of hunting, the nineteenth century was, in fact, the most discreditable period in its history. The fields were huge and paid little attention to the farmer; foxes, being in short supply because of poaching, were invariably bagged; with no traffic-ridden roads, no barbed wire, no artificial manures to steady the chase, hounds were forced on at a tremendous pace, the field riding, as if in a race, on unclipped horses many of which, their owners proudly boasted, died of exhaustion every season.

The march of progress and World War I brought foxhunters to their senses and when hunting was resumed after the war it was much more what those who, 200 years earlier, had first discovered the joys of the chase, had intended it to be.

Between the wars there were still plenty of people who maintained large establishments and foxhunting in those two decades was of a very high order: well organized, producing excellent sport, the country still ridable.

It was a miracle—the result, in fact, of a few dedicated and tireless enthusiasts—that hunting survived World War II. But it did, and during the last twenty-five years it has evolved as the sport that we know today. Lacking, perhaps, the style and bravura, and colour of previous centuries, it is, however, far more democratic and far more broadly based; and indeed gives pleasure to far more people than ever before.

This is due, first, to the fact that far more people today can actually afford to hunt, mounted, than even in the days before the war. Secondly, there is far less evidence of great wealth amongst the country landlords and so, with few exceptions, hunting is far less exclusive —far less a sport for the privileged few. Thirdly, more and more farmers come out hunting themselves, whereas before, so impoverished was their industry that not only could they not afford to hunt, but they were dependent upon the local hunt for their livelihood, which made it virtually impossible for them to complain to the hunt or even seek their co-operation. Were it not for the hunt they would have been bankrupt. Now many hunts are run by farmers.

Lastly, there has been, during the last twenty-five years, the formation of Supporters' Clubs which has meant that each year more and more people feel involved with their local hunt.

These Supporters' Clubs play a vital part in foxhunting. In some countries there is a danger of their playing almost too vital a part because they tend to dictate to the hunt. There have been cases where the continuity is much more in evidence in the Supporters' Club, where wealth is of no account whatever, than in the Mastership or Committee where money is still a major feature. In such cases the Supporters' Clubs become very powerful. The same thing has happened in football, but it is not a desirable situation because it is never good for any sport to be run from the side-lines.

The situation is, however, remarkably rare, fortunately, and for the most part the Supporters' Clubs do a wonderful job for hunting, many hunts being quite unable to exist without them, not only because of the part they play as ambassadors for foxhunting, popularizing the sport amongst a section of the community that has never before been interested and, even more important, providing a most useful antidote to those opposed to hunting; but most important of all laying, once and for all, the lie that hunting is an exclusive sport which can only be enjoyed by the privileged and wealthy.

Would such a situation ever have been envisaged 200 or even 100 years ago? It is, of course, unthinkable; but it may well be that hunting is much better for it. It could even be said that were it not for this development hunting would not have survived until today.

The fact of the matter is that the fox-hunter today has far greater responsibilities than in the past. He has responsibilities to the farmer, to the general public and to the sport itself.

In the last century he could enjoy his sport whenever he liked. The whole countryside was his playground. Now even in the most fortunate countries there are inevitably a few farmers who do not appreciate the hunt. Unless a proper responsibility towards agriculture is accepted many more farmers will be opposed to hunting and will refuse to allow the hunt over their land.

Never has it been more important that those who go out hunting should appreciate fully the importance of good relations between the hunt and the farmers, and have a proper understanding of the modern farmer's problems. Gates left open, seeds and growing crops ridden over, wire fences broken and so on: these are the things that make a farmer feel it just is not worth his while to allow the hunt over his land.

No less important is the actual relationship between farmers and the people who hunt. It is really the duty of hunting people to get to know the farmers in their country: not just those who actually come out hunting who may obviously be expected to support the hunt—though sometimes they are keener on the hunt going on others' land than their own!—but the many more who have nothing to do with the hunt, perhaps have no interest in hunting at all, and are even basically opposed to it. These are the farmers that hunting people should take the trouble to know and make friends with.

There is an obligation, too, to ensure that the general public is in no way incommoded, let alone offended, by the hunt. Too often people out hunting allow themselves to appear thoughtless, even arrogant. They ride on pavements; take up the whole road, making it impossible for cars to pass; they expect ordinary people to open gates or hold their horses and then forget to thank them. Such behaviour can only cause resentment, make people dislike the hunt, which is, of course, totally unnecessary.

The hunt has always been a colourful part of the countryside, respected, even loved, by local people. For generations hunting people have made it their business to see that the hunt is very much an integrated part of the countryside. With the developments of Supporters' Clubs this aspect should be increased. It would be unfortunate if the thoughtless behaviour of a few, often through ignorance, should be responsible for diminishing this good relationship.

Finally there is the responsibility of

ordinary hunting people towards their own hunt. To keep a hunt going today is by no means easy. The support of everyone is needed.

To begin with, there is the subscription. How much easier a Hunt Secretary's task would be if everyone paid their hunt subscription in good time so that he had no anxiety in meeting the regular weekly expenses.

Support also should be forthcoming from all the many money-raising efforts that every hunt has to indulge in to make sure that the hunt can remain viable and provide the sport that the members expect.

Those hunting should also respect at all times the Master or Masters, the Secretary and those in authority. Their task is difficult enough without factions, criticism which is as often as not unjustified when one realizes how much work is being done for no reward, and bad behaviour even if it is more often than not due to ignorance.

The Hunt Staff should also be respected and helped in every possible way, for they are doing an almost endless job for very long hours and usually for a wage that is quite unrealistic when one realizes not only how hard they have to work but how great is their responsibility.

A hundred years ago those who spent so much of their spare time enjoying the sport of foxhunting never had to give a moment's thought to such things as have been mentioned in the preceding paragraphs. The farmers were in no position to object. There were no 'antis'. The Master of the local hunt was monarch of all he surveyed.

But times have changed and taking everything into consideration it may be that they have not, as one might at first think, altogether changed for the worse. For more people, both mounted and on foot, now get pleasure from hunting than ever before. But with this enjoyment goes responsibility. The future of hunting depends upon an acceptance of this responsibility (see Plate 19).

* * *

Foxhunting (Alleged Cruelty) The Committee on Cruelty to Wild Animals, appointed by the then Home Secretary and Secretary of State for Scotland, reported in 1949 that foxhunting makes a very important contribution to the control of foxes, and involves less cruelty than most other methods of controlling them. 'It should be allowed to continue.'

'Foxhunting, the Father of' see WARDE, JOHN.

Fox Trot A four beat gait but not evenly spaced as the walk, the stride is not as long as in the running walk nor as speedy. It is between a square two beat and a square four beat. The left hind foot strikes ground followed quickly by the diagonal or right foot, then a slight pause, after which comes the right hind, then quickly followed by the left fore. In the United States of America the fox trot was accepted in early Plantation Horse Classes as a substitute for the running walk.

Frampton, Tregonwell (1641–1727) Had charge of the racing stud of William III, managed that of Queen Anne, and enjoyed like patronage in the reigns of George I and George II. Known as the Father of Racing.

Frederiksborg One of the oldest and best known breeds from Denmark where it is used for agricultural work and as a strong saddle horse. Of very good conformation, with deep body and short strong legs, it is chestnut in colour and stands up to 16 h.h. (163 cm).

Free Action Descriptive of horse's movement where there is plenty of propelling power behind and a proper use of the shoulders. A free mover uses shoulders, knees, pasterns, stifles and hocks to the best advantage and gets the fore feet well out in front.

Free Handicap   Two Free Handicaps are published at the end of the flat racing season by the handicapper to the Jockey Club, one for two-year-olds and the other for three-year-olds. The one for three-year-olds is now published for information only. The one for two-year-olds is run the following spring at the Newmarket Craven meeting over seven furlongs (1.4 km). There is no initial entry fee, hence the term.

Freeman, Frank   For twenty-five years huntsman to the Pytchley, Freeman was acclaimed by many to be the greatest huntsman of all time; some disputed this in favour of Tom Firr of the Quorn (*q.v.*). He died in 1947.

Free Return   A term meaning the right of an owner of a mare which has failed to conceive to send the same mare the immediately following season to the same stallion for service without payment of a further service fee.

Freiberger   A light to middleweight warm-blood horse with good action, bred in Switzerland, based on Norman and Postier Breton blood and Arab Shagya blood from Hungary.

French Bridoons   A term used for a simple mouth bit with a connecting link in the centre to prevent nut-cracker action.

French Clip   *see* STUD-FASTENING.

French Panel   *see* SAUMUR PANEL.

Fresh   A term descriptive of a horse which is alert and gay, somewhat excitable and probably short of exercise.

Fresh Fox   Where hounds of their own accord change from the hunted fox to another, the latter is termed a 'fresh fox'.

'Fresh-legged'   A term, used chiefly by dealers, indicating an unworn, and usually a young horse.

Frideriksborg   *see* FREDERIKSBORG.

Friesian   This was the most popular horse of the Middle Ages, being thickset, strong and heavy, thus answering the requirements of mediaeval warfare, when armour plate for man and horse increased in weight to resist the more powerful arrows of the long and cross bows. Later it developed into a strong and docile carriage horse, and is now much in use as an agricultural worker.

Fright   Many horses are extremely timid, hence it is never safe for a rider or driver to become careless and lose control. Defective sight is a common cause, and animals are often affected by the fear of fire, or the sight and smell of blood or nearby sudden movement.

Frog   'V'-shaped formation in the sole of the foot, having an elastic action and expanding laterally when carrying the weight of the horse.

Frog-cleft   A natural depression in the centre of the widest part of the frog.

Front   A term indicative of that portion of the horse which lies in front of the rider in the saddle.

Fronts   In jockey and butcher boots the fronts are closed into the legs to form the tongue in the neck or going-on position of the boots.

Fronts   *see* BROWBAND (FRONT).

Frost Nails   Nails fixed in shoes to prevent a horse from slipping. They are somewhat longer than those used ordinarily, and the heads need not be driven into the shoe, but may be flattened down to give a grip. (Also known as Pegs or Studs.)

Frozen Grass   This is undesirable as food. Horses at grass should be provided with hay in frosty weather.

Full Brother (or **Sister**) Progeny having both the same dam (*q.v.*) and the same sire (*q.v.*).

Full Cry Indicating that the whole or main body of any pack of hounds is in strong and relentless pursuit of its quarry in the open and is giving tongue.

Full Mouth A horse at six years old.

Full Panel One which follows the shape of the flap to within 2 in (5 cm) of the bottom edge. The part under the flap of the saddle is usually quilted.

Full Pass A movement on 'two tracks', exactly the same as 'head to the wall' or 'tail to the wall', but done in the open, without support from any boundary.

Fullered Shoe A shoe with a groove round the ground surface where the nail-holes are placed, and which grips the ground and makes for lightness. The inside edge should be concave to eliminate suction from the ground in deep going and to prevent over-reaches. It is the best shoe for the hunter. Flat (non-concave) shoes for a harness horse or a flat-footed hunter are generally fullered.

Fullering A groove in the ground surface of the shoe in which the nail-holes are placed.

Fulmer Saddle *see* SADDLE, DRESSAGE.

Fulmer Snaffle *see* AUSTRALIAN LOOSE RING SNAFFLE, *and Plate 6.*

Funk A temperamental horse which gets on its toes or breaks out in a sweat or shows other signs of nervousness on a hunting morning or when saddled for a race.

Furioso A Central European riding horse bred from the original 'Furioso' imported from England in about 1840 and which later included blood of many other English Thoroughbreds. The stock was distributed to studs throughout the old Austrian Empire.

Furlong A unit of distance used in racing, equivalent to 220 yd or $\frac{1}{8}$ mile (200 m).

Furniture The metal mountings on harness and saddlery. They may be galvanized, brass or plated.

Furze A poor food for horses. The green tips are sometimes collected, chopped and mixed with chaff, and are considered by some to be both fattening and appetizing. At one time furze or gorse was prepared by a machine called a Masticaton, which bruised it and made it palatable.

Futchells The fastenings of the splinter bar to the axle-tree bed of a coach, where the pole is inserted.

* G *

G. Gelding.

g. Grey.

G.D. (U.S.A.) Good track.

'G.R.' Accepted abbreviation for gentleman rider (*q.v.*).

G.S.B. General Stud Book (*q.v.*).

Gadfly *see* HORSEFLY.

Gags The term 'gag' denotes any bit used with a rounded leather cheek-piece passing through holes in the bit ring or through rollers, pulleys, etc., for the primary purpose of raising the head. There are numerous designs. Those used in place of a bridoon on a double bridle are the Duncan and Shrewsbury patterns.

Gag-twitch *see* TWITCH.

Gait Horse gait, at-gait, gaited-out all refer to animals pastured out for payment.

Gait Term for 'pace'. A horse normally has three gaits: walk, trot and canter. The American five-gaited (*q.v.*) horse also has rack (*q.v.*) and show gait.

Gaited Horse (U.S.A.) One which is schooled to artificial as well as natural gaits.

Gaiting Strap (U.S.A.) Strap running along inside the shafts of a trotting sulky from rear to front to prevent a horse moving sideways in its gait. Also known as Side-strap.

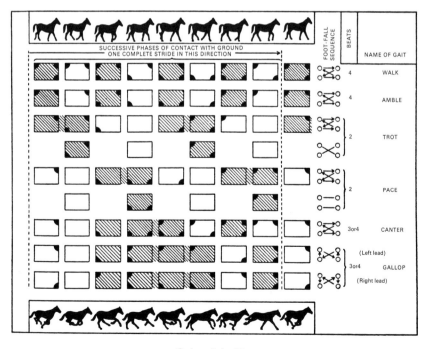

Gaits of the Horse

Galiceño It is claimed for this breed, which is now established in the U.S.A., that it originated in Galicia in north-west Spain and was among those which were brought by Cortès when he landed in South America. Referred to as a horse, though standing 12 to 13.2 h.h. (122–134 cm), the Galiceño is a tough, hardy and courageous type yet docile and easy to handle. It is found in all colours, but piebalds, skewbalds and albinos cannot be registered. *Breed Society:* The Galiceño Horse Breeders Association.

Gall A sore place caused by harsh or ill-fitting harness; usually found under the girth or the saddle.

Gallop A faster canter, the racing gallop being the fastest, where the sequence of the supporting legs is different, since the diagonal (second time) is dissociated and the pace is of four-time: near hind, off hind, near fore and (leading leg) off fore; or off hind, near hind, off fore and (leading leg) near fore (*see* CANTER, RHYTHM OF).

Gallop False *see* CANTER FALSE.

Galloped for Wind To ascertain whether a horse is sound in wind it is galloped in circles during which time, and immediately following, any defect in wind can be heard by an experienced person (*see* GRUNTING).

Galloping Disunited *see* CANTER DISUNITED.

Galloping Sheet *see* QUARTER SHEET.

Gallops, Training Stretches of grass, heath or downland of varying lengths where trainers gallop their horses in preparation for the racecourse. There are public and private gallops. The former are kept up by trainers having to pay so much per horse per season.

Galloway A riding pony, well-known for many years in Galloway, S.W. Scotland, standing about 14 h.h. (142 cm). Daniel Defoe, in his *Tour Through Scotland* in 1706 (Letter XII), wrote:

'Here (in Galloway) they have the best breed of strong low horse in Britain, if not in Europe, which we call pads (pacing as distinct from trotting saddle horses) and from whence we call *all* truss, strong, small, riding horses Galloways; these horses are remarkable for being good pacers, strong, easy-goers, hardy, gentle, well-broke, and above all, that they never tire; and are very much bought up in England on that account.' (The word truss probably means compact.) Also a term used in Pony or Galloway racing determining the height limit and, at one time, describing undersized Thoroughbreds used for racing outside the Jockey Club or National Hunt Rules.

Galloway (Show Classes) In Australia pony classes are limited in height to 14 h.h. (142 cm). Those exceeding 14 and not 14.2 h.h. (144 cm) are termed Galloways.

Galton's Law Sir Francis Galton (1822–1911) expounded a rule of ancestral contribution in breeding. The theory being that on an average both parents contribute one half to the issue's make-up, the four grand-parents a quarter each, the great-grand-parents one-eighth, etc. Galton's Law is often used as a stamina index amongst blood-stock breeders.

Galvayne, Sydney A renowned student of the horse, and a horse breaker and trainer who came to England from Australia in 1884 and introduced a humane system for the training of unbroken and vicious horses. He utilized scientifically the horse's superior strength against itself and stated that he had never had a failure. He held over 300 classes in Great Britain and, in 1887, appeared before Queen Victoria.

Galvayne Mark A brownish-coloured groove on the corner incisor teeth which appears when the horse is ten years old and runs down the length of the tooth: an indication of the approximate age of a horse between the ages of ten and twenty (when the groove will have reached the bottom of the tooth). It is named after Sydney Galvayne (*q.v.*), who first made use of the mark to determine age in a horse after ten years.

Galvayne Mark

Galvayne Strap   A device (often a piece of rope) to connect the head collar (*q.v.*) to the horse's tail. When a horse is tied in this manner he can only move in a circle and soon tires, which makes subjugation simple.

'Galway Blazers'   *see* 'BLAZERS, THE'.

Gambler's Choice (U.S.A.)   *see* TAKE YOUR OWN LINE.

Gambo   A two-wheeled farm cart used in Wales for carting hay.

Gammon Board   *see* BACKGAMMON BOARD.

Gammy Legs, Gummy Legs   The tendons below the knees and hocks should stand out clearly under the skin like taut cord. Should the line of the tendons be concealed owing to the legs being 'filled', or in a state of puffiness due to strain or hard work, the term gammy or gummy legs is used.

Garden-seat Bus   The last type of passenger horse-bus used on London streets. The outside passengers were accommodated on double seats facing the front of the bus, with a central gangway.

Garranos or Minho   A breed of pony in Portugal and western Spain of the same type but rather larger than the Sorraia (*q.v.*).

Garron (Gaelic, *gearran*)   A general name for the native ponies of Scotland and Ireland.

Garter   A narrow leather strap and buckle on hunting or riding boots which passes through a loop at the back and, in front, between the second and third buttons of the breeches. It is buckled on the outside of the leg. Fashioned in white buckskin for white hunting breeches, patent or black for patent 'tops' (*q.v.*), black for black butcher (*q.v.*).

Gascoigne, Chien de   A blue-mottled hound, said to be the oldest strain in France; the origin of the Holcombe (Lancashire) Harriers.

Gamgee   Cotton-wool tissue used under bandages on the legs.

Gaskin   The portion of the hind limb above the hock and extending upwards to the stifle. Often termed 'the second thigh'.

Gate (British Show Jumping Assn)   Swing gates must *not* be used, as they are dangerous (*see Plate 20*).

Gates, Opening   When a rider opens a gate the approach must be made from the hinge to the latch, with the reins and whip held in the hand away from the gate.

Gate Stop   Sharp brass or nickel stud fixed on the crook point of hunting whips.

'Gato'   The Criollo pony, joint hero with 'Mancha' of Tschiffely's Ride (*see also* CRIOLLO *and* TSCHIFFELY, A. F.).

Gaucho   South American cowboy or mounted horseman of mixed European and South American Indian blood. He is considered by many to be the world's finest rough-rider.

Gay   Said of a horse when the head and tail are carried gaily with an airy walk.

Gayoe   Ponies found in the Gayoe Hills at the northern end of the island of Sumatra.

Gayol *see* BATAK.

Gee *see* ARVE.

Gelderland   This horse originates from a very old native breed of the Dutch province of Gelderland, and was crossed many years ago with such stallions as English Thoroughbreds, Holsteins and Anglo-Normans. The modern horse is wide and deep, yet of beautiful build, with a very stylish action. Height ranges from 15.2 to 16 h.h. (154–163 cm), although larger animals are occasionally met with. A docile farm horse and an excellent saddle-horse and coach-horse.

Gelding   An emasculated male horse (*see* CASTRATION).

General Stud Book (G.S.B.) Founded in 1791 by James Weatherby and published ever since at regular intervals by the same family firm, Weatherbys. The G.S.B. includes all Thoroughbred mares and their progeny foaled in the British Isles. There is a new volume of the book every four years and an annual supplement showing the year's foalings. Vol. 37 was published in 1973 (*see* WEATHERBYS).

Generous   A horse that gives of its best, whether in racing, in any other sport or when used commercially.

Genet, Jennet   A small Spanish horse, or the offspring of a horse-sire and female ass, sometimes called a Hinny (*q.v.*). Also a type of horse known in the twelfth century—an ambling hack.

Gentle, to   The process of handling, quietly and with understanding, any horse, but usually applied to young animals.

Gentleman Rider (Racing)   An amateur rider or 'G.R.'. A rider who has never ridden for hire in a race. Amateurs cannot ride either on the flat or steeplechasing without a permit from the Jockey Club (*see* AMATEUR RIDER).

George III *see* BUCKHOUNDS, ROYAL.

George IV Phaeton *see* PARK PHAETON.

George V   He took a keen interest in racing, as did his father King Edward VII, but he did not have the same good fortune. Won the 1000 Guineas of 1928 with 'Scuttle'.

George VI   He was not so keen on racing as his father, George V, but he had more luck. In 1942 with the colt 'Big Game' and the filly 'Sun Chariot', both leased from the National Stud, he won four of the five classic races— all run at Newmarket in war time. The filly 'Sun Chariot' won the 1000 Guineas, the Oaks and the St Leger; and 'Big Game' the 2000 Guineas. 'Big Game' also started favourite for the Derby but failed to stay. Four years later the King's home-bred filly 'Hypericum', trained for him by Sir Cecil Boyd-Rochfort, won the 1000 Guineas.

German Dressage Weymouth *see* WEYMOUTH, DRESSAGE.

German Mouthpiece   A broad, comfortable mouthpiece covering a larger area of sensory nerves and so distributing the pressure rather than confining it to one area, as may be the case with a thin mouthpiece. The mouthpiece is often hollow.

German Panel *see* MELBOURNE FACINGS.

German Rein   Similar to the Market Harboro' Martingale. In Germany it is known as the 'English Rein'.

German Snaffle   A popular snaffle bit using a mouthpiece as described above. It is made with eggbutt cheeks or ordinary wire rings. In the latter case the holes in the mouthpiece through which the rings pass are specially small in diameter to prevent pinching the lips.

Gestation of Donkey Mare (Jenny) Approximately 12½ months.

Gestation of Mare   The period between conception and foaling, about 11 months (*see* FOALING TABLE, *page* 43).

Get   The progeny of any particular stallion.

Get Under, to   A term in jumping, whether steeplechasing or show jumping, in which the horse takes off too near the obstacle.

'Getting Hanged'   A coaching term for catching the thong of the whip in the bar or harness.

Getting Up   A horse does so by raising itself on its haunches with its fore-legs slightly extended in front and both feet on the ground, when it raises itself on its hindlegs. Where a horse falls on slippery ground, use sand, gravel, sack or rug to facilitate rising.

Gidran   A Hungarian breed larger than the Shagya, produced by crossing native mares with English Thoroughbred and half-bred stallions. A big saddle horse, about 16 h.h. (162 cm) with a beautiful, characteristic head and good conformation; usually chestnut or brown in colour.

Gig   A two-wheeled carriage to seat two people only; subject to much variety (*see* LAWTON, LIVERPOOL, MURRIETA, STANHOPE *and* TILBURY GIGS).

Gilbey, Tresham (1862–1947)   A noted polo player, polo pony breeder, past-President of National Pony Society.

Gilbey, Sir Walter (1831–1914)   The first baronet, and a well-known horseman, he wrote many books, including *Thoroughbred and Other Ponies, Horse Breeding to Colour, The Harness Horse, Horse Breeding in England and India, George Stubbs, The Old English War Horse or Shire Horse, Animal Painters.* He devoted much of his life to fostering interest in all breeds of horses, and was one of the founders of the Hunters'

Improvement and Light Horse Breeders' Society in 1885.

Giles, Godfrey Douglas (1857–1941)   Painter of military, battle and sporting scenes. Retired from the Indian Army as Major in 1884. Studied painting under Carolus Duran in Paris and exhibited in London. Accredited with being originator of hunting countries series, expanded later by Cecil Aldin (*q.v.*) and Lionel Edwards (*q.v.*).

Gilpin, Sawrey, R.A., F.S.A. (1733–1807)   Born in Carlisle, an important painter of animal and sporting pictures. Worked in London and studied under William Scott. Much of his work was commissioned by three important patrons, H.R.H. The Duke of Cumberland, the renowned English eccentric Colonel Thornton and Samuel Whitbread, the wealthy brewer. Also painted some historical works.

'Gimcrack'   A famous and very small Yorkshire horse, 'The Hero of the North', whose name is perpetuated in the Gimcrack Stakes for two-year-olds, run at the York summer meeting. The owner of the winner of this race is guest of honour at the annual Gimcrack Dinner, when he makes a speech giving his ideas for the improvement of racing.

'Gingering'   The practice of forcing an irritant, such as ginger or pepper, into the rectum to impel a high tail carriage. Rated as cruelty.

Gin-horse   A mill-horse.

Girth   The word descriptive of the circumference of a horse's body measured from behind the withers and around the lowest line of the body, e.g. 'A good girth', 'Lacking girth'.

Girth, Fitting Of   The placing of the girth is largely decided by the conformation of the back and withers. The girth should be as far back from the elbows as possible.

Girth Extension   A bifurcated strap about 14 in (356 mm) long, having two buckles and the bifurcations punched with holes. It is used to make an existing girth meet without difficulty when horses are fat after summer grazing.

Girth Galls   These can be very troublesome, and should not occur if care is taken in tightening girths. Horses in soft condition are particularly liable to develop them. A nylon cord or lampwick girth will rarely gall. When a horse comes up in soft condition from grass, the ordinary girth run through a section of motor tyre inner-tube or a sheepskin sleeve cut to the appropriate length gives effective prevention from galls. *Treatment* of sore: wash and keep clean, apply any healing ointment. The horse cannot be used for saddle work until a cure is effected.

Girthing   Care should be taken to girth up gradually. There should be at least two stages before mounting and one when in the saddle. Most horses are ridden with the girth too tight. If a horse has to be girthed tight, as before a race, stand in front of it and pull its forelegs towards you as high as they can be raised, to make sure that there are no puckers in the skin.

Girths   The main varieties are nylon or cotton cord, webbing, always used in pairs, lampwick, tubular web (i.e., two pieces of $1\frac{1}{4}$ in (31 mm) web joined in the centre and the join overlaid with pimple rubber; this gives a good grip and is popular as a pony show girth), elastic, used in pairs, and, best of all, leather. For racing, web girths, between 2 and $3\frac{1}{2}$ in (89 mm) wide, are used, or elastic. Most patterns can be inset with elastic to allow a little 'give'. Principal leather varieties are Atherstone (*q.v.*), Balding (*q.v.*) and Three-Fold. The FitzWilliam girth is now seldom used.

Girth Safes   Safes which prevent the girth buckles from penetrating the saddle flaps (*see* SAFES).

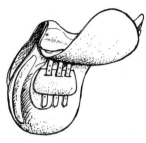

Girth Safe

Girth Sleeve   A sleeve of rubber or sheepskin passed over the girth to prevent galling.

Girth Straps   The straps to which the girth is attached on any saddle. There are usually three on a full-sized saddle; show saddles have an extra one upon the point of the tree; lightweight saddles have only one (*see* LONSDALE GIRTH STRAPS).

'Give a Lead'   A term describing when a horse and rider goes ahead to encourage a reluctant horse.

Give with the Hand   To open the fingers sufficiently to relax the tension of the rein, thus reducing the pressure of the bit on the bars of the mouth.

Giving the Office   *see* OFFICE.

Glanders (also known as **Farcy**)   A notifiable disease. *Symptoms:* a discharge from the nostrils, ulcers on the mucous membranes, abscesses in the angles of the lower jaw. *Treatment:* isolate and disinfect. It can be communicated from the horse to man and is incurable.

Glass-eye (U.S.A.)   *see* WALL-EYE.

Glitters, Lucy   A character in *Mr. Sponge's Sporting Tour* by R. S. Surtees (*q.v.*). A great horsewoman, she married Mr Sponge.

Globe Cheek Bit   This is usually a fixed mouth cob or pony riding curb, with a large eye and an even larger globe-like bottom ring (presumably to balance the bit). It is frequently seen in a good show pony bridle.

Gloster Bars   An arrangement fitted to the saddle comprising two shaped, padded and sprung bars which fit over the top of the rider's thighs. Intended to teach beginners jumping and for the incapacitated.

Goal Posts (Polo)   These are generally made of basket work and should be at least 10 ft (3 m) high, erected so that they collapse easily if collided with. They are usually painted a light colour at the base and dark at the top half. There is no cross-piece as in football or hockey, but a goal is held to be scored if a high ball passes between what would constitute the upward prolongation of the goal posts.

Goat-snatching   see KARABAIR.

Godolphin Arabian   Imported into England in 1730 from Paris by Mr Edwin Coke and now generally accepted as a pure-bred Jilfan Arabian standing just under 15 h.h. (152 cm). Later acquired by the Second Earl of Godolphin to become one of the three famous progenitors of the Thoroughbred (q.v.) and established the Matchem line (see BRUCE LOWE FIGURE SYSTEM, EVOLUTION OF THE HORSE and THE ENGLISH RACEHORSE).

'Goes well into Bridle'   Said of a horse who is not afraid of going up to its bit, and does not avoid its pressure by such means as throwing up its head, carrying it too high or too low, or going behind its bridle.

Go-Go Race   Pony Gymkhana event in the U.S.A., involving riding between poles placed 6 ft (1.8 m) and 12 ft (3.6 m) apart down the length of the arena.

Gogue, de   An extension of the principle employed by the Chambon (q.v.). It differs from the latter in that the horse can be ridden and jumped while wearing the martingale.

'Going'   A term indicating the nature of the ground over which a horse travels, whether hunting, racing or otherwise; e.g. 'going heavy', 'going good'.

'Going-amiss'   A racing term applied when a mare in training comes in season at the time of her race.

Going Gauge   see PILLING GOING GAUGE.

Going Short   A hesitating, short and uncertain gait, often indicating lameness or a tendency to such.

Golden Horseshoe Ride   First organized in 1965 by the *Sunday Telegraph*, later under the jurisdiction of the British Horse Society and Arab Horse Society with different venues each year. Competitors cover 50 miles (80 km) the first day and 25 miles (40 km) the second, under strict veterinary supervision. Also horses must have qualified previously over one-day rides of approximately 45 miles (72 km). To win a Golden Horseshoe an average speed, usually fixed at 9 mph (14.48 km/h), is required without veterinary penalty marks.

Golden Horse Society, The (Founded 1947)   *Objects:* to create an interest in the breeding and showing of Golden Horses, and to register suitable animals (*see* PALOMINO).

'Golden Miller'   Famous steeplechaser owned by the late Hon. Dorothy Paget. Foaled in 1927 by 'Goldcourt' out of 'Miller's Pride', he won 29 races, including the 1934 Grand National and the Cheltenham Gold Cup, which he won five years in succession from 1932–1936.

Gone Away   When a hunted fox has broken covert and is in fact running.

Gone in the Wind   An indefinite term, loosely applied to any affection of wind, more particularly whistling, roaring and broken wind. It indicates that a horse is 'unsound in wind'.

Gone to Ground   Said of a fox which has gone into a drain or earth.

Gooch Wagon   A very light and elegant four-wheel, single-horse vehicle of the spider phaeton type, designed and made by Mills & Sons. A pneumatic-tyred adaptation of this was their 'Viceroy'.

Goodall, Stephen (1757–1823)   Born in the reign of George II. He was a renowned huntsman with the Pytchley and the Quorn hunts. He weighed over 20 st (280 lb; 127 kg). His career, with that of his grandson, William, is described in *Huntsmen of a Golden Age*, by Daphne Machin Goodall.

Goodall, William (1817–1859) Grandson of huntsman Stephen Goodall (*q.v.*). Became huntsman at the age of 24 to the Belvoir Hunt, where he won great admiration and respect.

'Good big 'un will always beat good little 'un'   A popular but perhaps erroneous supposition. There is also the saying 'there is nothing to beat a good young 'un unless it's a good old 'un'.

Good Front   *see* GOOD REIN.

Good Head   Hounds are said to 'carry a good head' when they hunt fast on a wide front.

Good Horse   A 'Good Horse' is one with many good, few indifferent, and no bad points.

'Good Hunter'   A warranty in these words implies sound in wind, eyes and action, quiet to ride and capable of being hunted.

Good Nick   A term for good condition in a horse.

'Good Night' (after hunting)   The period at the end of a hunting day, even though it be in the early afternoon. It is customary on parting, however early, to say 'Good night'. After cub-hunting, 'Good day' or 'Good morning'.

Good Outlook   *see* GOOD REIN.

'Good Rein'   A term applied to a horse which, owing to the excellent position in which it carries its saddle, to its good sloping shoulders and generous length of neck with well set on and correctly carried head, gives its rider all that can be required in a 'well-fronted' horse. Also referred to as a 'good front' or a 'good outlook'.

Good Roof   A term denoting a good line of back and general excellence of body. Also called 'good top'.

Good Top   *see* GOOD ROOF.

Goose-rumped   Said of a horse when the slope from the highest point of the quarters runs acutely to the root of the tail (*see* DROOPING QUARTERS).

Goose-rumped

Gordon, Adam Lindsay (1833–1870) Born in the Azores and educated in England, Gordon emigrated to Australia in 1853. He achieved little success in various jobs but became well known for his bush ballads, galloping rhymes and songs of the open air, of steeplechasing, racing and hunting.

Gorse   Can be fed to horses when chopped (*see* FURZE).

'Go Spare'   When a horse goes off alone without its rider.

Gothland Pony   The oldest breed of pony in Scandinavia and originally not uniform in type. Although they run almost wild in the woods, selective breeding and strict judging has now resulted in a lightweight, elegant pony of 12–14 h.h. (122–142 cm); generally brown or bay, but black, chestnut, dun and palomino are also common colours. Most natural gait is the trot and annual trotting meetings are held in Gothland for the ponies.

Governess Cart   A light, low-hung, two-wheeled trap for a single horse or pony, and seating four persons facing, access being by a rear door, only one step from the ground. Also known as Tub-cart or car (*q.v.*).

Graded Horses   In B.S.J.A. competitions horses are graded according to the prize money they have won: Grade C: Nil–under £150; Grade B: £150–under £300; Grade A: £300 and over. For ponies: J.C. Nil–under £75; J.A. £75 and over.

Grade Horse   Indicating one which is not pure bred (U.S.A.).

Grade Thoroughbred   An American expression indicating that a horse has half or more Thoroughbred blood in its breeding.

Grade-up, to   In breeding when a stallion of superior blood is bred to an inferior type of mare.

Grading (Showjumping, B.S.J.A.)   *see* GRADED HORSE.

Grain (of leather)   The outside surface is known as the 'grain side'. In the currying process the finish is put on this side, sealing the pores and waterproofing the leather.

Grainger Martingale   *see* MARTINGALE, GRAINGER.

Grakle Noseband   A double noseband which prevents the horse from opening its mouth; this is designed for a horse which 'yaws', reaches for the bit with its mouth open, or swings its head. Named after the 1931 Grand National winner who wore one.

Grakle Noseband

Granddam   The mother of a horse's sire or dam (*qq.v.*).

Grand National, the   Most famous steeplechase in the world, run at Aintree (*q.v.*) on the outskirts of Liverpool over a course just over 4 miles (6 km) with 30 jumps including the water jump in front of the stands. Founded in 1837 by an innkeeper of Liverpool with the backing of the 2nd Earl of Sefton, then the owner of the course. It was not until 1847 that it acquired its present name of the Grand National Handicap Steeplechase. It is now always referred to as the National (*see Plate* 13). For results *see page* 390.

Grand Pardubice   Steeplechase in Czechoslovakia founded in 1874 by Count Kinsky, run over 4½ miles (6.9 km), with 31 jumps over much newly ploughed terrain.

Grandsire   The father of a horse's sire or dam (*qq.v.*).

Grant, Sir Francis, P.R.A.   (1810–1878)   His portraits won him the distinction of becoming President of the Royal Academy, but early in his career he had studied with John Ferneley Senr. (*q.v.*) and painted sporting scenes, the *Melton Hunt Breakfast* being one of his first Academy Exhibits in 1834.

Grape   A mangy tumor on the legs.

Grass   An excellent summer food, cooling to the blood. Its nutritive properties are not high, and it creates looseness of the bowels. Alone, therefore, it is not sufficient food for a horse in hard work, but is nature's perfectly balanced ration.

Grasscrack   A split from the wearing surface of the hoof upwards. Without being serious it can be stopped by passing a red-hot iron above the crack although the crack will usually grow out.

Grass Rings   Circular ridges on the hoof allegedly caused by a sudden change in a horse's diet (i.e. being brought in from grass) or from wet to dry standing conditions.

Grass Sickness   A sudden and fatal disease, the cause of which is unknown and for which effective treatment remains undiscovered. It affects large and small breeds alike and used to be nearly always confined to north of the Clyde, but now occurs in N.W. England, Wales, western Midlands and Devon and Cornwall.

Grass Yard   A paddock enclosed by wire netting, and perhaps an acre in extent, where hounds and puppies can be left in warm weather to bask in the sun and air themselves.

Grazing   The act of feeding on grass.

Grease   More common in heavy horses, particularly Shires, but may occur in light horses if cracked heels are not attended to; found chiefly in dirty stables. *Symptoms:* cracks in the heels which have become filled with 'cheesey' material with thick, foul, evil-smelling discharge. *Preventive treatment:* do not wash legs. *Treatment:* clip legs, damp daily with a 1 per cent zinc chloride lotion. Legs should be kept bandaged in cotton wadding to keep warm.

Great Horse, The   *see* SHIRE.

'Green'   Where the education of the horse is incomplete.

Green Meat   A general term indicating grass, lucerne, clover, green wheat or green barley. The feeding of such assists digestion and improves condition of coat.

Green Ribbon   Sometimes worn out hunting on the tail of a horse to indicate it is young and unschooled and therefore unpredictable.

Grey Colour   Where the body colour of a horse is a varying mosaic of black and white hairs with a black skin. With increasing age the coat grows lighter in colour. Grey is not strictly a colour, but a failure of pigment to produce colour. Nevertheless all grey racehorses are described as greys. Every grey Thoroughbred is descended from the Alcock Arabian (*q.v.*).

Grey-ticked   Where white hairs are sparsely distributed through the coat in any part of the body.

Grid   *see* TONGUE GRID.

Grief   Hunting term indicating a fall or falls.

Griffen   Term applied in India to a newcomer or novice pony.

Gripes   *see* COLIC.

Grisone, Federico   Italian nobleman who established a riding school in Naples in the mid-sixteenth century and was one of the first exponents of the use of combined aids, and of the use of the leg as opposed to the spur.

Grissel   A colour also known as 'Rount' (*q.v.*).

Grogginess   *see* KNUCKLING-OVER.

Groom   One who is engaged in the general care of the horse.

Grooming   Regular and thorough grooming is essential to a horse. It improves the appearance, keeps the skin in good order and contributes to the general health and well-being of the animal (see STABLE MANAGEMENT, *page* 315, *and Plate* 29).

Grooming Pad   A circular leather pad filled with hay, having an elastic hand loop. Also called a Massage or Strapping pad.

Groningen   A Dutch farm horse which can be used successfully as a heavy-weight saddle-horse and as a first-rate carriage horse. This horse has good conformation, a strong back and deep body, with legs and feet of excellent substance, and a very refined head and neck. Height ranges from 15.2 to 16 h.h. (154–163 cm), although larger horses are permitted. Despite a comparatively heavy weight the horse is primarily a light draught horse of pure breed and good pedigree.

Ground Line   The line of the base of an obstacle from which a horse judges its take-off.

'Growler'   A slang name for the four-wheeled, one-horse cab of the London streets; also called a Four-Wheeler.

Grow out   Term indicating that young stock may at maturity exceed the height limit of its type and/or breed.

Groy, Groi   A gipsy term for a horse.

Grullo   American colour description for a slate- or mouse-coloured horse, the most characteristic running into a blue. Nearly all grullos have barred legs and the dorsal stripe.

Grunting ('grunt to the stick')   Where, owing to the breed, such as heavy draught, or lack of opportunity, a horse cannot be galloped for wind (*q.v.*), it should be held by the head and a pretence made to hit it a violent blow in the stomach with a stick. If of faulty wind the horse, in its fright, will 'grunt to the stick'; if it makes no noise, soundness may be assumed. A hunter which grunts on landing over a fence may be the object of suspicion. Grunting to the stick is not universally accepted by the veterinary profession as being necessarily a proof that respiratory unsoundness exists (see BULL).

Guarantee   see WARRANTY.

Guard   Armed attendant on a mail coach (*q.v.*). On a stage coach (*q.v.*) this term also applied to the footman or 'cad' (*q.v.*), whose main job was to apply the brake.

Guard Rail   A stout pole placed before an open ditch in racing jumps, to make the horse 'stand back' and spread itself.

Gudbrandsal   see NORWEGIAN.

Guideless Pacing   A mare, 'Lady R.', in a match against time, with a flying start, paced, guideless, a mile (1.6 km) in 2 minutes 14⅖ seconds at Whitegate Park, Blackpool, 29th June, 1903.

Guide Terrets   Upright metal rings fastened into the top of the pad encircling the body of the wheelers in a team and through which the reins from the leading horse run.

Guinea   Money unit still used in racing and sales of horses. Equivalent of £1.05 (sterling) in modern coinage.

Guinea Hunter   Dealer's 'tout' and intermediary between buyer and seller, found in large numbers at Irish horse fairs and mostly of the gipsy or tinker fraternities.

Guineas, The   Colloquial name for the Two Thousand Guineas (*q.v.*).

Gulf Arab   see SHIRAZI.

Gullet   Lower end of a horse-collar.

Gullet Plate   A strengthening plate in the head of the saddle.

Gullet-plate   A device which is used in conjunction with a strap to prevent crib-biting.

Gum Dragon   Similar substance to gum arabic and used in the treatment and preservation of white buckskin hunting breeches, now rarely if ever used.

Gummy Legs   *see* GAMMY LEGS.

Gut, Twisted   Torsion or displacement of some portion of the intestine, generally proving fatal. Usually diagnosed by rectal examination and persistence of pain. Usually the result of irregular peristalsis and often associated with impaction of the large intestine.

Gymkhana, Mounted   A contest consisting of one or more mounted events, the winning of which depends largely upon the skill of the rider and the horse or pony. Such events are: musical chairs, bending, ball and bucket, etc.

Gyp Horse   A term used in some parts of the country to describe a horse, one of whose parents belongs to a heavy and the other to a light breed.

H.B. Stud Book HALF-BRED STUD BOOK (*q.v.*).

Hd. (Racing) Head.

H.H. Popular abbreviation for the Hampshire Hunt.

h.h. Hands high (*see* HANDS *and* HEIGHT).

H.I.S. Hunters' Improvement Society.

H.O.Y.S. Horse of the Year Show.

H.P. Horse-power (*q.v.*).

Habit Side-saddle costume for a lady or girl.

Hack This is not an established breed, but is a recognized type—the refinement of the riding horse, and not to be confused with the Hackney, which is a harness horse. The name 'Hack' is essentially British, and of ancient origin. Show Hack winners in England are mostly Thoroughbreds, or nearly so, and must be as near to perfection in conformation as possible, entirely without blemish, and have impeccable manners. *Breed Society*: The British Show Hack and Cob Association (*see Plate* 15).

Hack, Good A horse described as such is warranted sound in wind, eyes and action and quiet to ride.

Hack (Show—Ladies) A horse exceeding 14.2 h.h. (144 cm) and not exceeding 15.3 h.h. (155 cm), suitable to carry a lady riding side-saddle.

Hack (Show—Large) Exceeding 15 h.h. (152 cm) and not exceeding 15.3 h.h. (155 cm). To be ridden astride.

Hack (Show—Small) Exceeding 14.2 h.h. (144 cm) and not exceeding 15 h.h. (152 cm). To be ridden astride (*see Plate* 31).

Hack, to General term implying 'going for a ride'.

Hackamore The best-known form of single rein bitless bridle, it consists of two long metal cheeks, curved to embrace the nose by means of leather attachments acting on the chin and nose cartilage. Of Mexican origin introduced from Spain and deriving from the Spanish *jaquama* (the 'j in Spanish is pronounced as 'h') (*see Plate* 6).

Hackamore (Western) A type of breaking bridle which controls the horse by pressure on the nose.

Hack Bit Name given to a fancy cheek curb bit.

Hack Classes Competitions for the best Hack held at all important horse shows.

'Hackles Up' A hound is said to have its 'hackles up' when it is angry. The hair along its back and the back of its neck stands on end, and its stern curves stiffly over its back. Hounds have their hackles up when they are close to their fox and running for blood.

'Hack On' To ride one's own horse to a meet of hounds.

Hackney Carriage A carriage for hire, which requires a licence to ply.

Hackney Horse Harness Championship For results *see page* 379.

Hackney Horse, the The immediate ancestor of the Hackney Horse was the Norfolk Trotter. This horse, later known as the Norfolk Roadster (*q.v.*), was powerful, heavily built, and bred for the use of farmers and others in their daily work. It possessed great stamina and often carried both a farmer and his wife to market. In the nineteenth century, with the advent of the railway, the Roadster fell into disuse, but was revived later by the Hackney Breed Society. The chief characteristic of the Hackney is that the natural gait is trotting with spectacular action. Shoulder movement is free with high ground-covering knee action, the fore-leg being thrown well forward, not just up and down, with that slight pause which gives a peculiar grace of movement, the horse appearing to fly over the ground. Action must be straight and true with no dishing (*q.v.*) or throwing of hoofs from side to side. Hackneys possess a small convex head, small muzzle; large eyes and small ears; long, thick-set neck; powerful shoulders; compact body; short legs and well-shaped feet. Most usual colours are dark brown, black, bay and chestnut. The height varies between 14.3 and 15.3 h.h. (145–155 cm) and may sometimes reach 16.2 h.h. (165 cm). *Breed Society:* The Hackney Horse Society (*see Plate* 15).

Hackney Horse Society (Established 1883) *Objects:* to promote and improve the breeding of Hackney Horses, Hackney Ponies, harness and driving horses; to hold shows offering prizes in competition; and also to compile and publish Stud Books.

Hackney Pony, the The Hackney Pony is a smaller edition of the Hackney Horse. It is generally accepted that the appearance was through a 14 h.h. (142 cm) Hackney Pony stallion foaled in 1866 and sired by a horse of pure Yorkshire blood, though nothing is known of the history of the dam. Up to the beginning of the twentieth century, the pony was used by many tradesmen for delivery puposes. Nowadays it is seen mainly in the show ring, where the demand is for extravagant action. Characteristics are: long neck with good shoulders, and a compact body with hard limbs. Colours are mostly bays, browns and blacks. Chestnuts are rarely seen. *Breed Society:* The Hackney Horse Society (*see Plate* 15).

Hackney Pony Harness Championship For results *see page* 379.

Haemoglobinuria *see* AZOTURIA.

Haemolic Disease Produces the so-called 'jaundiced foal', which in the majority of cases dies within 7–10 days. Blood-test of the mare with preventative action is now possible.

Haflinger A Tyrolean breed of mountain pony, small but very thick-set, having plenty of bone, with a neat head which is carried close to the ground when climbing. Its great strength and surefootedness make it an excellent pack and draught pony and it is used frequently in agriculture and forestry. The village of Hafling in Tirol is said to be its original home. Haflinger stallions are reared in the Central Stud at Piber (Austria). Average height 14 h.h. (142 cm), with rather long body; colour chestnut with flaxen mane and tail. *Breed Society:* British Haflinger Association (*see Plate* 16).

Haggin Cup (U.S.A.) *see* WESTERN STATES TRAIL RIDE.

Hair, Feather The hair which all horses carry to a greater or lesser extent on the heels and legs. Shires and Clydesdales have a profuse growth, fine in texture, free from curl, and extending from the pastern almost to the back of the knee and hock. Light breeds have, on the fetlocks, a shorter growth of hair, which is removed by pulling. Hair on the heel, which is a sign of cold blood, should never be cut.

'Hairies' Derived from the hair on the heel. A friendly name for the heavier breeds which show some hair around the fetlocks. A term of affection used by troops in the First World War for Shire and similar type horses.

'Hairy' A straggly high fence of the 'bullfinch' type (*q.v.*).

Half-bred A term loosely applied to a horse which is an admixture of breeds; it is also applied to a Thoroughbred horse not eligible for entry in the General Stud Book.

Half-Bred Stud Book ('H-B' Stud-Book) Compiled by F. M. Prior, this illustrated book is a register of the produce of mares of winning blood in the female line which are not eligible for the General Stud Book. It contains the histories, pedigrees and racing performances of all the best-known half-bred families of racehorses. First published in 1914, the current edition, Vol. VIII (1972), is the last, as it is being superseded by the Register of non-Thoroughbred mares compiled by Weatherby's.

Half Brothers and Sisters   *see* BROTHERS AND SISTERS.

Half-pass   A movement on two tracks (*q.v.*) performed at the walk, trot or canter, where the horse travels sideways and forward, its head turned slightly to the side to which it is moving, legs crossing, shoulders preceding haunches in the oblique direction.

Half-pass

Half Pirouette   *see* PIROUETTE.

Half Pirouette Renversée   *see* PIROUETTE RENVERSÉE.

Half Speed   The usual pace of a horse doing fast work in training. It is rather more than half a horse's full speed, but the horse is not fully extended.

Half Volte   A figure consisting of a half circle of a given radius and an oblique following it, entailing a change of hand. It may be performed on either one or two tracks (*q.v.*).

Hall, Harry (Op. 1838–1886)   Sporting artist well known for his faithful portraits of hunters and racehorses. Also painted shooting, coaching scenes, etc. In style he owed much to the influence of J. F. Herring, Senr (*q.v.*).

Halt, the   To bring a horse to the halt, apply slight pressure with the legs behind the girth and on the reins.

Halter   A hemp head (*q.v.*) for leading an unbitted horse or tying up in a stall. The best type is a Yorkshire halter, which does not tighten up on the head as does the normal adjustable pattern, and is fitted with a cord throat-latch to prevent its being pulled across an eye. In the U.S.A. halters are usually of heavy leather with brass fittings.

Halter-classes   A term used in U.S.A. and elsewhere (but not in Great Britain), having the same meaning as in-hand classes (*q.v.*).

Hame-rein   A short rein of such a length that it passes over the points of the hames in certain cart-horse harness, where such points exist. It is customary to release this when a horse is pulling a load up an incline, thereby giving him full freedom to stretch his neck.

Hames   Detachable plated metal arms which link the traces and the collar (*see* NECK COLLAR).

Hame-strap   A strap fastening the hames at the top and keeping them in position on the collar.

Ham-fisted   *see* MUTTON-FISTED.

Hammer-cloth   A cloth covering the driver's seat or box in a state or family coach.

Hamshackle   To shackle a horse or cow by a rope or strap connecting the head with one of the forelegs.

Ham-string   The tendon that runs down the back of the second thigh to the point of the hock. The tendon of the gastrocnemius muscle, often termed the Achilles tendon—the most hard-worked in the horse's body.

Hand   The measurement by which the height of a horse is reckoned; it equals 4 in (10.16 cm) (*see* HEIGHT).

Hand Gallop   A fast smooth canter in which the horse settles down at a pace which does not quite approach its fastest speed.

Hand horse   Off side (*q.v.*) horse, or horse that is led in a postillion (*q.v.*) ridden pair.

Handicap (Polo)   Players are handi-capped on a basis of the number of goals they may be expected to score in a full game. The maximum is 10 goals, the minimum. The higher handicapped team concedes to the lower the dif-ference in the handicaps of each team, divided by 6 and multiplied by the number of periods of play.

Handicap (Racing)   A race in which the weights to be carried by the horses are adjusted by the Handicapper for the purpose of equalizing their chances of winning.

Handicapper   A Jockey Club Official who equates the weights to be carried by horses in races for the purpose of equalizing their chances of winning. He must attend the meeting to which he is appointed.

Handiness   The ability of a horse to turn quickly without reluctance.

Handlebar   A simplified form of Gloster bar for small children. It is a stout cane, leather-covered, easily attached to the head of a felt pad and acts as a 'life-line' and later as a support for the leg.

Handled   Said of a young horse which has been haltered and led before breaking.

'Handley Cross'   The immortal story by R. S. Surtees, published in 1843, of the adventures and misadventures of

John Jorrocks, a grocer, as Master of the Handley Cross Hunt in the 1830s (*see* SURTEES, ROBERT SMITH).

Handling   All foals should be handled from their earliest days, when they will grow up less shy and timid. They should be led from both sides, and should be accustomed to having the feet lifted.

Handling from the Near-side   Custom or habit causes practically every horseman to perform ninety per cent of his tasks from the near side, thus giving the horse a left-handed complex. A wise horseman will do everything possible from both sides. When leading a horse through traffic, the safest way is to keep to the left side of the road, therefore the horse must be taught to lead comfortably from the offside.

Hand-rubbing   Most useful for re-ducing fullness of the legs, as well as for warming when cold, or to alleviate pain. When rubbing, follow the direc-tion of the hair of the coat.

Hands, Good   Hands which rely on no greater strength than that of the fingers, which are light, and which know how to give and take to the pull of the horse on the bit. It is essential for the true horseman to possess good hands and a strong seat.

Hand Sale   Where the outstretched hand of the person making the offer is struck by the hand of the one accepting it on the sale of a horse.

Handy Hunter Class   Often included, though not officially recognized, in many smaller shows. Horses prove their obedience and handiness with obstacles that include hunting type jumps, gates to be opened and shut, slip rails removed, etc. Judging is on performance and time, not conforma-tion.

'Hanging Off'   An old coaching term used when one horse hangs away from his pair.

'Hang Up Your Bars'   An old road term applied to one who gives up coaching.

Hanoverian Bit   Any bit of any design with a double-jointed and ported mouth, and which is not attached to cheeks (*see Plate* 6).

Hanoverian Horse   Originating from the German Great Horse of the Middle Ages, the breed as known today owes much to the Hanoverian kings who, from the time of George I to 1837, sent over many Thoroughbreds to grade up the breed. There are two groups, the lighter of which is for riding, the heavier for harness, and both, in the show animal, must be strong in bone, but of good quality. A softer breed than the Trakehner (*q.v.*) (*see Plate* 16).

Hanoverian Mouth   A bit, either curb or more usually Pelham, having a fairly high port jointed to the mouthpiece on either side. The mouthpiece is one with metal rollers set round it.

Hansom

Hansom   A two-wheeled vehicle with the driver seated high up at the back. Originally designed by an architect named J. A. Hansom in 1834 as a huge clumsy carriage, it was improved into the shape latterly popular by a Mr J. Chapman. Used extensively as a public cab for hire, it was known as 'the gondola of London'.

Hantam   *see* HORSES AND RIDERS IN SOUTH AFRICA, *page* 304.

Haras   French word meaning a stud for breeding horses.

Harbourer   Through a great knowledge of venery and the habits of the stag, the Harbourer is appointed to advise the Master where it is likely that a warrantable stag may be found on the day of the hunt. By the size and shape of the slots (*q.v.*) of the stag, and by other signs, he is able to tell the probable age and weight of the quarry and where it may be found.

Hard and Fast   A term used by the American cowboy to denote the double half-hitching of the rope round the saddle-horn.

Hardel   To couple hounds. An old term now in disuse.

Harewood Horse Trials   Held in the autumn at Harewood House, Yorks, by permission of the late Princess Royal from 1953–1959 (*see also* HORSE TRIALS). For results *see page* 381.

Hark-to   Huntsman's cry calling one hound's attention to another which is speaking (acknowledging the scent). Also 'Hark-back' and 'Hark-forward'.

Harness   A comprehensive term given to the bridle, collar, pad, etc., for a driven horse; it is not applicable to a riding horse. There are different types for use with various vehicles. (*See diagram on page* xv.)

Harness, Black   A trade term applied only to harness used on horses other than for riding.

Harness, Brown   A trade term for that used on the ridden horse.

Harness Classes   Show classes generally embracing open driving, Hackney, Utility, Trade (Light and Heavy).

Harras   An Old English collective term for horses.

Harriers   A pack of hounds for hunting hares followed by a mounted field.

Harry Highover's Pelham   An early and once popular bit in which bridoon

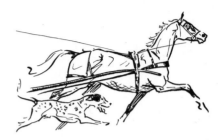

Harness
Above: left, Cart Harness; right, Breast Harness.
Below: left, Pair Harness; right, Gig Harness.

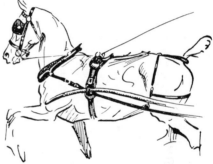

mouths were individually attached to the 2 in (5 cm) port of a curb bit.

Hart, Stag   A male deer at five years.

Hartwell Pelham   Now refers to a ported mouthpiece instead of the more usual mullen mouth. Older patterns had a bent mouthpiece.

Hat Guard   String of braid attached to the ring at back brim of a riding hat and also to the loop inside coat collar band. Rarely used today.

Hausman Gag   A metal gag used for veterinary purposes.

Haute École   *see* HIGH SCHOOL *and* CIRCUS HORSES.

Haw   The third eyelid, or nictitating membrane.

Hawick Common Riding   A picturesque ceremony held in Scotland during the first full week in June, and extending over several days. The date of origin is unknown, but the principal event, 'Cornet's Chase', re-enacts the capture of a standard from the English by the men of Hawick in 1514. The Cornet, a bachelor, is the standard-bearer; the chase is a gallop by Townsmen up the steep slope of Vertish Hill. Afterwards they ride the marches of the common to mark the bounds.

Hawkins, Jeremiah (1763–1835)   An eccentric sportsman, he was born in Gloucestershire and known as the Gloucestershire Mytton. He was immortalized 100 years ago by his picture on half the ale jugs in the country.

Passionately devoted to hunting, Jerry Hawkins had amazing endurance, and was in the habit of swimming the river Severn on his horse, when returning from a hunt. 'Nimrod' states that there was a ludicrous naïvety about him and that he was possessed of much goodness of heart.

Hay   Dried grass of most descriptions and clover, forming the staple bulk food of stabled horses and a supplementary food for others. Hay is called 'new' when it is less than one year old, and should not be fed in this state; after its first year it is known as 'old'.

Hay, Weights of   *see* WEIGHTS (FORAGE).

Hayes, Captain Matthew Horace (1842–1904)   Qualified as a veterinary surgeon at New Edinburgh Veterinary College in 1883 and took his Fellowship in 1891. He wrote extensively on horse subjects and his *The Points of the Horse* and *Veterinary Notes for Horse Owners* achieved great popularity.

Hay-net   A thick, corded net, usually tarred, into which the ration of hay is put and hung in the stall or box. It provides an economical method of feeding, for the hay cannot be thrown about and soiled, as it can when fed from the rack or from the ground.

Hay-net

Hay Tea   A very useful drink for a sick horse, being the equivalent of barley water to humans. Fill a stable pail three parts full with the best hay procurable, fill up with boiling water, place a cover over the pail and leave the hay to soak. When it is cold, drain off the water and give this as a drink.

Hazing-horse   A cowboy term for a horse that is engaged in bulldogging (*q.v.*). The rider uses it to keep the steer in a line to assist the competing rider to jump on to the back of the steer.

Head   A trade term for a leather or hemp head collar or head stall (*see* HALTER).

Head   The technical name for the hood of a carriage.

Head, Bridle   *see* BRIDLE HEAD.

Head (Distance)   When a horse wins a race by a head this means that the length of its head was in front of the second horse (*see* LENGTH).

Head-cap   *see* HOOD.

Head Carriage   The natural position of the head and neck expected of a horse of true conformation.

Head Collar, Head Stall   A leather head (*q.v.*) for leading an unbitted horse or for tying up in a stall. There are many patterns; the best have brass furniture. The browband should be of the buffed leather variety (*see Plate* 29).

Head Collar Rope   A rope attached to the head collar and running through a ring in the manger, with the other end fixed, preferably to a log of Lignum Vitae wood, in order that the rope may not become slack or get under the horse's legs. Rope or leather lines are superior to chains as the noise of the latter running through rings disturbs other horses. If the rope be well covered with soap when first used, this will treble its life. Also refers to a rope shank having a tarred 'eye' and used as a lead from a head collar or for tying up.

Headed Said of a fox (or other quarry) which has seen or heard someone or something causing it to deviate from its original line.

Headhalter (U.S.A.) *see* HALTER.

Head Lad In a racing stable he is responsible for stable management, morning work, feeding, minor ailments, etc. The word 'lad' is no indication of age for, from the nature and importance of the work involved, this necessitates the appointment of men of considerable and long experience.

Headland The uncultivated edge of a ploughed field, or the drier rim (close to the hedge) of a wet grass field.

Head Lap *see* HOOD.

Head of the Saddle, The The front arch.

'Headquarters' When applied to racing, this refers to Newmarket.

Head Shaking, Cause of Any form of ill-fitting bridle, or the maladjustment of a bridle, can give rise to head shaking, especially where the browband is pressing on the ears. Authorities on bridles should be studied, and the bridle—particularly the bit—should be fitted with great care and exactitude. Another cause of head shaking may be 'the staggers', or megrim (*q.v.*).

Head Shy A term for a horse that will not allow its head to be handled or its bridle put on. Usually due to rough treatment.

Head Stall *see* HEAD COLLAR.

Heads Up Said of hounds which are not feeling for the scent.

Head Terrets Fixed upright metal rings between wheelers' ears through which leaders' reins run but now more generally the rings are on the outside of wheelers' bridles. Objection to Head Terrets is too much pressure on poll (head) of wheeler, and when the horse throws its head up, it interferes with the leader.

Head to the Wall *see* TRAVERS.

Health Indications of good health are head erect and alert, eyes bright, ears pricked, good appetite, well-furnished body with skin supple and not tightly stretched, droppings fairly firm and not slimy.

Heart Room A term of commendation indicating depth through a horse's girth, combined with a broad and open chest ('deep through the girth' is also used).

Heat (on or in) Said of a mare or filly when in the condition to breed.

Heaves A defect of the wind, where a horse appears to heave twice on exhalation (*see* BROKEN WIND).

Heavy Horse Any one of the big draught horse varieties, Clydesdales, Percherons, Shire and Suffolk Punches.

Heavy Top Coarse neck, shoulders and light-boned limbs out of proportion to size of the horse.

Heel When hounds run the line of a fox in the reverse direction to which it was going. 'Running heel' or 'heel way'.

Heel Boot A leather boot cupped over the heel to protect that part against a blow from a hind toe.

Heel-bug A dermatitis affecting the heel and pastern and sometimes the face and muzzle also. The cause is uncertain but it is spread by the mud of certain locations which may carry an infection, or possibly set up an allergy. In some instances the cases are complicated by secondary infection by organisms. The fact that a number of horses crowded together in a muddy lane or gateway will sometimes contract the disease, apparently from infected horses, suggests the possibility of contagion. Another frequent cause in horses at pasture is sensitization to attack by the autumn harvest mite. White heels and white horses appear more susceptible but whether on account of photosensitization or because white heels are more often washed with soap and water is uncertain.

Heels   The lower back parts of the wall of the hoof.

Heels, Cracked   Similar to chapped hands in human beings, cracked heels are a form of eczema and are due to mud and wet. Washing the legs and heels is a cause, as it removes the natural oil and leaves the skin dry and brittle. *Treatment*: apply a lotion composed of lead acetate, zinc sulphate and glycerine. *Preventative*: apply vaseline to the heels occasionally. Never clip the hair out of the heels or use any water on the legs.

Height   The height of a horse is measured when the animal is standing naturally and easily on all four legs; it is taken from the highest part of the withers in a perpendicular line to the ground with the head and neck held in a straight line with the level of the back. It is important to measure the horse without shoes on level ground, preferably on a concrete floor. The horse is measured in hands (*q.v.*).

'Hell-for-leather'   To ride a horse 'all-out', pressed to its extreme. The expression may derive from a state of 'all of a lather'.

Hemp   The best halters are made of hemp, which also forms a good quality self-coloured night roller. Hemp is used by saddlers for sewing.

Henderson, Charles Cooper (1803–1877)   Born in Chertsey, England. A painter of coaching and harness pictures in oils and water-colours. Particularly successful with mail coach scenes at night, which combined animation with accuracy.

Hengest   A mediaeval term for a horse, usually a gelding.

Henry VIII   A good horseman, keenly interested in hunting and an indefatigable and adept performer at the joust. He took active measures to improve the size and stamina of the native horses by suitable legislation. He also imported Italian and Spanish breeding stock and established successful studs in different parts of the country.

Hereditary Diseases   Cataract, bone spavin, defective genital organs, navicular, parrot mouth, ringbone (high and low), roaring, shivering, sidebone, stringhalt.

Herring, Senior, John Frederick (1795–1865)   Probably the most prolific of all painters of racehorses and famous for portraits of 33 consecutive winners of the St Leger and 18 of the Derby. In his youth he was a stagecoachman on the Doncaster–Halifax route and was self-taught as an artist before studying with Abraham Cooper (*q.v.*). Though his pictures of Thoroughbreds tended to be static and lifeless, he attained great popularity and success. He lived in Doncaster, Newmarket and London before retiring to Tonbridge, where he painted attractive farmyard scenes with precise detail. His sons, John Frederick, Junr., Charles and Ben, also painted horses and sporting scenes; their work, though less able, is sometimes confused with J. F. Herring, Snr.

Herring-gutted   Said of a horse with a mean, weedy body which is flat-sided and runs upwards sharply from the girth to the quarters (*q.v.*).

Hickstead   Home in Sussex of All-England Jumping Course, established by Douglas Bunn in 1960.

Hidebound   The result of indigestion, worms, or some cause which contributes to horse getting out of condition. *Symptoms*: the coat 'stares', the skin becomes tight over the ribs, and there are general signs of malnutrition. *Treatment:* Discover the cause, as hidebound is not a disease. Investigate and treat for worms and build up with nourishing food.

High Blowing A very distinct sound heard sometimes at a gallop, often incorrectly suspected as a defect in wind, but it is due to fast movement causing excessive flapping of the false nostril (*q.v.*). Unlike 'roaring', it disappears as speed is increased. Sometimes termed 'cracking the nostrils'. Considered a merit by the S. American gauchos as denoting a horse of endurance.

'Highflyer" Phaeton An exaggeratedly high-hung phaeton, popular in Regency days.

High Jumping Record The official F.E.I. (*q.v.*) high-jumping record is 8 ft 1¼ in (2.47 m) achieved in 1949 at Viña del Mar by the Thoroughbred 'Huase' ridden by Capt. Alberte Larraguibel of Chile. The record for Great Britain is held by 'Swank' who cleared 7 ft 6⅛ in (2.28 m) ridden by W. Beard at the International Horse Show, Olympia, in 1937.

Highland Pony The Highland is the largest and strongest of the mountain and moorland breeds of ponies, and is found in the Highlands of Scotland and certain islands adjacent. It is of great antiquity, for it has been suggested that after the Ice Age, when Scotland was joined to the mainland of Europe, a movement of ponies took place, the larger remaining in Scotland and the smaller going farther south. The breed consists of three types: the smallest, 12.2 to 13.2 h.h. (124–134 cm), found on Barra and other outer islands; the intermediate, the well-known riding pony, 13.2 to 14.2 h.h. (134–144 cm); and the largest and strongest, the Mainland pony, standing about 14.2 h.h. (144 cm). The Highland, which has had an infusion of foreign blood, including Arabian, was originally bred

for working the crofts and for carrying deer, perhaps 20 st (280 lb; 127 kg), but has become increasingly popular as a riding and trekking pony. They are generally a good ride at the walk and trot, but are slightly heavy on the forehand. *Breed Society:* The Highland Pony Society (*see Plate 17*).

Highland Pony Society, The Founded 1923) *Objects:* to promote the general interests of the breeders and owners of Highland Ponies in the United Kingdom. Ponies are registered in the National Pony Stud Book. The Society holds classes at the principal Scottish Shows.

'High-lows' Low, laced boots cut rather higher than walking boots (but below the small of the calf) in order that leggings may ride comfortably over the tops.

'High-lows'

High School The classical Art of Riding, in accordance with traditions transmitted by the great equestrian masters of the past, and preserved and practised up to date, in the highest perfection, by the Spanish Riding School (*q.v.*), Vienna, and by the Cadre Noir, French Cavalry School, Saumur (*see* AIRS, ARTIFICIAL, CADRE NOIR *and* CIRCUS HORSES).

High School Horse One trained in accordance with the principles of the classical Art of Riding, and able to perform the classical or high school 'airs', such as Piaffe, Levade, Courbette, Capriole (*qq.v.*), etc.

High-tailing   Term for horses that gallop away suddenly with tails held high.

Highways   and   Locomotives (Amendment) Act 1878, Sec. 26 This Act calls for the use of a skidpan, slipper or shoe to be placed under the wheel of a wagon, wain, cart or carriage when descending a hill. The penalty for breaking this law is £2.

Hind   Female red deer.

Hind Hunting   *see* HUNTING SEASONS.

Hind Quarters   *see* QUARTERS.

Hinny   The progeny of a horse on a she-ass (*see* BARDOT).

Hip, Point of   The bony prominence a hand's breadth behind the last rib of a horse. This is in reality the external tuberosity of the pelvis and has no connection with the true hips or hip joint (*see* HIPS, RAGGED).

Hip Down   A term applied to the permanent result of a fracture of the angle of the haunch, the most prominent projection of the pelvis, which often occurs through the bone coming into contact with a gate or doorpost. A horse should always be faced when being led out of the stable, and should have a hand placed on either side of the bridle.

'Hipparchikos' (Greek, The Cavalry Commander)   The title of a work produced about 365 B.C. by Xenophon (*q.v.*) on his duties and training. It is the earliest known book dealing solely with cavalry training.

Hipparion   An early Pliocene Mammal with three toes. In the theory of evolution it is placed as one of the early ancestors of the horse.

Hippike   The Treatise on Horsemanship written in 365 B.C. by Xenophon (*q.v.*) 'to explain, for the benefit of

our younger friends, what we conceive to be the most correct method of dealing with horses'. This work remains a classic in basic principles.

Hippocampus   The sea-horse.

Hippodame   Obsolete term for a horse-tamer.

Hippodrome   The Greek name for a racecourse for horses and chariots.

Hippogriff   A fabulous creature like a griffin, with the hindquarters of a horse.

Hippoid   An animal resembling, or allied to, the horse.

Hippolith   A concretion found in the intestines of a horse.

Hippological Hethetica   Earliest-known book on the horse (c. 14th century B.C.), written on clay tablets by Kikkuli of Mitanni, an expert trainer of chariot horses.

Hippology   The study of horses.

Hippomanes   A small black fleshy substance found on head of newborn foal. Alleged to be an aphrodisiac. Sometimes known as foal-lap.

Hippopathology   The science of veterinary surgery.

Hippophagy   The act of feeding on horse flesh.

Hippophile   A lover of horses.

Hippophobia   A fear of horses.

Hippotomy   The anatomy or dissection of a horse.

Hips (Ragged)   A term given to the points of the hips of a horse when they are very prominent.

Hip Straps   Straps which pass over the rump of a cart horse to carry the breeching.

Hireling   A horse let out on hire.

Hissing   The sound made by a groom during the process of grooming, generally believed to prevent dust from entering the lungs and thought to have a soothing effect on the horse.

Hit and Hurry Competition (Show-jumping) Each competitor jumps the course in correct order for one minute. Three points scored for each obstacle cleared and one point for every obstacle knocked down.

Hitchcock Gag A neat head raiser consisting of a slip head with pulleys below the ears to which is attached a rounded leather rein controlled by the rider to put pressure on the corners of the mouth. As with any form of gag and bit, it has a strong controlling influence.

Hitch up, to To harness a horse or horses for driving (colloquial).

'Hit the Line' When a hound strikes the line of the hunted fox, it is said to hit the line.

Hobbles These are made of rope, leather bound where they come into contact with the horse, and consist of a loop round the neck, the ends passing between the forelegs to the hind pasterns, to which they are secured. This type is used when covering mares. Hobbles to prevent horses from straying resemble hound couples, fastening the forelegs together. There are patterns for securing all four legs for operations, etc. There is a pattern of service hobble made from cotton rope or buffalo hide where a strap, passing through the forelegs and encircling the mare's neck, is fastened to the hind hobbles. A quick-release device can be fitted to this pattern.

Hobby A description, originally given to a strong, active, rather small type of horse in the twelfth century, later applied to riding horses and hacks. It is still in use in some parts of Ireland.

Hobby-horse A stick with the figure of a horse, on which boys used to ride. One of the chief parts played in the ancient Morris-dance.

Hobbles

Hobday, Sir Frederick, F.R.C.V.S. (1870–1939) A distinguished veterinary surgeon. Educated at Burton Grammar School and the Royal Veterinary College, London. He served with the Royal Army Veterinary Corps in Italy and France, 1915–1918, was twice mentioned in despatches and was awarded the C.M.G. He was Principal and Dean of the Royal Veterinary College, London, from 1927 to 1937, during the period of rebuilding for which he was largely instrumental in raising funds; he was knighted in 1933. The author of several surgical books, he did pioneer work in veterinary anaesthetics, canine surgery and the operation for the relief of roaring (*see* ROARER) in horses with which his name is associated.

'Hobdayed' A familiar expression denoting the operation upon the larynx for roaring, practised by Professor Sir Frederick Hobday.

Hobson's Choice Tobias Hobson was an innkeeper, horse-dealer and carrier in Cambridge at the turn of the sixteenth century. Whatever horse the customer tried to choose he invariably got the next one in order, as fixed by Hobson. Hence the phrase 'Hobson's Choice' became a by-word for no choice at all.

Hock   The joint lying between the second thigh and hind cannon, corresponding with the human ankle. It is the hardest-worked joint in the whole horse's body and the most ingeniously constructed. It has two principal levers, the first being formed by the prolongation of the os calcis, equivalent to the human heel, which enables the gastrocnemius muscles to flex the hocks so violently that over half a ton of equine body is propelled over a fence and for some distance through the air. The second lever works on the pulley principle, the doubly grooved astragalus (the uppermost of the two rows of bones) revolving around the matching grooves and ridges on the lower end of the tibia. It is the extreme flexibility of the hock joints which enables the horse to change the position of the centre of gravity within the body and maintain balance at all gaits.

Hock-boot   A protective device consisting of a padded leather covering to strap on to the hock.

'Hocks, Well-let-down'   A greatly prized item of conformation. The closer to the ground the hocks are (if unblemished), implying short cannon bones, the better. The cannon bones of the hind legs are termed hind shanks, or shannon bones.

Hog-back   *see* ROACH-BACK.

Hogged Mane   A term used where the mane has been wholly removed.

Hog's Back (British Show Jumping Assn.)   A timber jump with the centre pole higher then those on the take-off and landing side (*see Plate* 20).

Hogtied   An American term for a horse which has all four feet tied to prevent it from rising.

Hoick! or **'Huick'**   A hunting cheer, pronounced 'Hike', and meaning 'Hark!'.

Hoick Holloa!   A cheer, pronounced

'Hike Holler', drawing hounds, or the huntsman's attention, to a holloa.

Hold   When a huntsman makes a cast, he is said to 'hold hounds round'.

Hold (Hunting)   Said of a covert in which lies a fox.

Holding (Racing)   A term indicating that the 'going' (*q.v.*) is soft or heavy. In hunting it is usually described as 'deep'.

Hold-up   To prevent foxes leaving a covert.

Holiday, Gilbert Joseph   (1879–1937)   Studied at the Royal Academy schools and became a talented sporting artist. His subjects included hunting scenes, polo and soldiering. After a fall with the Woolwich Drag, he was forced to work from a wheelchair.

Holloa (Hunting)   A high rousing cry given by one who has viewed a fox.

Hollow Back   A very pronounced form of back dipped behind the withers. Sometimes an indication of old age.

Hollow Back

Holstein   A good German breed, dating back to the thirteenth century, the Holstein is said to be of Andalusian (some think oriental) origin. The influence of the Thoroughbred is nearly negligible, but it is a fine, strong horse with good legs, free action and endurance, and is suitable for riding or driving. Although it is of rather slow growth, it enjoys a good reputation as a hunter (*see Plate* 17).

Home-straight   The run in to the finishing post on a racecourse.

Hood   A cloth covering for the head, ears and neck, used in cold weather for travelling horses. For wet weather a waterproof material is used. Known also as Head-cap and Head Lap.

Hood

Hoof   The horny covering of the sensitive foot, from the coronet downwards (*see* FARRIERY, *page* 115).

Hoof Oil   Should it be thought necessary, or should personal preference suggest, brush hooves with mixture of used car-oil or neatsfoot oil and Stockholm tar about 20–1. White and light coloured hooves should be brushed with neatsfoot oil to prevent brittleness. Can be purchased ready mixed (*see Plate* 29).

Hoof-pick   An implement, sometimes a folding variety, for removing dirt, stones, nails, etc., from the hoof (*see Plate* 29).

Hoofs and Horns   A monthly publication first published in 1948, circulated in Australia and New Zealand, concerning all activities of the horse.

Hook-fastening   *see* STUD-FASTENING.

'Hook-up' Stirrup Leathers   *see* EXTENSION STIRRUP LEATHERS.

Hopples   'Straps' of leather appertaining to the racing harness of a pacer. Hopples consist of loops on each leg, joined to permit adjustment to the correct length from front to hind leg and buckled by further straps on to the strap from the crupper to the saddlepad. In addition, a very thin breast collar is worn, the straps of which buckle on to the loops in which each front leg is placed. These four loops compel the horse to move at a lateral gait only. The loops should hang from 3 to 4 in (7.5–10 cm) above the hocks and the knees.

Horn   The outer surface of the hoof; which is also called the 'wall'.

Horn (Coaching)   The original horn used on mail coaches was issued by the Post Office and made of tin and 3 ft (1 m) in length (hence the expression 'yard of tin'), but mail guards took great pride in their blowing, and so usually provided their own horns which were made of either copper or brass to produce a softer tone. Apart from playing tunes, there were special calls warning of the coach's approach, and signals such as 'clear the road', 'Coming by', etc. Guards on road coaches also used these signals and tunes, as well as the grooms on private drags.

Horn (Hunting)   Usually made of copper with a nickel or silver mouthpiece, although some are made entirely of silver, the hunting horn is 9 to 10 in (20–25.5 cm) long (according to the maker). The huntsman indicates many of his directions to the hounds through his horn, using a combination of different notes or blasts.

Horn, Saddle   *see* SADDLE HORN.

Horn Basket   A basket or leather case on a coach for the guard's horn, umbrellas, etc.

Horn Case   An open end leather case fastened to the front of the saddle, to carry a hunting horn.

Horn Tumours   These form in the horny laminae, and are usually caused by the penetration of grit or other foreign matter, or by blows on the hoof wall. They may be up to ½ in (12.7 mm) in thickness, and cause absorption of the pedal bone for their accommodation.

Horny Sole   A plate of hard horn about ⅜ in (9.5 mm) thick, secreted by the sensitive sole and concave on its ground surface; its posterior position receives the horny frog. Its function is to assist in carrying the weight and to protect the sensitive parts immediately in contact with it.

Horse (Equus caballus)   The male equine animal.

Horse, to   To provide with a horse or horses; to set out on horseback.

'Horse and Hound'   A weekly periodical, first published in 1884. It combines an interest in racing, hunting and show world activities and is a medium for the expression of the views of horsemen throughout the world.

Horse and Pony Breeding and Benefit Fund   Founded in 1945 by R. S. Summerhays. *Objects:* to collect from Horse Shows, etc., a share of their profits or donations, and make collections there and obtain donations from individuals. To distribute such moneys to those causes which have for their purpose, and achieve in their efforts, the breeding and benefit of horses and ponies. Administered by a Committee and associated with the British Horse Society.

Horse-bier   A bier carried by two horses, for use at burials in hilly countries, one horse being harnessed in front, the shafts extending to the rear into which the following horse was harnessed. The coffin was placed between them on a platform on the shafts. There were no wheels.

Horse-block   *see* MOUNTING BLOCK.

Horse-boat   A ferry boat for conveying horses or carriages. In the U.S.A. refers to a boat drawn by horses.

Horse Box   The railway horse box is designed to hold two horses, the motor horse box will hold more. The latter is unequalled for general convenience, e.g. for a show, the horse arriving on the ground dry and in full bloom. When used for hunting, a horse which travels by motor horse box is saved many miles of road work, conserving its energy for the proper business of the day, and after the hunt it can be roughly bandaged and rugged up, and will be back in the stables in a minimum of time.

Horse-boy   Obsolete term for a stable-boy (often contemptuous).

Horse Brasses   *see* AMULETS.

Horse Bread   A mixture of beans, wheat, yeast and water kneaded together and baked and formerly used as a feed for horses.

Horse-breaker (-tamer)   One who breaks or trains horses by teaching them to carry a pack, rider or to draw a vehicle.

Horse-breeding Act, 1918   *see* STALLION LICENCES.

Horse-coper   *see* COPER.

Horse-corser   A jobbing dealer in horses.

Horse Dealer   One who is engaged in the buying and selling of horses for profit or on commission.

Horse Dealers' Job and Post Masters', Coach Proprietors' and Livery Stable Keepers' Provident Fund, The   Founded in 1839 to give permanent or temporary relief to members when in straitened circumstances, arising from age, sickness, accident or distress; and also to the widows and children of such in the event of the member's death.

Horseflesh This is widely eaten by certain Continental nations and others, and is given as food to dogs and cats. The reason why in Great Britain and the Scandinavian countries horseflesh is little eaten, may well be that the horse was sacred to Woden, hence to those of Scandinavian descent horseflesh was sacrificial meat. When Christianity came to Britain it had sometimes to be forced on the general populace, and, since the enforcers could never be sure whether horseflesh was being eaten as an ordinary meal, or whether it came from secret sacrificial pots, the eating of it was finally forbidden.

Horsefly Any of a family (Tabanidae) of dipterous flies, some of large size. Called also gadfly and breeze fly. The female sucks the blood of animals.

Horse-gentler East Anglian term for one who breaks in colts.

Horse Guards see HOUSEHOLD CAVALRY.

Horse Latitudes This term originated in the sixteenth century at the time of the Spanish Conquest of South America on the voyages from Spain to Mexico and Brazil, when a prolonged calm would cause shortage of water, necessitating throwing the horses overboard.

Horseman One who rides on horseback; one skilled in the riding and management of horses. Also a farm worker engaged in agriculture with horses.

Horseman's Sunday Service Originated by R. S. Summerhays in 1949, is held annually at Tattenham Corner, Epsom Downs, usually the Sunday following the St Leger (q.v.), when horses, ponies and donkeys, ridden or driven, are blessed. Similar services are held at other places through-out the country and in many parts of the world.

Horsemanship see RIDING, ART OF.

Horse Marines An old phrase of derision, 'Tell that to the Horse Marines' and said to one guilty of gross exaggeration. It has been said with some authority that they had existed from time immemorial in the capacity of Honorary Horse Militia attached to the Cinque Ports Defence Units and claimed now to be attached to the 5th Cinque Ports Battalion, Royal Sussex Regiment. The official journal of the Royal Marines mentioned that the 17th Lancers were known as the Horse Marines on account of service on board *H.M.S. Hermione* and it seems certain that there were many instances of marines serving in a mounted capacity (Java, 1811; Crimean War, 1854; Egyptian War, 1882; British Honduras, 1913).

Horsemastership A comprehensive term covering the care of the horse, in sickness, in health, and in all its activities whether for pleasure, utility or commercial uses.

Horse Net Light cord net placed over the muzzle of harness horses that bite at passers-by (see MUZZLE).

Horse of the Year Show Founded in 1949 and organized by the British Show Jumping Association (q.v.). The Show, as the name implies, seeks to find and proclaim the leading horse and pony of the year in all the usual show classes, as well as the leading jumper of the year. In consequence it is the last of the important shows and is held annually in October, originally at Haringey but now at the Empire Pool, Wembley, London.

Horseplay Rude, boisterous behaviour.

Horse-posts (Riding Posts) Term applied to the horse and rider carrying mails, especially those from main road coach stopping places to outlying country districts.

Horse-power   The power a horse can exert, or its equivalent, equals that required to raise 33,000 lb avoirdupois one foot per minute: a standard for estimating the power of engines. The calculation is said to be based on the performance of a Clydesdale horse. A Tractor Denominator is used in U.S.A. to test the power of draught horses in competitions. It records the total power exerted by a team of horses and also that of each member of the team.

Horserace Betting Levy Board   Set up by the Government under the Betting, Gaming and Lotteries Act to administer a levy for the benefit of horseracing. Decides how the money raised by the Levy should be spent in consultation with the Jockey Club. The Board is responsible to the Home Secretary, has a chairman and two members appointed by the Home Secretary, three members appointed by the Jockey Club, and two *ex officio* members, one representing the Horserace Totalisator Board (*q.v.*) and the other the Bookmakers' Committee.

Horserace Totalisator Board   Appointed under the Betting, Gaming and Lotteries Act of 1961 to administer the Tote. Under the Horserace Betting Levy Board it has a chairman, appointed by the Home Secretary, three other members, and a director general. It is successor in title to the Racecourse Betting Control Board established by the Racecourse Betting Act of 1928.

Horse Racing   Trials of speed between two or more horses.

Horses and Ponies Protection Association   Founded in 1937 to protect horses, ponies and donkeys from neglect and ill-treatment. Promotes propaganda for stricter supervision of slaughter houses and markets, better transport conditions by road, rail, sea and air, and the final banning of the Continental traffic in horses for slaughter.

Horse-sense   Sound common sense.

Horseshoe   Though of much earlier origin it appeared to arrive for general use in Europe in the tenth century and was introduced into England by William the Conqueror, his Marshal-Farrier being Henri de Ferrers.

Horseshoe Cheek   A fancy cheek in the shape of a horseshoe used on straight bar stallion show bits.

Horse Show   A horse show enjoys universal popularity whether it be the Royal International or a small village show. It is not known how horse shows originated, but they probably developed from fairs and other places where horses were assembled for sale. Except in the case of shows held by breed societies, the usual schedule, if time permits, includes such classes as Hunters, Hacks, Ponies, Hackneys and Show Jumping.

Horse-sick   A term applied to pastures which have become soured by horses grazing on them for too long, and which usually harbour red worm (*q.v.*).

Horse Sickness   *see* AFRICAN HORSE SICKNESS.

Horse-standard   Correct name for measuring-stick (*q.v.*).

Horse Trials   *   Sheila Willcox

Horse Trials, sometimes known as Eventing, is a sport which provides the all-round test for horse and rider. Originally the competition was a test for the officer's charger and on the Continent it is still known as the 'militaire'.

A Three-Day Event was first included in the Olympic Games programme in

1912, and although Britain entered a team for the Berlin Olympics in 1936 there were no national competitions in the United Kingdom until after the 1948 Olympic Games held at Aldershot and Wembley. The Duke of Beaufort realized the immense possibilities of the development of this sport in Britain and placed his estate at Badminton in Gloucestershire at the disposal of a committee to organize Britain's first national Three-Day Event. It was run on lines exactly similar to the Continental 'militaire', the first day being devoted to Dressage, the second to Speed and Endurance, and the third to Show Jumping.

The Dressage Test is of medium standard in that it requires that the horse is capable of good collected and extended paces, work on two tracks, counter canter and transitions from canter to halt. The standard has improved out of all recognition since the early years, and to win a current Three-Day Event the horse must produce a really good dressage test, go fast and clear on the second day and finally jump a clear round in the show jumping phase. The Speed and Endurance Test on the second day is divided into four phases and covers a distance of approximately 17 miles (27 km) in national events and 22 miles (35 km) in Olympic Games. The first phase, A, is Roads and Tracks, and competitors must complete it at a speed of 9 m.p.h. (14.4 kmh) (240 m per minute), an alternate steady trot and canter pace. Phase B is the Steeplechase course with ten or twelve obstacles over approximately $2\frac{1}{4}$ miles (3.6 km). The speed for the Optimum Time, the equivalent of the old maximum bonus points and now no penalties, is 755 yd (690 m) per minute or 26 miles (41 km) per hour. Penalty points are accumulated at the rate of 0.8 point for every second over the Optimum Time. Completing Phase B, competitors then face a second set of Roads and Tracks and again this Phase C must be completed at the speed of 9 m.p.h. (14.4 kmh). Penalties for ex-

ceeding the Optimum Time in Phases A and C are heavy, and for each second over the Optimum Time a competitor is penalized one mark up to the Time Limit, which is one fifth more than the Optimum Time. Exceeding the Time Limit entails elimination. The Optimum Time for Phase C starts as soon as the competitor crosses the finishing line of the Steeplechase Phase, and competitors sometimes fail to realize that if they complete Phase B in less than the Optimum Time they must also complete Phase C the equivalent number of seconds early. The time they have gained by completing the Steeplechase Phase B in less than the Optimum Time is added as a bonus to the 10-minute compulsory halt period before the start of the cross-country phase. This compulsory halt is included so that a veterinary panel can inspect each horse and ensure that he is fit enough to continue the competition. The panel will spin any horse showing signs of distress or lameness and this rule has been invaluable in preventing an unfit horse from facing the dangers and rigours of the fixed fences in the cross-country phase. Phase D, the Cross-Country, is the final phase of the Speed and Endurance Test, and it consists of 30 or more fixed obstacles cunningly sited so that the courage, skill and judgement of both horse and rider are thoroughly tested. It is over 4 miles (6.4 km) in length and must be completed for no penalty points at a speed of 624 yd (570 m) per minute or $21\frac{1}{2}$ miles (34.4 km) per hour. Penalty points are awarded at the rate of 0.4 points for every second over the Optimum Time. The cross-country fences will not exceed 3 ft 11 in (1.20 m) in height. Spreads must not exceed 5 ft 11 in (1.80 m) where there is both height and spread, and obstacles with a spread only must not exceed 11 ft 5 in (3.50 m) or a water jump 13 ft 1 in (4 m). They will include many problem fences where the riders have to decide on the best manner of approach and others which provide alternatives: a shorter route over a more difficult fence or a longer way round with less risk. Almost all cross-country courses will include a form of water-splash and this usually incorporates one or two fences as the horse enters or leaves the water. The cross-country course builders of today are extremely experienced and professional men and it is imperative for the riders to know how best to tackle the different obstacles if they are to complete this final phase successfully.

The final day is a Show Jumping Test, and is included merely to demonstrate that after a day of tremendous effort the horse is still fit enough to continue in service. The show jumping course is deliberately twisty and although no obstacle is more than 4 ft (1.22 m) in height and 12 ft (3.66 m) in spread it is a difficult enough test to conclude the Three-Day Event. The course must be negotiated at a fast canter of 437 yd (400 m) per minute. A competitor who exceeds the Time Allowed is penalized at a rate of a quarter of a mark for every second in excess of the Time Allowed up to the Time Limit, after which he is eliminated. The ultimate winner of the Three-Day Event is the competitor with the least number of penalty points calculated over the three phases.

A Three-Day Event is a severe test both of horse and rider. It demands of the horse the qualities of obedience, strength, courage and stamina, and from the rider intelligence, sympathy, judgement of pace and absolute common sense. It is a competition extraordinarily well suited to the British and Irish temperaments and both these countries have the additional advantage of their hunting heritage. Few other countries in the world can provide the wealth of talent, equine and human, so abundant in Britain and Ireland. British horses are second to none as potential international class Eventers for their inherent qualities are exactly what is required for Eventing. The British Thoroughbred or near-Thoroughbred from the hunting field is naturally high-couraged,

fast and a good jumper. The one doubtful factor is his temperament and for this one reason some competitors prefer to train an animal with a dash of common blood. There is no doubt, however, that the Thoroughbred horse who combines a good temperament with the qualities of courage, stamina and speed, is very hard to beat.

The British Horse Society is the governing body for Trials in Britain and since the Duke of Beaufort first offered Badminton as a venue for the Three-Day Event in 1948 there has been an increasing number of Trials organized all over the country. These, for the greater part, are One-Day Events, where dressage, show jumping and cross country are undertaken on the same day. The dressage test is ridden first and then either the cross country course or the show jumping at the discretion of the organizers. The Events cater for novice, intermediate and advanced grade horses, and sometimes run an open intermediate class which, as the name implies, is for both intermediate and advanced horses. A novice horse becomes intermediate when he has earned fifteen points and he upgrades to advanced standard when he has forty points. There are several Two-Day Events held during the season and these meetings are of immense value in providing an opportunity for the competitors to make an easier transition from One to Three-Day Eventing. They include a steeplechase course and several miles of roads and tracks before the cross-country course, and the competition quickly shows which horses and riders will be able to cope with the far greater demands of a Three-Day Event.

The important Three-Day Events in the Horse Trials calendar are Badminton in April, Tidworth in May, Burghley in September and Wylye in October. Tidworth is invaluable as an introductory Three-Day Event as the course is not as difficult as either Badminton or Burghley and is very well suited to the novice horse or rider. In

1974 a new Three-Day Event was introduced at Bramham Moor, bringing the total to five.

Badminton is an ideal venue for a Three-Day Event. The dressage arena is beautifully laid out in the main ring in flat parkland, and the estate's roads provide marvellous material for Phases A and C of the Speed and Endurance Test. The cross country course is imaginatively designed and constructed, requiring a bold horse and one who can gallop easily. The course rides fast and it is important to have a horse who can be ridden for no penalty points without straining himself at his top speed throughout the phase.

Until 1960 the Autumn Three-Day Event took place at Harewood, the Yorkshire home of H.R.H. the late Princess Royal. It was an event organized par excellence and was chosen as the venue for the European Championships in 1959. In 1960 the Marquess of Exeter offered his estate as an alternative to Harewood and since then Burghley has become Britain's second big Three-Day Event. Burghley requires a horse combining the quality of speed and the ability to cope with changing terrain, for it includes undulating trappy sections as well as open country.

The necessity for fit horses cannot be overstressed. The regrettable accidents which have occurred from time to time have been caused generally by an animal being forced to face an ordeal for which he is totally ill-prepared. A second reason for these unfortunate accidents at International meetings was the rule of the Fédération Equestre Internationale that teams should consist of three horses and riders, all of whom must complete the event to enable the team to qualify for an award. The inevitable result was that tired horses, or horses which had fallen and consequently were in no state to continue, were forced on in an attempt, all too often in vain, to safeguard the team as a whole. The Olympic Committee eventually changed this rule, and at present a team consists of four members and the three best scores count for the team. Until the Tokyo Olympic Games in 1964 women were barred from participation in the Three-Day Event. They were allowed in national Events and even the European Championships, but despite their obvious ability to take on the men at level terms and beat them, all efforts to effect a change of rule met with excuse after excuse. The decision to constitute a team of four eventually led to the change of rule to allow women members in a team and in 1964 the United States of America became the first nation to take advantage of the new ruling.

Britain began to participate in Horse Trials with little knowledge but a great deal of enthusiasm. The art of dressage, as practised by the Continentals, was not popular in 1948, but with instruction and advice from overseas, British competitors showed a gradual and steady improvement. This growing knowledge, coupled with an inherent talent for cross country riding, provided more than adequate winning material and from 1953 to 1957 Britain was undisputed king of the Event world. The Germans won the European Championship in 1959, and the Gold Medal at the 1960 Rome Olympic Games went to the Australian team who also took the Individual medal. Russia won the European Championship in 1962, and in 1964 the Gold Medal at the Tokyo Olympic Games went to the Italian team. The first World Championships took place in England at Burghley in 1966. Ireland won the team award and an Argentinian, Captain M. Moratorio, won the individual championship on 'Chalan'. From 1967 Britain entered her second golden era, winning the team awards at Punchestown in 1967, the Gold Medal in the Mexico Olympic Games in 1968, the team awards both at Haras du Pin in 1969 and at the World Championships in 1970, and the Gold Medal for the second successive Olympic Games in 1972 at Munich. Apart from these successes Britain took the Individual medals with Mary Gordon-Watson and her sensational horse 'Cornishman' at the European Championships at Haras du Pin in 1969 and at the World Championships in 1970. H.R.H. the Princess Anne won the European Individual Championship at Burghley in 1971 and Richard Meade took the Individual Gold Medal at the Munich Olympic Games in 1972 (see *Plates* 19 *and* 20).

*   *   *

'Horsing'   A mare 'in use' or 'in season', the period at which she is likely to breed.

Horsing Stone   *see* MOUNTING BLOCK.

Hostler (Ostler)   One who works with horses stabled or baited at an inn.

Hot Blood   The Thoroughbred and Eastern breeds—Arab, Barb, Turk, Syrian, etc., or an admixture of these.

Hot Shot, to   To use a battery-powered electric prod for training and moving horses in western America. Illegal and forbidden by racing authorities for 'big tracks' or recognized shows.

Hound Couples   A contrivance for attaching two hounds, and consisting of two hound collars and a distance chain and swivel. There is a lighter type for carrying rolled on the saddle.

Hound Gloves   Massage gloves made of horse hair.

Hound Hunt   A hunt in which, with but little scent, hounds doggedly hunt their fox by skill and perseverance.

Hound Jog   *see* HOUND PACE.

Hound Pace   The pace at which hounds normally travel on the road, about 6 miles (9.7 km) an hour; also known as 'hound jog' or fadge (*q.v.*).

Hound Show, First   Held by Cleveland Agricultural Society at Redcar in 1859.

'Hounds Please!'   A warning to the field to beware of hounds and get horses, etc., out of the way.

Household Cavalry   Consists of a mounted squadron of the Life Guards and of the Royal Horse Guards (The Blues) kept at the Hyde Park Barracks for such ceremonial duties as providing the Sovereign's Life Guard at Whitehall and the royal escort on such State occasions as the Opening of Parliament, visits of foreign Heads of State, etc.

Housing   An ornamental covering for a horse. A saddlecloth and the trappings of a horse (*see* SHABRACK). Also the large pad of leather which was fastened on to the hames or collar of a heavy harness horse. In dry weather this apron of leather stood stiffly up, but in wet it lay back on the horse's withers to keep him dry.

Hovels   Sheds in meadows designed to give shelter to horses when they are turned out. Doors are unnecessary, but there should be mangers and racks for hay. Attention should be paid to the state of the ground, as the condition into which it is sometimes allowed to get is bad enough to cause disease, particularly of the feet.

Howitt, Samuel   (1765–1822) An Essex man by birth and a prolific painter and etcher of animals and sporting scenes. He engraved 40 plates of *Field Sports of the East* and a set of 20 for *Orme's British Field Sports*.

Hucul (Huzul)   Mountain pony of Poland. Hardy, willing; used for pack and draught work. They have recently been introduced into England.

Huick!   *see* HOICK.

Humane Curb   A curb made of leather or elastic instead of the usual chain.

Humane Disposal of Surplus Ponies, Society for the Founded in 1971 to protect unwanted ponies, especially young stock and foals, from exploitation at public sales and elsewhere.

Humane Girth A three-fold leather girth having the buckles set on a sliding strap passed through a ring. Allows a little movement to conform to that of the horse.

Hummel A Nott Stag (*q.v.*).

Humour A pimply condition of the skin, caused by a heated state of the blood. *Treatment:* ensure that the bowels are kept open and that the corn ration is not excessive.

Hungarian Shagya (or Shagya Arabian) The best Hungarian breed; the Shagya is, in fact, a special Arab breed, the name being derived from a desert-bred Arabian stallion which founded the breed; the main stud in Hungary is at Babolna. It is an extremely hardy horse, mostly grey in colour, standing 14 to 15 h.h. (142–152 cm); it is an excellent mover, thriving on little food, and having most of the qualities of the Arab. The foundation stock consisted of pure-bred Arabians, and stock of undoubted Oriental blood and type, though not of authentic pedigree.

Hunloke Bit Incorrect name given to a Globe cheek curb bit.

Hunt A collective term for Master, hounds, servants and field.

Hunt The act of pursuing a fox is called a hunt or run.

Hunt The territory hunted by a pack, i.e. the country.

Hunt Button A button with a design, monogram or lettering distinctive to a particular Hunt, the right of a subscriber to wear it being vested in the Master. With scarlet, a brass button is worn; with a black coat, a black bone button having the design in white.

Hunt Cap, Velvet This has a gossamer body, comprising layers of calico and twill impregnated with shellac and ironed in layers to shape on wooden blocks, and is also made with a felt foundation for added strength. Some types are now made of fibreglass. The body is then covered with proofed velveteen or velvet, the lining being made of quilted silk padded with felt for added protection, the whole fitted with draw-cord for close fitting and cushioned protection. The cap is designed as protective headwear against falls and is ventilated with a screw-top button. The college-cap shape at the back gives added grip. When wet the cap should be dried naturally; artificial heat will soften and distort shape. The hunting bow at the back consists of two bows and two tails: the Hunt Master wears the tails (feathers) pointing upwards. Children's velvet hunt caps have one small bow and two tails. The velvet cap was worn when hunting only by Masters, ex-Masters, Field Masters, Hunt Secretaries, hunting farmers and children. In recent years it has been very generally adopted by women for hunting and riding and is also the accepted headgear for show jumpers of both sexes.

Hunt Cup Short title for the Royal Hunt Cup, the chief betting race of the Royal Ascot meeting in June, and run over 1 mile (1.6 km).

Hunter Not a breed, but a type, which is largely influenced by the nature of the country over which it is to be used. The Show Hunter, however, which is the ideal, is Thoroughbred, or nearly so; it has power and scope, giving a good length of rein, and a strong back and loins, hocks of great propelling power, with the best of galloping action. It must ride with balance and courage, carry its head in the right position, and be responsive to its rider. In hunter classes horses should be plaited and wear double bridles. *Breed Society:* Hunters' Improvement and

National Light Horse Breeding Society (*see Plate* 18).

Hunter, Bona Fide   A horse which has been regularly and fairly hunted and whose owner has been granted a 'Hunter's Certificate' by the Master of the pack concerned. A horse must be a 'Bona Fide Hunter' to compete in Point-to-Points and Hunt Steeplechases.

Hunter, Good   The warranty for a hunter is 'good hunter', which implies that the animal is sound in the wind and eyes, and is capable of being hunted (*see* WARRANTY, SOLD WITH).

Hunter (Show—Heavyweight)   A mare or gelding, 4 years old or over, capable of carrying more than 14 stone (196 lb; 89 kg). To be ridden astride.

Hunter (Show—Ladies')   A mare or gelding, 4 years old or over, suitable for carrying a lady side-saddle. To be ridden by a lady, side-saddle.

Hunter (Show—Lightweight)   A mare or gelding, 4 years old or over, capable of carrying not more than 12 stone 7 lb (175 lb; 79.37 kg). To be ridden astride.

Hunter (Show—Middleweight)   A mare or gelding, 4 years old or over, capable of carrying from 12 stone 7 lb to 14 stone (175–196 lb; 79–89 kg). To be ridden astride.

Hunter (Show—Small)   A mare or gelding, 4 years old or over, exceeding 14.2 h.h. (144 cm) and not exceeding 15.2 h.h. (154 cm). To be ridden astride or side-saddle, and to be judged as a hunter.

Hunters' Improvement and National Light Horse Breeding Society (Founded 1885)   *Objects:* to improve the breed and promote the breeding of Hunters and other horses used for riding and driving purposes.

Hunter Steeplechase   A race confined to hunters and amateur riders, run only in the second half of the steeplechasing season. It is confined to horses certified by an M.F.H. (*q.v.*) to have been fairly hunted during the season.

Hunter Trials   Competitive event held for horses and ponies across (as far as possible) a natural hunting country. Generally judged on performance and style within a specified time limit.

Hunt Heels   Heels for hunting boots are generally not more than $\frac{3}{4}$ in (19 mm) high. They are built square and longer in the waist of the boots than walking heels, and are cut at an angle more to the inside. This ensures that the stirrup irons are in the correct position when ridden right 'home'.

Hunt Hounds, to   To direct, control and assist hounds in pursuit of their quarry.

Hunting Boots   *see* DRESS.

Hunting-box, Lodge or Seat   A residence for hunting.

Hunting Gate   A narrow wicket erected for the use of riders.

'Hunting Jupiter'   The name given to Hugo Meynell (*q.v.*) by members of the Quorn Hunt of which he was Master from 1753 to 1800.

Hunting Monarch, First   In England this was King Penda of Mercia; his huntsmen lived near Pytchley Village.

Hunting Seasons   Cub hunting, August 4th–November 1st (approx.). Fox hunting, November–April. Deer (England and Wales): Red stag, Sika stag, Fallow buck, August 1st–April 30th; Red hind, Sika hind, Fallow doe, Roe doe, November 1st–February 28th; Roe buck, no legal close season. Deer (Scotland): Red stag, July 1st–October 20th; Roe buck, May 1st–October 20th; Fallow and Sika buck, August 1st–April 30th; Red and Sika hind, October 21st–February 15th; Fallow doe, October 21st–February 15th; Roe doe,

October 21st–February 28th. Harriers and Beagles, October–March (approx.). Coursing, September 15th–March 10th.

Hunting Spurs   *see* SPURS.

Hunting Tie   A specially shaped scarf of white linen or piqué worn round the neck, the ends being passed through a loop at the back of the neck then brought round and knotted in front, where they are crossed and held together with a plain solid safety pin. Also called a stock.

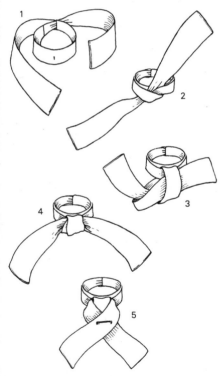

Hunting Tie (stock)

Hunting Whip   *see* WHIP, HUNTING.

Hunting Year   This runs from May 1st, when hunt subscriptions fall due.

Hunt Livery   The distinctive coat (usually scarlet), collar and buttons worn by the hunt staff.

Hunt Secretary   He fulfils (usually in an honorary capacity) the normal duties of a secretary but, in addition, he also acts, to a degree which varies according to the time he can spare and the inclination of the Master, as liaison between the Hunt and farmers, landowners and subscribers.

Hunt Servants   Huntsman (if professional), Kennel Huntsman (if any) and Whippers-in.

Huntsman   The Master, should he hunt his own hounds, may be the Huntsman, or a professional or any other person may be employed.

Hunt Subscriptions   These are payable in advance annually on May 1st. The amount varies according to the Hunt and the number of days normally hunted each week.

Hunt Supporters Clubs   Formed in support of local hunts by those keenly interested in the sport but often unable for various reasons to ride to hounds. Valuable work in marshalling cars, shutting gates and raising funds is performed by members.

Hunt Terrier   A small short-legged and very courageous terrier attached to most hunts and used to eject the hunted fox from any earth or drain which it may enter (*see* RUSSELL, REV. JACK *and* TERRIER MAN).

Hurdle Race   A race during the course of which a number of hurdles must be jumped. There must not be less than eight flights in a 2-mile (3.2 km) hurdle (the minimum distance for a hurdle race), and an additional flight for every extra $\frac{1}{4}$ mile (0.40 km) beyond 2 miles (3.2 km).

Hurlingham Polo Association Medium Championship (County Cup)   For results *see page* 382.

Hurlingham Polo Association Low-goal Championship (Junior County Cup) For results *see page* 382.

Hurlingham Polo Committee Since polo is no longer played at the Hurlingham Club, London, the control of the game is now vested in the Hurlingham Polo Committee which has jurisdiction of the game in England and the Commonwealth.

Huzul *see* HUCUL.

Hybrids Crosses between a horse on the one side and an ass, zebra, etc., on the other. Such offspring are, with very few exceptions, sterile.

'Hyperion' Owned and bred by the 17th Earl of Derby (*q.v.*), this chestnut by 'Gainsborough' out of 'Selene' was only 15.1 h.h. (153 cm) when he won the Derby and St Leger of 1933. The outstanding stallion of his generation, he was six times leading sire of the year. Died 1960.

Hyracotherium A lower Eocene Mammal, the size of a fox, with four toes; alleged to be the original ancestor of the horse.

Iberian Horse Ancestor of the Tarbenian horse (*q.v.*), which, at the beginning of the nineteenth century, was improved by the importation of Arabian stallions by Napoleon Bonaparte.

Iceland Pony The breed is not indigenous but is composed of immigrants, like the inhabitants who, being in disagreement with Norway's reigning king in the ninth century, migrated to Iceland, taking with them their household goods, farming stock and ponies. The Norwegians were later joined by settlers from the Western Isles, who brought with them ponies of Celtic stock; thus the Iceland is of mixed origin. There are two types: riding and draught, and for 1000 or more years the pony was the only means of transport. Short and stocky, with large heads, intelligent eyes, short thick necks with heavy mane and forelock, they stand 12–13 h.h. (122–132 cm). Predominantly grey and dun. Extremely hardy, they have keen sight, are docile and friendly, with a strong homing instinct. The best quality saddle horses pace (*q.v.*) and rack (*q.v.*).

'If Cash' or 'Any to Come' Bets When one or more selections are backed with the proviso that should there by any cash due from them it is placed on subsequent selections.

Imperial Crowner A bad fall.

Importation of Horses Particulars are available from the Ministry of Agriculture, Fisheries and Food in London, and the Department of Agriculture and Fisheries for Scotland in Edinburgh.

Impulsion A forward urge manifested by the energetic use of the hocks.

In blood Hounds which have killed recently are said to be 'in blood'.

Inbreeding The mating of brother and sister, sire and daughter, son and dam.

Incisors The front or biting teeth. The age of a horse is determined from them (*see* AGE).

'Incitatus' The racing stallion beloved by the Roman Emperor, Gaius Caesar (A.D. 12–41), who was usually known as Caligula. The horse was first called 'Porcellus' — Little Pig — but when it began to win races Caligula changed the name to 'Incitatus'—Swift-speeding—and his admiration for its qualities became an obsession. The horse was given a marble stable with manger of ivory and bucket of gold, trappings of purple cloth and a collar of jewels. The Emperor appointed the horse a citizen of Rome, then a senator and the final honour of a consulship was only prevented by the assassination of Caligula himself.

Independent Seat A rider is said to have an independent seat when he has reached such a degree of firmness, by balance and grip, that he is independent of the reins and stirrups as an aid to the correctness of the seat.

Indigestion, Cough due to *see* COUGHS *and* COLIC.

Indirect Rein An opposite or bearing rein; the action of this is to press against the horse's neck on the side opposite to the direction in which the horse is required to move; also called neck-reining. An artificial rein action.

Indoor Polo This is popular in the U.S.A., where international players and ponies participate in the winter. The game is played on tan, on an area approximately 300 ft by 150 ft (91.44 × 45.72 m), with the goal-posts 10 ft (3 m) apart; a leather-covered sponge rubber ball is used, and there are three players a side. It is a good schooling medium.

'In Front of the Bit' Said of a horse that hangs on the hand and pulls.

Inhaling   When it is desired to steam the head of a horse for medicinal purposes a small nosebag or metal bucket is employed and is suspended by a strap passing over the poll. A handful of hay, a dose of inhalant and about a pint of boiling water straight from the kettle form the mixture. Retain in position for ten minutes.

In Hand   A horse is said to be in hand when in flexes its jaw to the pressure of the rein. Many advise obtaining this flexion in the earliest stages of training by handling the bit reins while standing up, or walking with the horse.

In-hand   Indicating a led horse.

In-hand   Classes led into the show ring by rein and bridle or halter, unsaddled or without harness. They include stallions, mares and foals; also young stock and sometimes geldings. The term is used to distinguish the class from a saddle class or harness class.

Injured Jockeys Fund   The original fund was set up in 1964 following the grave injuries to the National Hunt jockeys Paddy Farrell and Tim Brookshaw. Public response was so generous that this fund was closed with the consent of the two injured jockeys, and the Injured National Hunt Jockeys Fund took its place, the purpose being to help any injured steeplechase jockey or their families. The fund has again been broadened in scope and is now able to help all jockeys, both flat as well as jumping. In its first nine years £80,000 has been distributed to help more than 60 jockeys and their families.

Injured National Hunt Jockeys Fund   see INJURED JOCKEYS FUND.

Insemination, Artificial   The process of serving or stinting a mare by artificial means as opposed to the natural act. This method, though used to a very great extent with cattle, is not generally used with horses.

Inside (Racing)   On a racecourse nearest the rails marking the inside perimeter.

Inspector of Courses (Racing)   An official appointed by the Jockey Club to see that racecourses are kept up to the standards laid down.

Insurance   Generally advisable for all horses and ponies and always for stables and contents. Various Insurance Companies specialize, and advice can be sought from the British Horse Society (*q.v.*). Under the Animals Act owners are liable for damage caused by their horses. Personal and Third Party insurance is advisable.

Instinct   *see* INTELLIGENCE *and* MEMORY.

Institute of the Horse and Pony Club, Ltd., The   (Founded 1925) *Objects:* to be an authoritative centre of information on all matters relating to the horse, its training and management; now absorbed by The British Horse Society (*q.v.*).

Intelligence   Experts differ entirely as to the intelligence possessed by a horse. Some claim that it has a very poor intelligence, and does everything from habit acquired by training, or in association with the comfort of the stable or the instinct for safety and protection. Others maintain that the horse is capable of applying its brain in a way that can only be attributed to great intelligence. One man will speak with feeling of the singleness of his horse's affection for himself in the stable and in the field, shown by whinnying; another will claim to get the same results within twenty-four hours if the horse be removed to his stables (*see* MEMORY *and* ELBERFELD HORSES).

Interfering   A general term used for the various ways in which a horse can injure itself by striking one foot or leg with another (*see* BRUSHING, FORGING, OVER-REACHING, SPEEDY CUTTING).

International Federation of Pony Breeders, The (Founded 1951) *Objects:* to make known the different breeds and types of ponies, their countries of origin and uses, and to investigate the markets and provide contact between breeders and intending purchasers. The first conference of the Federation was held at Cologne.

International Horse Show (C.S.I.) Any horse show which includes one or more competitions open to foreign riders who come as individual competitors authorized by their National Federation, at the invitation of the host National Federation, or by personal invitation. No team or individual competitor is ever sent officially to a C.S.I.

International Horse Show (C.S.I.O.) Any international horse show which, being authorized by its National Federation, and having obtained the consent of the F.E.I. (*q.v.*), is entered in the F.E.I. Calendar. Riders are sent to it officially by National Federations and with the approval of any Government departments which may be concerned.

International Horse Show, Royal One of the premier horse shows of the world, first held at Olympia, London, in 1907 and continuing there as an annual event up to and including 1939—with the exception of the First World War years 1915–1919, and also 1933. There were no shows during the Second World War years 1940–1944. In 1945 the show was held at the White City, London, as the 'National' show, no International competitors being able to enter owing to post-war difficulties. From 1946–1967 it was held at the White City as the International Horse Show, but in 1968 and 1969 it was held at the Wembley Stadium, London. In 1970 it went indoors to the Empire Pool, Wembley. Classes are open to Arabs, Hunters, Hacks, Cobs and Ponies under saddle, Hackneys (harness classes) and Jumpers. In 1957

the right to the prefix 'Royal' was granted.

'In the Money' Said of a racehorse, show horse or show jumper that receives any prize money offered in a race or class.

'In the Soup' When in difficulties— originally referred to hunting when a rider fell into a ditch or dirty water.

'In Velvet' Descriptive of a stag whose horns are growing (*see* VELVET).

In Whelp The state of a hound or other bitch when she is carrying her young.

Iodine, Tincture of An unbreakable tube of this should be carried by every hunting man for first-aid treatment for all cuts.

Iomud This Russian horse is descended from the same root as the Akhal-Teke breed (*q.v.*), but has been evolved by another Turkoman tribe, the 'Iomud'. The Iomud differs from the Akhal-Teke in being smaller, not so fast, and much more highly strung. These horses run in troops on the plains of Northern Turkmenia, and have great powers of endurance.

Irish Draught The indigenous breed of working horse in Ireland, now becoming scarce. Capable farm horses and natural jumpers, the mares crossed with a Thoroughbred stallion, produce top-class weight-carrying hunters.

Irish National Hunt Steeplechase Committee The governing body and recognized 'Turf Authority' responsible for controlling steeplechasing and hurdle racing in Ireland.

Irish Riff Term used for small lumps on horses' shoulders which sometimes occur within a few months of coming over from Ireland.

Irish Turf Club The governing body and recognized 'Turf Authority' responsible for controlling flat racing in Ireland.

I.R.M. Snaffle (India-rubber Mouth) Usually a mullen mouthpiece with a chain through the centre of the rubber as a precaution against its being bitten through. Jointed metal snaffles and straight bar or mullen mouthpieces sometimes can be obtained with the mouthpieces covered in rubber. When there is no solid metal centre to the mouth it is known as a 'flexible mouth'.

Iron   *see* STIRRUP IRON.

Isabella (Y'sabella)   Bred since the fifteenth century when Queen Isabella of Spain formed a stud of coloured horses for herself and her ladies to ride; some of these 'Golden Horses of the Queen' were given by the Queen to America, which was then being colonized by the Spaniards. Originally from Arab stock, they vary in colour from light to liver chestnuts with white mane and tail, more usually known now as Palomino (*q.v.*).

Italian Horse   In recent years several Italian Thoroughbred stallions of great merit have met with outstanding success on English racecourses and at stud. In the sixteenth and seventeenth centuries a Neapolitan breed became famous; it was apparently a light horse possessed of great speed, and was influenced strongly by Spanish horses. Today, Sardinia produces a pony of merit, and the Sicilian horse, an Arab type with Spanish and Italian influence, is also worthy of mention.

Italian Saddle   Either a saddle made by an Italian maker (i.e. Pariani) or a loose and now incorrect term applied to a spring tree, forward-cut jumping type saddle.

Itchy Mane and Tail   Irritation may be due to the presence of lice or an indication of psoroptic mange. It can also be brought about by the bites of flies, and in some animals by photosensitization (sensitivity to light, especially ultra-violet rays). The treatment must be adjusted to the cause (*see* SWEET ITCH).

J. Juvenile grade.

Jabbing   see JOBBING IN THE MOUTH.

Jack   see MULE.

Jackass   see ASS.

Jack-knifing   A term used in Buck-jumping when a horse clicks its front and hind legs together whilst in the air, or when it crosses them so that their positions are reversed. (Also called straight bucking.)

Jacks   A term sometimes used to indicate a bone spavin.

Jade, Jadey   A sluggish horse, a horse which lacks condition, courage and spirit.

Jaf   Hardy and active desert horses bred in Kurdistan, with hard tough hooves. The height varies.

Jagger   A pedlar's or pack horse; a small horse load in the north of England is known as 'a jaggin'. Many bridle paths once used by pack ponies carrying coal or lead are known as 'jagger' or 'jaggin' ways.

Jaggin   see JAGGER.

Jaivey   see JARVEY.

Jaquama   see HACKAMORE.

Jarde or **Jardon**   A callous tumour found on the outside of a horse's hock.

Jarvey   An Irish term for the driver of a hackney carriage. (Also 'Jaivey'.)

Jaundice   A yellow condition of the mucous membranes, visible in the eyes, mouth and nostrils. The urine is brown and discoloured by bile pigments. The cause is obstruction to the flow of bile into the intestines. It may result from hepatitis (inflammation of the liver substance), blocking of the bile duct, or thickening of the duodenum, the portion of small intestine into which the bile duct opens. Veteri-nary advice is urgently needed in even the mildest cases.

Jaunting Car   A two-wheeled Irish vehicle in which the passengers sit facing the sides of the road with their feet on platforms which fold up.

Jelly Dogs   Colloquial term for Beagles.

Jennet   Genet (see BARDOT, HINNY).

Jenny   A female donkey.

Jerk-line String   Jerk-line is a Western American term for any number from 6 to 20 horses strung out two abreast and the jerk-line string is a single line run from the lead to the driver on the wagon who 'steers' the team by certain jerks on the line.

Jerky   A small, low, American one-horse, four-wheeled vehicle of the buggy type which, when fitted with a top, is called a Surrey. The Jerky is now almost extinct, having in fact long been replaced by the first utility American motor-car. The name was probably acquired from folk-usage.

Jersey Act   A resolution introduced by Lord Jersey in the Jockey Club in 1913 and passed by his fellow members that Weatherbys, proprietors of the General Stud Book, should be advised to confine all future entries in the G.S.B. to animals whose pedigrees could be traced at all points to strains already appearing in pedigrees in earlier volumes of the G.S.B. It was aimed at preventing certain strains from the U.S.A. gaining admission, and was acted on by Weatherbys. It caused much ill-feeling among breeders in the U.S.A. and France, and when it was seen that some of the most successful racing families in France were not eligible after World War II it was modified by Weatherbys in 1949.

Jibbah   The term descriptive of the peculiar forehead of the Arabian horse, which should exhibit a bulge between the eyes up to a point between the ears and down across the first third of the nasal bone—a formation of the frontal and parietal bones in the form of a shield. This is the jibbah or dish-face. It is most pronounced in foals up to the second year, becomes modified at maturity, and is rounder and more prominent in mares.

Jibbing   A most objectionable habit where the horse refuses to move forward and, in some cases, runs backwards. This may be checked by quick circling two or three times and then pushing forward. When the horse is in harness, jibbing is a serious matter. The animal should have the near foreleg tied up with a strap or cloth round upper and lower part of leg and be harnessed to a cart for about an hour. A jibber should never be hit.

Jigetai   see KULAN.

Jigging   The action of a horse which refuses to walk and substitutes a short-paced uneasy trot.

Jingle   A cart with long shafts.

Jinked Back   A derangement of the nervous system. *Symptoms*: the horse shows a lack of control of the hind limbs, which is most obvious when the animal is turned suddenly, and varies in intensity from a slightly tottering gait in mild cases to falling with the hind quarters to the ground in severe cases. It is incurable and tends to become more severe with age. Also known as Chink Back.

Jobbing in the Mouth   The act, deliberate or involuntary, of catching a horse a sharp jerk in the mouth. In the U.S.A. the term is Jabbing.

Jobey Noseband   see BRINEKIND.

Job Horses   Horses (harness or otherwise) which are hired or 'jobbed' from a job master.

Job Master   One who offers horses for hire for riding or driving.

Job Masters' Provident Fund   see HORSE DEALERS', ETC., PROVIDENT FUND.

Jockette   Colloquial term for lady jockeys (*see* LADIES RACES).

Jockey   Any rider, whether professional or amateur, competing in a horse race.

Jockey   A thin sheet of metal curved to the shape of the front and rear tops of riding boots, and which, when slipped over the boot, guides it when being pulled on over the lower edge of the leg of the breeches.

Jockey, Dumb   see DUMB-JOCKEY.

Jockey Apprentices   see APPRENTICES ALLOWANCES.

Jockeys Association of Great Britain   The body representing jockeys in British racing.

Jockey Club, The   The governing body and recognized 'Turf Authority' responsible for controlling flat-racing and steeplechasing in Britain. Following the amalgamation of the Jockey Club and the National Hunt Committee in 1968 there are now about 100 members, and in addition half a dozen honorary members, and 20 ex-officio members. Granted a Royal Charter in 1970.

Jockey Club, The (U.S.A.)   Functions similarly to the Jockey Club in Gt. Britain and is responsible for stud processing. It produces the official Thoroughbred Stud Book.

Jockey Club Rules   The rules applying to this are issued by the Jockey Club and refer to all meetings held under its sanction. They are procurable in book form on payment from Weatherbys.

Jockey Club Stewards   There are now nine stewards of the Jockey Club, including a senior steward and two deputy senior stewards. The stewards have wide ranging powers as laid down in Rules 1–4 of the Rules of Racing.

Jockeys Hunting boots, usually of black waxed calf, with fitted polishing tops of various colours, black patent tops, or with scouring tops. (The latter have a matt finish and are cleaned with a top powder.)

Jockeys Small black deposits of grease and dirt which accumulate on the flaps and sweat flaps of a saddle. They should be removed as soon as they become apparent. In stubborn cases a mild solution of soda crystals will help.

Jockey's Valet   see VALET, JOCKEY'S.

Jodhpur Boots A type of boot to wear under Jodhpurs and similar to 'highlows' in height, with elastic sides or buckle-over front designed to protect the instep from undue pressure by the stirrup-iron.

Jodhpur Breeches A popular form of riding breeches, named from the Indian state of Jodhpur; the leg is extended, unbuttoned and unlaced, down to the ankle, rendering unnecessary high boots or leggings. They are worn with strappings and either without an opening at the ankle or with an opening held together with elastic or a zip fastener. Usually known as Jodhpurs.

Jodhpur Curb A curb with a large centre link which eliminates pressure upon a sore jaw. Sometimes called a cap curb.

Jodhpur Straps (or Garters) Leather straps used to hold jodhpur breeches in place below the knee. There are various patterns. No longer in common use.

Jogger Training vehicles for hackneys.

Jog-trot A gait somewhat short of a true trot, similar to jigging (q.v.).

Jointed Pelham A bit having a jointed mouthpiece.

Joint Evil A disease which may affect a foal at any time from birth until it is 18 months old, and which is caused by bacterial infection through the navel or through the mare's milk. *Symptoms:* an indisposition to suckle, a rise in temperature, stiffness of movement, signs of infection of the navel, lameness and bowel irregularity. *Treatment:* mainly preventive. This is a serious complaint and a veterinary surgeon should be consulted; even if a recovery is made, the animal is seldom of any value for work or show.

Joint Masters Two or more individuals sharing the Mastership of a pack of hounds.

Joint Measurement Scheme Sponsored by the British Horse Society, British Show Jumping Association, British Show Hack and Cob Association, Hackney Horse Society, National Pony Society and British Show Pony Society. A panel of measurers is prepared annually, grouped under counties for the measurement of horses and ponies under the Measurement Scheme rules. Measurement Certificates are then issued and are accepted at practically every show in the U.K., thus saving exhibitors and shows the time and trouble caused by measurements being made on the show-ground which, for various reasons, are often unsatisfactory. The rules allow adequate provision for objections to Certificates under rules laid down.

Joint Oil   see SYNOVIA.

Joint Racing Board A body consisting of the three senior stewards of the Jockey Club and the three Government-appointed members of the Horserace Betting Levy Board (q.v.), formed to discuss Racing policies.

Joints 'Hinge' joints are those which can be extended; 'ball and socket' joints are those in which the end of one bone rests in a socket in another.

Jones, Adrian (1845–1938) He occasionally drew or painted horse-portraits, but he is best known for the high place he achieved amongst contemporary sculptors of horses, with such impressive groups as the dominating Quadriga of Hyde Park Corner, the Cavalry Memorial at Stanhope Gate and the beautiful statue of 'Persimmon' at Sandringham.

Jorrocks, John   An eccentric and extravagant sporting grocer, a citizen of St Botolph Lane and Great Coram Street, London, invented by R. S. Surtees in 1831. The character appears in his books *Jorrocks's Jaunts and Jollities*, *Handley Cross* and *Hillingdon Hall*. Today he is probably the most quoted and best loved character in sporting fiction.

Jostling Stone   *see* MOUNTING BLOCK.

Joust   A combat between two mounted knights with lances. Often a mock combat as part of a tournament (*q.v.*).

Jowl   That portion of the head contained within the branches of the jaw bones.

Jowl Sweater   A form of cap with ear holes, overlapping under the throat and made from felt lined with oilskin, plastic or other waterproof material. Used to sweat off surplus fat which might make it difficult for a horse or pony to flex his head at the poll.

Juba Port   A rubber port which can be fastened on any mullen mouthpiece to prevent a horse getting his tongue over the bit. The bit should be adjusted fairly high in the mouth. A mullen mouth bit is always recommended for horses who have acquired this habit.

Judge (Racing)   An official appointed by the Jockey Club to place the first four horses in each race, or more if there are special prizes.

Judges, Panel of   Sometimes called a Jury. Most Societies and Associations maintain a panel of judges, qualified to judge general and special breeds; the British Show Jumping Association has a panel for show jumping classes under their rules. Lists are available to show executives.

Juger, se   French term meaning that the hindfeet touch down on the imprints left by the forefeet (*see* DÉJUGER, SE *and* MÉJUGER, SE).

Jumart   Erroneously believed to be the hybrid offspring of bull and mare or she-ass, or of a horse or ass and a cow.

Jumped   When a herd of wild horses are warned by a neigh from their leader (stallion) and gallop off, the American cowboy says they are 'jumped'.

Jumper's Bump   A term applied to the protuberance at the top of the croup, a formation erroneously supposed to increase a horse's power to jump.

'Jumping'   A coaching term for a wheeler which is cantering because it feels the pressure from the coach, which is 'overtaking' it.

Jumping Blind   A hunting term used to denote jumping through an untrimmed fence or over an overgrown (blind) ditch.

Jumping-lane   A long, narrow, fenced-in enclosure used in teaching a horse to jump. Different forms of jumps are placed at varying distances, and the horse can neither jump out of the lane, nor run out at the jumps; the exit is at the end of the lane. (Also known as a Weedon Lane.)

'Jumping Powder'   *see* STIRRUP CUP.

Jump-off (Barrage)   A jump-off is held to decide the winner of a show-jumping competition where there is a tie for first place.

Junior County Cup   *see* HURLINGHAM POLO ASSOCIATION LOW-GOAL CHAMPIONSHIP.

Jury   *see* JUDGES, PANEL OF.

'Justin Morgan'   Foaled in 1789, brought from Massachusetts to Vermont as a two-year-old, and named after his owner. A small bay stallion, his breeding was uncertain, but he is believed to have been sired by an English Thoroughbred, 'True Briton', out of a Wildair mare of Arabian extraction. His prepotency had an enormous influence on horse breeds in the United States and this horse was the founder of the Morgan Breed (q.v.).

Jute Rugs   Night rugs are usually made of jute. Jute is also used for the cheapest stable rollers. It is rarely a good investment in this respect.

Jutland   As the name suggests this horse originated from Jutland where it is still the most common breed. It came to the Danish islands at a very early date, and through skilful and consistent selection and with, at various times, infusion of Suffolk Punch (q.v.) and Yorkshire Coach Horse (q.v.) blood it has been improved to its present high level. The Jutland, which has an excellent temperament, is primarily an agricultural horse, although it is well suited for work in towns. It is of medium size, the body being of good width. The legs are massive with soft, smooth hair. It is generally chestnut in colour, but brown, bay, roan, black and grey Jutlands are also common.

Juvenile Show Jumping Grades   *see* GRADED HORSES.

* K *

Kabardin   These horses are found in the mountainous regions of the Caucasus, and are the result of the crossing of the native Mongol stock with Eastern sires of Persian or Arab blood. They are used both for saddle and pack work, and are exceptionally agile and sure-footed.

Kadir Cup, The   The competition for the Kadir Cup for pig-sticking in India was instituted in 1873 and first competed for in 1874 when it was won by Mr White of the 15th Hussars, on 'Hindoo'. It was competed for annually at the Meerut Tent Club meeting. With the exception of breaks during the Afghan war in 1879 and 1880 and the First World War in 1915 to 1918, the competition was held continuously until 1939. On the declaration of war in that year, the cup was left in the Royal Artillery Mess at Meerut and was subsequently taken to Kenya and later carried in the aeroplane of the Queen's Flight used by Princess Margaret on her return from there to England. The Cup is now displayed in the Indian Army Memorial Room at the Royal Military Academy at Sandhurst. The competition took its name from the rough uncultivated terrain by the banks of the Ganges-Kadir country, an ideal district for harbouring wild boar.

Kaolin Poultice   *see* ANTIPHLOGISTINE.

Karabair   Of mixed Mongol and Arab blood. This horse is a light saddle or pack horse of good conformation which is bred in the mountainous regions of Uzbekistan. The national game of 'goat-snatching' — in which one mounted man carries a goat while others try to take it from him in full gallop—has developed in this breed an exceptional agility and speed, while retaining a most tractable nature. Height 15.1–15.2 h.h. (153–154 cm).

Karabakh   This beautiful breed is found in the Caucasian districts and has greatly contributed in the past to the improvement of the Don horses (*q.v.*). They are similar to the highest class of Persian horse, that is to say they are predominantly Arabian in conformation, and with the dished face of the Arab as opposed to the straight profile of the Persian. Their characteristic golden colour is found nowhere else except in the Akhal-Teké (*q.v.*).

Karacabey   The native horse of Turkey bred at several state studs. Used for light agricultural work and as a saddle horse. Hardy and of good conformation. Height 15.3–16.1 h.h. (155–163 cm).

Kathiawari and Marwari   A pony found in Rajputna possessing some strong Arabian characteristics including inward-pointing ears and often with a long mane. All colours including piebald and skewbald. Height about 14.2 h.h. (144 cm).

Kave, Kaving   *see* PORTING.

Kay Collar   *see* RIM COLLAR.

Kazanka   A small Russian pony of some 13 h.h. (132 cm) in height allied to the Klepper (*q.v.*) (*see* VIATKA).

'Keep'   Pasture for grazing.

Keeper   Stitched leather loops to retain the straps of the bridle. Also the leather loop on the top end of a hunting whip to which the thong is attached.

Kehailan (Kehilan, Kehaylan, Koheilan, Koheili)   An Arabian generic term meaning pure-bred, and applied to the whole breed of pure Arabian horses.

Kelshie   *see* KLIBBER.

Kendrick Girth   A 1½ in (38 mm) twin-folded girth, joined in three places. Now virtually obsolete.

Kennel   A fox's bed above ground, or in a covert or hedgerow. To push him out is to unkennel him.

Kennel Huntsman   He is responsible for the management and feeding of hounds in kennel, and is often the first Whipper-in when the huntsman is an amateur.

Kennelman   One who works in the kennels under the huntsman or kennel huntsman.

Kennels   A collective term for the various buildings and yards comprising the quarters allotted to the pack.

Kentucky Derby   One of the three Classic Races in the U.S.A. (*q.v.*). It has been run annually without interruption since its inauguration in 1875, and its only change has been the lowering of the 1½ mile (2.41 km) distance to the present 1¼ miles (2.01 km), in 1896. The race is conditioned for three-year-olds and is run at Churchill Downs, Kentucky, on the first Saturday of May. For results *see page* 392.

Kentucky Futurity   An important class trotting race for three-year-olds, run annually at Lexington, Kentucky.

Kentucky Saddle Horse   *see* AMERICAN SADDLEBRED.

'Kept-up'   Said of a horse which is stabled during the summer: the converse of being turned-out or summered.

Keratoma   A horn tumour, i.e. a horny growth on the interior wall of the horn of the hoof. *Cause:* excessive activity of the horn-producing laminae following an injury, or the pressure of irritating matter in the foot, usually near the toe. *Symptoms:* inflammation and lameness; a fistula may form which will discharge pus. *Treatment:* all pressure should be removed from the area and a veterinary surgeon should be consulted.

Kerro Mouth   A wooden mouthpiece of lignum vitae employed in breaking bits but also found in Pelham form.

Kerry Pony   A robust and extremely hardy animal which, up to the beginning of the century, was in considerable demand for riding and driving.

Kersey   Coarse narrow cloth used for leg bandages and ankle boots (*q.v.*).

Key Bugle   A copper wind instrument, in appearance like a large cornet but with keys instead of valves. It was much used by musically disposed guards of the old stage coaches. Although it is said that they were prohibited on mail coaches, there are plenty of paintings by contemporary artists showing them in use.

Keys (Players)   Pieces of metal attached to mouthing bits to produce saliva and soften mouths.

Kiang   (*Equus heminus kiang*) The largest race of Asiatic wild ass inhabiting the Himalayas and Tibet, standing 13–14 h.h. (132–143 cm). Sandy red in colour with whitish underparts with a large heavy head, it resembles the Wild Horse, *Equus przevalskii przevalskii* (*q.v.*).

Kick Over the Traces   To throw off control, such as when a horse gets a leg over a trace.

Kicking   A vicious and dangerous habit. In the stable, pad the walls and door with rough leather packed with hay, straw or some soft padding. If kicking occurs when the horse is being ridden (when it is most dangerous), the head should be kept up, the corners of the mouth played on through the reins, and the whip applied to the shoulders. In harness, the habit is usually met with a kicking strap which passes through the loop above the crupper and is buckled at both ends of the shafts. It is not possible to prevent a horse which is being led, whether moving or stationary, from kicking.

Kicking Strap (in harness)   Only used if a horse is likely to kick (*see* KICKING).

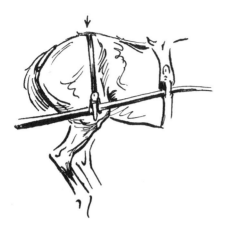

Kicking Strap

Kidney Link   The link at the bottom of the harness to which the pole chains are fastened.

'Kill, The'   When fox hounds roll over and kill the fox.

Kimberley Horse Disease (or **Walk-on Disease**)   Peculiar to Western Australia and the Northern Territory which includes the area known as the Kimberleys. *Symptoms:* loss of weight, somnolence, depression, yawning, muscle twitching about the head and neck, abnormal stance (leaning forward over the forelegs with hind legs extended, unco-ordinated gait, first dragging feet, particularly hind feet, later staggering, compulsive walking, usually in a straight line in the paddocks, but in circles in yards, often blundering into objects or fences. Jaundice and haemoglobinuria sometimes present in later stages. *Cause: Crotalaria retusa*, a plant that grows mainly on river flats subject to flooding. The poisonous principal is an alkaloid monocrotoaline. *Prevention:* keeping horses off areas where plant is prevalent.

Kimblewick; Kimbelwicke (U.S.A.)   A form of one-rein Pelham having a straight bit with small port, short cheek-piece and curb chain. Sometimes known as Spanish Jumping Bit (*see Plate* 6).

Kineton Noseband   A device attached to the bridle which by means of two semi-circles of leather-covered metal brings pressure upon the nose before there is any bearing on the bars of the mouth. Effective on a strong pulling horse. Sometimes called a 'Puckle' after its inventor who lived at Kineton.

King George V Cup   An individual Show Jumping award competed for annually under F.E.I. rules at the Royal International Horse Show, London. For results *see page* 405.

King George VI and the Queen Elizabeth Stakes   First run at Ascot in 1951 in celebration of the Festival of Britain, over 1½ miles (2.41 km) in July. For results *see page* 392.

Kink in the Tail   A permanent twist in the tail. It is unsightly, and may be cured by breaking and resetting the tail straight in splints.

Kiplingcotes Race   Founded by a body of foxhunters, and endowed by them in 1619, it is the oldest endowed race in the world. It is run over some four miles of old tracks and roads on the Yorkshire Wolds. There is evidence that the race was held 50 years earlier, for a husbandman on oath stated 'that he chauncinge to be at a Horse Runninge at Kypplingcote Eshe [Ashes or Ash] about Shrovetide last [1555] ...' Known as the 'Yorkshire Derby', the race was 'to be Ridd yearly on the third Thursday of March'. The winner takes the interest on the invested fund, the second, the entry fees, which may be greater in amount than that won by the winner. The race is open to any type of horse, each entry having to carry 10 stone. A veteran in attendance in 1875 stated: 'We have sometimes to cut through snow seven or eight feet thick for a passage for horses to run through, but we have always had our race ...'

Kirby Gate   Traditional venue 5 miles (8 km) from Melton Mowbray of opening meet of the Quorn Foxhounds.

Kirgiz   A breed of Russian Steppe horse from which has been developed the New Kirgiz used for saddle, harness and transport. Sure-footed and of outstanding stamina. Height 14.2–15.1 h.h. (144–153 cm).

Kladruber   A breed which takes its name from the place in Bohemia where it was bred at the Imperial Stud. It derived from Spanish horses imported to Austria and Bohemia from Spain and Italy, and from which it inherits typical characteristics of conformation, high action, a Roman nose and a long, heavy-crested neck. Selection was made in the direction of size, up to 17–18 h.h. (173–183 cm), and colour, black or white, forming the most imposing state carriage horses when used in teams of six or eight of one colour on State occasions.

Klebsiella   An equine venereal disease.

Klepper   Ponies supposed to have descended from native mares of the Baltic provinces of Livonia, Esthonia and of the islands of Dago and Oesel, crossed with eastern horses. Standing 13–15 h.h. (132–152 cm), they possess great strength and endurance, have a good outlook and a great ability in trotting. They are honest, and have a pleasing, intelligent countenance, being the reverse of mean, sour or pig-eyed.

Klibber   A saddle for Shetland ponies made of wood and used in the Shetland Isles. There is a basket on either side, called a 'Kelshie', used for carrying peat.

'Kluge Hans'   *see* ELBERFELD HORSES.

Knabstrup   An old Danish breed exclusively confined to spotted horses. It originated at the time of the Napoleonic wars. About 1808, Spanish troops stationed in Denmark left behind a spotted mare, 'Flaebehoppen', of exceptional speed and endurance, which became the foundation mare of the breed. There are now a number of stud farms in Denmark which foster the breed.

Knacker   A dealer in old horses. One who buys and slaughters worn-out horses. In East Anglia harness-makers were also called knackers as they used to dress their own leather and the horse-slaughterer and the harness-maker were in one business.

Knavesmire   The York racecourse.

Knee   The joint between the fore-arm and the cannon bone.

Knee, True   The stifle (*q.v.*), situated at the lower end of the thighs on the hindlegs, which corresponds to the human knee-cap (patella).

Knee-caps   A felt covering for the knees, reinforced with blocked leather and having two straps for fastening above and below the knee; used for walking exercise, or for travelling as protection against damage by slipping. The top strap should be tight, the lower one loose.

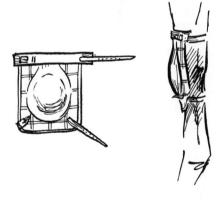

Knee-caps (Jumping)   A stout leather knee-cap lined with $\frac{3}{4}$ in (19 mm) foam rubber and having double, padded, elastic set straps on the top only. Used to school young horses over fixed timber, etc. Carter Pattern is the best known.

Knee-caps (Polo)   Protective devices designed to save acute distress to a rider through the bruises and abrasions that can result from efficient riding off (*q.v.*). Much used nowadays, especially in the U.S.A. and the Argentine.

Knee-caps (Polo)

Knee-caps (Skeleton)   There are various patterns, e.g. 'Freeknees'. Similar to a travelling knee-cap but lighter and without the rugging surround to the blocked caps. Used for jumping, exercise, etc.

Knee-halter, to   To couple the head to one foreleg by a rein or strap attached to the halter, closely enough to prevent the horse from moving freely.

Knee-roll   A pad or packing forming part of the front of the flap of a saddle. It can be of varying thickness and

Knee-roll

length to suit the rider's taste and is used for his greater security in the saddle and grip and steadiness while jumping.

'Knees and Hocks to the Ground'   A term denoting good short cannon-bones and shanks. (Also 'Well to the ground' and 'Near to the ground'.)

Knee Straps   A triangular piece of thin leather fitted with straps to wear round the knee when riding in trousers. The rough or 'flesh' side of the leather is on the outside to give better grip.

'Knifeboard' Bus   Early type of London horse-bus where the outside passengers (on the roof) sat back to back on long benches on either side. It was succeeded by the 'Garden-seat bus'.

Knobber, Knobbler   Male deer at two years old (terms now obsolete).

'Knocker'   A dealer's term of derision for a horse with cow-hocks (*q.v.*), sickled and standing far back. This last defect causes them to become soiled, while the cow-hocks, being so close together, 'knock' them clean.

Knots   Side-bones, formed by the ossification of the lateral cartilages on the anterior of the coronet.

Knuckling-over (also known as **Grogginess** or **Overshot Fetlock**)   Condition when the fetlock joints, fore and hind, protrude forward when the horse is at rest or collapse forward when it is in action; an indication of chronic lameness in the flexor tendons behind the joints. *Cause:* probably overwork with too heavy loads. *Treatment:* shoes off and prolonged rest (at grass in summer-time).

Kocholine   A jellylike grease for preserving all leather articles.

Konik   Several native breeds in Poland bear this name, which means 'small horse', and each breed has its own name. The Bilgoray Konik is said to be a direct descendant of the wild horse. In 1936 attempts were made to breed back to the wild horse from a stallion and mare which had the remarkable property of turning white in winter, and these met with some success. The Konik stands 11–14 h.h. (112–142 cm). The medium-sized pony is called 'Mierzyn', meaning between two sizes. The defects of size are more than compensated for by its many qualities. It is a small eater, making the most of poor food, extremely resistant to hunger, cold and all hardships, with amazing endurance and power for its size.

Kossiak A breeding herd of Russian Steppe Horses, consisting of about twenty mares and a stallion (*see* TABOON).

Koumiss, Kumis, Kumiss, Kumys Fermented liquor prepared from mare's milk.

Kournakoff Irons *see* COCK-EYED.

Kulan or Jigetai *(Equus hemionis kulan)* A type of wild ass found in Transcaspia, Turkestan, Mongolia and North China. In colour reddish yellow. Measures about 12.2 h.h. (124 cm).

Kumel A fox bed above ground.

Kurdistan A small horse found in the Kurdistan area of Persia (*see* JAF).

Kustanair A hardy Russian general-purpose horse, suitable for riding and draught work, descended from the ancient Kazakhs strain. There are three types: the steppe horse, massive, lacking in speed; riding type, lighter and adapted for riding; the basic type, a useful animal half-way between the other two. Average height: stallions, 15.2 h.h. (154 cm), mares 15 h.h. (152 cm). Bay and chestnut colour most common.

* L *

L (Racing) Length.

Lace Rein A rein in the handpart of which a lace is inserted and passed over and through in 'V' shapes. This rein gives a good grip.

Lacing *see* CROSSING FEET.

'Lad' One who looks after racehorses in stables, rides them in their work and accompanies them to race meetings. He may be of any adult age (*see* HEAD LAD).

Ladies' Races The Jockey Club sanctioned the introduction of Ladies' races for the first time on the flat at a meeting at Kempton Park on May 6 1972, the winner being Meriel Tufnell on 'Scorched Earth'. In 1974 women were allowed to compete against men in Amateur flat races. In 1975 applications for a professional jockey's licence will be permitted.

Lady's Phaeton *see* PARK PHAETON.

La Guérinière, François Robichon, de (1688–1751) Leading master of equitation in the mid-eighteenth century and considered the father of the modern classical school as known today. Author of *École de Cavalerie*, published in Paris in 1733.

Laid-on The place in a supposed line of scent at which a pack of hounds is urged to own the scent and to hunt on.

Lairage Horse transit camp.

'Lame Hand' A bad coachman. Also called a 'Spoon'.

Lameness, Intermittent In many cases, the cause may be rheumatism, in others, it may be the beginning of navicular disease (*q.v.*), or an unsuspected corn.

Laminae These appear as fine, very sensitive leaves, ranging between 500 and 600 according to the size of the foot, covering the external surface of the pedal bone and the lateral cartilages, and extending from the coronary cushion to the lower edge of the pedal bone. They interlock with the same number of horny laminae lining the interior surface of the wall, forming a secure union of the hoof with the sensitive foot.

Laminitis Inflammation of the sensitive laminae under the wall of the foot, caused by fast work on hard ground or by too much heating food and not enough exercise. If severe, it will cause structural changes within the hoof and 'dropped sole'. *Treatment :* give a bran mash, remove the shoes, stand the animal in a clay bed (*q.v.*) and consult a veterinary surgeon. Excellent results are often obtained nowadays from the injection of antihistamines. (Also known as Pony Gout.)

Lampas *Symptom :* a swollen condition of the roof of the mouth. *Cause :* sometimes associated with changing the incisor teeth in young horses. Often misdiagnosed when the condition of the mouth is normal, as an explanation of loss of appetite. *Treatment :* inadvisable, unless the diagnosis is confirmed by a veterinary surgeon.

Lampwick Girth A 3¼ in (8.3 cm) tubular wick suitable, owing to its weight and texture, for use in summer.

Lancer Bit A plain cheek curb bit with two rein slots; a military bit, sometimes used in polo. The 9th Lancer is made with an elbow. It is also useful for coaching where the leaders catch hold and carry the cheek.

Landau Invented at Landau, Germany, in 1757, this is an open carriage fitted with adjustable leather hoods for use as a closed vehicle when required. It was very popular in England from mid-Victorian times onwards, varying from the modest, single-horse type to the state (postillion-driven) landau.

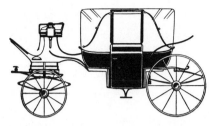

Landau

Landing The contact made by a horse with the ground on the far side of an obstacle.

Landing-side The far side (from the rider) of any obstacle to be jumped.

Landseer, Sir Edwin Henry, R.A. (1802–1873) Most famous Victorian animal painter. He received many royal commissions. His exceptional talents were often marred by sentimentality, but he painted many spectacular pictures, such as *The Hunting of Chevy Chase* and *The Stag at Bay.*

Lane Creeper A term applied to a New Forest Pony which leaves the Forest for the villages where it may cause damage to garden and other crops.

Lane-Fox Saddle A saddle much cut back at the withers.

'L'Année Hippique' The French edition of this annual was first published in 1943, and included a unique collection of some 300 articles and 8000 original photographs. Ceased publication 1972/3.

Laporte, George Henry (1799–1873) Painted animals, figures and hunting subjects. He was animal painter to the Duke of Cumberland. 43 engravings after his works were published in the Sporting Magazine (*q.v.*).

Lapping Traces Descriptive of where the inside trace of one leader passes the inside of the other and returns to its own bar.

Lariat A lasso used by riders and others for securing a steer or any other animal.

Lark To lark is to jump fences when hounds are not running, or on returning from hunting.

Lash A silk or whip-cord attachment to the end of the thong of a driving whip or hunting crop.

Latchford, Benjamin A well-known nineteenth century maker of bits, stirrup-irons and spurs, whose place of business was in Upper St Martin's Lane, London. He wrote *The Loriner* (1871). In the nineties spurs were known as Latchfords.

Latchfords Spurs. Jorrocks (*q.v.*) talks in one of his 'sporting lectures' of 'letting in the Latchfords'.

Lateral Aids Combination of two aids on the same side: left hand and leg; right hand and leg (*see* DIAGONAL AIDS).

Latigo Used on South American plantation saddles and is made of rawhide or other tough leather. The latigo is 4 or 5 ft (1·2–1·5 m) long, and there is one on each side of the saddle, hanging from a large ring. The latigo is threaded through the cinch ring back to the latigo ring and so on until there is just enough left to tie in. The whole is then pulled tight and tied to the latigo ring with a special type of knot.

Lawn Clippings Never feed these unless *absolutely* fresh — and then sparingly; to do otherwise invites a colic attack. They are, however, useful mixed in small quantities with chopped hay to entice a shy feeder.

Lawn Meet A meet of any type of pack, held at a house by the invitation of the occupier.

Lawton Gig Smart well sprung gig named after builder (*see* GIG).

Lay (Racing) To wager. To bet.

Lay on To put the main body of staghounds on the line after the tufters (*q.v.*) have driven the stag from covert. To set a pack of hounds on to where scent may be expected or on to the line of any hunted quarry.

Lazyback The back rest of the outside seat on a coach or a similar vehicle, which should be turned down when not in use. However, on a Road Coach it is fixed.

'Leadenhaller', A *see* BAG-FOX.

Leader Either of the two leading horses of a team ('near leader', 'off leader') or one driven horse which leads one or more.

Lead Harness Harness for leaders, as distinct from wheel harness.

Leading Jockey (Racing) The jockey winning most races in any given season. There are separate titles for flat racing and steeplechasing.

Leading Leg This always means the leading front leg, i.e. the leg strikes out forward during the 'second time' of the canter or gallop, while the three remaining legs are in support. In racing it is important that a horse should lead with his near-fore on a left-handed course, and with his off-fore on a right-handed course.

Leading on the Road The general idea is to lead on the right of the road against the traffic and walk or ride on the near side of the led horse, but this is little understood by motorists and is confusing to them and tends to dislocate the traffic. It is advisable, therefore, to lead on the *near* side of the road and from the *offside* of the horse, which cannot then swing its quarters into traffic, and is less likely to take fright with a man between him and the traffic. A horse should be trained from foalhood to lead from both sides.

Leading Reins Paddock lead reins are of web with a buckle and billet fastening, a snap hook, or a Y-fastening which passes through the bit rings and a central D before buckling. Leather lead reins are used for stallions in conjunction with a stallion chain. Paddock leads are 8 ft (2.43 m) long, stallion leads often considerably longer.

Leading Show Jumper of the Year *see* SHOWJUMPER OF THE YEAR, LEADING.

Lean Head One in which the muscles, blood vessels and bony protuberances show up distinctly. Usually neatly formed with a fine skin.

Leaping-head or **Leaping Pommels** *see* POMMELS.

Lease a Horse, to A recognized form of temporary ownership existing in breeding, racing, show jumping and showing. Length of term and monetary consideration a matter of negotiation.

Leasing Racehorse Horses may be leased from the owner for their racing career. The terms of the lease may be settled between the parties concerned, but the lease itself must be signed by the parties and lodged at the Racing Calendar Office.

Leasing Stallion A practical means of introducing the blood of a certain horse in some district for a season or more, whether to be travelled or otherwise. Also many are leased without reference to introducing the blood to any district but simply because of the lessee's particular fancy for the horse as a sire.

Leather Curb *see* HUMANE CURB.

Leather Punch A saddler uses a set of metal punches of varying sizes to make holes. A useful stable requisite is the hand type of punch, having the same action as a pair of pliers, with a revolving head fitted with variously sized punches.

'Leathers' Leather breeches.

Leathers, Stirrup Leather straps by means of which stirrup irons are attached to the saddle. The length of a leather can be gauged before mounting by placing the iron under the arm and extending the arm along the leather until the fingertips touch the side bar of the saddle. To make the stirrup irons lie where the rider may 'pick them up' readily, twist the leathers several times from right to left and then release.

Leech, John (1817–1864) Caricaturist and illustrator. He was a prolific contributor to *Punch*. He produced many coloured woodcuts of sporting subjects and illustrated most brilliantly *Mr Sponge's Sporting Tour* and *Handley Cross*, and other works by R. S. Surtees.

'Leery' Old time horseman's expression for a horse which, without being vicious or nappy, moves hesitatingly without much apparent heart in its work.

Left at the Post Term to describe a horse that is slow to take off at the start of a race and is left in the rear of other runners as they get away.

Left Half Pass A half pass to the left (*see* HALF PASS).

Left-hand Course A course where the horses run in an anti-clockwise direction, e.g. Aintree, Cheltenham, Doncaster and Epsom.

Leg, First The first half of a double event in betting.

Leg, Second The second half of a double event in betting.

Leg Boot A shaped rubber boot extending well above the knee which can be used in the same way as a leg bucket and with more safety.

Leg Bucket An oak or teak bucket, usually 17 in (43 cm) high, into which a horse's leg is placed for fomentation.

Legend of Eight Horses *see* EIGHT HORSES, LEGEND OF.

Leggings These are made in various leathers, pigskin, polo calf, box calf,

reversed calf (i.e. suède finish), and also in such materials as box cloth and canvas. They may be made to button or lace and hook, or to fix with metal thongs and slots, when they are known as 'Richmonds'. Leggings are worn with breeches and 'high-lows' (*q.v.*).

'Legs' The legs of riding boots, may be lined or single.

'Legs Out of One Hole' Descriptive of horses which are narrow chested and go close in front.

Leg Spray A circular piece of rubber hosing joined at the break by a T-connection to which a hosepipe can be fitted. The inside of the circle is perforated to allow water to be sprayed all round the leg. Used to combat puffy legs.

Leg-up The assistant should stand to the left of and somewhat behind the rider, and should grasp the rider's left leg (which should be sharply bent at the knee) above the ankle with the right hand. As the rider 'gives' or ducks to spring, the assistant should lift the leg firmly and somewhat sharply, enabling the rider to clear the saddle with his right leg and then sink into it. The rider's spring is essential to a neat and effective leg-up. When the rider is wearing highly-polished hunting boots, the groom should stand to the left of him and place both forearms, covered by the sleeves of his jacket, under the rider's boot; this prevents marking the polish.

Lemon-pied A hound having a white body with lemon-coloured markings.

Length The measurement from end to end of a horse used as a unit of distance in racing. The distance separating the leading horses at the finish of a race is judged in lengths, half-lengths, neck, head and short head.

Leopard-marking Where darker spots are widely distributed on a lighter background. One of the three group markings required by the British Spotted Horse Society (*see also* BLANKET-MARKING and SNOWFLAKE-MARKING).

'Lepper'   Colloquial Irish hunting term for a jumper—'A good lepper'.

'Let-down'   A term used to imply a well-conditioned and normal body, being the converse of 'tucked-up' (*q.v.*).

Leucoderma   A condition in which white patches appear on the hairless parts of the horse (round the eye and under the tail), due to a lack of pigment. They are unsightly and permanent, but not harmful.

'Leu-in' (Hunting)   To put hounds into covert.

Levade   High School movement in which the horse raises itself from the ground with the fore-feet and then draws them in whilst the hind quarters, deeply bent in the haunches, bear the entire weight of the body.

Levade

Level Mover   A horse that is true and level at the walk, trot, and canter, with the toes of the forelegs pointing to the front, and having the correct distance between the pairs of fore and hind legs, and firm and steady hocks.

Liberty   A horse shows liberty when it moves with freedom, using its shoulders and covering the ground freely.

Liberty Horses   Circus horses which perform evolutions in the ring, un-

handled and unridden, controlled only by the Ring Master. By reason of their presence, beauty and honesty of work and handy size Arab stallions are generally preferred.

Lice   Parasites found commonly on long-coated horses in poor condition, particularly in the early months of the year. Being blood suckers they aggravate the degree of debilitation shown and give rise to a blotchy appearance to the coat. *Symptoms :* the horse rubs itself on any convenient object and the hair comes away leaving smooth bare places more particularly at the poll, throat, crest, shoulder and flanks. *Treatment :* clip and singe to get rid of parasites and nits. Powder the line of the back with an animal parasitic dusting powder (not horticultural). The condition is unknown in well-groomed horses.

Licence, Racecourse   This must be renewed annually, and all meetings must be sanctioned by the Stewards of the Jockey Club. Applications for fixtures must be made to the Jockey Club by March 1st and must be accompanied by an audited statement of accounts for the preceding year.

Licence, Trainer   Every trainer of a horse running under the rules of Racing must obtain an annual licence (fee: one sovereign) from the Stewards of the Jockey Club. Applications must be sent in for consideration before March 1st. Any trainer running a horse without a licence is liable to a fine or to be made a disqualified person at the discretion of the Stewards. Women were first granted licences to train horses under Jockey Club rules in 1966.

Lichen   A somewhat similar complaint to Mallenders (*q.v.*) but more of a papular form, affecting the skin on the back of the legs. *Treatment :* as for Mallenders.

Lift   A hunting term used when the hounds are taken by a huntsman to a point where he thinks the fox has moved, or where the fox has been seen.

Ligamentum Nuchae The long ligament extending from poll to withers, which supports the head. It is divided into two parts, a funicular (rope-like) portion and lamella (fan-like) portion. It is the funicular portion which becomes necrotic and gives rise to poll evil (*q.v.*).

'Light Horse' An equestrian illustrated monthly founded in 1950 as *Show Jumping*. It was changed to its present title in 1951. It covers all aspects of light horse activities, especially show jumping, horse trials, point-to-points, bloodstock breeding and National Hunt racing. Published by D. J. Murphy, Ltd.

Light Horse The name of a group comprising hunters, hacks and riding horses in general, but not Thoroughbreds and light harness horses.

Lightness The horse's perfect obedience to the slightest indications of hand and leg, consequent to the disappearance of all resistances.

Light of Bone Insufficient circumference of bone immediately below the knee suggesting weakness: 'short of bone'.

Limekilns, The Situated at Newmarket on the eastern side of the town and well-known for its summer gallops. Normally open only in dry weather.

Limousin A half-bred horse of English blood, which derives its name from the region in France where it is bred. Big-boned, standing often 17 h.h. (173 cm), it represents a somewhat heavy-weight hunter, as it can gallop and jump, but, being late in development, it cannot be hunted before it is 7 years old. A similar breed is the Charolais, though smaller, 15–16 h.h. (152–162 cm), and lighter.

Linchpin The pin passed through the end of a vehicle's axle-tree to keep the wheel in place; it is still used as the sole means of securing the wheels of some farm waggons and carts.

Lincolnshire Handicap The first big race of the flat-racing season, now run at Doncaster, formerly at Lincoln. It is the first leg of the Spring Double, the Grand National being the second.

Lincolnshire Trotter A type of horse well-known at one time in the county. The breed or type probably became merged in the general light harness horse of the Eastern counties as typified by the Hackney of the period.

Line The trail of scent on which the pack hunt their fox.

Line-breeding The mating of individuals having a common ancestor some generations removed. It is used to intensify a desired hereditary virtue.

Linen Bearings A covering of linen sewn to the serge panel of a saddle.

Linhay (Cart-Linhay) An open farm shed for housing farm-carts.

Linseed The seed of flax, generally used in the form of mucilage, tea or gruel, and often added to moisten manger food when this is of a constipating nature. *Linseed Mash :* a pint of well-boiled linseed or linseed gruel is added to a bran mash. The gruel is made by soaking $\frac{1}{4}$ lb (113 g) of linseed in a bucket of cold water for two hours, bringing it to the boil and simmering it for several hours. Linseed gruel does not keep for more than one day.

Lipizzaner The breed was founded in about 1580 by the Archduke Charles, son of the Emperor Ferdinand I of Austria, who introduced Spanish, Italian and Arabian horses to breed a high-quality parade horse at Piber. Taking their name from Lipizza, the location of the stud farm, these horses are of amiable character, strong and well developed, with a rather long body on short legs and a heavily crested neck, large intelligent eyes with a convex face—a legacy of the Spanish horse.

They can be of any colour but only grey stallions are used in the famous Spanish Riding School of Vienna (*q.v.*). There are six lines: Conversano, Maetoso, Neapolitano, Pluto, Siglavy and Favory. The Lipizzaner with its grace and dignity makes a splendid harness horse. It is also used in agriculture and is also bred in Yugoslavia and Bulgaria.

Lip Markings   *see* FLESH MARKS. In any written description of the horse it should be stated whether they embrace the whole or a portion of either lip (*see Plate* 21).

Lip-strap   A thin leather strap fastened to one side of the ring of a curb-bit, threaded through a special link provided in the curb chain and buckled at the other end to the corresponding ring of the curb-bit. The strap keeps the curb chain from overhanging the lower lip, and the cheeks of the bit from turning. It also stops the horse from catching hold of the cheek of the bit with its lower teeth.

Lip Tattoo   Identification marks tattooed on the lips of horses. Sometimes also used on the ear. In some cases animals have suffered permanent nerve damage from this tattooing.

Lips   They should be thin and carried closed. A drooping under-lip is unsightly and is supposed to be a sign of lack of courage.

List   A dark stripe along the back (*see* DORSAL STRIPE). Also the particular place where the hair meets and runs in different directions on a horse's loins.

Lithuanian Heavy Horse   Used for city transport and agriculture in the U.S.S.R., this breed is based on the Zemaituka (*q.v.*). Predominant colours are grey, bay and chestnut; with deep chest and strong legs. Stallions 16.2 h.h. (164 cm). Mares 15·3 h.h. (155 cm).

Litter   A vehicle formerly used for the transport of invalids or the elderly. It contained a couch and was enclosed by curtains. It was carried by means of poles, by men or horses.

Litter   Straw bedding in stables.

Litter   The puppies produced by a hound bitch at one whelping.

Liverpool Bit   The most usual type of bit used for driving with three slots on the bar thus giving alternate amount of control on the horse's mouth.

Liverpool Bit

Liverpool Gig   Very similar to the Lawton gig (*q.v.*).

'Liverpool Horse'   A term implying that the horse referred to is capable of jumping the Grand National Course.

Livery, Horse At   The customer's property in a livery-stable as a boarder, fed, cared for, or turned out at the owner's request at an agreed sum per week, month or year.

Livery Cloth   A name given to the fine, faced wool cloth used in the manufacture of paddock clothing.

Livery Stables   A term applied to an establishment which offers to take in horses at livery, usually in conjunction with those at bait, or for hire (*see* BAIT).

Live with Hounds   A term meaning the ability of a horse to keep up with hounds when they are running very fast.

'Loaded' Shoulder   Excessive thickness of muscle lying over the region of the shoulder.

'Lobbing and Sobbing' When a horse rolls about and is blown after an exhausting gallop.

Lobuno Criollo (*q.v.*) term for dark smoky blue colour with black points.

Lock The amount of turn possible in the forecarriage and front wheels of a vehicle. While coaches have a quarter distance lock, many other carriages have a full lock allowing a turn in a small space.

Lockjaw *see* TETANUS.

Locote An outlaw horse of the West. The name derives from locote, a poisonous prairie weed which, if eaten, is said to turn a horse mad.

Locura A horse disease in Argentina known as horse madness. It causes partial or complete blindness and disorganizes nerve centres, paralysis sets in and death occurs within forty-eight hours. Animal vaccination is now used.

Lodging Rooms Hounds' sleeping quarters, containing benches about 1½ ft (45 cm) from the ground, running round three sides and almost completely occupying the floor space.

Lofts Over stables, lofts are often a cause of trouble to ears and eyes, owing to dust and particles of forage coming through crevices. It is better for the stable ceiling to be plastered.

Log-headcollar A solid block of lignum vitae wood, with a hole bored through the centre, through which a rope is passed and knotted. The other end is passed through a ring in the manger and allows limited scope for movement.

Loin Cloth A rainproof cloth placed over the loins when cart or van horses are likely to stand out in wet weather.

Loins That part of the back extending down to either side of the spinal vertebrae which lies immediately behind the saddle.

Log-headcollar

Lokai This breed from the foothills and valleys of Uzbekistan is a rather heavy harness-type. Like the Karabair (*q.v.*), the game of 'goat-snatching' has developed in these horses an amazing agility and speed, while retaining a docile disposition.

London Cart Horse Parade Society (Founded 1890). *Objects:* to improve the general condition and treatment of the London cart horses. The Society held an Annual Parade of cart horses in Regent's Park, London, on Whit Monday. In 1966 the Society was amalgamated with the London Van Horse Parade Society under the name of the London Harness Horse Parade Society (*q.v.*).

London Colour A trade term for the light colour usually used in new saddlery.

London Harness Horse Parade Society Founded in 1966 by the amalgamation of the London Cart and Van Horse Parade Societies (*qq.v.*). The

Annual Parade is now held on Easter Monday each year in Regent's Park, London.

London Tan   One of the shades in which saddlery leather is produced, being of a deeper brown shade than London Colour.

London Van Horse Parade Society (Founded 1904) *Objects :* the improvement of the general condition and treatment of van and light draught horses employed for business purposes, and the encouragement of drivers to take a humane and individual interest in the horses under their care. In 1966 it joined the London Cart Horse Parade Society to form the London Harness Horse Parade Society (*q.v.*).

Lone Eagle   *see* NORTON PERFECTION.

Longeing   *see* LUNGEING.

Longeing Rein   *see* LUNGEING REIN.

Longest Race   The longest races on the flat are the Queen Alexandra Stakes and the Brown Jack Stakes, both run over just over 2¾ miles (4.4 km) at Ascot in the summer. The longest race in France is the Prix Gladiateur of 4 miles (6.4 km).

Long Hay   Uncut hay which may be fed or made up into trusses, bales or stacks.

'Long in the Tooth'   A term descriptive of an old horse.

Long Jump Record   Held by Lt. Col. Lopez del Hierro of Spain on the Anglo-Arab 'Amado Mio' which jumped 27 ft 2¾ in (8.30 m) at Barcelona in 1951 under F.E.I. (*q.v.*) regulations.

Long Reining   The driving of a young horse by the trainer on foot. Most movements can be taught without the horse suffering the weight of the rider's body. It is said to produce more finesse in training before backing than is obtainable by lungeing, though this is debated by some experts. The trainer has good control due to the 'outer' rein

and should be able to place the horse where he will with complete control of pace.

Long Reins   These should consist of two separate webbing reins fitted with leather billets to prevent twisting, and each should be about 25 ft (7.6 m) long. They must not be fastened or buckled together. Tapered cotton plough lines are good substitutes, as these do not catch the wind and are easier to manipulate.

Long Tom   A racing term for a hunting whip. The trainer or his assistant carries one to encourage horses to start on the gallops.

Lonsdale, Hugh Cecil Lowther, Fifth Earl of (1857–1944)   M.F.H. Woodland Pytchley, Cottesmore and Quorn, he may be said to have been associated with all activities in the horse world throughout his long life. A dominant figure for years at the International Horse Show (*q.v.*) at Olympia.

Lonsdale Girth Straps   Straps which extend well beneath the saddle flap and used with a special short girth. This system removes the bulk of the girth buckles from under the thigh and is frequently employed on dressage and jumping saddles.

Lonsdale Waggonette   A luxurious form of waggonette with low-hung rounded body and folding hoods. Introduced by the fifth Earl of Lonsdale.

'Looker'   One who, for payment, 'watches' horses or cattle on unfenced marsh land which is surrounded by dykes. The name has been used for centuries on Romney Marshes, Sussex.

Loose Box   The average size is about 10 ft by 12 ft (3 × 3.65 m) and 12 ft (3.65 m) high. It has great advantages over the stall, which is old-fashioned but was built for economy where many horses were stabled. Horses thus stabled can move at ease, take limited exercise, and lying down and rising become simple movements which is not the case when horses are tied up in stalls.

Loose Box

Loose-headed Said of a horse which runs free of control, e.g., while out at grass.

Loose Rein A rein which hangs loosely, without contact between the horse's mouth and the rider's or driver's hands.

Lope The characteristic gait of a cowpony; an easy, uncollected canter.

Lop Ears Ears which tend to flop forwards and downwards or downwards to each side, giving a dejected appearance. Horses having such are usually quiet and generous, and many say that a lop-eared horse is never a bad horse. Many good racehorses are blemished in this way. Rare in Arabs.

Lord Mayor's State Coach Built in 1757 by Berry and Barker of Holborn, and in the Lord Mayor's Procession is drawn by six 'heavy horses' wearing the State harness made in 1833. It weighs 3 ton 16 cwt (3 t 725 kg). The body of the coach is supported on four black leather braces fastened with gilt buckles bearing the City Arms. The paintings on the panels are attributed to Cipriani, but this is not an established fact. Brakes were first fitted to the coach in 1951.

Loriner A manufacturer of bits, spurs, stirrups and minor steel adjuncts of a horse's harness.

Loriners Company, The The Masters, Wardens, Assistants and Commonalty of Loriners of the City of London, properly known as the Worshipful Company of Loriners; the Company ranks 53rd in order of precedence. The earliest known reference to this Livery Company is one made in 1245, relating to the representation of those concerned in the manufacture of bits, spurs and stirrups.

Losing Flesh Descriptive of a horse that is becoming debilitated, and suggests faults in management of feeding or watering, or the presence of worms, indigestion or bad teeth. It is necessary to ascertain the cause before giving treatment. If the horse is stabled, restriction of water is the usual cause.

'Lost Shoes' A Leicestershire term implying 'dead beat'.

'Lot of Horse in a Little Room, A' A reference to a horse that is close to the ground, compact, short-coupled, and has good bone.

Lowndes Pelham This is peculiar for the top loop of the cheek, which has a loose swivel sometimes known as a 'Sefton top'. This eliminates poll pressure and is frequently used on the cheeks of an egg link Pelham.

Lowther, Viscount In 1666, Lord Lowther took by road from Lowther Castle, Westmorland, the family pack of hounds for the purpose of hunting what is now the Cottesmore country, with which the Lowther family have long been associated.

Lowther Riding Bit In curb bits, this refers to the type of cheek where the curb rein ring drops from the hole in the cheek instead of being of the usual pattern which has a neck (*see* ARKWRIGHT BIT).

Lozenge A round piece of leather that may be fitted round a bit at the side of a horse's mouth. It is generally used to straighten a horse that hangs from its bit on one side, or to stop chafing at the angle of the lips.

Lucerne   A leguminous plant of great food value (*see* ALFALFA).

Lugging Bit   *see* ANTI-LUG.

Lundy Ponies   Of New Forest origin. Carefully selected mares and fillies were taken to the island in 1928 with two stallions, one being of 'mixed' blood, the other being a Thoroughbred.

Lungeing   (Previously known as Longeing.) An early stage in training when, by means of a single rein attached to the cavesson bridle, the young horse can be circled to left and to right, made to walk, trot and canter and to halt and get used to and obey words of command.

Lungeing Rein   (previously known as Longeing rein) This should be of tubular webbing, about 25 ft (7.6 m) in length, having a swivel billet at the bit end and a hand loop at the other. Can also be made with a swivel snap hook attachment. It is fastened to one of the rings on the noseplate of the breaking cavesson.

Lungeing Whip   A long whip with a light thong either made of cane or having a steel or fibreglass centre bound with gut. An essential part of lunging equipment.

Lung-worm   A species found in both horses and donkeys which, unless treated, progresses and causes parasitic bronchitis. Symptoms can be confused with other forms of lung trouble. The victim develops a hard dry cough and suffers an overall depreciation, loss of flesh with the typical unhealthy-looking condition of the coat.

The infestation can be passed on to other horses and donkeys. Prevention and treatment are to be found in dosage of equine lung-worm medicine under veterinary advice. Beyond loss of condition no other effects seem apparent.

Lurrie   Lancashire name for a flat-bodied four-wheeler (dray).

Lusitano   Originally the Portuguese Army horse, also used for light farm work and trained for the bull-ring. Usual colour is grey. Height: 15–16 h.h. (152–162 cm).

Lying Down   This should be encouraged by the provision of sufficient space and bedding.

Lymphangitis   Inflammation of the absorbent vessels, most frequently affecting the hind legs, and generally appearing on Monday morning after Sunday's rest, perhaps through overfeeding; it mostly affects sluggish and gammy-legged heavy horses. *Symptoms :* an attack is sometimes shown by a shivering fit or sudden and extreme lameness in one leg, showing great pain when touched and sometimes considerable swelling of the limb. *Treatment :* bandage with soft meadow hay, not too tightly twisted round the limb, commencing at the foot, rolling lightly and loosely up to the top of the affected part; when this is in position, soak with several pailsful of cold water, repeating every three or four hours. Feed on bran mashes with the addition of up to 4 oz (113 g) of Epsom salts and exercise whenever or as soon as possible. A veterinary surgeon may inject antihistamine, which often cuts short an attack.

* M *

M (Racing) Mile.

M. and M. Mountain and Moorland.

M.F.H. Master of Foxhounds.

M.F.H.A. Master of Foxhounds Association.

M.H. Master of Harriers.

M.R.C.V.S. Member of the Royal College of Veterinary Surgeons.

M.S.H. Master of Staghounds.

Macs Mackintosh racing breeches sometimes worn by jockeys when racing in bad weather.

'Made' A horse is said to be 'made' when its education for riding and/or driving is complete.

'Made-hunter' A hunter properly schooled to negotiate a hunting country with comfort and safety. One definition is said to run thus: the outline and shape of a cob, the spirit and breeding of a racehorse, the size and scope of a carriage-horse and the manners and action of a park hack.

'Made the Hit' Said of a hound when it has found the scent of the hunted fox (*see* OWN THE LINE).

Madison Square Garden *see* NATIONAL HORSE SHOW (U.S.A.).

Madrina *see* TROPILLA.

Magenis Snaffle The mouth has slits into which are set revolving rollers which work loosely (often miscalled McGuinness). Prevents a horse evading the bit by crossing the jaws. A popular bit for 'strong' horses (*see* Plate 6).

Mahogany Tops Brown leather tops to black hunting boots (*see* DRESS).

Maiden (Racing) A maiden for flat racing is a horse of either sex which has never won a flat race, except for minor exceptions like matches. Similarly, a maiden for steeplechasing is a horse of either sex which has never won a steeplechase or hurdle-race (point-to-points, matches etc. excepted).

Maiden Allowance A special allowance given in some races for a horse which has never won a race.

Maiden Mare and **Maiden** Different definitions exist. The Hunters Improvement and Light Horse Breeding Society give: 'a mare which has never been put to a stallion'; another: 'one carrying her first foal'.

Maiden Race A race confined to maiden horses at the start of the race (*see* MAIDEN (RACING)).

Mail Axle The safest type of axle, as introduced on mail coaches, in which the wheel is secured by three nuts.

Mail Coach Specially designed and painted as a Royal vehicle, i.e. black with maroon panels and scarlet undercarriage and wheels, and decorated with the Royal cypher. The mail coach was run under government contract before the invention of railways, and was introduced by John Palmer in 1784 to supersede the carrying of mails by men on horseback. The coach carried only nine passengers (four inside and five on top), as opposed to the sixteen on a road or stage coach (*q.v.*), no seats being available on the back since this area was occupied solely by the guard who had the mails under his care—as well as his feet—in the hind boot.

Mail Phaeton The heaviest type of phaeton for a pair, this was built on a perch, with mail axles and coach springing as in a mail coach.

Main Bar The largest of the three bars used in team driving (*see* 'BARS').

Maize This grain, rather less flesh-forming than oats, should be fed at least a year old, but, being very heating,

Mail Phaeton

it must be used with caution and is best fed with oats to horses in moderate and slow work. Flaked maize fed by itself is a good food for all classes of horses. In the U.S.A. it is always known as corn.

'Make and Break'   A term sometimes used for breaking in a young horse.

'Makes a Noise'   Unsound in wind, i.e. Whistling or Roaring.

Mallein Test   A test carried out for the detection of glanders in horses, mules or donkeys—usually suspects or in-contacts. It is applied by injecting mallein into or under the skin. Mallein is prepared from artificial cultures of *Pfeifferella mallei*—the casual organism of glanders—and its use is comparable to that of tuberculin for detecting tuberculosis in cattle.

Mallenders   Sub-acute or chronic inflammation of the skin at the back of the knee joint, with a water discharge causing the hair to stick out and eventually fall off, leaving a scurfy thickening of the skin; a common complaint in cart-horses when out of condition and those with thick gammy legs. *Treatment:* attend to condition, change diet, give a mild laxative, followed by a tonic, and dress the affected parts (which should not be washed) twice a week with a small quantity of 10 per cent oleate of mercury well rubbed in.

Mallet   Polo stick (*q.v.*).

Mameluke Bit   A curb bit with a ported mouth to the centre of which is attached a large ring. Also known as the Turkey Curb. Sometimes confused with the Turkish Curb, which is similar except for having loose eyes at the top of the cheek which reduce poll pressure.

Manada (South American)   A group or herd of wild mares collected by a mustang stallion. Depending upon the virility, courage and determination of the mustang concerned, this would vary from 6 or 8 to 50 or more. Manadas of about 100 have been quoted.

'Mancha'   A Criollo pony, joint hero with 'Gato' of Tschiffely's Ride (*see also* CRIOLLO, and TSCHIFFELY, A. F.).

Manchero   A Spanish word denoting one who not only journeys on horseback, but also makes the schooling, care and comfort of his horse his first consideration.

Manchester Team   *see* TRANDEM.

Mane   The long hair flowing from the top of the neck (crest).

Mane-drag   A comb affixed to a handle and used for trimming and dragging a rough mane.

Manège   A covered enclosure for the teaching of equitation or the schooling of horses.

Manège Figures   *see* SCHOOL FIGURES.

Mane Layer   A contrivance for making an unruly mane lie in place. It consists of two metal bars covered in rubber, hinged at one end and fastening with a butterfly nut at the other. The mane is placed between the bars and the weight of the device makes the mane lie flat.

Mane Thread   Heavy linen thread used in plaiting manes.

Mangalarga   A Brazilian horse descended from the Criollo (*q.v.*) and founded by a Portuguese Altér (*q.v.*) stallion about a hundred years ago. Height about 14.3 h.h. (145 cm).

Mange There are three forms: sarcoptic, psoroptic and symbiotic; the first being the most serious and notifiable by law. Mange is extremely infectious and the horse must be isolated and not worked. Sarcoptic usually starts on the head or neck, and later spreads everywhere. Psoroptic begins in the same way, but is due to a different mite. Symbiotic is usually confined to the legs and the root of the tail, and is the cause of stamping in the stable at night and the consequent loosening of the shoes and damage to the floor. Treatment is the same in all cases: isolate the affected animal and disinfect everything. Give a cooling diet and consult a veterinary surgeon.

Manger For feeding horses, these should be of iron or hard wood, wide enough to enable the horse to eat comfortably and deep enough to prevent the horse from wasting food by pushing it out with his nose. There are various designs, with or without a receptacle for water and a hay-rack attached; a manger is sometimes fitted into a wall-angle. Overhead hay-racks should be avoided, since falling dust and seeds may affect the horse's eyes.

Mangolds These should not be fed during the year they are grown (*see* TURNIPS).

Manipur A pony bred from time immemorial in Manipur State, Assam. Early manuscripts record that in the seventh century, the then reigning king of Manipur introduced polo played on ponies bred in that state. The pony is believed to be bred from Mongolian-Arab stock, and is small, 11–13 h.h. (112–132 cm), with a proportionate body, sturdy and sure-footed. The head is rather long, but of a gentle appearance, and set on a clean, strong muscular neck; the legs are of good quality with strong knees and hocks (*see* BURMESE or SHAN).

Manners A horse's obedience to the will of his rider, given in a generous, willing fashion.

'Man-o-War' The most famous of American racehorses. Foaled in 1917 near Lexington, Kentucky, he died of a heart attack 30 years later, having earned for his owner $1 million in prize money, stud fees and the sale of his foals. He was only once beaten in a race and was a most successful sire, one of his sons, 'Battleship', winning the 1938 English Grand National. In tail male he descended from the 1853 Derby winner, 'West Australian', and his dam was a daughter of the 1903 Derby winner, 'Rock Sand'.

Manual of Horsemastership The well-known Army *Manual of Horsemastership, Equitation and Animal Transport*, on which in pre-mechanized Army days the whole cavalry and artillery were trained.

Manure The accumulated excreta of the horse, a most valuable fertilizer.

Marchador Gaucho (*q.v.*) term for a fast rolling gait between a trot and a canter.

Mare The female equine animal which has attained the age of four years.

Care of the Mare and Foal ∗ I. M. Yeomans

Of first importance in the care of a mare and foal is the avoidance of breeding at all unless there are proper fields, fences and facilities available, and at least one person with some previous experience. Bloodstock breeding is usually in the hands of people able to afford to keep their mares at public studs or to employ good stud men at home to give the animals their entire attention, but sometimes a novice will set out to breed racing stock, and very frequently it is the novice who gets attracted by the idea of hunter or pony breeding. Basically the rules for breeding are the same for all types, with obvious modifications according to class. If the breeder will only decide always to take more trouble rather than less, and always to choose the safer way, he will stand a far better chance of success than the one who delights in being careless, using such futile phrases as 'They must look out for themselves here' or 'I do not believe in coddling animals'—which remarks you will find are never used by the successful breeder.

Breeding horses under suitable conditions is a delightful thing, under unsuitable conditions a constant worry and disappointment leading to considerable financial loss. Nobody with only one or two small paddocks should consider breeding a foal, not only because a brood mare eats an amazing amount of grass and needs constant change, but the foal will very soon be past the stage of running beside its mother and will need to be weaned and have a suitable companion and paddocks available away from the mare. Very many unfortunate foals have damaged themselves seriously and even fatally through trying to jump fences back to their mothers or to other horses. In addition to space, the fences must be considered. Many people have become so used to barbed wire that it is taken for granted, and hundreds of young horses are damaged by it yearly, frequently in a very serious manner, even young foals being exposed to the risk, which really is nothing less than cruelty. Barbed wire must have reduced the financial value of horses by thousands of pounds through the numerous accidents that have happened.

If we decide that our land and fences are good enough, the mare must be looked at with a cool, calm eye, and that fatal phrase, 'She *might* breed something good', forgotten. There are, of course, instances of the ugly mare, or the mare who could only win a little selling race, producing great stock, but these cases are so very rare and instances of failure so numerous that it is far better to start with a mare who is right in the greatest number of ways possible.

In the case of bloodstock, blood and performance and, most of all, performances of the tail-female forbears of the mare, are of the greatest consideration.

In the case of hunters it should be make and shape and, above all, soundness, also her record of temperament and endurance in her work.

In the care of the mare it is not only important to choose the right stallion for her, but also the right stud: not only has their care of the mare and foal to be of the highest standard, but they must be aware of the need for the greatest vigilance concerning the rise in rhinopneumonitis — contagious abortion — that has plagued many of the studs in the past few years; often traceable to imported mares, there have been 'storms' at some of the best Thoroughbred studs. Every mare that slips or has a dead foal or whose foal dies within a few days should be suspect and the veterinary surgeon called to have the foal's carcase clinically examined for the dread bug. (In 1971 there were more than usual found in a given number of carcases examined.) Until that time the mare must be isolated, washed down, her feet having special care, the bedding burnt and all contact with other mares avoided by attendants with unwashed boots, etc. When the mare has been passed clean it is quite safe for her to be covered a month later.

All responsible studs have all barren mares swabbed (uterine secretions collected by the veterinary surgeon and clinically examined) before service, and any that 'turn' may also be so examined. All are combining to stamp out the expensive and dismal trouble. But it may be felt that *some* of the smaller studs with less expensive stallions may not be following the code, thereby keeping the disaster alive. With small pony mares it is not usual to find the bug and it is difficult to examine them unless the vet has specially made small instruments. (Terrible results have happened with manual examinations of too-small mares.) No stallion owner should allow his horse to cover a barren mare unless it has been passed 'clean' by the vet. Only by our united efforts can we avoid the sad losses that have happened so often. Mares once cleaned up and breeding again need not cause any further worry.

Great progress has also been made by top veterinary surgeons into other causes of infertility in mares, such as the level of progesterone, but one might also say that the mare owner who thinks the mare must be vetted all the time is greatly mistaken; most mares do very nicely on their own and the less fiddling about with them the better in normal circumstances.

The ideal time for any mare to foal is about the first week in April (assuming, naturally, that she has been properly cared for and is not poor, a state no brood mare should reach) because flies are not much in evidence and the foal is able to spend most of its time lying down in peace, also the grass is growing to its best and will increase the mare's milk at the time when the foal needs more. Therefore, the mare should go to stud about the end of April. She should at the time be out and not muscled up with work, in good condition and free of worms: some Thoroughbred mares are covered when in training and win races afterwards, but this is not a very usual practice and is generally arranged because the mare has the maddening habit of going 'amiss' just on the very day she is in some special race.

On the mare's return from stud there is not much to be done as long as she has plenty of grass and a *frequent change of field*, clean water in a trough to avoid awkward slopes and the drag of muddy places to get water, which is very often polluted anyway. She should have a companion who is quiet and sensible and will not lead her in mad gallops, and she must be kept away from geldings. All stud grooms see red when a mare owner complains that the mare has 'turned' to the horse and, when asked, has to admit that there has been a gelding with her or over the fence, many geldings being surprisingly given to teasing a brood mare. In the warm weather the mare can stay out at night and, as long as she is quiet and peaceful, all is well.

The mare should never be allowed to go down in condition, and a deaf ear must be turned to those extraordinary people who, in spite of all the evidence against it, still say a brood mare should not be fat! About the first week in September, the mare should be given some oats daily (Thoroughbred mares are corn fed all the year), but in good weather she need not be brought in at night yet unless the season is bad; often horses will show signs of chill in the early autumn when it is wet because their coats have not yet had time to grow. Cod liver oil should be added to the mare's feed once a day, say from about September 1st. Practically all horses take it very readily, a convenient way being to rub it into dry bran and add it to the feed of crushed oats, barley and flaked maize. And here one must say that these are 'conventional' feeds as opposed to a newer type now widely used—cubes. It is better in all things not to get stubbornly fixed to an idea, remembering the need for variety in all things, because the brood mare needs to *enjoy* her feeds as well as eating because she must. However much one may know about feeds which have all the 'essentials', there still remains the importance of varying flavours and the freshness of things such as cod-liver-oil (which oxidizes on contact with air, so losing much of its first values), chopped carrots, *newly* crushed oats and (very important) good bran. The last named is a most important item in the brood mare's diet. She should have plenty of mashes, some made with boiled linseed, for two or three weeks before foaling, and some mash with the corn *every* day when the grass is past its best. She urgently needs a bran mash soon after foaling and for some hours later, about four or five in the first day perhaps, with boiled oats in the later ones and a sprinkle of flaked maize perhaps. The milk production has now to be considered, and tempting the appetite is as good as anything. This soft feeding will greatly help to avoid the constipation in new-born foals that has killed so many. Should the foal have this trouble and the owner has little or no experience, this is a time to call a vet *very* quickly, oil injections per rectum being of the greatest help. Tiny foals are not things for the inexperienced to risk. When the first milk has gone through the foal the droppings are bright yellow, and a sigh of relief can be given. If space is available a small plot of clover, or rye, or vetches, or lucerne, or a mixture, can be sown and cut green, and this is of top value to in-foal mares and those with foals.

The actual foaling is too large a subject to go into here, but as a rule a mare foals easily if properly prepared (not fed too 'hard' to the end, and having had less hay); but if she does not, it is likely to be serious, so do not hesitate to call a vet unless someone experienced is at hand. Even then mares' troubles are usually best dealt with professionally. Assuming the foal is born, the navel cord will break in its own good time, usually as the foal struggles about, and then the stump should *at once* be soaked in iodine (a tiny bottle poured over it is better than struggling with cotton wool) but *not* tied up—that is a blown theory. Then it is far best to shut the door, having seen that there is plenty of bedding under them, and leave mare and foal to get acquainted. If the inexperienced watch a new foal too much they get worried to death—the foal will try to get up and go head over heels seeming to need help, and this it should *not* have; there are trains of instincts in both mare and foal, and human handling of either breaks these and leads them to confusion and

what is foolishly called 'being awkward'.

The foal will not harm if it does not take a suck for an hour or two; 'helping' it is far from helpful really. A strong foal and a fond mare get together far better when left on their own; the very act of watching them is disturbing. Many foals have died through being over-stimulated and handled in the first 24 hours, which is their most dangerous time of life. It is also better not to open the door and start cleaning up too much. If there is a clean box next door into which they can be slipped easily, well and good; if not, they will not hurt if the bedding is thick and some clean straw put on top for the time being. It ought to be unnecessary to say that the box should have been well cleaned and the mare used to being in it; also that it should be safe for tiny foals—no spaces under mangers, for example, or buckets on the ground or spaces under the door.

The second day will probably see the foal a great deal rounder and safer on its legs, and the mare nice and calm. If the weather is really warm and the going normal, the mare can be led out for a little time in a nearby paddock and the foal allowed to skip around a bit, this being quite a usual practice for a day or so. The safest way is to 'handle' the foal out to the paddock, placing the right hand round its quarters and the left round its *chest*, but not its neck, which would press on the windpipe and frighten the foal. The off-side point of the shoulder bone fits into the left hand very conveniently and it should then be comfortable and safe. This way of handling the foal in and out is excellent and paves the way to leading it.

A tiny, soft headcollar of good design should be put gently on the foal when it is about four days old, fitting fairly closely, but naturally no attempt should be made to lead the foal on this for a few more days, during which time it should be handled all over its body and legs, but the hands must be kept away from its face, as this teaches it to draw back.

Most foals take no time at all at this age to handle but, if left even for a short time, it is a long process and wastes more and more time according to the greater age of the foal. At a fortnight the foal should lead reasonably well, but always keep the right hand ready to slip round its quarters in case of sudden rushing back, leading the foal with the left hand for safety and handiness for dropping round the chest again. Such a young foal needs careful and experienced handling. The skull is so soft that the animal should on no account be allowed to rush out on the rein and pull on the head collar. A foal should never be left un-handled, if for no other reason than it might get some cut that would have to be dressed, or some other trouble. Moreover, the horse that has been handled properly since birth is always the better animal in later life, but it must be *properly* handled.

In warm weather the mare can be turned out for a few hours with the foal, but if the ground be wet the latter should not be allowed to lie about too long in its first fortnight. All this is written on the basis of well-cared-for animals of the class that generally makes the good horses later on, but no doubt several cases can be quoted where mares have foaled in a thunderstorm alone in a stone quarry and have been all right. Choosing good weather, hunter mares and foals do well out at night providing the keep is good and they can have some oats every day, but it is well worth while to bring them in frequently and handle the foal again. At two or three weeks it should take no notice of having its feet picked up and should enjoy having its withers and chest scratched, and being brushed over.

The foal will start to eat oats, etc., at eight weeks; at that age it can digest it properly. It will have picked about at its dam's feed before this, but soon now it should be encouraged to eat on its own. Later the mare should be tied up while the foal has its own little feed in a safe heavy box on the ground (but do not go away and leave the mare too long so that the foal can hang itself!). Small pony foals would not be so encouraged, but Thoroughbreds or hunter types later expected to do hard work do well to start early. A handful of crushed oats, a little bran mash with it, a handful of flaked maize, some special cubes made for foals, are liked by many of them. It is as well to teach them about everything they will be offered—carrots in tiny bits and quite soon a little of the cod-liver-oil bran, freshly mixed. When weaning comes, foals do better when used to feeds, and when this sad day arrives, do it all in one go. Take the mare right off the place if at all possible; so many poor little foals are damaged by trying to get back to their dams. If the foal is kept overnight in the box it knows well and then goes out with another it *knows* already, it will soon settle, though it will call a lot when brought in for a night or two. Putting two foals in a box together is most unwise in the long run; the second 'weaning' is often worse than the first and two are involved! The great thing is to give a lonely foal a companion it knows already. The writer weans one foal at a time and puts it back with the mares and foals it has been running with, until soon there may be one mare with six or seven foals. Obviously this can only be done when they are all friends. It was interesting to read that the great 'Nijinsky' was reared at a stud that practises this method of weaning. It was forced on me during the War when a mare died in the middle of the season leaving a three-month-old (who grew up very well).

Worm dosing is usually carried out easily if the powder is disguised in a little mash with some black molasses in it, the molasses being a good source of iron for regular use. Feet should be trimmed into a correct shape regularly to preserve the angles of the fetlock joints, and the foal done well in its first winter. Colt foals do well if gelded at 10 to 12 weeks. It should not be believed that they do not get 'fronts'; this is quite untrue. Obviously the average hunter foal is not wanted as an awkward colt in the spring, when he may well get into trouble. Breeders who have taken to the early-gelded routine have been very thankful.

The main points in breeding are to be sure the place is suitable, to leave nothing to chance, to remember you are 'buying' an unseen article which may disappoint you, and that your dear little foal will soon be a big gay colt, awkward two-year-old, and even stronger three-year-old, unless, of course, you are breeding blood horses which sell at far younger ages, either as foals in December or yearlings the next autumn, but these must be of the right sorts and correctly produced, for bloodstock buyers are quite rightly very conservative. The thrill of seeing a colt you have bred 'first past the post' is a thing worth living for, the pleasure of collecting show rosettes with your home-bred colt or of seeing your pony foal grown into the family's most valued possession are both endless joys, but they will not come about without care and correct handling (see BREEDER'S FOALING TABLE, page 43).

*   *   *

Mare-colt   The name more usually applied by the moormen of Exmoor to fillies.

Maremmana, Maremma   Italian breed of general utility horse, bred in the lowlands north of Rome. Used by the mounted police and herdsmen of the Roman *Campagna*.

'Marengo'   The charger ridden by Napoleon throughout his Italian and Austrian campaigns and at the battle of Waterloo. The horse's skeleton is now housed at the National Army Museum, R.M.A., Sandhurst, Camberley, Surrey, England.

Mare's-nest   A supposed discovery which proves to be false.

Mark   The dark centre of the tooth of a young horse.

Market Harboro'   A type of improved draw rein having two straps running from the breast ring through the bit rings and fastening on to 'D's' set on the rein. It can be adjusted to permit the head whatever degree of elevation is desired.

Market Harborough   The centre for meets of the Fernie, Pytchley and Woodland Pytchley Hounds.

Markings, Face   Markings on the face and head include: *Face Markings*, covering the forehead and front of the face, extending laterally towards the mouth; *Muzzle Markings*, embracing both lips and extending to the region of the nostril; *Star Markings*, appearing on the forehead. The description should include reference to the shape, size, intensity and position; *Stripe Markings*, extending down the face, no wider than the flat anterior surface of the nasal bones; if it is a continuation of a star, they must be described as a star and a stripe co-joined, if separate and distinct, as an interrupted stripe; it should be specified whether the stripe is narrow or broad (see Plate 21).

Markings, Limb   Markings on the limbs include: *Coronet Markings*, where the hair immediately above the hoof is white; *Fetlock Markings*, comprising the region of the fetlock joint and downwards; *Heel Markings*, extending from the back of the pastern to the ergot; *Pastern Markings*, comprising the area immediately below the fetlock joint and downwards, and which may be elaborated as 'half pastern', or 'three-quarter pastern'; *Sock Markings*, extending to about half-way up the cannon bone; *Stocking Markings,* extending to the region of the knee or hock (*see Plate 21*).

Mark to Ground When hounds bay outside an earth or a drain in which is a hunted fox, they are said to 'mark the fox to ground'.

'Marocco' Elizabethan performing horse exhibited in London. At a command it would dance, rear, lie down and rap out with its foot numbers turned up by a dice. In 1600, ridden by its owner, Thomas Bankes, it climbed to the top of St Paul's. In Italy 'Marocco's' abilities were attributed to black magic and the horse and owner were ordered to be burnt to death. Bankes returned safely to England but 'Marocco's' fate is unknown.

Marshal (U.S.A.) Rider who leads parade past the Grandstand of entries in a race.

Marshall, Benjamin (1767–1835) Leicestershire-born sporting artist. First studied under L. F. Abbot the portrait painter, and later painted with outstanding talent hunters, racehorses, hacks and sporting groups. His pictures possess a unique English quality and fetch very high prices. After a coaching accident, he wrote sporting articles under the pen-names of 'Observator' and 'Breeder-of-Cocktails'. His son, Lambert, also became a sporting artist.

'Marshland Shales' One of the most famous of the early nineteenth-century Norfolk and Suffolk trotters from which many of the modern Hackneys are descended. 'Marshland Shales' was sired by 'Thistleton's Shales' out of 'Jenkins Mare' both of which went back to 'Original Shales' grandson of the 'Flying Childers'. 'Marshland Shales' was a 15 h.h. (152 cm) bright chestnut of great stamina; a prolific sire; capable of carrying 20 st (127 kg) and had, reputedly, trotted 20 miles (32 km) within the hour. George Borrow in *Lavengro* has a moving

description of 'Marshland Shales' in his old age (*see* 'ORIGINAL SHALES').

Martingale A device, in various arrangements, to regulate a horse's head carriage, claimed by Richard Berenger (d. 1782) to have been invented by an Italian Riding Master, Evangelista; it consists usually of a strap or straps, attached to the girth at one end, and at the other to the reins or the noseband.

Martingale, Bib A running martingale having the split filled in with baghide to prevent young racehorses becoming entangled in the martingale or catching it on their corner teeth. Also known as Web Martingale.

Bib Martingale

Martingale, Cheshire A standing type which divides at the breast, the two extension being connected directly to the bit rings by either buckles or snap hooks.

Martingale, Combined One in which both running and standing martingales are incorporated into one body and can be used together.

Martingale, Continental Of French origin, the body ends in a ring at the breast. A strap passes through the ring, fastening round the head behind the poll at one end, and attached to the noseband at the other. Used to assist in obtaining a lower head carriage and proper employment of the quarters.

Martingale, Grainger A martingale with the branches directly and permanently attached to a nosepiece. The latter is fitted above the bit but lower than the normal Cavesson noseband. There is a sliding fitment joining the branches which can be adjusted to give more or less freedom, as desired.

Martingale, Irish A loop of leather through which the reins pass, carried under the neck, thus preventing the reins being thrown over the horse's head in the event of a fall. There are usually two rings attached by a piece of double sewn leather $4\frac{1}{2}$ in (11.4 cm) long, but all-metal patterns are also made. Most racehorses run with Irish Martingales, which are also called 'Rings' or 'Spectacles'.

Martingale, Pugri A standing martingale, used only in polo, and made of turban (pugri) cloth. It is usually coloured, and all four ponies of the side wear the same colour. The cloth prevents cutting or 'nipping' of the

Martingales : A. Irish ; B. Pugri ; C. Standing ; D. Running

flesh, which, in the stress of the game, would happen with a leather martingale, and a further advantage is the slight elasticity of the cloth.

Martingale, Pulley A running martingale in which the rings are mounted on a cord passing through a pulley situated at just above breast level on the body. It allows a horse to make sharp turns, as in jumping competitions, without restriction against the opposite side of the mouth.

Martingale, Running A martingale which is divided at the breast into two branches, each culminating in a ring through which the rein is passed. It prevents undue raising of the head by exerting pressure on the reins and consequently on the mouth. When used with a double-bridle, the rings are attached to the curb rein.

Martingale, Standing This type of martingale runs from the girth to the noseband. The best type is made with an additional adjustment just above the breast. The top strap, in this pattern, should be lined with rawhide. This is the sort used in polo.

Martingale Ring A rubber ring fitted diagonally to encompass the point where the neckstrap and body of the martingale join. It keeps the neckstrap in place.

Martingale Split The branches of a running martingale fitted with a buckle and strap just beneath their point of junction. It is attached to the breast plate when it is desired to use a martingale as well as this latter. A similar standing attachment is also made.

Martingale Stop Leather stops fitted to the rein some 10–12 in (25–30 cm) from the bit. A rein so fitted should always be used with a running martingale, otherwise there is every possibility of the rings sliding forward and becoming caught on either the rein fastening or a corner tooth.

Martingale Triangles A metal, triangular-shaped fitting with a roller used in place of the ordinary running martingale rings, usually when a martingale is to be used on the curb rein of a double bridle or Pelham. The roller does not bend the leather as much as a ring.

Marwari A pony from Rajputana, India, similar to the Kathiawari (*q.v.*).

Maryland Hunt Cup Started in 1894 as a competition between members of the Elkridge Hunt and the Green Spring Valley Hunt. It was restricted to amateurs (but recently professionals have been permitted to ride without payment) over farmland and natural fences. Often spoken of in the U.S.A. as the Grand National. The course is now flagged, covers 4 miles (6.4 km) over 22 post and rail fences 5 ft (1.5 m). There has never been a grandstand, just natural hillside. No admission is charged and parking fees go to the local fire brigade. There was no purse until the last few years. For results *see page 393.*

Mash *see* BRAN MASH.

Mask A fox's head.

Massage Pad *see* GROOMING PAD.

Master *see* M.F.H.

'Master of Game, The' *see* DE FOIX, GASTON.

Master of Hounds, First Sir Rustyn Villenove was appointed Master of Hounds, *Magister Canum Regis*, to Henry IV at a salary of 12*d.* per day.

Master of the Horse John Russell was the first to hold this office in 1377, the reign of Richard II. Present holder is Henry Hugh Arthur Fitzroy, Duke of Beaufort, appointed 1951.

Masters of Foxhounds Association 'Headquarters' of the Masters of Foxhound packs, and publishers of the Foxhound Kennel Studbook. Founded in 1881 as the result of a dispute at

Boodle's Club in St. James's, London, where affairs concerning hunting were previously discussed and decided.

Mastication   When considering the state of a horse out of condition the mouth should be looked at and particular inspection made of the state of the molars (*q.v.*).

Masticaton   *see* FURZE.

Mastitis   Inflammation of the udder which can occur after foaling, at any time during which the foal is suckling, or immediately following weaning. During either of the first two the foal is much concerned, and unless the owner has had practical experience of this trouble veterinary advice should be sought.

Masuren Horse   Name given in Poland to the Trakehner (*q.v.*) or East Prussian Horse.

Match, A   A race between horses, the property of two different owners, on terms agreed by them.

Match Book, the Keeper of (Racing) *see* WEATHERBYS.

McClellan Saddle   American military saddle, named after the Civil War general, formerly the standard U.S.A. trooper's saddle. It was built on a solid tree, open along the side, had a deep seat, modified fan (*q.v.*) and hooded stirrups (*q.v.*).

McGuiness Snaffle *see* MAGENIS SNAFFLE.

McTaggart Saddle   A type of forward seat saddle designed by the late Lt.-Col. M. F. McTaggart. The head of the saddle is very high to give a pronounced dip to the seat. Now obsolete.

Mealy-nose   Descriptive of a muzzle mainly oatmeal in colour (*see* EXMOOR PONY).

Measurement Scheme *see* JOINT MEASUREMENT SCHEME.

Measuring-stick or **Horse-standard** A straight shaft of wood, with inches and hands marked upon it, having a sliding right-angle arm which is placed over the withers. As the arm is raised or lowered on the upright, it discloses the exact height. The best and most accurate have a spirit-level on the upper surface of the arm; there is a smaller size used for measuring hounds. A similar device is combined with an umbrella or a walking-stick, being contained in the hollow shaft, to be pulled out when required.

'Meat for Work'   An expression denoting the free keep of a horse in exchange for work.

Mecklenburg   A German breed which today is the product of 'The Association of Mecklenburg Warm Blood Breeders'; it was once a heavy type horse, and later, in the middle of the nineteenth century, it represented a good type of saddle horse.

Medicine Ball   Medicine administered in bolus form. To ball a horse, hold the animal's tongue to one side of the mouth, with one hand, to keep the mouth open. Hold the ball between three fingers of the other hand and place it far back on the mouth beyond the bulb of the tongue. Alternatively, using a balling iron or balling gun. When being swallowed, the ball may be seen passing down the neck. Balls are of various forms, viz. physic, cough, worm, etc.

Meet   The appointed place for a pack to meet on a hunting day.

Meeting   Any assembly of horses and jockeys at a given place for the purpose of racing.

Megrim   An affection of the brain resulting in a sudden loss of equilibrium. *Cause:* defective circulation due to a weak heart, a poor digestion, worms or congestion of the brain. *Symptoms:* the horse will sway, stagger and finally fall to the ground unconscious. The attack lasts about 5 minutes when the horse will rise, appearing slightly dazed. *Treatment*: remove all causes of restraint—bridles and collars, apply cold water to the animal's head and summon a veterinary surgeon. (The disease is popularly termed 'Staggers'.)

Méjuger, se French word meaning that the hindfeet touch down in front of the imprints left by the forefeet (*see* DÉJUGER, SE *and* JUGER, SE).

Melbourne Cup (Racing) The most important race in Australia and a handicap run over 2 miles (3.2 km). Founded in 1861. For results *see page 393*.

Melbourne Facings A saddle panel where a gusset is let in the rear to allow fuller stuffing of that part. Used in dressage saddles to ensure that the saddle remains level on the back. Sometimes called a German panel.

Melton A heavy coating originally a product of the West of England, which is extremely densely woven, thus ensuring both softness and shape. Often used for hunting coats, it was first made popular at Melton Mowbray (Belvoir, Quorn and Cottesmore hunts) from which town it takes its name.

Melton Mowbray The centre in Leicestershire for meets of the Belvoir, Cottesmore and Quorn Hounds.

Memory Horses are endowed with remarkable memories. In estimating this regard must be paid to the possible influence of instinct which in itself is most marked (*see* INTELLIGENCE).

Metacarpal Bone (Large) The cannon bone, the main bone of the front leg from the knee to the fetlock joint.

Metacarpals, Small (Splint Bones) Two in number, the small metacarpals are found at the posterior part of the large metacarpal bone, sometimes becoming attached to it by bony deposits.

Metatarsal Bone The cannon or shank bone, the main bone of the hind leg, between the hock and the fetlock.

Metrication (Racing) Racing weights and distances in the metric system are as follows: 1 stone (14 lb) = 6.350 kg; 1 lb = 454 g; 1 furlong (220 yd) = 0.2012 km; 1 mile = 1.6093 km; $1\frac{1}{2}$ miles = 2.4140 km; 1 yd = 0.9144 m. The decision of an official committee working in 1974 will be announced in due course, as to the introduction of metric measurements into racing in Great Britain.

Metropolitan Bit A term loosely describing a number of bits, e.g. Metropolitan Liverpool, Metropolitan Ashleigh, etc. In the trade it is used to describe those bits which are used by the Household Cavalry and which are inscribed *honi soit qui mal y pense*.

Metropolitan Drinking Fountain and Cattle Trough Association (Founded 1865) *Objects*: to provide Drinking Fountains for the people and Cattle Troughs for animals.

Metropolitan Police Mounted Branch It traces its origin to a small horse patrol, started in 1763 by Sir John Fielding, which was incorporated into the Metropolitan Police in 1836. The training headquarters at Imber Court in Surrey were opened in 1920 and here young horses are schooled for six months on an unhurried system based entirely on patience and reward before taking up official patrol duties. Women are now accepted for this branch.

Mettlesome Descriptive of a horse of spirit, courage and character—such an animal needs a skilled rider or driver.

Mewing A term used of a stag when shedding his antlers, usually at the end of April or the beginning of May.

Mews An area given over to stables. The word derives from the French *muer*, originally a place where moulting falcons were confined. In 1537 the royal stables at Charing Cross were called mews, having been built on a site where royal hawks were kept.

Meynell, Hugo (1735–1808) Became the second M.F.H. of the Quorn Hunt (from 1753–1800). Among his own field he was known as the 'Hunting Jupiter', and was one of the 'noble science' school, for he looked upon horses as machines which enabled him to keep company with his hounds.

Mézair Meaning half air, it is an obsolete movement, like a half *courbette* (q.v.) but lower and covering more ground.

Midden A dung-heap.

Middleton, Capt. 'Bay' (12th Lancers). Piloted the Empress of Austria (q.v.) when she hunted with fashionable packs in the Midlands. He was killed when riding his horse 'Night Line' in a House of Commons Point-to-Point race at Kineton.

'Midlands, The' Grass hunting countries, roughly in the Midlands, which include the following hunts: Bicester, Grafton, Pytchley, Quorn, Fernie, Belvoir, Cottesmore, Meynell, N. Staffordshire, Woodland Pytchley, Whaddon Chase, Atherstone, Warwickshire, N. Warwickshire, Rufford, Albrighton, Croome, S. Nottinghamshire, S. Staffordshire.

Midnight Steeplechase see MOONLIGHT STEEPLECHASE.

Mierzyn Lowland pony of Poland.

Mildew The most common of parasitic fungi appearing on growing grain or plants, this manifests itself as dark spots which eat into the plant and turn it to black powder.

Mildmay, Anthony, of Flete (1909–1950) Lord Mildmay was the most popular amateur rider of his time, and was twice unlucky not to win the Grand National. In 1936 he was out clear on his own horse 'Davy Jones' at the last but one fence when his reins parted at the buckle and his horse ran out at the final fence. In 1948 on his favourite horse, 'Cromwell', he finished third in spite of being attacked by cramp in the neck and riding almost blind in the last mile. He was tragically drowned when bathing near his home in Devon.

Miler, A A horse deemed to be well fitted to stay the distance with credit in a mile race on the flat.

Militaire see HORSE TRIALS.

Milk Mare's milk is not so rich as a cow's, but contains more sugar. When fed to a foal, cow's milk should be diluted with 3 parts of water to 2 of milk, and a little sugar added.

Milk Teeth Two incisors with which a foal is born, together with those which appear within the first few weeks.

Miller Brothers C. D., E. D. and G. A., these were great polo players and pig-stickers associated with the formation and subsequent history of the Roehampton Club, London.

'Milling' A coaching term for kicking.

Milord A carriage designed by David Davies of London with a cab-shaped body hung on four elliptic springs with a low driving seat. It became very fashionable in England and on the Continent (c. 1835).

Ming Horses Highly glazed models of horses, usually in fine white porcelain, produced in China during the Ming Dynasty, A.D. 1368–1644.

Minho see GARRANOS.

Mise en Main The relaxing at the jaw in the position of the ramener (q.v.).

Misfetched Mistaught: descriptive of an animal which has been badly broken and possesses some vice.

Misfit A horse not representative of, nor suited to, the work required of its breed, e.g. one bred for racing, but sold for hiring as a riding horse.

Mitbah The term descriptive of the peculiar angle at which the neck enters the head of the Arabian horse. The neck makes a slight angle at the top of the crest and from that point runs in a gentle curve to the head. The windpipe enters between the jaws in the same way. This gives the peculiar arched set to the neck and allows free movement of the head in every direction.

Mixed Pack A pack composed of dog hounds and bitches.

'Mob a Fox' A term describing the hunting of a fox without giving it any chance of escape; to surround it or 'gallop it down'.

Mock Feed A diet which includes no corn, for use when, for some reason, the horse cannot be exercised.

Model (U.S.A.) Term used for show class judged on conformation.

Moff A waggon which can be converted into a cart by the addition of sideboards.

Mohawk Attachment A straight bar covered with rubber ball washers, and two upturned hooks which catch upon the two eyes of Pelham cheeks, increasing twofold the bearing surface upon the tongue and the bars of the mouth. A Mohawk hook is fastened in the middle to a Pelham bar with a figure-of-S rubber ring, allowing the

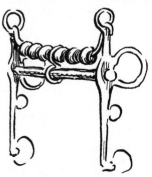

Mohawk Attachment

horse to push it out of line with its tongue, a rubber spring returning it to its place. The chief object of the bit is to put bit pressure on the bars of the mouth.

Molars The large grinding teeth of the horse which lie beyond the bars of the mouth. The grinding surfaces slope outwards towards the cheeks which are used to retain the food between the teeth. As a result the enamel of the teeth wears to sharp points on the outside of the upper row and inside of the lower row, rendering tongue and cheeks liable to laceration. This in turn inhibits perfect mastication. In such cases the services of a veterinary surgeon are required (*see* RASPING TEETH).

Monday Morning Complaint, Evil or Leg A complaint where the horse has puffed or filled legs, consequent upon standing idle on Sunday (*see* LYMPHANGITIS).

Mongolian A pony both domesticated and feral, the Mongolian is found all over the vast desolate area of Mongolia, reaching from Manchuria in the east to Turkistan in the west. Bred and kept in great numbers by the Buriats and other Mongolian tribes, it is extremely hardy and enduring and is in demand for export to China for racing and polo, and has been much crossed to produce the so-called China pony. Height is 12.2–13 h.h. (124–132 cm); the smallest are usually to the east of the China border, with the best ponies in the northern districts. The breed has a heavy head and shoulders, small eyes, a thick neck, deep chest, and well-sprung ribs, good quarters and loins, legs with plenty of bone, and feet iron-hard. Its temperament and tractability are uncertain. Though insignificant and of no equine beauty, its influence on the horse world has been considerable.

'Monkey' A betting term implying a wager of £500.

'**Moon-blindness**'   *see* OPHTHALMIA.

Moonlight Steeplechase This is said to have been run in 1803 from the Cavalry Barracks at Ipswich to Nacton Church, a distance of 4½ miles (7.2 km). There is complete lack of evidence that the event ever took place. Henry Alken (*q.v.*) painted a picture of the race and the first prints of this, in which the riders are seen to be wearing starched nightshirts, appeared in 1839. (Known also as The First Steeplechase on Record or The Night Riders of Nacton.)

Moray Car A two-wheeled carriage hung especially low for easy access by ladies.

Morgan An American breed of light horse produced from 'Justin Morgan' (*q.v.*), foaled in 1789. This horse was a bay standing 14.2 h.h. (144 cm): it reproduced its type, character and conformation with extreme exactness, and won great fame and popularity, resulting in the service of large numbers of mares. It was later bought by the U.S. Army (which established the Morgan Stud Farm), and died in 1821, having established America's most famous general-purpose horse. The defined height of the breed is now 14–15.1 h.h. (142–153 cm). Head is Arabian in type, deep through the body and showing great substance. This is combined with elegance. *Breed Society :* Morgan Horse Club (*see Plate 18*).

Morland, George (1763–1804) An artist of uneven talent. Horses figure frequently in the scenes of English rural life for which he is famed; hunting was an occasional subject. The countryman's horse 'in the rough' was Morland's choice; he had little use for a well-groomed Thoroughbred. His horses, like other animals, were painted as part of impoverished and unsophisticated country scenes.

Morning-Glory (Racing) A racehorse which goes well in its training gallops in the morning but badly on the racecourse.

Morocco (U.S.A.) Primary colour white and secondary colours black, brown, dun or sorrel. The morocco generally has an all-white body with the solid colour on the neck and head (*see* PINTO, PAINTED).

Morocco Saddle A military saddle used in the first half of the seventeenth century and later known as the Burford saddle.

Morven Park International Equestrian Institute Riding establishment in Leesburg, Virginia, U.S.A., founded in 1967. Co-sponsored by the U.S. Combined Training Association and Springfield (Mass.) College for training professional riding instructors.

The Mountain and Moorland Ponies of the British Isles *
Glenda Spooner

What are known as the native breeds of ponies are indigenous to the British Isles as is the moose to Canada and the ostrich to Africa. For all practical purposes they have occupied their self-chosen areas throughout our land for an incalculable length of time, but it was only, perhaps, towards the latter part of the nineteenth century that the horse world became particularly interested in them. Since then they have, as is the way with things, enjoyed varying degrees of fortune and, whereas in the early days of the twentieth century their fortunes were in decline, by mid-century they were enjoying prosperity undreamed of, with ponies being exported to the United States of America at hundreds of pounds a head; indeed some were sold for thousands. Perhaps even more remarkable than this is the fact that just at the turn of the half century, the export to various countries overseas of Mountain and Moorland ponies exceeded in value all other horses put together, with the exception of the Thoroughbred racehorses.

The breeds in this most distinguished group are the Welsh, Shetland, Dartmoor, New Forest, Highland, Exmoor, Fell, Dales and Connemara, and all have figured in the list of exports, but it has been a noticeable fact that for a variety of reasons the Welsh and Shetland have always led the way in numbers and value, closely followed by New Forest and Connemara, but all have their popularity.

Looking back over their long histories it is very noticeable that just as nature alters the conformation of an animal to suit its environment, so 'demand' influences breeding. When roads were made and wheeled traffic largely replaced the ridden horse and pony we find that Welsh Cob blood was introduced into the Fell and Dales Stud Books, for now that a pony was no longer needed to carry the lead over the moors to the sea ports but urgently required to trot in a gig at 10–15 m.p.h. to market, this was an obvious infusion of blood. In the same way Hackney blood was introduced into other breeds and of course Arab stallions, especially in Wales, have been used throughout the ages and the influence of this very prepotent blood can be seen in the Welsh and other breeds today. The introduction of Scotland's heavy and handsome Clydesdale to Highland ponies was done before the farms were mechanized, when a slightly larger 'halfway' animal was invaluable on any farm or small-holding. By now the staunch, sure-footed, strong pony is bred to be a good ride and performer across country. But so prepotent is the blood of the native pony, so ancient its lineage, that every one of the breeds have —despite very necessary upgrading from

time to time—retained their very definite type and characteristics. This is especially so with the Exmoors, some of whose breeders claim that they—the toughest of the lot—trace back to the European wild horse, whereas others assert that it is of no use to breed museum pieces and that they must move with the times and breed riding animals of all types and sizes.

It is the overseas trade that has played a very large part in the latter day prosperity of the ponies of Britain—that is the trade in high-class registered stock for which overseas buyers and breeders paid such large sums because they realized that these ponies are unique and are not obtainable anywhere else in the world. It remains to be seen whether these ponies which have gone overseas will retain, through the ages, their type and their characteristics; whether their breeders will have the necessary knowledge, and local conditions permit them to breed true.

The Second World War and the wholesale slaughter of these ponies for meat for human consumption, both during and after, reduced the herds on the mountains and moorlands to an alarming extent, but one factor which saved these ancient breeds from extinction was the fact that as foundation stock they were unsurpassed. Put to Thoroughbreds or Arabs, the mares of several of these nine breeds produce stock that fills our show rings and jumping arenas, the hunting field and Pony Club rallies. Indeed there is no equestrian activity which they are not capable of tackling. It is also an acknowledged fact that pony-blood is of the greatest possible value as the basis of a large proportion of our horses, for it gives brains, hardiness, surefootedness and the ability to look after both itself and its rider. It is, too, a most economical feeder and its powers of recuperation remarkable. It is on these native ponies that the youth of these Islands, as well as adults, have for generations learnt to ride, thereby having an immense advantage over those of other countries. So strong and sturdy are these ponies that most of them carry adults without any distress. It is not the least remarkable, therefore, that these ponies are in demand all over the world.

It is really rather wonderful that despite wholesale mechanization of transport, building encroachments on the land, and increasing scientific, agricultural and commercial demands and restrictions, these nine breeds of ponies still in fact inhabit the same localities where they have lived for centuries past: the moors of Dartmoor and Exmoor, the Black Mountains of Wales, the fells and dales of Northumberland, the forests of Scotland and Hampshire, the wilds of Connemara where the Atlantic rollers break on the Galway Bay, and the seaweed-covered beaches of the northern islands—haunts which saved the ponies when Henry VIII ordered all animals under 15 h.h. (152 cm) to be destroyed, and when two World Wars threatened to extinguish any animal that was not essential to the war effort.

We still find these ponies in their natural background, but also in private studs. On our showgrounds the cream of British ponies is to be seen, and what a wonderful sight it is! Their popularity both at home and abroad has escalated enormously. As much as £8000 has been paid for a 14.2 h.h. (144 cm) cross-bred gelding which, among other major awards, won the 'Ponies of Britain' Summer Show Ridden and Supreme Championships in 1971. The winner at the same show of the Youngstock Championship went to America for an alleged £4000 the following spring. Interest on the Continent has greatly increased as parents now realize how much better it is for children to ride ponies than horses. Practically all these larger ponies have a basis of native pony blood.

The Ponies Act 1969 (q.v.) instigated by the late Lord Silkin affords some protection, and has stopped the *legitimate* export trade in low-grade ponies, especially those not registered with any recognized Breed Society. The Act imposed minimum values under which ponies might not be exported, and raised these in 1973 to £120 for ponies under 12 h.h. (122 cm), and £160 for those over this height, except those of the Shetland breed whose minimum value is £60. The minimum values, when laid down in 1969, adequately protected those likely to be exported for breeding, riding or exhibition purposes, but with the increased demand and prices for horseflesh on the Continent today those values have been raised.

Pony trekking (q.v.) is booming. Undoubtedly this recreation saved our larger native breeds, i.e. Dales, Fell, Highland, Connemara, Welsh Cobs Section D and Welsh Ponies of Cob Type Section C (q.v.), which were in danger of extinction through lack of demand. Fortunately, these types are ideal for this work. The explosion in riding has also provided a valuable market, but, again, suitability is the key word. Increasingly, too, riders are realizing the value of crossing the larger native breeds with Thoroughbred and/or Arab blood to produce a higher performance while maintaining the toughness, sagacity and surefootedness of the natives. But it is the proportion of this alien blood which is all important (Shetland should not be crossed with any other blood).

While it is essential that the characteristics and attributes of our native ponies are retained, without doubt the majority are now bred in private studs all over the country. These can be seen at shows all over the country staging Mountain and Moorland classes, while cross-bred ponies flood the rings not only in show classes but also in working hunter pony classes which are increasingly popular. They also show the way across country both out hunting and in cross country events (*see* CONNEMARA, DALES, DARTMOOR, EXMOOR, FELL, HIGHLAND, NEW FOREST, SHETLAND, WELSH).

Mounties, The   *see* CANADIAN MOUNT-ED POLICE, THE ROYAL.

Mounting   There are four normal methods of mounting: placing the foot in the stirrup iron; using a mounting block (*q.v.*); having a leg-up (*q.v.*); springing up from the ground over the horse's neck and withers. The latter is the invariable practice of racing lads, and requires considerable agility. The spring must carry the body right on top of the neck and the right elbow must be well to the off-side. It is useful on many occasions, especially when there is a great hurry, as it can be performed while the horse is moving forward. The leg-up method is invariably used for jockeys in the paddock before a race.

Mounting Block   A small platform, some $2\frac{1}{2}$ ft (76.2 cm) high, approached by two or three steps, on which a rider stands when mounting a horse. The use of this is of the greatest comfort to both horse and rider. It had a permanent place in every stable-yard in Victorian times and of course in pillion days. Sometimes known as a Horsing Stone, Jostling Stone or Pillion Post.

Mounting Block

Moustache   A tuft of hair which appears on the upper lip of some heavy horses; it is considered a sign of underbreeding.

Mouth   In a horse, this comprises the lips, tongue, teeth, hard palate or roof which takes the form of ridges or bars running from side to side between the upper molar teeth, and the soft palate —a form of dense curtain hanging between the mouth and the throat, which, from its size, does not allow the horse to breathe through its mouth.

Mouth, Full   A term denoting that all the milk teeth have been finally replaced by permanent teeth. This state should be reached when the horse is five years old (*see diagram, page* 3).

Mouth, Good   Said of a horse which is 'on the bit', yet can be ridden with a light, soft, but firm pressure.

Mouth (of bit)   Usually refers to that part of any bit which is adjacent to the tongue and the bars of the mouth.

Mouthing   The preliminary process of accustoming a young horse to the bit and at the same time causing it to mouth and champ to make the essential saliva flow. There are various forms and designs of mouthing-bits (*see* MOUTHING-BIT).

Mouthing-Bit   A bit, made of wood or metal, and of either the bar or the broken mouth variety, with 'keys' or 'players' attached, which encourage a 'wet' mouth.

'Mucking Out'   The process of removing droppings and soiled bedding from a box or stall and sweeping it out.

Muck Sweat   Describes a horse which has been ridden to such an extent that it is in a lather and both dirt and sweat come out of its pores and impregnate its coat.

Mud Fever   Corresponding to chapped hands in humans, this is an inflammation of the heels, legs and sometimes the belly. *Cause:* mud and wet, and washing of legs after work, which removes natural oil. *Treatment:* apply lead lotion. *Prevention:* leave legs to dry and then brush out. Vaseline should be applied to heels and legs before hunting. Hunters' legs should not be clipped (*see* CRACKED HEELS).

'Mug's Horse' Said of a horse which is easy to ride even though it may look 'hot' and difficult.

Mule The offspring of a male ass and female horse; very rarely can a mule be bred from.

Mule Feet Feet with small frogs and high heels. Known also as club or boxy feet.

Mullen Mouth Half-moon mouth, otherwise known as a Mulling Mouth (*see* SNAFFLE BIT).

Munnings, Sir Alfred James (1878–1959), K.C.V.O., P.R.A. An artist of brilliant talent and great popularity who painted in a vivid and fluent style all types of horses and sporting scenes, as well as landscapes. His pictures of the modern Thoroughbred, especially of racehorses, were unequalled in his day. He was President of the Royal Academy of Arts from 1944 to 1949 and was relentless and reckless in his denunciation of 'modern art'.

Murgese A large robust Neapolitan horse of oriental origin.

Murrieta Gig Designed by C. J. de Murrieta, a member of the Coaching Club (*q.v.*). It had a more elegant but reduced form of the old curricle (*q.v.*) body suspended on a Stanhope Gig (*q.v.*) undercarriage. Fitted with a folding head.

Muscles Fibres which, attached by sinews to one bone which can be moved and one which is fixed, regulate the movement of joints by contraction or expansion. The longer the muscle, the greater the speed of movement. Where strength rather than speed is required, muscles are short and thick.

Muscovy, Anti-rearing This differs from the usual Chifney bit as the side rings are attached to knobs, which in turn are fitted loosely to a large bit ring (*see* ANTI-REARING BIT).

Muscular System of the Horse *see page* xii.

'Music' The cry of hounds when hunting.

Mustang The feral and semi-feral horses of the plains of W. America and the pampas of S. America. The name derives apparently from *mestengo*, i.e. 'stranger', which comes from the Spanish *mesta*, the name given to an association of graziers, one of whose functions was the appropriation of wild cattle which had attached themselves to the herd. Probably of Spanish origin, the horse, having been brought over by Cortès in 1519, was the first true specimen seen in the New World, and was of Spanish, Arabian and Barb blood. Seldom more than 14.2 h.h. (144 cm), it was scraggy and tough, of no quality and with an uncertain temperament, but it was hardy and courageous and possessed of a cast-iron constitution; it was represented by every known colour. Once domesticated, the Mustang made a useful light saddle horse, and was the original cow-pony. Today the true Mustang has been succeeded by the range horse, through crossing with a variety of strains—Arab, Thoroughbred, Standard Bred, Morgan, etc.

Mustard A counter-irritant for use in cases of colic or sore throat. Equal parts of mustard and linseed meal mixed in cold water make a good poultice.

Mute A hound which does not throw its tongue when on the line of a fox is said to be mute.

Mute An obsolete term for a pack of hounds.

Mutton Fat Chopped fine and melted makes a good ointment for hoofs and promotes the growth of horn; it is also a good dressing for the thongs of coaching whips.

Mutton-fisted Descriptive of a rider who is heavy-handed, but not necessarily rough.

Muzzle Protective covering for the nose, shaped like a bucket, made either of netting or leather, the latter with ventilation holes. It is attached and held in position by a slip-head. Net muzzles are used on harness horses which bite at passers-by. Leather muzzles are employed on horses addicted to dung-eating, eating bedding or tearing clothing. Muzzles are also constructed from wire mesh and recently from fibreglass. Both these materials have a longer life than leather which rots if the horse

Leather Muzzle

attempts to drink whilst wearing his muzzle (*see* BAR MUZZLE).

Muzzle That part of the head which includes the nostrils, lips, and bones, gums, and teeth.

Mytton, John (Jack) (1796–1834) An eccentric, inveterate gambler and a remarkable sportsman, commemorated in *The Memoirs of the Life of the Late John Mytton, Esq.* by Nimrod (*q.v.*). At one time he kept 28 hunters in his stable and hunted two countries. His feats of endurance were prodigious and his extraordinary exploits, many undertaken for bets, included driving his tandem across country at night and putting his gig at a closed turnpike. He died in penury of chronic alcoholism at the age of 38.

Mesh Muzzle

* N *

N.E.C.   National Equestrian Centre.

N.F.F.R.   No foal, free return (*q.v.*).

N.F.N.F.   No foal, no fee. An arrangement by which if no foal is produced from a mating no stud fee is payable.

N.H.   National Hunt. The National Hunt Committee has been absorbed by the Jockey Club.

Nk (Racing)   Neck.

N.P.S.   National Pony Society.

N.P.S.B.   National Pony Stud Book.

N.S.H.A.   National Steeplechase and Hunt Association (U.S.A.).

Nag   Derived from the word *negan*, Anglo-Saxon 'to neigh', this is an old term for a saddle horse but seldom used now.

Nagbut Snaffle   A jointed bit with a grid port in the centre to discourage tongue over the bit evasion. Light enough for racing.

Nagging   The process of training and schooling a horse for hunting or riding, and for good manners under all circumstances.

Nagsman   A horseman who, by his skill, rides to improve a horse, whether as a ride, or on account of some vice or bad manners. He is usually a professional attached to a dealer's yard.

Nail-bind   *see* SHOD TOO CLOSE.

Nails (Clenching)   For shoeing these must be made of the finest material (best Swedish Charcoal Iron) and shaped with the greatest of care. Otherwise the nail may deviate from its course when struck, or it may break, in either case probably resulting in serious trouble, causing the horse to 'stand by' for a long period.

'Nap' or **Nap Selection**   Each racing correspondent in Britain normally gives each day a Nap Selection, which he considers his best bet of the day at the probable odds.

'Nappy'   A horse which, either from stubbornness or bad temper, refuses to carry out any of the aids properly given, e.g. refusal to leave its stable or the company of other horses, an inclination to turn for home or to refuse to pass certain points.

Narragansett Pacer   From the founding of the American Colonies in the early seventeenth century until about 1800, when roads were sufficiently improved to take wheeled traffic, the customary means of travel was by a pacing horse. The most popular strain was developed in the Narragansett Bay area of Rhode Island. These horses, noted for their speed and comfort, were exported also to the West Indies and the Southern colonies. George Washington rode one in old age.

Narrow Behind   Where the croup and thighs are deficient in muscle, giving a narrow appearance when viewed from behind.

Nasal Gleet   An evil-smelling discharge from one nostril, resembling acute nasal catarrh. *Treatment* : isolate the animal and consult a veterinary surgeon.

National Equestrian Centre   The headquarters of the British Horse Society of Stoneleigh, Kenilworth, Warwickshire, opened in 1967.

National Foaling Bank, The   A foster mother service introducing owners of mares suitable for use as foster mothers to owners of orphan foals, or vice versa. It is organized for all breeds of horses. Similar services are organized for their members by the Thoroughbred Breeders' Association and the Hunters' Improvement Society.

National Horse Association of Great Britain (Founded 1922) *Objects* were to further the welfare of the horse and pony, and the interests of horse and pony owners and breeders. Absorbed by the British Horse Society (*q.v.*) in 1947.

National Horse Show (U.S.A.) Founded in 1883 and held annually in November at Madison Square Garden, New York City, as the premier horse show of the U.S.A. It features all classes including harness, equitation, international show jumping and displays of various descriptions. It is referred to colloquially as 'The National' and 'The Garden'.

National Hunt Committee (Racing) Formerly the governing body responsible for the conduct of steeplechasing and hurdle-racing in Britain, but now amalgamated with the Jockey Club (*q.v.*), which issues one rule book to cover both flat racing and steeplechasing.

National Hunt Trainers' Association A body formed to protect the interests of trainers of steeplechasers and hurdlers in Great Britain.

National Master Farriers and Blacksmiths Association (Founded 1905) *Objects*: to promote the welfare of those engaged in the Farriery and Blacksmiths' trade.

National Pony Society Originally known as the Polo and Riding Society, founded in 1893. *Objects*: to encourage the breeding and registration of Polo and Riding Ponies and to foster the breeds of Mountain and Moorland Ponies of the British Isles. The Society holds an annual pony show.

National Road Transport Federation An amalgamation of local Associations, originally composed of operators of horse-drawn vehicles.

National Steeplechase and Hunt Association Covers activities in the U.S.A. similar to those under the jurisdiction of the National Hunt Committee (*q.v.*) in Britain.

National Stud Established in 1916 at Tully in Co. Kildare, Ireland, when Lord Wavertree presented his entire stud of bloodstock to the nation, when it became Government sponsored. It was transferred from Ireland to Gillingham, Dorset, in 1943, and was expanded in 1949 when the West Grinstead Stud in Sussex was bought. At that time the National Stud had both brood mares and stallions, and it was hoped that it would breed racehorses good enough to stand later at the stud as stallions. The best of the yearlings were for many years leased for their racing career to the monarch. The stud bred some very high-class horses, including 'Blandford', sire of four Derby winners, and the classic winners 'Big Game', 'Carrozza, 'Chamossaire', 'Royal Lancer' and 'Sun Chariot'. There was regret among many when all the mares were sold in 1964 and it was decided that the National Stud, with its headquarters now at Newmarket, should be a stallion stud only and that it would no longer breed its own stock.

National Trainers' Association The body formed to protect the interests of flat-racing trainers in Britain.

National Trotting Association of Great Britain Founded in 1952 to promote the sport of horse-trotting races.

National Veterinary Medical Association of Great Britain and Ireland (Founded 1881) *Objects*: to promote and advance the interests of veterinary and allied sciences.

Nations' Cup Prix des Nations (*q.v.*).

Native Ponies Another name for Mountain and Moorland ponies (*q.v.*).

Navarre ('Cheval Navarrin', the Horse of Navarra) This owes its origin to the Andalusian (*q.v.*). Navarrin blood was dominant in the Tarbenian (*q.v.*).

Nave The wooden centre of a wheel from which the spokes radiate to the fellow or felloe (*q.v.*).

Navel Ill (Joint Ill)   This is not a specific disease, but a term applied to acute infectious diseases in the first few weeks of a foal's life. *Cause:* many different micro-organisms. Infection can be pre-natal, but very often it takes place at the time of foaling or shortly afterwards. *Symptoms* appear from six hours to seven days. The foal has a septicaemia (blood poisoning) causing depression and raised temperature, pulse and respirations. *Treatment:* call veterinary help immediately. Suitable antibiotics may save the foal. *Prophylaxis:* Whenever possible mares should be foaled on clean grassland. When the time of year makes this impractical, use a loose-box scrubbed with boiling water and washing soda. Blow-lamp every inch of brick, cement and woodwork, especially if there is recurrent foaling in the same box.

Navicular Bone   A small bone in the foot situated transversely behind the pedal bone, and which articulates with the latter and with the pastern.

Navicular Disease   A corrosive ulcer on the navicular bone, almost always confined to the fore-feet. *Cause:* concussion, i.e. too much strenuous work after a long rest, or hereditary weakness. *Symptoms:* lameness, pointing of the foot, when in the stable, to rest it. *Treatment:* roll the shoe at the toe, which should be thin, gradually thickening to about ¾ in (19 mm) at the heel. The horse cannot bear frog pressure. There is no cure (*see* UNNERVED *and* Plate 12).

Neopolitan Noseband   Similar to the Hackamore (Western) (*q.v.*). The loop encircling the nose is of metal with two metal shanks, allowing enormous leverage. A noseband of the same type but less severe is seen in Arabia.

Near Head   *see* POMMELS.

Near-side   A Committee appointed by the Royal College of Veterinary Surgeons strongly advised that the near- or left-hand side should be described as the 'left-side' and the off-side as the 'right-side'.

Neck (Racing)   A horse is said to have won by a neck when both its head and neck are in front of the following horse.

Neck Collar (Harness)   This consists of an outer cover of patent or other leather, and an interior stuffed with selected straw to form a cushion to fit the shoulder. The stuffing is strengthened with a roll or 'whale' shaped to form a recess into which are placed the hames (*q.v.*).

Neck Cradle   *see* CRADLE.

Neck Reining   *see* INDIRECT REIN.

Neck-strap   A circular leather strap worn at the base of the neck through which the martingale is passed and is held in position.

Neck Sweater   A hood covering the neck and throat made of heavy felt lined with oilskin, plastic or waterproof material. Used to sweat off a thick neck (*see* JOWL SWEATER).

Neigh   A call denoting surprise or pleasure, though in a stallion more often indicating the mating call.

Nelson Gag   A gag snaffle with cheeks. The bridle cheeks are fastened to eyes on the top of the bit cheek and not to the bit rings. As with most gags two reins should be used.

Nerve   Courage in the hunting-field; the reverse of 'nerves'.

Nerved (U.S.A.)   *see* UNNERVED.

Nettlerash   *see* URTICARIA.

Newcastle, William Cavendish, Duke of (1592–1676)   An ardent Royalist. When in exile he established a famous riding school at Antwerp and published there in French, in 1658, the first of many works on horsemanship: *La Methode et Invention Nouvelle de Dresser les Chevaux.* Translated into

English in 1667, after the Restoration, this became and still ranks as a classic work on equitation.

New Forest Hunt Club   Founded in 1789 for the purpose of hunting the New Forest country. In that year the Lord Warden of the New Forest (the then Duke of Gloucester) nominated Mr Gilbert's hounds to be the established pack of the country, in succession to his own, with prior rights to hunt the New Forest. Mr Gilbert's hounds had been granted permission to hunt the country since 1780, and in the season 1789–1790 they became a subscription pack under the New Forest Hunt Club. The Club is still in existence.

New Forest Pony   The New Forest is one of the nine breeds of ponies comprising the Mountain and Moorland group (*see page* 214). Its origin is uncertain, but in the days of Canute (*c.* 995–1035) mention was made of wild horses living in the forest which is in Hampshire in S. England. These ponies roam at will 60,000 acres of 'Forest' which is mostly bare land with heather and poor rank grass, which accounts for the breed's ability to live frugally and survive. From time to time foreign blood has been introduced. Queen Victoria, in 1852, lent her Arab Stallion 'Zora', which was in the Forest for eight years. These ponies are now extensively bred in private studs. *Height :* not exceeding 14.2 h.h. (144 cm). *Colour :* Any colour except Piebald or Skewbald. *Description :* A good riding type of pony. Head well set on. Neck a little short from throat to chest, but good laid-back shoulder giving plenty of length of rein. Short back, strong loins and quarters. Tail well set on, though not exaggeratedly high. Good fore-arm and second thigh, short cannon bones, good feet. Plenty of bone. Straight but not exaggerated action. *Type A.* Ponies 13.2 h.h.–14.2 h.h. (134–144 cm) of good bone and substance capable of carrying an adult but narrow enough for a child and fast for his size. *Type B.* Ponies up to 13.1 h.h. (133 cm), same basically as type A. Ideal children's riding pony but not up to quite so much weight, often showing more quality than the bigger ponies. *Breed Society :* The New Forest Pony Breeding and Cattle Society (*see Plate* 22).

New Forest Pony Breeding and Cattle Society (Founded 1906)   *Objects :* to improve and maintain breeding of pure-bred Forest animals. Ponies are entered in the National Pony Stud Book. The Society holds shows for pony stallions and other registered ponies, and periodical sales.

New Kirgiz   *see* KIRGIZ.

Newmarket   'Discovered' by James I in 1605 as a hunting, hawking and racing centre. Charles I continued the royal patronage of this sporting centre, as also did Charles II, whose first official visit after the Restoration took place in 1666, when he founded the Newmarket Town Plate (*q.v.*). Today Newmarket is generally considered the headquarters of flat racing in England. It is the biggest centre for the training of racehorses and a large number of studs surround the town. There are two racecourses — the Rowley Mile course, which is used in spring and autumn, and the July course, which is used in summer. The chief races are the 2000 Guineas and 1000 Guineas in the spring; and the Champion Stakes, the Cesarewitch and the Cambridgeshire in the autumn.

Newmarket Bandages   The name frequently given to stockinette bandages of many colours.

Newmarket Boots   Of the regulation hunting-boot height, these have a waterproof canvas leg, and a strap attached to the heel which passes over the instep and buckles on the outside of the foot.

Newmarket Bridle   A schooling bridle using a mullen mouth Wilson ring (i.e., 4 rings) snaffle. The reins are attached to the outer ring and a noseband connects the two inner rings. Pressure on the reins results in pressure on the nose which is consequently lowered.

Newmarket Cloths   Shaped pieces of box cloth which are sewn round a racehorse's legs to give support; usually round the forelegs between knee and fetlock.

Newmarket Sales   The principal sales of Thoroughbreds in England now take place at Newmarket, conducted by Tattersalls, the most important being the Newmarket October Yearling Sales and the Newmarket Houghton Yearling Sales in the autumn; and the Newmarket December Sales mostly for horses in and out of training at the beginning of December.

Newmarket Town Plate   No trainer, jockey, stable lad or groom can ride in this race but women are eligible. It is run over about 4 miles (6.4 km) on the Round Course at Newmarket with an entrance fee of £3 and a sweepstake of £1. The owner of the horse finishing last pays £1 to the owner of the horse finishing second. Each year the winner receives the year's sweepstake and the previous year's entrance fees. The weight carried is 12 st (76 kg). The race was instituted in 1665 by King Charles II.

New York Show   *see* NATIONAL HORSE SHOW, NEW YORK.

New Zealand   Horses were unknown in these islands until three were imported by a missionary the Rev. Samuel Marsden in 1814. Conditions are ideal for rearing Thoroughbreds which are renowned for their size, stamina and bone. Stock imported from the United Kingdom included in 1878 the famous 'Musket' who sired the successful 'Carbine' and 'Trenton', both sold back to England; and 'Sir Mordred' who went to the U.S.A. and headed there the winning sires list in 1894. Arabians which were first introduced in 1880 have recently become increasingly popular, with over 50 pure-bred stallions; also included in the Arabian Horse Registry of New Zealand are Anglo-Arabs and Part-breds. In 1969 the first Quarter Horses were imported; two years later the New Zealand Quarter Horse Association was formed, and numbers of the breed are rapidly growing.

Harness racing with trotters and pacers has become popular, with over 2000 horses competing at 133 meetings in recent seasons. Show jumping competitions have now reached international standards with a team being sent to the Olympic Games. The New Zealand Polo Association now numbers more than 20 registered clubs, and other equestrian interests such as endurance rides, rodeos and trekking have a considerable following. The New Zealand Pony Club Association (founded in 1946) has more than 10,000 members. Riders mostly use cross-bred ponies but there are also Welsh Mountain, Welsh and Shetland pony studs flourishing, and recently New Forest Ponies have been introduced.

New Zealand Rug   *see* RUG, NEW ZEALAND.

Nez Percé Indians   *see* APPALOOSA.

Nick   Indicating a mating likely to produce the desired type—'a good nick'.

Nicker   A call denoting pleasurable anticipation—to nicker or to whicker.

Nicking   The division and re-setting of certain muscles under the tail to give this a high carriage. Many American gaited horses undergo this operation.

Nicking   The practice whereby the blood of one family is combined with that of another to produce certain desired results, e.g. greater speed, better quality bone, greater or lesser height, etc.

Nidget A triangular horseshoe formerly used in Kent and Sussex.

Niggle A movement of the hands and reins to alter the horse's carriage or to induce a greater speed. The term is generally applied to jockeys when race riding. Also when 'playing' on a horse's mouth to prevent biting or to distract its attention.

Niggling A term used of a horse that persists in a very short, jerky trot.

Nigh (Colloquial)   Meaning near or left side.

Night Eyes   Another, but little used, name for chestnuts (*q.v.*).

Night Roller   *see* ROLLER.

Night Rug   *see* CLOTHING (NIGHT).

Nilgeri A knobbed riding cane frequently leather-covered.

'Nimrod'   *see* APPERLEY, CHARLES JAMES.

Nits *see* LICE.

Nobbling Interfering, by underhand methods, with a horse's chance in a race.

Nomination Race Each Hunt Point-to-point runs a Master's Nomination Race. This is an open race for bona fide hunters to be ridden by amateurs. Before entering, a nomination must be obtained from the Master of the Hunt concerned.

Non-hand-fed Mare A New Forest pony mare which has never been off the Forest except perhaps to be taken to the annual New Forest Pony Show.

Nonius A Hungarian breed named after its founder, an Anglo-Norman Stallion of that name. There are two types: 'Large Nonius', big-boned, rather massive and often 17 h.h. (173

cm) and 'Small Nonius' about 15 h.h. (152 cm); either type may come from one mare. Of a quiet disposition and an excellent action, they make good agricultural and military horses, though not very hardy. Usually dark bay in colour.

Norfolk Car A four-wheeled, one-horse vehicle with seats facing forward and back, being somewhat larger than the well-known dog-cart, but not measuring quite so high.

Norfolk Roadster A strong, short-legged, fast-trotting and tireless horse of a breed that dated back to the fifteenth century and became extinct in the 1930s, having been continuously exported to foreign countries. It had considerable influence on the Hackney (*q.v.*) especially through 'Marshland Shales' (*q.v.*) and 'Phenomenon'.

Norfolk Trotter   *see* NORFOLK ROADSTER.

Noriker A small type of cart horse used in Bavaria and Austria for agricultural purposes, originally bred in ancient times in the Roman province of Noricum. Height 16–16.2 h.h. (163–165 cm), heavy head on thick neck, straight shoulders, short ribbed and broad chested, generally chestnut or brown. There are two types, Oberlander and Pinzgauer (*q.v.*).

Northern Hackney Horse Club (Founded 1945)   *Objects:* to further the interests of The Hackney Horse and Pony.

North Swedish Horse   Originates from the ancient Scandinavian native horse. Medium sized, deep-bodied, long lived, strong constitution. Used for agriculture, forestry and in the Army. Height: mares 15.1 h.h. (153 cm); stallions 15.2 h.h. (154 cm).

Norton Perfection A racing bridle for a very hard pulling horse. The bit has four rings and two mouthpieces, one of which is very thin and sharp. To this latter is attached a low-fitting elastic noseband which is kept in place by thin straps fastening on the headpiece of the bridle. Sometimes called the 'Lone Eagle'.

Norwegian   One of the most interesting and distinctive breeds in Europe. There are two types: the Fjord of West Norway and the Gudbrandsdal Valley (Ostland Horse). The ancient original type seems to be the one of the west. The breed's usual colour is between cream and dun, with a dark dorsal stripe. Hardy and strong, this breed stands near the ground, has a thick neck and shoulders, good depth and width of barrel and broad chest. The second type was originally bred in the Gudbrandsdal Valley but is now seen all over the country and is bigger and stronger than the Fjord. Gudbrandsdal stallions exported in great numbers to Sweden were used in creating the North Swedish Horse (*q.v.*).

'Nose'   The ability of a hound to scent its hunted quarry, 'a good nose'.

Nose, Roman   This gives a convex line to the face as in, e.g., the Shire Horse.

Nosebag   Apart from being a portable manger, a nosebag can be most useful on a horse which needs to inhale.

Noseband   A broad leather band worn under the cheeks and above the bit, and usually described as the Cavesson (from the Franch *caveçon*) noseband. It should be adjusted to admit two fingers between the leather and the nose. Almost universally worn, it can be put on to provide an attachment for a standing martingale. To prevent a horse from opening its mouth too wide it is better to have a drop noseband (*q.v.*) fitted below the bit to act on the gristle of the nose.

Noseband, Cavesson   *see* CAVESSON.

Noseband, Crossed   *see* GRAKLE NOSEBAND.

Noseband, Drop or Dropped   Attached round the muzzle below the bit, this is used to prevent a horse from opening its mouth or crossing its jaws, thus evading the action of the bit. Pressure placed on the bit through the reins results in pressure on the nose through the noseband, and the resultant correct positioning of the head gives the rider more control.

Noseband, 'Flash'   *see* 'FLASH' NOSEBAND.

Noseband, Sheepskin (Shadowroll)   A noseband with a wide sheepskin covering on the front and chiefly used for racing; it is believed to keep the head from being thrown up, thus causing loss of balance. It also prevents the horse from noticing forward-cast shadows.

Nose-bleeding   *see* EPISTAXIS.

Nose Net   A muzzle made of light cord attached to the bridle in such a manner that, when the reins are pulled, it will tighten over the nostrils. It is sometimes placed over the muzzle of a puller as a check—it stops the horse from opening his mouth, and acts as a restraining influence (*see* MUZZLE).

Nott Stag   A West Country term for a stag which never grows horns; known in Scotland as a 'Hummel'.

Novice   A junior apprentice jockey.

Novice (In Show Classes)   Breed societies and shows impose regulations for inexperienced horses and ponies whereby they are eligible for novice classes if their cash winnings (including supposed value of cups) at previous shows up to a selected date is not more than a certain specified total. These regulations vary according to the authority making them.

Novice (Racing)   For hurdle races it is a horse which has not won a hurdle race at the time of closing, and for steeplechases a horse which has not won a steeplechase at closing. There are plenty of races confined to novice hurdlers or novice steeplechasers.

Number-boards   These are on all racecourses and give, by means of numbers corresponding with the day's race card (*q.v.*), the names of the horses running in any particular race, as well as the actual name of the jockey for each. They give, too, special information, e.g. that a certain horse will be wearing blinkers (*see* CHALK-JOCKEY).

Number Cloth   Every horse running in a race must carry a white linen saddle cloth bearing the number corresponding with its number on the race card. The cloth is supplied to the rider at the time of weighing out, and must be worn so that the number is clearly visible. The rider must put the cloth in the scale and include it in with his weight.

Numbers (Racing)   *see* NUMBER-BOARDS.

Numnah   A felt, rubber or sheepskin pad cut in the shape of, though rather larger than, the saddle and worn under it, having leather straps which hold it to the saddle. This prevents undue pressure from the saddle on a back which is sensitive, perhaps as the result of summering (*q.v.*) or other lack of condition. It is used for show jumping, eventing, etc., but continued use over a long period, as when hunting, can so overheat the back as to cause the very tenderness that its use sought to avoid; rubber is particularly bad in this respect, although the modern foam plastic does keep a back cool.

Nursery Handicap   A handicap race confined to two-year-old racehorses.

Nut-cracker   A horse that has acquired the rare habit of grinding his teeth.

Nut-cracker Action   The squeezing action, across the lower jaw, of a jointed snaffle.

Oaks, The The Oaks is the chief race of the season for three-year-old fillies only. It is run over 1½ miles (2.4 km) at the Epsom Summer Meeting over the Derby course. Founded in 1779, it was named after the nearby residence of the twelfth Earl of Derby and was won by his filly Bridget. The race was founded one year before the Derby. For results *see page 395.*

Oats White oats are generally preferred, although grey and black are good, provided they are heavy. New oats should be stored for a year before being fed. It is better to feed oats lightly rolled or crushed. They are very stimulating, and a horse in hard work requires about 14 lb (6.4 kg) per day.

Obedience In a horse obedience is the one great essential for the safety and comfort of the rider or driver.

Objection (Racing) Various causes may justify an objection being lodged after a race, as laid down in the Rules of Racing. Normally an objection is made in writing by the owner, trainer or jockey within five minutes of the winner weighing in. The stewards of the meeting may at the same time order an enquiry into the running of the race. There can be other objections made later on grounds which have nothing to do with an incident in a race, such as a horse's ineligibility to run in a particular race. In U.S.A. the term generally used is 'protest'.

Objection (Show Classes) Objections can be lodged for any alleged infringement of rules laid down by any society or show, which can require a specified amount to be lodged with each objection and call for this to be made within a specified time.

Objection Flags (Racing) A red flag with a white 'E' hoisted on the number board shows that an objection and/or enquiry has been lodged. A

white flag in place of the red flag with white 'E' indicates that the objection has been over-ruled; a green flag that the objection has been sustained.

Obvinka A bigger pony than the Russian Viatka (*q.v.*), very strong, hardy and fast; it stands 13 to 14 h.h. (132–142 cm).

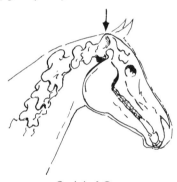

Occipital Crest

Occipital Crest The protuberance on the top of the head between the ears, i.e. the Poll.

Odd Coloured Descriptive of a coat in which there is an admixture of more than two colours tending to merge into each other at the edges of the patches, with irregular body markings. For two-colour coats, see Piebald and Skewbald.

Odd Feet Many otherwise good horses have odd feet, due to malformation or to varying causes. Although unlikely to cause unsoundness, they count as blemishes and faults in the show ring. They may indicate that a horse has previously suffered severe lameness, with consequent resting and lack of growth.

Odds The ratio between the amounts staked by the parties to a bet. Prices are offered or 'laid' on or against the chance of a horse winning a race.

Odds, Long Indication in betting that the chances of a horse winning or being placed are slender.

'Odds, Over the' When a backer obtains a longer price than that which is offered at the start of the race.

Odds, Short Indication in betting that the chances of a horse winning or being placed are good.

'Odds On' When the assumed chances of a horse winning are greater than even money.

Off When a horse has passed a certain year of its age, e.g. the fifth year, it is said to be 'five off'.

'Off, The' The actual start of a race. The starter's assistant raises a white flag to show that the horses are under starter's orders, and lowers it at the start of a race.

Official, The *see* THE O.K.

'Office', The The act of communicating to a horse the final indication for the 'take-off' in jumping.

Off-side *see* NEAR-SIDE.

Ogilvie, William Henry (1869–1963) A prolific writer of sporting verses. His best known collections on horses and hunting are *Galloping Shoes, Scattered Scarlet, Over the Grass,* and *A Handful of Leather.*

Oil Cake Linseed with oil extracted. It is permissible to feed it when a horse is shedding its coat, but it is a bad form of food at other times.

O.K., The American colloquial equivalent of the All-right (*q.v.*). Also in the United States called the Official.

Oldenburg The heaviest of the German 'warm blood' horses, often standing 17 h.h. (173 cm), with many characteristics of the 'cold-blood' horse such as flat hoofs, heavy head and neck, with flat ribs. It matures very early, but is not a hardy type, and lacks endurance. Today it is possessed of some Thoroughbred blood.

'Old Rowley' A nickname given to King Charles II, owner of the stallion of that name which he often rode at Newmarket (*see* ROWLEY MILE).

Olympic Games The Equestrian Section consists of: 1. The *Three-Day Event* (formerly known as The Military), which has three phases, as in the British Horse Trials (*q.v.*): (*a*) Dressage Test, (*b*) Cross Country, (*c*) Show Jumping. 2. *Show Jumping* comprising a Prix des Nations (*q.v.*) for teams and individuals. At Stockholm in 1956 lady riders took part in the Equestrian Section of the Games for the first time and are now eligible for all events. 3. *Grand Prix de Dressage.* In 1956 this was open to riders of both sexes for team and individual placings. At Rome in 1960 no team section was held. For results *see pages* 378, 381 *and* 405.

Olympic Games and International Equestrian Fund Provides money for equestrian teams travelling abroad to compete in the Olympics and International Competitions.

Omnibus *see* GARDEN-SEAT BUS, KNIFE-BOARD BUS, PRIVATE OMNIBUS.

Omnibus, Public *see* GARDEN-SEAT BUS, KNIFEBOARD BUS, SHILLIBEER.

Onager (*Equus hemionus*) An ass of Asiatic origin, to be found in Turkestan, Persia, N.W. India and Syria. Chestnut or dun in colour with white belly, legs and nose and a marked brown dorsal stripe. The legs are never striped.

One-day Event A modified version of the three-day event (*q.v.*). An increasing number of these have been held in different parts of Great Britain, the first in 1950. The programme is not always uniform but the steeplechase and track phases are always omitted. The show-jumping section is more frequently run after the dressage and before the cross-country. Sometimes the order is reversed but the programme is designed for completion in one day.

'One-sided Mouth' A mouth which is unresponsive on one side, and is inclined to set with the bit on one side and pull. The cause usually arises from a tenderness on the bars or lip corners which causes the horse to take the bit and pull to one side. Unless care be taken one side becomes calloused. Search for the cause and remove it by treatment, resting the mouth and bitting carefully.

One Thousand Guineas This race is for three-year-old fillies only and is run over a straight mile (1·6 km) at the Newmarket Spring meeting on the Rowley Mile course. The race was founded in 1814. For results *see page 396.*

One-track A term indicating that the hindlegs are moving strictly in line with their respective forelegs, near hind with near foreleg, off hind with off foreleg (*see* TWO-TRACK).

'On its Toes' A term describing a horse which is fidgety, excitable, keen, anxious and unwilling to keep to a walking pace.

'On the Bit' When a horse takes a light and temperate but definite feel on the reins it is said to be 'on the bit'.

'On the Leg' An expression to indicate that a horse is too long in the leg. This is generally associated with one which is shallow in the body. Implying the same defect is the expression 'Showing too much daylight'.

'On the Rails' (Racing) Said of a jockey who is riding closest to the 'rails' (*q.v.*).

Open A hunting term for a fox's earth which is not stopped.

Open The hound which first 'speaks' to a fox in covert is said to 'open' on it.

Open Country Hunting term indicating that the country hunted is virtually free from woodland.

Open Ditch (Racing) All steeplechase courses have two or more open ditches as opposed to plain fences which have no ditch on the take-off side. They have to be of dimensions approved by the Jockey Club.

Open Ditch (Racing)

Opening Meet The first meet of the regular season, generally held at the beginning of November. It is the first day on which the field wear scarlet coats or silk hats.

Open-rein (or **Opening-rein**) This refers to the use of one rein only for the purpose of guiding the horse, as, for instance, using the right rein to turn to the right—the left to the left. Also known as the direct rein.

Ophthalmia Inflammation of the deeper structures of the eye, characterized by pain, closing of the eyelids and a varying degree of discharge. *Periodic Ophthalmia* is a peculiar kind of inflammation of the eyes, sometimes known as 'moon-blindness'. It occurs in all breeds and is sporadic and unpredictable. In spite of the use of many experimental drugs none have been found to be satisfactory. *Specific Ophthalmia* is a recurrent disease of the eye involving the lens and adjacent structures with further damage resulting at each onset. The condition has been attributed to a virus, vitamin deficiency and other causes, but the true cause remains somewhat obscure.

Opportunity Race A race for young steeplechase jockeys over hurdles or fences, restricted to riders who have only ridden a certain number of winners.

Oriental Horses A loose term, now rarely used, to denote Arabs and Barbs imported from the Middle East to mate with home-bred horses in Stuart and Georgian times.

'Original Shales' Foaled in 1750 by 'Blaze' out of a Hackney mare bred by Robert Shales of Oxborough. Recognized as the progenitor of the modern Hackney (*q.v.*) (*see* MARSHLAND SHALES).

Orlov Trotter A famous breed of Russian trotters, originated in 1777 by Count Alexis Grigorievich Orlov and obtained by him through crossing English Thoroughbred, Arab, Dutch, Danish and Mecklenburg breeds, the first stallion, the Arab 'Smetanka' being put to a Dutch mare. There are now two types, the heavy, mostly black, and the lighter, generally grey and having pronounced Arab characteristics. A very handsome horse, with a small Arabian head, broad chest, longish back, good all-round quarters, strong muscular legs, and standing up to 17 h.h. (173 cm) (*see Plate 23*).

'Ormonde' The unbeaten horse belonging to the first Duke of Westminster. 'Ormonde' won the Triple Crown (*q.v.*) in 1886. He competed in sixteen races, and won over £28,000 in stake money. Later he turned roarer (*q.v.*), but is only known to have sired one roarer, 'Gold Finch'.

Orra Horse The product of a Highland mare and a draught horse, claimed to be a first-class utility animal.

Osbaldeston, George (Pronounced Osbal-*des*-ton) (1787–1866) Twice Master of the Quorn (1817–21 and 1823–27), Osbaldeston lived at Quorndon Hall. On a round course at Newmarket in 1831, for a bet of 1000 guineas, he rode 200 miles (321.8 km) on horseback in 8 hours 42 minutes. He rode in many matches across country; these included his ride on his own hunter, 'Clasher' against Dick Christian (*q.v.*) on 'Clinker' (*q.v.*). Osbaldeston tried his hand at every sport, and was famous at single wicket cricket.

Ostler *see* HOSTLER.

Ostrich Bit A bit perfected in Walsall for the American market. It has a hollow tube mouth in which rotates a longer mouth to which the rings are attached. It is secured to the bridle by 'eyes' from the main mouthpiece. It is always used with a leather chin strap. Mainly a racing snaffle and very useful on the sharp-cornered American tracks as it cannot slide through the mouth. A Pelham (*q.v.*) bit with the same mouthpiece was also made.

Our Dumb Friends League (Founded 1897) *Objects:* animal welfare.

Out at Elbow Of a hound, with elbows projecting outwards; not a straight mover. This is a weakness.

Outcrossing The mating of less closely related individuals, or unrelated individuals.

Outlaw A term for an incorrigible horse in Western U.S.A. A rogue.

'Out of Blood' Hounds which have not killed for some time are said to be 'out of blood', or 'short of blood'.

Outrider A mounted attendant who rides in advance of, or beside, a carriage. In the U.S.A. he is an official of the track, usually in hunt livery, who leads a parade of racehorses past the stands before the start of a race.

Outside, The (Racing)   Furthest from the rails. A jockey is often said to make his challenge on the inside or nearest the rails, or on the outside or furthest away from the rails.

Outsider (Racing)   A term implying a horse with little chance of winning a race in which it is engaged. Also a term of opprobrium, believed to be derived from the unfortunate passenger who was compelled to ride on the top of a stage-coach, exposed to all weathers.

Overalls   Tight dress riding trousers strapped under the instep and worn as full dress with a silk hat and tail coat in Hack classes.

'Over at the Knee'   A forward bend or curve of the knees which may be the result of excessive wear, but is often a matter of conformation. This was very marked in the case of the famous race-horse 'St Simon' as well as in many others. It is a disfigurement which would count against a show horse.

Over at the Knee

Overbent   Serious defective position of the head which approaches the chest to a point beyond the vertical. It may be caused by either the horse's attempt to evade the rider's control or the awkwardness of the rider.

Over-carted   A horse or pony drawing any vehicle which is too large (not necessarily too heavy), having regard to its size.

Overcheck (Driving)   A thin leather or cord check from the bit through the rings to the pad; used by Hackney Horse and Hackney Pony drivers.

Overcheck (on Hackney Buggy Harness)   Known among hackney people as 'top-rein', familiar to show spectators as the rein which is released from the hook on the pad when the horse comes to a standstill in the line-up, and which is fastened again at the moment of moving off.

Overcheck (on Racing Harness)   Used on pacers and trotters to keep the head up and the nose well forward, this position being an adjunct to speed.

Overcheck (Riding)   A thin leather or cord check, usually running from a small (broken or mullen) bridoon (*q.v.*) between the horse's ears to the saddle. This term is also used for a very thin (wire-mouth) gag snaffle, sometimes twisted, with cord cheeks used by nagsmen with a curb bit to raise the head.

Over-collected   Showing too much collection, the head position being behind the vertical.

Over-faced   Descriptive of a horse which is asked to jump beyond its powers, either in height or in number of jumps.

Overnight Declarations Office   This is the Jockey Club office, now at Weatherbys, Wellingborough, Northants, at which all horses have to be declared to run at the four-day stage before a race, and at which horses are withdrawn on the eve of a race.

Over-reach Boot   A circular rubber boot, sometimes laced, to prevent serious injury to the coronet when a horse over-reaches.

Over-reach Boot

Over-reaching This is caused by the rim of the toe of the hind shoe striking down against the heel of the fore-foot. *Prevention:* a smooth concaved toe in the hind shoe or, in exceptional cases, a specially made shoe (*see* FULLERED SHOE). *Protection: see* OVER-REACH BOOT.

Over-ride Term to describe hunt followers who ride too close to hounds when they are running.

Over-ride, to To ride a horse either at an excessive pace or for too long a period having regard to its physical condition.

'Over-the-Bridge' A dealer's term applied to steeplechasing.

'Over the Sticks' A slang term applied to steeplechasing.

Overo (U.S.A. and South America) Bay, black, brown, dun, roan or sorrel (chestnut) with white as a secondary colour extending in an irregular pattern. Legs are a combination of colour, always one colour white. The white extends upwards from under the belly, the dorsal (back) region being coloured. The head is partially or fully white. Glass or blue-eyes are a characteristic (*see* PINTO, PAINTED).

Overshot Fetlock *see* KNUCKLING-OVER.

Overshot Mouth *see* PARROT MOUTH.

Owner According to the Rules of Racing the owner of a racehorse, broadly speaking, may be a part-owner or a lessee but not a lessor.

Owner Partnership In racing a horse can be owned by one to four persons. Details of all partnerships, the name and address of every person having any interest in a horse, and the relative proportions of such interest must be supplied, signed by all parties, and lodged at the Racing Calendar Office. All partners are jointly and severally liable for every stake or forfeit.

Own the Line A hound which is on the fox's line is said to 'own the line'.

Ox Fence, Oxer An ordinary hedge, up to about 3 ft (91 cm) in height, with a guard rail set about a yard out from it on one side.

Oyster Feet Flattish feet marked with ridges as on an oyster shell. This is sometimes a natural condition, but often it appears after laminitis. Not to be confused with grass rings (*q.v.*).

P.B.A.R.   Part-bred Arab Register.

P.C.   Pony Club.

P.O.A. (U.S.A.)   Pony of the Americas.

P.O.B.   Ponies of Britain.

P.u.   (Racing)   Abbreviation for 'pulled up'; a horse which for some reason or other is pulled up by its jockey and does not complete the course.

Pace   A company or herd of asses. The original word was *passe*.

Pace   Army requirements are: walk 4 mph (6.43 km/h); trot 8 (12.8); canter 9 (14.4); slow gallop 12 (19.3); gallop 15 (24.1).

Pace-maker   A horse which leads and sets the pace in a race. In long distance races other than handicaps, a trainer often puts in a pace-maker to ensure a true-run race, a well-known example being 'Mail Fist' and 'Brown Jack' (*q.v.*) in the Queen Alexandra Stakes at Ascot.

Pacer   A horse which, instead of trotting with a diagonal action, moves like a camel, near-fore and hind together, followed by off-fore and hind. A very comfortable gait for long distance riding, and popular in America for shows and trotting races. The old English name of Ambler describes a horse with this action.

Pacing

Pacing   A term describing a form of racing in great vogue in the United States and to a lesser extent elsewhere (*see* AMBLE *and* PACER).

Pack   An undefined number of hounds kept for hunting.

Packhorse   A horse used for carrying packs, either the kit of a horseman or merchandise. In ancient times, packhorses were the chief, and often the only, means of transportation for goods.

Pad   The centre-piece of a set of harness, bridging the horse's back.

Pad   The foot of a fox. To 'pad a fox' is to follow the pad marks, i.e. to track it.

Pad (Harness)   The saddle used in double harness. It should have a top of patent leather on an under-panel of oiled leather, and its pattern should match the blinkers and padcloths (*q.v.*).

Pad (Roller)   A rectangular piece of felt, one inch in thickness, may be strapped under rollers, if the latter are not stuffed and regulated properly.

Padcloth   A cloth covering a horse's loins.

Padding   Flock is used as stuffing in good saddle and roller panels.

Paddock   An enclosed area of grassland which is used for rearing young horses, for turning out working animals when not required, and for restoring sick or lame horses to health or soundness. The term is synonymous with pasture though the latter suggests something of greater area. A paddock should afford a good growth of sweet and rich herbage and have a sound and safe surface and fence.

Paddock (Racing)   Every racecourse must have a railed-off paddock where the horses are paraded after they have been saddled, and where the jockeys assemble and mount.

Paddock Bucket A smaller version of the oak stable bucket for paddock use.

Pad-groom The correct term for a hunt servant. Livery: white cord breeches; top boots with flesh-coloured tops.

Pad-horse An obsolete term for a horse used for riding on the road: an easy-paced horse.

Pad-saddle A thick felt saddle without a tree. Pad-saddles of better quality are made with a fore-arch in place of a full tree, and there are models using an abbreviated tree made in leather and used for exercise in training stables.

Pad-tree The wooden or metal frame to which harness-pads are attached.

Pails, Oak Stable see BUCKETS, STABLE.

Pair Two horses driven abreast.

Palfrey In mediaeval times a light horse, as distinct from a war-horse, especially a small saddle-horse which could amble (*q.v.*).

Palio of Siena see SIENA RACES.

Palmer, Lynwood (1868–1939) Educated for the Diplomatic Service but went to Canada ranching and horse breeding. Artistic talent and a dedication to horses led to Canadian commissions for equestrian pictures. He went to New York and after a lapse of eleven years returned to England where he became established as a sporting artist, painting pictures for Edward VII and George V. He possessed a remarkable gift for capturing the individuality and character of Thoroughbred horses and also included picturesque landscape effects as background. Several of his pictures are owned by the Royal Jockey Club, Newmarket. In addition Palmer was a leading authority on horsemastership and driving, shoeing and care of the horse's foot.

Palomino The 'Golden Horse of the West' is not a breed, but a colour type, which is golden in its varying shades, with chalk white mane and tail. Usually no other white is allowed except on the face although the British Palomino Society allows white markings provided they are not so extensive as to give the impression of skewbald colouring. The origin of the Palomino is remote but probably Arab and may date back to the Homeric age; the first mention of it states that it was much favoured by the kings of Yemen, whilst Queen Isabella of Spain, the sponsor of Columbus, encouraged their breeding, and the horses were known in Spain as 'Y'sabellas'. The present name is believed to derive from Juan de Palomino who received one of these horses from Cortès. They are now used extensively for saddle, parade and spectacular purposes. *Breed Societies:* (In America) The Palomino Horse Breeders' Association of America, and The Palomino Horse Association. (In England) The British Palomino Society (*see* ISABELLA *and Plate 23*).

Pan American Games These events, based on the Olympic model, are limited to nations in North, South and Central America and were first held in 1951 and then every four years in the year preceding the Olympic Games. For dressage results *see page* 378; for show jumping results *see page* 406; for three-day event results *see page* 382.

Panel (Saddle) see SADDLE PANEL.

Pannade The curvet (*q.v.*) of a horse.

Papes Pattern A method of securing any type of rug by means of straps from the rear flanks joined to a central belly ring, from which a further strap passes through the forelegs and is secured at the breast.

Parabola (Show Jumping) The arc through the air made by a horse on clearing any obstacle, from the point of leaving the ground to the point of contact with it.

Parade-ring   Area where horses are paraded before a race.

Paradise (and Horses)   The followings lines are by the German author Friedrich Bodenstedt (1819–1892):

'Das Paradies der Erde
Liegt auf dem Rucken der Pferde,
In der Geshundheit des Leibes,
Und am Herzen des Weibes.'

(Paradise on Earth
Lies on the back of Horses,
In the health of the body
And on a woman's heart.)

Parafilariasis   A skin complaint found in horses mostly in the southern regions of the U.S.S.R. This disease is unknown in Great Britain.

Parallel Bars (British Show Jumping Assn.)   A spread fence consisting of two lines of poles set parallel to each other.

Parallel Bit   *see* FENNERS BIT.

Pariani   *see* ITALIAN SADDLE.

Pari-mutuel   A system of reciprocal betting similar to the totalisator; the only form of betting authorized in France since 1891. The odds returned are determined by dividing the total amount invested on a race by the number of winning units, less the percentage taken.

Park Course   A term to describe a racecourse which is entirely closed, like Kempton Park and Sandown Park in England, in contrast to Epsom which is partly open to the racing public without payment.

Park Drag   *see* DRAG.

Park Hack   Such a horse must be perfect in symmetry, manners and paces, with an easy and graceful walk, trot and canter. It may be of any colour except washy or mealy, its temper and mouth must be good in every respect, and it should stand 15–16 h.h. (152–163 cm).

Park Phaeton   A low-hung phaeton for ladies' driving, otherwise known as a George IV, Lady's or Peter's Phaeton.

Park Phaeton

Park Railings (Hunting)   Any iron railing.

Parliamentary Horse   It was illegal for mail coaches (*q.v.*) to be driven at a gallop but if one horse of the team was trotting the coach was within the law. Mail contractors therefore paid high prices for fast trotters, one of which they liked to include in each team. This trotter was known as the 'parliamentary' horse.

Parrot Mouth

Parrot Mouth   A malformation of the upper jaw, where the front (incisor) teeth overhang the lower jaw, preventing proper contact between the upper and lower incisor teeth and therefore inducive to digestive trouble. The condition also prevents a horse from grazing. A congenital deformity, often known as 'overshot'.

Parthenon Frieze   A masterpiece of Greek sculpture dating from the mid-fifth century B.C. Carved on the top of the outer wall of the Cella of the Parthenon at Athens it represents the ritual procession of the Pan-Athenaic festival, with many horses of different types. A part of the Frieze can be seen in the British Museum.

Paso Corto   *see* THE HORSE WORLD IN THE UNITED STATES OF AMERICA, *page* 351.

Paso Fino   Small type of saddle horse originating in Columbia, Peru and Puerto Rico (*see* THE HORSE WORLD IN THE UNITED STATES OF AMERICA, *page* 351).

Paso Largo   *see* THE HORSE WORLD IN THE UNITED STATES OF AMERICA, *page* 351.

Pass   *see* HALF-PASS.

Passage   A high school air, consisting of a very cadenced, lofty trot, with the moment of suspension clearly marked.

Passe   *see* PACE.

Passmore and Cole Bars   A pattern of safety stirrup bars designed to release the leather in the event of a fall.

Pastern   That part of a horse's leg which lies between the fetlock joint and the coronet.

Pastern, Long (Suffraginis Bone) *see* PASTERN, SHORT.

Pastern, Short (Coronet Bone)   Together with the suffraginis the coronet forms the pastern joint. Two branches of the Flexor Pedis Perforatus tendon are attached one on either side, to the lateral surface of the coronet bone.

Pastern Bone, Split   *Symptoms:* sudden and extreme lameness. *Treatment:* complete rest (in slings) and plaster of Paris strapping. A veterinary surgeon should be consulted; a suspected split will be clearly shown by X-ray.

Past Mark of Mouth   A term meaning a horse is 'aged' (*q.v.*).

Patch   A well-defined irregular area of hairs differing from the general body colour. The colour, shape, position and extent should be given on any written description (*see Plate 21*).

Pate (obsolete)   The head of a fox.

Patent Safety   Meaning a horse (generally a hunter) that will carry its rider with maximum safety and comfort.

Pato   A traditional mounted game played in South America (*see* HORSES IN SOUTH AMERICA, *page* 308).

Pattern Races   The principal weight-for-age flat races of the season, published in a Pattern Race Book, by authority of the Jockey Club, the Irish Turf Club and the Société d'Encouragement (the French equivalent of the Jockey Club).

Peacock Safety Irons   A type designed for children. The outside leg of the iron is removed and replaced with a stout rubber ring. Children should be made to change the irons from side to side, otherwise constant pressure on the tread, as is exerted when mounting, will cause it to bend and the child will be unable to maintain a correct leg position.

Peacock Safety Iron

'Peacocky'   Descriptive of a very high neck carriage with the head bent strongly at the poll: a narrow and flash-looking appearance which attracts the unwary buyer.

Peas   Almost as nutritious as beans, and having somewhat the same composition, peas are weight for weight cheaper, and are often substituted for beans. They should be fed (in limited quantities only) at least one year old, and should be clean and free from perforations.

Pechorsky, Pechora   Hardy and active small draught horse, bred in the valleys of the river Pechora in northern U.S.S.R. Used as a packhorse and for drawing sleighs.

Peck   A term denoting the act of stumbling. This can be at any gait and is commonly used when a horse stumbles on landing over a fence; hence the term 'Pecked on landing'.

Pedal Bone   This is crescent-shaped and somewhat resembles the hoof. It lies with the navicular bone and lower portion of the coronet bone, within the hoof, to form the pedal or foot joint.

Peel, John (1776–1854)   A Cumberland yeoman farmer who hunted his own hounds in that country for 46 years. Lived at Ruthwaite near Ireby and is buried in Caldbeck churchyard. Acquired fame through the popular song 'John Peel' written by Woodcock Graves in 1832.

Pegasus (Greek mythology)   The winged horse, offspring of Poseidon and Medusa, the Gorgon. He was caught by Bellerophon with a golden bridle and ridden by him to kill the Chimera. From a mark where his hoof struck Mount Helicon sprang Hippocrene, the River of the Muses.

Pegasus Club   Composed of members of the Bench and the Bar, this club holds a point-to-point meeting annually on a different course.

Pegs   *see* FROST NAILS.

Peg Sticking (U.S.A.)   *see* TENT PEGGING.

Pegu Pony   A small hardy Indian pony, stout, with strong limbs and feet, and capable of carrying a heavy load.

Pelethronius   King of the Lapithae, in Thessaly, said to have invented bridles.

Pelham   Any bit designed to combine in one the action of a double bridle, i.e. curb and bridoon (*q.v.*) (*see Plate 6*).

Pelham Roundings   Curved leather couplings joining the bridoon and curb rings on a Pelham bit so that one rein can be used instead of two.

Penalty (Racing)   In certain races, e.g. Maidens (*q.v.*) at Closing (*q.v.*), penalties can be incurred by horses winning between the closing of the entries and the running of the race concerned, in which they will have to carry more weight. Penalties vary considerably and conditions for these vary with different races. There are no penalties for the Classics (*q.v.*) and certain other races, nor can they be incurred by horses which have only been placed but have not won.

Penalty Seconds (Show Jumping)   Time added in speed contests for faults incurred while jumping the course.

Pendulous Lip   Where the under lip hangs low and lifeless.

Peneia Pony   Bred in the Greek province of Eleia, used for farm and pack transport. The stallions are used for breeding hinnies (*q.v.*). Height varies between 41 in and 14.1 h.h. (104–143 cm).

People's Dispensary for Sick Animals, The   Founded in 1917 by the late Mrs Maria Elizabeth Dickin, C.B.E., and incorporated in 1923, the P.D.S.A. claims to be the only society founded exclusively for the free treatment of sick and injured animals of people unable to afford professional fees. Through its Dispensaries, Animal

Hospitals, Mobile Caravans and home treatment it attends to nearly one million cases a year. It is supported entirely by voluntary contributions.

Perch The main timber in the undercarriage of coaches and some other old-time carriages, the perch runs from the front to the back of the vehicle, and usually curves downwards.

Perch-bolt This passes through the fore axle-tree bed and the fore transom holding the perch on a coach.

Percheron One of the most popular heavy draught horses, the Percheron originated in the La Perche district of France some hundred years ago. Known, used and admired in Great Britain, America, Canada and throughout the British Dominions, it is possessed of low draught, having a short compact body of tremendous depth. It stands on short legs, and in colour is grey or black, of great bone, yet, in spite of its bulk and weight, it is very active and is claimed to be the most economical of all heavy breeds. It has good hard blue feet with flat, flinty bone and clean legs. Stallions should be not less than 16.3 h.h. (166 cm), mares not less than 16 h.h. (163 cm). *Breed Society*: The British Percheron Horse Society (*see Plate 25*).

Percheron Horse Society, The British (Founded 1919) *Object*: to establish and maintain the purity of the breed of Percheron Horses in the United Kingdom.

Perioplic Ring Situated around the extreme upper border of the coronary band, this is composed of papillae like those of the coronary band, but smaller in size. It secretes the periople, a thin varnish-like horn covering the exterior of the wall.

Periplantar Shoe *see* CHARLIER SHOE.

Permit Holder Under Jockey Club Rules for steeplechasing and hurdle racing only trainers who train solely for themselves and immediate members of their family can be granted a permit to train, as opposed to a full training licence (*see* LICENCE, TRAINER).

Persian Arab *see* PERSIAN HORSE.

Persian Horse Known as a breed for many centuries B.C., the Persian is claimed to be descended from the Tarpan (*q.v.*); it is also suggested by some that the Persian was the ancestor of the Arab. In any event, it is a typical oriental breed, beautiful and full of quality, high-spirited and speedy, and consequently was much appreciated by Islam warriors. Today there are found in Persia several different breeds, such as the Persian Arab, the Turkoman, the Shirazi, the Yamoote, the Bokara Pony, and the Jaf.

Peruvian Ambler Mainly of Barb descent, extremely agile and sure-footed, their main pace being the amble (*q.v.*) (*see* HORSES IN SOUTH AMERICA, *page* 309).

Petachial Fever An acute feverish condition accompanied by purple bleeding from the mucous membranes of the eyes and nose. Generally the aftermath of another disease, its prognosis is poor. Veterinary advice essential.

'Peterborough' To fox-hunters, this meant the Peterborough Royal Hound Show, which was founded in 1878; held annually since then, the show has become established as the premier foxhound show of Great Britain, and is now incorporated in the East of England Show.

Peter's Phaeton *see* PARK PHAETON.

Peytrel or **Poitrel** Breast plate armour for the horse.

Phaeton A four-wheeled carriage for personal driving of which there are many varieties (*see* MAIL, DEMI-MAIL, PARK, EQUIROTAL, SIAMESE and SPIDER PHAETONS).

Phill-horse or Thill-horse   A shaft-horse.

'Phiz'   *see* BROWNE, HABLOT KNIGHT

Photo-finish   A device whereby the finish of a race is photographed from both sides of the course to enable the judge to decide with certainty the first four or more in a race to finish.

Physic Ball   *see* MEDICINE BALL.

Piaffe   A passage (*q.v.*) done on a particular spot without gaining ground. The action should be lofty, slow and cadenced (*see* PASSAGE).

Pickaxe   A slang name for a team of five horses with 2 wheelers and 3 leaders; also used for 1 wheel-horse and 2 leaders, as opposed to unicorn, i.e. 1 leader and 2 wheelers.

'Picked-up'   Racing term indicating a shortening of the reins by the jockey to balance and poise his mount for an increase in pace.

Pick Hounds Up   To lift hounds.

Pick-me-up   To a pint of warm old ale, add: tincture of ginger, 1 tablespoon; tincture of calumba, 1 tablespoon; compound tincture of gentian, 2 tablespoons; and compound tincture of cardamom, 1 tablespoon. A more simple tonic is ¼ pt (0.14 l) of whisky to ¾ pt (0.43 l) of water or milk.

Pie   A foxhound colour, lighter than the rich Belvoir Tan. There are three shades, lemon pie, hare pie and badger pie.

Piebald   Where the body colour consists of large irregular patches of black and white. The line of demarcation between the two colours is generally well defined. Piebalds and Skewbalds are termed Pintos in the U.S.A. and are separately named according to colour-grouping (*see* MOROCCO, OVERO *and* TOBIANO).

Pigeon-toed   *see* PIN-TOES.

Pig-eye   A small eye, undistinguished in character and having a mean, uninterested and unintelligent outlook.

Pigskin   The most desirable leather for the seat of a saddle, on account of its durability and elasticity.

Pig-sticking   The sport of hunting wild boar on horseback with a spear, developed by British Officers in India at the beginning of the nineteenth century from the more ancient sport of spearing bear. The greatest centres were in the thick grass-grown old beds of the great rivers, i.e. the Jamna and the Ganges of the United Provinces, called the Kadir country, and in the Central Provinces, especially around Muttra. It was also carried on in parts of the Punjab, of Bengal, and in North Africa. Doyen of clubs was the Meerut Tent Club, founded before the Mutiny. The premier competition was for the Kadir Cup (*q.v.*), an individual event instituted in 1873; the Muttra Cup is given for the best team results each season. A smallish animal of the polo pony type is best for this sport, which requires the highest degree of skill and courage in both horse and rider.

Pigtail   In an American 'train' of fifteen mules, each animal is tied to a short rope with loops braided in each end. This rope is called a pigtail, and is fastened to the rear end of the saddle of the mule in front, whilst the halter of each animal is passed through the open loop of the rope with a knot which can be easily pulled loose in the case of an emergency.

Pilentum   Open carriage with the doorway very near the ground. Made in different sizes to carry four or six people and drawn by one or two horses (*c.* 1834).

Pillar or Pillars   Training of the horse by the aid of pillars may have originated in classical times as Eumenes (died 316 B.C.), when besieged at the fort of Nora by Antigonus, feared his

Highland Pony

PLATE 17

Holstein

Hunter

PLATE 18

Morgan

(*above*) Hunting: going to draw

PLATE 19

(*below*) Show Jumping

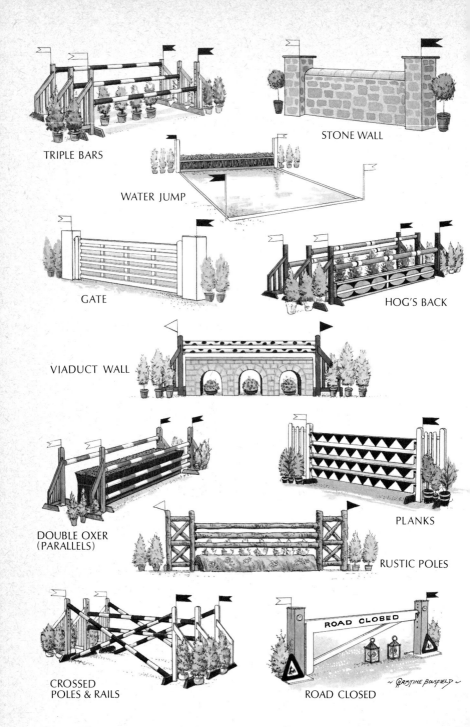

TRIPLE BARS

STONE WALL

WATER JUMP

GATE

HOG'S BACK

VIADUCT WALL

DOUBLE OXER
(PARALLELS)

PLANKS

RUSTIC POLES

CROSSED
POLES & RAILS

ROAD CLOSED

~ CHRISTINE BOUSFIELD ~

PLATE 20   Show Jumps

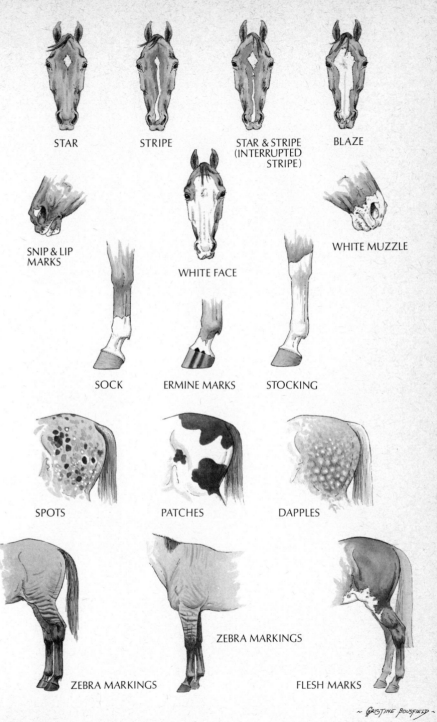

STAR STRIPE STAR & STRIPE
(INTERRUPTED
STRIPE) BLAZE

SNIP & LIP
MARKS WHITE FACE WHITE MUZZLE

SOCK ERMINE MARKS STOCKING

SPOTS PATCHES DAPPLES

ZEBRA MARKINGS ZEBRA MARKINGS FLESH MARKS

~ CHRISTINE BOUSFIELD ~

PLATE 21 Markings

(*above*) New Forest Pony

PLATE 22

(*below*) Welsh Cob

(*above*) Orlov Trotter

PLATE 23

(*below*) Palomino

PLATE 24

(left) Polo

(right) Polocrosse

(below) American
Trotting
Championship

Percheron

PLATE 25

Shetland Pony

(*left*) Pony Trekking

PLATE 26

(*below*) Private Drag

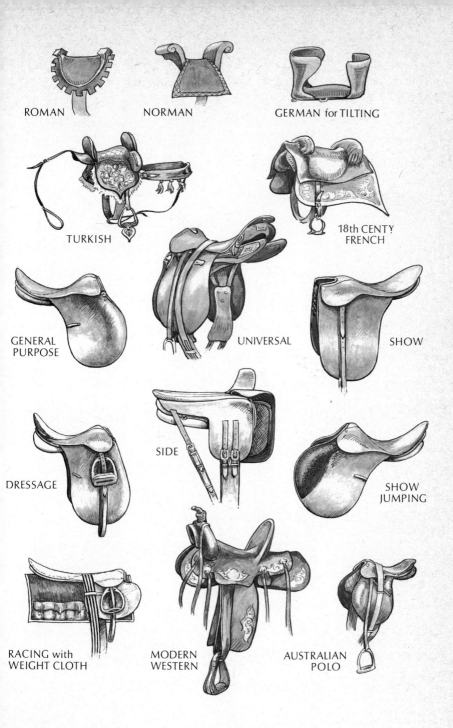

ROMAN

NORMAN

GERMAN for TILTING

TURKISH

18th CENTY FRENCH

GENERAL PURPOSE

UNIVERSAL

SHOW

DRESSAGE

SIDE

SHOW JUMPING

RACING with WEIGHT CLOTH

MODERN WESTERN

AUSTRALIAN POLO

PLATE 27   Saddles

(*above*) Shire

PLATE 28

(*below*) Show Pony

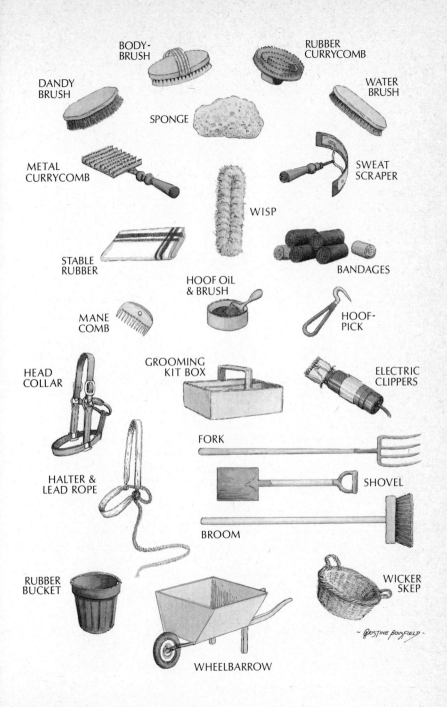

DANDY
BRUSH

BODY-
BRUSH

RUBBER
CURRYCOMB

WATER
BRUSH

SPONGE

METAL
CURRYCOMB

SWEAT
SCRAPER

WISP

STABLE
RUBBER

BANDAGES

HOOF OIL
& BRUSH

MANE
COMB

HOOF-
PICK

HEAD
COLLAR

GROOMING
KIT BOX

ELECTRIC
CLIPPERS

FORK

HALTER &
LEAD ROPE

SHOVEL

BROOM

RUBBER
BUCKET

WICKER
SKEP

WHEELBARROW

~ Christine Bousfield ~

PLATE 29   Stable Equipment

(*above*) Tennessee Walking Horse

PLATE 30

(*below*) English Thoroughbred

(*right*) Riders of the
Spanish Riding
School of Vienna

PLATE 31

(*below*) Small Hacks
at the Royal Windsor
Horse Show

Welsh Mountain Pony

PLATE 32

Wild Horse and Foal

horses would suffer from lack of exercise. He therefore invented a method of working them in their stalls by placing a pulley in the stable beams and, with a running rein, pulling up their fore parts. Assistants in the rear urged the horses into motion on the one spot. Pignatelli, the famous Neapolitan master of equitation, to save the fatigue of holding the lunge rein, and having no manège (q.v.), used to tie his horses to a tree and work them round it. Antoine de Pluvinel de la Baume (1555–1620) copied this idea in France by a post or pillar, later adding a second one. Pillars are still used in training the horses of the Spanish Riding School in Vienna (q.v.).

Pillar Reins　A pair of brass-mounted reins, attached to stall-posts or pillars, to secure a horse when backed into its stall. When the horse is to be saddled it should be turned round and placed with the reins attached to pillars (q.v.).

Pillars　The supporting posts to the divisions between stalls to which pillar-reins are attached (see PILLAR REINS).

'Pillars of the Stud Book'　The three Arabian sires to one of which all entries in the General Stud Book trace their descent: The Byerley Turk (1689), The Darley Arabian (1704), The Godolphin Arabian (1730) (qq.v.).

'Pill-box'　A slang name popularly applied to a brougham of the smallest build, seating two persons within. It was particularly favoured by West End doctors (see BROUGHAM).

Pilling Going Gauge　An instrument designed to test the state of the 'going' (q.v.) on racecourses.

Pillion　A type of saddle attached to the hinderpart of an ordinary saddle on which a second person (usually a woman) could ride. Extensively used in the Middle Ages. There are records of Queen Elizabeth I riding behind her Master of the Horse to St Paul's

Cathedral. The pillion is stated to have been out of use since about 1830.

Pillion Post　see MOUNTING BLOCK.

Pindos Pony　Bred in the Greek mountainous regions of Thessaly and Epirus for riding and light farm work. Height 12–13 h.h. (122–132 cm).

Pinerolo　Famous Italian Cavalry School near Turin, founded in 1823. It became the Royal Cavalry School. Federico Caprilli (q.v.) in this century became its most renowned instructor.

Pin-firing, Point-firing　To some extent the place of this as a treatment has been taken by blistering. Pin-firing is a method to stimulate the growth of tissues, and consists in the application of pointed irons, which are subjected to great heat, to the affected part. The treatment may be graduated from a mere puncturing of the skin to a penetration as deep as the bone.

Pin-toes　Toes which turn inwards; horses having such never strike themselves and the fault can often be cured by shoeing.

Pink Eye　Influenza: similar to an ordinary cold, but far more serious. As the attack develops, the fever increases and the mucous membrane of the eye becomes pink. Treatment: consult a veterinary surgeon.

Pink (Hunting)　Incorrect term for the colour of scarlet hunting coats. Origin of term uncertain, but possibly based on the fact that 'Mr Pink' was a fashionable nineteenth-century hunting tailor.

Pint Pot, Muzzle in a　A popular phrase descriptive of a muzzle so small and refined as to be capable of being 'put in a pint pot'; e.g. the best type of Arabian horse has such a muzzle.

Pinto, Painted　The word derives from the Spanish pintado (painted), and in this application has a similar meaning to the English piebald or skewbald, as it implies a colouring which is the result of a combination of albinism (whiteness), melanism (blackness) and erythrism (redness) of the skin. Pintos are separately named according to colour-grouping (*see* OVERO *and* TOBIANO), but these colourings can be found in many breeds so the Pinto cannot be said to form one distinctive breed. It is, however, known as a distinctive American horse which has a reputation for toughness and endurance; having a natural camouflage, it was popular with the Red Indians. Breeding results demonstrate the Pinto strain to be very potent, reproducing itself fairly constantly (*see* THE HORSE WORLD IN THE UNITED STATES OF AMERICA, *page* 351). *Breed Association:* Pinto Horse Association of America.

Pinto Horse Society   Formed in United States of America by enthusiasts, to encourage the development of pinto coloration into a breed of its own by type selection.

Pinzgauer   A medium-sized draught horse of the Noriker (*q.v.*) breed which is characterized by being spotted.

Pipe   A branch or hole of a fox-earth.

Pipe Opener   A gallop to clear a horse's wind.

Pirouette   A movement where the forelegs describe a complete circle of which the centre is occupied by a hindleg serving as a pivot. It may be performed at the walk, at the piaffe, at the canter; each of those paces must remain unimpaired in executing the movement which is called *half pirouette* when the rotation of the shoulders stops at half circle.

Pirouette Renversée   A movement where the hindlegs describe a complete circle of which the centre is occupied by a foreleg serving as a pivot. It is performed only at the walk. It is called *half pirouette renversée* when the rotation of the quarters stops at half circle.

Unlike the pirouette, it does not figure in the F.E.I. dressage tests.

Pithing   A speedy and painless way to kill a horse, this consists of running the blade of a knife between the joints of the vertebrae at the axis. Death is practically instantaneous.

Pitter   *see* COLLIER.

Pit Ponies   Not used before the nineteenth century, but when colliery 'lift' cages were installed they worked underground in large numbers. Size, and therefore breed, were determined by the height of the pit workings. Shetland, Welsh, Fell, Dartmoor, Exmoor, Norwegian and Iceland ponies were used. In recent years with increased mechanization few ponies are still working underground.

Place (Racing)   Any horse placed by the judge first, second or third in a race is a 'placed' horse. No horse passing the winning post after the judge has left his box can be 'placed'.

Place Betting   Backing a horse for a place—three places with eight or more runners and two places with five to seven runners. Bookmakers tabulate their own rules on place betting with various contingencies, but normally a backer should receive one quarter the odds for a place with eight or more runners and one-third the odds for a place with five to seven runners.

Plaited Reins   This usually refers to plaited handparts, as all plaited reins cannot well accommodate a running martingale. The hand parts are usually plaited from five strands.

Plaiting   *see* CROSSING FEET.

Plaits   Worn most generally in the show ring by hunters, hacks, show and working ponies and Hackneys to smarten the neck and general appearance and to add refinement.

Plaits (Hack)   Similar to plaits for a hunter (*q.v.*), but the mane can be shorter and the plaits smaller and neater.

Plaits

Plaits (Hackney) The mane is hogged on each side of the neck, leaving a very thin line of mane in the centre. This is plaited in a considerable number of small plaits with yellow, green or red wool.

Plaits (Hunter) The mane must be a fair length and not pulled too short; the plaits, five, or at the most six, in number, should be turned back underneath and sewn with thread of the same colour as the mane.

Plaits (U.S.A.) Usually called braids. Great difference of opinion as to correct number. It is likely to run to 9–13 on a gelding and 8–12 for a mare. Mares are supposed to have even numbers of braids, geldings odd.

Plantar Cushion A mass of fibro-fatty tissue, filling up the space behind the pedal bone and forming the bulb of the heel, this acts as a shock absorber.

Plantation Walking Horse *see* TENNESSEE WALKING HORSE.

Plate (Racing) A very light shoe used for racing. If a horse is wearing the heavier exercise shoes as opposed to racing plates in a race he will not show his best form.

Plate (Racing) Races are either sweepstakes or plates. In the former entry fees, forfeits etc. are added to

the prize money and distributed to the owners of the placed horses. In a plate the racecourse guarantees so much prize money, but keeps the entrance fees etc. for itself (*see* SWEEPSTAKE).

'Plate, In the' Descriptive of a rider when sitting in the saddle.

Plater A term for a horse which runs in a selling race (*q.v.*), so is normally of a low standard.

Platten Shoe *see* FARRIERY, *page* 117.

Players *see* KEYS.

Pleven A breed of Hungarian horse of mixed ancestry but of considerable distinction. It exhibits Arab characteristics, having been based mainly on that breed. Average height about 15.3 h.h. (155 cm).

Plough A hunting term implying wheat fields, seed, stubble and fallows.

Ploughs The arable parts of East Anglia are known as 'the ploughs', hence: 'To hunt on the ploughs'.

Pluvinel, Antoine de (1555–1620) (Antoine de Pluvinel de la Baume) Riding instructor to the King of France, Louis XIII, and author of *The Instruction of the King in the Art of Riding*, printed in 1626, which is in the form of a dialogue between the King as his pupil and the author as riding instructor.

Pneumonia The general cause of this serious complaint is almost certainly a neglected severe cold or chill, and every effort must be made to bring relief and comfort pending the arrival of the veterinary surgeon whose attendance should be sought at once. The symptoms will be evident: severely laboured breathing, shivering, a dejected and miserable animal.

Poached (Hunting) Where the take off in front of a jump—or in gateways—is muddy and cut-up.

Point   The point of a run is the greatest distance between any two points measured in a straight line. The *actual* distance, however, is termed 'as hounds ran' (*q.v.*).

Point-firing   *see* PIN-FIRING.

Pointing   The resting of either foreleg: an indication of leg or foot trouble, and a reliable sign of navicular disease (*q.v.*).

'Pointing your Leaders'   Giving the leaders in a coach team the hint that you are intending to alter direction to right or left.

Point-to-points   Races confined to horses which have been regularly and fairly hunted with any recognized pack of hounds. For all races (except those confined to the hunt promoting the meeting, i.e. 'Members' Races') the owners must obtain a Master of Hounds certificate for each horse which must be registered at the Racing Calendar Office before the horse is eligible to be entered.

Each hunt normally has its own point-to-point meeting annually on a course chosen by the Committee. A race for lady riders is often included at a meeting, and unlike the men's races, it is not necessary for the women riders to be amateurs. Women may also ride at the same weights as men in races confined to the hunt promoting the meeting as well as those confined to adjacent hunts. Originally all these races were run over a natural country from one point to another, but now most of the fences are made up. The minimum distance is 3 miles (4.8 km). The longest race is the Ralph Grimthorpe Gold Cup of $4\frac{1}{2}$ miles (7.2 km) at the Middleton in Yorkshire. There are about 185 point-to-points in England, Scotland and Wales during the season, which lasts from February to early June (*see Plate* 13).

Points   A term elaborating a colour, e.g. 'Bay with black points' indicating a bay with black mane, tail and lower portion of the legs.

Points   Ready-knitted tips for the whip.

Points of the Horse   *see page* xi.

Poisons   Some plants are poisonous— yew, laburnum, St John's wort, hemlock, ragwort and deadly nightshade being the most dangerous. Acorns, rhododendrons, damsons, meadow saffron, bluebell, horse-tails, green bracken, celandine and some buttercup, white clover, vetches, ground ivy, water drop wort, foxglove, maple and coniferous trees if eaten in quantity are also poisonous. Weeds such as dog's mercury, fat hen and water figwort, thornapple, henbane and cowbane are also harmful but are usually absent from paddocks. Fool's parsley (*Arethusa cynapium*) is poisonous, but although a common field weed is usually avoided.

Poitevine   A heavy horse bred in the Landes district of France, originally being brought from Norway, Denmark and Holland. Slow, dull disposition, dun in colour. The mares are used almost solely to breed very large mules to the big Poitou jackass (*q.v.*).

Poitou Ass   An ass which sometimes attains 15 h.h. (152 cm) and sometimes has 9 in (228 mm) of bone below the knee. It has enormously large ears, which cannot be carried upright but poke outwards, and which have the hair inside forming a series of curls called 'cadenettes', regarded as a sign of pure breeding. The usual colours are dark brown and black, but greys are seen. Bred to cart mares, Poitou jacks throw very good heavy-type mules, some of which stand over 16 h.h. (162 cm) (*see* POITEVINE).

Pole   The timber on each side of which a pair of horses, or the wheelers of a team, are put.

Pole (Aids for Pacer and Trotter)   A pointed wooden pole placed on the side opposite that to which the horse pulls. It is buckled to one of the rings on the saddle-pad and the pointed end is pushed through a ring on the head-piece, protruding a few inches beyond the nose of the horse.

Pole Chains These are used in coaching and a few carriages to put-to wheelers (*see also* POLE PIECES).

Pole Head A movable steel fitting on the pole of a coach (and some other vehicles) to which pole chains or pole pieces are attached.

Pole Hook The hook on the end of a coach pole to carry the bars. In coaching parlance it is known as the 'Swan-neck'.

Pole Pieces Strong leather straps used in most private carriages for putting-to a pair, in place of chains (*see* POLE CHAINS).

Pole Pin This secures the pole in place when fitted between the futchells (*q.v.*).

Poleys Pads on a western saddle.

Poling Poling-up or Pole-piecing: the act of attaching pole chains or pole pieces to the horses' hames.

Polish Arab The Polish have a great reputation as horse breeders and their horses have always been in big demand in Europe, while their cavalry in the seventeenth century was in-vincible. The horses had eastern blood in them, Arab, Barb, Turkish, Persian, etc., but the Arab has been held by them in the highest regard since the sixteenth century. Many great families of Poland founded studs of Arabian horses long ago, e.g. the Sangussgo Stud in 1506, while the name of Count Potocki and his stud are well known to Englishmen. Several studs in America have been founded on Polish Arabs, while the famous and beautiful Arab Champion in England—'Skowronek' —came from the Antoniny Stud in Poland. A characteristic feature of Polish Arab breeding was the constant introduction of fresh blood by im-porting the most valuable horses direct from the Arabian desert and by selec-tion from racing at Levow. During the 1960s Polish Arabs have been increas-ingly purchased by breeders in many parts of the world, especially the United States, Great Britain and Germany. *Breed Society:* The Arab Horse Breed-ing Association of Poland (*see* THE ARABIAN HORSE (*page* 11).

Polish Half-bred The nature of the Polish country, wide agricultural lands, the type of soil, not always good roads and the distance from railways, ren-dered heavy draught horses such as Percherons and Shires unsuitable and, in consequence, Polish breeders, with care and system, developed a cross-breed to suit their requirements, using the English Thoroughbred, Arab or Anglo-Arab to bring stamina and ac-tion. Before the 1939 war, this was done on a highly selective basis and a very good type of half-bred was pro-duced, and half-bred stud books or registers were kept. Types vary with provinces and general requirements.

Polish Thoroughbred The term indicates a horse of pure English Thoroughbred stock as bred and de-veloped in Poland. The first English Thoroughbreds were introduced to Poland early in the nineteenth century and the Polish Horse Racing Associa-tion was formed in 1841. Breeding was at first confined to a few wealthy families, but many good brood mares were imported from England, France, Germany and Austria and also the stallion 'Flying Fox' from England at a cost of 37,000 guineas. Training stables on English lines became established. The two World Wars decimated the horse population of Poland but today the Thoroughbred is being bred ex-tensively in Government studs.

Poll The area of a horse's head be-tween the ears; the seat of Poll Evil (*q.v.*).

Pollard, James (1792–1867)   Son of Robert Pollard, an engraver and sporting artist. Painted angling and shooting scenes, but became particularly popular for his vast number of pictures of coaching and driving subjects, there being more coaching prints after Pollard than any other artist. His style was meticulous and seldom varied; often his human figures are curiously elongated and much of the charm of his picture lies in the interesting London backgrounds and provincial inns.

Poll Evil   Arises from necrosis of the ligamentum nuchae (*q.v.*) in the region of the poll, with or without necrosis of the occipital process of the skull. Complete excision of the funicular portion of the ligamentum nuchae from the upper third of the neck usually secures healing within three months. In fine weather the horse may graze out after the operation and be brought in for dressing, as hanging the head assists drainage. The condition may arise from striking the poll on the frame of the stable door or other object, or it may result from a *Brucella* infection.

Poll Pad or Guard   A felt pad which slides on to the headpiece of a head collar or bridle to prevent injury should the horse throw up his head whilst travelling in a horse-box.

POLO

History   The origin of polo is lost in the mists of antiquity, but records exist of games played in 525 B.C. The cradle of the game appears to have been Persia (where a game resembling lawn tennis was played mounted and was called Chaugan), and Manipur, in Assam. It was introduced into England by the 10th Hussars in 1869, and the first public game in this country was played at Hounslow in that year, although the game had already been adopted by Assam tea planters in India in 1850. America took up the game in 1883. Since the abolition of the height limit, Argentina has become the leading country in the breeding of polo ponies. India was formerly the nursery of all British players, but the position altered between the wars, although first-class polo is still played in the Native States. Argentina is now the leading polo nation.

The polo ground is 300 yd (274 m) long, 160 yd (146 m) wide if boarded, 200 yd (182 m) wide if unboarded. In U.S.A. and Argentina these dimensions are sometimes slightly larger. Polo boards must not exceed 11 in (27.9 cm) in height, and are fixed on either side of all British and U.S. grounds. They are used to some extent in Argentina, but never in India. The goal posts are 8 yd (7 m) apart.

Duration of Play   The full game is 8 chukkas (*q.v.*) in Argentina, and only 6 in Great Britain and the U.S.A. Each chukka is timed to last 7 minutes, then a bell is rung but the game goes on until the ball goes out of play, or the umpire stops the game when fair to both sides.

In case of a tie the game goes on with additional chukkas until a deciding goal is scored.

There are intervals of 3 minutes between chukkas, and 5 minutes at half-time.

Ends are changed each time a goal is scored—this has been found fairest when there is a wind.

Handicaps   Each player is handicapped (on an 8-chukka basis) from minus 2 up to 10 goals (the best players). The aggregate handicap of the four players in a team is the team handicap. In all matches played under handicap conditions during the season the higher handicapped team shall concede to the lower handicapped team the difference

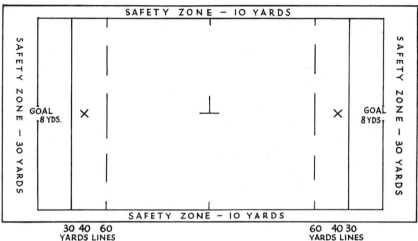

Layout of Boarded Polo Ground

in the handicaps divided by six and multiplied by the number of periods of play of the match.

Ponies normally play two chukkas in an afternoon with a rest of at least one chukka in between.

There is no limit to the height of ponies.

Rules These are laid down by national bodies, such as the Hurlingham Club in Britain, the U.S. Polo Association in the U.S.A., and the Argentine Association in that country, but all are now similar in essentials. They are all designed to combat dangerous play in a game which is essentially 'dangerous' in itself. There is no off-side rule.

Fouls (a) A player following the ball on its exact line has the Right of Way over all other players. Any other player who crosses the player on the right of way close enough to be dangerous, commits a foul. Penalties vary according to the degree of danger and closeness of the cross.

(b) No player may hook an opponent's stick unless he is on the same side of the opponent's pony as the ball.

(c) Dangerous riding or rough handling is not allowed—a player may ride an opponent off, but must not charge in at an angle.

Penalties The following penalties may be given:

(a) Penalty 1. A goal is given if the cross is dangerous or deliberate in the vicinity of the goal. The ball is then thrown in 10 yd (9.1 m) in front of the goal without ends being changed.

(b) Penalty 2. Free hit from 30 yd (27 m) opposite the centre of the goal—defenders to be behind the back line and outside the goal posts which they must not ride through when the ball is hit.

(c) Penalty 3. Free hit from 40 yd (36 m) same conditions as (b).

(d) Penalty 4. Free hit from 60 yd (54 m)—none of the defending side to be nearer than 30 yd (27 m) when the ball is hit.

(e) Penalty 5a. Free hit from the spot where the foul took place— no defender to be nearer than 30 yd (27 m).

(f) Penalty 5b. Free hit at the ball from the centre of the ground, none of side fouling to be within 30 yd (27 m) of the ball, the fouled being free to place themselves where they choose.

Corners are not taken as in Association football—instead, a free hit is given 60 yd (54 m) from the goal from a spot opposite where the ball was hit behind the line, none of the defending side to be nearer than 30 yd (27 m).

There is no 'off-side' in Polo.

Umpire, Referee and Good Judges The rules shall be administered in a match by two umpires, who shall be mounted to enable them to keep close to the play, and by a referee who shall remain off the field of play in a central position. By mutual agreement between captains of teams, one umpire and, if desired, also the referee, may be dispensed with. In this case, the decision of the umpire shall be final; where there are two umpires, and they disagree, the decision of the referee shall be final.

Polo Positions Forwards, Nos. 1 and 2; half-back, No. 3; back, No. 4. All positions are instantly interchangeable as the game dictates. Each member must mark the opposite number in any line-up or hit in.

Start of the Game At the beginning of the game the two teams shall line up in the middle of the ground, each team being on its own side of the half-way line; numbers 1, 2, 3 and back face their respective opponents. The Umpire shall bowl the ball underhand and hard between the opposing ranks of players, from a distance of not less than 5 yd (4.6 m), the players remaining stationary until the ball has left his hand.

Stoppage of Play Play is stopped only at the conclusion of a chukka when the ball has gone out of play (or, in the last chukka, promptly on time), or for infringement of the rules or an accident or the fall of a pony. Play is not stopped for a player being thrown, provided he is not seriously hurt.

Tie In the event of a tie the last chukka is extended beyond the final bell until the ball goes out. If it still remains a tie, the game continues by chukkas until one side scores a goal.

How a Goal is Scored A goal is scored when a ball passes between the goal posts and over and clear of the goal line. If a ball is hit above the top of the goal posts, but in the opinion of the umpire between those posts produced, it shall count as a goal.

Tactics These vary according to the capacity and temperament of the team. A diamond formation attack, careful marking and, above all, long and accurate hitting are essentials of modern polo.

Equipment The necessary equipment for the pony in polo is as follows: boots or bandages on the pony's four legs, to protect them against the stick or the ball; a pelham or double bridle; a standing martingale and saddle.

Polo Headgear

Polo headgear: the wearing of a helmet of the 'Pigsticker' type, or a Polo Cap, is compulsory for safety purposes. Made of three-ply natural cork body of thirty pieces of natural cork laminated into three layers, the cap is fitted with college-cap back, trimmed with deep leather, which is fitted with draw cord and anti-concussion cross tapes. Both cap and helmet type are fitted with adjustable chinstrap and rubber pad in the top of the crown, the latter finished with four large rubber ventilators. The rider must also have a left-hand glove, a polo whip about 42 in (106 cm) which a player can use without taking his hand from the rein, boots, which are brown unlaced top boots, and breeches.

Polo stick: the shaft, about 51 in (129 cm) long is generally of either malacca (stiff) or whangee (whippy), the former being preferred everywhere outside India. The head is usually cylindrical and made of bamboo root or other light, tough wood such as persimmon, but there is no official definition of shape or size. Often termed Mallet in the U.S.A. The size of the ball shall not exceed 3¼ in (8.25 cm) in diameter, and the weight of the ball shall be within the limits of 4¼ to 5 oz (127–141 g). The balls are made of willow and bamboo, and the practice ball (excellent for schooling purposes and use in riding school or for practising on rough grass) is made of unburstable foam rubber (*see Plate* 24).

*   *   *

Polo Breast Girth   Similar to an Aintree breast girth but made of leather, often padded with sheepskin and having a slot sewn on at the centre of the breast, through which a martingale can be passed.

Polo Brown Calf   High polishing leather, vegetable tanned, for Polo Boots and Leggings.

Polo Championship Cup   For results *see page* 382.

Polo Club (Oldest)   This is the Cachar Polo Club (India), founded in 1859 by some British planters in Assam who, since about 1850, had been taking part in local polo. For other clubs *see page* 417.

Polocrosse   A mounted combination of polo and lacrosse which began as an indoor game in England in the 1930s. In 1939 it became immensely popular as an outdoor game in Australia with three players a side, using a soft ball and a polo-type stick with a net at the end. Ponies are limited to 15 h.h. (152 cm). In Australia the standard field is 160 yd long by 60 yd wide (146 × 54 m), goal posts 14 ft (4.27 m) high and 8 ft (2.43 m) apart (*see Plate* 24).

Polo International Matches   The rules of the host nation are honoured. The chief trophies are the Cup of the Americas and the Westchester Cup (*q.v.*) first competed for by Hurlingham and Meadow Brook (U.S.A.) Clubs in 1886. America beat England for the first time in 1909 and since this time England has won only once, in 1914. Games are also played between Argentina and the U.S.A. Since 1946 representative English teams have played as follows, *in England*: 1951 3 matches *v.* an Argentine side, for the Coronation Cup. England won. 1953 6 teams competed for the Coronation Cup. Argentina won. 1971 and 1972 U.S.A. beat England in a match for the Coronation Cup. *Abroad:* England played in a triangular contest with Argentina and U.S.A. in 1966. Won by Argentina.

Polo Inter-Regimental Tournament   For results *see page* 383.

Polo Inter-Services Championship Cup   For results *see page* 384.

Polo Pit   An enclosed 'cage' with sloping floor, used for instructing beginners in the correct use of the stick for hitting purposes. The learner sits astride a saddled wooden horse in the centre of the pit and the ball returns to him after striking.

Polo Pony   A type rather than a breed. The height has varied from about 12–13 h.h. (121–132 cm) in the sixteenth century up to 16 h.h. (163 cm) and over, the height limit having now been removed. Variations in breeds include Manipur ponies from Assam, mountain ponies from the Himalayas, Arabs and English Thoroughbreds. At the end of the nineteenth century, a start was made to breed polo ponies by small Thoroughbred sires and good foundation pony mares selected for performance. Requirements: a long neck with good flexion at the junction of the head, good shoulders, a short strong back with well-sprung ribs, elbows well away from the body, exceptionally powerful quarters, and hocks well-let down. Ponies must have courage and playing temperament. *Breed Society:* The National Pony Society.

Polo Pony Boots   Made of felt and leather with elastic fastenings. They envelop the leg from just below the knee and from some 5 in (12 cm) below the hock to the hoof, giving all-round protection for treading, blows from the stick, etc.

Pommels   There are two pommels on a side-saddle and they are known as the leaping or lower pommel (detachable) and the top pommel or near head (fixed).

Ponies Act, 1969   Presented by the late Lord Silkin in the House of Lords, ratified 1970, whereby it is not lawful to ship any pony to any port outside the United Kingdom unless the Minister of Agriculture (or in Scotland, the Secretary of State) is satisfied that the pony is intended for breeding, riding or exhibition. In 1973 the pony had to be of not less value than £120 if not exceeding 12 h.h. (122 cm), or if over that height £160; ponies of the Shetland breed must be of not less than £60. Any pony being exported must be rested immediately before being loaded on the vessel or aircraft.

Ponies of Britain, The   Originally registered as a charity when the late Sir John Crocker Bulteel, then Clerk of the Royal Ascot Racecourse, asked Mrs Glenda Spooner to stage a show in the Paddock at Ascot. The first show was held in 1953. Thereafter the late Miss Gladys Yule joined Mrs Spooner as Joint Founder and was Chairman until her death in 1957. Under the Chairmanship of Mrs Spooner it now runs three major shows a year (the

Stallion, Scottish and Summer) together with cross-country events, instructional courses and lectures; runs an extensive Approved Trekking and Riding Holidays Scheme, and is extremely active in promoting the fair treatment of all animals with particular reference to equines.

Ponies of the Americas   A new and very popular breed of pony in the U.S.A., which in 10 years spread from coast to coast. It is a cross of Arabian (*q.v.*), Quarter Horse (*q.v.*) and Appaloosa (*q.v.*) with the colour and markings of the latter. Height limit is 11.2 h.h. (113 cm) to 13.2 h.h. (134 cm). In breeding one parent must be a registered Pony of the Americas. In official show classes the rider must be 17 years old or under.

'Pony'   A betting term implying a wager of £25.

'Pony'   An illustrated monthly magazine exclusively for young riders in all their activities. It is specially devoted to British pony breeds, breeding, showing, etc. Founded in 1949 and published by D. J. Murphy, Ltd.

Pony   In the early part of the century the definition of a pony was 'a small horse less than 13 hands'. The show pony is an animal not exceeding 14.2 h.h. (144 cm). It should be noted, however, that a polo pony, to which no height limit applies, is always a pony, yet an Arab horse, to which the same also applies, is always a horse, however small it may be. The height designation of a show Hackney is that a pony must not exceed 14 h.h. (142 cm), and a Hackney horse must exceed that height. The general understanding is an animal of about 14 h.h. (142 cm) (*see* SHOW PONY).

Pony Club, The   Founded in 1929 to encourage young people to ride and enjoy sport connected with horses and ponies and to receive skilled instruction. Membership is open to all under 17 years and Associate Members between 17 and 21 years. Its success is phenomenal and branches are found in most English-speaking countries. The number of members now approaches 100,000, and it is represented in no less than 20 countries, the largest association of riders in the world.

Pony Express Established in 1860 by William H. Russell and Pike's Peak Express Co. as a fast mail service from St Joseph, Missouri, to San Francisco. Five hundred horses were distributed across the continent between 190 relay stations about 12 miles (19 km) apart. A rider rode three stages and was allowed only two minutes to change horses. The ponies travelled at the gallop and, in spite of snow, floods and marauding Indians, the mails had to get through. It is recorded that one express rider covered 380 miles (610 km) and was in the saddle 36 hours. The ponies used were mainly of native Western stock and the distance of nearly 2000 miles (3210 km) was covered in ten days. The service, however, lasted only eighteen months, as it was never successful commercially.

Pony Gout *see* LAMINITIS.

Pony Racing No longer officially held; formerly under the authority of the Pony Turf Club which no longer exists. It was confined to Thoroughbred ponies not exceeding 15 h.h. (152 cm) and half-breds which also ran under these rules.

Pony Trekking A form of cross-country holiday riding evolved sometime in the mid-twentieth century to give opportunity for riding through beautiful country in England, Scotland, Wales and other countries. Parties are organized, and the mountain or moorland ponies supplied from centres to which riders return, usually daily, and where they are accommodated at overall agreed charges (*see Plate* 26).

Porlock Pony A term given to a cross-bred pony which is found in Exmoor forest.

Port An indentation of greater or less depth in the centre of the mouthpiece of a bit, giving the horse sufficient room for its tongue.

Porting A term used by grooms for horses which paw their bedding to the rear of the stall and strike the floor with their fore-feet. Also known as Kaving.

Posnam Horse Heavy harness warm-blood type, bred west of Warsaw. With an infusion of Thoroughbred or Masuren (*q.v.*) blood, it makes a useful riding horse.

Post American term for rising at the trot.

Post and Rails Timber obstacle with various methods of attaching rails to posts fixed in the ground.

Post Betting *see* BETTING.

Postboy An attendant who, in posting days, rode one of a pair to a carriage, or, with another postboy, rode the leader or wheeler.

Postboy Waistcoat A long and waisted garment usually cut high at chest opening and with 'flaps' on all four pockets.

Post-chaise A postboy-driven closed carriage of posting days.

Post Entry No late post entries are allowed under the Rules of Racing, entries for all races closing at a time laid down in the Racing Calendar (*q.v.*).

Post Horse A horse which, in posting days, was let out for hire to the public for post vehicles.

Postillion A man who drives from the saddle, riding the near horse of a pair or team.

Posting A term indicating the rider rising from the saddle at the trot.

Posting In pre-railway days, posting was the method of travel used by the wealthy, who travelled in hired vehicles of various types, which gave them the privacy unobtainable in the stage coaches. Horses used for this purpose were travelled a certain distance or stage, usually about 10 miles (16 km), depending on the nature of the country, and either worked back with a vehicle travelling in the opposite direction or were ridden back by a postboy.

Post Master   The owner, in posting days, of post horses (*q.v.*).

Post Race   A race for which a person under one subscription, was able to enter two or more horses, and run any one or more of them, as the conditions prescribe. No longer in use.

Potatoes   Though possessing only a small amount of flesh-forming material, potatoes are said to be about one-third as nutritious as oats. When steamed or boiled, and fed mixed with chopped hay and straw and a small portion of oats, they are capable of maintaining in good condition a horse doing slow work. They may also be fed raw, but should be pulped first.

Pouch   The leather wallet slung over the shoulder of the guard to a coach. Among the small items carried was a small clock with a face exposed through a window cut in the leather surface.

Poultice Boot   A heavily constructed foot boot, with a sole of leather or wood. The remainder consists of canvas and straps into which the fomentation is placed. A more practical rubber poultice boot is now made.

Poultry Fund   A small cap made by most hunts, usually at each meet, on all present, including foot followers, to compensate owners of poultry for damage done.

Pound   A small stout timber-built fenced enclosure in which police or local authority retain temporarily straying horses, ponies or other animals (*see* CORRAL).

Prad   A Victorian term for a horse.

Prairie Schooner   *see* CONESTOGA WAGON.

Prance   The action of a horse when bounding or springing gaily.

Pratt & Co.   Managers of Cheltenham and other racecourses.

Preakness Stakes   The Preakness, one of the three Classic Races (*q.v.*) in the U.S., has had a most chequered career since its introduction as a $1\frac{1}{2}$-mile (2.4 km) event at Pimlico, Maryland, in 1873. It was abandoned after the 1889 renewal at $1\frac{1}{4}$ miles (2.01 km) then revived as a $1\frac{1}{16}$-mile (1.7 km) contest at Gravesend in New York in 1894. The race was run at a mile when it returned to Pimlico in 1909. The present $1\frac{3}{16}$-mile (1.9 km) distance was not finally adopted until 1925. Two divisions of the Preakness were staged in 1918. The race is scheduled for the middle of May, and is conditioned for three-year-olds. For results *see page* 398.

Prefix   In some Breed Societies, prefixes and affixes are much used by breeders as a means of establishing permanently the chosen names to all animals bred by them. Such prefixes and affixes are registered with the Breed Society and are transferable on sale.

Pregnancy Diagnosis in the Mare This is carried out by two methods, Physical and Biochemical.

PHYSICAL For use by the veterinary surgeon only and falls into two categories: (*a*) manual examination of the uterus through the wall of the rectum; (*b*) vaginal examination, either by noting by means of a speculum changes that take place in the walls of the vagina during pregnancy, or by microscopic examination of a smear from the vaginal mucosa.

BIOCHEMICAL *Urine Test* A small quantity of fresh urine is collected in a clean stoppered bottle and sent to the appropriate laboratory. The test shows greatest accuracy when carried out during the 120–150-day period of pregnancy, when it is accurate in over 90 per cent of cases.

Blood Serum Test This is applicable to mares between the 45–90-day period of pregnancy. Blood has to be collected from a vein of the mare and sent to a laboratory.

Preliminary Canter All horses leaving the paddock before starting for a race canter down to the start except when there is a parade, as before The Derby, Grand National, Gold Cup, etc., when they canter to the start after the parade.

Premium Stallion A stallion which has been awarded, through its Breed Society, an annual premium to travel an allotted district, to serve mares in that district at a very small fee.

Prepotency The strong power of transmitting hereditary features and qualities.

President's Cup An annual trophy first given in 1965 by Prince Philip, on his taking office as President of the Fédération Equestre Internationale (*q.v.*), for the country gaining the most total points in a year in Nations' Cup Competitions (*q.v.*). For results *see page* 406.

Prestashka A galloping mate to a Russian trotter driven to a wagon or droshky (*q.v.*).

Price Odds quoted on a horse in a race.

Prick Ears Short, pointed ears normally directed to the front, and giving an alert and expectant appearance.

Pricked Descriptive of a foot when a nail has been driven into the sensitive area of the foot, usually the sensitive laminae.

Pricker Obsolete term for one who follows hounds on horseback. Also a whipper-in (*q.v.*).

Pricker Boots Leather boots studded with tacks to prevent a horse tearing his leg bandages. Used in racing stables but nevertheless a barbaric and dangerous article.

Pricker-pad (or shield) A cruel device to deal with a one-sided mouth. It consists of a washer, the inside of which is studded with sharp points and is attached to the side of the snaffle against which the horse leans. Now obsolete and replaced by the Brush Pricker.

Pricket A male deer, at 2 years of age, with its first horns.

Prime Age A horse is at its prime between the ages of 6 and 10 years.

Prince of Wales Cup (Show Jumping) Up to 1914 known as King Edward VII Cup. Competed for annually under F.E.I. rules at the Royal International Horse Show, London, by teams of four amateur riders of the same nationality. For results *see* page 406.

Prince of Wales Spur A modern spur with drooping neck (with or without rowel) secured to the boot with a single strap through loop ends.

Prince of Wales Spur

Prince Philip Mounted Games Inaugurated in 1957 at the suggestion of H.R.H. the Duke of Edinburgh with the object of providing members of the Pony Club with a competition for good and well trained ponies that do not necessarily have to be of high quality or great value. The events are for Pony Club teams of five riders and preliminary meetings are held during the summer. Finalists compete at the Horse of the Year Show in October for the Prince Philip Cup.

Prior's Half-bred Stud Book   *see* HALF-BRED STUD BOOK.

Private Omnibus   A closed vehicle of varying size with seats arranged as in a waggonette (*q.v.*).

Private Omnibus

Private Pack   Where the Master, unsupported by subscriptions, bears the entire expenses of the Pack.

Prix Caprilli   A test judged on riding ability and not as a dressage test. Often used in various forms in Riding Club Competitions.

Prix des Nations (F.E.I.)   International Team Show Jumping Competition. The full team consists of four riders, men or women, from each country, the score of the best three competitors in each of two rounds to count.

Produce Classes   Those classes open to mares and racing stock as potential breeding stock, e.g. colts and fillies.

Produce Race   These races, now extinct in Britain, were for the produce of mares, and the horses which ran in them were entered before they were foaled and ran usually as two-year-olds or three-year-olds.

Professional (non-racing events under F.E.I. rules)   Any person aged 18 and over who accepts remuneration for riding, training or hiring out Competition horses in Show Jumping, Dressage or Three-day Events ranks as a Professional; also any one aged 18 or over who sells more than three International Competition horses in one year without permission of his national federation or allows his name or photograph to be used for advertising purposes.

'Prop, to'   Describes slowing-up action of a horse reluctant to take off at a fence.

Prophet's Thumb Mark   A pronounced dimple mark occasionally found in the neck of horses. This is believed by some Eastern races to be a sign of great luck to an owner, and his horse is in consequence greatly treasured.

Proppy   A stilty mover not flexing at the knees or pastern joints, probably straight in the shoulders.

Proprietor   One who owns a team and drives his own coach.

Protest (U.S.A.)   *see* OBJECTION.

'Provinces'   The term applied to a hunting country anywhere in England, Scotland or Wales, except in the Midlands and the Shires (*q.v.*) in England.

Prussia-side Stirrup Iron   A pattern of iron, unlike those commonly used in the United Kingdom (the sides of which do not vary in width). It narrows gradually on either side from the tread upwards, as far as the eye which receives the stirrup leather.

Przevalski   *see* WILD HORSE.

Puckle Noseband   *see* KINETON NOSEBAND.

Pudding   Oatmeal porridge as boiled and fed to hounds.

'Puddle' A shuffling, 'footy' action seen in many underbred, common horses and those with worn legs and unsound feet.

'Puffer' One who runs up the price of a horse at an auction on behalf of the seller but who has no intention of buying (sometimes called a Trotter).

'Puffing the Glims' An expression used to denote a method of making a horse look less than its age by cutting a small hole through the skin of the hollow above the eye and blowing through a quill to fill the cavity.

Pugri   *see* MARTINGALE, PUGRI.

Puissance (Show Jumping)   *see* TEST COMPETITION.

Pulled Tail A fashion where the hair at the side of the dock, from the upper to the lower end, as well as any excessive growth on top, is removed by pulling to give a slim and tidy effect.

Puller A horse pulls through having had its mouth spoiled, and therefore made insensitive, or from excitement (mostly in company with other horses). Methods to combat this are many and varied, but most of them are ineffective unless the rider is a good horseman. The elementary rule is 'give and take'.

Pulse A horse's pulse is normally 36 to 40 beats, and is taken either where the submaxillary artery passes under the jaw on either side or at the radial artery inside the foreleg, on a level with the elbow.

Pump Handles Two curved iron handles at the rear of a coach to hold when jumping up.

Punter One who backs a horse or bets on a horse to win or gain a place in a race.

Puppy Walker Someone who takes care of one or two hound puppies at about ten weeks old until the following February or March, when they are returned to the kennels. Essentials for these puppies are absolute freedom and good suitable food, thus giving them every chance to develop well. Lord Yarborough at Brocklesby (1746) was the first M.F.H. to start the system of 'walking puppies' and of keeping hound pedigrees.

Pure-bred A breed which is unsoiled, and unmixed by any alien blood.

Purgatives Before administering these it is important to diet the horse with bran mashes and no other food for 48 hours. Linseed oil: dose $\frac{1}{2}$–1 pt (0.28–0.57 l), according to the size of the horse. Epsom Salts: $\frac{1}{2}$ lb (226 g) is a full dose; $\frac{1}{4}$ lb (113 g) should be given to stabled horses every Saturday night.

Purges Opening medicines of which there are many varieties.

Purging Diarrhoea, due to a sudden change of diet, to red worm in the intestines, to a chill or to excitement. *Treatment:* if due to injurious matter in the stomach or intestines, give $\frac{1}{4}$ pint (0.14 l) of linseed oil to lubricate and pass out irritant matter, then 1 to 4 drachms chlorodyne and $\frac{1}{2}$ oz (14 ml) of bismuth carbonate given in flour gruel. A frequent sequel is constipation, and small doses of salts in mashes should be given to counteract this.

Pur Sang Pure-bred (*q.v.*), e.g. *le pur sang arabe* = pure-bred Arab; *le pur sang anglais* = the Thoroughbred.

'Puss' The name by which the hunted hare has been known to many generations of those who hunt with harriers.

Puszta Hungarian plains, the great feeding grounds for herds of horses and cattle.

Put-down A horse or hound is put-down when it is destroyed on account of old age, ill health or injury. In shooting a horse, the muzzle of the pistol or revolver should not quite touch the skin where the lowest hairs of the fore-lock grow.

Putting-to   Fox earths which are closed with the fox inside during the morning of a hunting day are said to be 'put to'. The process of closing the earth is 'putting-to'.

Putting-to   The act of harnessing a horse to a vehicle.

* Q *

Quad A slang term for a horse.

Quadrille The first 'horse-dances' recorded date back to 700–650 B.C. when quadrilles of two, four and eight riders took part. For many centuries these were neglected, but in the early part of the sixteenth century a great revival took place which lasted until the latter part of the nineteenth century. The art was courted by most of the nobles throughout Europe, musicians composed special music to suit the superbly caparisoned horses and their riders whose displays reached great elegance and showed the highest skill. Though far less practised in England, quadrilles were encouraged and performed in the reign of Elizabeth I. They have recently been revived. A Quadrille competition now takes place at the Horse of the Year Show (*q.v.*).

Quagga (*Equus quagga*) This member of the equine family is thought to be extinct. Like the Zebra, the species was peculiar to South Africa, but it bore more resemblance to a horse than does the former, being easier to break, and having a good mouth. The striped markings were distinct on the head and neck, but faded away behind the withers, and disappeared altogether about the middle of the back. One of the last known of the species was a stallion owned by Lord Morton in 1870.

Quarrelling Some horses have various vices when at grass with others: kicking and/or biting other horses, or an individual horse to which a dislike has apparently been taken, chasing them away and generally dominating them, especially when supplementary food is placed in the paddocks. Such behaviour can be very detrimental to other horses, possibly depriving them of necessary food, upsetting their nerves (bearing in mind that one of the objects of turning out to grass is to rest the horse) and this behaviour can obviously lead to acci-dents. Any horse showing these tendencies should be watched carefully and if interference with others appears to be marked the culprit should be isolated.

Quarter Part of the hoof between the toe and the heel.

Quarter Horse, American An American-bred horse able to run a quarter-of-a-mile (0.4 km) at great speed on the race-track. The origin of this breed was in Virginia, U.S.A., where in the early days of settlement race-tracks were cut in the virgin forest; these tracks were usually about a quarter-of-a-mile in length, hence 'Quarter Horse', synonymous with a quick starter and fast sprinter. Bred originally from a Thoroughbred stallion 'Janus' and native mares. Now also much used for roping, cutting and other cattle and ranch work. The stud book was founded in 1940 (*see* THE HORSE WORLD IN THE UNITED STATES OF AMERICA, *page* 350).

Quartering An abbreviated form of grooming, in which the roller is not removed. Eyes, nose and dock are sponged, and rugs turned back so that the quarters and then the forehand can be groomed. The term also indicates the application of the water-brush on soiled and ruffled hair on the lower part of the quarters, caused by the horse lying down during the night.

Quarter Marks Fancy patterns made solely for appearance on the quarters of a horse, mostly seen on racehorses and show horses. The hair is brushed in parts with a wet brush in the reverse direction from the way in which it grows, thus forming a design. A stencil plate may be used to achieve a specific pattern.

Quarter Marks Marks placed a quarter and three-quarters of the way along each side of a riding school, for convenience in drilling a ride and schooling.

Quarter Sheet   A rectangular sheet varying in length between 3 ft 6 in (1.06 m) and 4 ft (1.21 m) for use in the paddock or when at exercise. In the paddock it is kept in place by a light 'race' roller and breast girth, at exercise the front corners are folded back under the girth straps. In this context it is also known as a galloping sheet. It can vary in weight according to the time of year and is also made in waterproof sheeting. A fillet string (*q.v.*) should be used to prevent the sheet being blown up.

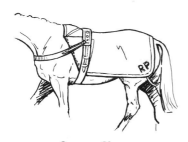

Quarter Sheet

Quarter Strap   Harness passing over a horse's quarters to meet the breeching.

Quarter Straps   An American term, the English equivalent being a loin strap or trace bearer (*q.v.*). In single harness, a loin strap buckles on to the shafts, whereas in pair harness it is across the loins and acts as a trace bearer. The State harness of the Lord Mayor of London's coach (*q.v.*) is fitted with loin straps. The loin strap is a form of kicking strap (*q.v.*).

Quarters   The area lying between the rear of the flank and the root of the tail, stretching downwards to the top of the gaskin.

Quarters, False   A longitudinal depression in the wall of the hoof, caused by the failure of the coronet to secrete the horny crust; this failure is the result of some injury such as a tread or a quittor (*q.v.*). An unsoundness.

Quarters and False Quarters   A slang term long since in disuse and described by Malet in his *Annals of the Road* under 'General Road and Slang Terms' as a term for 'Ruts and very deep ruts'.

Quarters In   *see* TRAVERS.

Quarters Out   *see* RENVERS.

Queen Elizabeth II Cup (Show Jumping)   An individual award open to ladies only. Competed for annually under F.E.I. rules at the Royal International Horse Show, London. For results *see page* 407.

Queen's Birthday Parade, The   *see* TROOPING THE COLOUR.

Queen's Plate, The   Canada's oldest race, established in 1860, and considered the most fashionable event of the year. The purse of $100,000 and 65 per cent of all entry fees go to the winner, plus 50 guineas. The race was for three-year-olds and over up to 1938, when it was restricted to three- and four-year-olds. It is now open to Canadian-bred three-year old colts, geldings and fillies. The distance has been altered several times over the years. Prior to 1886 it was a 1½-mile (2.4 km) race; then from 1887 it was run over 1¼ miles (2.01 km), until 1924 when shortened ‚to 1⅛ miles (1.81 km). In 1957 the distance was lengthened again to 1¼ miles (2.01 km) which will remain. For results *see page* 399.

Quiddor   A horse that drops food from its mouth in the process of mastication. *Cause*: invariably major abnormalities of the teeth; a veterinary surgeon should be consulted.

Quintain   A mediaeval game in which riders on horses tilted at a bar swinging from a horizontal cross-piece erected on a pole.

Quirt (Spanish *cuarta*)   A blacksnake whip or bullwhip (American terms).

Quittor   A fistulous sore at the coronet, usually developing from a neglected suppurating wound, being generally the outcome of not allowing the escape of matter formed under the sole after irritation by grit or a punctured wound from nails, etc. The sole should be opened with a draw knife. The cure depends upon a drastic operation for the removal of part of the lateral cartilage of the affected side of the foot. In all true cases of quittor this cartilage is involved.

Quoiler   A name for thill harness, the shaft horse in a waggon team being the thill horse (*see* THILL).

Quotation (Racing)   Odds offered about a horse by a bookmaker.

* R *

R.C.   Riding Club.

Ref (Racing)   Refused.

R.I.H.S.   Royal International Horse Show.

R.o. (Racing)   Ran on or ran out.

R.P.C.   Riding Pony Colt (N.P.S.)

R.P.G.   Riding Pony Gelding (N.P.S.).

R.P.M.   Riding Pony Mare.

R.P.S.   Riding Pony Stallion.

R.S.P.C.A.   Royal Society for the Prevention of Cruelty to Animals.

Race   A thin white mark running down the face. (Also known as stripe, rache or rase.)

Race Card   The official programme for each day's racing, issued by order of the clerk of the course, and containing the time and conditions of each race, with details of all horses still in the race, their numbers, colours, owners, trainers, ages if appropriate, weights to be carried, and pedigrees.

Racecourse Association   An association of all the racecourse owners of Britain, divided into three areas—Midland, Northern and Southern.

Racecourse Betting Control Board Originally established under the Racecourse Betting Act of 1928 to organize and control the Totalizator. It has now become the Horserace Totalizator Board, which is responsible to the Horserace Betting Levy Board for the Totalizator.

Racecourse Paddock   A railed-in enclosure to which all horses running at the meeting are brought before their races. The horses' attendants are provided with badges bearing numbers corresponding with those on the Race Card.

Racecourse   Security   Services These are under an Inspector of Security.

Racecourse   Technical   Services This is a subsidiary of the Horserace Betting Levy Board (*q.v.*) and is responsible for the Photofinish and Race Timing, the Camera Patrol, Public Address Services on courses, and starting stalls and barrier gates.

Race Exercise Saddle   A name given to exercise saddles used in racing stables. They resemble a steeplechase saddle in appearance, but are not cut so far forward. Usually serge-lined and made on a very strong tree.

Racehorse   A horse bred for racing (*see* GENERAL STUD BOOK).

The Racehorse and Racing in Great Britain   *
Bill Curling

Racing in Britain is of two kinds—flat racing and steeplechasing. Flat racing is much the older in origin and can fairly be said to date as an organized sport from the sixteenth century; steeplechasing from 1830 when the St Albans Steeplechase was run for the first time. There are over sixty racecourses in use in Britain, some of which cater for flat racing and steeplechasing, some for flat racing only and some for steeplechasing only.

The principal courses on which there is flat racing only are Chester; Epsom, the home of the Derby; Goodwood in Sussex; Newmarket in Suffolk; and York. The principal course for steeplechasing only is Cheltenham, the home of the Cheltenham Gold Cup, the Champion Hurdle and the National Hunt meeting. The principal courses on which there are both flat racing and steeplechasing and sometimes mixed meetings are Ascot, which belongs to H.M. The Queen and at which the Royal meeting is held in June; Ayr in Scotland; Chepstow in Wales; Doncaster, the home of the St Leger; Liverpool, the home of the Grand National; Newbury in Berkshire; Newcastle on Tyne; and Sandown Park in Surrey, the home of the Eclipse Stakes.

The flat racing season normally starts at Doncaster towards the end of March and ends in the first half of November. The steeplechasing season is longer, beginning with a few small jumping meetings at the end of July or the beginning of August and finishing normally at the end of May. The close season for steeplechasing is thus less than two months, and for flat racing over four months.

The Jockey Club is now responsible for the conduct both of flat racing and of steeplechasing. Formerly the National Hunt Committee was responsible for over a century for the conduct of steeplechasing, but it amalgamated with the Jockey Club in 1968, losing its separate identity. The amalgamation followed the setting up of the Horserace Betting Levy Board in 1961, as a result of which a small proportion of the money betted on racing is now funnelled back into racing through the Levy Board. The Jockey Club and the National Hunt Committee were formerly responsible for racing and its various services. Now the Levy Board, with perhaps £4 to £5 million a year to distribute, takes part in all decisions concerning racing finance and has been responsible for financing the photo finish, the camera patrol, the racecourse commentary system, racecourse security, the Forensic Laboratory at Newmarket for dope testing and research, the Racing Industry Benefit Scheme, various schemes for the improvement of racecourses, starting stalls, a substantial sum towards the cost of transporting race-horses to meetings, and a sum of over £2 million for prize money. The Joint Racing Board, consisting of members of the Jockey Club and of the Levy Board, meets regularly to consider various aspects of racing policy.

As a result of the advent of the Levy Board, racecourse amenities and services have improved greatly and racecourses have been encouraged to hold more meetings, so that with the exception of Sundays there are now few days on which there is not some race meeting. In round figures, between 4 million and 5 million people go racing annually on over sixty racecourses on which about 5000 races are run annually, the total number of runners exceeding 50,000. The total annual prize money is about £5 million. There are now slightly more steeplechase meetings than flat race meetings, but the number of runners on the flat slightly exceeds the total number of runners at steeplechase meetings. There are some 11,000 racehorses in training, trained by 700 trainers.

So much for the bare statistics of racing as it is conducted in Britain today. The charm of English racing is in its great variety. In the United States all flat race courses are flat, left-handed and oval in shape. In Britain some are left-handed like Chester, Epsom and York; some are right-handed like Ascot, Goodwood and Sandown Park; Chester is almost circular; Epsom and Goodwood are downland courses with a sharp decline leading to the final half mile; Doncaster, Newbury, Newcastle and York are almost flat except for the hill on the far side of Doncaster; and there is similar variety with the steeplechase courses, with the Grand National Course at Aintree almost flat in ugly surroundings on the edge of Liverpool, and in complete contrast to Cheltenham set in a bowl of the Cotswolds with Cleve Hill as a superb backcloth.

There is evidence of horse racing of a sort in Britain from the tenth century, but it is not till the sixteenth century that there are records of annual prizes being given for racing. Two of the earliest are a Silver Bell raced for in the Forest of Galtres near York from 1530, and a Silver Bell raced for annually on Shrove Tuesday on the Roodeye at Chester beside the north bank of the River Dee, where Chester races are still held. Later in the sixteenth century it is on record that Queen Elizabeth I watched racing at Salisbury in the year of the defeat of the Spanish Armada.

However, credit for popularizing horse racing in Britain must go to the Stuarts. James I came to Newmarket for the first time in 1605, liked it, and started it on its way as a centre for hunting, hawking and racing; but it was not until the days of the Restoration under Charles II that racing really came into its own. He loved Newmarket, founded the Newmarket Town Plate (q.v.) there in 1665, rode in it himself and won the race twice. In those early days it was won by high-class horses. Now it is not run under Jockey Club rules and is monopolized by girl riders. More important, it was in the seventeenth century that English racing men began importing Arab stallions from the east to mate with home-bred mares to improve the speed, stamina and looks of the English country-bred horses. Charles II went further and imported a number of Arabian mares to mate with the Arab stallions. These were known as Royal mares.

The three Arab stallions from which all Thoroughbreds now descend in tail male were, however, not brought to England until after the death of Charles II in 1685. The three in order of arrival were the Byerley Turk, the Darley Arabian and the Godolphin Arabian; and the key names in their male lines are 'Herod' in the case of the Byerley Turk, 'Eclipse' in the Darley Arabian, and 'Matchem' in the Godolphin Arabian. Up to about 1770 breeders of racehorses used to mate imported Arabs with home-bred mares or descendants of the Royal mares, but it was then found that the best racing results were being obtained by using home-bred stallions

with home-bred mares, and Arab stallions gradually ceased to be used for racing purposes.

In the early days races were run in heats over distances of 2 to 4 miles (3.2–6.4 km) and horses were not asked to race till they were four years of age or five. Gradually races of shorter distance became more popular and horses were asked to race as three-year-olds, so that when the St Leger, the oldest of the five classic races for three-year-olds, was founded in 1776 at Doncaster, it was of 2 miles (3.2 km), this being subsequently reduced to just more than 1¾ miles (2.8 km). In 1779 the Oaks for three-year-old fillies only was run for the first time on Epsom Downs, and 1780 saw the first running of the Derby at Epsom. The original Derby distance was only a mile (1.6 km), but this was soon altered to its present distance of 1½ miles (2.4 km)—the same as the Oaks. The other two classic races, the 2000 Guineas and the 1000 Guineas, were both founded at the beginning of the nineteenth century and are both run at Newmarket over a straight mile. The 2000 Guineas for colts and fillies was first run in 1809, and the 1000 Guineas for fillies only in 1814. The Guineas are run in April, the Derby and Oaks at the beginning of June, and the St Leger in September. It was at this period that the first of the well-known two-year-old races was founded—the July Stakes first run at Newmarket in 1786, only six years after the founding of the Derby.

The Racing Calendar giving race results and pedigrees of runners and details of races to come was first published by John Cheny in 1727, so that it can be said that from that date racing has been well authenticated. The first volume of the General Stud Book (q.v.) giving details of Thoroughbred mares and their produce and of Thoroughbred stallions, made its appearance in 1791. This was produced by James Weatherby, who relied largely on the earlier Racing Calendars of John Cheny, Heber and the York historian William Pick for much of his early information. The Weatherby family, owners of the General Stud Book, have produced the present Racing Calendar ever since.

At the beginning of the nineteenth century there was a multiplicity of small meetings and racing was very laxly run; but the Jockey Club, which originally only had jurisdiction over Newmarket meetings, gradually assumed control over other meetings, and, under first Lord George Bentinck and then Admiral Rous, its influence spread and it did much to clean up the Turf in Victorian days.

During the nineteenth century steeplechasing was very much the poor relation of flat racing, in spite of the quick popularity of the Grand National run for the first time in 1837. Steeplechasing was also bedevilled by lax control in the middle of the nineteenth century, but with the formation of the National Hunt Committee it became more popular again. Between the two World Wars the founding of the Champion Hurdle at Cheltenham and the Cheltenham Gold Cup brought it more to the forefront, and the advent of television has made people realize what a spectacular sport it is. It has, in fact, increased greatly in popularity in the last fifteen years, aided by the sponsorship of steeplechases and hurdle races on most National Hunt courses.

Television, while bringing home to people how spectacular a sport steeplechasing is, has undoubtedly had an adverse effect on attendances, as has the introduction of betting shops. Total racecourse attendances for 1965 were approximately 5.2 million. Five years later the total was down to 4.1 million. But for help from the Levy Board an alarming proportion of British racecourses would no longer be viable, in contrast to France and the United States where Tote monopolies have brought great prosperity to racing.

In contrast to the immediate post-war years when French owners won many of our principal races, the large French prizes have induced a lot of British owners to run their best horses in France in recent seasons with satisfactory results, while a number of leading American owners continue to support racing in Europe.

There continues to be a very strong demand for British bloodstock, which is exported to all parts of the racing world, and the number of commercial breeders has increased in the last two decades, though death duties and high taxation have sadly thinned the ranks of private owner-breeders on which the long range prosperity of the Turf depends. Until prize money in Britain bears a closer relationship to the cost of keeping a horse in training, this trend will surely continue (*see also* THE ENGLISH THOROUGHBRED).

*   *   *

Racehorse Owners' Association
The only organization which looks after the interests of flat and jumping racehorse owners in Britain.

Racehorse Trainers' Association
see NATIONAL TRAINERS' ASSOCIATION.

Racers Old-time phrase for footgear cut as jockey boots and made of the lightest black calf with painted tops. Minimum weight about 5 oz (141 g). Used only for flat racing.

Rache *see* RACE.

Racing (Rules of) Published annually by Weatherby & Sons on behalf of the Jockey Club.

Racing Abbreviations Bbv = Broke blood vessel. F = Fell. Hd = Head. L = Length. M = Mile. Nk = Neck. Pu = Pulled Up. Ref = Refused. Ro = Ran on, Ran out. Sh = Short head. Ss. = Started slowly. t = tubed. tnp = took no part. t.o. = tailed off. uns =

unseated rider. w.r.s. = whipped round start.

Racing Calendar, The It is published weekly by Weatherbys on behalf of the Jockey Club, giving details of races, entries for races, handicap weights, Jockey Club notices, etc., and other information of interest to those professionally engaged in racing. Often known as 'The Calendar'.

Racing Calendar Office The office appointed by the Jockey Club, which is at present at Weatherbys, Wellingborough, Northants, to which all entries for races, acceptances, declarations of forfeit and lodgement of official documents are normally made.

Racing Colours Declared essential on the Turf and first registered in October 1762; the Duke of Cumberland selected 'purple', still part of the Royal colours (*see* COLOURS OF THE ROYAL FAMILY). All colours (jacket and cap) must be registered with Weatherby & Sons, and are exclusive to the owner. They are worn by jockeys when riding in a race.

Racing Girths Either narrow web, web inset with elastic, or all elastic. Except when mounted to a very light saddle, are always used in pairs.

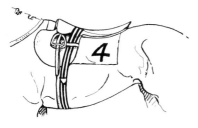

Racing Girth

Racing Season The flat racing season in Britain normally starts in the second half of March and ends in the middle of November. Steeplechasing starts at the end of July and ends at the beginning of the following June.

Racing Seat The special position in the saddle adopted by jockeys for race riding. Leathers are very short and the seat is far forward and clear of the saddle.

Rack A single-footed pace, each foot coming down singly and with great speed, a steady 1-2-3-4 with no pauses (*see* RACKING-BOOTS).

Rack A stag-hunting term for a gap in a hedge caused by continued passing of the deer.

Rack, Hay This should be situated with its top on a level with the manger, to avoid dust, etc., falling on to the horse and irritating the eyes and nose.

Rack Chain A galvanized chain with spring hooks or, sometimes, a safer type of 'Y' piece which prevents any possibility of the horse catching his lips or nostrils in the springs. The chain is used to restrain the horse during grooming.

Racking Placing hay in the feeding rack.

Racking-boots Heavy rubber caps strapped over the fore feet of American Five-Gaited (*q.v.*) horses to protect them against injury through being struck by the hind feet when racking too fast (*see* RACK).

Rack-up, to To tether a horse to a ring in the wall.

Rag (or Rake) A company or herd of young colts.

Ragged Hips Prominent and unsightly hip-bones ('hat-racks'), poorly fleshed and muscled.

Rails (Racing) The very stout, white-painted, timber posts and rails surrounding and containing all racecourses.

Railway Crossing (British Show Jumping Assn.) Two gates with a red disc in the centre of each. The gates are provided with wings.

Rake *see* RAG.

Rake a Horse, to To slide the rider's legs and spurs to and fro on a horse's sides; a practice inducing artificial bucking for rodeo purposes.

Ralli Cart A two-wheeled trap similar to a dog-cart but with shafts continued along the floor to the rear of the vehicle and usually having curved sides, built to the design of Mr Ralli, Ashstead Park, Surrey in 1898.

Ramener Head position close to the vertical allowed by the flexion of the poll and the first two cervical vertebrae. It must be obtained by the advance of the entire body toward the head, not by the retraction of the head toward the chest.

Ram-headed A convex profile line of the head, the name applied by Arabs to the head of a Barb.

Random Three horses driven in single file.

Ranelagh Club Now liquidated, this was formerly a slightly more 'countrified' club than Hurlingham, noted for its clubhouse, Barn Elms, residence of the Earl of Walsingham, which later became the headquarters of the Kit-Cat Political Club. It was noted also for its excellent cuisine and wines and for the exotic waterfowl and its beautiful gardens. It was the headquarters of the Coaching Club, and one of pre-war London's polo centres.

Range Pony A comprehensive term, used on *estancias* in South America and on cattle ranches in North America for ponies used in cattle work (also known as 'cow ponies').

Rangy A term describing a horse with plenty of size and scope.

Rapping Pole A pole held at either end when training a show jumper; it is raised slightly as the hind legs are about to come over, in such a way that the horse receives a slight rap which should encourage it to lift its legs higher on future occasions. This painful practice is banned at shows run under the B.S.J.A. (*q.v.*).

Rarey, John Solomon (1827–1866) A horsetamer and farmer from Ohio, who came to England in 1858 and 'cured' many violent tempered racehorses. He attained his ends by a process of exhaustion, and, though the method subdued a horse for a time, it was not invariably permanent. This treatment must not be compared with Galvayne's humane method.

Rase *see* RACE.

Rasper A term denoting a very big fence, e.g. a double oxer.

Rasping Teeth The molar teeth of horses, especially after about eight years, may become long and sharp on surfaces which escape wear during mastication. Removal of the sharp edges requires the use of an adjustable gag and a variety of rasps. Rasping teeth is no job for the amateur, as serious injury to the mouth can be produced. A veterinary surgeon should be asked to examine the teeth of all horses which show difficulty in chewing and especially those which 'quid' their food; that is to say, those which leave the manger wet with chewed food dropped into it.

Rat-catcher Informal, but permissible, hunting dress. Hunting bowler, stock, tweed riding coat, any non-flashy coloured waistcoat, breeches (fawn for choice), brown boots; spurs and crop optional.

Rate, to To scold or rebuke a hound.

Rat Tail One with little or no hair on the dock.

'Rat Tails' Used at one time to pull on riding boots, but now fitted only on 'Jockeys'. The modern practice is to fit tugs inside the boots.

Rattle (Hunting) Said of hounds when they are pressing hard on a fox.

Also the note sounded on the horn at a kill.

Rave, Raves   The framework of rails or boards added to the sides of a cart to enable a greater load to be carried.

Ray   List or dorsal stripe (q.v.).

Razor-backed   With a sharp and prominent backbone.

'Ready'   To ready a horse is to prepare it for some particular event, whether racing or a show.

Rearing   A most dangerous habit. Do not pull on the mouth when the horse goes up, but lean forward, lower one rein as near to the foot as possible and pull round in a circle. It is wise to have a tight martingale. The horse should be given a thorough veterinary overhaul, and this should include the teeth.

Reata   An American term for a rope used as a lasso.

Reata Strap   A strap used to hold the rope or lasso to the saddle when coiled.

Recklinghausen's Disease   Rare condition in horses causing deterioration of the hardness of the bone. Possible cause may be over-feeding of vitamin concentrates.

Records   *see* HIGH JUMPING RECORDS.

Red Flag (Show Jumping)   Used to show the right-hand limit of the obstacle to be jumped.

Redopp   Obsolete term describing a movement where the horse canters on two concentric circles, haunches in.

Red Ribbon   On the tail of a horse in the hunting field, this indicates a kicker (Rogue's badge).

Red Worm   Most harmful of all the bowel parasites which attack the horse, these are reddish in colour and up to $\frac{1}{2}$ in (12.7 mm) long but not always visible in the droppings. Often in company with larger strongyles which may be even more dangerous. *Symptoms:* loss of

flesh, anaemia, hollow flanks, dropped abdomen and dry coat. *Treatment:* Special drugs are required and some new medicaments of value have been introduced. It is always wise to leave treatment of this condition in veterinary hands.

Refuse, to   To stop in front of any obstacle. To rein back or to circle in front of a fence, resulting in a horse crossing its track, is counted as a refusal in both show jumping and eventing.

Register of Non-Thoroughbred Mares   Compiled by Weatherby & Sons in place of the Half-Bred Stud Book (q.v.).

Regularly Ridden   Implying in a written description that a horse is quiet to ride.

Rein, Running   A gag rein, running from the rider's hands through any snaffle bit, thence to the girths.

Reinagle, Philip, R.A. (1749–1833)   Of Hungarian origin, he painted many scenes of horse and hound, also some angling and shooting pictures. The eccentric sportsman, Col. Thomas Thornton of Yorkshire, was his patron.

Rein Aids   The opening rein, neck rein and the three reins of opposition called direct rein of opposition (affecting particularly the haunches); counter-rein of opposition in front of the withers (with particular effect on the shoulders); counter-rein of opposition behind the withers (acting on shoulders and haunches). They may be combined in countless ways and serve principally to determine direction. Other rein aids control speed and obtain halt and rein-back; still others position the horse by the attitude they give to its head and neck.

Rein Back   A natural retrograde pace on alternate diagonals (*see* BIPED). For it to be correct, the two feet of the same diagonal must be lifted and put down together; foot-dragging, head-raising, hollowing out of the back are serious faults. In the U.S.A., the term is usually shortened to 'back'.

Reins Leather ones can be plain, plaited, laced or with rubber hand-parts, and stitched, hook-studded or buckled. Some are made of webbing mainly for show jumping. The length of a full-size rein is approximately 5 ft (1.5 m). Children's reins should be very much shorter. Widths of reins vary between ½ in (12.7 mm) and 1 in (25.4 mm).

Reins in both Hands The normal way of conducting a horse.

Reins in one Hand There are a number of recognized ways of controlling a horse thus, varying with the different schools of practice.

Rein Stops Really 'martingale stops'. These are pieces of leather fixed to the rein some 10 in (25.4 cm) from the bit to prevent the rings of a running martingale sliding so far forward as to catch on either the rein fastening or even over a tooth.

Rejoneador A mounted matador.

Remounts A term applied generally to all horses taken in for service in an Army Unit.

Remouthing The process of remaking a spoiled mouth. It usually consists of re-starting and repeating the process applied when breaking a young horse.

Remuda Western American term for herd of broken horses used daily on a ranch.

Rendlesham Benevolent Fund (Racing) A fund to help steeplechase trainers and jockeys in necessitous circumstances. Administered by Weatherby & Sons (q.v.).

Renvers Also called *quarters-out* or *tail to the wall*, it is a half-pass performed along the wall, hindlegs on the track, forelegs on an inner track, head slightly flexed in the direction of the movement,

the horse's body at a 35° to 45° angle to the wall followed (*see* HALF-PASS and TRAVERS).

Repository A place for the sale of horses.

Resin Back *see* ROSINBACKS.

Respiration Normal rate at rest is 12 or 13 per minute.

Rest All working horses require periodic rest—one day a week for those in ordinary work, but hunters should have more. It is not desirable to leave a resting horse in the stable for two or three days as the legs may 'fill'. After the first day it should be lightly exercised.

Rest-horses *see* SPARES.

Restiveness This results from high spirits, temporary excitement, or vice. Treat the offender kindly but firmly. Where the horse gives trouble when physicked or groomed, a fore-leg should be held or tied up, and the animal must then stand quietly.

Restoratives Stimulants used in cases of exhaustion—brandy, beer, bread and milk, beef tea, linseed tea, etc. (*see* PICK-ME-UP).

Retainer (Racing) Any time after a jockey ends his apprenticeship he is free to make his own riding arrangements and receive retainers (if sufficiently successful), from any owner or 'Stable', at a fee to be agreed upon, half being paid in advance, the balance on termination of agreement—usually at end of season. A good jockey may have a second or third retainer.

Rhenish German Heavy Draught *see* RHINELAND HEAVY DRAUGHT.

Rhesus A condition of the blood of a brood-mare which taints her first milk which, if taken by the foal, is likely to cause death from jaundice. Pre-natal blood tests should be taken.

Rhineland Heavy Draught A strong massive horse originally bred in West Germany and the Brabant, but with the mechanization of agriculture and transport numbers have dwindled and it no longer ranks as an official breed. The Rhenish Stud Book now concerns itself with registered warm-blood horses, small horses and ponies and it is hoped eventually that with suitable stallions a new breed of Rhenish riding horse may be evolved. Also known as Rhenish German Heavy Draught Horse.

Rhinopneumonitis Upper respiratory tract infection.

Rhum Pony Represents the most ancient-known strain of the Highland pony (*q.v.*). Samuel Johnson described them on the island of Coll as: 'very small, but of a breed eminent for beauty'. There are very few ponies on the island now, and though there has been some admixture of Highland stock, they are more compact than the mainland type. They are mostly mouse-dun or chestnut, and often have very pale manes.

Ribbed Up, Well A term descriptive of a deep, short body, well rounded and with well-sprung ribs.

'Ribbons' A driving term for reins.

Ribbons Popular term for coloured rosette show awards. To win, to be 'in the ribbons'.

Ribs In *all* breeds, generous, rounded and well-sprung ribs are essential. There are (in pairs) 8 true and 10 false ribs.

Richards, Sir Gordon (b. 1904) In 1933 Richards passed Fred Archer's record (1885) of riding 246 winners in one season by riding 259. On 26th April, 1943, when riding 'Scotch Mist' at Windsor racecourse, he rode his 2750 winner, thus breaking the then record also held by Fred Archer. In September 1956, Yorkshire-born American jockey, John Longden, exceeded Sir Gordon's total of 2780 victories. American jockeys, unlike English, can flat-race throughout the year. Sir Gordon, 26 times champion jockey, was knighted in 1953, being the first professional jockey to be so honoured.

Richmond Royal Horse Show Society Founded in 1892, holding an annual show at Richmond, Surrey. Now amalgamated with the South of England Agricultural Society (*q.v.*).

Richmonds see LEGGINGS.

Ride A lane cut through a wood (*see* 'TALLY OVER').

Rider One who, by the proper application of aids, controls and directs his horse with safety and natural comfort (*see* RIDING, ART OF).

Ride Work, to To ride racehorses at training headquarters during their regular routine of preparation for the racecourse.

Ridge and Furrow Pasture land of regular wavy formation, the result of ploughing and drainage in the days of strip farming.

Ridgeling see RISLING.

'Riding' An illustrated monthly journal for all interested in horses, riding and driving, this covers all activities of the horse world, with a young riders' section. First published by Country Life Ltd., in June 1936.

Riding, Art of A rider must so conduct himself in the saddle that, by hands, legs, seat and balance, by lightness of touch, rhythm of movement and mental understanding, the horse and rider proceed in safety to themselves and in complete accord (*see* THE PRINCIPLES OF RIDING, *page* 269).

The Principles of Riding   *   Cherrie Hatton-Hall, F.B.H.S.

Skill in riding involves, like all sports, a knowledge of technique, and its execution demands balance through acquired suppleness and plenty of practice. Certain moral qualities such as patience, sympathy and understanding of both the psychological and mental make-up of the horse are also necessary to give rewarding results and a lifelong interest in this great art. Whatever motivates the wish to learn to ride, it is important that a correct start is made to ensure maximum comfort, safety and enjoyment for rider and horse. To trust to luck or prowess by climbing on to a friend's horse is asking for trouble—not only is it unsafe but, worse still, causes untold discomfort and confusion to the horse. Good horsemanship means less effort for the horse and greater pleasure shared by the rider.

Where to Ride Lessons from a qualified instructor are essential. Once bad habits are developed through apprehension, they are extremely difficult to correct later on. There may be a choice of several riding schools in the vicinity. The British Horse Society at the National Equestrian Centre, Stoneleigh, Warwickshire, will supply for guidance a booklet entitled 'Where to Ride', with a list of schools approved by them from Stage I to Stage IV. If possible the prospective beginner should take along someone with experience to make an inspection, visiting several establishments and finally choosing one with a pleasant friendly atmosphere but capable instructors. The yard should be neat and tidy with well-fed and cared-for horses and ponies, and with a well-organized programme. Facilities should include a large covered school where riding can take place in all weathers, and also some land should be available to ride outside.

Certain articles of clothing are necessary, such as a properly fitted hunting cap or bowler. While falls are to be avoided at all costs, precautions against accidents must be taken. Borrowing hats is never satisfactory as they rarely fit. A pair of jodhpurs or breeches and boots give greater comfort than jeans or trousers, as they prevent pinching, but are not essential. Gloves also should be part of the equipment and tidy hair and neatness generally will also give a feeling of self-confidence.

Ideally the first lessons (probably a course of about six separate hours depending on the age and aptitude of the beginner) should be private. A qualified instructor with a well-trained lunge horse is best. The horse should have a well-designed and fitted saddle, and comfortable paces. Half an hour of riding for the first three or four lessons would be sufficient, to prevent overtiring muscles causing stiffness and soreness. It is better to have two or three short periods a week, if possible, rather than one long one. The rest of the hour lesson can be profitably spent in the stables, under supervision, handling horses, grooming, and tacking-up, especially if the learner has had no previous experience.

The Seat Learning the basic principles of posture related to balance are begun on the lunge horse, thus acquiring some feel for following the movement at the walk, slow trot and in simple transitions. Security in the saddle and control are based on balance made possible through suppleness.

Correct mounting and dismounting, adjustment of girths and stirrup leathers are practised at this stage. During movement balance is three-dimensional, forward and backwards, lateral or from side to side, and up and down from the oscillations of the horse's back. To absorb this the rider must be so poised in order to have supple flexible joints, especially the loins, hips, knees and ankles. Correct adjustment of the stirrup leathers to this end is essential to allow flexion of these joints. A relaxed but upright upper body must be maintained without contraction or stiffness, enabling the rider to follow the movement of the horse, therefore, he or she must be sitting squarely on the seat bones in the deepest part of the saddle, which should be closest to the horse's centre of gravity —that is, just behind the withers at the halt. The legs should 'hang' down close to the horse's sides with relaxed thighs, the stirrup iron on the ball of the foot and the heel just below the level of the toe, without being forced in any way. The length of stirrup leather will vary slightly according to individual conformation of the rider, but must allow flexion of knee, hip and ankle joints. There should be a straight line from the ear, shoulder, hip and heel as a general guide to the outline of the rider. A neck strap should be used to help maintain balance, and can gradually be dispensed with as confidence and balance improve. Suppling exercises which are related to individual requirements should be introduced but used with discretion to achieve positive results. This should include progressive work without stirrups. Once rising trot is established confidence usually develops, but this must not be practised to the exclusion of developing feel for movement and softness at sitting trot. After several lessons the rider may be given the reins. It is quite normal to want to use the arms and hands to maintain balance, as this is their natural function in everyday life. The development of a firm independent seat without resorting to the use of the hands is the first objective in learning to ride. To start with it will be difficult to keep them still. At this stage on the lunge, complete relaxation, comfort and confidence should be established without having to worry about control.

The Aids Knowledge of the simple aids which are the rider's means of communication with the horse must be introduced. The natural aids are the weight of the body, the legs, the hands, the voice. To understand fully the importance and effect of a firm independent seat, capable of following the movements with a feel for balance in relation to the movement of the horse, it is helpful to consider the mechanism of the horse. In order to carry the weight of the rider, a horse has to readjust his balance to the new load. If this is continually shifting about, either forwards or backwards or laterally, in a direction contrary to the horse's centre of gravity, loss of control of his limbs is inevitable. Hence, if a horse increases his pace and the rider tries to stop him by pulling the reins, leaning forward and bracing against the stirrup irons, the result will be to go faster rather than slower, because of opposing aids and increased loss of balance. Therefore the adjustment of the rider's body weight and the ability to control it at all paces, both on turns and circle, and maintenance of quietness and softness in the saddle, are the major factors in security and control. Independent use of the hands and legs will require much practice to develop co-ordination and harmony, and should be started while still on the lunge, where the instructor is in control. A trained horse will respond to the rider's requests and this is the best means of teaching a beginner to feel and learn.

The leg aids have two functions, to create impulsion and control the hind quarters. Once the rider is capable of keeping the legs still and close to the horse's sides, he can start to apply them as aids, making sure that the weight still goes down into the heel and that the shoulders and upper body do not fall forward and stiffen. Leg aids should be applied inwards and forwards, and not in repetitive kicking from front to back. The hands, which control impulsion and the forehand, at this stage of the rider's training should maintain a passive role, the main endeavour being to follow the movement by understanding the action of the horse's head and neck.

At the walk, the horse's head and neck move up and down from the shoulder; therefore the rider's arms, with elastic elbows, soft shoulders, fingers closed round the reins, should endeavour to follow the movement with a lightly stretched rein. While trotting, the head and neck of the horse should remain still; this will cause problems for the rider to start with, as the hands should be quiet but not fixed in any way. A straight line from the horse's mouth over the top of the thumb to the elbow, which must be bent, is a guide to the attitude which will eventually allow independent and positive use of the hand as an aid at a later stage. In the canter, the head and neck move slightly, and as at the other paces constant contact has to be developed through practice and feel, the rider's seat remaining close to the saddle.

Practical Application After about six hours of work on the lunge, the rider should start to join a class. This must be in an enclosed space with not more than three or four others, one of whom should be a more experienced rider as leading file and demonstrator. During this period the main objective is practice of the previous lessons, with sometimes what appears to be retrograde results with the problems of controlling independently even a trained horse! However, work at transitions, changes of direction and keeping correct distance will help to improve balance and co-ordination. It is better, if possible, to ride the same horse as on the lunge for the first few times, to maintain confidence. Careful observation of a more experienced rider and constant correction to posture will still be continued. If the school is large enough, cantering down the long side can be started, and also work over trotting poles, to develop feel for greater movement. Change of horses is very valuable once confidence and balance are sufficiently established to cope with the variation without apprehension. The object of work in the school is to improve technique through knowledge of the aids and paces of the horse, and to understand the association of sensations, which by training make the horse give himself both physically and mentally under all circumstances to the demands of his rider.

Once several hours have been spent in the school, the rider should be taken outside, hacking on a quiet horse accompanied by an instructor. Riding is essentially an outdoor sport—at first the wide open spaces, and probably a little more impulsion, will cause slight apprehension, but the importance of work over undulating ground in developing balance, co-ordination and initiative cannot be over-estimated. The pupil will become aware of the different strides, impulsion, rhythm, training, mouth and temperament of every different horse he rides.

After between twelve and eighteen lessons the rider should be able to show some control and maintain balance at slow paces. Variation between work in the school and outside will complement each other, developing all-round ability.

The learner should now be ready to start jumping, which should be done under instruction in an enclosed area. Stirrup leathers will need to be a couple of holes shorter to allow more weight on the knees. The upper body is inclined forward from the hips, without the seat being lifted out of the saddle to any degree. Practice at the trot in the jumping seat is the first essential, holding a neck strap to start with until balance is maintained with ease. Trotting poles placed 4 ft 6 in (1.36 m) apart will increase the bounce in the horse's stride and teach the rider to absorb it by closing the angles of hips, knees and ankles without resort to the hands or reins in any way. Then a small fence 2 ft (60 cm) high can be placed 8 ft (2.4 m) from the last trotting pole. The rider should approach at a trot, sit softly, look ahead and enjoy the bounce! Once this exercise has been accomplished without resort to the hands to maintain balance, a small single fence can be attempted from canter, which will give the rider a feeling of accomplishment.

To ride a highly sensitive Thoroughbred horse under all conditions with ease, grace and harmony should be the challenge to those learning to ride, in order to fulfil the ideal epitomized in the words, 'there is no secret so close as that between a rider and his horse'. This endeavour will provide a lifelong interest.

*   *   *

Riding Classes, Children's   The British Show Pony Society recommends height limits for *Open Classes* as follows:
1   Not exceeding 12.2 h.h. (124 cm) as suitable for, and to be ridden by, a child not exceeding 12 years.
2   Exceeding 12.2 h.h. (124 cm) and not exceeding 13.2 h.h. (134 cm) to be ridden by a child not exceeding 14 years.
3   Exceeding 13.2 h.h. (134 cm) and not exceeding 14.2 h.h. (144 cm) to be ridden by a child not exceeding 16 years. In *Leading Rein Classes* the pony must not exceed 11.2 h.h. (113 cm) and the child must not be under the age of 3 years. *Novice Pony Classes, Side-saddle Classes, Pairs of Ponies Classes* and *Working Hunter Pony Classes* all have their own special rules.

Riding Clubs, The Association of Over 400 Riding Clubs in the British Isles are affiliated to the British Horse Society which supplies information, lectures, films etc., and co-ordinates their activities which culminate in the Riding Club Championships at the National Equestrian Centre, Stoneleigh, Kenilworth, Warwickshire.

Riding Establishments Act 1964 Regulates the keeping of riding establishments and enacts that no person shall keep a riding establishment except under licence. Requirements to justify this are detailed and the powers of local authorities of inspection, prosecution, etc., are indicated. The Act came into operation on 1st April, 1965. In 1970 further powers were granted to local licensing authorities, providing the issue of Provisional Licences valid for three months and including such regulations as not allowing responsibility for riding establishments by anyone under 16 years old, or hiring out any horse aged three years or under or heavy in foal.

Riding for the Disabled Association, The Established as a charity in 1969 to encourage riding for the physically and mentally disabled. Regional groups have been formed all over the country. *Headquarters:* National Equestrian Centre, Stoneleigh, Kenilworth, Warwickshire.

Riding Machine   *see* ROSINBACK RIDING MACHINE

Riding-posts   *see* HORSE-POSTS.

Riding Off (Polo) A player may be 'ridden off' the ball provided that his opponent comes into him not at an acute angle and applies side-to-side pressure. Charging at an angle greater than roughly 45 degrees is prohibited as dangerous.

Riding School   An enclosed space, open or covered, for the exercising and schooling of horses. The dimensions should be approximately 180 ft (54 m) by 60 ft (18 m).

Rig   A horse with a retained testicle. Such horses are mischievous and a nuisance when running loose with mares, and some are liable to get mares in foal. It can also refer to a horse inadequately operated upon or to one having some abnormality at birth.

Rig   An equipage or turn-out for driving.

Righthand Course   One where the horses run in a clockwise direction, as at Sandown Park and Ascot.

Rigid Tree   A saddle tree not of the spring type is termed rigid, denoting its lack of resilience.

Rim Collar   Used in hackney harness, the groove (in which the hames rest) showing on the inside (the neck side). A Kay collar, named after its designer, is neater than a rim collar as the groove does not show and the lining is carried smoothly from back to front.

Rim Firing A cowboy practice of putting a burr under the saddle blanket to make the horse buck harder in rodeo buckjumping contests.

Ring, The (Racing) Bookmakers collectively are known as 'The Ring'.

Ringbone A bony formation in the pastern region, which may be 'high' or 'low' according to position; the latter may be partly contained within the hoof. *Causes:* hereditary tendency, prolonged work and concussion on hard roads, and in some cases a blow. *Symptoms:* enlargement and heat in the pastern. *Treatment:* rest, consult a veterinary surgeon. *Recommended:* the use of an open Rocker or Rocker-bar Shoe (*see* SHOE, ROCKER-BAR).

Ringer (Racing) A horse which is substituted for another.

Ringing Fox One which persists in running in circles and never moving far from the home covert.

Rings *see* MARTINGALE, IRISH.

Rings on Feet Ridges running round the outside walls of the hoof. They should be regarded with suspicion as they may be the result of laminitis. They are sometimes caused by the horse having been turned out on damp land. If the coronet has been blistered, rings may appear on the hoof, but will grow out.

Ringworm A highly contagious disease of the skin caused by a fungus. *Cause:* contagion. *Symptoms* include loss of hair, usually in round patches of variable size over any part of the body, but commencing usually on head and neck, gradually extending. *Treatment:* isolation—everything must be disinfected, and each patch dressed with iodine or some strong fungicide. An internal form of treatment is now in common use and meets with considerable success. Ringworm is communicable to human beings and care must be taken to wash carefully after applying dressings. The affected horse should not be ridden.

Riot When hounds hunt any animal or bird other than their proper quarry, they are said to riot.

Risen Clench When a clench (*q.v.*) rises and protrudes from a shoe through wear; it is vital that this is attended to immediately to prevent injury to a horse and it is advisable to obtain a new set of shoes.

Rising A term used in giving the age of a horse. A horse that is, for example, nearly five years old is said to be 'rising five', and if just over five, it is said to be 'five off'.

Risling, Ridgeling A horse which has its reproductive organs only partially developed (*see* RIG).

Ritt *see* EARS, IDENTIFICATION MARKS.

Roach-back

Roach-back A prominent malformed convex spinal column, also known as a hog-back.

Roached Mane Equivalent term in the U.S.A. for hogged mane (*q.v.*).

'Road Closed' Jump recognized by The British Show Jumping Association and in popular use—usually a 'gallows' arm with the words painted boldly in contrasting colours (*see Plate* 20)

Road Coach (Stage Coach) The public passenger-carrying vehicles which were run like those transporting the mails but carrying many more passengers—twelve on top and four inside. In order to attract custom road coaches were painted gaily, also having the names of destinations and stopping places on their panels and hind boots. Since payment had to be made at toll-gates they were considerably slower than the mail coaches (*q.v.*), but the fares were considerably cheaper.

Roadster A saddle-horse of the hackney type—in great demand in the early part of the century. In the United States of America this is a light harness horse, usually standard bred (trotter), driven to a light four-wheeled road cart (also termed a roadster).

Roan Barbary The horse of King Richard II, believed to have been imported from the East. It was of great beauty and uncertain temper, but much loved by the King. It has been immortalized in famous lines by Shakespeare in *The Tragedy of King Richard II*.

Roan Colour Where there is an admixture of white hair with the body colour, lightening the general effect of the latter. *Blue roan*: where the body colour is black or black-brown, the admixture of white hair giving a blue tinge; the limbs from the knee and hock downwards are black. *Bay or Red roan*: where the body colour is bay or bay-brown, the admixture of white hair giving a reddish tinge; the limbs as above. *Strawberry or Chestnut roan*: where the body colour is chestnut, the admixture of white hair giving a pinkish-red ringe.

Roarer A term describing a horse with an affection of the larynx, and which makes a noise when galloping. This noise is not to be confused with 'whistling', which is a modified form of roaring (*see* TRACHEOTOMY).

Rockaway A town carriage of the Brougham type, although the driver's seat is placed lower and is joined to the body of the vehicle. An extension of the roof projects over the driving seat.

American Rockaway

Rock Salt Blocks of iodized or plain salt should always be available for horses to lick, and are appreciated by most. It is necessary from a health point of view and a licking block is a convenient form. Sometimes known as Salt-lick.

Rockwell Bridle A bit having metal loops of figure 8 shape round the mouthpiece on the inside of the bit rings. To these loops is fastened a nosepiece, usually elastic, which is supported by a central strap fastening at the poll. Prevents a horse poking his nose, getting tongue over the bit and has a restraining effect on hard pullers. Sometimes known as Crocker's bit.

Rodeo (Spanish, *rodear*—to go round) Originally a round-up of cattle on American ranges, now mainly applied to special shows where cowboys give exhibitions of skill in various forms of their work, and compete in riding buckjumpers and steers, and in steer roping and steer wrestling.

Rodzianko Gag *see* ROLLER MOUTH

Rogue A vicious horse and not just bad mannered.

Rogue's Badge Denotes blinkers worn by racehorses, but all horses running in them are not necessarily rogues. They are sometimes worn to stop horses from staring about them. Winkers on harness are not rogues' badges. In hunting a red tail-ribbon (*q.v.*) is a rogue's badge.

Roll Cantle A roll of leather on the back of an American saddle which the rider uses to help raise himself into the saddle.

Roller A form of girth made of leather, hemp and webbing, and used with a night or day rug to keep it in place. It is fastened with one or two buckles and has two panels to fit on either side of the spine. There are various patterns, including the arch type which eliminates pressure on the spine.

Roller Bolts Four upward projections on the splinter bar to which the traces of a pair, or of the coach wheelers, are attached.

Roller Mouth A bit with rollers set round the mouthpiece. It is useful on strong horses, the movement of the rollers assisting mouthing of the bit, and discouraging a horse's 'taking hold' of it. When used with gag rings it is sometimes called Rodzianko's gag, after the late Paul Rodzianko. The rollers can also be referred to as 'cherries'.

Roll-up A new Tote bet, introduced in 1973, in which Tote betters try to forecast successfully the first six in correct order in a roll-up flat race on a Saturday. Unit 5p. Discontinued in the same year.

Roman Nose *see* NOSE, ROMAN.

Rooster Pull An American cowboy game played at one time; with his horse travelling at a high speed, the rider had to lean down and seize the neck of a 'rooster' buried in the ground, pull it loose and then race round a large circle.

Roots A hunting term implying any field of turnips, swedes, beet, mangolds, potatoes, etc.

Rope Horse A horse qualified by training to hold a rope tight enough to prevent a steer from rising after it has been thrown.

Rope Shoes These have a groove on the ground surface in which rests a tarred rope, the purpose being to lessen the possibility of the horse slipping on smooth pavements. Special long-headed nails are used.

Rosebery, Archibald Philip Primrose, 5th Earl of The only Premier to have owned a Derby winner while Prime Minister. He won with 'Ladas' (1894) and 'Sir Visto' (1895) when Prime Minister. He won the race a third time with 'Cicero' in 1905 when no longer Premier.

Rosette A show ring award consisting of ribbons of one or more colours, presented for championship, or reserve to championship. Special, First, Second, Third, Fourth, Very Highly Commended, Highly Commended, or Commended. Cups, money prizes and other awards may be added. In Britain red usually signifies first place and blue second, with some important exceptions; these include the Royal International Horse Show (*q.v.*), Bath and West Show (*q.v.*), Pony Club events and many shows in the West Country. In the U.S.A. blue ranks first and red second, but Canada reverses these colours.

'Rosinante' The horse of Don Quixote de la Mancha, the 'Knight of the Melancholy Countenance', hero of Cervantes' romance satirizing the excesses of the last ages of chivalry. Used as a term to denote that a horse is in the last stages of usefulness.

Rosinback Riding Machine (or **Mechanic**) A crane-like device used in the circus in training bareback riders. The rider is suspended from the head of a moving crane by a rope attached to a leather belt that encircles the waist, thus preventing a fall when loss of balance takes place.

Rosinbacks   The circus name given to bareback riding horses on which artistes stand and perform various acrobatic and other acts. The term originated from the fact that resin is rubbed into the horse's back, mainly around the quarters, to prevent the performers from slipping. It is essential for the horse to have a wide, level and un-dipped back. It must have plenty of bone, and the gait, speed and level pace at which it canters are of great importance (see CIRCUS HORSES).

Ross, Martin   see ROSS, VIOLET.

Ross, Violet (1862–1915)   Under the nom-de-plume 'Martin Ross', with her cousin, Edith O. Somerville (*q.v.*), she was the author of many books on Irish sporting life, including the well-known *Some Experiences of an Irish R.M.*

Rostopchin Saddle Horse   see RUSSIAN SADDLE HORSE.

Rotten Row   A straight and broad riding track in Hyde Park, London, extending from Hyde Park Corner to Alexandra Gate, and popularly known as 'The Row'. Made, probably about 1690, by William III to take him from Westminster to his palace at Kensington, it then had a surface of sorts, was lit by oil lamps, and was known as King's or Lamp Road. About 1734 it was converted to a soft surface. Apart from the obvious possible reference to the latter ('rotten' = 'soft'), there are various theories as to the origin of the name. One is that it is a corruption of *Route du Roi*, referring to the way taken by the Plantagenet kings from Westminster Palace to the Royal hunting forests; this route covered what are now Birdcage Walk, Constitution Hill and Rotten Row. Another suggestion is that after George II had constructed the South Carriage Road—a shorter distance—the older way, now called Old King's Road, became the haunt of idlers, whence derived its nickname—which had certainly come into use by

1770 at the latest. A third theory is that the name derived from the Teutonic *rotteran*, to muster, since William III and the Hanoverians occasionally mustered troops in the Row. It was referred to in the *Sporting Magazine* in 1837 as Rontine (alias Rotten) Row.

Rough Country   Any country which is not easy to ride across, i.e. woodland, moorland, or many hills.

Roughing Off, Roughing Up.   A course adopted immediately preceding the act of turning a horse out to grass, including the alteration of diet by omitting stimulants, cessation of grooming and exercise, and gradual removal of rugs, etc.

Rough-shoeing   The insertion of frost-nails into shoes to secure a better hold on ice-bound surfaces.

Rouncey   Mediaeval term for a riding horse of the small cob type.

Round Action   Showing little liberty or dash in movement. Many high-movers have this fault, and cover the ground very slowly in harness.

Rounder, The   A Round the Clock (*q.v.*) bet taking three selections in which the 'If Cash' (*q.v.*) on the remaining two is a double instead of singles.

Rounding   Cutting off the points of hounds' ears when they are puppies. A fashion of no practical value, it is no longer practised.

Round the Clock   A bet taking three or more selections and can be a win only or an each-way bet.

Round-up   The collection of cattle off the ranges in the American and other ranchlands for branding, selecting for sale, etc. They are held periodically among some of the mountain and moorland breeds in the British Isles.

Round   An early English term (and a modern American one) for a horse which is roan or flesh-coloured, intermixed with white or peach. Originally known also as grissel.

Rous, Admiral the Hon. Henry John (1795–1877) Called 'The Dictator of the Turf', Admiral Rous was official handicapper for a long period. He once said, when he was handicapper, that 'Eclipse' (*q.v.*) was about good enough to win a £50 Selling Plate. The Rous Memorial Stakes were named after him (*see* THE RACEHORSE AND RACING IN GREAT BRITAIN).

Rouse (Stag Hunting) A term denoting that a stag has been set a-foot in cover.

Rowel A 'wheel' inserted at the head of a spur. There were many different designs of varying severity in action. Very little used in modern practice and then only mild in action except with western horses in the U.S.A. when rowels are severe and used too much.

Rowlandson, Thomas (1756–1827) Esteemed for his countless drawings and water colours of English life, in many of which horses are depicted, Rowlandson is most widely known for work of caricature or cartoon nature, notably the famous illustrations for the *Tours of Dr. Syntax*. Sporting prints designed and etched by Rowlandson include hunting and racing sets; e.g. *High Mettled Racer*, a set of four published 1879.

Rowley Mile The last mile of the Newmarket course, over which are run the 1000 and 2000 Guineas. Named after Charles II's well-known stallion 'Old Rowley' (*see* NEWMARKET *and* OLD ROWLEY).

Royal Agricultural Society of England, The Founded in 1839, the Society held an annual Royal Agricultural Show in different parts of the country, popularly known as 'The Royal'. It is now permanently sited at Stoneleigh, Warwickshire.

Royal College of Veterinary Surgeons The governing body of the veterinary profession in Great Britain and Ireland, under Royal Charter granted in 1844. The Membership diploma (M.R.C.V.S.) granted by the College entitles the holder to be placed on the Register of Veterinary Surgeons maintained by the College and to practise the art of veterinary surgery and medicine. The Fellowship diploma (F.R.C.V.S.) is granted to members of not less than two years' standing on presentation of a thesis based on original research or observation. Candidates for Fellowship will be required to: (1) Submit a thesis; or (2) pass examinations; (3) under the provisions of by-law 105, apply for permission to submit published work as evidence of meritorious contributions to learning. Candidates for award by thesis must first be accepted as a provisional candidate and then submit with the application the proposed course of study.

Royal Colours *see* COLOURS OF THE ROYAL FAMILY.

Royal Dublin Society *see* DUBLIN SHOW.

Royal George Gag An alternative but incorrect term for a Nelson gag (*q.v.*).

Royal International Horse Show *see* INTERNATIONAL HORSE SHOW.

Royal Mares Arab and Barb mares imported into England in the seventeenth century for the Royal Stud. These, with certain others, became the foundation mares of the English Thoroughbred.

Royal Mews Situated in Buckingham Palace Road, London. When the Royal Stables were destroyed by fire in 1537 Henry VIII ordered his Stud to be housed in the Mews of the King's Falcons at Charing Cross. The mews were moved to the present site in 1825.

Royal Society for the Prevention of Cruelty to Animals, The (Founded 1824) *Objects:* to prevent cruelty to animals and to promote kindness to animals.

Royal Windsor Horse Show Club, The (Founded 1943) *Objects:* to benefit charities and to promote the well-being of horses. The Society holds an Annual Horse Show at Windsor in May.

Royal Winter Fair   Held in Toronto, Canada, founded in 1925 and now an important event in the International Show Jumping scene of North America.

Rubber, Stable   A twilled linen square used in grooming.

Rub-down   Should be given to a horse which is brought in sweating, or wet from rain. Dry straw should be used, followed by one or two dry stable rubbers. Most important parts are the ears, throat, chest, back and loins.

Rug, New Zealand   A weatherproofed canvas rug used on horses (which may be hunter clipped) turned out in the winter. There are a number of varieties, the best being those kept in place without the use of a surcingle (*see* EMSTON).

New Zealand Rug

'Rugby' on Horseback   *see* BUZKASHI.

Rugby Pelham Bit   A term embracing various types of Pelham (usually mullen mouth) which have a loose top ring attached closely to the cheeks. Similar to the Berkeley.

Rugby Saddle Panel   A short leather panel with an interior of felt.

Rugged Up   A term applied to a horse wearing either day or night rugs. It is important to see that the rugs fit well and are not buckled up too tightly.

Rule of the Road (in Britain)   Ride on the left and lead on the left (keeping yourself between the led animal and the traffic). B.H.S. safety suggestions: after dusk ride with stirrup light showing white to the front and red to the rear. Wear reflective arm-bands or belt.

Rumble   *see* DICKEY.

Run   An action found in a badly broken horse, a compromise between a canter behind and a trot in front. In U.S.A. a term applied to Thoroughbreds and Quarter Horses at the fastest gait a horse can execute.

Run   A hunting term referring to every occasion during which a quarry is hunted by hounds. The distance is measured by a straight line from the point of find to the point of kill; 'as hounds ran' gives the actual distance covered.

Runciman   Those bearing this name may assume that it is derived from the obsolete word runcy or rouncey (*q.v.*). Thus Runciman would mean a runcy-keeper or runcy-dealer.

Runcy   *see* ROUNCEY.

Runnable Stag   *see* WARRANTABLE.

Runners (Racing)   All the horses in the list of those entered in a race, actually taking part in that race.

Runners (Saddlery)   Leather loops on saddlery (especially the bridle), that slide up and down and through which the strap ends pass.

Running   When hounds are actually in pursuit of a fox.

Running Iron   A $\frac{1}{2}$ in (12.7 mm) iron rod, slightly curved at one end and used by cowboys for branding cattle before the introduction of the modern branding iron.

'Running Loose' A term descriptive of a racehorse which, owing to a general lack of confidence in its ability to win a race, shared by the personnel at the stable where it is trained, runs unbacked by the latter.

Running-out A term implying that a horse is out at grass.

Running-out The action of a horse skirting round an object instead of jumping it, either when racing over fences, or when jumping in the show ring.

Running Up Light Descriptive of a horse which has badly muscled quarters and sunken flanks: the result of poor condition.

Running-walk An accelerated flat-footed walk, 6–8 m.p.h. (9.6–12.8 km). Tennessee Walking Horses (*q.v.*) are the best performers of this gait.

Russell, Rev. 'Jack' He inherited a love of field sports from his father, the vicar of Iddesleigh, who kept his own pack of hounds and was a fearless rider. For some years he kept a pack of Otterhounds and eventually founded the North West Devon Hunt. When 76, in 1871, he gave up his hounds after having hunted otter and then fox for 50 seasons. However, he still followed, and when he became vicar of Torrington he started a Harrier Pack although then over 80 years of age. He was the originator of the Jack Russell terrier, the prototype of the hunt terrier (*q.v.*).

Russian Saddle Horse Called also the Orlov-Rostopchin breed, this was formed by crossing the Orlov Trotter with the Rostopchin saddle horse, the latter being bred about 1800 by a great Russian breeder, Count Rostopchin, from Arabs and English Thoroughbreds in Moscow. His studs were bought later by the Russian Government.

Russian Steppe These horses belong to a Mongolian group of many strains. All, however, represent the same type, standing 13–14 h.h. (132–142 cm), with strong constitutions, rather heavy, ugly heads on ewe necks. The legs are very short, strong and muscular with small hard hoofs. All varieties are hardy and resist all weathers; they find grass and moss under the snow in long winters. They possess great speed and stamina and can carry weight. A 15-stone (210 lb; 95.25 kg) Cossack will gallop a 13 h.h. (132 cm) pony. Cossack D. Pieszkow covered nearly 6000 miles (9656 km) in 6 months riding a Steppe horse. In modern times these horses are used as saddle horses by Mongolian tribes or as agricultural horses by peasants.

Rust A parasitic fungus growing on plants and grasses in the form of a yellowish powder, often having serious results when fed to horses.

Rustic Gate Parallels (British Show Jumping Assn.) Gates of rustic material and colour, requiring a horse to negotiate both height and spread.

Rustle, to (U.S.A.) To herd, round up or steal horses or cattle.

Rutter's Twitch *see* TWITCH, HUMANE.

Rutting Season The stags' mating season—October.

Rye Inferior to oats as a feed, but better and safer than barley.

Ryegrass A very good food in the form of hay, especially for heavy horses. It is best fed with clover.

* S *

S.A.N.E.F. South African National Equestrian Federation (*see* HORSES AND RIDERS IN SOUTH AFRICA, *page* 305).

S.B.A. Stud Book Argentino.

Sh (Racing) Short head.

Ss (Racing) Started slowly.

Sack A sack of corn equals four bushels (145 l).

Saddle A pad is occasionally called a saddle by harness makers. In cart-harness a pad is always called a saddle.

Saddle This came into use in the fourth century and was either invented by the Byzantines or 'adopted' by them from the hordes of Barbarian horsemen which threatened the Roman Empire (*see Plate 27*).

Saddle, Astride or Cross One used by anyone riding astride, as distinct from side-saddle.

Saddle, Dressage A saddle specifically designed for this specialized branch of riding. The seat is dipped but generally shorter than that of a jumping saddle. The head of the saddle is straight as opposed to being sloped to the rear. The flaps are fairly straight in cut and the panel offers a little knee and thigh support. The best known English design is the Fulmer (*see Plate 27*).

Saddle, Felt A saddle with a girth attached—very useful for a tender backed horse, but as this design comes right down on the withers, and is hot and inclined to draw, it is not recommended for long rides, or for hunting. It is, however, very useful for young riders, as it provides a secure seat.

Saddle, General Purpose A modern spring tree saddle not quite so exaggerated in cut as the jumping saddle. It is used for hunting and cross-country work and can also be used for elementary dressage (*see Plate 27*).

Saddle (Harness) Made as a miniature riding saddle, this can be of many designs, and carries the back band, shaft tugs and belly band.

Saddle, Hunting A term generally applied to the conventional 'English' saddle made on a rigid tree and with very little dip to the seat. The term can, of course, be applied to any saddle used for hunting. This type is still used but the tendency is for more and more people to use a saddle of a 'general purpose' pattern which gives greater support and positions the rider more correctly in relation to the movement of the horse.

Saddle, Jumping A spring tree, characteristically deep-seated saddle, cut well forward and having knee rolls incorporated into the panel. Its design positions the rider over the centre of gravity and assists him to remain with the movement of the horse. It is cut further forward than a 'general purpose' saddle and is usually lighter. There are some modern jumping saddles which employ Lonsdale girth straps (*q.v.*) (*see Plate 27*).

Saddle, Pariani Pariani was the name of Italy's foremost saddlemaker, the reputed originator of the spring tree saddle.

Saddle, Polo Slightly deeper, with a high cantle, and shorter and wider than the English hunting saddle (*see Plate 27*).

Saddle, Racing A small saddle with flaps cut well forward, weighing from 8 oz–2½ lb (226 g–1.12 kg). Steeplechase saddles are, in general, larger and can be made on a weighted tree if the rider has to carry much extra weight. Racing saddles are rarely made with stirrup bars, the leathers being passed round the tree itself. Plastics and fibreglass are increasingly used in the manufacture of lightweight trees (*see Plate 27*).

Saddle, Santini One of the first British-made jumping saddles on the Italian pattern. Designed by Piero Santini (*q.v.*).Now superseded by more modern designs.

Saddle, Short A 'half' saddle built on a fore-arch rather like a driving pad and about 12 in (30.4 cm) long. Used in training stables for horses with sore backs caused by the cantle of badly fitting saddles.

Saddle, Showing Of closer fit than a hunting saddle, with straighter flaps and designed to show the horse's front to the best advantage. A show saddle is usually fitted with an additional girth strap emerging from the point of the tree to enable the saddle to be fitted farther back. The best show saddles have the bars extended farther to the rear which permits the rider's knee to rest on the flap. With normally positioned bars the leathers, and the rider's leg, would be too far forward. Used in the U.S.A. for gaited saddle horses, Tennessee Walking Horses (*q.v.*), Arabians and Morgans (*q.v.*) and more artificial breeds. Hunters and show-jumpers use English saddles (*see Plate* 27).

Saddle, Side A lady's saddle upon which she sits with both legs to one side, usually the left or near side. The saddle has two projections or pommels on that side; over one of these the rider rests the right leg, and under the lower pommel she places the left leg. The seat of this saddle is often made of doeskin (*see* SIDE-SADDLE *and Plate* 27).

Saddle, Stock Used by mounted herdsmen and cowboys of the American West and Mexico; with a deep seat, high cantle (*q.v.*) and pommel horn for attaching rope or lariat, full cut flaps, fastened by double leather cinches (*q.v.*) pulled tight by slide knots.

Saddle, Toptani A modern spring tree show jumping saddle designed by Count Ilias Toptani.

Saddle, Universal The name given to the British Army Trooper Saddle (used by all mounted Units). A skeleton saddle panel is protected by a folded blanket. It has proved an excellent saddle for all types of backs in every condition (*see Plate* 27).

Saddle Airer A stand for holding a saddle after use; the front of the saddle goes downwards, and the flaps are held well open and thus exposed to the air.

Saddle Bars Metal fittings beneath the skirts of the saddle to which the stirrup leathers are attached. Most bars are fitted with a safety catch, or thumb-piece, at the rear. Very few horsemen would recommend that this should ever be used in the 'up' or 'locked' position, and it might indeed be dangerous used in this way. It is, therefore, largely superfluous but remains as a relic of the various patterns of, so called, safety bars which were once popular. The bars on a good saddle should be forged steel; on cheaper saddles the bars are cast and, therefore, likely to fracture. Bars on modern spring tree saddles are recessed to avoid bulk under the thigh.

Saddle Bracket A wall-bracket in the saddle-room on which saddles are placed.

Saddlebred, American *see* AMERICAN SADDLEBRED.

Saddle Channel The aperture between the two panels, which runs between all well-fitting saddles and horses' backs.

Saddle Cloth A shaped rectangular cloth, often in a cotton or linen check, placed under the saddle.

Saddle-flaps Leather sides of a saddle made of cowhide, and with which the rider's knees come into contact (*see* SWEAT FLAPS).

Saddle Horn A fitting on the front of American stock or western saddles, around which the line is twisted when a steer is roped. The 'horn' is made of metal covered with leather, and slopes forward with the top, which is enlarged at the front, also projecting forward, facilitating the quick release of the rope.

Saddle Horse A wooden trestle-like stand upon which one or more saddles can rest securely for cleaning or storage.

Saddle-linen Unbleached linen used to line saddle panels and bearing surfaces. Should always be put over serge and not used on its own. It protects the serge from wear and is more easily kept clean.

Saddle Marks When clipping marks should be left in the natural position of the saddle to protect the back. Nothing looks worse than a saddle mark showing with the saddle fitted in front of it. Also a term for patches of white hair under the saddle—probably caused by galls. These patches are used as identification marks.

Saddle Panel The cushion between the tree and the horse's back. It can either be made of felt covered in leather, or it can be stuffed with wool and covered in serge, serge-covered linen, or leather lined. The latter form is used for most modern hunting, jumping saddles, etc. Felt panels are often used in show saddles. Foam plastics or similar materials are now sometimes used. A panel can be made, according to the tree, in any of four shapes: full panel, Rugby or short, Saumur or Witney, Continental. The last two are those most used in modern saddles and because of their knee rolls and general construction afford more security to the rider and allow him to be in closer contact with the horse.

Saddlers, Black The trade term applied generally to makers of cart and carriage harness, as distinct from saddles, bridles, etc. (see SADDLERS, BROWN).

Saddlers, Brown The trade term applied generally to makers of saddles,

bridles, etc., as distinct from harness (see SADDLERS, BLACK).

Saddlers' Company, The 'The Wardens or Keepers and commonalty of the mystery or Art of Saddlers.' The exact date of formation is unknown, but the Company probably existed in Anglo-Saxon times; a document in possession of the Dean and Chapter of Westminster showed its existence many years before 1154. The first Hall was destroyed in the Great Fire of 1666, the second in 1821, and the third was destroyed by enemy action in 1940. All had been rebuilt on the same site. The Company ranks 25th in order of precedence among the City Livery Companies.

Saddle Serge A special, white wool cloth used for lining saddle panels.

Saddle Sheepskin A sheepskin numnah used under the saddle to give greater comfort to the horse or a cover fitting over the saddle to give more security and comfort to the rider. Although comfortable, sheepskin is very hot. A sheepskin pad saddle was made but is now rarely seen.

Saddle Soap Applied with a damp sponge in cleaning, 'feeding' and preserving saddles, bridles and harness. Glycerine soap can also be used for similar purposes.

Saddle Sores Caused by bad riding or a badly fitting saddle and harness. Prevention being better than cure, particular care must be taken to see that the saddle fits correctly. A horse just up from grass should not have on a saddle for more than one hour at a time until his back has hardened.

Saddle Stuffing The wool flock used to stuff the panels of a saddle.

Saddle Tree The frame upon which the saddle is built. At one time the tree was always of beech reinforced with steel plates, but nowadays strips of wood laminated in moulds are largely used and reinforced with a light alloy. This method gives greater strength and a lighter tree.

Safes   A term used in the saddlery trade referring to any piece of shaped leather which keeps undue pressure from the animal, usually behind a buckle which would otherwise cause a gall. Girth buckle 'safes' save the saddle flap.

Safety Bars   Stirrup bars employing a device, often activated by a spring or swivel, designed to release the stirrup leather in the event of a fall. They are seldom used today. The best known patterns, apart from Passmore and Cole, were Allfreys, Beaufort, Cotswold, etc. Christie's bar, a plain one tapering upwards at the rear, is used on Australian trees and is probably the most practical of all the types.

Safety Catch   A movable 'latch' on the metal bar holding the stirrup leather to the saddle. In an emergency the leather is released from the saddle for the rider's safety.

Safety Chain   This can be fastened round the felloe of the near hind wheel to hold it if the skidpan breaks or jolts off.

Safety Stirrups   There is a variety of patterns, every one permitting the foot to be freed in the event of a fall.

Saiffin   A Mongolian pony imported into China Treaty Ports for racing purposes.

Sainfoin   see SANFOIN.

St Christopher   Traditionally Patron Saint of all who travel and thus the Patron Saint of horsemen.

St Hubert   Patron Saint of Huntsmen. Hubert was the son of Bertrand, Duc d'Aquitaine, but became so fond of the chase he neglected his religious duties until one day a stag with a crucifix between its horns threatened him with eternal perdition, which resulted in

his speedy reformation. The feast of St Hubert is still celebrated in certain districts of France where hounds and hunt attend Mass each year on November 3 and are blessed.

St Leger   The oldest in origin of the five classic races, it was founded in 1776 and is run annually in September on the Town Moor, Doncaster, in Yorkshire. It is for three-year-old colts and fillies over a distance of about 1 mile 6½ furlongs (1.81 km). The St Leger received its name as a compliment to Lt-General St Leger of Park Hill, Doncaster, a leading local sportsman of the 1780s. The first winner was a grey filly, Hollandaise. For the first years of its existence it was run over a 2-mile (3.22 km) course. For results *see page* 400.

Sais, Syce   An Indian groom.

Sales, Bloodstock   Various bloodstock sales are held during the year. The chief ones are conducted by Tattersalls at Newmarket in England and by Goffs in Ireland. In England there are also bloodstock sales at Ascot and Doncaster.

Salisbury, Emily Mary, Marchioness of (1749–1835)   Claimed to be the first woman M.F.H. She was Master of the Hertfordshire Hunt from 1793 until her seventieth year in 1819.

Saliva Tests (Racing)   Where the running of a racehorse is suspect, the stewards of a meeting can order the saliva and urine of a horse to be tested for evidence of doping. The samples are sent to the Forensic Laboratory at Newmarket for testing.

Sallenders   A complaint similar to mallenders (*q.v.*), the only difference being in situation, as sallenders is found at the front and the bend of the hock. *Treatment:* as for mallenders.

Salmon Marks   A rarely-used expression denoting a certain amount of white hair on the quarters and back.

Salt   Small quantities stimulate the appetite and should be added to the scalded oats and bran given to foals.

'Salted'   A horse in South Africa which has recovered from an attack of African Horse Sickness or has been immunized against it. Colloquially implies acclimatized, tough, hardened etc.

Salt-lick   Shaped blocks of salt which can be fitted into holders. Minerals are often added (*see* ROCK SALT).

Salt Marshes   Marshland affects the quality of the bone, tending to make it spongy and soft. It is beneficial to horses recovering from laminitis or ailments which set up foot troubles.

Salts   Purgatives (of which Epsom Salts are the most frequently given) are much used for keeping the digestive organs in condition.

Salt Water   (Sea Water)   Benefit is derived from exercise in salt water, which strengthens the sinews and cools the limbs. Swimming is beneficial to a lame horse as it provides for the exercise of joints and muscles without risking concussion in the injured limb.

Sandbath   A natural or artificial hollow in which horses delight to roll.

Sandcrack   A split in the wall of the hoof which starts near the coronet or below and penetrates the sensitive parts within, which bleed. It may occur in any part of the hoof, but it usually appears in the front of the hind hoof and on the inside quarter of the fore hoof. *Cause :* severe exertion or faulty horn secretion. *Treatment :* there are various methods with which the veterinary surgeon and the farrier are both concerned, but often a notch is made at the top of the crack with a hot iron and a blister applied to promote the growth of new horn. Clips or clamps holding the sides of the crack together are also used (*see Plate* 12).

Sandalwood   A very hardy pony bred in the Indonesian islands of Sumba and Sumbawa used for bareback racing. Named after the sandalwood which was the biggest export from the islands. Height 12.1–13.1 h.h. (123–133 cm).

Sandwich Case   Used when hunting, this is enclosed in a leather canteen and attached to the saddle by 'D's.'

Sanfoin, Sainfoin   A grass from which the best hay is made. It can be fed alone, or as hay having a predominant sanfoin content in a seeds mixture. The plant thrives well only on chalk or limestone soils, and, being drought-resistant, grows best in dry summers.

Santini, Piero (1881–1960)   A major in the Italian Cavalry Reserve. He won the *Croce di Guerra ad V.M.* (Military Cross for Valour, World War I). He was a noted Italian horseman and writer whose books, *Riding Reflections* (1932); *The Forward Impulse* (1937); and *The Riding Instructor* (1952) introduced the doctrine of Federico Caprilli (*q.v.*) on the Italian system of forward riding, thus revolutionizing modern cross-country and show-ring riding.

Sardinia Pony   Originally bred in a semi-wild state in the island of Sardinia, these hardy ponies stand between 13 and 14 h.h. (132–142 cm). Bay in colour, they are good work and ride ponies.

Sartorius, Francis (1734–1804)   Son of John Sartorius Senr. (*q.v.*) and achieved more widespread recognition, painting many race-match pictures, portraits of hunters and racehorse portraits, including several of 'Eclipse'. Having been taught by his father, he inherited many of the same limitations of technique.

Sartorius, John (Senr.) (1700–1780)   Son of a Nuremburg engraver, he became established in England *c.* 1720, the first of four generations of this family who used British field sports as their subject. He painted several racehorses in a stiff primitive style for some influential owners. English records of sport are considerably enriched by the

work of the Sartorius family who ig-
nored Continental influence and
brought an English approach to sporting art.

Sartorius, John Nost (1759–1828)
Son of Francis Sartorius, and the most
gifted of this family. His backgrounds
and composition of his pictures of
racing, hunting and portraits of horses
are pictorially more pleasing and technically better painted. Many prints
were made after his works. One of his
sons, John Francis (1775–1830), also
painted sporting subjects.

Satchel   A leather pouch worn by a
coachguard and containing a timepiece.

Saturation   A theory strongly believed in by many breeders, but without any foundàtion in fact, that a mare
repeatedly served by the same stallion
will produce offspring more and more
resembling the sire, through the constant interchange of blood between the
unborn foal and its dam.

Saucer Shoe   A shoe which has had so
much of its bearing surface hollowed
out that it bears only on the outer surface of the wall of the foot; injurious,
and may induce coronitis.

Saugor (Cavalry School)   The home
for many years of the Indian Army
Equitation School, Saugor, in the
Central Provinces, was the Indian
counterpart of Weedon (*q.v.*). It was
closed in 1939.

Saumur   A town in western France,
home of the French cavalry school
founded in 1814. In 1593, in the reign
of Henri IV, a well-known riding
academy had been founded there, and
in 1768 Saumur became the garrison
of the Carabiniers de Monsieur, a
crack troop made up of remarkable
horsemen. Today the home of the
Cadre Noir (*q.v.*).

Saumur Panel   A type of saddle panel
(*q.v.*) giving knee support. It is sometimes made of felt-covered leather.

Also known as French panel and Witney panel.

Sausage Boot   A stuffed
leather ring strapped
round the coronet as a
prevention against a cap-
ped elbow, caused when
lying down, by pressure
of the inner heel of the
shoe on the elbow.

Sausage Boot

Savage   Horses proved to be savage to
humans are very dangerous and should
be destroyed. 'To savage' denotes the
act of biting another horse or a human.
Savaging is almost certainly hereditary.

Sawdust   Often used as bedding, sawdust must be spread thickly to be rest-
ful, and drains must be stopped to avoid
choking. It is the least 'attractive' in
appearance of all forms of bedding, but
the most comfortable.

Scamperdale Pelham Bit   An angle
mouth, straight bar bit made popular by
Sam Marsh, a well-known twentieth-
century horseman. It is thought that
greater control is obtained by reason
of the fact that the cheeks come into
contact with a part of the horse's mouth
not hitherto affected. Its main advantage is in having the mouthpiece
turned back at each end, bringing the
cheek piece farther to the rear, and
away from the area where chafing is
likely to occur.

Scandinavian Horses   These include
the Fjord Horse of Norway, the Gudbrandsdal, and the native ponies of
Sweden, Finland and the Baltic States.
Their appearance and ancestry suggest
relation to the same group comprising
the ponies of the British Isles and
N.W. Europe generally. The Finnish
horse of today is of medium size, very
active and of great staying power. It
has a tough constitution, strong feet
and legs, and a thick muscular body.
The horse in Sweden was originally
introduced from the Baltic regions and
is generally supposed to have originated
from a type of horse from the Ukraine.

Scarlet, Hunting (Incorrectly termed Pink) Its origin is uncertain, but the custom was possibly originated by Henry VIII, who clothed his huntsmen and yeomen-prickers in habits of scarlet cloth. It is more likely, though, that it began in the days of Queen Anne, when scarlet coats were usually worn by country gentlemen who would naturally ride to hounds in them. It is likely that it became widely popular when military men from service in the Peninsular wars rode in their smart scarlet coats in the hunting field and established a fashion which exists to this day. Other coloured hunting coats often followed the livery of the family pack, as in the Beaufort green (for the hunt servants) and the Berkeley tawny yellow.

Scawbrig Bridle A bitless schooling bridle.

Scent, Fox's Hounds rarely see the fox, and hunt it by a scent which the fox gives off from glands just under the brush (chief source) and from the pads (feet). This is imparted in the form of an oily substance to any object touched by the fox but the hounds receive it as it is carried on the air in the form of gas molecules. The scent is best when the temperature of the ground is higher than that of the air. A vixen in cub leaves no scent and is therefore practically immune from being hunted.

'Sceptre' One of the greatest race mares in the history of the British Turf. Won four of the five classic races of 1902—the 2000 and 1000 Guineas, the Oaks and the St Leger. She only finished fourth in the Derby. Bred by the Duke of Westminster, she was sold as a yearling after his death for the then record sum of 10,000 guineas to R. S. Sievier, who won the four classics with her.

Schedule The published terms, conditions and requirements of all classes at any horse show.

Schleswig Horse Bred on the abundant pastures of Schleswig Province, this breed is a heavy type of horse claiming long ancestry, for, in the Middle Ages, a saddle horse to carry heavily armoured knights was required, and later breeding was well patronized by German rulers. The end of the nineteenth century saw the formation of the Schleswig Horse Breeders' Society, to control the breeding of two types, one for artillery, the other for heavy haulage. The Province had been Danish at one time, and a dash of the heavy Danish horse can be found from time to time.

School The area, open, enclosed or enclosed and covered, used to exercise or train a horse, ridden or otherwise. Also the exercise done by a horse with or without its rider for education or training.

Schooled A steeplechaser, hurdler or hunter which has been ridden at home over fences which it is likely to meet in its work.

School Figures These include the diagonal change of hand, counter change of hand, reversed change of hand, the 'doubler', half-volte, volte or circle, figure of eight, serpentine, and many others.

Schooling *see* BREAKING.

School Paces Collected paces (walk, trot, canter) loftier in step and more perfect in cadence than normal paces.

School Riding Riding exercises of the classical school; alternatively, any work done in a riding school (*see* MANÈGE).

Scissors Horse scissors used for trimming have curved blades, occasionally bent shanks and always blunted points Tail scissors are long and straight, like paperhanger's scissors, and are used only to cut the tail to the required length.

Scorrier Snaffle Also called Cornish Snaffle. A 'strong' bit having four rings, the inner pair being set in slots within the serrated mouthpiece. The construction encourages a strong squeezing action against the lower jaw (*see Plate* 6).

Scowling The act by a horse of laying back the ears and perhaps showing the whites of the eyes.

Scratching An expression used when a cowboy rides a buckjumper at a rodeo—he spurs the horse's sides with a continuous raking motion backwards and forwards; this is compulsory in all rodeo bucking contests.

Scratching (Racing) Taking a horse out of a race for which there is a declaration of forfeit because it is lame, unfit, etc.

Screw A derogatory term implying an inferior, unsound or worn-out horse. A superior horse can be termed a screw if suffering from some unsoundness which does not affect his usefulness, e.g. whistling.

Scrotum The purse or sac which holds the testes, placed between the thighs.

'Scrub, to' A term descriptive of the action of a rider during a race trying to get the best out of a horse who is lazy or unwilling, or nearing the end of his tether. A horse often has to be 'scrubbed along' to keep his place in a field. It should be noted that the whip is not in fact applied to the horse's flank but is used to encourage extra speed.

Scurry A show jumping competition recognized by the British Show Jumping Association. It is judged on time, over medium-sized obstacles, and the course must be clearly marked by flags. The competitor is judged over the whole course, and to the time he takes is added 6 seconds for any fault over an obstacle; refusals are not penalized, as they will already have increased the competitor's time. The shortest total time—i.e. time of round plus time for faults—wins.

Scurry (U.S.A.) A short quick hunting run or race on horseback.

Scut The tail of a hare.

Seam The amount of a horse load.

Season, Racing *see* RACING SEASON.

Seasons, Hunting *see* HUNTING SEASONS.

Seat The position of the rider in the saddle.

Seat, Balanced A rider's seat on a horse is said to be balanced when he is completely independent of any need of support by the reins and when he is able to follow the horse's movements smoothly and without disturbance.

Seat, Forward First put into practice by Captain Federico Caprilli of the Italian Army. The knee, firmly and immovably in one and the same place on the saddle, is the central pivot. The knee should be pointed and the leathers sufficiently short to give a definite 'feel' of the stirrups. The lower leg is bent backwards to a point where the foot remains behind a perpendicular line drawn from the knee downwards. The toe is held up and pointing outwards with heel down. The rider does not sit in the saddle but rides on the fork and during a jump rests on the stirrup irons. He leans forward with hollow loins and not with a rounded back.

Seat, Hunting The hunting seat of the past and up to the early years of this century was that of long leathers, sitting right down in the saddle behind the line of balance, leaning forward at the take-off and lying right back on landing. The modern seat has become increasingly the balanced seat required in scientific equitation. This indicates the shorter stirrup leather and consequent pointed knee, with lower leg drawn slightly back—the rider sitting forward at the jump, and on landing the whole tendency is to sit balanced lightly and considerably 'off' the saddle.

Seat, Western   Straight, upright and long-legged seat typical of the cowboy type. All balance and no grip, even on a bucking broncho, and rider never posts (rises to the trot).

Seated Shoe   Where the sole of a horse's foot tends to weakness a seated shoe is used which is slightly hollowed, thus avoiding pressure on the sole and throwing all the shoe's bearing surface on the wall of the foot.

Seating   The hollowed-out part of the bearing surface of a shoe so that a 'seated' shoe bears only on the wall of the foot (*see* SEATED SHOE).

Seat of Saddle   The part between the head and the cantle on which the rider sits.

Seaweed   In a concentrated powder form this is used as a feed additive. It is said to increase bone, promote growth and general health and prevent laminitis.

Second Horse   Often desirable for the huntsman and for followers, a second horse is ridden by the 'Second Horseman' who, in following the Hunt by devious routes, attempts to meet the first horse and its rider, when a change of mounts is effected. He must take the second horse slowly, without jumping, and by the shortest way, and he should time his arrival, if possible, for when the first horse is tiring.

Second Horseman   Traditionally introduced by Lord Sefton in 1800–1802 (*see* SECOND HORSE).

Second Thigh   *see* GASKIN.

Second Wind   *see* COMES AGAIN.

Seedy Toe   *Cause:* inflammation of the coronet which affects the horn of the hoof and causes separation of the crust. *Symptoms:* it can be detected by tapping the feet, when a hollow sound will be heard, and lameness is bound

to appear. *Treatment:* rest with cooling medicine will reduce the inflammation. No permanent results can be obtained, however, unless the horn of the foot which has grown over the cavity formed inside be cut away and the new horn encouraged to grow. After the horn is cut away, the coronet may be blistered and the cavity stopped with Stockholm tar.

Seeling   Obsolete term for white hairs when they start to grow in a horse's eye-brows.

Sefton Top   *see* LOWNDES PELHAM.

Segundo, Don Juan   A Spanish authority on bridles, bits and spurs, he wrote a treatise on the subject, dedicated to King George IV (*see* SEGUNDO BIT).

Segundo Bit   This refers to one of the series of curb and pelham bits invented by Juan Segundo. Common to all these bits is the large heart-shaped port designed to accommodate the tongue. In all cases the cheeks revolve independent of the mouthpiece.

Selby, James (1844–1888)   A well-known and popular professional driver of London coaches. He was proprietor of the Old Times Coach running between London and Brighton. In 1888 he made history by winning a £1000 bet for accomplishing the double journey in under eight hours.

Selby Apron   Worn below the Selby coaching cape and fastened at the waist with a strap and buckle. Named after James Selby (*q.v.*), a famous coachman of the last century.

Selby Cape   A short, loose, double-breasted, sleeved cape of box-cloth, worn, when coaching in bad weather, outside the apron so as to shoot off the rain.

Selfing   A term for breeding true to type.

Selling Handicap   *see* HANDICAP *and* SELLING RACE.

Selling Race It is a race in which every horse running, if a loser, may be claimed, and if the winner, must be offered for sale by auction in accordance with the rules governing selling races. Selling races are generally for racehorses of small ability.

Semi-mail Phaeton *see* DEMI-MAIL PHAETON.

'Send-on' Expression used to indicate that hunters are sent to a meet in advance of their riders.

Senner An almost extinct breed of pony living in the Teutoburg Forest of Hanover.

Sensory Nerves These exist all over the body, and when touched, actuate movement of various muscles and produce locomotion.

Serge *see* SADDLE SERGE.

Serpent Tail A term used when the curve of the dock is concave instead of convex.

Service The mating of a mare with a stallion (*see* STINT).

Service Boots *see* COVERING-BOOTS.

Service Collar A padded leather collar to protect the mare from being bitten by the stallion during service.

Service Hobbles *see* HOBBLES.

Sesamoiditis Inflammation of the sesamoid bones behind the fetlock joint. *Cause:* faulty conformation or turned-out toes, the latter causing the horse to go close at the fetlocks. *Symptoms:* lameness and heat. There is usually swelling and the condition is likely to become chronic. *Treatment:* rest and blister or pin fire. No certain cure.

Sesamoids Two small bones situated at the back of the fetlock, forming part of that joint. The two branches of the suspensory ligament are attached to these bones.

Set-fair A term applied, especially in racing stables, to putting down a horse's bed.

Setfast or Sitfast A hard painful swelling on the back probably caused by an ill-fitting saddle or by pressure on an incompletely healed sore. A hard lump will be apparent which will increase in size the longer it is neglected. The setfast must be cut out by a veterinary surgeon, and if the roots are not completely removed it will not heal.

Set Tail A cruel fashion, current in the United States of America, of breaking and setting the tails of saddle horses to give a high and showy tail carriage. The operation is painful and deprives the horse of the use of the tail as a protection against flies.

Setter Apparatus worked with a movable arm, placed under the axle of a vehicle to raise the wheels when they are being washed.

Seymour, James (1702–1752) Hunting, racing and other sporting scenes and sporting portraits by Seymour are almost as well known as those by his friend John Wootton (*q.v.*), and some were engraved. A Londoner of good family and means, Seymour took up professional painting after losing money on the Turf. Though his horses have stiffness of all the artists of this early period, his best work proves him a talented draughtsman.

Shabrack (or Shabraque) A trooper's housing or saddle-cloth (*see* HOUSING).

Shabraque *see* SHABRACK.

Shadbelly (Swallowtail or Cutaway) Tight fitting double breasted hunting coat in either scarlet or black, with high-cut front and sides cut away into tails. Named after hard-riding members of the Pytchley Hunt.

Shadowroll *see* NOSEBAND, SHEEPSKIN.

Shafts   The bars between which a horse is harnessed in any single-horse vehicle.

Shagya Arabian   *see* HUNGARIAN SHAGYA.

Shan Pony   *see* BURMESE.

Shanderidan   A four-wheeled pair-horse vehicle of the waggonette type used for private parties attending race-meetings and picnics. Brakes were operated by the coachman's hand by means of a long lever.

Shandrydan   A light two-wheeled cart associated with Ireland. In that country the name is sometimes used to denote shabby or rickety conveyance.

Shanks   *see* CANNON BONE.

Shannon Bone   The cannon bone of the hind leg.

'Sharatz'   Piebald charger of Prince Marko of Serbia in the fourteenth century. Their exploits together against the Turkish oppressors figure in many legends and epic poems of the Balkans.

Shayer, William J. (1811–1860)   Born in Southampton, son of William Shayer Senr, an artist of rural and animal scenes. Painted animal, sporting and coaching subjects. The roads of Southern England generally formed the background of his coaching scenes.

Sheath   A loose fold of skin, situated in front of the scrotum, investing the front and free portion of the penis, and having the anterior end open.

Shedding Coat   *see* CASTING COAT.

Sheet Calendar   *see* RACING CALENDAR.

Shelly   A term applied to the hollow in newly cut incisor teeth.

Shelly Feet   Brittle and thin-soled feet predisposing to lameness. Such feet are hard to shoe.

Shelt   A Highland pony used by deer-stalkers to carry the carcase.

Shelter   During the winter months horses at grass will rarely use a shed, no matter how bad the weather, but a shelter of some kind should be provided for the summer as a refuge from fly torment.

'Sheltie'   *see* SHETLAND PONY.

Shetland Pony (Popular name 'Sheltie')   The smallest of all breeds of ponies, this is nevertheless probably the strongest member of the equine world in relation to its size. Its origin is unknown, but records of its existence in the Shetland Isles to the north of Scotland date back many centuries. The diminutive size is thought to be due to poor living and the severe climate, although ponies of this type bred in the south of England would appear to increase but little in size. The pony is generally used in the Shetland Isles as a saddle and pack pony. Great demands from coal pits caused breeding to flourish but no attempt at selective breeding was contemplated until 1870. It is very docile, lovable and hardy, and makes a good riding pony for children. Of pleasing appearance with a small head and muzzle, neat short ears and large 'kindly' eyes; the compact little body is supported by short legs. The mane is abundant and the thick tail is carried high. Height limits: 4 years and over 42 in (106.6 cm); 3 years and under 40 in (101.6 cm). (The height of a Shetland is usually described in inches rather than in the customary hands.) Colouring varies—black, brown and bay being prominent, but there are also piebalds and skewbalds. *Breed Society:* The Shetland Pony Stud Book Society. (*See Plate* 25).

Shetland Pony Stud Book Society (Founded 1891)   *Objects:* to encourage the breeding of pedigree Shetland Ponies.

Shillibeer   In 1829 George Shillibeer (1797–1866), an Englishman who had been a coach-builder in Paris, put on the road the first public omnibus in

England. It started from 'The Yorkshire Stingo' at Paddington, London, and ran to the Bank of England and back at a single fare of one shilling. It was roomy, comfortable, and was drawn by three horses abreast. It met with immediate success, and Shillibeer put others into service, calling them 'Omnibuses'. Many competitors followed his example, and Shillibeer was ruined. He had also, when practising as an undertaker, introduced a form of hearse bearing his name.

Shim   A dialect word for a white mark and often used instead of blaze (*q.v.*) in East Anglia.

Shin Boot   A foreleg boot worn by steeplechasers to prevent the shins being knocked when jumping.

Shippon   A stable.

Shirazi   A pony found in Persia and known also as the Gulf Arab. (*See* PERSIAN HORSE.)

Shire   In height and weight the Shire is the greatest of England's agricultural and trade horses, and is believed to be a survival of the type known in mediaeval times as the Great Horse used in battle when riders with armour could weigh in all as much as 30 st (420 lb; 190.5 kg). The Shire possesses great strength and stamina allied to docility and was developed for heavy draught work on the land and on the road. Standing over 17 h.h. (173 cm), weighing one ton to 22 cwts (1.016–1.117 t), though slow workers they can pull immense weights. Bays and browns predominate but blacks and greys are also seen. Shoulders should be deep and oblique, wide across the chest with full-muscled hindquarters. Shires often have a considerable amount of white on feet and legs, which also carry a lot of fine silky hair (feather *q.v.*). Recently there has been a revival of interest in the breed and several horses have been exported to the United States. Breed Society: the Shire Horse Society (*see Plate* 28).

Shire Horse Society (Founded 1878) *Objects:* to promote the Old English Breed of Cart Horse.

Shires, The   Part of the Midlands. These include Leicestershire, Rutland, Warwickshire, Northamptonshire and parts of Lincolnshire.

'Shires, The' (Hunting)   Shire Packs are: Pytchley, Quorn, Fernie, Belvoir and Cottesmore.

Shivering   *Cause:* a weakness of the nervous system which affects the muscles of the legs. *Symptoms:* slightly resemble those of stringhalt (*q.v.*), as the hind legs move stiffly from the ground, and a shiverer cannot be backed without the muscles twitching and, in many cases, the tail being moved up and down. An unsoundness, hereditary and incurable.

Shod Too Close   An expression denoting that a nail has been driven so close to the sensitive part of the foot that it presses against the latter. Known also as nail-bind.

Shoe, Box   A shoe with a 'lid' to retain a dressing for a wound of the sole.

Shoe, Feather-edged   A shoe where the inside edges are narrowed, bevelled and rounded to avoid brushing. The wall of the foot on the inside protrudes over the shoe.

Shoe, Half-   This is used to allow for the expansion of the heels where contraction has been suffered and to bring pressure to bear on the frog if possible.

Shoe, Rocker-bar   A shoe with a curved surface which has a rocking action, used in ring-bone or side-bone cases affected by ankylosis (*q.v.*).

Shoe, Roller-toe   A shoe designed to prevent stumbling.

Shoe, Three-quarter   This is used to prevent the development of corns, to prevent or protect capped elbows when the horse is lying down, and also in severe cases of brushing and cutting.

Shoe-boil   Capped elbow (*q.v.*).

Shoeing   The art of making, fitting and fixing shoes to the feet of a horse.

Shoeing Block   A tripod used in shoeing on which the horse's foot is placed for certain processes. Known also as a foot-stool.

Shoeing-cage   *see* TRAVE.

Shoeing Forge   Where only horse-shoeing is practised the Forge is known as a Shoeing Forge or Farrier's Shop, the workers being Farriers, consisting of a Fireman and Doorman (*qq.v.*).

Shoes, Removal of   Shoes should be removed about every three weeks, otherwise the horse suffers from pinching caused by the growth of the horn of the hoof.

'Shooting Your Wheelers'   Sending the wheelers (*q.v.*), or leaders in a coach team into their collars in order to draw the weight of the load.

Short   'Going short' meaning restricted front action indicating some discomfort or even lameness.

Short-coupled   A term denoting a horse that is short and deep in the body with well-sprung ribs.

'Short of Blood'   *see* 'OUT OF BLOOD'.

Short of Bone   *see* CANNON BONE.

Short of a Rib   Where there is a marked space between the last rib and the point of the hip, and showing a sign of slackness over the loins. A condition found in horses of defective conformation, i.e., too long a back, hindquarters standing too far back.

Short Tommy   A short, stiff leather thong, some 3 ft (0.9 m) in length, for use on wheel-horses of a coach. Often used by box-seat passengers while the coachman was using his thong on the leaders of the team to extricate the coach from ruts and boggy patches. About 1828 Short Tommy happily fell into disuse owing to the improving state of the roads.

Shoulder, Point of   The point immediately over the joint between the extreme lower end of the shoulder blade and the humerus, or upper arm.

Shoulder, Sloping   This runs obliquely from the point of the shoulder to the withers. In theory the more sloping the shoulder, the better the ride.

Shoulder, Straight   A less oblique type than the above. The harness horse should have shoulders tending to straightness, being a draught horse, where the position and set of the neck collar is very important. A Hackney intended for show must have oblique shoulders for the up-and-out action which is now demanded.

Shoulder-in   A two-track movement where the horse, evenly bent from head to dock around the rider's inside leg, travels in the direction of its convex side, legs crossing.

Shoulder Lameness   To test for lameness pull each leg forwards and backwards two or three times. If the horse rears or flinches he is probably in pain. For a further test, trot him up and down hill. Lameness in the shoulder will become more acute when ascending the hill, whereas foot lameness will be more visible on the downward trot. In spite of general opinion to the contrary among horsemen, shoulder lameness is comparatively rare. In fore-limb lameness very careful attention must always be paid to the foot before diagnosing shoulder lameness.

'Shouldering the Pole'   An old coaching term describing the act of one of the wheelers (*q.v.*) pushing the pole against its partner.

Show Bridle (Riding)   A very light, elegant bridle, either hook studded or more probably sewn to the bits. Snap billets can also be used as a means of attachment.

Show Bridle (Stallion)   A substantial brass-mounted bridle with swelled noseband and cheeks. It can be fitted with a coloured front and leather or brass rosettes.

Showing Too Much Daylight   *see* 'ON THE LEG'.

Show Jumper of the Year, Leading   Annual competition at the Horse of the Year Show (*q.v.*), Wembley. For results *see page* 407.

International Show Jumping   *   Dorian Williams, M.F.H.

It can hardly be denied that show jumping has never been more popular than it is today. Television audiences number anything between nine and thirteen million for such shows as The Horse of the Year Show; and to show that the enthusiasm is not limited to Britain, on the last morning of the Olympic Games in Munich in 1972 by 9 o'clock in the morning, despite the almost arctic cold, no less than 70,000 people were in their places in the Olympic stadium.

It is not easy to analyse the reasons for this popularity. Certainly it can be as exciting as any sport. It is spectacular, often dramatic. It is a sport mercifully free from graft: there is no pulling or doping or jiggery-pokery. Everyone who comes into the arena comes in to win. The horse is a noble and attractive animal and has always inspired affection and admiration.

Courage is needed, of course, as well as skill. Above all, thanks largely to television, show jumping has produced names which have become known all over the world. One does not have to be a horseman to have heard of d'Inzeo, Steinkraus or Harvey Smith. Pat Smythe, Marion Mould, Ann Moore have been the darlings of the crowds far beyond their own shores.

It must be admitted, too, that the standard of show jumping is now very high, and there is always a place for anything that is absolutely top class. If one goes to a show in England, America, Germany, Italy and many other coun-tries, one is assured of seeing the very best jumping.

So high has the standard become, in fact, that in some countries there is a real danger of there being two leagues. In other words, certain countries such as Germany, the United States, Italy and Britain are capable of producing riders of a calibre superior to those in other countries. Fortunately such nations as Spain, Portugal, Brazil, the Argentine, France and Ireland are all capable of producing individual riders of top-class ability and so they are more than able to hold their own in the biggest inter-national shows. In team events, however, they do not find it so easy, for while they may be able to produce one or two riders of the calibre of Broome, Winkler, Mancinelli, if not their superior, they have difficulty in finding a whole team which is good enough to hold its own against a team from Britain, the United States, Italy or, of course, Germany.

There is no doubt that during the seventies Germany has established itself as the leading show jumping nation, though—it must be emphasized—not in such a way that they completely domi-nate the scene. It should be remembered that the United States was only beaten by Germany by half a point in the 1972 Olympics at Munich, and that in the same year Britain beat Germany in the President's Cup which can virtually be considered the World Championship. Nor did a German rider win a medal in the Individual Show Jumping event at Munich.

Nevertheless their strength is very real both in the calibre of their riders and in the horses they ride. The latter are very powerful, usually with Hanoverian blood in their veins, and superbly schooled and trained, most of them at their national school at Warendorf. Their power behind the saddle, their strength in the quarters and loins is responsible for their great jumping ability; their discipline for the accuracy of their jumping. The German riders, too, are for the most part noticeably disciplined in their style of riding, so much so that both in dressage and jumping one refers to the Germanic style. That it is effective is beyond all doubt. Whether it is altogether attractive is another matter. Certainly many people do not find it so, believing it to be too rigid, with the horses inevitably over-bent.

The United States riders, too, are disciplined, but in a quite different style. They are all trained by the great Hungarian authority, Bert de Nemethy, whose production of smooth, fluent perfectionists, both in horses and riders, has long been the envy of other countries.

The Americans are fortunate in having beautiful big three-quarter bred quality horses, with great scope, a turn of foot and exceptional suppleness. It has been suggested that they are produced almost too much in a mould and if things go wrong they can come completely unstuck. There may be a germ of truth in this, and it is certainly true that they have more often come very close to winning the really big events than actually winning them; though one must conclude that their classical style of riding has given so much pleasure that in the long run they have been a greater influence for good in riding styles than that of many who may have won more competitions.

For a quarter of a century the Italian scene has been dominated by the d'Inzeo brothers, which is not surprising since they were pupils of their father who was himself a pupil of the immortal Caprilli. It could be said that compared with, say, Britain, Germany, France or the United States, riding in Italy is still a somewhat exclusive sport and, therefore, is less broadly based than in other countries which inevitably means there are fewer riders of international calibre available. This means that for many years the burden has been borne by the d'Inzeo brothers, supported more recently by Graciano Mancinelli and Vittorio Orlandi. But one cannot help wondering a little what will happen in Italy when at last the d'Inzeos disappear from the show jumping scene.

Britain's strength rests on the extraordinary reservoir of riders capable of representing their country which is available to the international selectors. It is not unusual for between twenty and thirty British riders to show jump for Britain in any one year. This is probably at least twice as many as in any other country. Typically British, the riders tend to be very independent and, therefore, there is no obviously British style. For instance no two riders could be more different in style than Harvey Smith and David Broome, yet both are consistently extremely successful.

Perhaps the greatest problem in Britain is that there are so many shows: over 2000 between March and October; and each year indoor jumping in the winter becomes more and more popular. The risk, therefore, is that both riders and horses tend to get stale, the latter even jumping themselves into the ground so that when they are still comparatively young they are no longer reliably sound, and cannot be risked in big competitions. It is for this reason that so often the year before an Olympics the British Team seems to be invincible, yet when the Olympic year comes the selectors are scratching to find a team of really sound on-top-of-their-form horses. The riders have unique experience; but even the most experienced rider in the world cannot succeed without top-class horses.

A country that is often underrated is France. It has a magnificent Olympic record and has produced some of the most famous names in show jumping: in particular d'Oriola, twice Olympic Gold Medalist, 1952 and 1964; and Janou Tissot (née Lefebvre), Ladies World Champion 1970 and 1974. They are fortunate, too, in having generous sponsors and a Government that is allegedly putting more money into equestrianism than any other country.

Eastern Europe also produces good jumpers, but they lack, one feels, international competition. The same could be said for South Africa and Australia where show jumping is taken very seriously and is of a very high order. It is unfortunate, indeed, that for reasons of quarantine and distance, Europe and the Americas are denied seeing the best riders from these countries. Even more unfortunate that South African and Australian riders are virtually denied the opportunity of a tilt at the best American and European riders. They could, without doubt, more than hold their own.

To a lesser extent the same applies to the South American countries. They have great potential, but with rare exceptions they seldom get further than the Pan American Games; yet Chile, it

should be remembered, won two Silver medals in the Helsinki Olympics in 1952, Mexico having won the Gold in 1948, while some of the best jumpers in the world have come from the Argentine, and Brazil produced Nelson Pessoa.

In conclusion, healthy as international show jumping is, one has to ask oneself whether in the long run show jumping will benefit from the enormous prices now paid for show jumpers, the greatly increased prize money and the prevalence, more and more, of countries using horses from other countries in their teams; to such an extent that in a recent International Horse Show at Rome over 70 out of 100 entries came from England or Ireland, while 20 out of 50 in the Grand Prix de Dressage in Munich were German bred.

It is fortunate that show jumping has such an active and vigilant organizing body, the F.E.I. (*q.v.*). Even more fortunate that the F.E.I. has had as President H.R.H. Prince Philip, Duke of Edinburgh. It is not easy to assess his contribution to the sport (*see also* SHOW JUMPING, ABBREVIATED RULES *and Plates* 19 *and* 20).

*   *   *

Show Jumping, Abbreviated Rules
Under F.E.I. Rules: 1. There are no marks or faults for style. 2. Knocking down a fence with either fore or hindlegs—4 faults. 3. Refusals: these are cumulative, and the third refusal in the whole round eliminates the competitor. First refusal—3 faults; second refusal —6 faults. 4. Fall of horse or rider—8 faults. 5. A certain speed for each competition is required, and the time allowed for the course is announced. Exceeding the time allowed is penalized at the rate of $\frac{1}{4}$ fault for every second or part of a second. The time limit is double the time allowed, and exceeding the time limit is always penalized by elimination. *Under B.S.J.A. Rules:* 1. There are no marks or faults for style. 2. Each fence is judged separately.

3. The winner is the competitor making the least number of faults during the round. 4. Knocking down fence with either fore or hindlegs—4 faults. 5. Refusals: first—3 faults; second—6 faults; third—elimination. Refusals are cumulative, and the third refusal in the whole round eliminates the competitor. 6. Fall of horse or rider—8 faults. 7. Time: the course has to be completed within the time allowed which is based on the number of yards per minute required by the conditions of the competition. Exceeding the time allowed is penalized at the rate of $\frac{1}{4}$ fault for every second or part of a second. The time limit is double the time allowed. Exceeding the time limit is penalized by elimination.

Show Jumping Results *see pages* 403 *and* 407.

Show Pony Classifications for showing (*a*) The best pony, mare or gelding, not exceeding 12.2 h.h. (124 cm), suitable for and to be ridden by a child not exceeding 12 years. (*b*) Exceeding 12.2 h.h. (124 cm) and not exceeding 13.2 h.h. (134 cm), and to be ridden by a child not exceeding 14 years. (*c*) Exceeding 13.2 h.h. (134 cm) and not exceeding 14.2 h.h. (144 cm), and to be ridden by a child not exceeding 16 years. If these classes are found unsuitable certain other classes and ages are defined by the British Show Pony Society (*q.v.*) and can be substituted. Local and novice classes are encouraged, as is also the showing of ponies, mounted, in leading rein classes and as pairs. No ponies under four years may be shown under saddle. Must combine ideal conformation with quality allied to the temperament suitable for a child rider. Quiet good manners are rightly considered of paramount importance. By judicious upgrading of native pony stock, especially the Welsh pony, with an infusion of Arabian and/or Thoroughbred blood, today's child's pony has no equal in the world. A small quality head, sloping shoulder, short back and sound limbs are demanded with brilliant floating action. The general impression should be of great elegance, but it should always maintain substance and that indefinable 'pony' character (*see Plate* 28).

Show Presentation (Arabs, In Hand) *Stallions :* No pulling, plaiting or trimming of manes or tails, no thinning or clipping of heels. Quarter-markings undesirable. The Arab's natural beauty must not be altered. Show bridle brown stitched leather with fixed noseband, brass buckles, coloured or plain browband, stallion bit half-moon or straight bar with fixed rings. Leather or white webbing lead attached to bit according to stallion's behaviour. *Mares :* As above as to plaiting, pulling,

trimming, etc. Lightest possible leather bridle and bit, brass-mounted head collar. Lead as above.
(Arabs, Under Saddle) *Stallions, Mares and Geldings :* Mane and tail unpulled and unplaited. Light, short-cheek double bridle with $\frac{1}{2}$ in (12.7 mm) or $\frac{3}{8}$ in (16 mm) rein. No martingale. Fairly straight-fronted leather saddle.
Anglo-Arabs and Part-bred Arabs —as for Hunters, below.)
(Hunters, In Hand) *Stallions :* Manes plaited (7 or 9, or if preferred, as many as possible), tails pulled or plaited, heels and long hair on lips and back of jaw trimmed. Brown, brass-mounted stallion bridle, stitched leather with fixed noseband, half-moon or straight bit, plain (uncoloured) browband. Lead of leather or white webbing attached to bit. *Mares :* Double bridle with plain browband or snaffle, but former preferable. Curb bit only and chain of the double permissible.
(Hunters, Under Saddle) *All Hunters :* Manes plaited, tails pulled or plaited as above. Double bridle, no martingale, fairly straight-fronted, leather saddle. As for Arabs, the value of quarter-markings for hunters is debatable.
(Hacks, Under Saddle) Manes plaited, tails pulled or plaited. Heels and lips trimmed. Double bridle preferable, but Pelhams permissible. No martingale. Reins $\frac{1}{2}$ in. (12.7 mm) or $\frac{3}{8}$ in (16 mm). Light leather saddle somewhat straight cut to set off shoulder. Coloured browbands permissible (usually made of strips of different coloured plastic). Elegance of appearance and turn-out is of utmost importance. *Note :* Hacks are not normally shown in hand.
(Cobs, Under Saddle) Pulling, plaiting and trimming for mares and geldings as for hunters, but cobs are usually shown with hogged manes. *Note :* Cobs are not shown in hand.
(Show Ponies, In Hand) Manes pulled, plaiting optional but desirable, tails pulled or plaited, heels and chins trimmed. Bridle or head collar, narrow

stitched with brass fittings on head collar, coloured browband, leather or white webbing leading rein. Bits for *young stock*: snaffle half-moon showing bit, joiners for leading rein. *Brood Mares*: double bridle or curb bit only, or snaffle. Unbroken *young stock* should be shown in head collar without bit to prevent possible damage to mouth. Elegance of appearance and turn-out important.

(Show Ponies, Under Saddle) *Leading Rein Class*: Novice and Child's First Pony, snaffle bridle only may be used. Single rein. Leather saddle, or felt with tree if child is really small. Leather or white webbing leading rein. *12.2 h.h. Class*: Double bridle with two reins if child is a capable rider, or Pelham, with single rein, with joiners from snaffle to curb bit, or Kimblewick. Coloured or plain browband. No martingale. Leather saddle with white narrow webbing girth. *13.2 to 14.3 h.h. Class*: As above, but with double rein bridle. *All classes*: Single rein ½ in (12.7 mm); double ½ in (12.7 mm) top, ⅜ in (19.05 mm) bottom recommended. Elegance of appearance and turn-out important. *Note*: The British Show Pony Society permits plain snaffle if considered suitable by owners, but spurs are forbidden.

(Hackneys, In Hand) Plaiting, pulling and trimming as before. Show bridle, black stitched leather with fixed noseband and brass buckles, coloured or plain browband. Stallion bit, half-moon or straight bar with fixed rings. Lead, either leather or white webbing, attached to bit. *Yearlings*: Manes plaited, to be shown in a halter. *Two- and Three-year-old Fillies and Brood Mares*: Manes plaited, bridle with short-cheeked curb bit. *Two- and Three-year-old Colts and Stallions*: Manes plaited. Stallion tack with brown side and bearing reins.

(Hackneys, Under Saddle) Manes thinned (never hogged) to produce even length of 4 to 5 in (101–127 mm), plaited 12 to 20 (much smaller than for hunting); tails should not be cut, plaited or thinned, but washed well and brushed; heels, ears and lips trimmed. Maximum weight of shoes: ponies not exceeding 14 h.h. (142 cm), 1½ lb (0.67 kg); horses exceeding 14 h.h. (142 cm), 2 lb (0.9 kg). Lightweight black leather harness with brass mountings. Reins brown, toned to dark shade. Black browband with a small brass chain preferred. No martingales. Kay collars (*q.v.*) correct for all two-wheeled vehicles and pairs. Optional for lead horse in a tandem to wear either a Kay or a breast collar, but former is preferable. Breast pieces essential with Kay collars, optional with breast. Overcheck usually worn. Lightweight holly whip preferred.

Show Saddle Designed for showing hunters or any other riding horse or pony. The flap is cut sharply away in front, roughly perpendicular to the ground, the idea being to expose and show the slope of the horse's shoulder to its fullest advantage.

Show Waggon A lightweight vehicle having bicycle wheels with fine wire spokes and pneumatic tyres, and to which Hackneys are usually driven at shows.

Shrewsbury Gag A small ringed gag used with a curb bit.

Shy Feeder A horse with a fickle appetite needing to be tempted with small varied feeds—a little salt added is helpful. Such a horse should have most of its ration at night when all is quiet and there is nothing to disturb or distract it.

Shying This may be a dangerous vice at any time. Many theories have been advanced as to the cause, including defective eye-sight, fear and temper inherited from ancestors, nervousness, intended playfulness, etc.

Siamese Phaeton Unlike the ordinary phaeton (*q.v.*) it had two identical seats one behind the other.

Sick *see* VOMITING.

Sickle-hocks Bent and weak-looking hocks which somewhat resemble a drawn-out sickle in shape.

Sickle-hocks

Side Bone A bony formation of either lateral cartilage of the foot—common in heavy horses, but also found in the lighter breeds. *Cause:* may be hereditary, or through narrow feet or high calkins. *Symptoms:* a hard lump and heat can be felt on the coronet on either side of the heel. *Treatment:* if the horse is lame, consult a veterinary surgeon who may blister or fire the affected parts.

Side Reins These are attached to the roller for training purposes, and are used by some trainers when lungeing young horses.

Side-saddle Its history is somewhat obscure. In the fifth century B.C. women are depicted as riding astride and also sitting sideways on the off side. There is a spirited pottery figure of a woman playing polo sitting astride, made in A.D. 620 during the T'ang dynasty. Nicetas (1118–1205), the Greek historian, deplored the fact that women no longer rode, as formerly, on a side-saddle, but had started to ride indecently astride. In early times in Britain women rode astride, but there is evidence that a form of side-saddle was known and used about the mid-twelfth century. An historian during the time of Richard II (1367–1400), however, wrote: 'Likewise noble ladies used high heads and coronets, and robes with long trains, and seats or side-saddles on their horses, by the example of the respectable Queen Anne, daughter of the King of Bohemia, who first introduced this custom into this kingdom; for before women of every rank rode as men do, with their legs astride the backs of their horses'. But this side-saddle was not the side-saddle as we know it today. The rider sat sideways on the horse with her feet supported by a little footrest known as a *planchette*, and in contemporary pictures both near- and off-side are used. This style of saddle was used only for formal and state occasions; women still rode astride for hunting and long journeys. About 1500 Catherine de Medici, a keen hunting woman, is supposed to have introduced pommels on the top of the saddle, one on the off side, one on the near, to form a crutch in which to wedge the right leg and probably also—as the gossip of the day, Pierre Brantôme, reported—to show off her own very shapely legs. About 1830 the French riding master, Jules Charles Pellier or François Baucher (*q.v.*), added on the near side a third pommel about the level of the stirrup bar, to act as a leaping head. Originally about 6 in (15 cm) long, it was later lengthened and curved to fit the shape of a woman's left thigh and give her real security in a side-saddle, and by 1860 it was being generally used. This invention made the off-side pommel unnecessary and so this gradually for several years became smaller and finally disappeared. In the early part of the twentieth century side-saddles were again considerably modified in design to meet the modern forward style of riding (*see* SADDLE, SIDE).

Side Steps A term used to indicate any movement on two tracks, where the horse proceeds sideways to a certain extent.

Side-stick   A strong stick fastened at one end to the bit and at the other to the surcingle, a device used when grooming a confirmed biter.

Side-strap   *see* GAITING STRAP.

Side-wheeling   The roll of a pacer from side to side when in motion (lateral fore and hind legs striking the ground in pairs).

Siena Races   Correctly known as The Palio of Siena, this race was first run in 1482 to celebrate the return of 'reformer citizens' to the government. In 1659 it was established and held twice yearly, in July and August, after 1701 (wars, etc., excepted). The course is round the main square and the race is preceded by a procession of great pageantry in fifteenth-century costumes. The riders represent different districts in the town and there is enormous local interest and intrigue. The Palio is the Latin word for the painted silk banner presented to the winner.

Sight   The seriousness or otherwise of bad sight is governed by the use to which a horse is put, e.g. a pony 'blind of an eye' may not be played at polo.

Silage   Grass and other green vegetable matter preserved by the addition of diluted molasses—not greatly used as a feed for horses, but of considerable nutritive value.

Silks   Silks or racing silks are the jockey's jacket and cap, whether for racing on the flat or steeplechasing. Real silk has been almost entirely replaced by satin nylon (lightweight) which is more hard wearing and easier to launder, and is available in no less than 120 colours or shades.

Silver Ring   The cheap and secondary betting enclosure on a race-course where the smaller bookmakers operate.

Silver-sand   Where this is used for cleaning non-rustless bits and irons, it must be used in conjunction with a burnisher.

Simplex Irons   Australian pattern safety stirrup-iron. The outside section is shaped forward in a half moon and allows the foot to be released in an emergency.

Sinews   *see* TENDONS.

Singeing   The burning of the hair is sometimes used in conjunction with clipping (*q.v.*) and is carried out by lamp or gas flame. Since the introduction of electrical clipping machines singeing is much less practised. The long bristle-like hairs about the eyes, nostrils or lips should never be singed or cut.

Singe Lamp   A flat, triangular metal container with a wick at the wide end. The wick is dipped into methylated spirits and lighted for singeing 'cat- ·hairs' (*q.v.*), etc.

Single Bank   A bank with a ditch on one side.

Single-foot   A very fast walk of short steps with only one foot on the ground at a time. The horse must not break into a trot, but it must travel at the highest possible speed.

Single-trees   *see* BARS.

Sinking Fox   A very tired hunted fox.

Sire   Male parent of a horse or foal.

Sire, to   To beget.

Sitfast   *see* SETFAST.

Skeleton-break

Skeleton-break   A four-wheeled vehicle built for breaking horses to double harness; it has no body work behind the box seat but a small platform on which an assistant can stand.

Skeleton of Horse and Man in Action, Comparative *see page* xvi.

Skeleton Bridle A harness bridle without winkers (*q.v.*).

Skeleton Kneecaps *see* KNEECAPS.

Skeleton of the Horse *see page* xii.

Skep *see* SKIP.

Skewbald Where the skin bears large irregular patches of white hair and any definite colour except black. The line of demarcation is generally well defined (*see* PIEBALD).

Skid-pan An iron shoe or platform on which the tire of a wheel rests, fastened to a four-wheeled vehicle by a strong chain, which locks the near hind wheel on steep hills. It is seldom used in these days as, unless the hill is very bad, and the load very heavy, the brake is usually adequate. The fitting of a skid-pan is compulsory under Bye-laws of the Highways and Locomotives (Amendment) Act, 1878, on certain hills, in which case an extract from the Act is posted on a board at the crest of the hill. Penalties for infringement are imposed. Also called a Slipper, Drag-shoe or Wagon-lock.

Skin In the horse, this consists of two porous layers. The upper one is insensible to pain, the lower is sensitive, being composed of nerves and blood vessels.

Skip A wicker basket used in stables for collecting the droppings. Also known as a skep. A modern and more practical variety is made of rubber (*see Plate* 29).

Skirt A hound which does not follow the true line of the fox, but cuts off corners, is said to skirt, or to be a skirter.

Skirt The lower and forward part of the saddle which covers and protects the rider from the metal spring bar.

'Skowronek' A famous Arabian stallion bred at Volhynia in Poland in 1909. A grey horse, by 'Ibrahim' out of 'Yaskoulka', he was imported to England by the late Walter Winans and bought from him by H. V. Musgrave Clark and was subsequently acquired from him by the late Lady Wentworth. His blood has had great influence on modern Arab breeding in England.

Skull Caps (Racing) Under Rule 146 skull caps of a pattern approved by the stewards of the Jockey Club must be worn.

Skyros Pony A very small ancient breed on the Aegean island of Skyros, used in local agriculture. Measures only 9.2 h.h.–11 h.h. (92–111 cm).

Slab-sided *see* FLAT-SIDED.

Slack in the Loins A horse of weak loins. The last rib is short and too far from the point of the hip.

Sleep Horses sleep little and lightly, dozing for short spells only. Some horses never lie down—the reluctance to do so is a bad and incurable habit. Some old horses are unable to do so owing to the stiffness of the spine.

Sleepy-foal, The A condition, often fatal, in which the young foal is sleepy and lethargic. Early diagnosis is vital.

Slick Saddle An American saddle without any safety devices.

Slings A special form of harness employed to suspend, and thereby rest, a very lame horse or one with badly damaged legs or feet. It consists of very stout canvas to encircle the belly, with a breast collar and breeching to retain this in place. The upper ends of the canvas have stout metal bars with rings attached, and pulleys with ropes or chains are attached to the roof. Also valuable for raising a cast horse.

Slings

Slip Head The head strap and cheek-piece which supports the bridoon in a double bridle.

Slipper *see* SKID-PAN.

Slipping Point The point at which the rider starts to time a horse to get him into his stride for a jump.

Sloan, James Todhunter ('Tod') (1874–1933) An American jockey who in 1897 brought the 'crouching' style of flat-race riding—the extreme forward seat with very short leathers—from America. His judgement of pace was unerring, and he practised the art of waiting in front of his field. Sloan died in obscurity, but this 'seat' is now universal for flat-racing.

Sloped Head The head of a modern jumping or general purpose saddle has the points sloped forward at an angle of about 45°. The result is to place the stirrup bar, and therefore the rider, that much further forward.

Slot The foot or footprint of a deer.

Slug A lazy horse, always requiring to be urged. The term is not applied to a

sick horse showing these inclinations (*see* JADE).

S. M. Pelham (Solid Mouthpiece) A bit with a wide, flat, ported mouth-piece on which the cheeks move independently in a restricted arc.

Smith, Horace Dayer (1878–1957). Appointed Royal Riding-master to Queen Elizabeth II (then Princess Elizabeth), 'Cadogan' Smith was associated with horses for three-quarters of a century. A well-known horse-dealer and show ring judge, winner of a great number of prizes, he bought and sold nearly twelve thousand horses. He taught the Queen and various members of the Royal Family to ride. He was the author of *A Horseman Through Six Reigns*.

Smith, Thomas Assheton (1776–1858) Founder of the Tedworth Hunt. When Master of the Quorn, he jumped Billesdon Brook 'in a place like a ravine' which required 34 ft (10 m) to cover it, with a fence on the landing-side. He once remarked that 'there is no fence you cannot get over *with* a fall'.

Smith, Tom (1790–1878) Master of Hambledon, Craven and Pytchley hunts, Smith wrote *Extracts from the Diary of a Huntsman,* in which is a description of his famous 'all-round-my-hat' cast consisting of a closed loop, starting on the up-wind, or the least likely side of the check.

Smudish A breed of ancient origin from Lithuania. Its appearance is extremely characteristic. The prevailing colour is dun, with a light mane and tail —mouse colour and, more rarely, bay are also found. All have a dark dorsal stripe to the tail. The head is small with intelligent eyes widely spaced, the neck arched, short and muscular, with thick wavy mane. The powerful forehand is a distinguishing mark. Legs are strong and clean, though light in bone, and the hoofs are hard and well-shaped; height 13–15 h.h. (132–152 cm). Generally compact, sturdy, well-made animal of very high reputation in Poland, Lithuania, Baltic countries and Russia.

Snaffle Bit   A bit consisting of a single-jointed or unjointed mouthpiece. The latter may have a straight or curved (half-moon or mullen) bar. The ring can be either circular or D-shaped which minimizes the risk of the lips being pinched (*see Plate* 6).

Snaffle Bridle   A common term for a bridle with any snaffle bit attached (*see Plate* 6).

Snatch   A once popular term for stringhalt (*q.v.*).

Snip   An isolated white marking situated between or in the region of the nostrils. Its size, position and intensity should be specified when a written description is given (*see Plate* 21).

Snowflake-marking   In which white spots appear on a darker background. This is one of the three group-markings required by the British Spotted Horse Society (*q.v.*) (*see also* LEOPARD-MARK-ING, BLANKET-MARKING *and Plate* 21).

Snubbing-post   A post round which a rope is wound to check the motion of a horse.

Soaping   The sweat of a horse is peculiar in its white soapy richness. It is easy to see on parts such as the neck and between the hind limbs, where lathering is particularly profuse in a highly strung and excited animal.

Sobre Paso   *see* THE HORSE WORLD IN THE UNITED STATES OF AMERICA, *page* 351.

Sociable   A low, pair-horsed, four-wheeled vehicle with doors, driven from a box-seat, for four people sitting opposite each other.

Society   Horses are gregarious and at times suffer from lack of company. It is therefore advantageous to introduce another animal such as a goat or donkey.

Society of Master Saddlers   A section of the Retail Leather Goods and Saddlery Association, Ltd. Its aims are to protect, encourage and advance the interests of the retail saddler.

Sock   A white mark extending from the coronet, a short way only up the leg (*see* STOCKING *and Plate* 21).

Soft Palate   This somewhat misleading term is applied to the condition in which a horse during a race or after excitement—or in rare instances when standing in the stable—suddenly experiences great difficulty in breathing and may even roll about in the throes of impending suffocation. The cause is usually either a temporary paralysis of the soft palate (the soft portion of the palate immediately behind the hard palate lining the roof of the mouth), or it may be due to a soft, oedematous swelling of the soft palate, probably induced through some form of allergy. Improvement has been found in some cases by removing a triangular portion of the soft palate. It is likely that this condition is associated with the rather mythical condition believed to be caused by 'swallowing the tongue'.

Soil   The nature of the soil affects the development of horses. Heavy cold clay is bad for all horses except Shires. For lighter breeds, dry sandy sub-soil under rich loam, and sub-soils of limestone and chalk are preferable.

Soil, to   To feed (possibly green food) in a stall in order to fatten a horse.

'Soiling'   Deer enjoy wallowing in muddy water, generally in recognized 'soiling pits'. They frequently 'soil' when they are hunted.

Sokolsk   A breed of working horse in Russia and Poland founded in the mid nineteenth century, later improved in 1920 by chestnut Norfolk-Breton stallions from France and by Anglo-Norman and Ardennais blood. A good tempered, hardy and almost clean-legged type, generally chestnut, about 15.1–16.1 h.h. (153–163 cm).

Sold at Halter Old-time dealer's expression indicating that the buyer bought the horse as he found it, without warranty or veterinary examination.

Sole-bruise Arises through picking up a stone in the foot. Thin brittle soles or those with weak frogs are much more sensitive to such trouble. *Treatment:* shoe with a piece of leather between sole and shoe.

Solid Nickel The metal from which the cheapest bits and irons are made. It is rustless but rapidly assumes a yellow colour when left unwrapped. It is a soft metal, very easily broken and therefore unreliable.

Somer Fifteenth-century term for a pack-horse (*see* SUMPTER).

Somerville, Dr Edith Oenone (1858–1949) Farmer, organist, philanthropist, artist and M.F.H., she is best known as an author, collaborating with her cousin Violet Ross (*q.v.*) in many books featuring Irish sporting life. The most famous is *Some Experiences of an Irish R.M.*

Sore Back *Causes:* bad stable-management and horse-mastership, resulting in ill-fitting saddles causing pressure or friction on particular parts of the back, slack girths, working unfit horses, etc. *Prevention:* make sure the back is hard; make sure the saddle fits;' make sure the rider is sufficiently competent to sit square without rolling in the saddle. *Cure:* rest is the only cure for a soreback.

Sore Shins *Periostes,* or inflammation of the covering of the bone, which occurs mostly in young racehorses, due to concussion or vibration or both. *Symptoms:* the parts afflicted become swollen and very painful, and, unless relieved, may terminate in disease of the bone (*necrosis*). *Treatment:* rest and cold water applications, but a veterinary surgeon should be consulted.

Sorraia The native pony of western Spain and Portugal, resembling the Przevalski wild horse (*q.v.*). Frequently dun in colour with dark dorsal stripe and often with stripes on the legs.

Sorrel In U.S.A. a chestnut colour of lighter red or golden tones.

Sound Horse, A Taplin, an old time horse-doctor, described it as one which 'should possess a perfect state of both frame and bodily health, without exception or ambiguity, the total absence of blemishes as well as defects, a freedom from every imperfection and from all impediments to sight and action'.

'Soup-plate' A term denoting a horse with big round feet out of proportion to the size of the animal and usually found to be low on the heel.

Horses and Riders in South Africa   *   Jean Edmunds

A vast country of plains, deserts and mountains, forests and fertile valleys. A land where wild game teemed, but human beings were few—and horses non-existent. That was South Africa in 1652 when Jan van Riebeeck of the Dutch East India Company landed at what is now Cape Town to establish a refreshment station. Today the picture is entirely different, and visitors to South Africa are often surprised to find several horse and pony breeds flourishing, plus a wide range of horse activities in full swing.

The first South African horses were bred from Javanese ponies imported by van Riebeeck and succeeding Dutch governors of the Cape from the Far Eastern Colonies. Later Arabs were introduced from various sources. In 1789 a lucrative export trade in cavalry mounts to India was begun. British rule at the Cape meant the importation of British Thoroughbreds. Lord Charles Somerset, governor from 1814 to 1826, was a prime mover in this, bringing out 34 Thoroughbred stallions at his own expense. From the original imported ponies, the new Thoroughbred cross produced the small, incredibly tough Cape Horse (or 'Hantam', after two prolific horse-breeding areas). This was the cavalry mount of India and the Crimea.

But horse-sickness epidemics between 1854 and 1893, plus foolish horse-breeding schemes (farmers went crazy about fashionably bred but weedy imported Thoroughbreds) brought about the downfall of this useful animal. The Anglo-Boer War (1899 to 1902), with its terrible toll of horses, put the final touch to the ruin of the Cape Horse.

But a tremendous step forward in the welfare of horses and other animals in Southern Africa was made in 1908. The Onderstepoort Veterinary Research Institute near Pretoria was built, and Swiss-born veterinary surgeon Arnold Theiler, later knighted for his services to science, established laboratories there. Sir Arnold and his researchers concentrated on African diseases affecting animals, particularly horsesickness. Their first preventative inoculation against this disease was improved steadily over the years, and by 1966 at least nine antigenically different virus types, all capable of causing horsesickness, had been found, and a polyvalent vaccine issued to combat them all. Onderstepoort sends out literally millions of doses of vaccine annually throughout Africa and elsewhere, for horsesickness and other animal diseases. The vaccine must be injected for at least three years running to ensure immunity against most strains of horsesickness virus. Onderstepoort is the only veterinary training centre in Southern Africa. Some 250 applications are received every year from would-be students, but only the best 46 are accepted, and about 38

graduate at the end of the five-year course.

Due in no small part to the activities of Onderstepoort, the twentieth century has seen a gradual resurgence of horse-breeding and horse activities in South Africa. Today there are dozens of Thoroughbred studs producing race-horses of high quality, Arab studs with the best blood lines, and a phenomenal interest in breeding and showing the flashy, eye-catching American Saddle Horse.

The South African horse world, however, is virtually split down the middle. On one side of the fence is the world of the Thoroughbred and allied breeds, with interest centred on racing, show jumping, dressage, eventing, polo and show classes. On the other is the world of gaited American Saddle Horses and their farmer-breeders with their special show classes—in hand, under saddle and in harness.

There is keen interest in racing in South Africa, where flat racing continues all the year round. Biggest centres are Natal (there is a magnificent training complex at Summerveld), with superb racecourses at Durban and Pietermaritzburg, Cape Town and Johannesburg. Other racing takes place at Port Elizabeth and Bloemfontein. Sponsorship in South African racing is increasing—a further incentive to breeders.

All South Africa tries to pick the winner of the Durban July (q.v.), biggest race of the year. Among other big races are the Cape Metropolitan Handicap and the generously sponsored Holiday Inns' Handicap. The annual yearling sales are held at the Milner Park showgrounds in Johannesburg at approximately Easter time. Over 500 future racehorses, representing some 120 breeders, come under the hammer, but this by no means represents the total of Thoroughbreds born every year. Many a useful racehorse has never seen the sale ring.

Hurdle racing is catching on fast in South Africa and these races are often held at the end of a normal afternoon's flat racing. Amateur riders, many of them show jumpers, have taken a keen interest in this sport—some very successfully.

When horses finish racing in South Africa they are frequently available for purchase quite cheaply by overseas standards. Scores of them pass on to the show jumping arena, polo field, show ring and dressage arena. All the top show jumpers look automatically for Thoroughbreds and it is said that, as a result, they are probably among the world's finest jumpers on speed. Alas, opportunities for international competition are almost negligible. Due to stringent anti-horse-sickness regulations, horses from Africa are banned in Europe. This is deeply regretted by South African show jumpers, as those who took horses to compete in Britain and on the Continent before the ban more than held their own. The only international competitions open to show jumpers are those in Rhodesia and Mozambique. And Springbok (national) colours are only awarded to riders representing South Africa in the jumping teams in Mozambique.

Every year three or four top international jumpers are invited to fly out to South Africa and take part in the indoor Horse of the Year Show in Johannesburg in September. Despite the restrictions and the long miles between big centres (1000 miles (1600 km) from Cape Town to Johannesburg), the standard of jumping is very high; and at the key shows, like the Rand Easter, Horse of the Year and sponsored Derby meeting in Johannesburg, and the Pietermaritzburg, Port Elizabeth and Cape Town fixtures, exciting performances are seen in both speed and precision events.

National show jumping championships for seniors and juniors are held annually. Bob Grayston, doyen of the South African show jumping ring, was the first champion on 'Guardsman', back in 1955. And the gallant part-Hackney 'Gunga Din', owned by Mrs Gonda Betrix (formerly Butters), holds the distinction of having won both the senior (in 1961 with Miss Butters) and junior (1964 with Miss A. Rauch) national titles. There are also hotly contested annual inter-provincial team show jumping contests for both seniors and juniors, where the strongest hands are usually held by the Western Province and Transvaal.

Horse trials, a relatively new sport in South Africa, have their senior and junior individual and inter-provincial team championships too, but the dressage championships are for senior and junior individuals only.

Major George Iwanowski, a Johannesburg professional, has won the dressage championship six times on South African-bred Lipizzaners. These various championships are held at different big centres every year.

Show jumping, horse trials, dressage and certain show classes in South Africa are controlled by the South African National Equestrian Federation (Sanef) which is affiliated to the F.E.I. Show classes are similar to those in Britain. There are hack, hunter and riding horse and sometimes polo pony classes for seniors, and show pony/horse and hunter classes for children and juniors. Other events, which do not come under Sanef, are 'utility mount', 'schooled horse' and 'Lady's riding horse'. Thoroughbreds dominate the senior classes, and many juniors have them too.

The top South African show ponies are predominantly Welsh in type. Pure and part-bred Welsh Mountain ponies and a few Section Bs are being bred in increasing numbers. A nation-wide equitation scheme for children (13 years and under) and juniors (14 to 17 years), based on the American equitation classes, was introduced in 1971, sponsored by an oil company, and good results became apparent within the first year.

Johannesburg, and the area surrounding it, is the main centre for show jumping, showing, dressage and eventing, although Natal also has many dressage devotees, and in South-West Africa there is a large German community which is very dressage- and horse trials-minded.

Turnout and schooling at the bigger shows is extremely good, and it is improving in the country areas, many of which are American Saddle Horse orientated.

Several thousand horses and ponies are kept in stables, many professionally run, on the outskirts of the 'Golden City'. Many riding establishments hold their own shows and there is a show or event somewhere in the Johannesburg area at least every weekend. By contrast, in some remote country districts the agricultural shows are the biggest events of the year. Every agricultural society, however humble, has its own permanent show grounds, with an arena, grandstand and stabling for horses, together with sheds and pens for other animals, exhibition halls and so on.

Also in Johannesburg is the Inanda Polo Club, scene of games against visiting teams from South America and New Zealand. Polo is played extensively in Natal and the Orange Free State. Polo crosse is becoming more and more popular, and interest in it was further stimulated by a visiting team from Australia who played in South Africa in 1972.

A sport much enjoyed in the country areas is 'gymkhana'—tentpegging and similar mounted activities.

The Rand Hunt is one of South Africa's two drag hungs (the other is the Cape Hunt). Hounds bred at the Rand Hunt kennels outside Johannesburg are supplied to farmers' hunt clubs all over the country, and play a large part in destroying jackal and other vermin.

The once famous South African mounted police have dwindled to a small section at the Police Training College in Pretoria, used mainly for ceremonial duties and displays, but there is an increasing interest in horses in the Defence Force.

At the headquarters at Voortrekkehoogte outside Pretoria, ample provision is made for horse sports, and army trainees can take part in showing, show jumping, polo and tentpegging.

All student officers at the Military Academy at Saldanha Bay in the Cape are required to ride. And at Welgegeund, the army stud farm near Potchefstroom, Transvaal, horses are being bred, mainly from Arab and Thoroughbred blood (shades of the old Cape Horse?) for border patrol work, parades and competitions.

Almost 1000 pure and part-bred Arabs are in the books of the Arab Horse Society of South Africa, and visiting judges have been impressed with their quality.

The Boerperd ('Farmer's horse'), a stocky, attractive, 'do anything' little fellow, strongly resembling both the American Morgan Horse and the Welsh Cob, seems, unfortunately, to be losing ground to the American Saddler. Other 'minority groups' include Hackneys, Quarter Horses, Percherons and the coal-black Flemish horses prized by many Western Cape farmers.

But no breed in South Africa today, apart from the Thoroughbred, makes the same impact as the American Saddler. Purebred only since the 1940s when the first mares arrived from the U.S.A. (a few stallions were imported pre-war), Saddlers are booming today. Prices paid for imported horses compare with those paid for racehorses, and despite the efforts of many small breeders, producing and showing Saddlers is really a sport for the wealthy.

Biggest event of the year in the Saddler world (controlled by the Saddle Horse Breeders' Association) is the national championships at Bloemfontein, where these peacocks of the show ring with their tremendous presence are shown in hand, under saddle and in harness. Over 400 Saddlers (all pure-bred) compete at Bloemfontein—and these are only the very best. The training, showing and turnout follows American lines, and though indisputably artificial and flashy, the show ring Saddle Horse, whether three- or five-gaited, is a sparkling sight.

And Saddlers can make useful pleasure horses, hunters and jumpers if trained 'Sanef-style'.

'Increasing, flourishing, enthusiastic' —these are the words to describe the South African horse world today. And the future of the sport, both from the horseman's point of view and from the spectator's, looks bright.

* * *

Horses in South America * M. Popp

It is almost impossible to condense South America under one heading where horses are concerned, or anything else for that matter. There are thirteen different countries on the South American continent, the majority with widely varying customs and conditions, topography and climate.

Each country has developed its own type of horse or pony, adapted to local conditions, although actually most of these do claim, to a greater or lesser degree, among their ancestors horses brought over by the Spaniards in their conquest of South America. There were a few Arabs among these horses but they were mainly Barbs and the horses of Andalusia, these being a mixture of the local Iberian pony of obscure origin, crossed with Barbs and Arabs brought over by the Moors in the days when they were the over-lords of Spain.

Speaking very generally, and despite mechanization and modern methods of farming, the horse in South America is still a working animal, kept for his usefulness and judged accordingly. Probably this is the main difference from Europe, where, apart from racing, horses are generally for pleasure-riding or are show animals. This detail is an important one because where a horse is needed for work there is little or no use for one that is not absolutely sound and a good doer, no matter how attractive he may be otherwise. The horses, except for Thoroughbreds, live out and grow up under completely natural conditions, the method of breaking-in and age at which this is done varying in accordance with local custom.

Other things common to most South American countries are the Thoroughbred horse and a love of racing, which is almost universally popular. Breeding Thoroughbreds has changed from a fascinating hobby into a major industry, run on the most modern lines. This is especially true in the Argentine. Two-year-old Thoroughbred Sales are now attended by buyers from all over South and Central America, as well as from the U.S.A. and Canada. The original stock was brought from, mainly, the U.K. and France. Top quality sires are still imported when necessary and occasionally mares when a particular line needs strengthening. In recent years some good horses have been acquired in the U.S.A.

According to statistics of the Argentine Stud Book (S.B.A.—Stud Book Argentino) which registers all pedigree Thoroughbred, Arab and Anglo-Arab stock, in 1971 there were over 7500 Thoroughbred foals registered. The total number of Thoroughbreds registered in 1972 was between 65,000 and 70,000.

There are few heavy draught horses, none at all in most of the northern part of the Continent, where work that cannot be done by tractors etc. is relegated to mules or oxen. Many years ago in the more southerly countries of South America there were considerable numbers of heavy horses—principally Percherons, Shires, Clydesdales and Suffolk Punches. Today only the Percheron—actually a later arrival on the South American scene than the other 'heavies' —and its crosses survive in any number in the Argentine and Uruguay, and to a lesser degree in Chile. In the Argentine there are still a very few Suffolk Punches.

Of coach-horse breeds the heavy category of the Anglo-Normando breed is the most popular and numerous. Hackneys are little used now except for driving classes at shows where one or two good ones may still be seen. There are a considerable number of crosses of these heavier horses with light breeds.

To return to light horses and in terms of sport, polo is tremendously popular with a generally high standard for both players and ponies. A great advantage is that the cost of the keep of ponies is relatively low and there is an almost unlimited supply of prospective polo-ponies to be had at reasonable prices. The Argentines are still leading in the game and it is said that one may see more first-class polo played there in a season than anywhere else in the world. Their top ponies are mostly Anglo-Argentinos and some Thoroughbred, but many a budding player gets his first experience of the game on whatever stock horses happen to be available at the time.

Show jumping is growing steadily in favour as a sport, with an increasingly high standard among riders, particularly those from Argentina, Brazil, Chile, Ecuador, Peru and Venezuela. There are numerous national and Inter-American jumping events and those countries are usually well represented in most big European events and, of course, the Olympic Games. The lighter weight of the Anglo-Normando and the heavy-weight category of the Anglo-Argentino are sought after for jumping. A limited number of Hanoverian horses are also being used, some Thoroughbreds and the very occasional Anglo-Arab. Broadly speaking, to date the best have been the Anglo-Argentinos.

A game with a limited but growing number of fans is 'Pato', a traditional gaucho game, which was prohibited for some time owing to danger to life and limb of the players. The name 'pato' (duck) comes from the fact that, in the game as it was originally played, an unfortunate live duck was used . . . the game is faintly reminiscent of Rugby on horse-back. Now a substitute for the duck is used, an object roughly the same size and weight with grips by which it can be held, but it still must be picked up off the ground at a gallop. The Criollo pony with his short legs, extraordinary manouvrability, good initial acceleration and even temperament is ideal for the game.

Anglo-Argentino Horse Often called the Argentine Horse (Caballo Argentino) where formerly this was only applied to the Criollo. The Anglo-Argentino breed originated by the crossing of Thorough-bred stallions with Criolla mares. Successive crosses of Thoroughbred stallions, as well as registered Anglo-Argentino stallions, have finally produced a breed with approximately three-fifths to four-fifths Thoroughbred blood. They are strong, well-built animals, showing quality as well as toughness, agile, with excellent legs and feet and a fine turn of speed. They make excellent stock horses although they are not quite so agile or as hardy as the Criollo or the Arab. In colour chestnut, bay and brown seems to predominate. The breed is divided into categories—under 16 h.h. (162 cm) and over 16 h.h. The first form the backbone of the top Argentine polo-ponies and the larger heavier type is popular for all show jumping and riding events and could give a good account of themselves in the English hunting field (*see Plate* 4).

Anglo-Normando This breed originated in France but has been bred for many generations in South America, particularly in the Argentine where it has adapted very well to local conditions. The breed is divided into two groups, the heavier being for driving, the lighter for riding. The latter group is well liked by the Cavalry and mounted police and for show jumping. The Anglo-Normando is a strongly built horse, courageous with a rather sluggish temperament; it lacks the quality of the Anglo-Argentino but has more bone. A long-backed animal, it does not stand up well to hard work on sandy, stony or broken ground (*see* ANGLO-NORMAN).

Arab In the past the Arab was not a popular breed in South America and owed its existence in that continent to a handful of enthusiasts in Argentina, Brazil and Uruguay who spared no trouble or expense to obtain the best desert stock. The first to import pure Arab breeding stock from Arabia were the brothers Senores Alfonso and Hernan Ayerza, who in the 1880s and '90s brought back to the Argentine from the desert a few of the finest Arabs they could obtain, which became the foundation stock for their respective studs. That the breed was not at first popular proved its salvation as there was no financial incentive to breed from anything but the best. In the last few years their popularity has grown considerably as people are beginning to appreciate the value of the Arab's iron-hard legs, powers of endurance and perfect action. The breed has gradually adapted itself to the needs of the land; for example, in Brazil the Arab tends to be smaller and shorter in the leg than in the Argentine and Uruguay where the country is not so hilly. Arabs and Anglo-Arabs are now being sought after to improve other breeds. They make an excellent cross with the Anglo-Argentino and Criollo. In 1972 there were approximately 600–700 registered pure-bred Arabs in the Argentine.

Criollo The Argentine cow-pony, famous for his toughness, reliability and sure-footedness. He is descended entirely from the horses brought by the Spaniards in their Conquest of South America. These were mainly Barbs, a few Arabs and the local Spanish horses from Andalusia. Since the time of the Spaniards the Criollo lived the real hardship of a natural life. Survival of the fittest produced great hardiness and the ability to withstand exposure to great heat or cold. Their thick skin and coat enable them also to be less worried by flies and other insects than most horses.

The Criollo comes in many colours, dun with black stripes down the back; blue and red roan; mealy bay; brown, black and skewbald. They thrive everywhere, from the lush green country of Argentine's central and northern provinces, the south of Brazil, Uruguay and Chile, to the dry, rugged, sandy hills and plains of Patagonia. Height is from about 13.2 to 14.3 h.h. (134–145 cm).

Peruvian Ambler (Caballo de Paso Peruano) This horse claims descent from the horses brought over in the Conquest of Peru, which were mainly of Barb origin. In type the Caballo de Paso is similar to the Barb, but slightly bigger with longer legs and higher tail carriage, the legs fine boned, strong and clean. These horses are extremely agile and sure-footed, an absolute necessity for their rugged country. Their main pace, the amble, is most comfortable and can be surprisingly fast. Every year there are competitions to find the best Caballo de Paso. These are enthusiastically supported by admirers of the breed. There is as yet no registry for this breed.

Falabella Miniature Horse This minute breed has a maximum height of 30 in (76 cm) and is named after the man who started the breed in the Province of Buenos Aires, Argentina. They are friendly, gentle little creatures and much in demand as pets for children (*see* FALABELLA).

＊ ＊ ＊

Southern Hound The last areas in which this type of hound was maintained in its purity were Devonshire, the Sussex Weald and Wales. In type it was a slightly built hound, in colour a light tan to yellow.

South African National Equestrian Federation (SANEF) The body affiliated to the F.E.I. (*q.v.*), which controls show jumping, horse trials, dressage and certain show classes in South Africa.

South of England Agricultural Society An agricultural society founded in 1967 by the amalgamation of the Sussex County Agricultural Society, the Tunbridge Wells and South-Eastern Counties Agricultural Society and the Royal Counties Agricultural Society. It also incorporates the Richmond Royal Horse Show. The permanent show ground is at Ardingly, Sussex.

South Wales and Monmouthshire Agricultural and Horse Shows Association (Founded 1944) *Objects:* to encourage and improve Horse and Agricultural Shows, to encourage interest in, and a better understanding of, the horse amongst the general public, and to encourage the breeding and showing of all classes of horses and ponies.

Sovereign A carriage closely resembling the Clarence (*q.v.*) but more ornate in design.

Sowar (Under-horseman) A trooper in an Indian Cavalry Regiment.

Spahis Originally irregular light cavalry units in the Turkish army but the term was applied to certain native cavalry regiments, the officers being French, in Algiers and Tunis. Disbanded in 1963.

Spanish When the Saracens invaded Spain and brought with them Arabs and Barbs, this greatly improved the native stock. Subsequent crossings of this Spanish horse resulted in the Spanish jennet, famous for its beauty, great docility and obedience, possessing width of chest, powerful shoulders, Roman nose, long arched neck with full flowing mane, goose-rump, and extraordinarily high action. This action was appreciated in the Vienna High School, where they excelled at the Spanish Walk. Later the Spanish horse deteriorated, except for the Andalusian breed (*q.v.*) which, until recently, provided a large proportion of remounts.

The most important stud is now at Jerez, where warm-blood horses are bred.

Spanish Jumping Bit Another name for the Kimblewick (*q.v.*).

Spanish Riding School of Vienna, The Evidence exists of an open manège in the sixteenth century on the premises of the Imperial Palace in Vienna which was later replaced by a covered arena. Between 1729–1735 in the reign of Emperor Charles VI the present Spanish Riding School was completed to the magnificent design of Fischer von Erlach. Here equitation based on the sixteenth- and seventeenth-century Italian and French riding masters was, and still is, actively taught and practised in its purest classical form, movements of which still include Airs Above the Ground, i.e. the Levade (*q.v.*), Capriole (*q.v.*) and Courbette (*q.v.*). The training of selected riders covers several years. The name Spanish derives from the horses of Andalusian, Arab and Barb origin, imported from the Spanish Court of Queen Isabelle in the sixteenth century, which were the foundation stock of the Lipizzaner (*q.v.*) stallions now used exclusively in the School; these are selected on performance. During World War II the horses were evacuated from bombed Vienna to Upper Austria and in 1945, owing to the intervention of the U.S.A. Army Commander, General Patton, they were returned to the Spanish Riding School and to the breeding farms at Lipizza, which ensured the continuation of four hundred years of classical equitation (*see Plate* 31).

Spanish School A designation for the Spanish Riding School of Vienna.

Spanish Walk An artificial air in which the horse lifts its forelegs very high and stretches them out straight in front. A spectacular movement, much favoured in the circus, but not recognized as classical high-school.

Spares   A racing term for horses in partial training and not doing work with the main string.

Spares   Spare coach horses for a road coach, which were kept at the allotted 'changes' on the coach route.

Spatterdashes   Long gaiters or leggings of leather or cloth etc. to keep the trousers or stockings clean when riding.

Spavin, Bog   A puffy swelling or distension of the capsular ligament on the inside, and slightly to the front, of the hock. It is caused by strain, but is not serious unless it is accompanied by inflammation, and need not cause lameness. *Treatment:* rest; cold applications, followed after pain has disappeared by embrocation.

Spavin, Bone   A bony growth inside and just below the hock joint. *Cause:* concussion. *Symptoms:* the horse will shorten his stride and drag his toe. *Treatment:* rest, or mild blistering should be employed, and shoes with high wedge heels and roll toes fitted (*see Plate* 12).

Spavin, Knee   A bony growth at the back of the knee on the inner side, which occurs mostly in race-horses. *Cause:* a blow or strain. *Symptoms:* a distinct swelling at the knee, and the horse will show signs of pain. *Treatment:* as for bone spavin (*q.v.*).

Spavin, Occult   A serious complaint, difficult to detect, in which a growth occurs between two bones of the hock, just below the joint on the inner side. *Symptoms:* no enlargement is noticeable, though the horse will probably go lame. *Cause:* concussion or strain. Horses with sickle or cow hocks are susceptible. *Treatment:* rest and raise the heels of the shoe. Blistering will be necessary.

Speak   Hounds do not bark, but speak.

Spectacles   *see* MARTINGALE, IRISH.

Speed   In a horse this depends on type, conformation and condition. The approximate speed at which the Derby is run is 35 mph (56 km/h) and the time for the Grand National averages about 28 mph (45 km/h). The steeplechase section of a three-day event (*q.v.*) is 25.73 mph (41 km/h) maximum, 22 mph (35 km/h) required. The same figures for the cross-country section are 21.27 mph (34 km/h) and 16.75 mph (26.95 km/h). The speed of the collected walk should be approximately 90 yards a minute (82 m/min); of the ordinary trot, 200 yards a minute (182 m/min); of the collected trot, 220 yards a minute (201 m/min), and for 'trotting out' at least 300 yards a minute (274 m/min) (*see also* FASTEST SPEED (RACEHORSE).

Speedy Cut Boot   A boot made specially high to prevent speedy cutting.

Speedy Cutting   An injury to the hock, knee or cannon bone. *Cause:* a blow from the opposite foot, peculiar to high steppers such as Hackneys, and which generally occurs in green or weak horses, or those with bad conformation. *Treatment:* as for a bruise or wound.

Spider Phaeton

Spider Phaeton   The lightest type of phaeton for a pair or single.

Spiffing   A coper's trick of blowing black snuff into the left nostril to start a jibbing horse.

Spire   A three-year-old stag.

Spiti   A characteristic breed of Indian hill pony of Mongolian origin, taking its name from the Spiti tract of very mountainous country in the Kangra district between Kulu and the central spine of the Himalayas. Breeding is mostly in the hands of the Kanyat tribe of high-caste Hindus. The pony is small, tough, thickset, up to weight and very sure-footed. It has an intelligent head, with remarkably sharp ears, a strong short back, short legs and hard round feet. The neck is short and thick, shoulders are sturdy and straightish, ribs well sprung and quarters developed. It thrives only on the Himalayas, and is apparently tireless and indestructible. Height 12 h.h., (122 cm), colours grey and iron-grey (*see* BHUTIA).

Spiv, Spivvey   An unattached groom who will 'do' a spare horse at race meetings (describing himself as a 'paddock assistant'); he will box one bought at a sale or lead horses to and from race meetings, sales and shows.

Splash Board   An upright protection in front of the coachman's feet in some vehicles; it may be of thick leather or wood.

Splint   A small bony growth which forms between the splint bone and the cannon bone in either the fore or the hind limbs. It seldom causes trouble in a horse over 6 years old, except as a result of a blow. *Cause:* generally due to the legs having been jarred unnecessarily when the horse was still young, also to bad conformation. *Symptoms:* lameness. *Treatment:* apply cold water bandages or a cooling lotion, but in persistent cases employ blistering or pin-firing.

Splint Bones   *see* METACARPALS, SMALL.

Splinter Bar   A cross-timber fixed to the front of a vehicle to which the wheelers of a team are attached by their traces.

Split Quarter Strap   A strap carrying a short breeching body.

Split Up Behind   A term applied when the quarters, viewed from behind, show from the dock to the top line of the gaskins, instead of the cheeks lying firm and close together; a wide dividing line.

Spoke Brush   A long, narrow brush with thick, hard bristles, used for washing carriage wheels.

Spokes   Wooden or metal bars connecting the inside rim of the wheel with the centre portion.

Sponge   Separate sponges should be used for the eyes and nostrils, and for the dock and sheath. 'Elephant ear' sponge is a special close-texture, small, flat sponge favoured in tack cleaning (*see Plate* 29).

Sponsored Events   Races or classes at race-meetings or shows which are supported by cash contributions from other sources than the racecourse or show concerned.

Sponsorship   Earliest race sponsor was William Blenkiron in 1866; he gave £1000 for a two-year-old race named after his Middle Park Stud.

Spoon   *see* 'LAME HAND'.

Spoon Cheek   A shortened and flattened cheek to a snaffle bit. A 'full spoon cheek' extends above and below the mouthpiece, a 'half spoon' extends only beneath the mouthpiece.

'Sport of Kings'   An expression referring to horse racing. Originally applied to hawking.

Spots (Body)   Small, more-or-less circular collections of hairs differing from the general body colour, distributed in various parts of the body.

Spotted Horse *see* APPALOOSA.

Spread Fence An obstacle designed to test a horse's ability to jump width as well as height.

Spreading *see* STRETCHING.

'Spreading a Plate' An expression indicating that a shoe has become loose in its seating.

Spring Bar The name refers to the stirrup bar which has a spring-mounted safety catch or thumbpiece.

Spring Double The Lincolnshire Handicap, now run at Doncaster, and the Grand National, run at Aintree, constitute the Spring Double, for which bookmakers often make an ante-post book.

Springer (Racing) A horse which suddenly springs into prominence in the betting on a race. A 'market springer' is a horse suddenly well backed in the betting market.

Springhalt *see* STRINGHALT.

'Springing' An old coaching term for galloping.

Spring Mouth A jointed snaffle bit without rings which can be fastened on to an existing snaffle by spring clips to make the action more severe. It often has a serrated mouthpiece and is sometimes known as a 'Butterfly'.

Spring Tree A saddle tree having two highly tempered lengths of steel set into the head and extending to the cantle. It makes the seat of the saddle resilient, gives to the movement of the horse's back and enables the rider's seat and back aids to be more easily

Spring Tree

transmitted. Used in modern jumping, general purpose and dressage saddles. Showing and racing saddles do not have spring trees.

Sprinter A horse that gallops at great speed up to 6 furlongs (1.2 km) but can stay no further.

Sprung Hock *Symptoms :* swelling at the back of the hock causing lameness, with fever and pain. *Cause :* strain or concussion. *Treatment :* remove the shoe, apply a cooling lotion, and give a mild dose of purging medicine. Keep on a low diet, put in slings (*q.v.*) in a bad case. Consult a veterinary surgeon.

Spur Boxes Sometimes set in the heels of boots such as jodhpur boots, and dress boots worn with overalls (*q.v.*). These spurs are known as box-spurs.

Spur Rests A small triangular block of leather sometimes fitted at the top back of a riding boot counter to keep the spur point parallel with the ground.

Spurrier One who makes spurs.

Spurs An artificial and supplementary aid, believed to have been used first by the Assyrians. There are different types for hunting and racing, and also military types. The designs are numerous, and neck lengths vary with fashion. Modern spurs are of the loop and single strap pattern; others are kept in place by ankle straps. Box-spurs, worn with riding trousers, fit into a hole at the back of the heel of the boot, which keeps them in place without a strap.

Spurs (Polo) Blunt spurs only are permitted.

Spurshields Square-shaped safes (*q.v.*) which go beneath the top strap of the spur straps.

Squaring Tail Skill is required to cut the ends of the hairs on the tail perfectly level. Tie a string round the ends before attempting the cutting.

Squatter's Rights, to Take (U.S.A.)
To be thrown.

Stable   A building for housing horses.
There are several advantages in housing a horse in a stable: the horse can be cleaned and groomed more easily when the utensils are close to hand; he can be clipped and rugged in winter, and extremes of cold and heat are avoided. It should be noted, however, that should the stable door be left open, the horse would not remain within, on even the coldest of nights (see STABLE MANAGEMENT).

Stable, Construction of   The essentials are light, air and good drainage.

Stable-connections   A racing term implying those connected with a horse running in a race, e.g. the owner, trainer, and stable staff at its training quarters.

Stable Management   *   Mary Rose, F.B.H.S.

Good stable management is largely a matter of common sense, good time-keeping, cleanliness, hard work and meticulous attention to detail.

Whether you are putting up your own stables or buying buildings already constructed, there are certain considerations to bear in mind. The site of the buildings should provide good dry foundations with free drainage. If the nature of the ground does not provide good drainage, then drains must be provided for in the plans. The building site chosen should provide pure air, good light and a good water supply.

The best soil to build on is that with a sub-soil of gravel or deep sand, as this gives a firm dry base with good drainage. The second best would be any rocky formation, and the worst site would be on stiff clay, deep loam or peaty or marshy soils.

The buildings themselves should be sheltered from the most severe prevailing winds and should not be overshadowed by other structures to the extent of excluding pure air and sunlight. Buildings are best arranged in echelon or parallel lines or large open squares. Small enclosures or squares permit less free supply of air and give greater chance of contagion when any form of sickness is present.

Buildings should be constructed of solid, fire-resistant materials and be well insulated. Brick or concrete block construction, for example, is less of a fire risk than wooden buildings. Corrugated iron, though cheap, is noisy and, unless very well insulated, very cold in winter and hot in summer. If used for roofing, it should have an inner roofing of wood. Walls, which should be at least 12 ft (3.66 m) high, should be damp-proofed. Roofs should slope not more than 45°, maintain an equable temperature in hot and cold weather, be durable, noiseless and non-inflammable.

Floors should be laid on solid foundations, preferably raised above the outside ground level. They should be impervious to moisture, smooth, durable, non-slippery, and should not strike cold to the horse when he lies down. If concrete is used it must be given a rough facing. Asphalt is too easily affected by heat and cold to make a good flooring, and it gets slippery when wet. 'Dirt' or 'clay' floors are good, but must be relaid each year. 'Tartan', a composition floor, is excellent, but prohibitively expensive.

The best size for loose boxes for hunters is 12 ft by 14 ft (3.66 × 4.27 m). Boxes 10 ft by 12 ft (3.04 × 3.66 m) or even smaller are suitable for ponies. Standing stalls should be 5 ft 6 in (1.67 m) wide and 11 ft (3.35 m) long from wall to heel post.

Ventilation is of first importance in

stable buildings as horses need a plentiful supply of pure air to stay healthy. The air in the building must be changed often, but the means of ventilation must not cause draughts. Windows are the prime means of ventilation and should be arranged along both outer walls of the stable, one for each loose box or stall. Windows should be protected with iron bars on the inside, and should open inwards from the top, being hinged in the centre. Other means of ventilation include louvre boards, cowls and tubes.

Doors are also a means of ventilation, if they are the Dutch door type with top and bottom portions opening separately. All stable doors should be at least 8 ft (2.44 m) high and 4 ft (1.22 m) wide. They should be hinged, opening outwards, or hung on rollers. Door latches should be strong and fit flush to the door. Two latches are necessary on Dutch doors, one at the top and one at the bottom of the lower half of the door, in addition to a bolt on the top half of the door.

The fewer fittings in a stable the better. Rings, fitted firmly and flush to the wall for the hay net and the water bucket, and one at breast level for tying the horse to, are necessary. Mangers, which should be broad and shallow with a broad rim, should be fitted at about 3 ft 6 in (1.07 m) from the ground, and should have completely smooth surfaces and all corners well rounded.

If automatic water bowls are fitted, they should be sited away from the manger and the hay rack, or hay net. All electric light fittings should be of a special 'stable' type and should be placed outside the loose boxes where the horse cannot interfere with them.

Horses are creatures of habit and thrive best when cared for according to a fairly strict routine. So far as you possibly can, always feed at the same time each day.

Cleanliness is very important in stables. Not only should the loose boxes be properly mucked out every day, but the droppings should be picked up at regular intervals, and the manger and water bucket (or water bowl) should be sponged out every day. Passageways and aisles should be swept at least twice daily and kept clear. The yard should be raked or swept and kept looking neat and tidy. Any grass should be kept properly trimmed, weeds removed, and so on. Nothing creates slovenliness in the care of animals so quickly as ill-kempt surroundings.

All stable tools and equipment should be kept clean and in their assigned place. Whatever bedding you use — straw, shavings, sawdust, peat etc. — keep it fresh and stacked neatly, preferably at a little distance from the stable building to avoid fire hazards, and keep the muck heap out of sight, and neatly stacked. Not only is a neatly built muck heap less of an eye-sore, but also the heat generated will kill flies, whereas a spread-out heap will encourage them.

Set a daily routine and stick to it. Check horse often during the day, but allow him plenty of time for real rest and quiet. Learn to observe your horse, and always move quietly around him, speaking before entering the box or touching the horse.

Grooming is of vital importance to the health of your horse. Grooming is the daily attention needed by the feet and coat of the stabled horse. Grooming removes waste products from the skin, stimulates circulation of blood and lymph and improves muscle tone. It is necessary to maintain condition, prevent disease, ensure cleanliness and to improve the appearance of the horse. The necessary tools are: hoof pick, for cleaning out the feet; dandy brush, for removing heavy dirt and caked mud; body brush for removing dust, scurf and grease from the coat, mane and tail; currycomb, either metal or rubber, to clean the body brush — the rubber variety may also be used on horses with heavy coats and helps to remove caked mud and dirt; the water brush, used damp, to lay the mane and tail — also used in washing the feet; two sponges, for cleaning eyes, nose and dock; a wisp, woven out of hay, used to promote circulation and for massage; a mane and tail comb, usually metal, used to help in pulling manes and tail; a stable rubber, for final polishing; and a sweat scraper, used to remove excess water from the coat after washing the horse.

The stabled horse should be brushed off and have his feet picked out, eyes, nose and dock sponged each morning before exercise. This is called 'quartering'. He should receive a thorough grooming (approximately forty-five minutes), including extensive use of the body brush and the wisp, after work. This is sometimes known as 'strapping'. He should be lightly brushed off each evening when day rugs are changed for night rugs, before evening feed. This is called 'setting fair'.

Horses or ponies kept at grass should have their feet picked out daily and be brushed with a dandy brush only. The body brush removes the natural oils from the coat and should not be used on horses living outside. Horses kept at grass also appreciate the sponging of eyes, nose and dock regularly.

Grooming machines are in wide use today and many excellent models are on the market. They should be used every second or third day on a horse, and he should be hand groomed and wisped on the other days.

In hot climates horses are regularly bathed after work. Bathing is not a short cut to good grooming. Never bath a horse unless he can be thoroughly dried. If the horse is sweaty after work, he will enjoy a bath; but do not wash him until you have walked him cool, if not dry. After bathing, which should be done with warm water and a wash mixture or mild soap, give him a thorough brushing, using the body brush.

Looking after your horse's clothing is also very important. Winter rugs and blankets should be sent to be cleaned and mended before being stored, preferably in chests between sheets of newspaper and with a plentiful supply of moth balls, for the summer. Summer sheets should be washed frequently, and always washed and mended before being stored for the winter.

Keeping your tack clean and in good repair is part of good stable management. Ideally, tack should be cleaned each time it is used. Using warm, but never hot, water, wash all leatherwork thoroughly, without getting it too wet. If saddle lining is leather, wash it too; if it is serge, brush thoroughly with dandy brush; if it is linen, sponge off lining. Undo all buckles on the bridle as you wash it. Take it apart completely about once a week. When all the dirt has been removed, soap the leatherwork thoroughly, with glycerine, or other good-quality saddle soap. Use a practically dry sponge and work soap well into both sides of the leather. Avoid making a lather, which will happen if sponge is too wet. Liberal soaping protects leather and stitching. Wash and dry all metal work and then clean with metal polish and rub up with burnisher.

Never wash leather with soda or with hot water. Do not place leather too close to artificial heat. Do not use saddle soap on top of dirt. Keep saddle pads clean by regular brushing or washing to avoid causing sore backs. Keep clean tack neatly hung on bridle and saddle rack in tack room.

A plentiful supply of fresh water is very important for all horses. Horses can suffer greatly from thirst and will lose condition very quickly if deprived of sufficient, pure water. Horses require from 6 to 10 gal (27–45 l) of water a day, in order to make the 6 gal (27 l) of saliva necessary for mastication.

If water is supplied to the stabled horse in a bucket, it must be washed out at least twice a day, and refilled three or four times, or more if necessary, during the day. Many stables are fitted with automatic water bowls, which are very labour-saving, but must be kept scrupulously clean and checked at least once each day. The disadvantage of this method of watering is that it is impossible to tell if the horse is drinking properly and so an early indication of sickness may be missed.

Recently a new method of automatic water bowl has been introduced in the United States, which consists of a pipe connected directly to the main water supply pipe and projecting about 3 ft 6 in (1.07 m) above ground level inside the loose box, in a corner. The bowl is larger than most automatic waterers and the advantage is that the water, drawn into the bowl by pressure of the horse's nose on a pedal in the bowl, is always the same temperature, winter and summer, and is always fresh, since it drains out of the bowl back into the ground, below the frost line, immediately the pedal is released. This equipment has the added advantage of draining in 35 seconds and therefore cannot freeze.

Horses kept at grass should either be watered from a river or stream, provided it is running water with a gravel bottom and a good approach, or from a trough in the field. If a trough is used, it should have no sharp edges or projections and should have an outlet in the bottom for easy emptying so that it can be kept clean. Good stable management is vitally important to the physical and mental health and well-being of the stabled horse. It means caring enough about the horses in your charge to take the extra trouble necessary to observe each one carefully and treat him as an individual, and always with kindliness, gentleness and authority (see FEEDING, and Plate 29).

* * *

Stable Rubber A twill linen cloth about 26 in by 33 in (66 × 83 cm) used in grooming (see Plate 29).

'Stables' A term used in the army and in racing stables for the first and last work of the day in the stables—'Morning stables', 'Evening stables'.

Stag A male deer at 4 years of age and over (see WARRANTABLE).

Stag An unbroken colt or gelding over one year of age, although the term is often applied to a horse castrated late in life.

Stage Coach see ROAD COACH.

Stage Wagon A big clumsy vehicle for cumbersome loads, drawn by six, eight and even ten heavy horses. Wheels were big and very broad with the idea of improving roads by flattening the ruts.

Staggart A now obsolete term for a male deer at 4 years.

Staggers see MEGRIM.

Stag Hook The hook of a hunting whip is made from stag horn.

Staghunting see HUNTING SEASONS and RUTTING SEASON.

Stain Another term for foil (q.v.).

Stake and Bind A useful and familiar fence consisting of strong but thin vertical stakes interlaced horizontally with supple saplings (see CUT AND LAID).

Stake Money The total money allotted and contributed for a race, out of which the winner and placed horses are paid.

Stale An over-trained or over-raced horse which has become lethargic and uninterested in its work.

Stale The act of equine urination.

Stale see JADEY.

Stale Line The line of a fox which has passed some time earlier.

Stalking-horse A horse behind which a sportsman hides while stalking game.

Stalled A term descriptive of a horse which is surfeited with food and leaves some in his manger.

Stallion   A horse, not under four years, capable of reproducing the species. An entire—ungelded horse.

Stallion Hound   A dog hound in a pack, used as a sire.

Stallion Licence   Under the Horse Breeding Act of 1918 the Ministry of Agriculture and Fisheries demands, with certain exceptions, that colts and stallions used for service are licensed from the age of two years. Inspection by officially appointed veterinary surgeons must certify that the animal is free from hereditary disease.

Stallion Tack   Leather roller, crupper side reins, bridle and lead run worn when being exercised or shown.

Stalls   Compartments, open at the rear, in which horses must be haltered. Main disadvantages of stalls are: the risk of becoming cast (*q.v.*), slipping the head-stall and freeing itself, and the possibility of gorging from an open corn bin. Chains stretching from the two pillars at the entrance to the stall will minimize this latter risk.

Stalls (Racing)   *see* STARTING STALLS.

Standard, A (Show Jumping)   If the show is running late or there are many clear rounds a competitor, after he has made a certain number of faults, may be required to retire from the event.

Stand Back, to   A term used when a horse takes off some way in front of a jump. The opposite of 'get under' (*q.v.*).

Standardbred   The official name of the famous American trotting and pacing horses, bred with extreme care and scientific efficiency. The father of the breed was Rysdyk's 'Hambletonian', foaled in 1849, and descended from the English Thoroughbred 'Messenger'. He also had the Norfolk Trotting blood of 'Bellfounder', which claimed the blood of the Darley Arabian. Characteristics of the breed are similar to those of the Thorough-bred with modifications due to differences in gait and work. Though it is heavier limbed and more robust than the Thoroughbred, with longer body, shorter legs and greater endurance, its average height is 15.2 h.h. (154 cm), 16 h.h. (162 cm) rarely being found. A Standardbred possesses unequalled heart and stamina, and runs heat after heat at top speed without flagging. Its activities are now almost entirely confined to race tracks (*see* THE HORSE WORLD IN THE UNITED STATES OF AMERICA, *page* 350).

Standing Over   A term descriptive of a horse that appears to 'give' at the knees. The defect is not detrimental (except in the show ring), unless it is caused by overwork.

'Stands Near the Ground'   Said of a deep-bodied, short-legged horse.

Stand Up A Horse, to   To place a horse, when in hand, standing level on all four legs, enabling a judge to assess conformation.

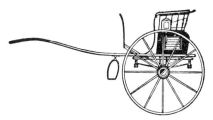

Stanhope Gig

Stanhope Gig   The seat (designed for two persons) rests on the boot or locker foundation. The vehicle was named after the Hon. F. Stanhope.

Stanhope Phaeton   A light phaeton for a pair or for one horse, this has a full lock for turning in a limited space, and seats four people, all facing forwards.

Star   Any white mark on the forehead. Size, shape, intensity, position and coloured markings (if any) on the white should be specified if a description is being given (*see Plate* 21).

Starch Bandage Dip an ordinary linen bandage into liquid starch, and apply to the injured limb whilst still wet. When dry, it will become hard and will hold the limb as though it were in a splint.

Star Gazer A horse which holds its head too high and is liable to take its fences blindly; though a dangerous horse to ride, a star gazer will seldom refuse a fence.

Staring Coat The general state of the coat when a horse is out of condition, suffering from worms or ill: dull hair, not lying flat but 'staring'.

Starling An obsolete term for brown or blackish grey colouring mixed with white.

Start, The In flat racing in Britain now there are two usual modes of starting a race, either by the mechanical barrier start or by starting stalls. If the barrier start is being used, the starter calls over the runners and their places in the draw, previously drawn by lot at the Overnight Declarations Office, and gives orders for the jockeys to move into position. When they are in position the white flag is raised, denoting that the field is under starter's orders, the starter releases the gate as soon as he considers a fair start can be made, and the white flag is lowered.

Should the tapes of the barrier be broken prematurely by a horse or jockey or should the starting barrier not work properly, the starter can always declare a 'no start' and order the jockeys to return to the start by means of a red re-call flag. The procedure is the same with starting stalls. The white flag is raised when all the runners are in their correct stalls, and lowered when the stalls are opened simultaneously by the starter operating the opening mechanism.

With steeplechasing and hurdle rac-ing, the starter merely releases a single strand of rubber, which acts as the barrier, and there is no draw for the start.

Starter An official who obtains an annual licence from the Jockey Club, by whom he is employed. His duty is to give the orders necessary to secure a fair start. He has the power to remove an unruly horse from his place in the draw, to order a horse to be held behind the other runners in a barrier start, and to order a horse to be withdrawn if it refuses to enter its starting stall. He can fine jockeys who misconduct themselves at the start.

Starting Gate First used in Great Britain in 1900, this is a mechanical removable barrier used to assist the starter in securing a fair start to the race. The gate consists of strands of rope (tapes) stretched across the course at the starting point and secured to posts at either end. The ropes are spaced one above the other at intervals of 2 ft (0.6 m) (the lowest being 4 ft (1.2 m) from the ground). These tapes fly up when the starter releases the catch from his position on the platform (*see* STARTING STALLS).

Starting Price (Racing) The starting price of a horse is the odds quoted about him by a bookmaker at the time of the start of a race. Representatives of the two daily sporting papers the *Sporting Chronicle* and the *Sporting Life* decide on the starting prices of all horses in a race at the time of the start. These prices are telephoned to London from the course and distribut-ed by press agencies to all newspapers, bookmakers and clubs who pay for the service. Starting prices normally rule all off-the-course bets unless the bets are ante-post.

Starting Stalls Movable sets of stalls into which horses are placed at the starting point of a race. The front gate is opened mechanically when the starter presses an electric button, releasing the horses. These stalls are now used at almost all flat races in Great Britain.

State Coach   Used by nobility only for state occasions. Equipped with great splendour and fitted with glass side panels so that the four occupants could be easily visible.

Stayer   A horse that can gallop at a racing pace over $1\frac{1}{2}$ miles (2.4 km), or farther.

Steed   A popular poetical description for a horse or stallion, infrequently used by horsemen; a spirited horse.

Steeplechase   A race in which the horses have to jump fences, open ditches and, under Jockey Club rules, a water jump. There are regulations governing the height of fences, etc.

Steeplechase Meetings   The first organized steeplechase meeting was held in 1830 at St Albans in Hertfordshire; the first steeplechase at Aintree was run in 1836, and the first Grand National (though not so called at the time) was in 1837.

Steeplechaser   A horse which races over fences, as opposed to a flat racer or a hurdler.

Steeplechasers   Boots of a slightly sturdier type than racers (*q.v.*), with fitted 'polishing tops', and a minimum weight of about $1\frac{1}{4}$ lb (0.56 kg).

Steeplechases, Early   Old manuscript records show that in 1752 a match was run over $4\frac{1}{2}$ miles (7.2 km) of country in Ireland between O'Callaghan and Blake, the course being from Buttevant Church to the spire of St Leger Church. In 1792, a steeplechase was held in Leicestershire, the competitors being hunting men, Lord Forester, Sir Gilbert Heathcote and Mr C. Meynell this was a match not between two horses only). In 1810, the first steeplechase over a made course was run at Bedford. The 3-mile (4.8 km) race was run in heats over eight fences but unfortunately there were only two runners. Mr

Spence on 'Fugitive' winning from a Mr Tower on 'Cecilia'.

Steeple-hoof   A condition in which the toe of the hoof wears out more quickly than the rest of the foot, causing it to tilt forward. It may lead to deformity in front legs. Hereditary.

Stepping   A horse with high action is called a stepper or a high stepper. This may be a natural action, but can be developed by artificial means and careful schooling.

Sterility   The cause of sterility in a horse may be constitutional or physical (undue fat or acidity). The animal should be examined by a veterinary surgeon, as a minor operation may remove the cause.

Stern   A hound's tail.

Sternum   The breast-bone.

Steward   An official supervising at a race meeting or horse show. On a racecourse there are at least three stewards. At horse shows many stewards may be engaged within the show arena, in the collecting ring, stables and elsewhere.

Steward's Secretary   Racing official, employed by the Jockey Club, whose duty it is to help and advise the stewards of a meeting, who in Britain are always unpaid volunteers. Steward's secretaries have largely the duties of stipendiary stewards but can only advise the stewards.

Sticky   A horse which 'boggles' at its fences, half-refuses and jumps from a standstill or trot; an uncertain fencer.

'Stiff-necked'   A straight running fox.

Stifle   The junction of the tibia and patella, corresponding to the knee in a human being. The joint is subject to (1) a disease similar to rheumatoid arthritis, for which treatment is of little use as the trouble appears progressive, and (2) a condition in which the patella slips out of its groove. The latter is a fairly common condition in youth.

Stifle Lameness *Symptoms:* the horse raises its quarter on the side it is lame. The step will be shorter and the horse will 'save' the lame leg by bending only slightly the stifle, hock and fetlock. *Treatment:* if lameness be due to sprain, apply fomentations, if to dislocation, a veterinary surgeon should be consulted to get the joint back into position.

Stile (British Show Jumping Association) 5 ft (1.52 m) wide with wings 6 ft (1.83 m) high prolonging the width of the fence.

Stings Stings from bees and wasps will result in reckless and perhaps dangerous galloping about. *Treatment:* keep the horse quiet in the stable, remove the sting and apply strong ammonia. If the sting be in the mouth, dangerous swelling may occur, and a veterinary surgeon should be consulted.

Stint The right to pasture one or more horses on common land.

Stint The service of a mare to which she is holding; 'has been stinted to (stallion)'.

'Stipe' (Racing) Slang for a steward's secretary or stipendiary steward.

Stipendiary Steward *see* STEWARD'S SECRETARY.

Stirrup, Hooded Describes a stirrup with front section covered as used with a Western stock saddle.

Stirrup Cup Liquid refreshment offered to a rider, usually a hunting man or woman, when mounted, and sometimes referred to as a 'jumping powder'.

Stirrup Iron (derivation *stigan* to mount, *rap* rope). A metal fitting into which the rider's foot is placed. The period of introduction is unknown but it was a barbarian invention. It appears to have been known in the second century and was in use by the dreaded Huns of Attila. Various patterns, sizes and metals are used. Stainless steel and named metals such as Eglentine, Kangaroo, etc., are reliable. Solid nickel is not recommended.

Stirrup Leathers *see* LEATHERS.

Stirrup Webs Lightweight tubular webs used instead of leathers for racing.

Stock *see* HUNTING TIE.

Stocked A term used to denote that a mare has been served; it also refers to a field that is being pastured.

Stockholm Tar *see* TAR.

Stocking White on the leg extending from the knee or hock to the coronet (*see* SOCK, *and Plate* 21).

Stockton Bit (of Pelham type) Has a mouthpiece which slides and revolves through the cheek.

Stock Whip A whip with a short stock but very long thong, used by mounted stockmen when driving cattle on ranges.

Stomach The connecting medium between the gullet and the small intestine, the stomach inclines to the left of the abdominal cavity, and is very small compared with the size of the animal. For this reason horses should always be fed little and often. They will graze for as many as 20 hours out of the 24.

Stone-cold A term applied, in racing, to a horse which has run itself out, is unresponsive and quite unable to 'come again'.

Stone-horse A stallion (*q.v.*).

Stone Wall (British Show Jumping Association) This should be not less than 11 ft (3.35 m) wide and 3 ft (0.91 m) high, and the rails placed above the wall should be at whatever height is required in the competition (*see Plate* 20).

Stoop A fox is said to stoop when it lowers its nose to the ground on a scent.

Stophound A slow form of harehound in Stuart times which could eventually be stopped by the huntsman (who ran with them), by flinging his pole in front of leading hounds.

Stopping Earth   The closing of a fox-earth with gorse, branches, etc., after the fox is known to have left, and to prevent its return. Blackthorn faggot, bound with wire, is the most effective barrier.

Stopping the Feet   It is believed that cow-dung applied to the soles is beneficial when the horn of the sole is dry and the foot brittle. The best way of stopping the feet, however, is by smearing mutton fat on the walls and soles, or by standing the horse in a clay bed.

Stopping Out   Fox earths which are closed when the fox is out of them during the night preceding a hunting day are said to be 'stopped out'; the process is known as 'stopping out'.

Stops   Metal projections on the shafts which keep the harness of a single horse at the proper point of contact with the shafts. They carry much of the weight of the vehicle when descending a hill.

Stops   *see* REIN STOPS.

Stoves   It is not necessary to heat the stable, but the coach-house and harness room should be kept warm. A solid-fuel boiler in the harness room provides warmth as well as hot water.

Stowed   *see* EARS, IDENTIFICATION MARKS.

Stradstick   *see* BARS.

'Straight, The'   The straight 'run in' to the winning post from the final bend in any racecourse. The length of the 'straight' varies on every racecourse in Great Britain.

Straight Mover   *see* LEVEL MOVER.

Strangles   A highly contagious disease of the nose and throat which may occur in other parts of the body and which is caused by a streptococcal organism.

Cause: as a result of travelling, horses may be infected from railway and motor boxes, from mangers, headstalls, bedding, buckets, etc. *Symptoms:* apathy, rise of temperature, the membrane of the eye appears unhealthy and of a red colour, there is a watery discharge from the nostrils which thickens rapidly and the glands under the throat become very swollen and tender, and ultimately burst. *Treatment:* isolation, on account of the contagious nature of the disease, in a roomy and airy box which must be free from draughts. Keep the horse warm with rugs and flannel bandages. Apply eucalyptus ointment and encourage the swellings to maturity by application of a stimulating liniment. Antibiotics are now used with marked success. Food must be soft and easily digested and the patient must be encouraged to eat. The horse will be under the influence of the disease for some 4 to 6 weeks, convalescing for not less than two months, and re-conditioning will occupy a long period. Wind trouble may result.

Strap, Balance   The balance strap is attached to the centre of the off-side cantle of the side-saddle and runs on top of the girth and around under the belly in order to steady the saddle.

Strapper   A groom or other stable assistant engaged in the grooming and general preparation of horses for riding and driving.

Strapping Pad *see* GROOMING PAD.

Strappings   A term applied to ceremonial harness, including saddles and bridles.

Strappings   These are sewn on riding breeches and jodhpurs extending above and below the knee. They are sometimes referred to as 'grips' or 'patches'. The best are made of finest buckskin dressed from the skins of small wild deer from Yanau in Southern China. The roughly dressed skins are exported to England where they undergo dressing similar to that which produces chamois leather. They are in small supply and costly, but there are two substitutes: Cape Buck, similar in appearance to buckskin, but not so soft or subtle; and Mock Buck, made from various types of heavyweight sheepskin for cheaper quality strappings. All strappings lengthen the life of breeches and tend to assist the knee-grip.

Straw   *see* WEIGHTS (FORAGE).

Strawyard   Horses being rested or recovering from an illness are often turned into a yard deeply bedded in straw, and if possible leading out of a box or boxes. This assures exercising room, and they keep warm and can be handled and examined with a minimum of difficulty. The yard should be kept dry and rotting manure removed.

Strelets   This breed originated when selected native mares from the mountainous regions of the Ukraine were crossed with Anglo-Arab, Turkish, Persian or pure Arab sires. The Strelets are now breeding true to type. This breed can be described as a large Arab with all the excellent attributes of that ancient race. A supreme riding horse and is particularly valuable for cavalry needs.

Stretching   The practice of causing harness horses, especially Hackneys, to stand with their front legs stretched forwards, and the hind legs stretched backwards. In the U.S.A. many saddle horses are trained to stand in the same way. The position makes the true height deceptive as it tends to lower it. Also known as camping and spreading.

String   A term applied to two or more racehorses out at exercise together.

Stringhalt   A disease of nervous origin affecting the abductor muscle and causing one or both hind legs to be lifted in a jerking action, higher than the natural gait. The disease is incurable and gets worse with age; a veterinary operation gives partial relief

only. An unsoundness. (Once known as springhalt.)

Stripe   A narrow white mark down the face, not wider than the flat anterior surface of the nasal bones (*see Plate* 21).

Stripe   *see* RACE.

'Stripe, The'   Colloquial term for the dorsal stripe (*q.v.*).

Stub   A wound on the sole of the foot. *Cause :* treading on a sharp and uneven surface, or more commonly on the projecting end of a sapling or bush. *Treatment :* if severe, remove the shoe and apply a bran poultice. Otherwise, remove the shoe, plug the wound with tar to keep out the dirt, and rest the horse. A dose of anti-tetanus serum should be given if the horse has not been permanently immunized.

Stub-bred   Foxes born above ground rather than in an earth.

Stubbs, George, A.R.A. (1724–1806) Son of a Liverpool currier, he received only a few weeks' professional training from Hamlet Winstanley. First made his living by painting portraits, but an obsessive interest in anatomy led to his patient dissection of horse carcases in 1758 in a remote Lincolnshire farmhouse and the publication in 1766 of *The Anatomy of the Horse* with engravings by his own hand. This work ranks as a vital reference for every artist of repute who came after him. He became known as 'Mr Stubbs the Horse Painter' and his portraits of famous Thoroughbreds of the day are outstanding. From 1760 he lived in London and received immediate and influential commissions as an artist of animal and sporting subjects. His pictures of hunting scenes are rare, though *The Grosvenor Hunt* painted for Lord Grosvenor is a masterpiece but he also excelled in such tranquil studies as his nine compositions of *Mares and Foals*. His undeniable genius as a painter of animals reaches its quintessence in several paintings of *A Horse attacked* *by a Lion* and in the picture of *A Cheetah and a Stag with Two Indians.* In addition to oils he also worked in enamels, first on copper and then on stoneware tablets made for him by Josiah Wedgwood. Stubbs published a number of mezzotint engravings. His natural son, George Townley Stubbs, was an engraver.

Stud   A breeding establishment where may be found mares and foals, with or without a stallion.

Stud, At   A stallion standing at a given place or travelling, whose services are offered to mare-owners at a fee.

'Stud and Stable'   A monthly illustrated racing magazine, founded in 1961, principally for owners and breeders of horses. It has racing news and views from home and abroad, and features on racing personalities, studs, veterinary subjects, sales, etc.

Stud Book   A record book of all pedigree stock whether of Thoroughbreds (General Stud Book) or of other breeds.

Stud-bred   A foreign term referring to horses of certain breeds that have a stud book of their own.

Stud-fastening   A metal stud by which the reins may be fastened to the rings of the bit. Satisfactory cleaning of the bit is facilitated by virtue of the simplicity and ease with which the rein is detached. Also known as a hook-fastening and French clip.

Stud Groom   The chief executive in charge of a breeding stud, although the term is often applied to one who has charge of a few horses, e.g. hunters.

Studs   These are inserted in the shoe to give a better holding surface (*see* FROST NAILS).

Stumbling   A result of debility, low condition, faulty conformation of forehand or forelegs, bad shoeing, lameness, tiredness or bad horsemanship.

Stumer   Slang for a horse who is not doing its best to win a race; a worthless horse in a particular race.

Substance   The thickness of a piece of leather. Best quality leather should have plenty of substance which enables it to accept and retain more grease during the dressing stage. Show bridles, etc., are made of leather having less substance, and being lighter cannot be expected to wear as well as a heavier hunting bridle.

Sucker   A foal of either sex up to weaning time or, if unweaned, until ranking as a yearling.

Sudadero   A leather flap on a Western saddle, behind which the stirrup leather runs, protecting the rider's leg from friction.

Suffolk   Known always as the Suffolk Punch, this breed is always chestnut colour, and together with the Percheron, is the only clean-legged heavy draught horse breed in England. Associated with the county of that name, the Suffolk Punch is said to date back to 1506 and every specimen today traces its descent in direct male line, in unbroken chain, to a horse foaled in 1760. The breed has received an infusion of foreign blood from time to time giving, perhaps, finer forehand and greater activity. Suffolk Punches are economical to keep, doing well on little food, are active and docile, stand about 16 h.h. (162 cm) with great width in front and behind. They have a very strong 'pull', are round and impressive, yet of friendly appearance, and are able to trot freely in spite of their bulk. *Breed Society:* The Suffolk Horse Society.

Suffolk Cob   *see* LINCOLNSHIRE TROTTER, the definition of which is probably applicable in this case.

Suffolk Horse Society, The (Founded 1878) *Objects:* to maintain the purity of the breed and to promote the general interest of members of the Society. It holds an annual Show and Sales.

Sulky A very light two-wheeled single-seated cart with skeleton body, used for racing trotters and pacers. In the U.S.A. it is known as Bike (*q.v.*).

Sullivan, Con A nineteenth-century Irish horse-whisperer, who tamed many high-spirited and dangerous blood horses, generally reckoned 'savages'.

Sumba Ponies bred on the islands of Sumba and Sumbwa in Indonesia. They are trained to dance with bells attached to their knees to the rhythm of tom-toms. Hardy and intelligent, usually dun with dorsal stripe, dark mane and tail. Height varies, about 12.2 h.h. (124 cm).

Summering A term applied to the summer period during which hunters or any horses are turned out at grass for rest and green feed.

Sumpter A horse for carrying burdens.

Sun-bonnets Formerly much used on draught horses in hot weather, these are not of much use unless a current of air passes under the bonnet.

Sunfishing The action of a buck-jumper when it twists its body into a crescent while in the air.

Sunstroke Horses are susceptible to sunstroke. *Symptoms:* sudden collapse with apparent insensibility, quick breathing and listlessness. *Treatment:* apply cold water to the head and spine, and protect from the sun. Keep cool and quiet in the stable and feed on roots and green food, with cooling medicine.

Suppletrees *see* BADIKINS.

Supporting Rein This supports the intention of the opposite rein during any movement off a straight line, e.g. on circling to the right, the right rein indicates the direction required; the left rein assists this indication, prevents the bit being pulled through the mouth and at the same time limits the extent of the circling.

Surcingle Often confused with a roller. A surcingle is a 2½-in (63 mm) or 3-in (76 mm) piece of web passing over the saddle and secured by a strap or buckle. Invariably used with race-saddles. It can also be a hemp or jute surcingle sewn to a rug as a method of keeping it in place.

Surfeit *Symptoms:* an eruption akin to nettle rash, causing irritation and loss of hair. Small blisters which burst sometimes appear all over the body, causing acute irritation. *Cause:* over-feeding, impaired condition and exposure to heat. *Treatment:* cut corn and feed green food. Apply a cooling lotion to the affected parts. An injection of antihistamine may help recovery.

Surrey

Surrey A light, four-wheeled American carriage with two separate seats mounted on a flat bottom. Most had flat cloth tops with fringes.

Surrey Clarence *see* CLARENCE.

Surtees, Robert Smith (1803--1864) A sporting author and qualified solicitor who bought a practice in London. Surtees subsequently abandoned law, founded *The New Sporting Magazine* (1831), and created the world-famous sporting character John Jorrocks (*q.v.*), who was the quintessence of cockney vulgarity, good-humour, absurdity and cunning. The chief works of this author are: *Hawbuck Grange, Mr Facey Romford's Hounds, Mr Sponge's Sporting Tour, Hillingdon Hall, Handley Cross, Country Life, Ask Mamma, The Horseman's Manual, Plain or Ringlets, Jorrocks's Jaunts and Jollities, The Analysis of the Hunting Field.*

Suspensory Ligament   Found between the two splint bones, under the back tendons, it runs from the two small flat bones of the knee nearly to the fetlock, above which it divides, but the two parts join about the middle of the pastern.

Swage Buckle   A flat, oval buckle of brass or white metal, with the tongue set on a central bar. Used for headcollars, etc.

Swaged Side Stirrup Irons   Where the sides gradually taper towards the eye, also known as graduated sides. Claimed to be the strongest form of stirrup iron.

Swales Gag   A veterinary gag to keep the mouth open.

Swales Three in One Bit   A riding Pelham and also a driving bit featuring various mouthpieces. The mouthpiece and cheeks revolve in two rings set round the mouthpiece. There is no poll pressure but considerable curb action is obtained.

Swallowing Tongue   It is very doubtful if a horse could possibly swallow its tongue. Horses often come to a sudden slowing down during a hard race and may make sounds suggestive of choking. Although horses breathe through the nostrils and only through the mouth in emergencies (and sometimes under anaesthesia) any obstruction at the root of the tongue, such as might be caused by a relaxed, soft palate, will cause difficulty in breathing. If the tongue is ever involved it can only be the thick 'bulb' at the hinder end of the tongue and not the flattened, spatulate anterior portion. Bandaging this part of the lower jaw has been said to produce good results but it is difficult to explain why (see SOFT PALATE).

'Swallows His Head'   A term used by cowboys when a broncho in the act of bucking gets its head right down between its forelegs, arches its back strongly and springs from the ground with great force.

Swallowtail (Coat)   see SHADBELLY.

Swan-neck   see BARS, and POLE HOOK.

Swan Neck   Where at its lower end the neck tends to become ewe-necked (q.v.).

Sway-backed   Descriptive of a horse which has wrenched the lower part of its back below the short ribs, a defect which is often accompanied by stringhalt. Such a horse cannot back a load. Also termed 'bobby-backed'.

Sweat Flaps   An under-flap to keep sweat from the saddle flaps; it also prevents buckles from causing discomfort to the horse.

Sweating   The natural result of normal exercise in warm weather or excessive exercise in any temperature. Nervous horses will often sweat before a race and others on their return to stables. This is sometimes a sign of weakness. Make every effort to 'dry off' to avoid a chill and give only a small drink of water, and hay. An effective cure is to put straw on the horse's back, cover with a rug and leave him for half an hour (see ANTI-SWEAT SHEET).

Sweat Scraper   A half-moon strip of metal to which a handle is attached. Most useful for the quick removal of the outer layer of excessive sweat from a horse after a race, polo or on returning wet to the stables. The metal edge can have a projecting rubber piece attached, the use of which avoids damage to prominent bones and is more comfortable to the horse (see Plate 29).

Swedish Ardennes   This strong compact breed was first introduced in 1837, and is now used mostly for forestry work. Very little hair on legs, low to the ground. Height: 15.2–16 h.h. (154–162 cm). More popular than the native draught horse found in the north (see also SCANDINAVIAN).

Swedish Warm-blood (Swedish Half-bred) Originally based on East Prussian, Hanoverian and Thoroughbred blood, it has evolved into a quality all-purpose riding horse, and also performs well in harness with good, fine action. *Height:* about 16.2 h.h. (164 cm).

Sweepstake (Racing) A race in which the entrance fees, forfeits and other contributions of owners go to the winner and placed horses, and are added to the prize money as opposed to a plate, in which the owners' entrance fees, etc., are kept by the racecourse.

Sweet Itch A summer disease of horses mainly affecting the crest, withers and croup. Now known to be allergic in origin, the causes covering a wide range from pollen of grasses to hens' eggs. *Symptoms:* intense irritation, rubbing and loss of coat with bare bleeding areas. There is no known cure, but for alleviation the horse should be stabled during the summer months. Horses purchased during the winter months may give no indication whatever that they are subject to this most distressing disease.

Swell-fork *see* SWELLS.

Swells A padded roll known as the swell-fork, forming part of the Western Saddle and running down from the centre of the front of the saddle to either side, giving considerably added security to the seat of the rider of a bucking horse. Rodeo specifications require a 14-in (35 cm) swell.

Swing Bars, Swingle Bars, Swingletrees, Singletrees *see* BARS.

Swing Horse The middle horse in a random, or the middle pair in a six-horse team (*see* RANDOM).

Switch-tail Undocked tail with the terminal hairs pulled to a point.

Swopping Ends A term used when a buckjumper bends to a half circle or loop in the air.

Syce, Sais An Indian groom.

Syndicate (Racing) A syndicate of not more than twelve persons may share an interest in a racehorse under Jockey Club rules provided that the legal ownership of the horse is vested in not more than four members of the syndicate, who are treated as joint owners and are subject to all the liabilities, duties and privileges of joint ownership. Under Rule 45 all syndicates have to be approved and registered by the stewards of the Jockey Club, for which there is a registration fee of £5.

Syndication of Stallions Generally involves a horse's capitalization into 40 shares (40 being the number of mares normally covered by a stallion in a season) and the offer of some, or all, of these shares for sale.

Synovia Commonly known as joint oil, this is secreted by the membrane lining the capsular ligament. Together with the articular cartilage, it prevents friction and ensures the easy working of the joints.

t (Racing) Tubed.

T.B. Universally accepted abbreviation for the Thoroughbred horse.

tnp (Racing) Took no part.

t.o. (Racing) Tailed off.

T.P.R. Temperature (*q.v.*), pulse (*q.v.*), respiration (*q.v.*).

t.y.o. (Racing) Indicates a two-year-old.

Tables The polished surface of the front (incisor) teeth formed by contact with the teeth in the other jaw. The shape of the tables gives an indication of age.

Tables (Show Jumping) *see* BARÊME.

Taboon Russian term for a large-scale breeding of Steppe horses (*see* KOSSIAK).

Tack A stable word for saddlery; an abbreviation for tackle (harness).

Tackle Spur Straps A pair of straps fitting on to spur and boot by means of studs and a buckle on the former.

Tack Room A room fitted with saddle racks and bridle holders for keeping saddlery and harness when not in use. Often contains glass-fronted cupboards for storing bits.

Taffy Australian term for a dun colour. Correctly taffy is liver chestnut with a yellow or silverish mane and tail.

Tag The tip of a fox's brush.

Tail This includes the whole of the dock and hair.

Tail Bandage A flex-woven cotton bandage put on to keep the tail slim and neat. Elastic bandages are often used, but they should not be damped or put on too tightly or they will damage the hair and cause discomfort. In polo, bandages are worn on tails to prevent the hair being caught by the stick in course of play.

Tail Carriage This should be high and gay, which is a sign of quality and breeding. It is best exemplified in the high-caste Arabian, which is unmistakable and has a character of its own.

Tail Going Round A sign of distress, excitement, irritability or exhaustion often noticeable during racing and show jumping and in the in-season mare.

Tail Guard

Tail Guard Made of rugging or leather, to cover the dock completely, and designed to prevent damage to the tail when the horse is travelling.

Tail Hounds Those which are some distance behind the main pack when running.

Tail Notches Horses grazing on common land sometimes have notches cut in the hair of their tails to facilitate identification.

Tail String *see* FILLET STRING.

Tail to the Wall *see* RENVERS.

'Take Hold' A phrase indicating that a horse is taking the bit strongly, and pulling through the reins against the rider or driver.

Take-off   The horse's act of lifting the forehand and striking off from the hocks when jumping; also the place from which the horse takes off when attempting a jump.

Take-off Side   That side of any obstacle to be jumped, and which is nearest to the rider.

Take with the Hand   To close the fingers sufficiently to increase the tension of the reins and consequently the pressure of the bit.

Take Your Own Line (Show Jumping)   A competition in which fences are given different values, from 10–100, and competitors are allowed to select which fences they jump, aiming to collect as high a score as possible in a given time. Fences knocked down are not penalized but their score is not counted. In the U.S.A. it is known as Gambler's Choice.

'Taking the Bump'   *see* TROT, RISING AT THE.

Taking Your Own Line   A term used in foxhunting for a rider who does not remain with the field.

Tallet   A hay-loft.

'Tally Ho!' 'Tally O!'   A hunting cry indicating that a fox has been seen. Unless the huntsman is within speaking distance, a shrill scream known as 'View Holloa' is substituted.

'Tally Over', 'Tally Ho Over'   A hunting cry indicating that a fox has crossed a ride in a wood.

Tan   The bark of trees, being the residue after treatment by tanneries. A good flooring for riding schools, being soft, springy and cool to the feet if kept slightly damp, and useful on floors of boxes when a horse is suffering from foot trouble. This type of flooring should be sprinkled with agricultural salt to keep it damp.

Tanbark (U.S.A.)   *see* TAN.

Tandem   Two horses driven one ahead of the other.

Tandem Cart   A dog-cart or other two-wheel trap used for driving a tandem.

T'ang Horses   Funeral pottery horses, lively and spirited in fashion, made during the T'ang Dynasty of A.D. 618–906 in China and executed as substitutes for living animals to accompany their dead masters in their tombs.

Tanghan   A pony living on the borders of Nepal and Tibet, 13–14 h.h. (132–142 cm), used mainly for riding.

Tantivy   At full gallop, riding headlong. The term originally represented the sound of a horse's feet. Sometimes erroneously applied to a flourish on the hunting horn.

Tapedero   Hooded stirrup cover on a cowboy saddle.

Tap Root   The main root of a female pedigree traced back to the origin.

Tar   Stockholm or Fir-tar should be applied on tow for plugging feet in cases of thrush (*q.v.*).

Tarbenian   This is a famous breed from the neighbourhood of the small, quiet town of Tarbes at the foot of the Pyrenees and which originated in the Iberian horse. The strain was improved at the beginning of the nineteenth century by Arab stallions imported by Napoleon Bonaparte. Later the Bourbons imported English Thoroughbred stallions which augmented the height, and thus was created the Bigourdan horse. The introduction of the Thoroughbred was thought by French connoisseurs to be a rather disastrous influence and the tendency was to add more Arab blood. The Tarbenian of today is merely an Anglo-Arab (*q.v.*), bred for more than a century on the plains around Tarbes. The breed is light boned, about 15 h.h.

(152 cm), of good conformation and beautiful action. It is possessed of great courage, speed and intelligence, and is unexacting in food requirements. The breed produced many excellent cavalry horses as a result of these fine qualities.

Tares   An excellent green food, but it must not be fed too liberally as it is liable to produce lymphangitis (Monday Morning Evil).

Tarpan   This was the original primitive wild horse of Europe including the southern Russian steppes, there being both a forest and a steppe strain. During the sixteenth century the Tarpan disappeared from Western Europe altogether, surviving only in some regions of Prussia, Poland and Lithuania until the end of the eighteenth century. The last specimens were found in Bialowieza in 1780 and were transferred to Count Zamoyski's Reserve. Proving expensive to maintain they were, in about 1887, distributed among the peasants and could still be found in remote regions of eastern Europe until the end of World War II. Professor T. Vetulani decided to regenerate the forest variety, and all primitive horses with Tarpan characteristics were transferred to the forest at Popielno, Poland where there are now two wild herds and a number of domesticated Tarpans at the breeding and research station. Professor Lutz Heck started experimental mongrel cross breeding with Przevalski stallions (*q.v.*) on light Konik (*q.v.*) mares at Munich Zoo and in the second generation succeeded in producing a horse strongly resembling the original Tarpan.

Tarporley Hunt Club   The club was founded in 1762 to hunt hares, but later changed to fox-hunting. Membership is limited to forty and since 1799 the qualification for membership is property, family or residence in Cheshire. Since 1775 the Club has held a yearly race meeting, except during war years, and since 1874 steeplechases were substituted for flat races. Hunting songs were written year by year specially for the Club by the well-known sporting poet Rowland Eyles Egerton Warburton (*q.v.*) (1804–1891), and were sung after supper at Club Meetings, which are still held at the Swan Hotel at Tarporley.

Tat   A native-bred Indian pony.

Tattenham Corner   The last bend on the Epsom race-course. The winning chances of many horses running in the Derby are made or marred at this sharp left-handed turn.

Tattersall, Richard (1724–1795) Founder of the firm of that name, Tattersall migrated to London from the Yorkshire-Lancashire border. Tattersalls are now bloodstock auctioneers, their activities being almost confined solely to the sale by auction of Thoroughbreds at Park Paddocks (Newmarket).

Tattersall Bit   A colt's circular bit with or without players or keys. Often called a foal bit or sometimes a yearling bit.

Tattersall's Committee   Formed in 1795. It took the name from the fact that it met at Tattersall's auction room which was then at their Knightsbridge premises. It has the authority to settle all questions relating to bets, commissions for bets and any matters arising either directly or indirectly out of wagers or gaming transactions on horse racing, to adjudicate on all cases of default, and, at its discretion to report defaulters to the Jockey Club.

Tattersall's Ring   The chief betting ring on any race-course to which bookmakers and the public are admitted on payment.

Tattersall's Sales   The family and firm of Tattersall's, founded in 1766, have been associated with public sales of hunters, Thoroughbreds and other horses at Knightsbridge, London, up to 1939, and Newmarket, since the early eighteenth century.

Tattoo   For identification purposes the lips or gums are sometimes tattooed.

'Tatt's'   Colloquial abbreviation of Tattersall's Auction Sales (*q.v.*) when at Knightsbridge, London.

T Cart   Similar to a Stanhope Phaeton (*q.v.*), and formerly very popular for driving polo ponies in single harness, especially in India.

Team   Used alone, this term is understood to mean a four-horse team; a four-in-hand; a pair of wheelers behind a pair of leaders.

Teaser   A substitute stallion, often of little value, presented to a mare at a stud to test whether she is ready for mating to a more popular and valuable stallion.

Teeth   In each jaw there are six front or biting teeth (incisors), and twelve back or grinding teeth (molars), and between these, in both jaws of horses, lie two tushes, or tusk-like teeth. They are rarely seen in mares (*see also* AGE, AGEING *and* AGE, TO TELL THE, *and* DIAGRAMS *on page* 3).

Teething, Cough due to   *see* COUGHS.

Telegraph Springs   Coach springs or beds, invented by John Warde (*q.v.*), and first used on the coach 'Manchester Telegraph', hence the name.

Temper   This is due to heredity, to ill-treatment or to teasing. Where heredity is the cause, it may be useful to note, for breeding purposes, that the sire has more to do with the transmission of a disposition to future stock than has the dam.

Temperature   The normal temperature for a horse is 100.5° F (38° C); a rectal reading should always be taken. *Method:* shake the mercury to 95° F (35° C), or below. Raise the dock and insert the bulb of the thermometer

(which should be vaselined); rotate the instrument until three-quarters of its length is within. Leave in position for the time stated on the glass of the thermometer.

Temperature   The temperature in stables should maintain an average of about 55° F, if the horse is clipped and suitably rugged.

Tendon Boots   Specially designed boots made to support the tendons.

Tendons   Amber-coloured fibrous structures, forming bands and cords which attach the muscles to the bones of the legs. They are light, but of great strength. Tendons (also called sinews) are brought into action by the contracting and relaxing of the middle or fleshy part of a muscle.

Tendons, Bowed   An advanced form of leg sprain. Tendons should be approximately parallel to the cannon bone, but bowed tendons spring outwards and assume the shape which the term implies.

Tendons

Tendons, Sprained   More often the connective tissue of the tendon sheath is affected, very seldom the tendon itself.

Tendons, Strained A laceration of the tendon fibres, causing heat and lameness, found most frequently in the forelegs. *Cause:* heavy work, especially in the case of cart-horses. *Treatment:* complete rest, with the application of cold water bandages. When the swelling has subsided, blistering should be undertaken, and the horse turned out to grass.

Tennessee Walking Horse The name indicates the special purpose for which it is bred, i.e. to carry farmers and planters of the southern states of the U.S.A. at a comfortable walking pace over plantations. Also known as the Plantation Horse, which now refers to the Pleasure rather than the artificial Show type. Like the Morgan breed, it owes its foundation to one prepotent sire, in this case 'Black Allan' (foaled 1886), a standardbred trotter of mixed Hambletonian and Morgan ancestry. Heavier and more powerful than the American Saddle Horse, the Walking Horse is larger, stouter, more robust, and less elegant, having a large plain head, rather short neck, massive, solid body and quarters, and heavier limbs. The prevailing colours are black and chestnut, although roans are found frequently, and white markings are conspicuous. Intelligent and well-mannered temperament. Characteristic running walk, fast, easy and enduring, for which careful training is required, otherwise it develops into a 'pace'. Height 15.2–16 h.h. (154–162 m) (*see* THE HORSE WORLD IN THE UNITED STATES OF AMERICA). *Breed Society:* The Tennessee Walking Horse Breeders Association (*see* Plate 30).

Tent Club The general name given to clubs, especially in India, which were devoted to the sport of pig-sticking (*q.v.*). The premier club of India and of the sport was the Meerut Tent Club. Other famous clubs were the Muttra Tent Club and the Delhi Tent Club.

Tent Pegging A spectacular equestrian sport, which originated in India.

A soft, white wooden peg, bound with wire, is placed in the ground at an angle, leaving roughly 9 in by 4 in (23 × 10 cm) showing, and it has to be taken with a lance or sword at full gallop. It was popular in the Army until recent years. In the U.S.A. it is known as Peg Sticking.

Tersky Russian horse bred and developed in the Stavropol region (N. Caucasus) as the result of crossing Russian Arab stallions (Streletsky) with pure-bred Arabian (Karbardin) mares. They possess good temperament and action, with great powers of endurance. Average height about 15.1 h.h. (153 cm).

Terrets The two rings attached to the pad through which the driving reins pass. The centre piece is not a terret, but a bearing rein hook or pillar.

Terrier Man One who accompanies the hunt (mounted or unmounted), and has a terrier, either in a carrier on his back, or on a leash. If the fox goes to ground the terrier must be available to go into the earth. He must also be ready to go with the pack into an extra thick covert (e.g. close-growing gorse).

Test (Puissance Competition) To test horses' ability to jump large obstacles. The course consists of 6–8 obstacles, height varying, except for a jump-off (*q.v.*), between 4 ft 6 in (1.4 m) and 5 ft 3 in (1.6 m).

Tetanus A disease, also known as Lockjaw, caused by the bacillus *Clostridium tetani* entering a wound. Foals are susceptible from birth and should receive an appropriate dose of serum, as should horses wounded in the foot and lower limbs at all times. Punctured wounds are more dangerous than surface, open wounds. *Symptoms:* the temperature rises to 103° F and 105° F, there is a general stiffening of the limbs, and the membrane of the eye extends over the eyeball. The horse is in a nervous state, and later the jaws become set and nourishment can be taken only by sucking. *Treatment :* the horse should be kept quiet in a dark box, the wound dressed with disinfectant and a veterinary surgeon called immediately. Avoid placing the hand or fingers in the horse's mouth. *Prevention :* an anti-tetanus serum should always be injected as soon as possible after a deep wound has been inflicted. Such an injection is advisable before castration. Tetanus toxoid given in three doses will be an effective preventive for several years.

Tevis Ride   *see* WESTERN STATES TRAIL RIDE.

Thatch   An excellent roofing for stables, as it is cool in summer and warm in winter. It is necessary, however, to guard against the danger of fire. Thatch does not wear as well as many other types of roofing, and needs frequent repairing. Also it is well to remember that it harbours insects.

'Thief'   A racing term for a dishonest horse, i.e. one which does not reproduce his good home form in public.

Thill   A two-wheel cart harness horse as opposed to a lead chain horse. A shaft horse is termed a Thiller. In Eastern Counties and some other parts of England, however, the term denotes also cart horses in tandem or team.

'This Grass'   An expression used when referring to the age of a horse, e.g. 'three years old this grass', meaning this coming spring.

Thongs   Plaited leather, with a loop to fasten to whip keeper and a lash at the other end. The best-known types are the Beaufort and the Melton. The length varies between 1 and 2 yd (0.9–1.8 m).

Thorns   After hunting, every care should be taken to trace and remove any thorns from the horse's legs, as they cause considerable irritation and soreness.

Thoroughbraces   Strong leather braces connecting the rear and front C-springs and supporting the body of a C-spring-hung carriage or coach.

Thoroughbred Breeders Association Founded by Lord d'Abernon in 1917. *Objects :* to encourage and ensure co-operative effort in all matters pertaining to the production and improvement of the Thoroughbred horses and the interests of their breeders.

The English Thoroughbred   *   Bill Curling

The Thoroughbred, the best known of all English breeds, and one of the most beautiful and fleetest animals in the world, traces its ancestry in male line through about thirty generations to three Arabian stallions imported into England between 250 and 300 years ago—the Byerley Turk in 1689, the Darley Arabian in 1704 and the Godolphin Arabian in 1730.

It was during the seventeenth century that English racing men began importing Arab stallions from the east to mate with home-bred mares to improve the speed of English-bred horses, and Charles II went further and imported a number of mares of eastern blood to add to the mares he had inherited. He received also as presents mares of oriental blood from Spain. These were all known as Royal mares and were mated with the Arab stallions. On the female side all horses in the General Stud Book now trace to thirty or so tap-root mares, some of which were Royal mares and some were not. The whole idea was to breed faster horses, and gradually it became apparent by the second half of the eighteenth century that the fastest horses were not the pure bred Arabs, but horses who were the result of mating home-bred stallions with home-bred mares with Arab blood in the first place predominant.

Colonel Byerley after riding his Arabian at the battle of the Boyne in 1690 retired in the same year to live at Goldsborough Hall in Yorkshire, where his gallant charger begat 'a middling horse' called 'Jigg', who sired 'Partner', who in turn sired 'Tartar', described as 'a strong chestnut near fifteen hands [152 cm] high'. Tartar was a useful racehorse, but his chief claim to fame was that he was the sire of 'Herod', who was bred by the Duke of Cumberland in 1757 and was a marvellous sire, getting the winners of over £200,000—a very big sum in those remote days. From 'Herod' in direct tail male descend through the 1836 Derby winner 'Bay Middleton' and the 1849 Derby winner 'The Flying Dutchman' many of the best French racehorses, including 'Bruleur', 'Ksar', 'Tourbillon' and 'Djebel', and horses well known in this country like 'My Babu', 'Le Lavandou', 'Le Levanstell', and the 1969 Ascot Gold Cup and Prix de l'Arc de Triomphe winner 'Levmoss'.

The Byerley Turk thus started his career at stud in 1691. At the beginning of the eighteenth century another Yorkshireman, Mr J. Darley of Aldby Park, near York, asked his brother who was in Asia Minor to buy him an Arabian horse to stand at stud, and in 1704 the horse arrived in England. A bay, 15 h.h. (152 cm) high, he was of little use for racing and as a stallion covered few mares apart from his owner's until Mr Childers of Doncaster in about 1715 sent his mare 'Betty Leedes' to him, and the result was 'Bartlets Childers', sometimes known as 'Bleeding Childers', since he was a blood vessel breaker. 'Bartlets Childers' begat 'Squirt', who begat 'Marske', the sire of the immortal 'Eclipse', from whom descend in tail male some ninety per cent of the horses who race in Britain today.

The third progenitor of the three male lines was the Godolphin Arabian who was bought in Paris in 1729 by Mr Edward Coke of Derbyshire. Mr Coke died four years later and his Arab stallion, described as 'a lop-eared bay, just under 15 hands', was then bought by Lord Godolphin and stood at the latter's home Gog Magog near Cambridge for 20 years. His sons included 'Cade', who begat 'Matchem', from whom descends 'West Australian', foaled in 1850 and first winner of the 2000 Guineas, the Derby and the St Leger—the Triple Crown. 'West Australian' had two sons responsible for sire lines which have continued to the present—'Solon' and 'Australian'. From 'Solon' is descended 'Hurry On', sire of three Derby winners who were failures at stud, but also of the Ascot Gold Cup winner 'Precipitation', whose son 'Sheshoon' has been a success at stud and has two or three promising young stallions to represent him.

'Australian' was responsible for a succession of good horses in America. From his line came 'Fairplay' and the brilliant 'Man o' War' (q.v.), from whom descend such as 'Relic', 'Roan Rocket' and 'Silver Shark'. The 'Matchem' line, as it is sometimes called, looked like dying out in this country during World War II, but now it is more strongly represented again. The 'Herod' line (Byerley Turk) between the two world wars was strong in this country, thanks to 'The Tetrarch', 'Tetratema', 'Mr Jinks' and others. Now that branch of the 'Herod' family has died out in Britain, and the line here depends on the descendants of the Tourbillon horses 'Djebel' and 'Goya II', both of whom raced with distinction for a leading French owner M. M. Boussac.

The ramifications of the Darley Arabian male line are much more complicated. They all trace back in this country to Eclipse's two sons 'King Fergus' and 'Pot 8 O's'. From 'King Fergus' through the 1850 Derby winner 'Voltigeur' and the 1875 Derby winner 'Galopin' descends the great 'St Simon'. Horses like 'Charlottesville', 'Charlottown' and 'Ribot' descend from 'St Simon'. From 'Pot 8 O's' horses like 'Relko', 'Reliance II', 'Fairway', 'Nearco' and all the other descendants of 'Phalaris' descend through the 1880 Derby winner 'Bend Or'. From 'Pot 8 O's' also descend the sons and the grandsons of the mighty 'Hyperion' through the 1834 Leger winner 'Touchstone'.

Horses like 'Alycidon' and 'Alcide' descend also from 'Pot 8 O's', but through 'Birdcatcher' and 'Sir Hercules'. The first common male line ancestor of Hyperion's son 'Aureole' and Alycidon's son 'Alcide' is 'Whalebone', winner of the 1810 Derby for the Duke of Grafton over 160 years ago. There are 10 generations between 'Whalebone' and 'Aureole', and 12 between 'Whalebone' and 'Alcide', so in human terms they are no longer significantly related in tail male.

The British have for long had a great reputation as breeders of livestock, whether horses, cattle, pigs, sheep or dogs; but certainly the Thoroughbred racehorse with its beauty of appearance and movement is outstanding. Today the head is refined, long, arched neck, pronounced withers, sloping shoulders with the back short, body deep and ribs well sprung, generous quarters with tail well set on. The legs are clean and hard with hocks well let down. The action is outstandingly free with a great stride indicative of speed. Height varies from 15 h.h. (152 cm)—16.2 h.h. (164 cm) with an average of about 16.1 h.h. (163 cm). This brief outline of Thoroughbred breeding gives no idea of the popularity of the Thoroughbred racehorse in Britain today (see page 263). Suffice it to say that the latest register of Thoroughbred stallions gives details of over a thousand stallions in Britain and Eire, and the latest volume of the General Stud Book lists over 12,000 brood mares. It is the English Thoroughbred over the years that has been the progenitor of the breed all over the world.

It should also be emphasized that it is not only on the turf that the Thoroughbred reigns supreme, but also in many other spheres of equestrian sport the breed has produced top-class performers, especially in the all-round test of international Three-Day Events and, of course, in the hunting field. Thoroughbred blood used as a cross has proved immensely valuable in producing show jumpers, dressage horses and hacks, etc., and in many cases the Thoroughbred of undiluted blood has also often been successful in these different spheres (see THE RACEHORSE AND RACING IN GREAT BRITAIN, and Plate 30).

*   *   *

Thoroughbred, Polish   see POLISH THOROUGHBRED.

Thoroughbred Stallions, Register of First published in 1910 and compiled by F. M. Prior who continued to do this for thirty-eight years, after which it was published every other year by the Register of Thoroughbred Stallions, Ltd. It is now published by Turf Newspapers. Its object is to record the name of every Thoroughbred or near Thoroughbred stallion, with pedigree, owner's name and certain other details. The more important horses have full-tabulated pedigrees with performances, and record of winners.

Thorough-pin Found above and on either side of the hock, it is a distension of the sheath of the tendon. *Symptoms:* fluid distension of tendon sheath. *Causes:* strain, or hereditary predisposition. *Treatment:* rest is essential and massage helpful. The fluid can be drawn off surgically, and high-heeled shoes will provide relief. The fluid distension can be pushed through to the other side, hence the old name which was 'Through-pin'.

Thorough-pin Truss A device designed to apply pressure to the affected area (*see* THOROUGH-PIN).

Three-Day Event Held in England at Badminton, Tidworth, Burghley, Bramham Moor and Wylye (*see* HORSE TRIALS *and results on pages* 380–382).

'Three Feet of Tin' A coaching term for the horn used by guards on Royal Mail coaches. Also known as 'Yard of Tin' (*see* COACH-HORN).

Three-gaited Saddlehorse (U.S.A.) Saddlehorse or hack trained only to the ordinary gaits of walk, trot and canter, as distinct from the five-gaited American Saddlehorse (*q.v.*). Three-gaited are shown with hogged manes and stripped tails.

Three-parts Brothers and Sisters *see* BROTHERS AND SISTERS.

Three-quarters Brothers and Sisters *see* BROTHERS AND SISTERS.

Three-year-old A gelding, filly or colt is termed a 'three-year-old' between the third and fourth anniversaries of its birth, but a race-horse is so described between January 1st of the third year after birth and December 31st of the same year; e.g. a Thoroughbred foaled in April 1970 would officially become a three-year-old on January 1st, 1973 (*see also* AGE OF HORSES).

Throat A muscular tube lined with mucous membrane and containing the gullet.

Throat Cap Form of throat-covering worn by Hackneys (*q.v.*) to encourage wasting and fining down of the neck.

Throat Lash, Throat Latch A narrow, buckled strap which is part of the bridle head, running under the throat. It should only be tight enough to prevent the bridle from slipping over the horse's ears.

Throttle Upper part of the horse's throat or gullet, the wind pipe directly behind and beneath the jowl.

'Throwing Their Tongues' When hounds vocally acknowledge the presence of a fox in covert.

'Thrown' When a horse is cast on to straw or any other bed for an operation, it is said to be 'thrown'.

Thrush An inflammatory condition of the frog of the foot characterized by discharge and a foul smell, and even lameness in advanced cases. *Causes:* neglect in the care of the feet; dirty bedding and badly drained stables; frog not in contact with the ground leading to degeneration. *Treatment:* Wash the foot thoroughly with disinfectant. Dry off and apply a dry antiseptic dusting powder deep into the diseased parts and cover with a wad of carbolized tow to keep the powder in place. Renew powder twice daily. Provide a clean dry floor. Recovery is generally swift.

Thruster An aggressive rider to hounds who, though mostly selfish and without consideration of others, may be one who makes himself conspicuous by his boldness and courage in riding his own line.

Thumb of the Prophet, The Indentation on the neck of an Arabian horse made, according to legend, by Mahomet's thumb.

Thurlow Bit A pattern where, instead of the usual 'eye' or top loop in the top of the cheek, there is a slit about $1\frac{1}{2}$ in (37 mm) long in which the cheek slides.

Tibia *see* FIBULA.

Ticks These usually appear between the thighs, under the mane and the root of the tail when horses are neglected or turned out at grass. *Treatment:* dress with paraffin oil or sulphur ointment.

Tick-tack A method of signalling by hand and sign used by bookmakers and their agents on a race-course. By this method, prices are quoted and bets laid.

'Tied-in Below the Knee' Where the measurement immediately below the knee is less than the measurement taken lower down towards the fetlock joint. A bad fault and the horse is necessarily light of bone. A horse can also be 'tied in under the hock' giving an impression of a bad, slightly bent, hind leg.

Tiercé A special form of betting in France conducted under pari-mutuel principles, the object being to select the first three to finish in a specific race which is chosen every Sunday or public holiday as the Tiercé Race.

'Tiger' The name given to a groom of small stature who rode behind a cabriolet (*q.v.*), standing on the platform and holding on by the straps.

Tiger-trap Rails set at an angle over a deep ditch; either one set of rails or two sets forming an inverted 'V'.

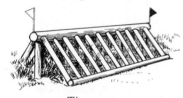

Tiger-trap

'Tilbury' The horse traditionally supposed to have been ridden by Queen Elizabeth I when reviewing her troops at Tilbury. It became fashionable for other Elizabethans to prefix 'Tilbury' to the names of their horses—Tilbury Rose, Tilbury Tip, etc.

Tilbury Gig A gig with the body supported at the back by three upright rails, and having seven springs. It was named after its designer.

Tilbury-tugs Where these are used, the shafts do not go through loops but drop into a metal reinforced tug opened

at the top to receive them, and over which the belly band passes to keep them in place. They are not confined in their use to a Tilbury gig but are used on a number of vehicles. The chief advantage in their use is that they prevent the up and down play of the shafts.

Tillemans, Peter (1684–1730) A Fleming or Dutchman who, from the age of 20, lived in England (mainly at Richmond) painting sporting scenes and horses. Though best known for attractive compositions that include a number of people and horses, like views of racing at Newmarket, he has some good equestrian portraits attributed to him. For a while he shared the studio of his friends Wootton and Seymour, who are thought to have owed more than a little to his help.

'Timber' Any fence made of timber, e.g. a post and rail fence.

Timber Splitters A term applied to horses skilled in picking their way through 'burns' with speed and safety.

Time Test (Racing) Official scale for calculating weight and time is: 1 length = 3 lb (1.36 kg); head (or short head) = 1 lb (0.45 kg); neck = 1 lb: 1 lb is taken to equal 1/15 of a second. For calculating weight, 1 lb = 0.06 second; 2 lb (0.9 kg) = 0.13 second; 3 lb = 0.20 second; 10 lb (4.5 kg) = 0.66 second; 15 lb (6.8 kg) = 1 second.

Timor Small pony bred in the island of Timor, Indonesia. Robust, agile and of great endurance. Usually dark coloured, about 12 h.h. (122 cm).

Tips A form of shortened shoe designed to protect the toes of a horse out at grass.

Tire An iron or rubber hooping confining the felloes of a wheel.

Tits A slang term for light horses. Little horses.

'**Tittup**' A term describing a false, fidgety, up-on-the-toes action; not a true-gait. To 'tittup down the road', 'Tittupping into a jump'.

Toad Eye The typical prominent eye of the true Exmoor Pony (*q.v.*), due to the puffiness of the upper and lower lids, both being of a distinct mealy colour.

Tobiano (U.S.A.) Primary colour white, secondary colours black, brown, dun or sorrel. Mane and tail are the same colour of the region from which they stem. All four legs are white, and head is entirely dark or with white marks. Glass-eye not characteristic (*see* PINTO, PAINTED).

Todd Bridle Similar to the Rockwell (*q.v.*) but having the mouthpiece joint covered in strong rubber, from which two pieces of elastic are taken to encircle the upper jaw and form a noseband. This latter is kept in place by a central strap running up the face fastened at the poll. Prevents the tongue being placed over the bit by raising the latter in the mouth.

Tom Thumb Bit A name given to a Weymouth bit when the cheek is very short, about 2½ in (63 mm). The action is correspondingly mild.

Tonga Draught A form of pair-horse draught, used in India, similar to the curricle (*q.v.*). In Tonga draught the necessary elevation is given to the end of the pole by inclining it upwards from the bottom of the body of the cart.

Tongue 'Giving tongue', the cry of hounds when hunting.

Tongue Grid A metal port suspended in the mouth, above the bit, by a slip head. Prevents the tongue getting over the bit.

Tongue over Bit The bit should normally lie on the tongue and if the horse will not permit this, the proper placing of its head and general control become greatly marred.

Tongue over Bit Device Two leather circles fitting round the mouth-piece, preferably of the mullen type, connected by an adjustable nose strap. To prevent this lying too low there is a central fastening attached to the ordinary cavesson. It raises the bit in the mouth and is often effective.

Tongue Port *see* JUBA PORT.

Tongue Strap A racing device to keep the tongue down. It is a slotted strap through which the tongue is passed, the strap then fastening under the lower jaw. It can cause great pain if adjusted too tightly. The Jockey Club rules that no tongue strap shall be less than 1 in (2.5 cm) wide.

Tony Collings Memorial Challenge Trophy Awarded to the British rider gaining the most points at any Three-day Event or Horse Trials organized by or affiliated to a national federation during the season.

'**Tooling**' (a four-in-hand) A slang expression for driving a team.

Tooth Rasp A rasp or file for removing the sharp edges of teeth.

Tooth Rasping A simple operation (known as floating in the U.S.A.) designed to remove the sharp edges which develop on the molar (grinding) teeth consequent upon constant lateral movement in mastication. The points so formed lacerate the gums and tongue and so prevent proper digestion of food. A long-handled rasp is employed and the operation is facilitated by the use of a gag.

Top Boots Any form of hunting boot whether black or brown.

Top Hats Tall hats came into fashion again at the end of the eighteenth century and the top hat as known today was first made by John Hetherington, a hatter, of Charing Cross in 1797, from fine silk shag. The style became universally popular and soon appeared in the hunting field where it is still correct wear.

Top-latch The leather thong that binds together the top ends of the hames or seals on the horse-collar.

Top Line Term referring to line of back from withers (*q.v.*) to end of croup (*q.v.*).

Top Pommel or Near Head *see* POMMELS.

Top-rein *see* OVERCHECK (ON HACKNEY BUGGY HARNESS), *also* OVERCHECK (ON RACING HARNESS).

'Tops' A term for contrasting tops of riding boots. A fashion originated by cavaliers who used to turn down the tops of their boots to expose the coloured linings.

Top Weight Heaviest weight (of jockey and lead), carried by the horse which is allotted the highest weight in a handicap.

Tor di Quinto Situated just outside Rome, this Italian cavalry school was an adjunct of Pinerolo (*q.v.*). It was used as an international training ground for officers specializing in cross-country riding. After motorization in 1945 the stables became an equestrian museum.

Torisky, Toric Strong muscular Russian horse originally bred in the Toric Stud in Esthonia and developed from the Klepper (*q.v.*).

Totalisator A mechanical device showing the number and amounts of bets staked on a race. The minimum unit for an ordinary win or place is 30p. The total pool on each race, less the Horserace Totalisator Board's percentage, is divided equally in proportion amongst holders of winning tickets of the pool in which the person bets. Popularly known as 'the Tote'.

Tote *see* TOTALISATOR.

Tote Double A daily double usually takes place on the third and fifth races

in the programme. The stake is 50p, and the backer nominates the number of the horse in the third race, for which he secures a ticket. Should this horse win, he nominates his choice for the fifth race, for which he receives a transfer ticket. The total pool subscribed for the double is then equally divided amongst the number of winning tickets.

Tote Forecast Bet for which the punter has to nominate the first two horses — in correct order — in races where three, four, five or six horses are declared to run overnight; and in either order where seven, eight, nine or ten horses are declared overnight. A forecast pool also operates where a field of eleven or more runners declared overnight is reduced to ten or fewer by late withdrawals. Minimum stake 30p.

Tote Place Pool A pool separate from the win pool operated by the Tote, which allows the punter to back a horse for a place only in fields of six and upwards. Minimum stake 30p.

Tote Treble A daily treble on the second, fourth and sixth races in the programme. The stake unit is 25p and the mode of operation and payout follows the Tote Double method (*q.v.*).

'Touched in the Wind' A horse which is unsound in wind to a slight extent only.

Touch the Horn To blow the hunting horn.

Tournament A contest which reached its greatest popularity between the twelfth and fifteenth centuries. Mounted armoured combatants with blunted lances or swords engaged for a prize bestowed by the 'Queen of Beauty' or lady of the tournament. It was derived from *tourner*, to turn (French), because the riders rode in a circular arena and were, according to the rules, obliged to make many turns.

'Towelling' An old coaching term for the flogging of coach-horses.

Town Moor (Racing) The Doncaster racecourse: *c.f.* Knavesmire, the York Racecourse, and The Roodeye, the Chester racecourse.

Towne, Charles (1763–1840) Rural scenes of great beauty painted by this Liverpool-born artist often included horses. Racing was also one of his important subjects.

'To You' A ditch on the near-side of a fence about to be jumped is a ditch 'to you'.

Trace-bearer A leather strap passing over and between the pad and the crupper with end loops to hold the traces in position; used on any pair-horse harness.

Trace-clipping *see* CLIPPING.

Trace Horse A spare horse to assist in drawing vehicles up an incline (*see* COCKHORSE).

Traces The means of harnessing a draught horse, this consists of two thicknesses of strong leather, with adjustment usually at the shoulder end. There are various means of attachment according to the type of vehicle.

Tracheotomy An operation of great service in roaring (*q.v.*), or where some difficulty in breathing is experienced owing to abscesses in the throat, as in Strangles (*q.v.*). An opening is made through the skin and flesh into the trachea or windpipe, about 9 to 12 in (23–30 cm) from the angle of the throat, and a plated metal tube is inserted which must be removed and cleaned two or three times a week. The operation is simple and effective.

Track The prints of a horse's hooves on soft going are known as the 'track'. The riding-school term for making a horse follow the correct path is 'keeping a horse to the track' (*see* ONE-TRACK *and* TWO-TRACK).

Tracks, Circular Tracks left by a horse moving in a circle.

Trail-ride A term given to cross-country rides much favoured by American riders—also known as Bridle-trail.

Trail Riders of the Canadian Rockies, The Order of the Established in the early 1920s and sponsored by the Canadian Pacific Railway, this Order holds annual summer meetings at remote beauty spots to encourage the riding of trails on horses through the Rockies, and the finding of new trails and to foster good fellowship and the preservation of old customs.

Trainer *see* LICENCE, TRAINER.

Trainers' Association *see* NATIONAL TRAINERS' ASSOCIATION and NATIONAL HUNT TRAINERS' ASSOCIATION.

Trakehner The famous Trakehnen Stud was founded in 1732 by Frederick William I of Prussia with a number of mares and stallions of different breeds, the intention being to furnish horses for the Royal Mews. At first breeding was not very successful but later under qualified direction quality improved until Trakehnen became the 'Newmarket' of East Prussia. Although a few Eastern sires were used with success, one of the most potent stallions was the Thoroughbred 'Perfectionist' by 'Persimmon' out of 'Perfect Dream'. In his three years at the stud he left 32 stallions and 37 brood mares out of 131 foals. The East Prussian or Trakehner horse, now bred extensively also in West Germany, stands about 16–16.2 h.h. (162–164 cm), of excellent conformation and action with a good temperament. The hardiness of the breed was proved by the exceptionally difficult trek to the west made by survivors in the winter of 1944–45 at the end of World War II.

Trakener or Trakehner A type of fence used in cross-country and other events. It is a ditch spanned by rails in the centre.

Trakener

Trandem Three horses driven abreast; known as a Manchester team.

Transom Plates Plates above and below the axle-tree beds on a coach.

Trap A name loosely applied to any two-wheeled horse-drawn vehicle. Also a horse-cloth.

Trapaderos The fancy swinging pieces on cowboys' stirrups.

Trappings A term applied to ceremonial harness including saddles, bridles and ornamental coverings.

Trave A stout wooden cage used for shoeing difficult horses. A shoeing-trave.

Travelling Head Lad He is appointed by the trainer to be in charge when horses go to race meetings.

Travers Also called *quarters-in* or *head to the wall*, it is a half-pass performed along the wall, forelegs on the track, hindlegs on an inner track, head slightly flexed in the direction of the movement, the horse's body at a 35° to 45° angle to the wall followed (*see* HALF-PASS and RENVERS).

Traverse Screened-off portion of smithy where horses were actually shod.

Tread, Stirrup *see* AGRIPIN.

Treads Wounds on the coronet. *Cause:* another horse treading on the coronet, as is likely when one horse leads another; the condition is seldom self-inflicted. It may develop seriously if neglected. *Treatment:* cleanse the wound with warm water and paint with collodion; if serious, it should first be poulticed and dressed with carbolized oil. Treads which bruise the lateral cartilages develop into side bones (*q.v.*).

Treble A bet naming three horses in different races to make one wager.

Tree, Saddle *see* SADDLE TREE.

Trees, Boot Leather riding boots after wear should be treed-up immediately. Trees were formerly made of wood but now metal and plastic are used. Tightly rolled newspapers used as stuffing make a good emergency substitute, the boots then being hung up by the loops to dry.

Trekking *see* PONY TREKKING.

Trencher-fed Hounds which are trencher-fed are not kept in kennels. Each one is looked after by some farmer, subscriber or other person, and on hunting days is collected and taken to the Meet.

Tricorne A cocked hat with the brim turned up on three sides, introduced in the 1770s for riding and driving.

Triella A bet associated with the television coverage of racing in which the punter has to forecast the first two in the first three races covered by television at certain Saturday meetings.

Triple Bars (British Show Jumping Assn.) Three bars of increasing height with a wide spread (*see Plate* 20).

Triple Crown A triple crown winner is a horse which wins the Two Thousand Guineas, The Derby and the St Leger. For results *see page* 402.

Triple Crown (U.S.A.) A winning sweep of the three major races, the Kentucky Derby, the Preakness Stakes and the Belmont Stakes is considered a most distinguished feat. Only nine horses have been able to accomplish this. For results *see page* 402.

Trippler   Gaucho term for a horse with a fast rolling gait between a trot and a canter.

Troika   A Russian term for a team of three horses driven abreast, usually in an open carriage called a Calèche, which is similar to a Victoria.

Trooping the Colour   This takes place on the official birthday of the Sovereign on the Horse Guards Parade, and is part of the ceremony correctly known as The Queen's Birthday Parade.

Tropilla (South American)   From six to twelve horses, the property of each individual Gaucho (*q.v.*). Only male horses are ridden, but a mare, usually piebald, is made leader (Madrina) and wears a specially toned bell round her neck. The riding horses become *amadrinada*, i.e. they will seldom stray from the bell-mare.

Trot   A natural two-beat pace on alternate diagonals (*see* BIPED *and* ACTION), the two beats separated by a period of suspension during which the horse is completely off the ground; the greater the speed the longer is the period of suspension. The speed of the ordinary trot is 220 yd (201 m) per minute.

Trot, Collected   In this, the horse should carry itself between its rider's legs and hands, full of impulsion and rhythm, have a good head-carriage, and be light in hand.

Trot, Extended   The horse should not trot fast, but should move with

Extended Trot

long, extended strides which must on no account be hurried, and should make itself long, with the head and neck carried forward of the collected position.

Trot, Rising at the   The rider, instead of sitting down in the saddle and feeling each hoof beat as each diagonal pair of legs meets the ground, rises in the saddle to one hoof beat, misses the next, and comes down again. Also called 'trotting light', 'posting' or 'taking the bump'.

Trotter   Any horse that moves with a two-beat diagonal gait at considerable speed.

Trotting Championship, The American   Held at the Roosevelt Raceway, Westbury, Long Island, New York. From 1946 to 1951 it was over 1 mile (1.6 km) but now covers 1¼ miles (2.01 km) (*see Plate* 24).

'Trotting Light'   *see* TROT, RISING AT THE.

Trotting Out   Trotting faster than the ordinary trot, at a speed of at least 300 yd (274 m) per minute.

Trotting Racing (Harness)   Horses draw light gigs or sulkies competing at the trot. Two types of gait are recognized, the true-trotter which is diagonally gaited and the pacer which is laterally gaited. In recent years in Great Britain the sport has regained some popularity. Permanent tracks have been laid down in Prestatyn in North Wales, Glasgow, Stirling, Edinburgh and at Kendal, Westmorland. Harness racing is much enjoyed in the U.S.A., with the Standàrdbred (*q.v.*). Many important meetings are held, the Triple Crown being the Yonkers Futurity in New York, the Hambletonian at Du Quoin and the Kentucky Futurity at Lexington.   *Society:*   (in Britain) National Harness Racing Club.

Trotting Vanner   A typical tradesman's small horse of pre-motor days, much used by the old railway companies. Of indiscriminate breed, it was usually a hard-wearing, short-legged type, and was formerly a light-legged cart-horse, very active and capable of a sharp trot. Dealers called them 'Vanners'.

True Arm Humerus bone on the foreleg of a horse.

Trumble A two-wheel 'tip' cart used on farms.

Trying-board A device which is used at studs to discover whether the mare is ready to breed. She is presented to the stallion and each stands on opposite sides of the trying-board, which should be made of wood 3 in (75 mm) thick, and be 4½ ft (1.37 m) high from the ground, with a roll-top. Railway sleepers, suitably 'stacked', make efficient trying-boards.

Tschiffely, Aimé Felix (1895–1954) Born in Switzerland later becoming a naturalized Argentinian, he earned great fame by riding two Argentine Criollo horses, 'Mancha', 16 years old, and 'Gato', 15 years, some 10,000 miles (16,000 km) from Buenos Aires, South America, to Washington, U.S.A., in two and a half years, starting on St George's Day, 1925. Great hardships were endured, including extremes of heat and cold and hunger. 'Gato' died at the age of 36, 'Mancha' at 40. Modelled in their own skins, they are to be seen in the Colonial Museum, Buenos Aires. The expressed object of the journey was to prove the stamina of the Criollo breed of ponies (q.v.), which Tschiffely believed to be dying out.

Tub-cart, Tub-car *see* GOVERNESS CART.

Tubed Horse A roarer which has had a tube inserted in its windpipe by a tracheotomy (q.v.).

'Tucked-up' A term descriptive of a wasp-waisted appearance with the loins drawn up behind the ribs. Such a tightly drawn-up condition of the abdomen points to illness, overwork, excitable temperament or improper management.

Tufters A stag-hunting term: several couples of experienced hounds are drafted from the pack (which is temporarily kennelled) and taken into covert to rouse and push the stag into the open, and the pack is then laid on the line of exit.

Tugs Circular-shaped, stoutly made loops which connect the shaft to the backband and meet the traces in pair and team horses.

Tumbril A farm cart, although in some parts of England the term refers to a large trough on legs for feeding horses and cattle in the field.

Turf, The Racing as a whole is referred to sometimes as the Turf; e.g. a credit to the Turf is the same as a credit to racing.

Turf Board, The The Turf Board is a body set up by the Jockey Club (q.v.) and the National Hunt Committee (q.v.) to co-ordinate and direct policy for meetings with members of the Horserace Betting Levy Board (q.v.). It now consists of the chairman, who is also senior steward of the Jockey Club, the two deputy senior stewards of the Jockey Club, six stewards, and the three Jockey Club members of the Levy Board. The senior steward of the Jockey Club and the two deputy senior stewards meet the chairman of the Levy Board and the other two Government-appointed members of the Levy Board in the Joint Racing Board (q.v.) to discuss racing priorities.

Turf Pony Term used in the nineteenth century before the advent of racing grandstands. Owners and other visitors to race meetings rode 'turf ponies' alongside the rails during races.

Turk   The Turkish horse was once considered the best saddle horse in the world. It is of characteristic oriental type, having a great amount of Persian and Arab blood; the species bred in Anatolia has the highest reputation. Today the most typically indigenous Turkish horses are Kurdistan ponies, bred near Sivas, where the custom is to cross mares with Arab sires, thus producing a useful working pony, 14–14.2 h.h. (142–144 cm).

Turkey Curb   *see* MAMELUKE BIT.

Turkoman Horse   *see* PERSIAN HORSE.

Turn on the Forehand   *see* PIROUETTE RENVERSÉE.

Turn on the Quarters   *see* PIROUETTE.

Turn-out   A two- or four-wheeled vehicle.

'Turned' or 'Turned to the Horse'   A term used to indicate that a mare's last service at stud will be unproductive of a foal.

Turned Out   A term implying that a horse is put out at grass and not stabled, usually for the summer or at any period.

Turnips   When of good quality, these are useful in supplementing the food of horses standing idle or doing little work. They are best fed raw but pulped.

Turpin, Dick (1706–1739)   He was born at Hempstead, Essex, where his father, John Turpin, kept the Bell Inn. Around Dick Turpin has been built a picture of a romantic highwayman, and he and his black mare (possibly fictitious) are featured in many tales. In fact, he was an unsavoury character. He was wild in his early youth, and it was not long before he joined a band of knaves whose robberies terrorized the countryside. To this he added sheep-stealing and footpad robbery. Later he took to highway robbery on horse-back, sometimes using a hackney coach, and he worked in many parts of the country. The ultimate hue and cry for him was so strong that he retired from the road, became a respected horse-dealer in Yorkshire under the assumed name of John Palmer, rode to hounds and was liked in local society. He was arrested for stealing a race-horse named 'White Stockings', and he was executed. The famous ride is apocryphal.

Tushes   *see* TEETH.

Twici, William   Huntsman to Edward II (1284–1327), who hunted in the Ashdown Forest and wrote the earliest treatise on English hunting.

Twicing   The practice adopted by some trainers of long-distance horses when, on the training gallops, another horse is jumped in at about half-way.

Twins   They are nearly always slipped. It is a rare event for a mare to give birth to living twins, and those which do survive are sometimes weakly.

Twist   *see* WAIST OF SADDLE.

Twisted Snaffle or Bridoon   A pattern where the mouth of the bit has serrated edges.

Twitch

Twitch   A method of minor restraint applied to control a restive horse for a specific purpose, such as administering medicine, performing minor operations, clipping, etc. A small loop of soft rope, fastened to the end of a long wooden handle, is passed over the upper lip, or the base of the ear, and the handle is turned until the loop becomes fast round the loose flesh. *Gag Twitch*. An alternative form of the above. A stout, loop-ended cord with the loop at the top corner of the lip passing over and behind the ears. The cord is then taken down the other side of the face and under the upper lip (but above the upper incisors), the end being passed through the loop and pulled to the desired tightness. The less twitches are used the better. They tend to make a horse head shy (*q.v.*).

Twitch, Humane This consists of slightly serrated wooden 'handles' held by a hinge and buckle and strap, also known as Rutter's Twitch.

Two-Day Event *see* HORSE TRIALS.

Two Thousand Guineas Normally the first of the five classic races of the year, it is run over a straight mile (1.6 km) at the Newmarket Spring Meeting, and is open to three-year-old colts and fillies. For results *see page* 402.

Two-time A pace of two-time is marked by two hoof-beats at each stride.

Two-track A two-track movement is one in which the hindlegs follow a separate track from that made by the forelegs.

Two-tracking An American expression describing a movement in which a horse gains ground to the front and to one side simultaneously, without turning the neck or body.

Two-year-old A colt, gelding or filly having attained the second but not having reached the third anniversary of its birth. A racehorse is so described, however, from January 1st of the second year of its birth until December 31st of the same year.

Two-year-old Racing Initiated by Sir Charles Bunbury and the Jockey Club at Newmarket about 1770.

Type Hunter, cob, show pony, etc., as opposed to Breed, e.g. Thoroughbred, Arab, Shetland, etc.

Tyres (Pneumatic) These were first fitted to carriage wheels in 1845 by the Duke of Northumberland and are said to have served him for one thousand miles (1600 km) of travel.

uns (Racing)   Unseated rider.

U.S.C.T.A.   United States Combined Training Association.

Ukrainian   ,The Ukrainian saddle horses have been developed at the Stud Farms of the Ukrainian S.S.R., in the same manner as English hunters. Large mares of the West European saddle horse type are mated with Thoroughbred stallions. Average height is 16 h.h. (162 cm).

Unbreakable Stirrup Leathers (Red) This generally refers to a brand of leathers made from buffalo hide and practically unbreakable.

Under-bitted   *see* EARS, IDENTIFICATION MARKS.

Undercarriage   The foundation of a vehicle below the bodywork.

Under-reach   In trotting action the front of the toe of the fore-shoe comes into contact with and scrapes away the hind toe almost up to the coronet. *Prevention:* a square-shaped toe in the fore-shoe, with two clips and the front edge of the shoe well rounded off. A flat hind shoe with a heavy toe should be used.

Undershot   A deformity in which the lower jaw protrudes beyond the upper. If the incisors do not meet satisfactorily, the ability of the horse to graze is impaired.

'Under Starter's Orders' (Racing) Every horse is under starter's orders when the white flag is raised, and is con-

Undershot

sidered to have started in the race once this has happened.

Under-weight   By so mishandling his weight (whatever it may be) in the saddle a rider is said to ride overweight. By light, active and alert riding he may, whatever his weight, ride underweight.

'Under the Whip'   *see* WHIP HAND.

Unentered   A hound which has not finished one cub-hunting season is described as being unentered.

Unicorn   A team of three, with two wheelers and one leader.

'United'   A horse is said to be cantering 'united' when the leading foreleg and the leading hind leg appear to be on the same side. A horse should always canter 'united'.

The Horse World in the United States of America   *

Francis McIlhenny Stifler

In a country as vast as the United States horse activities are innumerable and breeds are many and varied.

Racing   Thoroughbred racing is advised by the Jockey Club, New York, but the Jockey Club exerts no jurisdiction nor authority except in maintaining the integrity of The Stud Book. The 57 official running tracks police themselves by the T.R.A. (Thoroughbred Racing Authority) Security. The number of tracks increases slowly but surely and betting increases even faster. The Commonwealth of Pennsylvania founded in 1680 by the English Quaker, William Penn, for years had no running races except at hunt race meetings and point-to-points, but today there are many trotting and also running tracks with pari-mutuel (totalisator) betting. New York State enacted a statute to permit 'off-track' betting, but no other state has legalized it, although illegal betting with furtive bookmakers is more and more open.

Most of the major tracks are a mile (1.6 km) oval or longer but there are some half-mile (0.8 km) tracks still operating. Formerly there were often courses for steeple-chasing or hurdling just inside the 'in-field' but steeple-chasing is declining at the big tracks although it still flourishes at the hunt race meetings. Every track has its stakes race or races but the 'big three' races for 'The Triple Crown' remain: the Kentucky Derby; the Preakness Stakes at Pimlico, Maryland; and Belmont Stakes at Belmont Park, New York.

The breeding of Thoroughbreds is an important industry no longer confined to Kentucky, Virginia and Pennsylvania. Stud farms are found in most states, with major operations on the West Coast and in Florida. In volume XXV of the Jockey Club covering 1966–69 there were nearly 90,000 applications for registration of foals and every year 25,000 or more applications are made. Volume XXVI will be based on more than 100,000. This is a big segment of world Thoroughbred breeding.

Steeplechasing seems at the moment to be dwindling in popularity and many major tracks have dropped it. Of the several dozen tracks in the major Eastern metropolitan area, only three have any steeplechasing today.

Hunt Races—Jumping Races There are also in the U.S.A. flat, brush, hurdle and timber races at country meetings usually sponsored by a hunt club or the masters of private packs. The greatest is the Maryland Hunt Cup (*q.v.*), one race of 4 miles (6.4 km) over timber fences some of which are 5 ft (1.5 m) high. No rider is permitted to accept money for riding any race, although he may be otherwise a professional horseman. This is recent. Formerly all were amateurs by the strict Olympic standards.

Such races, and some others at the major tracks such as hurdle races, are under the jurisdiction of the National Steeplechase and Hunt Association. In 1972 there were nearly 200 races under N.S.H.A. guidance. Of these 48 were flat races (hunt races are usually on turf in natural fields); 21 were over brush jumps; 88 were over hurdles including 25 at the major tracks; and 26 were over timber, most of those at about 3 miles (4.8 km).

Foxhunting Foxhunting has a great following with more than 130 packs in spite of the encroachments of high-speed highways and the proliferation of dwellings. Some packs have had to move farther from expanding cities. The Rose Tree Foxhunting Club, recognized 1859, has moved from Media, near Philadelphia, west to Red Lion near York, Penna, and now starts cubhunting later and finishes the season earlier to please the tobacco farmers. Most U.S.A. packs use American hounds who eat less, are taller and have more tongue than English, but a few still adhere to 'the Peterborough type'. More rural packs are flourishing and some permit no guests on weekends or holidays to keep down the size of the fields. Suburban hunts are faced with the alternative of moving farther afield or changing to drag.

Polo The sport of polo, which was for a while waning, is waxing again under the jurisdiction of the U.S. Polo Association, and in 1972 there were 129 member clubs, including outdoor and indoor.

The two most important matches are usually considered to be the National Handicap of 20 to 25 goals and the National Open for 18 to 22 goals; both are held at Oak Brook, Illinois. Other major matches are held in the following states: California, Arizona, Illinois, Ohio, Texas, New York, Virginia, Kansas, Wisconsin, Pennsylvania, Delaware, Maryland, Massachusetts, Colorado, Connecticut, Vermont, South Carolina, Minnesota, Oklahoma and New Mexico; and some polo of some sort will be found in every state in continental U.S. and also in Hawaii.

Combined Training Combined training and Three-Day Events are popular as in Europe with Dressage, Cross-country and Stadium jumping. The major competitions which would rival Badminton or Burghley are: Woodstock, Green Mountain, Vermont; Ledyard Farm, Myopia, Massachusetts; Foxcatcher Hounds, Fair Hill, Maryland; Pebble Beach, California; Potomac, Maryland; Round Top, Radnor Hunt, California; and Concord Mountain, California, Malvern, Penna. These are all three-day. There are many others of two days and of one day. These are under the auspices of the USCTA and the AHSA.

Show Jumping Jumping classes for both amateur and professionals are a part of almost all general shows. The high spots are the international team competitions at the Pennsylvania National, Harrisburg, Penna; the National, Madison Square Garden, New York; and the Royal Winter Fair at Toronto, Canada. Individual members often show at the Washington D.C. International, the Philadelphia Show and elsewhere. The United States Equestrian Team both in show jumping and in Three-day Events operates with no government subsidy, depending on donations of money and loans of horses by individuals, but still puts up an impressive record in various parts of the world. The riders are strictly amateurs. The U.S. team won two Olympic Silver Medals in the Three-Day

Event at Tokyo in 1964 and in Mexico in 1968, and in Munich in 1972 they took the silver in show jumping. At the Royal International Horse Show in London the King George V Trophy has four times been won by American riders. This is one of the top show jumping competitions of the world. Grand Prix jumping is growing in the U.S.A. and Canada. The top money event is the American Gold Cup currently held in Philadelphia. Total purse $30,000; $9000 to winner.

Trail Riding Trail riding is popular all over the U.S.A. The endurance rides started in Vermont in 1932 with the 100-mile (161 km) Green Mountain Trail ride. Events are held under strict veterinary supervision. Mileage is usually 35–35–30 or 40–40–20 over three days. The Western States Trail Ride of 100 miles (161 km) in 24 hours is held annually in California, and properly attracts many entries and much attention. This ride is almost always won by a pure-bred Arabian, although horses of many breeds compete. Canadian entries are common in U.S. endurance rides and the Green Mountain Ride prize often goes to Canada, again usually to a pure-bred Arabian, over the Vermont's favourite Morgans.

The Harness Horse In the past 25 years the number of Hackney horses has diminished in the U.S.A., as have imports. However, the number of Hackney ponies has increased. Recently there has been a great revival of general driving at shows, rallies and marathons, and sometimes there is a combination. These are mainly in the East. The greatest marathon is in connection with the Devon Horse Show. In 1972 100 vehicles were judged at Blackburn Farm (actually an estate), then did 6 miles (9.65 km) on the road and were finally judged on the Devon Show grounds. There were singles for ponies and horses, pairs or tandems, unicorns, randoms, trandems, and four-in-hands and finally commercial or farming vehicles.

Pony Clubs U.S. Pony Clubs, of which there are now nearly 250 with over 8500 members in 20 regions, are direct descendants of those in Great Britain and organized on similar lines: teaching children how to ride properly, how to care for horses and training them to take part in equestrian events in a spirit of real sportsmanship. The members are mostly the children of horsemen or foxhunting parents who live in open suburban country.

4-H Clubs 4-H (for Head, Hands, Heart, Health) Clubs are for children of farmers but they are much broader than just equitation with activities connected with cattle, sheep, hogs, poultry, field crops, handicrafts, etc. They hold horse shows in every state, usually with divisions for English saddle riding and also for Western stock saddle riding.

Veterinary Schools The U.S. facilities for research in animal diseases are famous and the veterinarian has a high professional status. Some first obtain their medical degree and then take postgraduate work to become veterinarians. For a while there was an increase in the drugging of racehorses and show horses. Happily it is disappearing under strict rules of the Jockey Club, the American Horse Shows Association, the federal Department of Agriculture and state laws and local ordinances. A few years ago a winner of the Kentucky Derby was denied his laurels and winner's purse because he showed traces of butazolodin which is neither a stimulant nor a depressant but simply an analgesic. 'Bute' is allowed for show horses, but no medicament to pep up or quieten down. The leading Veterinary Schools are in connection with the most important colleges or universities, most notably the University of Pennsylvania.

Horse Breeds Breeds of horses used under saddle such as Arabians, Quarter Horses, Morgans, Saddlebreds, Tennessee Walking Horses, Appaloosas, Palominos and Pintos and the Pony of the Americas, have devotees in various parts of the country. All breeds—as well as colours—that are eligible to show have their own breed associations. The American Horse Shows Association is in overall authority over recognized shows and among other things in its Rule Book is a list of all breed headquarters. The A.H.S.A. evaluates judges by two categories: Registered (Senior) and Recorded (Junior). It also approves Registered and Recorded Stewards who must know all the details of the Rule Book. It also approves the list's Technical Delegates. There are more than 1200 judges in the U.S.A., many eligible for one division only; in fact there is currently only one man, Joseph Vanorio, of Park Ridge, New York, registered in every division recognized by the A.H.S.A.

The Arabian Horse Since World War II there has been an enormous increase in the numbers and popularity of the Arabian horse all over the U.S.A. Today more than 10,500 pure-bred Arabians are registered annually. There has been an important introduction of Polish-bred horses and Egyptian blood lines, especially within the last decade. With breeders living as far apart as Maine and California, there has been in some cases an unfortunate diversion from the classic Arabian conformation of the small fine head, deep chest, short back and high-set tail. Big prices are paid for first-class animals; high stud fees are charged. Arabian classes at shows include various divisions with Park, English pleasure, Western, costume and driving events. The breed societies are: International Arabian Horse Association and the Arabian Horse Registry of America.

The Morgan Horse The Morgan Horse (*see* JUSTIN MORGAN *and* MORGAN HORSE) continues to grow in popularity, having spread from its original home in Vermont and New England as far as the West Coast. The versatility shows for the breed are unique and still unchallenged by any other breed. Ideally each horse would be shown in one day in each of 13 classes, the winner gaining the highest total points. That has become impractical so today each entry must show in at least two classes of each division. The divisions and classes are:

Park Division   most elegant performance, saddle, fine harness, in hand.

Pleasure Division   more relaxed than Park, English saddle, stock saddle, trail.

Racing Division   ¼ mile (0.4 km) walking race, ½ mile (0.8 km) trotting race to a bike, ½ mile running race in silks.

Utility Division   Hunter — over fences, stock horse, Road driving 4-wheeled vehicles, Draught—pulling weighted sledge.

Breed Society: American Morgan Horse Association.

American Quarter Horse   The Quarter Horse (*q.v.*) continues to increase in numbers. Today in the United States there are more Quarter Horses registered than Thoroughbreds. There are a vast number of quarter-mile races, with purses that often exceed those of Thoroughbred running races. There are two distinct types of Quarter Horse: the racer and the 'bulldog' working type. The latter is in demand for ranch work and for competing in shows and rodeos in reining, roping, cutting and other Western activities. This versatile breed is also used for polo, hunting and show jumping. The breed society is: American Quarter Horse Association.

American Saddlebred   The American Saddlebred (*q.v.*) (originally nicknamed the Kentucky Saddle Horse) continues to find adherents in most states. In addition to the three- and five-gaited subdivisions there are also Fine Harness and, more recently, the Pleasure division, the latter being less formal than the older 'park' category. Three-gaited have hogged manes and stripped tails. Five-gaited have full manes and tails that are 'set'. Pleasure horses have full manes and tails but no setting, and hooves are

shorter. The breed association is: American Saddle Horse Breeders Association.

Tennessee Walking Horse   The popularity of the Tennessee Walking Horse has spread far beyond its native Tennessee and North Carolina and it is found from coast to coast. It is three-gaited, but the middle gait is not the trot. It performs a flat-footed walk, a running walk with a great overreach of the hind hooves, and a canter. It was originally developed for comfortable riding requiring no rising (posting), as well as for driving and general farm work. Today's show animals command high prices. Forty years ago a useful 'plantation horse' might bring $40; today's show champions may be bought for $50,000. The Breed Association is: Tennessee Walking Horse Breeders' Association of America.

Standardbred   The Standardbred (*q.v.*) Trotter or Pacer had a registry for years but since 1932 nearly 200,000 Standardbreds have been entered, and trotting and pacing races have spread all over the country. Horses are raced in harness to a small two-wheeled 'bike' with wire spokes and pneumatic tyres. Races used to take place in daylight, many in connection with country fairs. In 1972 in the U.S. and Canada more than 60 tracks had 'extended meetings' at night, racing under lights. In the nineteenth century 2.20 was considered a good time for a mile. Today the record for trotting a mile is 1.54 and for pacing 1.52. The Standardbred is a rugged horse whose ancestors used to do three heats in an afternoon. Besides his track proficiency he can make a good hunter, a pleasure saddle horse, and is always an excellent driving horse. He has a more placid disposition than the Thoroughbred or saddlebred. The breed association is: the United States Trotting Association.

The Appaloosa   The Appaloosa (*q.v.*) is a versatile breed that will perform well at cattle work, jumping, in harness, and makes a good polo pony and a reliable hunter and often a sensational jumper. Some shows have an Appaloosa division and there are many breed shows for Appaloosas only. The early coarseness too often evident has been softened and refined by Thoroughbred and Arabian outcrosses, but the progeny must always conform to the Appaloosa colour and marking to be eligible for registration. The breed association is: Appaloosa Horse Club.

Palomino   The Palomino (*q.v.*) is a colour rather than a breed. Palominos have been outstanding jumpers, Quarter Horses, Saddlebreds and compete in all kinds of Western classes for cattle work. One parent must always be a registered Palomino. They are all-purpose horses, very showy, great parade horses but of every breed and conformation.

Breed Associations are: Palomino Horse Breeders of America, this group has the largest registry. A competing group is the Palomino Horse Association.

Paso Fino   The Paso Fino originated or was developed in Columbia, Peru, Puerto Rico and Florida, and is gaining a foothold in continental U.S.A. Two breed clubs have members in various parts of the country. The horses must *never* trot. They perform the *paso largo* and *paso corto*, and sometimes the *sobre paso* and *andadura*. They are from 13 to 15.2 h.h. (132–154 cm), and weigh between 700 and 1100 lb (317–454 kg). The *paso fino* gait, sometimes called *fino-fino*, is very slow with extreme collection and a steady unbroken rhythm. The *paso corto* is a more relaxed gait suitable for trail or pleasure with only mild collection—faster than the walk. The *paso largo* is the speed form of the gait and adherents claim that the Paso Fino can pass other horses at a canter while he continues to do the *paso largo*. The same 1 2 3 4 rhythm must be maintained and the rider should appear motionless in the saddle as at all paso gaits. The *sobre paso* is the most relaxed form of the gait with little or no style but the horse must not hang his head. The rein is completely loose. This is not a showring gait. The *andadura* is executed when the horse is pushed for top speed, not into a gallop but rather into a sort of pace. This is not a comfortable gait. The Paso Fino can walk in a free manner and some have a delightful canter. Speed at a gallop is never part of showing. The breed headquarters: American Paso Fino Pleasure Horse Association, Inc.

Pony of the Americas   The Pony of the Americas (*q.v.*) is a relatively new breed, being a blend of Appaloosa, Arabian and Quarter Horse. Today one parent must be a registered P.O.A., but the other may be the same or Appaloosa, Arabian, Quarter Horse, Shetland, Welsh or Thoroughbred. They must be 11.2 h.h. to 13.2 h.h. (113–134 cm) at maturity. At the end of 1971 there were nearly 15,000 P.O.A.s registered and that in only 18 years. The breed association is: Pony of the Americas Club, Inc.

The Pinto   The Pinto (*q.v.*) is a colour rather than a breed. There are two eligible markings: the Tobiano (*q.v.*) with white legs, white over the withers and smooth patches of colour on neck, chest, flank and buttocks. The Overo (*q.v.*) has

Total Registration of Horses in the U.S.A.

Breed	In 1973	Total
Quarter Horse	76,325	931,112
Thoroughbred	26,760	612,759
Appaloosa	18,419	199,200
Arabian	13,000	107,000
Standardbred	11,393	391,970
Tennessee Walking Horse	7196	150,000
American Saddle Horse	4013	148,533
Morgan	3052	51,291
Pinto Horse	2195	20,790
Pony of the Americas	1370	21,583
Paso Fino	247	1873
Palomino	134	8480

more solid colour with patches of white. Legs are usually coloured. They make good polo ponies, hunters and jumpers and seem to have uniformly good temperaments. Breed association: Pinto Horse Association of America.

* * *

United States Trotting Association Governing body of trotting harness races founded in 1938.

Unkennel   see FIND.

Unmol (meaning 'priceless') A type of pony bred in the Northern Punjab and now practically extinct, save for a few maintained by local maliks who have infused Thoroughbred and Arab blood. Supposed by tradition to be descended from the horses brought by Alexander the Great when he invaded India. The type is very strong, elegant and shapely, with a compact body and long mane.

Unnerved   The nerve supply to the foot is sometimes severed in the case of a horse suffering from chronic foot lameness. This method is often resorted to as a relief from the painful navicular disease (*q.v.*). The equivalent American term is 'nerved'. An unnerved horse is unsound.

Unsaddling Enclosure   Situated in the paddock adjoining the weighing room with separate places for the first three horses finishing a race. Immediately after pulling up, the riders of the first three horses ride into the unsaddling enclosure. Other jockeys dismount in the main part of the paddock.

Unseen   A term applied to horses bought on a verbal or written description without being seen by the buyer. The full expression is 'Bought sight unseen'.

'Upsides' (Racing)   A racing term used of horses at exercise together, almost in line.

Unskid   To remove the skid from the wheel of a coach or other heavy vehicle, necessitating backing the wheelers (*see* SKID-PAN).

'Up to their Bits'   A coaching term for going freely.

Up to Weight   A term denoting that a horse has the substance and stamina to carry the weight of a rider with ease.

Urticaria (Nettlerash)   A non-contagious skin disease, sudden in onset and characterized by the appearance of small raised areas distributed throughout the coat. *Cause:* errors in diet, or stings and bites. *Treatment:* administer a purgative, give bran mashes and reduce heating food. An injection of an antihistamine usually hastens recovery.

* V *

V.E.E. Venezuelan equine encephalitis (*q.v.*).

V.W.H. Abbreviation for Vale of White Horse (*see* LIST OF HUNTS, *page* 411).

Valet, Jockey's An assistant attendant who has the care of the clothes, silks, saddles, etc., of jockeys. At a big race meeting there will be several jockeys' valets present, each one looking after a number of jockeys, who rely on their valets for their smart turn-out.

Valeting Room (Hunting) A room for the use of whippers-in for cleaning and drying hunting clothes and boots.

Van Horse Parade Society *see* LONDON VAN HORSE PARADE SOCIETY.

Vanner *see* TROTTING VANNER.

Vaquero Mexcican cowboy.

Vardo A gypsy van.

Varmint A familiar hunting term for a fox.

Vaulting on *see* MOUNTING.

Vaulting Roller A roller having handgrips for the gymnastic exercise of vaulting on, off or over a horse.

Velvet The hairy skin through which blood is supplied to the horns of a stag when these are growing. During this period, the horns are very sensitive. When growth is complete, in late August, the 'velvet' peels off.

Venezuelan Equine Encephalitis A mosquito-borne virus disease that is usually fatal to horses and can cause flu-like symptoms in humans. Little known outside South America until 1969, then it spread to countries further north.

Ventilation Of great importance in stables. It is essential that sufficient pure air be admitted, but horses are particularly susceptible to draughts.

Verderers Persons appointed to protect the rights and privileges of Commoners, e.g. New Forest Verderers (*see* AGISTERS).

Vertebrae The segmented portions of the spinal column.

Vestland *see* FJORD.

Vetch A leguminous plant of the pea variety grown with rye, which supports it. If cut when in flower it makes good green fodder or hay.

Veterinary Boot A leather boot often with an adjustable, hinged shoe on the sole allowing the frog to receive pressure but protecting the rest of the foot.

Veterinary Certificate A statement of the physical condition of a horse consequent upon an examination made by a veterinary surgeon. In 1973 the Royal College of Veterinary Surgeons and the British Veterinary Association advised their members to avoid the use of the terms 'sound' and 'soundness' because of the difficulties of legal interpretations of these terms. Advice was given on a standard form of examination for horses on behalf of intending purchasers, and on the certificate which should be issued thereafter.

Veterinary Chest The only contents required are some linen and crêpe bandages, for use in emergencies such as bleeding; a two-minute thermometer for rectal use; and a packet of cotton wool; a disinfectant (preferably T.C.P.) and ointment such as zinc and castor oil. Any wound, however slight, should necessitate an antitetanic injection and no time should be wasted in amateur doctoring. Embrocations may do more harm than good, especially when rubbed into the wrong part of the body or limb. Colic may be serious and requires immediate veterinary diagnosis. Drenching horses is almost outdated and in unskilled hands may give rise to pneumonia.

Veterinary Colleges and Schools
There are now seven of these in the British Isles, namely: The Royal Veterinary College and Hospital, University of London; The School of Veterinary Medicine, Cambridge University; The Faculty of Veterinary Science, Liverpool University; The Royal (Dick) School of Veterinary Studies, Edinburgh University; The University of Glasgow Veterinary School; The School of Veterinary Science, Bristol University; and The Veterinary College of Ireland. The course of training in each extends to at least five years and after graduation leads to the award of the diploma of Membership of the Royal College of Veterinary Surgeons, London (*see* VETERINARY SCIENCE AND THE VETERINARY PROFESSION, *below*).

Veterinary Science and the Veterinary Profession   *

R. H. Smythe, M.R.C.V.S.

The governing body of the veterinary profession in the British Isles is the Royal College of Veterinary Surgeons, whose headquarters are at 32 Belgrave Square, London, S.W.1. A Royal Charter was granted in 1844 to the graduates of the two veterinary schools then in existence, forming them into a body incorporate. It declared the practice of veterinary medicine to be a profession. It provided also for the government of the profession by the formation of a Council and for the systematic examination and enrolment of graduates. Unqualified practice became illegal on July 30 1949, except for certain minor treatment and operations. Unqualified persons who satisfied the Council of the Royal College of Veterinary Surgeons that certain requirements contained in the Act had been met were permitted to continue the practice of veterinary surgery through their lives or until their name was removed from a new register which was called 'The Supplementary Veterinary Register'. A person registered in the Supplementary Register could not take or use the title 'Veterinary Surgeon' or anything which might lead to the belief that he was registered in the Register of Veterinary Surgeons. Such a person was entitled to call himself a 'veterinary practitioner'.

In 1966 a new Veterinary Surgeons Act was passed which came into operation on March 15, 1967. It dealt largely with the reconstitution of the Council, but it retained the recognition orders in respect of the veterinary schools previously included.

Since 1948 the education of veterinary students has been carried out in universities, many of which have acquired land and buildings in rural areas which have been converted into Field Stations where tuition can be given in natural farm surroundings.

The original 'one portal system' of examination, whereby every teaching centre was visited by the same teams of examiners in order to maintain a similar level of graduates from each of these, has been abolished and each university school today has its own examiners although the system of examination is open to supervision and approval by the Royal College. Graduates who fulfil the requirements of the university schools and acquire the necessary degrees are accepted by the Royal College of Veterinary Surgeons as members and are entitled to use the abbreviation M.R.C.V.S. in addition to those signifying degrees granted by their respective universities.

The chief veterinary schools in Great Britain are situated at the Universities of Bristol, Cambridge, Edinburgh, Glasgow, Liverpool, London and Dublin (Trinity College and National University of Ireland).

The Fellowship of the Royal College of Veterinary Surgeons may be awarded to existing graduates by Thesis, Examination or by Election by the Council of the R.C.V.S. for meritorious contributions to learning.

The training of veterinary students within a university for the membership diploma involves a course of study covering a period of five years and is most comprehensive. It includes in addition to the basic sciences a thorough training in veterinary anatomy, animal management, veterinary hygiene and dietetics, pharmacology, bacteriology, pathology, parasitology, medicine and surgery. Additional Postgraduate Diplomas may also be awarded to members of the R.C.V.S. in Veterinary Radiology and Veterinary Anaesthesia.

In addition, the following diplomas in the field of Veterinary Science are currently awarded by universities in the United Kingdom—Diploma in Animal Health (London), Diploma in Applied Parasitology and Entomology (London), Diploma in Bacteriology (London and Manchester), Diploma in Tropical Medicine and Diploma in Veterinary State Medicine (Edinburgh).

Equine Veterinary Practice Although the number of horses in Great Britain fell during the 1960s to a very low level and veterinary students were unable to acquire any great amount of practical experience in equine practice, horses have now become popular again with countless human families, and there is a tendency in certain areas to restore the Shire horse to favour and use wherever this may be a practical possibility. The increase in the equine population arises out of the great interest taken in equitation by the younger generation and by others who specialize in dressage and show jumping, as well as by countless juveniles who are attracted by gymkhanas and open-air competition.

It seems probable that the number of horses and ponies kept privately in this connection will increase. Even to suggest that the keeping of a horse or pony more valuable or more successful in competition than one's neighbour's adds to one's social prestige may not court favour in residential areas, but the fact remains that while a pony could have been purchased cheaply some years ago it is now worth a large sum of money in the competition world, and the interest centred around the family representative is considerably increased. In both town and country practices the relationship between the veterinary surgeon and the horse-owning family has bcome very close.

Veterinary students will accordingly require as much practical acquaintance with the horse as possible, and with this in view some of the veterinary schools have now included in their extra-mural tuition the art of riding and the principles of horsemanship, coupled with a practical riding school and club. The majority of veterinary surgeons who have special knowledge of equine management, medicine and surgery have acquired it as the result of post-graduate training and experience. The duties of the equine practitioner fall under three main headings—clinical veterinary medicine, including and with emphasis upon preventive medicine; surgical diagnosis and treatment including operative procedure; the diagnosis and treatment of lameness and the use of X-rays in diagnosis.

The examination of horses for soundness both in relation to purchase and insurance has acquired an additional importance now that horses and ponies have increased so greatly in value. Few insurance companies can afford to issue policies for horses worth very large amounts of money without veterinary assurance that no unusual risk is apparent. Even then, the premiums may be above what the owner is willing to pay and the uninsured horse becomes even more dependent upon an efficient veterinary service. This applies particularly to stallions which may be valued in enormous sums, racehorses, hunters and show jumpers, all of which are exposed to special risks.

Surgery Probably one of the most important features having an influence upon the success of modern equine surgery is the development of the range of antibiotics. The other, nearly as important, is the revolutionary change in the administration and safety of anaesthetics.

Chloroform inhalation, which served its purpose during many generations, has practically gone out of use and its place has been taken by such inhalants as halothane, usually in conjunction with either the intravenous or intramuscular injection of a fluid carrying reliable anaesthetic properties. The effect of such injections can be removed almost instantly after the completion of the operation by the injection of an antidote. Local anaesthetics are still employed in minor surgery, usually in conjunction with a sedative injection.

The use of intravenous anaesthetics does away with a deal of the preliminary casting and struggling which was necessary when using chloroform alone as the anaesthetic, and the recovery period is shortened and the after-effects of the anaesthesia are now negligible.

Operation upon the larynx for the purpose of relieving roaring and kindred conditions continues to be performed with a fair measure of success.

Although the anatomical structure of the horse's intestine does not lend itself to a great deal of surgery, the abdomen with the aid of antibiotics and modern aseptic surgery, together with improvements in anaesthesia, can be subjected to laparotomy without undue risk. Caesarian section has been successfully carried out in the mare but only as a last resort.

Operation for retained testicle is frequently performed through the flank when it cannot be found in the usual position.

Much more is known today concerning the equine eye and disorders of vision. The use of modern ophthalmic instruments makes correct diagnosis of eye conditions much easier.

The universal use of antitetanic serum and toxoid in every case when the skin has been broken makes tetanus merely a terrible disease of the past. The only remaining difficulty is to make horse-owners realize that any wound, however slight, can produce symptoms and death, all of which can be avoided by vaccination.

The employment of X-rays in the diagnosis of lameness, fractures and the presence of foreign bodies, particularly within the foot, is now everyday practice. Unfortunately, owing to the bulky construction of the equine body, its use in spinal conditions other than in the cervical region is difficult; nor is it generally practicable in intestinal conditions.

Attempts are being made by the younger generation of veterinary surgeons to decry the operation of 'firing' limbs for the relief of certain forms of lameness. In spite of this many of the older and more experienced equine practitioners consider that in some types of lameness the operation, carried out under total anaesthesia, is still the most satisfactory method available.

Heat therapy and also the rhythmic contraction of muscles produced by application of an electric current are employed by many veterinary surgeons for the relief of certain forms of lameness, while high frequency treatment also has its supporters.

Medical Treatment In recent years a great many new drugs and methods of treatment have superseded many of the older methods and the stomach tube has to be used far less frequently. The knowledge regarding the causation of disease, pathology in general, and the treatment of parasitic diseases inside and outside the body, has undergone marked improvement. Antibiotics have become more numerous and varied, and more is known regarding the specific use of these in infection due to varied organisms.

The laboratory is made use of more than ever before, not only for the accurate determination of the type of parasitic invasion but also in connection with bodily secretions and excretions and the condition of the blood. The presence of alkaloids in the blood and saliva can be detected, especially in racehorses. Vaccination now covers other conditions, particularly the influenzalike conditions associated with loss of form and cough. In the racing world as well as in connection with shows, jumping competitions and the like, the spread of these diseases may be prevented and there need be no falling-off in entries as hitherto occurred.

Scheduled diseases, including epizootic lymphangitis and glanders are now things of the past, and more recently parasitic mange has disappeared. Ringworm appears to be rather more prevalent, but successful methods for its treatment have now come into use.

Certification The common forms of certificate granted by veterinary surgeons are as follows:
Certificates of Soundness. This constitutes one of the most highly technical and responsible duties asked of the veterinarian since it calls for a large measure of knowledge of the horse and experience of serviceability. The examination required for this certificate necessitates a complete 'overhaul' of the animal, as far as such is practical. The completeness and thoroughness of these examinations has added a new verb to the English language, namely 'to vet', implying an exhaustive overhaul. Subsequent to the examination the horse is certified as either 'Sound' or 'Unsound'. In the latter case a list of the defects found to exist is incorporated in the report. The certificate also includes a complete description of the animal to which it refers, including the important considerations of height and age.

While the interpretation of such a certificate presents no special problem to the experienced horseman, it is apt to prove both puzzling and inadequate to the needs of the novice. In such a case it is often preferable to ask a veterinary surgeon for a written 'opinion' on a horse rather than the more formal certificate of soundness. 'Opinions' include not only a statement of such defects as exist, but also a report on the extent to which they are of importance and are likely to affect future usefulness in relation to the work required of the horse.

Life Certificates of Measurement. These are granted under a Joint Measurement Scheme (*q.v.*) initiated by certain of the recognized horse societies. The rules require that such measurement of a horse or pony be made by a veterinary surgeon appointed to the official panel of recognized measurers under the scheme.

Professional Etiquette Veterinary surgeons are governed by certain rules of professional conduct, the infringement of which may lead them into serious trouble with the Royal College. It is interesting to note that for the most part the rules are framed for the protection of the public generally.

It is not always understood that under these rules it is forbidden for veterinary surgeons to take over the treatment of a sick or lame horse which is already in the care of a professional confrère. Should an owner be dissatisfied with the service given by his veterinary surgeon or feel that progress towards recovery is too slow, he has three courses of action open to him:

(1) To instruct his veterinary surgeon to discontinue attendance on the case. Having done this—preferably in writing—he is at liberty to call in someone else.

(2) To ask for a 'second opinion' on the case, i.e. the calling in of a second veterinary surgeon to consult with the one already in attendance. The latter cannot with reason object to such a course of action. Either the veterinary surgeon attending or the owner may nominate the second surgeon to be called in.

(3) To inform his veterinary surgeon that he wishes a 'consultant' called in. Again, the veterinary surgeon in at-

tendance cannot reasonably object. A man of outstanding ability and knowledge of equine medicine and surgery is

then asked to attend the case either to advise on or to supervise diagnosis or treatment.

*   *   *

Veterinary Surgeon   Under an Act of Parliament of 1844, this term is reserved exclusively for Members or Fellows of the Royal College of Veterinary Surgeons. Its use otherwise is illegal, the intention being to enable persons in need of veterinary aid to distinguish between practitioners trained at a veterinary school or college and the unqualified (*see* VETERINARY COLLEGES AND SCHOOLS).

Viatka   In Viatka (Russia) and in the northern parts of the Kazan provinces, mares were bred to Esthonian ponies known as Kleppers, with a strong admixture of oriental blood, and later Finnish blood was introduced. The Viatka pony consists of two varieties, 'Obvinka', the taller and better pony, and 'Kazanka'. The Viatka stands 13–14 h.h. (132–142 cm), and is very strong, hardy and fast, of good looks and conformation.

Vice   Any chronic objectional habit acquired by a horse but particularly the following: kicking, biting, rearing, jibbing, bolting, crib-biting, wind-sucking, weaving, dung-eating and clothing-tearing.

Vice (Polo)   A pony showing any vice is not permitted to be ridden in a game.

'Viceroy'   *see* GOOCH WAGON.

Victoria

Victoria   An open carriage only partly protected by a hood, universally popular from the 1870s onwards.

Victoria, Queen (1819–1901)   Upon the death of William IV in 1837 the Royal Stud at Hampton Court was sold, but it was later re-formed for Queen Victoria by Charles Greville, and such famous horses as 'Sanfoin', 'La Flèche', 'Diophantus', etc., were bred there. During her girlhood and early married life, she was a keen horsewoman and her diaries have many affectionate references to particular horses and ponies and to the pleasure she derived from riding. The Queen attended several race meetings, and was seen at Newmarket and Ascot, but after the death of the Prince Consort in 1861, she never went racing again.

Victoria Club   A London Club for Bookmakers where 'Call-overs' (*q.v.*) take place on races which have ante-post betting.

Vienna Riding School   *see* SPANISH RIDING SCHOOL.

View   To see a fox.

View Holloa   (pronounced 'holler') The scream given to reach the huntsman when a fox is viewed (*see* 'TALLY-HO!').

Villitis   *see* CORONITIS.

Vis-à-vis   An open four-wheeled vehicle without hood or side doors, and with the seats facing each other. Sometimes called the Barouche-Sociable. Similar to the Victoria or Calèche (*q.v.*).

Vives   *Symptoms:* inflammation and swelling of the parotid glands situated below the ear. *Cause:* usually the same as for strangles—catching cold, overheating, etc. *Treatment:* apply a fomentation and rub in a belladonna liniment. Feed slops and add salts to the drinking water.

Vixen   A female fox (*see* SCENT, FOX'S).

Volte   A circle 20 ft (6 m) in diameter. May be performed on one or two tracks (*q.v.*); in the latter case either haunches in, with the pirouette (*q.v.*) for a limit, or haunches out, with the pirouette renversée (*q.v.*) for a limit.

Voltige   The exercise of vaulting, which consists of jumping off and on a galloping horse, and which may comprise a number of more or less difficult acrobatic exercises on the horse. A regular turn to be seen in the circus.

Vomiting   For anatomical reasons, the act of vomiting is almost impossible for the horse. When it does occur, it is a serious development, indicative of a major injury to the stomach.

Voronezh Harness Horse   A Russian breed of substance and bone. Capable of pulling heavy loads. Very hardy breed which is able to live well in poor conditions. Forelegs are set on straight, hoofs are large and feet carry a lot of feather. Average height of stallions 15.25 h.h. (154.5 cm); mares 15 h.h. (152 cm). The breed was developed from the Bitiug carthorse which can be traced back to the time of Peter the Great when Dutch stallions were sent to Voronezh.

Vuillier Dosage System   This system hinges on Galton's Law (*q.v.*) of ancestral contribution in bloodstock and was propounded by Colonel Vuillier, a French Cavalry officer, in the 1920s. He traced the pedigrees of hundreds of good horses to the 12th generation, at which stage a horse has 4096 ancestors, and he based calculations on this figure. He computed that fifteen stallions and one mare appeared in the various pedigrees with approximately the same frequency. He then worked out the average influence of each of these 16 names in the numerous pedigrees which he dissected, and thus fixed a standard dosage desirable in the make-up of the ideal racehorse. This system no longer has influence among breeders.

Vulcan Mouth   When the mouth of the bit is of Vulcanite, it is not flexible, as is rubber, but is recognized as being a softer mouth than steel.

* W *

W.A.H.O. World Arabian Horse Organization (*q.v.*).

W.C.F. Worshipful Company of Farriers.

W.H.P. Working Hunter Pony.

W.P-B.R. Welsh Part-bred Register.

W.P.C.S. Welsh Pony and Cob Society.

w.r.s. (Racing) Whipped round start.

W.S.B. Welsh Stud Book.

W Mouth Snaffle *see* Y MOUTH SNAFFLE.

Waggoner One who conducts a wagon.

Waggonette, Wagonette An open vehicle with the backs of the passenger seats to the wheels with one or two seats crosswise in front, from the right hand one of which a single horse or pair are driven. Popular for country use with a pair or single.

Waggonette Brake *see* BRAKE.

Wagon, Waggon A four-wheeled vehicle for carrying heavy goods. A chariot.

Wagon-lock A kind of iron shoe which is placed under the rear-wheel of a wagon to retard motion when going downhill (*see* SKID-PAN).

Wain A wagon.

Wainwright A wagon-maker.

Waist of Saddle The narrowest part of the seat just behind the head. The waist, also known as the 'twist', should be as narrow as possible to avoid spreading the rider's thighs.

'Waler' The abbreviation of New South Wales, where this mixed type of horse was originally bred in Australia. It is a comprehensive term covering a variety of types. The foundation stock was of Dutch origin with other breeds, including Arab and Barb. The Waler has always found favour as a riding horse and is largely used as a range pony. It is an outstanding jumper and has a reputation as a Rodeo buck jumper (*see* THE HORSE IN AUSTRALIA *page* 19, *and Plate* 4).

Walk A pace of four-time, the sequence of hoof-beats being: near hind, near fore, off hind, off fore. A horse should be a good walker and put his feet fairly and squarely on the ground, all feet moving in a straight line (*see* ACTION).

Walk (Puppy) Foxhound puppies, when boarded at farms, etc., are said to be 'at walk'.

Walk, Collected In this, the horse should carry itself between the rider's legs and hands full of impulsion, have a good head-carriage and be light in hand. The speed should be approximately 90 yd (82 m) per minute.

Walk, Extended In this, the horse should walk fast with long extended strides, which must not be hurried, should make itself long, with the head and neck carried well forward of the collected position, on a long but not loose rein, control being maintained.

Walk, Free A walk on a loose rein, the horse's head being free, with a long rein.

Walking Horse Class An event in horse shows in the U.S.A. for Plantation or Tennessee Walking Horses (*q.v.*).

Walking Out Taking a hound pack out on foot in the kennel, paddock or elsewhere.

Walking Out Boot A leather boot enveloping the hoof and having a thick sole. It is useful for giving a horse with a damaged foot a little gentle exercise.

Walk-over   If only one horse should arrive at a race meeting to run for a certain race it is allowed to 'walk-over' in order to receive the prize money. Both horse and jockey must conform to the orthodox procedure, weigh-out, mount at the appointed time, canter past the stands and return to the unsaddling enclosure, be unsaddled and weighed-in.

Wall-eye   The term used exclusively where there is such a lack of pigment, either partial or complete, in the iris as to give a pinkish-white or bluish-white appearance to the eye. It is not indicative of blindness. Known also as China or Blue Eye, and in the U.S.A. as Glass-eye.

Wallis   Obsolete term for withers (*q.v.*).

Wall of Hoof   That portion (also known as the crust) which is visible when the foot is placed flat on the ground. It is divided theoretically, and for the purpose of description only, into toe, quarters, and heel. At the heel it turns inwards and forms bars which run on each side of the frog at the ground surface towards the toe. The wall is thickest at the toe, becoming thinner as it reaches the quarters. It contains 17 per cent to 24 per cent moisture and has an externally smooth, fibrous-like appearance. These fibres are small horny tubes, filled with, and matted together by, a gelatinous matter; they run from the top of the hoof to the bottom in an oblique fashion.

Walsall   The Midlands town which is the centre of the saddlery, bit making, saddlery furniture, etc., industries. Walsall production is entirely wholesale, and much is exported abroad.

'Wap-John'   An old stage-coachman's term of contempt for a gentleman's coachman.

Warbles   *Symptoms:* hard lumps occurring in the saddle region during spring and early summer. *Cause:* the presence of the maggot of the Warble fly. *Treatment:* keep the saddle off and apply fomentations to bring the lumps to a head. When the maggot is evicted, the cavity must be dressed with iodine.

Warburton, Rowland Eyles Egerton (1804–1891)   Known as 'The Poet Laureate of Hunting', he rode Thoroughbred horses which he bred, and published his 'Hunting Songs' in 1846, and other verses between 1855–1879, many appearing in *Bailey's Magazine*. He was blind for 17 years.

Ward, James, R.A. (1769–1859)   An artist of versatile and original talent, who was appointed engraver in mezzotinto and painter to H.R.H. the Prince of Wales (George IV) in 1794. During his long life he exhibited 298 pictures at the Royal Academy. Noted for horse portraits, hunting pictures and landscapes.

Warde, John (of Squerries, Westerham, Kent)   Born in 1752, he hunted much of the Berkshire and Oxfordshire countries between 1776–1798, and the Pytchley between 1798–1826. 'The Father of Foxhunting', he was one of the first to practise the modern fast style of hunting. He invented the Telegraph Springs (*q.v.*).

'Ware Wire'   A warning—pronounced '*Wor* wire'—flung over the shoulder by one hunting man to another on sighting wire in a fence.

Warmblood   A term which in general applies to horses possessing some Arabian blood in their make-up, i.e. Thoroughbreds, Hanoverians. Coldblood indicates such horses as Shires, Clydesdales and Percherons.

Warned off Newmarket Heath (Racing)   When the Jockey Club warns a person off Newmarket Heath that person is considered disqualified, and as long as the disqualification lasts is not allowed under Rule 205 of the Rules of Racing to (1) act as steward or official at any recognized meeting; (2) act as authorized agent under the Rules of

Racing; (3) enter, run, train or ride a horse in any race at any recognized meeting or ride in trials; (4) enter any racecourse, stand or enclosure; (5) except with the permission of the Stewards of the Jockey Club, be employed in any Racing Stable.

Warrantable (or runnable)   A male deer should strictly not be hunted until 5 years old, at which age he is termed warrantable.

Warranty   The buyer of an unsound horse has no case in law unless there be evidence of express warranty or fraud. Generally the seller only warrants a horse to be what it appears to be and, if the purchaser makes no inquiries as to its soundness or qualities, and the horse proves to be unsound or otherwise undesirable, he cannot recover in damages, the assumption being that he purchased at a cheaper rate in consequence (see AUCTION).

Warranty, Sold With   Horses sold with warranty as good hunters must be 'sound in wind and eyes, quiet to ride, have been hunted and be capable of being hunted'. Good hacks must be 'sound in wind and eyes, quiet to ride and not lame'.

Warts   Excrescences of the skin occurring most frequently on the nose, inside the hind leg and on the sheath. They are unsightly but not necessarily detrimental unless in a position to be rubbed by tack or assume a malignant form. Also called Angleberries. *Treatment:* those of a benign nature can usually be brought under control by a silk thread drawn tightly round the base or a stick of caustic potash carefully applied.

Washing Horses   This is generally regarded as a bad practice and is unnecessary if grooming is efficient, but it is resorted to in special circumstances such as generalized skin disease and in the tropics where horses are often hosed down after exercise.

Due precautions must be taken to prevent a chill following an all-over wash (see STABLE MANAGEMENT).

Water (for Drinking)   All drinking water should be clean. Soft water is best; rain water, if free from impurities, is excellent, as is river water, but that drawn from wells should, if very hard, be boiled first to soften it.

Water (Hunting)   A ditch or stream having no fence on either side, but containing water.

Water Brush   An item of grooming kit with longer bristles than a body brush. It is used damp on the mane and tail and is good for dry brushing of the head and legs, but is applied wet for quartering (see STABLE MANAGEMENT, and Plate 29).

Water Jump (F.E.I. Rules)   No obstacle is permitted before, in the middle of, or beyond the ditch full of water. A guard rail or hedge is usually fixed on the take-off side. The landing side must be marked by a white strip of wood or other material. Under B.S.J.A. rules a water jump may have a pole over it (see Plate 20).

Watering   Opinions vary as to whether horses should be watered at regular fixed intervals or not. The general modern practice is to leave water available to the stabled horse, the supply being changed twice daily. Horses should not be watered immediately preceding fast work but they rarely suffer if allowed to drink in moderation at any time when they are hot.

Water Out, to (U.S.A.)   To cool off a trotter (or pacer) after a race by walking it about, allowing it occasional drinks of water.

Waterproof Clothing   A suit consisting of a shaped rug, hood and surcingle of twilled waterproof material, generally used for horses which are travelling in the rain.

Wattle (Hunting)   A hurdle.

Wax Creams (for cleaning boots and shoes)   These contain the same ingredients as wax pastes (*q.v.*) except that they are emulsified by a neutral soap. For this reason they have not such a high wax concentrate when applied.

Wax Pastes (for cleaning boots and shoes)   Consist of sugar, cane wax, carnauba and beeswax, with colouring matter in a solvent base of turpentine (or white spirit, when the former is unobtainable).

Weaning   Foals soon start to masticate and supplement their milk diet with grass. The time for weaning is to some extent governed by circumstances, such as the condition of the mare and foal, quantity and nutritive value of the grass, resentment of the mare to the foal's attentions, but it usually takes place between the fourth and fifth month after the birth of the foal.

Wear   A horse is said to 'wear itself well' if it carries the head and tail up and puts life into its action. An alternative term is 'to carry both ends'.

Weatherbys   1773 is now considered the date when Weatherbys came into being although the Mr Weatherby who started the General Stud Book and his relation Mr James Weatherby, who was first Keeper of the Match Book for the Jockey Club, were not at the time working together. The latter, however, held office from 1777 until his death in 1793, and a member of the Weatherby family has been Keeper of the Match Book to the Jockey Club ever since. Weatherbys act as Secretaries to the Jockey Club and publish the Racing Calendar on their behalf. They own and publish the *General Stud Book* and the *Registered Names of Horses*. They act as the Jockey Club civil service for racing. In 1963 a General Stud Book Office was also opened in Dublin.

Weaving   A stable habit of nervous origin. *Symptoms:* the horse rocks to and fro continually and may lift each forefoot in turn as it sways its head and forehand. Should be stabled in a box rather than a stall as the habit is disturbing to other horses, which may catch it. *Treatment:* two bricks suspended on cords at the half-door of the loose-box are said to be effective, as the horse hits its head first on one brick, then on the other as it rocks.

Web   This implies the whole structure of the horse shoe, and the word is usually applied to the width of the actual shoe, e.g. 'bend upwards half the web of the toe'.

Web Martingale   *see* MARTINGALE, BIB.

Webbs, Race   *see* STIRRUP WEBS.

Wedging   *see* BEANING.

Weed   A derogatory term for a horse of poor and mean conformation and one usually lacking in stamina and carrying no flesh. Generally a Thoroughbred, or of Thoroughbred type.

Weedon (Northamptonshire)   One time headquarters of Army Cavalry training until 1940 and largely responsible for teaching the art and science of modern equitation in England.

Weedon Lane   *see* JUMPING-LANE.

Weedon Snaffle   A bit having a broad, flat and curved mouthpiece of 2 in (50 mm) wide and with eggbutt rings into which are punched slots to carry the bridle head. Its construction enables it to lie flat across the tongue and bars and to cover a greater area of sensory nerves. Now little used.

Weedy   A description of a long-legged animal with a mean body and generally unimpressive appearance. Such a horse does not stand up to work, is difficult to get—and keep—in condition, and tends to knock its legs about in fast work.

Weighing-in   Immediately after dismounting at the end of a race, every jockey must present himself to be weighed by the Clerk of the Scales (*see* WEIGHTS).

Weighing-out   Every jockey must be weighed for a specified horse by the Clerk of the Scales, at the appointed place, not less than 15 minutes before the time fixed for the race (*see* WEIGHTS).

Weight Calculation   Can be ascertained approximately by the following formula:

$$\frac{\text{Girth}^2 \times \text{Length}}{300} = \text{Total weight in lb}$$

Girth measurement to be taken around barrel in inches. Length from elbow upwards to point of buttock in inches.

Weight Carrier   A horse capable of carrying a minimum of 15 st (210 lb; 95.2 kg). Strength, bulk of frame and big limbs are watched for in the show ring, though these are worth nothing without quality, heart room and action.

Weight Cloth   A leather and felt cloth carried on a horse's back under the saddle. The outside of a weight cloth has a series of narrow flat pockets in which lead weights of ½ lb or 1 lb (0.2 or 0.4 kg) can be inserted in order to increase the jockey's weight to the required amount.

Weight For Age Race   The official definition in the Rules of Racing is 'any race which is not a handicap or a selling race'. As in practice this lends itself to contradictions it may be said to be 'an event open to horses of different ages in which the runners carry different weights according to their ages'. For this purpose the age is reckoned as dating from January 1st, and only years and not months are taken into consideration when allotting weight for age. As it is considered that the difference between the older and the younger horses becomes less as the year advances, a scale, varying with each month, has been published by the Jockey Club for the guidance of Clerks of the Course, but it is not obligatory to

make use of this. This scale was due for revision in 1974.

Weights (Forage)   Agricultural products are now sold by law by avoirdupois weight in tons, cwt, lb, etc. A bale of hay weighs approximately 50 lb (22.7 kg), a bale of straw approximately 40 lb (18.1 kg), both varying according to density.

Weights (Racing)   All horses must carry a certain weight in races either according to the conditions of the race or according to the weight allotted by the handicapper, in the case of handicaps. In flat racing the conditions of a race shall not provide for a weight of less than 7 st (98 lb; 44 kg), and in no case shall any allowance reduce this weight below 6 st 7 lb (91 lb; 41 kg). For steeplechases and hurdle races no horse shall carry less than 10 st (140 lb; 63.5 kg) except in long-distance steeplechases when the lowest weight may be 9 st 7 lb (133 lb; 59 kg). According to Rule 109 inexperienced cross-country riders can claim a special allowance in the less valuable steeplechases and hurdle races. In weighing out, a jockey includes in his weight everything carried by the horse except the jockey's skull cap, whip, bridle, plates, rings or anything worn on a horse's legs.

Weights (Show Jumping)   Under F.E.I. rules all competitors carry a minimum of 165 lb (75 kg), including saddle. This also applies under B.S.J.A. rules, but in certain competitions for Associate Members the minimum weight is 154 lb (70 kg).

Weights of Horses   A pony about 13.2 h.h. (134 cm) weighs 480–600 lb (220–300 kg); small hunter about 15 h.h. (152 cm), 814–946 lb (370–430 kg); show jumper about 16 h.h. (162 cm), 1034–1144 lb (470–520 kg); middle-weight hunter about 16.3 h.h. (165 cm), 1144–1232 lb (520–560 kg); heavy hunter about 16.3 h.h. (165 cm), 1276–1540 lb (580–700 kg). Three-fifths of the weight of a horse is distributed on the forelegs, two-fifths on the hind.

Weights on the Foot The practice of shoeing harness horses heavily, causing them to give an exaggerated bend to the knees.

Wellington Snaffle Best known of the hinge or solid cable link mouthpiece, the links are five in number, and the mouthpiece folds around the bars of the mouth.

'Well Let Down' Said of hocks, when they are long and low, and drop straight to the ground.

Well-ribbed Up A term signifying that the front or true ribs are flat, with the back or false ribs well 'sprung' or hooped behind the saddle.

Well-sprung *see* WELL-RIBBED UP.

Welsh Cob (Section D in Welsh Pony and Cob Society Stud Book) An old established breed whose virtues are known far beyond Great Britain. Its foundation is in the Welsh Mountain Pony, the history of which goes back beyond the time of record-keeping. It has had a great influence on trotting animals throughout the world and has also had an influence on the Fell Pony. As a riding cob, it stands 14–15 h.h. (142–152 cm) but there is no official height limit. It provides a good mount for all riders including the elderly. The action should be free and active. A natural and bold jumper, with strength and stamina, it makes a useful hunter for heavy and trappy country. The body is deep and strong, the legs short with powerful hocks. Perhaps the best of the breed come from Cardiganshire. A heavy type, with some feather at the heels, is found in various parts and is very impressive and powerful. *Breed Society:* The Welsh Pony and Cob Society (*see Plate* 22).

Welsh Mountain Pony (Section A in Welsh Pony and Cob Society Stud Book) One of the most popular and perhaps the most beautiful of the nine breeds forming the Mountain and Moorland group; its origin is so remote as to be incalculable. Truly indigenous to the mountains of Wales, its rough existence and ancestry produce the qualities of intelligence, pluck, soundness and endurance for which the breed is famed. Though not exceeding 12 h.h. (122 cm), it will carry adult weight without apparent effort. As a child's pony, in or out of the show ring, it is popular and successful. Mares have had much to do with producing many breeds such as polo ponies, Hackneys, hunters and Welsh Cobs. The Mountain Pony (it must not be confused with the Welsh pony, which is larger) has a small neat head, big eyes well apart, a dished face-line, the muzzle fine and tapering and soft to the touch. The neck should be of a good length and the shoulders graceful, deep and well laid (though the withers must not be pronounced), the back strong and short, with the tail set high and carried gaily. *Breed Society:* The Welsh Pony and Cob Society (*see Plate* 32).

Welsh Pony (Section B in Welsh Pony and Cob Society Stud Book) Must not be confused with the Welsh Mountain Pony (*q.v.*) or the Welsh Cob, being in fact a combination of both within the limits of 12.2 and 13.2 h.h. (124–134 cm). It makes an excellent child's pony, combining great quality with bone and substance. *Society:* The Welsh Pony and Cob Society.

Welsh Pony and Cob Society (Founded 1901) *Objects:* to encourage the breeding of Welsh Ponies and Cobs.

Welsh Pony, Cob Type (Section C in Welsh Pony and Cob Society Stud Book) Most well-known of the Welsh breeds which came from intermingling of Cob blood with that of ponies. The whole impression should be of strength for its size (not exceeding 13.2 h.h. (134 cm) but without coarseness and retaining pony appearance. An excellent ride and drive pony. *Society :* The Welsh Pony and Cob Society.

Welter Handicap   One in which the minimum weight that can be allotted is 7 st 7 lb (105 lb; 48 kg).

Welter Weight   In racing, this means a big weight.

Wentworth, Baroness Judith Anne Dorothea Blunt-Lytton (1873–1957) Renowned as a breeder of Arabian horses, and for many years, up to the time of her death, the owner of the Crabbet Park Stud at Crawley, Sussex, which she inherited from her parents, Lady Anne and Wilfred Scawen Blunt. She was a distinguished poet and writer.

Westchester Cup   The Premium International Polo Trophy for competition between England and the U.S.A. The first contest was played in 1886 at Meadowbrook in America. Losers of the best of three matches contest challenged the winners in their own country. No competition held since 1939. For results *see page* 384.

Western States Trail Ride An annual endurance ride, starting at Lake Tahoe, California, covering 100 miles (161 km) over the rugged Sierra Nevada Range, which attracts about 200 riders. The course must be completed in 24 hours, which includes three one-hour stops for veterinary checks and a 15-minute final check before the finish. The Tevis Cup goes to the entry covering the course in the fastest time and the Haggin Cup to the horse in the best condition amongst the first 10 to finish.

Weymouth Bit   This usually consists of a straight mouthpiece with a port, or it can be a straight bar or mullen mouth. The cheeks vary in length but normally correspond to the width of the mouth. The mouthpiece slides up and down, within the cheeks, a matter of half an inch or so. The bit is worn in conjunction with a thin jointed snaffle to form the double bridle.

Weymouth, Dressage   This bit is made on the German pattern with a fixed cheek, obligatory in advanced tests and with a very broad mouthpiece in which the port is slightly offset forward. The bridoon is usually, but not always, one with small eggbutt cheeks and again has a broad, flat mouthpiece. Because of the mouth construction this is a mild bit.

Whalebone   Before 1946, when the killing of the Greenland whale was prohibited by International Law, whalebone was used as the centre of good-quality whips of all sorts. It has now been replaced by fibreglass and nylon. Cheaper whips are lined with steel.

Whanghee   A yellow riding cane having rings or knots closely spaced and made from the stem of Chinese or Japanese plants allied to the bamboo.

Wheat   Indigestible to horses, as also is wheat straw.

Wheel-bar   *see* SPLINTER BAR.

Wheel Harness   Harness for the wheelers (*q.v.*), as distinct from lead harness.

Wheeler Irons   A pattern of safety stirrup having a revolving tread.

Wheelers   Team horses nearest to the vehicle, as opposed to the leaders.

Wheelwright   A man who makes wheels on wheeled vehicles.

Whelps   Unweaned hound puppies.

Whicker   *see* NICKER.

Whiffle-tree (or Whipple-tree) Another name for Swingle-tree and Bars (*q.v.*).

Whinny   A horse's call of pleasure and expectancy.

Whip, Coaching   Sometimes called a team whip, though the coaching term is 'crop'. It is made of holly and the total length is more than that of the normal driving whip. The stick is shorter than that of the latter, but the thong is long enough to reach the leaders on the hocks.

Whip, Cutting Made of fibreglass, nylon or steel, covered with gut or plaited kangaroo leather and carried mostly for racing and hacking.

Whip, Dog-leg A driving whip having a near right-angle bend in the shaft. Lightly held, the head of the thong will hang down correctly for instant use.

Whip, Hunting Incorrectly called a hunting crop, this is made of steel, cane or fibreglass, which may be covered in braided nylon, or gut, or with plaited kangaroo hide, with a thong and a silk or cord lash attached to the top end, and, at the lower end, a buckhorn handle for opening gates.

Whip (Trotting) Whalebone whip in one piece, limited in the U.S.A. to 4 ft 8 in (142 cm).

Whipcord (Cloth) A strong and durable cloth with a more pronounced rib than gabardine. It is used for riding coats or breeches and is ideal both for wear and because animal hairs do not cling to the clear surface of the cloth. It was originally made with drab and white twill, the finished twill resembling plaited whipcord, hence the name.

Whip-cord *see* LASH.

Whip Hand, 'Under the Whip' Terms signifying off-side horse of pair or team. The off-side is generally said to be under the whip, as it is in the better position to be reached easily by the whip and can therefore be kept up to work if required. It is customary to put the sluggish horses on the off-side.

Whipper-in, First The Huntsman's principal assistant.

Whipper-in, Second The Huntsman's second assistant.

Whippletrees or Whiffletrees *see* BARS.

Whip Reel A circular wooden block attached to a wall and used to hang driving whips of the quill top variety. By use of the block, the semi-circular shape at the upper end is maintained.

Whip Reel

Whirlicote A conveyance for women riders, which preceded the side-saddle. Stow's Commentaries record that 'Richard the Second, being threatened by the rebels of Kent, rode from the Tower of London to the Miles End, and with him his mother, because she was sick and weak, in a *whirlicote*'; and this is described as an ugly vehicle of four boards put together in a clumsy manner. In the following year Richard married Anne of Bohemia, who introduced riding upon side-saddles, and so 'was the riding in those whirlicotes forsaken, except at coronations and such like spectacles'.

Whisk *see* DANDY BRUSH.

Whiskey, Whisky An early form of gig with a chair body.

Whisperer A horse-whisperer, one who tames high-spirited and dangerous horses, often reckoned as savages (*see* SULLIVAN, CON).

Whistling An affection of the larynx or throat due to paralysis of the left vocal chord, whistling is a form of roaring, but with a higher note. Frequently it is the forerunner of more pronounced roaring. *Cause and treatment : see under* TRACHEOTOMY.

White Very pale colour or absence of any pigment in the hairs of the coat is designated white but in reality many white horses are simply grey horses in old age when white hairs increasing with age replace the black hairs with which the horse was born.

'White Castor'   A slang term for a white coaching hat.

'White of the Eye'   Where some part of the white sclerotic of the eye shows between the eyelids.

White Face   When the white covers the forehead and front of the face, extending laterally towards the mouth, it is described as a white face. The extension may be unilateral or bilateral (*see Plate* 21).

White Flag (Show Jumping)   This is used to show left-hand limit of the obstacle to be jumped.

White-horse   The name applied to the figure of a horse on a hillside, which is formed by the removal of the turf to show the underlying chalk. There are several of these to be seen in England, the most famous perhaps being at Uffington, Berks. It is traditionally supposed that this commemorates Alfred the Great's victory at Ashdown in A.D. 871. It is likely that all commemorate some event deemed worthy of lasting recognition.

White Legs   An old doggerel, of which there are many versions, on white-legged horses:

Four white legs, keep him not a day,
Three white legs, send him far away,
Two white legs, give him to a friend,
One white leg, keep him to the end.

White Line   The band of soft horn secreted by the papillae and found on the lower border of the sensitive laminae, this is the bond of union between the wall and the sole, and its presence indicates the amount of wall the farrier has in which to place the nails. Nails may enter the white line but must not penetrate beyond it.

Whole Coloured   Where there are no hairs of any colour, other than the main colour of the horse, on the body, head or limbs.

Whorl   A circle or irregular setting of coat hairs.

Whyte-Melville, George John (1821–1878)   A sporting novelist, poet and soldier. The most quoted (with Adam Lindsay Gordon) among the Victorian poets of the horse and the chase and an authority on the science of hunting. One of his most quoted poems is 'The Old Grey Mare'. He met with a fatal accident while hunting.

Wid   A dealer's term, little used now, indicating that a horse is unsound in wind.

Wide Behind   When both hind legs from the feet to the quarters are separated beyond the normal.

Wild Goose Chase   A type of race in the seventeenth century, in which the riders, after covering 240 yd (219 m), had to follow and keep behind the leader. He could take any course he liked and the others had to follow him and one another at agreed distances (i.e. two lengths, or three lengths). Triers (judges), who rode alongside, whipped those that transgressed. The chase, in its equal spacings, resembled the flight of wild geese.

Wild Horse *(Equus przevalsii przevalskii poljakoff)*   More correctly known as the Asiatic or Mongolian wild horse, it was discovered in 1881 by the Russian explorer Professor M. M. Przevalski and is considered to be the ancestor of all living breeds of horses and ponies. These horses had been known from time immemorial to inhabit an area some 200 × 100 miles (5178 km²) in northern Sinkiang—Mongolia, being referred to by early travellers. Today the Asiatic Wild Horse measures about 12.2 h.h. to 14.2 h.h. (124–144 cm in height). Bay/dun is the predominating colour, often with a dark dorsal stripe; it is of compact build with strong legs, and a thick neck. The eye is placed high up in the head, the ears short and pointed. The mane short and upright and the lower half of the tail, only, covered with thick black hair. The Survival Service Committee is actively trying to prevent the extinction of this ancient breed and the governments of the U.S.S.R., China and Mongolia have forbidden any further hunting. About 200 of the horses are now to be found throughout the world, many in zoos including Whipsnade. The largest herd is at Prague and a stud book is kept (*see Plate* 32).

Wilson Snaffle A variety of bits, all of which have four rings, come under this heading.

Wind A hound is never said to smell a fox, but to wind it.

Wind, Testing For To test for soundness in wind, gallop the horse on a circle, first on one rein and then on the other. The defect is best detected from the saddle. Alternatively, listen carefully at the nostrils when the horse is halted. The fitter the horse, the less noise it will make (*see* GRUNTING).

Wind, Thick in the This often occurs when a horse is gross and fat. In this condition, an animal should not be given severe or fast work, for this may lead to whistling (*q.v.*). A thick wind may be the sequel to bronchitis, or may be a temporary condition, but so long as it persists it is an unsoundness.

Wind, to Obsolete term applied to blowing the horn.

Windgalls *Symptoms:* soft, round, painless swellings which appear above and behind the fetlock joint on both sides of the limb. They are unsightly but otherwise of little consequence. *Cause:* strain and overwork. *Treatment:* rest.

Windsor Greys The popular name given to the horses at the Royal Mews, Buckingham Palace, and which are so familiar in all State processions. George I, because of his interest in the famous Hanover Stud, introduced Hanoverian Cream horses into England, and they were used as Royal carriage horses. Later, before World War I, a small stud was in being in Windsor, having been started from stallions and mares supplied from the Hanover Stud. The war interfered with the supply of stock and the stud gradually diminished, until it was finally disposed of. Some of the horses were sold, some were given to cavalry regiments, and some were destroyed. After the war, grey horses were bought for the Royal carriages, and five were presented by the Queen of the Netherlands. The term 'Windsor Greys', frequently used to refer to these horses, is incorrect, as there is no such breed. The expression arose from press and public references to the 'horses from Windsor' when they appeared in London on various State occasions, later becoming 'Greys from Windsor' and then 'Windsor Greys' (*see Plate* 10).

Windsor Horse Show, Royal Founded in 1944 by the Windsor Horse Show Club (*see Plate* 31).

Windsucker A horse may, for no apparent reason, draw or suck in air and swallow it with a gulping sound. This is a disagreeable and harmful vice, and an unsoundness. *Treatment:* feed from the ground, remove all fittings from the box, and put a muzzle on the horse. This vice is similar to crib biting (*q.v.*).

Windsucker's Bit A straight, tubular mouth with holes pierced through it.

Wingey A north country term to describe a horse of uncertain temperament.

Wings Extensions at the sides of an obstacle in show-jumping.

Winkers *see* BLINKERS.

'Winston' The chestnut gelding owned by the Mounted Branch of the

Metropolitan Police Force and ridden for several years by Queen Elizabeth II (and also when she was Princess Elizabeth) at the ceremony of Trooping the Colour. Winston was by 'Erehwemos' and, as a seven-year-old, came from Yorkshire in 1944 to the Mounted Branch Training Establishment at Imber Court, Surrey. His fine presence and perfect temperament earned him national popularity and he is commemorated for posterity on the Coronation Year crown piece and on the Great Seal of the County Palatinate of Lancaster where Queen Elizabeth is depicted riding 'Winston'. He was killed in a street accident in 1957.

Wintering Out   Leaving a horse unstabled throughout the winter.

Wire   In a fence, wire constitutes a grave menace to all who follow hounds mounted, whether it is plain or barbed.

Wire-cutters   These may be of varying pattern, and are carried in a leather holster on the front of the saddle and used during a hunt for cutting any wire. Cutters should be carried only by Hunt Officials, and be used with great discretion.

Wire Fund   In some hunts a cap of a small amount is taken from all mounted and unmounted followers to provide money for the removal, temporarily or permanently, of wire in fences.

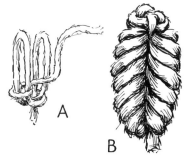

A. *Method of making wisp*
B. *Completed wisp*

Wisp   A grooming device made of rope, hay or straw, coiled in the form of a figure of eight to make a pad. Used to improve the skin and coat, to stimulate circulation and form muscle (*see Plate 29*).

Wither Pad   Usually consists of two pads of knitted wool or other soft yielding material, joined together and placed under the saddle, one at each side. This method, which leaves an air passage, is preferable to the use of one pad doubled up over the wither. Recommended for emergency and not for permanent use. Generally denotes that the horse is carrying a badly fitting saddle. Admirable for the prevention or relief of wither pressure. Used to great advantage if there is any likelihood of the withers being wrung.

Withers   These commence at the dip at the base of the crest line of the neck, should be reasonably high and pronounced at the uppermost point of the shoulder, and should slope away gradually into the back. Good lean withers on a saddle horse are most desirable, as they ensure correct placing of the saddle.

Withers, Fistulous   An abscess above the vertebrae at the withers, extending down between the shoulder blades. *Cause:* a blow, or a bite from another horse, or an ill-fitting collar or saddle. *Symptoms:* pain followed by swelling. In most cases the swelling bursts, and the skin may heal, but this will be only temporary, for the abscess is bound to recur owing to the difficulty of draining it. *Treatment:* this is a very serious condition, and a veterinary surgeon should be called. He may be able to remove all diseased tissue by operation.

Withers, Pinched   Withers are said to be pinched when the saddle grips, rather than lies, on them.

Withers, Wrung   An old term for withers which are wrung or bruised by an ill-fitting saddle, although the skin is not broken.

Witney Panel   see SAUMUR PANEL.

Wobbler   Victim, usually a young horse, of a condition in which varying degrees of paralysis, usually of the hindquarters are apparent. The cause is still unknown.

Wolf Teeth   Rudimentary teeth which, when present, occur in front of the upper and lower molar teeth on either side of the jaw, especially the upper one. Suggestions that they are the cause of bad eyesight, unthriftiness, shying and bolting can be dismissed. The best opinions seem to agree that they need not be removed.

Wolstenholme, Dean, Senr (1757–1837). **Wolstenholme, Dean, Jnr** (1798–1882)   Father and son, the Wolstenholmes were both very important and admirable painters of sport—particularly hunting—whose works are rated very highly for their representations of the old English sporting scene. Many beautiful prints after them show a great similarity in technique, and in the case of original paintings there is sometimes doubt as to who was the painter.

Women Jockeys   see LADIES' RACES.

Woodland   A very large covert, or series of coverts (see COVERT).

Wootton, John (c. 1677–1765)   Talented sporting artist who also painted landscapes and battle scenes. Received training from Jan Wyck, the Dutch-born artist, and under the patronage of the Second Duke of Beaufort, studied in Italy. Painted huge hunting scenes for such stately homes as Althorp and Longleat and was also much in demand for portraits of the racehorse of the day.

Working Canter   Term introduced in 1974 into dressage tests, taking the place of the ordinary canter.

Working Hunter   Show Class for horses 15.2 h.h. (154 cm) and over, to be judged 40 per cent for jumping performance, 60 per cent as for Hunter Classes. Fences to be a minimum of six in number and a maximum of 3 ft 9 in (110 cm) in height.

Working Hunter Pony   Judged in the Show Ring on 50 per cent marks jumping, 20 per cent marks style and maners, 30 per cent marks type, conformation and action.

Working Trot   Term introduced in 1974 into dressage tests, taking the place of the ordinary trot.

'Workman'   A good coachman (colloquial).

World Arabian Horse Organization Created in 1970 with the object of acquiring and promoting information in all countries concerning the Arabian breed and its derivatives, to safeguard their interests and to maintain throughout the world the purity of the blood of horses of the Arabian breed.

World Championship Three-Day Event   Held every four years. For results see page 382.

World Dressage Championship for results see page 378.

World Driving Championship   A competition in three phases taking four days. 1 Presentation; 2 Dressage; 3 Marathon; 4 Obstacle Driving. First held at Munster, West Germany in 1972. For results see page 379.

World Ladies' Show Jumping Championship (F.E.I. Rules)   For results see page 407.

World Men's Show Jumping Championship (F.E.I. Rules)   For results see page 407.

Worley, William   Born in 1765, Worley had charge of the Royal Paddocks at Hampton Court during the reigns of George IV and William IV, and during the lifetime of Queen Adelaide.

Worms   Horses, particularly when young, suffer frequently from worm infestation, and horses grazing together on a limited acreage should be dosed at regular intervals under veterinary supervision. The commonest worms to cause emaciation and anaemia are the strongyles. Of these there are several varieties, but the most common are *Strongylus tetracanthus*, the red worm, usually about 10–15 mm in length, and *Strongylus armatus*, a greyish worm, rounded and about 3–4 cm. The latter may pass their larval stage in the arteries supplying the intestines and cause colic and diarrhoea. Ascarids are larger round worms, possibly 4 in (10 cm) in length, inhabiting the large bowel and seldom causing noticeable effects. Tapeworms are not common but those in horses are flattened, about 1–2 cm in width and 5–6 cm in length. Different kinds of worms require different treatment and this is best administered by a veterinary surgeon.

Worry, to   Killing by biting and shaking of the quarry by hounds.

Wrangler (U.S.A.)   A cowhand or cowboy.

Würtemberg   Hardy   warmblood German horse bred principally at Marbach. Evolved from admixture of several breeds including Arab, Oldenburg, Nonius and Anglo-Norman, resulting in a useful all-purpose cob.

Wykeham Saddle Panel   An arrangement of shaped felt pads which can be removed or added to, in order to vary the fitting.

* X *

Xanthos   The colour given to the chariot horses of the Greeks, probably chestnut, yellow or dun.

'Xanthus'   With 'Balios' he drew the chariot of Achilles. Both horses were immortal and 'Xanthus' was given the power of speech and foretold the death of Achilles.

Xenophon (*circa* 430–350 B.C.)   An Athenian soldier, writer, historian and horseman, who wrote *Hipparchikos*—The Cavalry Commander—and *Cynegeticus*—a treatise on hunting (on foot) with and without dogs. He led the Ten Thousand Greeks from Mesopotamia to the Black Sea after the defeat of Cyrus at Cunaxa in 401 B.C., which he has described in the *Anabasis*. Most of the principles of horsemanship and stable management which he propounded hold good to this day.

'Xerxes'   One of Mr Jorrocks' hunters, 'a great rat-tailed brown', sold to Captain Doleful and the subject of a law suit. When driven in tandem he took the lead in front of 'Arterxerxes' (*q.v.*) (*see also* JORROCKS, 'HANDLEY CROSS', R. S. SURTEES).

Y.S.R. Young Stock Register.

Y Mouth Snaffle A snaffle having a double-jointed mouthpiece. Each mouthpiece has a long and a short side. The joint of the top one is on the near side, and that of the bottom on the off side. A severe bit. Known also as a W mouth snaffle.

Yaboo An Afghan pony.

Yamoote *see* PERSIAN HORSE.

'Yankee' (Racing) A bet on four selections which makes six doubles, four trebles and an accumulator (*q.v.*). It may be each way or win only, as desired.

Yard An open space adjoining and used in connection with stables. The word is also used comprehensively to express the business or premises of a horse dealer; a dealer's yard.

'Yard of Tin', 'Three Feet of Tin' The horn used by guards of the old Royal Mail Coaches (*see* COACH-HORN). Exactly 36 in (91.4 cm) long.

Yaud An old mare, or a decrepit horse.

Yawing The action of a horse which, when ridden, fights with its head to reach outwards and downwards (*see* GRAKLE NOSEBAND).

Yearling A colt or filly having attained the first, but not the second anniversary of its birth. Alternatively, a race-horse, from January 1st of first year of birth, until December 31st of same year.

Yearling Bit A name given to a Tattersall's bit, but more often to a straight or jointed breaking bit with keys.

Yearling Headcollar A light headcollar ⅞ in or 1 in (19 or 25 mm) in width with adjustment at head, nose and throat.

Yeld A Scottish term applied to brood mares which are not in foal (*see* EILD).

Yellow-bounder A hired post-chaise usually painted bright yellow.

Yellows *see* JAUNDICE.

Yerk, to To lash or strike out with the heels; also to crack a whip (Dialect).

'Yoi' (Hunting) 'Yoirouse 'im', 'Yoi wind 'im' are huntsmen's cheer to encourage hounds.

Yorksman A substitute for Gloster Bars (*q.v.*), using two corn sacks and a rolled blanket with a surcingle running its length. Sometimes used when riding a young horse for first time.

Yorkshire Boot A protective boot or covering for the fetlock to prevent injury to a horse liable to brush. Made from a piece of Kersey horse clothing, 12 in by 9 in (30 × 23 cm), it is wrapped round the fetlock and tied above that joint with tape, the margin above this being folded down over the tape to form a double protective fold over the joint itself (*see* BRUSHING, BRUSHING BOOTS).

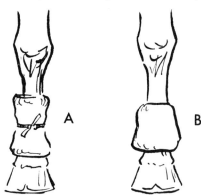

Yorkshire Boot

Yorkshire Coach Horse This breed originated in the East Riding of Yorkshire and for a great number of years was indistinguishable from the Cleveland Bay (*q.v.*). At the end of the eighteenth century the Yorkshire Coach Horse emerged as the demand for a bigger and more flashy type of harness horse for the many elegant vehicles appearing in the fashionable part of London increased. The Thoroughbred was used on the Cleveland Bay and there was also some infusion of Arab and Barb blood. Standing about 16.1–16.3 h.h. (163–165 cm), bay and brown the predominating colours. A long body on comparatively short legs gave the horse the appearance of being close to the ground. The Yorkshire Coach Horse disappeared about the middle of the present century.

Yorkshire Gallop   A gallop which is between a half speed (*q.v.*) and a trial.

Yorkshire Halter   A good type of hemp halter having a throat latch. It cannot pull over against an eye.

Young Entry   Before cub-hunting, young hounds are said to be 'unentered'. During cub-hunting they are taught to hunt the fox and nothing else, and at the end of cub hunting are 'entered', at which time they are about 18 months old.

Y'sabella   *see* ISABELLA.

* Z *

Zebra   Related to both the horse and the ass, the zebra more closely resembles the latter in several characteristics, notably size of the ears, and is white in colour with black stripes, vertical on the body and horizontal on the legs. Found only in Africa from Ethiopia through the grasslands of Central Africa, to the mountainous regions of Cape Province, and is also to be found in Angola. Uncertain of temper, even when trained from its earliest days, the Zebra is difficult to domesticate. There are three main types: *Grevy's*, the largest of the species averaging about 13 h.h. (132 cm), inhabits certain regions of Ethiopia, Somaliland and northern Kenya. It is distinguished by its enormous ears and stripes broader on the neck than on the body. The *Mountain* is found in the highlands of Cape Province and Botswana. It has more ass-like ears than Grevy's, shows rather more breeding and averages 10 h.h. (101 cm). *Burchell's Zebra* is a larger animal than the Mountain type but has smaller and completely white ears, a longer mane and fuller tail. It is found on the plains north of the Orange River extending to north-east Africa.

'Zebra Marks'   Striping on the limbs, neck, withers or quarters of horses (*see Plate* 21).

Zeeland Horse   The prototype of the Zeeland Horse, a product of the Netherlands, goes back to the earliest times. The Zeeland Horse has been in great demand since the Middle Ages; it has proved to be of great use in agricultural work, and equally successful in horse-artillery. It is said to bear cold and heat, and to show great adaptability under all circumstances; it is quiet and meek but possessed of great stamina. The main characteristics are the snub-nosed head with straight profile; flat forehead; large intelligent eyes; short ears, pointing forward; broad deep chest; very muscular loins, with flanks wide apart; plenty of bone with excellent feet and good carriage.

Zemaituka   A tough breed of ancient origin, standing from 13 to 15 h.h. (132–152 cm) and indigenous to the wide grasslands of western Lithuania. The ancestral roots ˜seem to be the Tartar Pony of the Steppes (Przevalski or Mongolian) and the Arab, the latter having refreshed the breed even down to recent times. The Zemaituka is renowned for staying power and almost indestructible legs and feet. It can live as frugally as any horse to be found. The prevailing colour is dun, with light mane and tail. A compact, sturdy, and well-made pony, full of latent fire and energy. Both the Lithuanian and Latvian breeds of harness horses are based on the Zemaituka.

Zig-zag   A timber jump with short units of posts and rails placed at angles to each other. The horse jumps either over the point of the 'V', or over the angled sides.

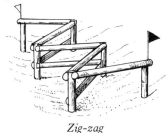

Zig-zag

Zmudzin   A Polish pony (*see* KONIK).

RESULTS SECTION

* * *

Dressage	378
Driving	378
Harness	379
Horse Trials	380
Polo	382
Racing	384
Show Jumping	403

DRESSAGE CHAMPIONSHIP RESULTS

European Dressage Championship
1973 *Team:* W. Germany
      Individual: Dr R. Klimke, 'Mehmed',
      W. Germany
1974 *No competition*
1975
1976
1977

European Junior Dressage Championship
1973 *Team:* W. Germany
1974 *No competition*
1975
1976
1977

Olympic Games Grand Prix de Dressage (*see also page* 229)
1912 *Team: No competition*
      Individual: Count G. Bonde, 'Emperor', Sweden
1920 *Team: No competition*
      Individual: Capt Lundblad, 'Uno', Sweden
1924 *Team: No competition*
      Individual: General Linder, 'Piccolomini', Sweden
1928 *Team:* Germany
      Individual: Baron von Langen, 'Draufgaenger', Germany
1932 *Team:* France
      Individual: Comdt Lesage, 'Taine', France
1936 *Team:* Germany
      Individual: Lt Pollay, 'Kronos', Germany
1940 *No competition*
1944 *No competition*
1948 *Team:* France
      Individual: Capt H. M. Moser, 'Hummer', Switzerland
1952 *Team:* Sweden
      Individual: H. St. Cyr, 'Master Rufus', Sweden

1956 *Team:* Sweden
      Individual: H. St. Cyr, 'Juli', Sweden
1960 *No team awards given*
      Individual: Sergei Filatov, 'Absent', U.S.S.R.
1964 *Team:* W. Germany
      Individual: H. Chammartin, 'Woermann', Switzerland
1968 *Team:* W. Germany
      Individual: Ivan Kisimov, 'Ikhor', U.S.S.R.
1972 *Team:* Russia
      Individual: Liselott Linsenhoff, 'Piaf', W. Germany
1976

Pan American Games Dressage Championship (*see also page* 235)
1951 *Team:* Chile
      Individual: Capt J. Larrain, Chile
1955 *Team: Not held*
      Individual: Capt H. Clavel, Chile
1959 *Team:* Chile
      Individual: Patricia Galvin, U.S.A.
1963 *Team: Not held*
      Individual: Patricia Galvin, U.S.A.
1967 *Team:* Chile
      Individual: Kyra Downton, U.S.A.
1971 *Team:* Canada
      Individual: Christilot Hanson, Canada
1975
1979

World Dressage Championship
1974 *Team:* W. Germany
      Individual: Dr R. Klimke, 'Mehmed', W. Germany

World Junior Dressage Championship
1974 *Team:* W. Germany
      Individual: M. Fassbender, 'Veneziano', W. Germany

DRIVING CHAMPIONSHIP RESULTS

European Driving Championship (F.E.I. Rules)
1971 *Team:* Hungary
      Individual: I. Abonye, Hungary
1972 *No competition*

1973 *Team:* Switzerland
      Individual: A. Dubey, Switzerland
1974 *No competition*
1975
1976
1977

World Driving Championship
(*see also page* 371)
1972 *Team:* Gt Britain
Individual: A. Dubey, Switzerland

1973 *No competition*
1974 *Team:* Gt Britain
Individual: S. Fülöp, Hungary

HARNESS CHAMPIONSHIP RESULTS

Hackney Harness Horse Championship
1900 Mel Valley Princess
1903 Forest King
1904 Heathfield Squire
1905 Fylde Sabrinetta
1906 Menella
1907 Coker's Rosador
1908 Radiant
1909 Authority
1910 Londesborough
1911 Gaythorne
1912 Argo
1913 King of the Air
1914 Gay Boy
1915 Adbolton Black Prince
1916 Adbolton Black Prince
1917 *No Award*
1918 *No Classes*
1919 *No Classes*
1920 Park Carnation
1921 Dark Legend
1922 Knight Commander
1923 Knight Commander
1924 Glenavon Charm
1925 Edgware Duke
1926 Stella Vane
1927 Holland Lavendula
1928 Knight Batchelor
1929 A.1's Conquest
1930 Modern Maid
1931 Modern Maid
1932 Modern Maid
1933 Modern Maid
1934 Fleetwood Viking
1935 Fleetwood Viking
1936 Nork Spotlight
1937 Fleetwood Viking
1938 Nork Spotlight
1939 Nork Monoplane
1946 Black Magic of Nork
1947 Black Magic of Nork
1948 Basing Belle
1949 Holywell Florette
1950 Holywell Florette
1951 Holywell Florette
1952 Holywell Florette
1953 Walton Diplomat
1954 Hurstwood Lonely Lady
1955 Hurstwood Superlative
1956 Hurstwood Superlative
1957 Hurstwood Superlative

1958 Hurstwood Superlative
1959 Hurstwood Superlative
1960 Craigweil Maybole
1961 Craigweil Maybole
1962 Marden Midas
1963 Sherwood Forest Queen
1964 Marden Midas
1965 Craigweil Maybole
1966 Craigweil Maybole
1967 Outwood Florescent
1968 Outwood Florescent
1969 Outwood Florescent
1970 Outwood Florescent
1971 Outwood Florescent
1972 Outwood Florescent
1973 Outwood Florescent
1974 Brookacres Light Mist
1975
1976
1977

Hackney Harness Pony Championship
1903 Mel Valley Princess
1904 Ryburn Masher
1905 Mel Valley Princess
1906 Tissington Kit Cat
1907 Tissington Kit Cat
1908 Mel Valley's Wonder
1909 District Sensation
1910 Mel Valley's Masterpiece
1911 First Edition
1912 Mel Valley's Flame
1913 Kitty Melbourne
1914 Tissington Bauble
1915 Tissington Bauble
1916 Tissington Bauble
1917 Tissington Bauble
1918 *No Classes*
1919 *No Classes*
1920 Axholrne Venus
1921 Axholme Venus
1922 Miss Freda
1923 Axholme Venus
1924 Miss Freda
1925 Penwortham Claudius
1926 Billet Doux
1927 Billet Doux
1928 Billet Doux
1929 Jix
1930 Eastertide
1931 Nork Magnet

Hackney Harness Pony Championship (contd)	
1932 Nork Magnet	1957 Highstone Nicholas
1933 Barcroft Belle	1958 Highstone Nicholas
1934 Nork Magnet	1959 Highstone Nicholas
1935 Nork Magnet	1960 Highstone Nicholas
1936 Barcroft Belle	1961 Highstone Nicholas
1937 Onyx Zenophen	1962 Highstone Nicholas
1938 Cassilis High and Mighty	1963 Marden Finality
1939 Cassilis High and Mighty	1964 Marden Little Nick . .
1946 Harlock Chiquita	1965 Marden Little Nick
1947 Harlock Chiquita	1966 Marden Finality
1948 Harlock Chiquita	1967 Vulcan Sir Richard
1949 Bossy	1968 Vulcan Sir Richard
1950 Bossy	1969 Vulcan Sir Richard
1951 Bossy	1970 Marden Little Swell
1952 Hurstwood Autocrat	1971 Marden Finality
1953 Oaklands Parader	1972 Marden Finality
1954 Oakwell Sir James	1973 Marden Finality
1955 Oakwell Sir James	1974 Marden Finality
1956 Oakwell Sir James	1975
	1976
	1977

HORSE TRIALS RESULTS (THREE-DAY EVENTS)
(see also page 164)

Badminton Horse Trials
1949 Mr J. Shedden, 'Golden Willow'
1950 Capt J. A. Collings, 'Remus'
1951 Capt H. Schwarzenbach,
    'Vae Victus', Switzerland
1952 Capt M. A. Q. Darley, 'Emily Little'
1953 Maj L. Rook, 'Starlight'
1954 Miss M. Hough, 'Bambi'
1955 Maj F. W. C. Weldon, 'Kilbarry'
1956 Lt-Col F. W. C. Weldon, 'Kilbarry'
1957 Miss Sheila Willcox,
    'High and Mighty'
1958 Miss Sheila Willcox,
    'High and Mighty'
1959 Mrs Sheila Waddington (Willcox),
    'Airs and Graces'
1960 Mr Bill Roycroft, 'Our Solo', Australia
1961 Mr Lawrence Morgan, 'Salad Days',
    Australia
1962 Miss Anneli Drummond-Hay,
    'Merely-A-Monarch'
1963 Cancelled. Owing to weather only a
    one-day event held
1964 Capt J. R. Templer,
    'M'Lord Connolly'
1965 Maj E. A. Boylan, 'Durlas Eile'
1966 Cancelled owing to weather
1967 Miss C. Ross-Taylor, 'Jonathan'
1968 Miss Jane Bullen, 'Our Nobby'
1969 Mr Richard Walker, 'Pasha'
1970 Mr Richard Meade, 'The Poacher'
1971 Lt Mark Phillips, 'Great Ovation'

1972 Lt Mark Phillips, 'Great Ovation'
1973 Miss L. Prior-Palmer, 'Be Fair'
1974 Capt Mark Phillips, 'Columbus'
1975
1976
1977

Burghley Horse Trials
1961 Miss Anneli Drummond-Hay,
    'Merely-A-Monarch'
1962 No competition (European
    Championship)
1963 Capt H. Freeman-Jackson,
    'St. Finbarr'
1964 Richard Meade, 'Barberry'
1965 Capt J. J. Beale, 'Victoria Bridge'
1966 No competition (World
    Championship)
1967 Miss Lorna Sutherland, 'Popadom'
1968 Miss Sheila Willcox, 'Fair & Square'
1969 Miss Gillian Watson, 'Shaitan'
1970 Miss Judy Bradwell, 'Don Camillo'
1971 No competition (European
    Championship)
1972 Miss Janet Hodgson, 'Larkspur'
1973 Capt. Mark Phillips, 'Maid Marion'
1974 No competition (World
    Championship)
1975
1976
1977

European Championship—
Three-day Event
1953 *Team:* Gt Britain
 Individual: Maj A. L. Rook,
 'Starlight', Gt Britain
1954 *Team:* Gt Britain
 Individual: Mr. A. E. Hill, 'Crispin',
 Gt Britain
1955 *Team:* Gt Britain
 Individual: Maj F. W. C. Weldon,
 'Kilbarry', Gt Britain
1956 *No competition*
1957 *Team:* Gt Britain
 Individual: Miss Sheila Willcox,
 'High and Mighty', Gt Britain
1958 *No competition*
1959 *Team:* Germany
 Individual: Maj. H. Schwarzenbach,
 'Burn Trout', Switzerland
1960 *No competition*
1961 *No competition*
1962 *Team:* U.S.S.R.
 Individual: Capt J. R. Templer,
 'M'Lord Connolly', Gt Britain
1963 *No competition*
1964 *No competition*
1965 *Team:* U.S.S.R.
 Individual: M. Babierecki, 'Volt',
 Poland
1966 *No competition*
1967 *Team:* Gt Britain
 Individual: Maj E. A. Boylan,
 'Durlas Eile', Eire
1968 *No competition*
1969 *Team:* Gt Britain
 Individual: Miss M. Gordon-Watson,
 'Cornishman V', Gt Britain
1970 *No competition (World
 Championship)*
1971 *Team:* Gt Britain
 Individual: H.R.H. Princess Anne,
 'Doublet', Gt Britain
1972 *No competition*
1973 *Team:* W. Germany
 Individual: A. Evdokimov, 'Jeger',
 U.S.S.R.
1974 *No competition (World
 Championship)*
1975
1976
1977

European Junior Championship—
Three-day Event
1967 *No team placing*
 Individual: A. Sonchon,
 'Roi d'Asturie', France

1968 *Team:* France
 Individual: R. Walker, 'Pasha',
 Gt Britain
1969 *Team:* U.S.S.R.
 Individual: H. Bolten,
 'Lausbub XIII', W. Germany
1970 *Team:* W. Germany
 Individual: N. Barkander, 'Pegasus',
 Sweden
1971 *Team:* Gt Britain
 Individual: C. Brooke, 'Olive Oyl',
 Gt Britain
1972 *Team:* Gt Britain
 Individual: B. Clement, 'Quel Pich',
 France
1973 *Team:* Gt Britain
 Individual: Virginia Holgate,
 'Dubonnet', Gt Britain
1974 *Team:* W. Germany
 Individual: Miss S. Ker, 'Peer Gynt',
 Gt Britain
1975
1976
1977

Harewood Horse Trials
1953 Miss V. I. Machin-Goodall, 'Neptune'
1954 Miss P. Molteno, 'Carmena'
1955 Lt-Col F. W. C. Weldon, 'Kilbarry'
1956 Miss Sheila Willcox,
 'High and Mighty'
1957 Mr I H. Dudgeon, 'Charleville'
1958 Herr Ottokar Pohlmann,
 'Polarfuchs', W. Germany
1959 *No competition (European
 Championships)*
1960 *No competition
 (For subsequent results see* Burghley
 Horse Trials)

Olympic Games Three-Day Event
(*see also page* 229)
1912 *Team:* Sweden
 Individual: Lt A. Nordlander,
 'Lady Artist', Sweden
1920 *Team:* Sweden
 Individual: Count Moerner,
 'Germania', Sweden
1924 *Team:* Holland
 Individual: Lt Voort van Zijp,
 'Silver Piece', Holland
1928 *Team:* Holland
 Individual: Lt Pahud de Mortanges,
 'Marcroix', Holland
1932 *Team:* U.S.A.
 Individual: Lt Pahud de Mortanges,
 'Marcroix', Holland

Olympic Games Three-Day Event (contd)

1936 *Team:* Germany
Individual: Capt Stubbendorf, 'Nurmi', W. Germany
1940 *No competition*
1944 *No competition*
1948 *Team:* U.S.A.
Individual: Capt B. M. Chevallier, 'Aiglonne', France
1952 *Team:* Sweden
Individual: H. G. von Blixen-Finecke, 'Jubal', Sweden
1956 *Team:* Gt Britain
Individual: P. Kastenman, 'Illuster', Sweden
1960 *Team:* Australia
Individual: Lawrence Morgan, 'Salad Days', Australia
1964 *Team:* Italy
Individual: M. Checcolli, 'Surbean', Italy
1968 *Team:* Gt Britain
Individual: Capt Jean-Jacques Guyon, 'Pitou', France
1972 *Team:* Gt Britain
Individual: Richard Meade, 'Lauriston', Gt Britain
1976

Pan American Games Three-Day Event
(*see also page* 235)

1951 *Team:* Argentina
Individual: Capt Julio C. Sagasta, Argentina
1955 *Team:* Mexico
Individual: Walter Staley Jr, U.S.A.
1959 *Team:* Canada
Individual: Michael Page, U.S.A.
1963 *Team:* U.S.A.
Individual: Michael Page, U.S.A.
1967 *Team:* U.S.A.
Individual: Michael Plumb, U.S.A.
1971 *Team:* Canada
Individual: Manuel Mendevil, Mexico
1975
1979

World Championship— Three-Day Event

1966 *Team:* Eire
Individual: C. Moratorio, 'Chalan', Argentina
1970 *Team:* Gt Britain
Individual: Miss M. Gordon-Watson, 'Cornishman V', Gt Britain
1974 *Team:* U.S.A.
Individual: B. Davidson, 'Irish Cap', U.S.A.
1978

POLO RESULTS

Coronation Cup
1974 U.S.A.

Hurlingham Polo Association Medium Championship (County Cup)
1967 Buccaneers
1968 Buccaneers
1969 Jersey Lilies
1970 Lushill
1971 San Flamingo
1972 Los Locos
1973 San Flamingo
1974 San Flamingo
1975
1976
1977

Hurlingham Polo Association Low-goal Championship (Junior County Cup)
1967 Windsor Park
1968 Tidworth
1969 Cowdray Park
1970 Cheshire

1971 'La Ema'
1972 Kerfield
1973 Rhinefield
1974 Langley Priors
1975
1976
1977

Polo Championship Cup
1876 Royal Horse Guards
1877 Monmouthshire tied with Tyros
1878 Monmouthshire
1879 Hurlingham
1880 Ranelagh
1881 Sussex
1882 Sussex
1883 Sussex
1884 Freebooters
1885 Sussex
1886 Freebooters
1887 Freebooters
1888 Sussex
1889 Sussex
1890 Sussex

Polo Championship Cup (contd)

1891	Sussex
1892	Sussex
1893	Sussex
1894	Freebooters
1895	Freebooters
1896	Freebooters
1897	Rugby
1898	Rugby
1899	Rugby
1900	Old Cantabs
1901	Rugby
1902	Freebooters
1903	Rugby
1904	Old Cantabs
1905	Roehampton
1906	Roehampton
1907	Freebooters
1908	Old Cantabs
1909	Roehampton
1910	Old Cantabs
1911	Eton
1912	Old Cantabs
1913	Quidnuncs
1914	Old Cantabs
1915–18	*No tournament*
1919	Freebooters
1920	Freebooters
1921	Freebooters
1922	Argentine Federation
1923	Robots
1924	Eastcott
1925	Eton
1926	Harlequins
1927	Hurricanes
1928	Hurricanes
1929	El Gordo
1930	Hurricanes
1931	Merchiston
1932	Osmaston
1933	Jaipur
1934	Aurora, U.S.A.
1935	Kashmir
1936	Templeton, U.S.A.
1937	Goulburn, Australia
1938	Texas Rangers, U.S.A.
1939	Jaguars

This Championship Cup ceased to be competed for at the outbreak of the Second World War. Since then its place has been taken by the **Cowdray Park Open Gold Cup.**

1956	Los Indios
1957	Windsor Park
1958	Cowdray Park
1959	Casarejo
1960	Casarejo
1961	Cowdray Park
1962	Cowdray Park
1963	La Vulci
1964	Jersey Lilies
1965	Jersey Lilies
1966	Windsor Park
1967	Woolmers Park
1968	Pimms
1969	Windsor Park
1970	Boca Raton
1971	Pimms
1972	Pimms
1973	Stowell Park
1974	Stowell Park
1975	
1976	
1977	

Polo Inter-Regimental Tournament

1878	5th Lancers
1879	5th Lancers
1880	16th Lancers
1881	16th Lancers
1882	5th Lancers
1883	7th Hussars
1884	7th Hussars
1885	7th Hussars
1886	7th Hussars
1887	9th Lancers
1888	10th Lancers
1889	9th Lancers
1890	9th Lancers
1891	9th Lancers
1892	13th Hussars
1893	10th Hussars
1894	13th Hussars
1895	13th Hussars
1896	9th Lancers
1897	Inniskillings
1898	Inniskillings
1899	7th Hussars
1900–2	*No tournament*
1903	17th Lancers
1904	17th Lancers
1905	Inniskillings
1906	20th Hussars
1907	20th Hussars
1908	11th Hussars
1909	11th Hussars
1910	Royal Horse Guards
1911	4th Dragoon Guards
1912	Royal Horse Guards
1913	15th Hussars
1914	12th Lancers
1915–19	*No tournament*
1920	17th Lancers
1921	17th Lancers
1922	17th Lancers
1923	17th/21st Lancers
1924	17th/21st Lancers

Polo Inter-Regimental Tournament (contd)
1925 17th/21st Lancers
1926 17th/21st Lancers
1927 Royal Artillery
1928 17th/21st Lancers
1929 17th/21st Lancers
1930 17th/21st Lancers
1931 Queen's Bays
1932 Royal Artillery
1933 Royal Scots Greys
1934 7th Hussars
1935 3rd Brigade Royal Horse Artillery
1936 12th Lancers
1937 10th Hussars
1938 Royal Scots Greys
1939 10th Hussars
1940–57 *No tournament*
1958 7th Hussars
1959 Royal Wiltshire Yeomanry
1960 3rd Royal Horse Artillery
1961 3rd Royal Horse Artillery
1962 Royal Horse Guards
1963 Life Guards
1964 Royal Artillery
1965 Queen's Own Hussars
1966 Queen's Own Hussars
1967 Life Guards
1968 3rd Carabiniers
1969 3rd Carabiniers
1970 Royal Hussars
1971 Blues and Royals
1972 17th/21st Lancers
1973 Queen's Own Hussars

1974 Queen's Own Hussars
1975
1976
1977

Polo Inter-Services Championship Cup
1967 Queen's Own Hussars
1968 Life Guards
1969 3rd Carabiniers
1970 5th Inniskilling Dragoon Guards
1971 Royal Scots Dragoon Guards
1972 Royal Scots Dragoon Guards
1973 Army in Britain
1974 U.S.A.
1975
1976
1977

Westchester Cup
(*see also page* 366)
1886 Gt Britain
1900 Gt Britain
1902 Gt Britain
1909 U.S.A.
1911 U.S.A.
1913 U.S.A.
1914 Gt Britain
1921 U.S.A.
1924 U.S.A.
1927 U.S.A.
1930 U.S.A.
1936 U.S.A.
1939 U.S.A.

RACING RESULTS

Ascot Gold Cup
(*see also page* 16)
1807 Master Jackey
1808 Brighton
1809 Anderida
1810 Loiterer
1811 Jannette
1812 Flash
1813 Lutzen
1814 Pranks
1815 Aladdin
1816 Anticipation
1817 Sir Richard
1818 Belville
1819 Anticipation
1820 Champignon
1821 Banker
1822 Sir Hildebrand
1823 Marcellus
1824 Bizarre
1825 Bizarre

1826 Chateaux Margaux
1827 Memnon
1828 Bobadilla
1829 Zinganee
1830 Lucetta
1831 Cetus
1832 Camerine
1833 Galata
1834 Glaucus
1835 Glencoe
1836 Touchstone
1837 Touchstone
1838 Grey Momus
1839 Caravan
1840 St Francis
1841 Lanercost
1842 Beeswing
1843 Ralph
1844 The Emperor
1854 West Australian
1855 Fandango

Ascot Gold Cup (contd)

1856	Winkfield	1913	Prince Palatine
1857	Skirmisher	1914	Aleppo
1858	Fisherman	1915–18	*No race*
1859	Fisherman	1919	By Jingo
1860	Rupee	1920	Tangiers
1861	Thormanby	1921	Periosteum
1862	Asteroid	1922	Golden Myth
1863	Buckstone	1923	Happy Man
1864	The Scottish Chief	1924	Massine
1865	Ely	1925	Santorb
1866	Gladiateur	1926	Solario
1867	Lecturer	1927	Foxlaw
1868	Blue Gown	1928	Invershin
1869	Brigantine	1929	Invershin
1870	Sabinus	1930	Bosworth
1871	Mortemer	1931	Trimdon
1872	Henry	1932	Trimdon
1873	Cremorne	1933	Foxhunter
1874	Boiard	1934	Felicitation
1875	Doncaster	1935	Tiberius
1876	Apology	1936	Quashed
1877	Petrarch	1937	Precipitation
1878	Verneuil	1938	Flares
1879	Isonomy	1939	Flyon
1880	Isonomy	1940	*No race*
1881	Robert the Devil	*1941	Finis
1882	Foxhall	*1942	Owen Tudor
1883	Tristan	*1943	Ujiji
1884	St Simon	*1944	Umiddad
1885	St Gatien	1945	Ocean Swell
1886	Althorp	1946	Caracalla II
1887	Bird of Freedom	1947	Souverain
1888	Timothy	1948	Arbar
1889	Trayles	1949	Alycidon
1890	Gold	1950	Supertello
1891	Morion	1951	Pan II
1892	Buccaneer	1952	Aquino II
1893	Marcion	1953	Souepi
1894	La Flèche	1954	Elpenor
1895	Isinglass	1955	Botticelli
1896	Love Wisely	1956	Macip
1897	Persimmon	1957	Zarathustra
1898	Elf II	1958	Gladness
1899	Cyllene	1959	Wallaby II
1900	Merman	1960	Sheshoon
1901	Santoi	1961	Pandofell
1902	William the Third	1962	Balto
1903	Maximum II	1963	Twilight Alley
1904	Throwaway	1964	*No race*
1905	Zinfandel	1965	Fighting Charlie
1906	Bachelor's Button	1966	Fighting Charlie
1907	The White Knight	1967	Parbury
1908	The White Knight	1968	Pardallo
1909	Bomba	1969	Levmoss
1910	Bayardo	1970	Precipice Wood
1911	Willonyx	1971	Random Shot
1912	Prince Palatine	1972	Erimo Hawk
		*	*Run at Newmarket (2½ miles)*

Ascot Gold Cup (contd)
1973 Lassalle
1974 Ragstone
1975
1976
1977

Belmont Stakes
(*see also page* 29)
(*Horses foaled outside North America have their country of origin after their name*)
1867 Ruthless
1868 General Duke
1869 Fenian
1870 Kingfisher
1871 Harry Bassett
1872 Joe Daniels
1873 Springbok
1874 Saxon, England
1875 Calvin
1876 Algerine
1877 Cloverbrook
1878 Duke of Magenta
1879 Spendthrift
1880 Grenada
1881 Saunterer
1882 Forester
1883 George Kinney
1884 Panique
1885 Tyrant
1886 Inspector B
1887 Hanover
1888 Sir Dixon
1889 Eric
1890 Burlington
1891 Foxford
1892 Patron
1893 Comanche
1894 Henry of Navarre
1895 Belmar
1896 Hastings
1897 Scottish Chieftain
1898 Bowling Brook
1899 Jean Bereaud
1900 Idrim
1901 Commando
1902 Masterman
1903 Africander
1904 Delhi
1905 Tanya
1906 Burgomaster
1907 Peter Pan
1908 Colin
1909 Joe Madden
1910 Sweep
1911–12 *No race*
1913 Prince Eugene
1914 Luke McLuke

1915 The Finn
1916 Friar Rock
1917 Hourless, England
1918 Johren
1919 Sir Barton
1920 Man o' War
1921 Grey Lag
1922 Pillory
1923 Zev
1824 Mad Play
1925 American Flag
1926 Crusader
1927 Chance Shot
1928 Vito
1929 Blue Larkspur
1930 Gallant Fox
1931 Twenty Grand
1932 Faireno
1933 Hurryoff
1934 Peace Chance
1935 Omaha
1936 Granville
1937 War Admiral
1938 Pasteurized
1939 Johnstown
1940 Bimelech
1941 Whirlaway
1942 Shot Out
1943 Count Fleet
1944 Bounding Home
1945 Pavot
1946 Assault
1947 Phalanx
1948 Citation
1949 Capot
1950 Middleground
1951 Counterpoint
1952 One Count
1953 Native Dancer
1954 High Gun
1955 Nashúa
1956 Needles
1957 Gallant Man, England
1958 Cavan, Ireland
1959 Sword Dancer
1960 Celtic Ash
1961 Sherluck
1962 Jaipur
1963 Château Gay
1964 Quadrangle
1965 Hail to All
1966 Amberoie
1967 Damascus
1968 Stage Door Johnny
1969 Arts and Letters
1970 High Echelon
1971 Pass Catcher
1972 Riva Ridge

Belmont Stakes (contd)
1973 Secretariat
1974 Cannonade
1975
1976
1977

Canadian International Championship
(*see also page* 59)
1938 Bunty Lawless
1939 Sir Marlboro
1940 Cerisse III
1941 Bunty Lawless
1942 Shepperton
1943 Shepperton
1944 Be Brief
1945 Tulachmore
1946 Kingarvie
1947 Brown Hostess
1948 Canada's Teddy
1949 Arise
1950 Nephisto
1951 Bull Page
1952 Beau Dandy
1953 Navy Page
1954 Resilient
1955 Park Dandy
1956 Eugenia II
1957 Spinney
1958 Jack Ketch
1959 Martini II
1960 Rickey Royale
1961 Our Jeep
1962 El Bandido
1963 The Axe II
1964 Will I Rule
1965 George Royal
1966 Royal George
1967 He's a Smoothie
1968 Frenetica
1969 Vent du Nord
1970 Drum Top
1971 One For All
1972 Drole Rolf
1973 Secretariat
1974 Dahlia
1975
1976
1977

Derby Stakes, The
(*see also page* 88)
1780 Diomed
1781 Young Eclipse
1782 Assassin
1783 Saltram
1784 Sergeant
1785 Aimwell

1786 Noble
1787 Sir Peter Teazle
1788 Sir Thomas
1789 Skyscraper
1790 Rhadamanthus
1791 Eager
1792 John Bull
1793 Waxy
1794 Daedalus
1795 Spread Eagle
1796 Didelot
1797 Br. c. by Fidget
1798 Sir Harry
1799 Archduke
1800 Champion
1801 Eleanor
1802 Tyrant
1803 Ditto
1804 Hannibal
1805 Cardinal Beaufort
1806 Paris
1807 Election
1808 Pan
1809 Pope
1810 Whalebone
1811 Phantom
1812 Octavius
1813 Smolensko
1814 Blücher
1815 Whisker
1816 Prince Leopold
1817 Azor
1818 Sam
1819 Tiresias
1820 Sailor
1821 Gustavus
1822 Moses
1823 Emilius
1824 Cedric
1825 Middleton
1826 Lapdog
1827 Mameluke
1828 Cadland
1829 Frederick
1830 Priam
1831 Spaniel
1832 St. Giles
1833 Dangerous
1834 Plenipotentiary
1835 Mündig
1836 Bay Middleton
1837 Phosphorus
1838 Amato
1839 Bloomsbury
1840 Little Wonder
1841 Coronation
1842 Attila
1843 Cotherstone

Derby Stakes, The (contd)

1844	Orlando	1900	Diamond Jubilee
1845	The Merry Monarch	1901	Volodyovski
1846	Pyrrhus the First	1902	Ard Patrick
1847	The Cossack	1903	Rock Sand
1848	Surplice	1904	St Amant
1849	The Flying Dutchman	1905	Cicero
1850	Voltigeur	1906	Spearmint
1851	Teddington	1907	Orby
1852	Daniel O'Rourke	1908	Signorinetta
1853	West Australian	1909	Minoru
1854	Andover	1910	Lemberg
1855	Wild Dayrell	1911	Sunstar
1856	Ellington	1912	Tagalie
1857	Blink Bonny	1913	Aboyeur
1858	Beadsman	1914	Durbar II
1859	Musjid	†1915	Pommern
1860	Thormanby	†1916	Fifinella
1861	Kettledrum	†1917	Gay Crusader
1862	Caractacus	†1919	Grand Parade
1863	Macaroni	1920	Spion Kop
1864	Blair Athol	1921	Humorist
1865	Gladiateur	1922	Captain Cuttle
1866	Lord Lyon	1923	Papyrus
1867	Hermit	1924	Sansovino
1868	Blue Gown	1925	Manna·
1869	Pretender	1926	Coronach
1870	Kingcraft	1927	Call Boy
1871	Favonius	1928	Felstead
1872	Cremorne	1929	Trigo
1873	Doncaster	1930	Blenheim
1874	George Frederick	1931	Cameronian
1875	Galopin	1932	April the Fifth
1876	Kisber	1933	Hyperion
1877	Silvio	1934	Windsor Lad
1878	Sefton	1935	Bahram
1879	Sir Bevys	1936	Mahmoud
1880	Bend Or	1937	Mid-day Sun
1881	Iroquois	1938	Bois Roussel
1882	Shotover	1939	Blue Peter
1883	St Blaise	1940	Pont l'Eveque
*1884	St Gatien	†1941	Owen Tudor
	Harvester	†1942	Watling Street
1885	Melton	†1943	Straight Deal
1886	Ormonde	†1944	Ocean Swell
1887	Merry Hampton	†1945	Dante
1888	Ayrshire	1946	Airborne
1889	Donovan	1947	Pearl Diver
1890	Sainfoin	1948	My Love
1891	Common	1949	Nimbus
1892	Sir Hugo	1950	Galcador
1893	Isinglass	1951	Arctic Prince
1894	Ladas	1952	Tulyar
1895	Sir Visto	1953	Pinza
1896	Persimmon	1954	Never Say Die
1897	Galtee More	1955	Phil Drake
1898	Jeddah	1956	Lavandin
1899	Flying Fox	1957	Crepello
		1958	Hard Ridden

Derby Stakes, The (contd)

1959 Parthia
1960 St Paddy
1961 Psidium
1962 Larkspur
1963 Relko
1964 Santa Claus
1965 Sea Bird II
1966 Charlottown
1967 Royal Palace
1968 Sir Ivor
1969 Blakeney
1970 Nijinsky
1971 Mill Reef
1972 Roberto
1973 Morston
1974 Snow Knight
1975
1976
1977
* Divided after a dead heat.
† The Epsom Summer and Doncaster Meetings were abandoned, in consequence of the War, and the New Derby Stakes, New Oaks Stakes, and September Stakes, run at Newmarket, were substituted for the Epsom Derby and Oaks and Doncaster St Leger.

Durban July Handicap

(*see also page* 101)
1897 Campanajo
1898 Campanajo
1899 Talma
1900 Verdant Green
1901 Apollo
1902 Chaos
1903 Peerless
1904 Nymagee
1905 Chère Ami
1906 Bonnie Dundee
1907 Corriecrian
1908 Corriecrian
1909 King's Favourite
1910 Sir Caulin
1911 Nobleman
1912 Lombard
1913 Caged Bird
1914 Rhanleigh
1915 Winnipeg
1916 Margin
1917 Fanous
1918 Pamphlet
1919 Goldwing

1920 Pamphlet
1921 Longstop
1922 Collet
1923 Eunomea
1924 Oriel
1925 Bird of Prey
1926 Moosme
1927 Hussein
1928 Glen Albyn
1929 Gifted
1930 Full Dress
1931 Agrippa
1932 Findhorn
1933 Legacy
1934 Sun Tor
1935 Eccentric
1936 Petersfield II
1937 Ballyjamesduff
1938 Extinguisher II
1939 Silver Spear II
1940 Kipling
1941 Sadri II
1942 Silver Phantom
1943 Piccadilly Jim
1944 Monteith
1945 St Seiriol
1946 St Pauls
1947 Brookhill
1948 Monasterevan
1949 Milesia Pride
1950 Milesia Pride
1951 Gay Jane
1952 Mowgli
1953 Flash On
1954 C'est Si Bon
1955 Preto's Crown
1956 Spey Bridge
1957 Migraine
1958 Excise
1959 Tiger Fish
1960 Left Wing
1961 Kerason
1962 Diza
1963 Colorado King
1964 Numeral
1965 King Willow
1966 Java Head
1967 Sea Cottage and Jollify (dead heat)
1968 Chimboraa
1969 Naval Escort
1970 Court Day
1971 Mazarin
1972 In Full Flight
1973 Yataghan
1974 Ribovilla
1975
1976
1977

Eclipse Stakes
(see also page 103)
1886 Bendigo
1887 No race
1888 Orbit
1889 Ayrshire
1890 No race
1891 Surefoot
1892 Orme
1893 Orme
1894 Isinglass
1895 Le Justicier
1896 St Frusquin
1897 Persimmon
1898 Velasquez
1899 Flying Fox
1900 Diamond Jubilee
1901 Epsom Lad
1902 Cheers
1903 Ard Patrick
1904 Darley Dale
1905 Val d'Or
1906 Llangibby
1907 Lally
1908 Your Majesty
1909 Bayardo
*1910 Lemberg
     Neil Gow
1911 Swynford
1912 Prince Palatine
1913 Tracery
1914 Hapsburg
1915–18 No race
1919 Buchan
1920 Buchan
1921 Craig an Eran
1922 Golden Myth
1923 Saltash
1924 Polyphontes
1925 Polyphontes
1926 Coronach
1927 Colorado
1928 Fairway
1929 Royal Minstrel
1930 Rustom Pasha
1931 Caerleon
1932 Miracle
1933 Loaningdale
1934 King Salmon
1935 Windsor Lad
1936 Rhodes Scholar
1937 Boswell
1938 Pasch
1939 Blue Peter
1940–5 No race
†1946 Gulf Stream
1947 Migoli
1948 Petition

1949 Djeddah
1950 Flocon
1951 Mystery IX
1952 Tulyar
1953 Argur
1954 King of the Tudors
1955 Darius
1956 Tropique
1957 Arctic Explorer
1958 Ballymoss
1959 St Crespin III
1960 Javelot
1961 St Paddy
1962 Henry the Seventh
1963 Khalkis
1964 Ragusa
1965 Canisbay
1966 Pieces of Eight
1967 Busted
1968 Royal Palace
1969 Wolver Hollow
1970 Connaught
1971 Mill Reef
1972 Brigadier Gerard
1973 Scottish Rifle
1974 Coup de Feu
1975
1976
1977
* Dead heat.
†At Ascot.

Grand National
(see also pages 4 and 144)
1837 The Duke
1838 Sir Henry
1839 Lottery
1840 Jerry
1841 Charity
1842 Gaylad
1843 Vanguard
1844 Discount
1845 Cureall
1846 Pioneer
1847 Matthew
1848 Chandler
1849 Peter Simple
1850 Abd el Kader
1851 Abd el Kader
1852 Miss Mowbray
1853 Peter Simple
1854 Bourton
1855 Wanderer
1856 Freetrader
1857 Emigrant
1858 Little Charley
1859 Half Caste
1860 Anatis

Grand National (contd)

1861	Jealousy	1918	Poethlyn
1862	Huntsman	1919	Poethlyn
1863	Emblem	1920	Troytown
1864	Emblematic	1921	Shaun Spadah
1865	Alcibiade	1922	Music Hall
1866	Salamander	1923	Sergeant Murphy
1867	Cortolvin	1924	Master Robert
1868	The Lamb	1925	Double Chance
1869	The Colonel	1926	Jack Horner
1870	The Colonel	1927	Sprig
1871	The Lamb	1928	Tipperary Tim
1872	Casse Tête	1929	Gregalach
1873	Disturbance	1930	Shaun Goilin
1874	Reugny	1931	Grakle
1875	Pathfinder	1932	Forbra
1876	Regal	1933	Kellsboro' Jack
1877	Austerlitz	1934	Golden Miller
1878	Shifnal	1935	Reynoldstown
1879	Liberator	1936	Reynoldstown
1880	Empress	1937	Royal Mail
1881	Woodbrook	1938	Battleship
1882	Seaman	1939	Workman
1883	Zoedone	1940	Bogskar
1884	Voluptuary	1941–45	*No race*
1885	Roquefort	1946	Lovely Cottage
1886	Old Joe	1947	Caughoo
1887	Gamecock	1948	Sheila's Cottage
1888	Playfair	1949	Russian Hero
1889	Frigate	1950	Freebooter
1890	Ilex	1951	Nickel Coin
1891	Come Away	1952	Teal
1892	Father O'Flynn	1953	Early Mist
1893	Cloister	1954	Royal Tan
1894	Why Not	1955	Quare Times
1895	Wild Man from Borneo	1956	E.S.B.
1896	The Soarer	1957	Sundew
1897	Manifesto	1958	Mr What
1898	Drogheda	1959	Oxo
1899	Manifesto	1960	Merryman II
1900	Ambush II	1961	Nicolaus Silver
1901	Grudon	1962	Kilmore
1902	Shannon Lass	1963	Ayala
1903	Drumcree	1964	Team Spirit
1904	Moifaa	1965	Jay Trump
1905	Kirkland	1966	Anglo
1906	Ascetic's Silver	1967	Foinavon
1907	Eremon	1968	Red Alligator
1908	Rubio	1969	Highland Wedding
1909	Lutteur III	1970	Gay Trip
1910	Jenkinstown	1971	Specify
1911	Glenside	1972	Well To Do
1912	Jerry M	1973	Red Rum
1913	Covertcoat	1974	Red Rum
1914	Sunloch	1975	L'Escargot
1915	Ally Sloper	1976	
1916	Vermouth	1977	
1917	Ballymacad		

Kentucky Derby
(*see also page* 183)
(*Horses foaled outside North America have their country of origin after their name*)
1875 Aristides
1876 Vagrant
1877 Baden Baden
1878 Day Star
1879 Lord Murphy
1880 Fonso
1881 Hindoo
1882 Apollo
1883 Leonatus
1884 Buchanan
1885 Joe Cotton
1886 Ben Ali
1887 Montrose
1888 Macbeth
1889 Spokane
1890 Riley
1891 Kingman
1892 Azra
1893 Lookout
1894 Chant
1895 Halma
1896 Ben Brush
1897 Typhoon II
1898 Plaudit
1899 Manuel
1900 Lieut Gibson
1901 His Eminence
1902 Alan-a-Dale
1903 Judge Himes
1904 Elwood
1905 Agile
1906 Sir Huon
1907 Pink Star
1908 Stone Street
1909 Wintergreen
1910 Donau
1911 Meridian
1912 Worth
1913 Donerail
1914 Old Rosebud
1915 Regret
1916 George Smith
1917 Omar Khayyam, England
1918 Exterminator
1919 Sir Barton
1920 Paul Jones
1921 Behave Yourself
1922 Morvich
1923 Zev
1924 Black Gold
1925 Flying Ebony
1926 Bubbling Over
1927 Whiskery
1928 Reigh Count

1929 Clyde Van Dusen
1930 Gallant Fox
1931 Twenty Grand
1932 Burgoo King
1933 Brokers Tip
1934 Cavalcade
1935 Omaha
1936 Bold Venture
1937 War Admiral
1938 Lawrin
1939 Johnstown
1940 Gallahadion
1941 Whirlaway
1942 Shut Out
1943 Count Fleet
1944 Pensive
1945 Hoop Jr
1946 Assault
1947 Jet Pilot
1948 Citation
1949 Ponder
1950 Middleground
1951 Count Turf
1952 Hill Gail
1953 Dark Star
1954 Determine
1955 Swaps
1956 Needles
1957 Iron Liege
1958 Tim Tam
1959 Tomy Lee, England
1960 Venetian Way
1961 Carry Back
1962 Decidedly
1963 Château Gay
1964 Northern Dancer
1965 Lucky Debonair
1966 Kauai King
1967 Proud Clarion
1968 Forward Pass
1969 Majestic Prince
1970 Dust Commander
1971 Canonero II
1972 Riva Ridge
1973 Secretariat
1974 Little Current
1975
1976
1977

King George VI and Queen Elizabeth Stakes (*see also page* 184)
1951 Supreme Court
1952 Tulyar
1953 Pinza
1954 Aureole
1955 Vimy
1956 Ribot

King George VI and Queen Elizabeth Stakes (contd)
1957 Montaval
1958 Ballymoss
1959 Alcide
1960 Aggressor
1961 Right Royal V
1962 Match III
1963 Ragusa
1964 Nasram II
1965 Meadow Court
1966 Aunt Edith
1967 Busted
1968 Royal Palace
1969 Park Top
1970 Nijinsky
1971 Mill Reef
1972 Brigadier Gerard
1973 Dahlia
1974 Dahlia
1975
1976
1977

Maryland Hunt Cup
(*see also page* 209)
1894 Johnny Miller
1895 Sixty
1896 Kingsbury
1897 Little Giant
1898 The Squire
1899 Reveller
1900 Tom Clark
1901 Garry Owen
1902 Garry Owen
1903 Princeton
1904 Landslide
1905 Princeton
1906 Princeton
1907 Garry Owen
1908 Judge Parker
1909 Sacandaga
1910 Sacandaga
1911 Pebbles
1912 Conbe
1913 Zarda
1914 Rutland
1915 Talisman
1916 Bourgeois
1917 Brosseau
1918 Marcellinus
1919 Chuckatuck
1920 Oracle II
1921 Mazarin
1922 Oracle II
1923 Red Bud
1924 Daybreak
1925 Burgoright

1926 Billy Barton
1927 Bon Master
1928 Bon Master
1929 Alligator
1930 Brose Hover
1931 Soissons
1932 Trouble Maker
1933 Captain Kettle
1934 Captain Kettle
1935 Hotspur 2nd
1936 Inshore
1937 Welbourne Jake
1938 Blockade
1939 Blockade
1940 Blockade
1941 Coq Bruyere
1942 Winton
1943–45 *No race*
1946 Winton
1947 Winton
1948 Peterski
1949 Pine Pep
1950 Pine Pep
1951 Jester's Moon
1952 Pine Pep
1953 Third Army
1954 Marchized
1955 Land's Corner
1956 Lancrel
1957 Ned's Flying
1958 Ned's Flying
1959 Fluctuate
1960 Fluctuate
1961 Simple Samson
1962 Mountain Dew
1963 Jay Trump
1964 Jay Trump
1965 Mountain Dew
1966 Jay Trump
1967 Mountain Dew
1968 Haffaday
1969 Landing Party
1970 Morning Mac
1971 Landing Party
1972 Early Earner
1973 Morning Mac
1974 Burnmac
1975
1976
1977

Melbourne Cup
(*see also page* 211)
1861 Archer
1862 Archer
1863 Banker
1864 Lantern
1865 Toryboy

Melbourne Cup (contd)

1866	The Barb
1867	Tim Whiffler
1868	Glencoe
1869	Warrior
1870	Nimblefoot
1871	The Pearl
1872	The Quack
1873	Don Juan
1874	Haricot
1875	Wollomai
1876	Briseis
1877	Chester
1878	Calamia
1879	Darriwell
1880	Grand Flaneur
1881	Zulu
1882	The Assyrian
1883	Martini-Henri
1884	Malua
1885	Sheet Anchor
1886	Arsenal
1887	Dunlop
1888	Mentor
1889	Bravo
1890	Carbine
1891	Malvolio
1892	Glenloth
1893	Tarcoola
1894	Patron
1895	Auraria
1896	Newhaven
1897	Gaulus
1898	The Grafter
1899	Merriwee
1900	Clean Sweep
1901	Revenue
1902	The Victory
1903	Lord Cardigan
1904	Acrasia
1905	Blue Spec
1906	Poseidon
1907	Apologue
1908	Lord Nolan
1909	Prince Foote
1910	Comedy King
1911	The Parisian
1912	Piastre
1913	Posinatus
1914	Kingsburgh
1915	Patrobus
1916	Sasanof
1917	Westcourt
1918	Night Watch
1919	Artilleryman
1920	Poitrel
1921	Sister Olive
1922	King Ingoda

1923	Bitalli
1924	Backwood
1925	Windbag
1926	Spearfelt
1927	Trivalve
1928	Statesman
1929	Nightmarch
1930	Phar Lap
1931	White Nose
1932	Peter Pan
1933	Hall Mark
1934	Peter Pan
1935	Marabou
1936	Wotan
1937	The Trump
1938	Catalogue
1939	Rivette
1940	Old Rowley
1941	Skipton
1942	Colonus
1943	Dark Felt
1944	Sirius
1945	Rainbird
1946	Russia
1947	Hiraji
1948	Rimfire
1949	Foxzami
1950	Comic Court
1951	Delta
1952	Dalray
1953	Wodalla
1954	Rising Fast
1955	Toparoa
1956	Evening Peal
1957	Straight Draw
1958	Baystone
1959	MacDougal
1960	Hi Jinx
1961	Lord Fury
1962	Even Stevens
1963	Gatun Gatun
1964	Polo Prince
1965	Light Fingers
1966	Galilee
1967	Red Handed
1968	Rain Lover
1969	Rain Lover
1970	Baghdad Note
1971	Silver Knight
1972	Piping Lane
1973	Gala Supreme
1974	Think Big
1975	
1976	
1977	

Oaks, The
(*see also page* 228)
1779 Bridget
1780 Teetotum
1781 Faith
1782 Ceres
1783 Maid of the Oaks
1784 Stella
1785 Trifle
1786 The Perdita Filly
1787 Annette
1788 Nightshade
1789 Tag
1790 Hippolyta
1791 Portia
1792 Volante
1793 Caelia
1794 Hermione
1795 Platina
1796 Parissot
1797 Niké
1798 Bellissima
1799 Bellina
1800 Ephemera
1801 Eleanor
1802 Scotia
1803 Theophania
1804 Pelisse
1805 Meteora
1806 Bronze
1807 Briseis
1808 Morel
1809 Maid of Orleans
1810 Oriana
1811 Sorcery
1812 Manuella
1813 Music
1814 Medora
1815 Minuet
1816 Landscape
1817 Neva
1818 Corinne
1819 Shoveler
1820 Carolina
1821 Augusta
1822 Pastille
1823 Zinc
1824 Cobweb
1825 Wings
1826 Lilias (aft. Babel)
1827 Gulnare
1828 Turquoise
1829 Green Mantle
1830 Variation
1831 Oxygen
1832 Galata
1833 Vespa
1834 Pussy
1835 Queen of Trumps
1836 Cyprian
1837 Miss Letty
1838 Industry
1839 Deception
1840 Crucifix
1841 Ghuznee
1842 Our Nell
1843 Poison
1844 The Princess
1845 Refraction
1846 Mendicant
1847 Miami
1848 Cymba
1849 Lady Evelyn
1850 Rhedycina
1851 Iris
1852 Songstress
1853 Catherine Hayes
1854 Mincemeat
1855 Marchioness
1856 Mincepie
1857 Blink Bonny
1858 Governess
1859 Summerside
1860 Butterfly
1861 Brown Duchess
1862 Feu de Joie
1863 Queen Bertha
1864 Fille de l'Air
1865 Regalia
1866 Tormentor
1867 Hippia
1868 Formosa
1869 Brigantine
1870 Gamos
1871 Hannah
1872 Reine
1873 Marie Stuart
1874 Apology
1875 Spinaway
*1876 Enguerrande
     Camelia
1877 Placida
1878 Jannette
1879 Wheel of Fortune
1880 Jenny Howlett
1881 Thebais
1882 Geheimniss
1883 Bonny Jean
1884 Busybody
1885 Lonely
1886 Miss Jummy
1887 Rêve d'Or
1888 Seabreeze
1889 L'Abbesse de Jouarre
1890 Memoir
1891 Mimi

Oaks, The (contd)

1892 La Flèche
1893 Mrs Butterwick
1894 Amiable
1895 La Sagesse
1896 Canterbury Pilgrim
1897 Limasol
1898 Airs and Graces
1899 Musa
1900 La Roche
1901 Cap and Bells II
1902 Sceptre
1903 Our Lassie
1904 Pretty Polly
1905 Cherry Lass
1906 Keystone II
1907 Glass Doll
1908 Signorinetta
1909 Perola
1910 Rosedrop
1911 Cherimoya
1912 Mirska
1913 Jest
1914 Princess Dorrie
†1915 Snow Marten
†1916 Fifinella
†1917 Sunny Jane
†1918 My Dear
1919 Bayuda
1920 Charlebelle
1921 Love-in-Idleness
1922 Pogrom
1923 Brownhylda
1924 Straitlace
1925 Saucy Sue
1926 Short Story
1927 Beam
1928 Toboggan
1929 Pennycomequick
1930 Rose of England
1931 Brulette
1932 Udaipur
1933 Chatelaine
1934 Light Brocade
1935 Quashed
1936 Lovely Rosa
1937 Exhibitionist
1938 Rockfel
1939 Galatea II
†1940 Godiva
†1941 Commotion
†1942 Sun Chariot
†1943 Why Hurry
†1944 Hycilla
†1945 Sun Stream
1946 Steady Aim
1947 Imprudence
1948 Masaka

1949 Musidora
1950 Asmena
1951 Neasham Belle
1952 Frieze
1953 Ambiguity
1954 Sun Cap
1955 Meld
1956 Sicarelle
1957 Carrozza
1958 Bella Paola
1959 Petite Etoile
1960 Never Too Late II
1961 Sweet Solera
1962 Monade
1963 Noblesse
1964 Homeward Bound
1965 Long Look
1966 Valoris
1967 Pia
1968 La Lagune
1969 Sleeping Partner
1970 Lupe
1971 Altesse Royale
1972 Ginevra
1973 Mysterious
1974 Polygamy
1975
1976
1977
* Divided after a dead heat.
† Run at Newmarket.

One Thousand Guineas
(see also page 230)

1814 Charlotte
1815 Selim filly
1816 Rhoda
1817 Neva
1818 Corinne
1819 Catgut
1820 Rowena
1821 Zeal
1822 Whizgig
1823 Zinc
1824 Cobweb
1825 Tontine
1826 Problem
1827 Arab
1828 Zoe
1829 Mouse filly
1830 Charlotte West
1831 Galantine
1832 Galata
1833 Tarantella
1834 May Day
1835 Preserve
1836 Destiny
1837 Chapeau d'Espagne

One Thousand Guineas (contd)

1838 Barcarolle	1895 Galeottia
1839 Cara	1896 Thais
1840 Crucifix	1897 Chelandry
1841 Potentia	1898 Nun Nicer
1842 Firebrand	1899 Sibola
1843 Extempore	1900 Winifreda
1844 Sorella	1901 Aida
1845 Picnic	1902 Sceptre
1846 Mendicant	1903 Quintessence
1847 Clementina	1904 Pretty Polly
1848 Canezou	1905 Cherry Lass
1849 Flea	1906 Flair
1850 Exotic filly	1907 Witch Elm
1851 Aphrodite	1908 Rhodora
1852 Kate	1909 Electra
1853 Mentmore Lass	1910 Winkipop
1854 Virago	1911 Atmah
1855 Habena	1912 Tagalie
1856 Manganese	1913 Jest
1857 Impérieuse	1914 Princess Dorrie
1858 Governess	1915 Vaucluse
1859 Mayonaise	1916 Canyon
1860 Sagitta	1917 Diadem
1861 Nemesis	1918 Ferry
1862 Hurricane	1919 Roseway
1863 Lady Augusta	1920 Cinna
1864 Tomato	1921 Bettina
1865 Siberia	1922 Silver Urn
1866 Repulse	1923 Tranquil
1867 Achievement	1924 Plack
1868 Formosa	1925 Saucy Sue
1869 Scottish Queen	1926 Pillion
1870 Hester	1927 Cresta Run
1871 Hannah	1928 Scuttle
1872 Reine	1929 Taj Mah
1873 Cecilia	1930 Fair Isle
1874 Apology	1931 Four Course
1875 Spinaway	1932 Kandy
1876 Camelia	1933 Brown Betty
1877 Belphoebe	1934 Campanula
1878 Pilgrimage	1935 Mesa
1879 Wheel of Fortune	1936 Tideway
1880 Elizabeth	1937 Exhibitionist
1881 Thebais	1938 Rockfel
1882 St Marguerite	1939 Galatea II
1883 Hauteur	1940 Godiva
1884 Busybody	1941 Dancing Time
1885 Farewell	1942 Sun Chariot
1886 Miss Jummy	1943 Herringbone
1887 Rêve d'Or	1944 Picture Play
1888 Briar Root	1945 Sun Stream
1889 Minthe	1946 Hypericum
1890 Semolina	1947 Imprudence
1891 Mimi	1948 Queen Pot
1892 La Flèche	1949 Musidora
1893 Siffleuse	1950 Camaree
1894 Amiable	1951 Belle of All
	1952 Zabara

One Thousand Guineas (contd)
1953 Happy Laughter
1954 Festoon
1955 Meld
1956 Honeylight
1957 Rose Royale II
1958 Bella Paola
1959 Petite Étoile
1960 Never Too Late II
1961 Sweet Solera
1962 Abermaid
1963 Hula Dancer
1964 Pourparler
1965 Night Off
1966 Glad Rags
1967 Fleet
1968 Caergwrle
1969 Full Dress II
1970 Humble Duty
1971 Altesse Royale
1972 Waterloo
1973 Mysterious
1974 Highclere
1975
1976
1977

Preakness Stakes
(see also page 252)
1873 Survivor
1874 Culpepper
1875 Tom Ochiltree
1876 Shirley
1877 Cloverbrook
1878 Duke of Magenta
1879 Harold
1880 Grenada
1881 Saunterer
1882 Vanguard
1883 Jacobus
1884 Knight of Ellerslie
1885 Tecumseh
1886 The Bard
1887 Dunbine
1888 Refund
1889 Buddhist
1890–93 No race
1894 Assignée
1895 Belmar
1896 Margrave
1897 Paul Kauver
1898 Sly Fox
1899 Half Time
1900 Hindus
1901 The Parader
1902 Old England
1903 Florcarline
1904 Bryn Mawr

1905 Cairngorm
1906 Whimsical
1907 Don Enrique
1908 Royal Tourist
1909 Effendi
1910 Layminster
1911 Watervale
1912 Colonel Holloway
1913 Buskin
1914 Holiday
1915 Rhine Maiden
1916 Damrosch
1917 Kalitan
1918 War Cloud (1st div.)
     Jack Hare (2nd div.)
1919 Sir Barton
1920 Man o' War
1921 Broomspur
1922 Pillory
1923 Vigil
1924 Nellie Morse
1925 Coventry
1926 Display
1927 Bostonian
1928 Victorian
1929 Dr Freeland
1930 Gallant Fox
1931 Mate
1932 Burgoo King
1933 Head Play
1934 High Quest
1935 Omaha
1936 Bold Venture
1937 War Admiral
1938 Dauber
1939 Challedon
1940 Bimelech
1941 Whirlaway
1942 Alsab
1943 Count Fleet
1944 Pensive
1945 Polynesian
1946 Assault
1947 Faultless
1948 Citation
1949 Capot
1950 Hill Prince
1951 Bold
1952 Blue Man
1953 Native Dancer
1954 Hasty Road
1955 Nashua
1956 Fabius
1957 Bold Ruler
1958 Tim Tam
1959 Royal Orbit
1960 Bally Ache
1961 Carry Back

Preakness Stakes (contd)
1962 Greek Money
1963 Candy Spots
1964 Northern Dancer
1965 Tom Rolfe
1966 Kauai King
1967 Damascus
1968 Forward Pass
1969 Majestic Prince
1970 Personality
1971 Canonero II
1972 Bee Bee Bee
1973 Secretariat
1974 Little Current
1975
1976
1977

Queen's Plate
(*see also page* 258)
1860 Don Juan
1861 Wild Irishman
1862 Palermo
1863 Touchston
1864 Brunette
1865 Lady Norfolk
1866 Beacon
1867 Wild Rose
1868 Nettie
1869 Bay Jack
1870 John Bell
1871 Floss
1872 Fearnaught
1873 Mignonette
1874 Swallow
1875 Trumpeter
1876 Norah P
1877 Amelia
1878 King George
1879 Moss Rose
1880 Bonnie Bird
1881 Vice Chancellor
1882 Fanny Wiser
1883 Rhody Pringle
1884 Williams
1885 Willie W.
1886 Wild Rose II
1887 Bonnie Duke
1888 Henry Cooper
1889 Colonist
1890 Kite String
1891 Victorious
1892 O'Donaghue
1893 Martello
1894 Joe Miller
1895 Bonniefield
1896 Millbrook
1897 Ferdinand

1898 Bon Ino
1899 Butterscotch
1900 Dalmoor
1901 John Ruskin
1902 Lyddite
1903 Thessalon
1904 Sapper
1905 Inferno
1906 Slaughter
1907 Kelvin
1908 Seismic
1909 Shimonese
1910 Parmer
1911 St Brass
1912 Heresy
1913 Hearts of Oak
1914 Beehive
1915 Tartarean
1916 Mandarin
1917 Belle Mahone
1918 Springside
1919 Ladder of Light
1920 St Paul
1921 Herendesy
1922 South Shore
1923 Flowerful
1924 Maternal Pride
1925 Fairbank
1926 Haplite
1927 Troutlet
1928 Young Kitty
1929 Shorelint
1930 Aymond
1931 Froth Blower
1932 Queensway
1933 King O'Connor
1934 Horometer
1935 Sally Fuller
1936 Monsweep
1937 Goldlure
1938 Bunty Lawless
1939 Archworth
1940 Willie the Kid
1941 Budpath
1942 Ten to Ace
1943 Paolita
1944 Acara
1945 Uttermost
1946 Kingarvie
1947 Moldy
1948 Last Mark
1949 Epic
1950 McGill
1951 Major Factor
1952 Epigram
1953 Canadiana
1954 Collisteo
1955 Ace Marine

Queen's Plate (contd)
1956 Canadian Champ
1957 Lyford Cay
1958 Caledon Beau
1959 New Providence
1960 Victoria Park
1961 Blue Light
1962 Flaming Page
1963 Canebora
1964 Northern Dancer
1965 Whistling Sea
1966 Titled Hero
1967 Jammed Lovely
1968 Merger
1969 Jumpin Joseph
1970 Almoner
1971 Kennedy Road
1972 Victoria Song
1973 Royal Chocolate
1974 Amber Herod
1975
1976
1977

St Leger
(see also page 283)
1776 Allabaculia
1777 Bourbon
1778 Hollandaise
1779 Tommy
1780 Ruler
1781 Serina
1782 Imperatrix
1783 Phenomenon
1784 Omphale
1785 Cowslip
1786 Paragon
1787 Spadille
1788 Young Flora
1789 Pewett
1790 Ambidexter
1791 Young Traveller
1792 Tartar
1793 Ninety-three
1794 Beningbrough
1795 Hambletonian
1796 Ambrosio
1797 Lounger
1798 Symmetry
1799 Cockfighter
1800 Champion
1801 Quiz
1802 Orville
1803 Remembrancer
1804 Sancho
1805 Staveley
1806 Fyldener
1807 Paulina

1808 Petronius
1809 Ashton
1810 Octavian
1811 Soothsayer
1812 Ottrington
1813 Altisidora
1814 William
1815 Filho da Puta
1816 The Duchess
1817 Ebor
1818 Reveller
1819 Antonio
1820 St Patrick
1821 Jack Spiggot
1822 Theodore
1823 Barefoot
1824 Jerry
1825 Memnon
1826 Tarrare
1827 Matilda
1828 The Colonel
1829 Rowton
1830 Birmingham
1831 Chorister
1832 Margrave
1833 Rockingham
1834 Touchstone
1835 Queen of Trumps
1836 Elis
1837 Mango
1838 Don John
1839 Charles XII
1840 Launcelot
1841 Satirist
1842 Blue Bonnet
1843 Nutwith
1844 Faugh-a-Ballagh
1845 The Baron
1846 Sir Tatton Sykes
1847 Van Tromp
1848 Surplice
1849 The Flying Dutchman
1850 Voltigeur
1851 Newminster
1852 Stockwell
1853 West Australian
1854 Knight of St George
1855 Saucebox
1856 Warlock
1857 Impérieuse
1858 Sunbeam
1859 Gamester
1860 St Albans
1861 Caller Ou
1862 The Marquis
1863 Lord Clifden
1864 Blair Athol
1865 Gladiateur

St Leger (contd)

1866	Lord Lyon
1867	Achievement
1868	Formosa
1869	Pero Gomez
1870	Hawthornden
1871	Hannah
1872	Wenlock
1873	Marie Stuart
1874	Apology
1875	Craig Millar
1876	Petrarch
1877	Silvio
1878	Jannette
1879	Rayon d'Or
1880	Robert the Devil
1881	Iroquois
1882	Dutch Oven
1883	Ossian
1884	The Lambkin
1885	Melton
1886	Ormonde
1887	Kilwarlin
1888	Seabreeze
1889	Donovan
1890	Memoir
1891	Common
1892	La Flèche
1893	Isinglass
1894	Throstle
1895	Sir Visto
1896	Persimmon
1897	Galtee More
1898	Wildfowler
1899	Flying Fox
1900	Diamond Jubilee
1901	Doricles
1902	Sceptre
1903	Rock Sand
1904	Pretty Polly
1905	Challacombe
1906	Troutbeck
1907	Wool Winder
1908	Your Majesty
1909	Bayardo
1910	Swynford
1911	Prince Palatine
1912	Tracery
1913	Night Hawk
1914	Black Jester
*1915	Pommern
*1916	Hurry On
*1917	Gay Crusader
*1918	Gainsborough
1919	Keysoe
1920	Caligula
1921	Polemarch
1922	Royal Lancer
1923	Tranquil
1924	Salmon-Trout
1925	Solario
1926	Coronach
1927	Book Law
1928	Fairway
1929	Trigo
1930	Singapore
1931	Sandwich
1932	Firdaussi
1933	Hyperion
1934	Windsor Lad
1935	Bahram
1936	Boswell
1937	Chulmleigh
1938	Scottish Union
1939	*No race*
*1940	Turkhan
*1941	Sun Castle
*1942	Sun Chariot
*1943	Herringbone
*1944	Tehran
1945	Chamossaire
*1946	Airborne
1947	Sayajirao
1948	Black Tarquin
1949	Ridge Wood
1950	Scratch II
1951	Talma II
1952	Tulyar
1953	Premonition
1954	Never Say Die
1955	Meld
1956	Cambremer
1957	Ballymoss
1958	Alcide
1959	Cantelo
1960	St Paddy
1961	Aurelius
1962	Hethersett
1963	Ragusa
1964	Indiana
1965	Provoke
1966	Sodium
1967	Ribocco
1968	Ribero
1969	Intermezzo
1970	Nijinsky
1971	Athens Wood
1972	Boucher
1973	Peleid
1974	Bustino
1975	
1976	
1977	

* Run at Newmarket.

Triple Crown
(*see also page* 341)
1853 West Australian
1865 Gladiateur
1866 Lord Lyon
1886 Ormonde
1891 Common
1893 Isinglass
1897 Galtee More
1899 Flying Fox
1900 Diamond Jubilee
1903 Rock Sand
1915 Pommern
1917 Gay Crusader
1918 Gainsborough
1935 Bahram
1970 Nijinsky

Triple Crown (U.S.A.)
(*see also page* 341)
1919 Sir Barton
1930 Gallant Fox
1935 Omaha
1937 War Admiral
1941 Whirlaway
1943 Count Fleet
1946 Assault
1948 Citation
1973 Secretariat

Two Thousand Guineas
(*see also page* 345)
1809 Wizard
1810 Hephestion
1811 Trophonius
1812 Cwrw
1813 Smolensko
1814 Olive
1815 Tigris
1816 Nectar
1817 Manfred
1818 Interpreter
1819 Antar
1820 Pindarrie
1821 Reginald
1822 Pastille
1823 Nicolo
1824 Schahriar
1825 Enamel
1826 Dervise
1827 Turcoman
1828 Cadland
1829 Patron
1830 Augustus
1831 Riddlesworth
1832 Archibald
1833 Clearwell
1834 Glencoe

1835 Ibrahim
1836 Bay Middleton
1837 Achmet
1838 Grey Momus
1839 The Corsair
1840 Crucifix
1841 Ralph
1842 Meteor
1843 Cotherstone
1844 The Ugly Buck
1845 Idas
1846 Sir Tatton Sykes
1847 Conyngham
1848 Flatcatcher
1849 Nunnykirk
1850 Pitsford
1851 Hernandez
1852 Stockwell
1853 West Australian
1854 The Hermit
1855 Lord of the Isles
1856 Fazzoletto
1857 Vedette
1858 Fitz Roland
1859 Promised Land
1860 The Wizard
1861 Diophantus
1862 The Marquis
1863 Macaroni
1864 General Peel
1865 Gladiateur
1866 Lord Lyon
1867 Vauban
1868 Moslem (walk-over after dead heat
     with Formosa)
1869 Pretender
1870 Macgregor
1871 Bothwell
1872 Prince Charlie
1873 Gang Forward
1874 Atlantic
1875 Camballo
1876 Petrarch
1877 Chamant
1878 Pilgrimage
1879 Charibert
1880 Petronel
1881 Peregrine
1882 Shotover
1883 Galliard
1884 Scot Free
1885 Paradox
1886 Ormonde
1887 Enterprise
1888 Ayrshire
1889 Enthusiast
1890 Surefoot
1891 Common

Two Thousand Guineas (contd)

1892 Bonavista	1935 Bahram
1893 Isinglass	1936 Pay Up
1894 Ladas	1937 Le Ksar
1895 Kirkconnel	1938 Pasch
1896 St Frusquin	1939 Blue Peter
1897 Galtee More	1940 Djebel
1898 Disraeli	1941 Lambert Simnel
1899 Flying Fox	1942 Big Game
1900 Diamond Jubilee	1943 Kingsway
1901 Handicapper	1944 Garden Path
1902 Sceptre	1945 Court Martial
1903 Rock Sand	1946 Happy Knight
1904 St Amant	1947 Tudor Minstrel
1905 Vedas	1948 My Babu
1906 Gorgos	1949 Nimbus
1907 Slieve Gallion	1950 Palestine
1908 Norman III	1951 Ki Ming
1909 Minoru	1952 Thunderhead II
1910 Neil Gow	1953 Nearula
1911 Sunstar	1954 Darius
1912 Sweeper II	1955 Our Babu
1913 Louvois	1956 Gilles de Retz
1914 Kennymore	1957 Crepello
1915 Pommern	1958 Pall Mall
1916 Clarissimus	1959 Taboun
1917 Gay Crusader	1960 Martial
1918 Gainsborough	1961 Rockavon
1919 The Panther	1962 Privy Councillor
1920 Tetratema	1963 Only for Life
1921 Craig an Eran	1964 Baldric II
1922 St Louis	1965 Niksar
1923 Ellangowan	1966 Kashmir II
1924 Diophon	1967 Royal Palace
1925 Manna	1968 Sir Ivor
1926 Colorado	1969 Right Tack
1927 Adam's Apple	1970 Nijinsky
1928 Flamingo	1971 Brigadier Gerard
1929 Mr Jinks	1972 High Top
1930 Diolite	1973 Mon Fils
1931 Cameronian	1974 Nonoalco
1932 Orwell	1975
1933 Rodosto	1976
1934 Colombo	1977

SHOW JUMPING RESULTS

British Jumping Derby
(see also page 49)

1961 S. Hayes, 'Goodbye III', Ireland
1962 Miss P. Smythe, 'Flanagan', Gt Britain
1963 N. Pessoa, 'Gran Geste', Brazil
1964 S. Hayes, 'Goodbye III', Ireland
1965 N. Pessoa, 'Gran Geste', Brazil
1966 D. Broome, 'Mister Softee', Gt Britain
1967 Miss M. Coakes, 'Stroller', Gt Britain
1968 Miss A. Westwood, 'The Maverick VII', Gt Britain
1969 Miss A. Drummond-Hay, 'Xanthos', Gt Britain
1970 H. Smith, 'Mattie Brown', Gt Britain
1971 H. Smith, 'Mattie Brown', Gt Britain
1972 H. Snoek, 'Shirokko', W. Germany
1973 Mrs A. Dawes, 'The Maverick VII', ('Mr Banbury'), Gt Britain

British Jumping Derby (contd)
1974 H. Smith, 'Salvador', Gt Britain
1975
1976
1977

British Show Jumping Association National Championship
1947 Lt-Col N. H. Kindersley, 'Maguire'
1948 S. Hayes, 'Limerick'
1949 S. Hayes, 'Sheila'
1950 S. Hayes, 'Sheila'
1951 A. Oliver, 'Red Admiral' and 'Red Knight'
1952 D. Beard, 'Costa'
1953 Lt-Col H. M. Llewellyn, 'Foxhunter'
1954 A. Oliver, 'Red Admiral'
1955 Ted Williams, 'Larry' and 'Sunday Morning'
1956 Ted Williams, 'Montana' and 'Pegasus XIII'
1957 T. H. Edgar, 'Jane Summers'
1958 P. McMahon, 'Tim II'
1959 A. Oliver, 'John Gilpin'
1960 H. Smith, 'Farmer's Boy'
1961 D. Broome, 'Discutido'
1962 D. Broome, 'Wildfire'
1963 H. Smith, 'O'Malley'
1964 Miss E. Broome, 'Jacopo'
1965 P. Robeson, 'Firecrest'
1966 A. Fielder, 'Vibart'
1967 D. Broome, 'Mister Softee'
1968 Miss M. Coakes, 'Stroller'
1969 A. Oliver, 'Pitz Palu'
1970 A. Oliver, 'Sweep III'
1971 Miss M. Mould, 'Stroller'
1972 Miss A. Ross, 'Trevarrion'
1973 D. Broome, 'Sportsman'
1974 P. Nicholls, 'Timmie'
1975
1976
1977

European Junior Championship (F.E.I. Show Jumping)
1957 Gt Britain
1958 Gt Britain
1959 Gt Britain
1960 Gt Britain
1961 W. Germany
1962 Gt Britain
1963 Gt Britain
1964 Italy
1965 Gt Britain
1966 Italy
1967 Gt Britain
1968 Gt Britain
1969 Switzerland
1970 Gt Britain
1971 Ireland
1972 Belgium
1973 Switzerland
1974 Austria

European Ladies' Championship (F.E.I. Show Jumping)
1957 Miss P. Smythe, 'Flanagan', Gt Britain
1958 Miss G. Serventi, 'Doly', Italy
1959 Miss A. Townsend, 'Bandit IV', Gt Britain
1960 Miss S. Cohen, 'Clare Castle',
1961 Miss P. Smythe, 'Flanagan', Gt Britain
1962 Miss P. Smythe, 'Flanagan', Gt Britain
1963 Miss P. Smythe, 'Flanagan', Gt Britain
1964 *No competition*
1965 (World Championship)
1966 Miss J. Lefebvre, 'Kenavo', France
1967 Miss K. Kusner, 'Untouchable', U.S.A.
1968 Miss A. Drummond-Hay, 'Merely-a-Monarch', Gt Britain
1969 Miss I. Kellett, 'Morning Light', Eire
1970 *No competition*
1971 Miss A. Moore, 'Psalm', Gt Britain
1972 *No competition*
1973 Miss A. Moore, 'Psalm', Gt Britain
1974 *No competition (World Championship)*
1975
1976
1977

European Men's Championship (F.E.I. Show Jumping)
1957 H. G. Winkler, 'Sonnenglanz', W. Germany
1958 F. Thiedemann, 'Meteor', W. Germany
1959 Capt P. d'Inzeo, 'Uruguay', Italy
1960 *No competition (World Championship)*
1961 D. Broome, 'Sunsalve', Gt Britain
1962 C. David Barker, 'Mister Softee', Gt Britain
1963 G. Mancinelli, 'Rockette', Italy
1964 *No competition (World Championship)*
1965 H. Schridde, 'Dozent II', Germany
1966 N. Pessoa, 'Gran Geste', Brazil
1967 D. Broome, 'Mister Softee', Gt Britain

European Men's Championship (contd)
1968 No competition
1969 D. Broome, 'Mister Softee', Gt Britain
1970 No competition
1971 H. Steenken, 'Simona', W. Germany
1972 No competition
1973 P. McMahon, 'Pennwood Forge Mill' Gt Britain
1974 No competition (World Championship)
1975
1976
1977

King George V Cup (F.E.I. Show Jumping)
(see also page 184)
1911 Capt D. d'Exe, 'Piccollo', U.S.S.R.
1912 Lt Delvoie, 'Murat', Belgium
1913 Lt Baron de Meslon, 'Amazone', France
1914 Lt Baron de Meslon, 'Amazone', France
1915–19 No show
1920 Capt de Laissardière, 'Grey Fox', France
1921 Lt Col G. Brooke, 'Combined Training', Gt Britain
1922 Major Count Antonelli, 'Bluff', Italy
1923 Capt de Laissardière, 'Grey Fox', France
1924 Capt Count Borsarelli, 'Don Chisciotte', Italy
1925 Lt-Col Malise Graham, 'Broncho', Gt Britain
1926 Lt F. H. Bontecou, 'Ballymacshane', U.S.A.
1927 Lt X. Bizard, 'Quinine', France
1928 Lt A. G. Martyr, 'Forty Six', Gt Britain
1929 Lt Gibault, 'Mandarin', France
1930 Lt J. A. Talbot-Ponsonby, 'Chelsea', Gt Britain
1931 Capt J. Misonne, 'The Parson', Belgium
1932 Capt J. A. Talbot-Ponsonby, 'Chelsea', Gt Britain
1933 No show
1934 Lt J. A. Talbot-Ponsonby, 'Best Girl', Gt Britain
1935 Capt J. J. Lewis, 'Tramore Bay', Eire
1936 Cmdt J. G. O'Dwyer, 'Limerick Lace', Eire
1937 Capt X. Bizard, 'Honduras', France
1938 Major J. C. Friedberger, 'Derek', Gt Britain
1939 Lt-Col A. Bettoni, 'Adigrat', Italy

1940–46 No show
1947 J. P. d'Oriola, 'Marquis III', France
1948 Lt-Col H. M. Llewellyn, 'Foxhunter', Gt Britain
1949 B. Butler, 'Tankard', Gt Britain
1950 Lt-Col H. M. Llewellyn, 'Foxhunter', Gt Britain
1951 Capt K. Barry, 'Ballyneety', Eire
1952 Sen don Carlos Figueroa, 'Gracieux', Spain
1953 Lt-Col H. M. Llewellyn, 'Foxhunter', Gt Britain
1954 Fritz Thiedemann, 'Meteor', W. Germany
1955 Lt-Col Cartesegna, 'Brando', Italy
1956 W. Steinkraus, 'First Boy', U.S.A.
1957 Capt P. d'Inzeo, 'Uruguay', Italy
1958 W. H. Wiley, 'Master William', U.S.A.
1959 W. H. Wiley, 'Nautical', U.S.A.
1960 D. Broome, 'Sunsalve', Gt Britain
1961 Capt P. d'Inzeo, 'The Rock', Italy
1962 Capt P. d'Inzeo, 'The Rock', Italy
1963 T. Wade, 'Dundrum', Ireland
1964 W. Steinkraus, 'Sinjon', U.S.A.
1965 H. G. Winkler, 'Fortun', W. Germany
1966 D. Broome, 'Mister Softee', Gt Britain
1967 P. Robeson, 'Firecrest', Gt Britain
1968 H. G. Winkler, 'Enigk', W. Germany
1969 T. Edgar, 'Uncle Max', Gt Britain
1970 H. Smith, 'Mattie Brown', Gt Britain
1971 G. Wiltfang, 'Askan', W. Germany
1972 D. Broome, 'Sportsman', Gt Britain
1973 P. McMahon, 'Pennwood Forge Mill', Gt Britain
1974 F. Chapot, 'Main Spring', U.S.A.
1975
1976
1977

Olympic Games Show Jumping
(see also page 229)
1912 Team: Sweden
     Individual: Capt J. Cariou, 'Mignon', France
1916 Not held
1920 Team: Sweden
     Individual: Lt T. Lequio, 'Trebecco', Italy
1924 Team: Sweden
     Individual: Lt A. Gemuseus, 'Lucette', Switzerland
1928 Team: Spain
     Individual: Capt F. Ventura, 'Eliot', Czechoslovakia
1932 Team: No award given
     Individual: Lt T. Nishi, 'Uranus', Japan

Olympic Games Show Jumping (contd)

1936 *Team:* Germany
    Individual: Lt K. Hasse, 'Tora',
    Germany
1940 *Not held*
1944 *Not held*
1948 *Team:* Mexico
    Individual: H. M. Cortes, 'Arete',
    Mexico
1952 *Team:* Gt Britain
    Individual: P. J. d'Oriola, 'Ali Baba',
    France
1956 *Team:* W. Germany
    Individual: H. G. Winkler, 'Halla',
    W. Germany
1960 *Team:* W. Germany
    Individual: R. d'Inzeo, 'Posillipo',
    Italy
1964 *Team:* W. Germany
    Individual: P. J. d'Oriola, 'Lutteur',
    France
1968 *Team:* Canada
    Individual: W. Steinkraus,
    'Snowbound', U.S.A.
1972 *Team:* W. Germany
    Individual: G. Mancinelli,
    'Ambassador', Italy
1976

Pan American Games (F.E.I. Show Jumping)
(see also page 235)
1951 *Team:* Chile
    Individual: Capt A. Larraguibel, Chile
1955 *Team:* Mexico
    Individual: Lt R. Vinals, Mexico
1959 *Team:* U.S.A.
    Individual: Not awarded
1963 *Team:* U.S.A.
    Individual: Mary Mairs, U.S.A.
1967 *Team:* Brazil
    Individual: Jim Day, Canada
1971 *Team:* Canada
    Individual: Elisa P. de las Heras,
    Mexico
1975
1979

President's Cup (F.E.I. Show Jumping)
(see also page 253)
1965 Gt Britain
1966 U.S.A.
1967 Gt Britain
1968 U.S.A.
1969 W. Germany
1970 Gt Britain
1971 W. Germany
1972 Gt Britain

1973 Gt Britain
1974 Gt Britain
1975
1976
1977

Prince of Wales Cup (F.E.I. Show Jumping)
(see also page 253)
1909 France
1910 Belgium
1911 Russia
1912 Russia
1913 Russia
1914 Russia (won outright)
1915–19 *No show*
1920 Sweden
1921 Gt Britain
1922 Gt Britain
1923 Italy
1924 Gt Britain
1925–28 *No show*
1929 Gt Britain
1930 Gt Britain
1931 France
1932 France
1933 *No show*
1934 France
1935 Gt Britain
1936 France
1937 Irish Free State
1938 Gt Britain
1939 Gt Britain
1940–46 *No show*
1947 France
1948 U.S.A.
1949 Gt Britain
1950 Gt Britain
1951 Gt Britain
1952 Gt Britain
1953 Gt Britain
1954 Gt Britain
1955 Italy
1956 Gt Britain
1957 Gt Britain
1958 U.S.A.
1959 U.S.A.
1960 U.S.A.
1961 Italy
1962 W. Germany
1963 Gt Britain
1964 Gt Britain
1965 Italy
1966 *No competition*
1967 Gt Britain
1968 U.S.A.
1969 W. Germany
1970 Gt Britain

Prince of Wales Cup (contd)
1971 Gt Britain
1972 Gt Britain
1973 W. Germany
1974 Gt Britain
1975
1976
1977

Queen Elizabeth II Cup
(F.E.I. Show Jumping)
(*see also page* 258)
1949 Miss Iris Kellett, 'Rusty', Eire
1950 Miss Jill Palethorpe, 'Silver Cloud', Gt Britain
1951 Miss Iris Kellett, 'Rusty', Ireland
1952 Mrs G. Rich, 'Quicksilver III', Gt Britain
1953 Miss Marie Delfosse, 'Fanny Rosa', Gt Britain
1954 Mlle J. Bonnaud, 'Charleston', France
1955 Miss Dawn Palethorpe, 'Earlsrath Rambler', Gt Britain
1956 Miss Dawn Palethorpe, 'Earlsrath Rambler', Gt Britain
1957 Miss Elisabeth Anderson, 'Sunsalve', Gt Britain
1958 Miss Pat Smythe, O.B.E., 'Mr Pollard', Gt Britain
1959 Miss A. Clement, 'Nico', W. Germany
1960 Miss S. Cohen, 'Clare Castle', Gt Britain
1961 The Lady S. Fitzalan-Howard, 'Oorskiet', Gt Britain
1962 Mrs. B. J. Crago, 'Spring Fever', Gt Britain
1963 Miss J. Nash, 'Trigger Hill', Gt Britain
1964 Miss G. Makin, 'Jubilant', Gt Britain
1965 Miss M. Coakes, 'Stroller', Gt Britain
1966 Miss A. Roger Smith, 'Havana Royal', Gt Britain
1967 Miss B. Jennaway, 'Grey Lag', Gt Britain
1968 Mrs Frank Chapot, 'White Lightning', U.S.A.
1969 Miss Alison Westwood, 'The Maverick VII', Gt Britain
1970 Miss A. Drummond-Hay, 'Merely-a-Monarch', Gt Britain
1971 Miss M. Mould, 'Stroller', Gt Britain
1972 Miss A. Moore, 'Psalm', Gt Britain
*1973 Miss A. Dawes, 'Mr Banbury', ('The Maverick VII'), Gt Britain
Miss A. Moore, 'Psalm', Gt Britain
1974 Mrs J. Davenport, 'All Trumps', Gt Britain
* Dead heat

1975
1976
1977

Show Jumper of the Year, Leading
1949 Miss Pat Smythe, 'Finality'
1950 S. Hayes, 'Sheila'
1951 A. L. Beard, 'Eforegiot'
1952 R. W. Hanson, 'Snowstorm'
1953 A. Oliver, 'Red Admiral'
1954 Miss D. Palethorpe, 'Earlsrath Rambler'
1955 Ted Williams, 'Sunday Morning'
1956 Ted Williams, 'Dumbell'
1957 Ted Williams, 'Pegasus XIII'
1958 T. Edgar, 'Jane Summers' and Miss P. Smythe, 'Mr Pollard'
1959 H. Smith, 'Farmer's Boy'
1960 Ted Williams, 'Pegasus XIII'
1961 D. B. Barker, 'Lucky Sam' and Miss C. Beard, 'Mayfly'
1962 Miss P. Smythe, 'Flanagan'
1963 A. Fielder, 'Vibart'
1964 Mrs C. D. Barker, 'Atalanta'
1965 H. Smith, 'Warpaint'
1966 A. Fielder, 'Vibart'
1967 H. Smith, 'Harvester'
1968 A. Fielder, 'Vibart'
1969 T. Edgar, 'Uncle Max'
1970 Miss M. Mould, 'Stroller'
1971 A. Oliver, 'Pitz Palu'
1972 Miss A. Moore, 'Psalm'
1973 D. Broome, 'Sportsman'
1974 G. Fletcher, 'Tauna Dora'
1975
1976
1977

World Ladies' Championship
(F.E.I. Show Jumping)
1965 Miss M. Coakes, 'Stroller', Gt Britain
1970 Miss J. Lefebvre, 'Rocket', France
1974 Mrs J. Tissot (*nee* Lefebvre), 'Rocket', France

World Men's Championship
(F.E.I. Show Jumping)
1953 F. Goyoaga, 'Quorum', Spain
1954 H. G. Winkler, 'Halla', W. Germany
1955 H. G. Winkler, 'Halla', W. Germany
1956 Lt R. d'Inzeo, 'Merano', Italy
1960 Capt R. d'Inzeo, 'Gowran Girl', Italy
1966 P. J. d'Oriola, 'Pomone B', France
1970 D. Broome, 'Beethoven', Gt Britain
1974 H. Steenken, 'Simona', W. Germany

LIST OF HUNTS

FOXHOUNDS

ENGLAND AND WALES

ABER VALLEY Snowdonia.

ALBRIGHTON Staffordshire and Shropshire.

ALBRIGHTON WOODLAND Shropshire, Staffordshire and Worcestershire.

ASHFORD VALLEY The Weald of Kent and the Ashford–Tenterden–Headcorn district.

ATHERSTONE Greater part in Leicestershire and Warwickshire.

AVON VALE Melksham, Devizes and Trowbridge.

AXE VALE Seaton, Axminster and Honiton.

BADSWORTH Adjoining Grove and Bramham Moor in Yorkshire.

BANWEN MINERS West Glamorgan.

BARLOW North-east Derbyshire, and small part of Yorkshire.

BEAUFORT'S, DUKE OF Gloucestershire, Somerset and Wiltshire.

BEDALE North Riding of Yorkshire.

BELVOIR (*beevor*) (DUKE OF RUTLAND'S) Leicestershire and Lincolnshire.

BERKELEY Gloucestershire. Adjoining Cotswold and Ledbury, and in the east the Beaufort.

BERKSHIRE, OLD Berkshire and Oxfordshire. Adjoining the Heythrop in the north, the V.W.H. (Cricklade) in the west, and the Craven in the south.

BEWCASTLE Borders of Scotland, Northumberland and Cumberland.

BICESTER (*bister*) AND WARDEN HILL Oxfordshire, Buckinghamshire and Northamptonshire.

BILSDALE Thirsk, Stokesley and Helmsley, Yorkshire.

BISLEY AND SANDHURST Surrey and Hampshire.

BLACKMORE AND SPARKFORD VALE Dorset and Somerset.

BLANKNEY Lincolnshire and Nottinghamshire.

BLENCATHRA Cumberland.

BORDER North-west Northumberland, and Roxburghshire.

BRAES OF DERWENT South Northumberland and north-west Durham.

BRAMHAM MOOR The West Riding of Yorkshire, adjoining the York and Ainsty in the north and east and the Badsworth in the south.

BRECON Breconshire, but does not include Tallybont and district.

BROCKLESBY Lincolnshire.

BURTON The northern half of Lincolnshire.

CAMBRIDGESHIRE Cambridgeshire, Huntingdonshire and Bedfordshire.

CARMARTHENSHIRE Best centres, Carmarthen, St Clears, Whitland and Llanboidy.

CATTISTOCK (*catstock*) Dorset and small part of Somerset.

CHESHIRE Most of Cheshire.

CHESHIRE FOREST The Wirral Peninsula.

CHIDDINGFOLD, LECONFIELD AND COWDRAY Surrey and Sussex.

CLEVELAND North Riding of Yorkshire.

CLIFTON-ON-TEME Worcestershire and Herefordshire.

COLLEGE VALLEY Northumberland.

CONISTON Partly in Westmorland, partly in North Lancashire.

CORNWALL, EAST Liskeard district.

CORNWALL, NORTH From Boscastle and Padstow Bay, on the north coast, to Fowey in the south.

COTLEY Devon, Somerset and Dorset.

COTSWOLD Gloucestershire.

COTSWOLD, NORTH Gloucestershire and Worcestershire.

COTSWOLD VALE FARMERS' Around Cheltenham and Gloucester.

COTTESMORE (*cotsmore*) Rutland, Leicestershire and Lincolnshire.

CRAWLEY AND HORSHAM Sussex, from Rudgwick to the sea.

CROOME AND WEST WARWICKSHIRE Worcestershire, Warwickshire and Gloucestershire.

CUMBERLAND Wholly in Cumberland.

CUMBERLAND FARMERS' Around Penrith and Carlisle.

CURRE Monmouthshire, around Chepstow.

CURY The Lizard Peninsula to the sea.

DARTMOOR Devon.

DAVID DAVIES Montgomeryshire.

DERWENT   The North Riding of Yorkshire.

DEVON, EAST   South-east Devon.

DEVON, MID   The Dartmoor district.

DEVON, SOUTH   Throughout South Devon.

DORSET, SOUTH   Dorset. Best centres, Dorchester and Blandford.

DULVERTON, EAST   South-east edge of Exmoor.

DULVERTON, WEST   North Devon and West Somerset.

DURHAM, SOUTH   County Durham. Best centres, Darlington and Stockton.

EGGESFORD   Devon. Best centres, Eggesford and Okehampton.

ENFIELD CHACE   Hertfordshire and Middlesex.

ERIDGE   Sussex. Best centres, Tunbridge Wells and Crowborough.

ESKDALE AND ENNERDALE   Cumberland, Westmorland and Lancashire.

ESSEX   Best centres, High Roding, Harlow, Ongar and Dunmow.

ESSEX, EAST   North-west and East Essex.

ESSEX FARMERS'   Mostly between rivers Crouch and Blackwater.

ESSEX AND SUFFOLK   Partly in Essex and partly in Suffolk.

ESSEX UNION   South-east Essex around Billericay and Chelmsford.

EXMOOR   Devon and Somerset.

FARNDALE   North Riding of Yorkshire. Best centres, Castleton and Kirby Moorside.

FERNIE   South Leicestershire.

FITZWILLIAM (MILTON)   Northamptonshire and Huntingdonshire.

FLINT AND DENBIGH   The western parts of Flintshire and Denbighshire.

FOUR BURROW (*forbrer*)   The Truro, Falmouth and Helston districts of Cornwall.

GARTH AND SOUTH BERKS   Principally in Berkshire, with corners of Surrey, Hampshire and Oxfordshire.

GELLIGAER FARMERS'   North-east Glamorganshire and parts of Monmouthshire.

GLAISDALE   The North Riding of Yorkshire. Best centres, Glaisdale, Lealholm, Danby End and Roxby.

GLAMORGAN   Cowbridge district of Glamorganshire.

GOATHLAND   The North Riding of Yorkshire.

GOGERDDAN   The west of Cardiganshire.

GOLDEN VALLEY   Herefordshire and Radnorshire.

GOSCHEN'S, MR   West Sussex, Hampshire and Surrey.

GRAFTON   South Northamptonshire and North Buckinghamshire.

GROVE AND RUFFORD   Nottinghamshire, Yorkshire and Derbyshire.

HAMBLEDON   Hampshire.

HAMPSHIRE ('H.H.')   Aldershot to Winchester and Basingstoke to West Meon. Best centre, Alton.

HAYDON   The south-west corner of Northumberland.

HEREFORDSHIRE, NORTH   Hereford, Leominster and Bromyard.

HEREFORDSHIRE, SOUTH   Between Hereford, Ross-on-Wye, Peterchurch and Whitchurch.

HEYTHROP (*heethrop*)   Oxfordshire and Gloucestershire.

HOLDERNESS   The East Riding of Yorkshire.

HURSLEY   Part of Hampshire and Wiltshire between Winchester, Salisbury and Southampton.

HURWORTH   Between South Durham and North Yorkshire.

IRFON AND TOWY   North Breconshire.

ISLE OF WIGHT   Newport, Ryde, Shanklin, Sandown and Freshwater.

KENT, EAST   Canterbury, Folkestone and Ashford.

KENT, WEST   Sevenoaks and Tonbridge.

LAMERTON   West Devon and north-east Cornwall.

LEDBURY   Herefordshire, Worcestershire and Gloucestershire.

LEDBURY, NORTH   North of Ledbury and Malvern, on the borders of Herefordshire and Worcestershire.

LLANDILO FARMERS'   Carmarthenshire and Glamorgan.

LLAGEINOR   Glamorgan.

LLANGEITHO   Mid-Cardiganshire.

LLANGIBBY   Monmouthshire.

LONSDALE, NORTH   The portion of North Lonsdale not including Low Furness and the Duddon Valley.

LUDLOW   Shropshire, Herefordshire and Worcestershire.

LUNESDALE   North, south and east Westmorland and parts of North Lancashire and the West Riding of Yorkshire.

MELBREAK   West Cumberland.

MENDIP FARMERS'   Bristol, Bath, Wells, and Shepton Mallet.

MEYNELL (*menel*) AND SOUTH STAFFORDSHIRE Derbyshire, South Staffordshire and Warwickshire.

MIDDLETON   The North and East Ridings of Yorkshire.

MILVAIN (PERCY)   Northumberland.

MONMOUTHSHIRE   The northern half of Monmouthshire and small coverts in Herefordshire.

MORPETH   South Northumberland.

NEW FOREST   Hampshire, and a small part of Wiltshire.

NORFOLK, WEST   Best centres, East Dereham, Swaffham, Fakenham and King's Lynn.

NORTHUMBERLAND, NORTH   Cornhill-on-Tweed, Berwick and Wooler.

NOTTINGHAMSHIRE, SOUTH   Nottingham, Newark and Bingham

OAKLEY   Bedfordshire, Buckinghamshire, Northamptonshire and Huntingdonshire.

PEMBROKESHIRE   North of Milford Haven, in Pembrokeshire.

PEMBROKESHIRE, SOUTH   The Tenby and Pembroke districts with some coverts in Carmarthenshire.

PENDLE FOREST AND CRAVEN   *see* HARRIERS.

PENNINE   The Pennine Range, from Malhamdale and Wharfedale to Edale and Derwentdale.

PENTYRCH   East Glamorgan, between Cardiff and Pontypridd.

PERCY   Northumberland.

PERCY (WEST)   Northumberland.

PORTMAN   Dorset, Wiltshire and Hampshire.

PUCKERIDGE AND THURLOW   Hertfordshire, Essex, Suffolk and Cambridgeshire.

PYTCHLEY   Northamptonshire and Leicestershire.

PYTCHLEY, WOODLAND   Northamptonshire.

QUORN   Mainly in Leicestershire, with coverts in Derbyshire and Nottinghamshire.

RADNORSHIRE AND WEST HEREFORDSHIRE North-west Herefordshire and parts of Radnorshire.

ROYAL ARTILLERY   Wiltshire. Between West Lavington, Wylye, Salisbury and Tidworth.

SALTERSGATE FARMERS'   Yorkshire. Between Whitby and Pickering.

SEAVINGTON   Dorset and Somerset.

SENNYBRIDGE AND DISTRICT FARMERS'   Breconshire, around Sennybridge and Brecon.

SHROPSHIRE, NORTH   Shrewsbury, Wem and Wellington.

SHROPSHIRE, SOUTH   South of Shrewsbury.

SHROPSHIRE, WEST   Around Oswestry.

SILVERTON   The Exeter district of Devonshire.

SINNINGTON   The North Riding of Yorkshire.

SNOWDON VALLEY   Caernarvonshire.

SOMERSET, WEST   Between the Brendon Hills and the sea.

SOMERSET VALE, WEST (formerly QUANTOCK FARMERS')   From Bridgwater to the Quantock Hills.

SOUTHDOWN   The Sussex seaboard.

SOUTH WOLD   Lincolnshire. Extending from Louth, adjoining the Brocklesby, to Boston in the south, and from the sea to the Burton country in the west.

SPOONER'S AND WEST DARTMOOR   Chiefly on Dartmoor.

STAFFORDSHIRE, NORTH   North of Stafford town, bordering Shropshire, Cheshire and Derbyshire.

STAINTONDALE   North Riding of Yorkshire, between Scarborough and Whitby.

STEVENSTONE   North Devon.

SUFFOLK   West Suffolk.

SURREY AND BURSTOW, OLD   Surrey, Sussex and Kent.

SURREY UNION   The North Downs from Horsham to Guildford.

SUSSEX, EAST, AND ROMNEY MARSH   Battle, Hastings, Bexhill, Eastbourne and West Kent.

TALYBONT   Breconshire, bordering Monmouthshire.

TANATSIDE   East Montgomeryshire to borders of Shropshire.

TAUNTON VALE   The Taunton district of Somerset.

TEDWORTH   Wiltshire and Hampshire.

TEME VALLEY   Radnorshire, Herefordshire and Shropshire.

TETCOTT   Devon and Cornwall.

TETCOTT, SOUTH   The borders of North-west Devon and Cornwall.

TICKHAM   North Kent.

TIVERTON   Devonshire, with a small part extending into West Somerset.

TIVYSIDE   North Pembrokeshire and South Cardiganshire.

TORRINGTON FARMERS'   Devonshire, between Dolton and Barnstaple.

TOWY AND COTHI   North Carmarthenshire. Best centres, Cilycwm and Llandovery.

TREDEGAR FARMERS'   The south-west district of Monmouthshire.

TYNE, NORTH   The Wark and Falstone districts of Northumberland.

TYNEDALE   Northumberland.

ULLSWATER   Westmorland and Cumberland.

UNITED   Shropshire and Montgomeryshire.

VALE OF AYLESBURY   Buckinghamshire.

VALE OF CLETTWR   North-east Carmarthenshire.

V.W.H.   Gloucestershire and Wiltshire.

VINE AND CRAVEN   Hampshire with a small portion in Berkshire and Wiltshire.

WARWICKSHIRE   Warwickshire, Gloucestershire, Worcestershire and Oxfordshire.

WARWICKSHIRE, NORTH   Entirely in Warwickshire, from Rugby to the Worcestershire border.

WESTERN   West Cornwall.

WEST OF YORE   Yorkshire, west of River Yore from Ripon northwards.

WEST STREET   Kent, Sandwich, Dover and Herne Bay districts.

WHADDON CHASE   Buckinghamshire.

WHEATLAND   South Shropshire.

WILLIAMS-WYNN'S, SIR WATKIN   Denbighshire, Flint, Cheshire and Shropshire.

WILTON   South of Salisbury to the North Dorsetshire border.

WILTSHIRE, SOUTH AND WEST   Shaftesbury and Warminster.

WORCESTERSHIRE   Central Worcestershire from the Hereford to the Warwickshire borders.

YNYSFOR   South Caernarvonshire and North Merionethshire.

YORK AND AINSTY, NORTH   The West Riding and North Riding of Yorkshire. Best centres, Harrogate and Boroughbridge.

YORK AND AINSTY, SOUTH   North, west and south of York.

YSTRAD   Aberdare and Rhondda Valleys.

ZETLAND   South Durham and North Riding of Yorkshire.

SCOTLAND

BERWICKSHIRE   Best centres, Duns, Coldstream and Greenlaw.

BUCCLEUCH'S, DUKE OF   Roxburghshire, Selkirk and Berwickshire.

DUMFRIESSHIRE   Best centre, Lockerbie.

EGLINTON   Ayrshire. Best centres, Ayr, Troon and Kilmarnock.

FIFE   Best centres, Cupar and St Andrews.

JED FOREST   Roxburghshire. Best centres, Jedburgh and Hawick.

LANARKSHIRE AND RENFREWSHIRE   Almost wholly in Renfrewshire, adjoining the Eglinton.

LAUDERDALE   In Roxburgh, Berwick, Selkirk and Midlothian.

LIDDESDALE   Roxburghshire.

LINLITHGOW AND STIRLINGSHIRE   Midlothian, West Lothian and Stirlingshire.

LOCHABER AND SUNART FARMERS'   Inverness-shire and Argyllshire.

IRELAND

AVONDHU HUNT CLUB   Co. Cork, Waterford and Tipperary.

BALLYMACAD   North Co. Meath, bordering on Cavan and Westmeath.

BERMINGHAM AND NORTH GALWAY   North of Co. Galway and South Mayo.

CARBERY   Entirely in Co. Cork.

DOWN, EAST   Between Strangford Lough and Carlingford Lough.

DUHALLOW   Co. Cork. Best centre, Mallow.

DUNGANNON   Private foot pack.

GALWAY, COUNTY ('THE BLAZERS')   Best centres, Loughrea and Athenry.

GALWAY, EAST   Co. Galway and Co. Roscommon.

ISLAND   Wexford. Best centres, Gorey, Ferns and Enniscorthy.

KILDARE   Kildare and Dublin, with portions in Meath and Wicklow.

KILKENNY   Best centre, Kilkenny.

KILKENNY, NORTH   Best centre, Freshford.

LAOIS (QUEEN'S COUNTY)   Queen's County. Best centres, Abbeyleix, Athy, Maryborough and Stradbally.

LIMERICK   Co. Limerick.

LOUTH   Louth, Meath, Dublin, Cavan and Monaghan.

MACROOM   Mid Co. Cork.

MEATH   Throughout Co. Meath. Small part in Westmeath.

MUSKERRY   Co. Cork. From Carrigrohane Bridge to Macroom.

ORMOND   South Offaly and North Tipperary.

SCARTEEN (THE BLACK AND TANS)   Tipperary and Limerick.

SHILLELAGH AND DISTRICT   Co. Wicklow.

SOUTH UNION   Co. Cork.

STRABANE   On the borders of Counties Tyrone and Donegal.

TIPPERARY   Co. Tipperary.

TIPPERARY, NORTH   From Coolbawn in the north, southwards to Killaloe.

UNITED HUNT CLUB   Co. Cork.

WATERFORD   Between the sea and the Comeragh mountains.

WATERFORD, WEST   Centres are Cappoquin, Lismore and Ardmore.

WESTMEATH   Westmeath County.

WEXFORD   Co. Wexford.

WICKLOW   South Co. Wicklow and North Co. Wexford.

STAGHOUNDS

ENGLAND

DEVON AND SOMERSET   West Somerset and North Devon.

NEW FOREST BUCKHOUNDS   The centres are Lyndhurst, Brockenhurst and Stoney Cross.

QUANTOCK   The Quantock Hills.

TIVERTON   Almost wholly in Devon, south of the Taunton–Barnstaple railway.

IRELAND

COUNTY DOWN   Best centres, Belfast, Ballynahinch, Newcastle and Downpatrick.

WARD, UNION   North Co. Dublin and South Co. Meath.

HARRIERS

ENGLAND AND WALES

ALDENHAM   Hertfordshire, Buckinghamshire and Bedfordshire.

AXE VALE   see FOXHOUNDS, *page* 408.

BOLVENTOR   Cornwall.

CAMBRIDGESHIRE   Within the territories of the Puckeridge and Thurlow and Cambridgeshire Foxhounds.

CLIFTON FOOT   North Somerset.

COTLEY   see FOXHOUNDS, *page* 408.

DART VALE AND HALDON   The greater part of South Devon from the Dart Valley to the Exe.

DUNSTON   South Norfolk.

EASTON   East Suffolk.

EDMONSTONE   Midlothian and East Lothian.

ERYRI   Caernarvonshire and Anglesey.

HIGH PEAK   Bakewell and Buxton, Derbyshire.

HOLCOMBE   Central Lancashire.

MINEHEAD   West Somerset and Exmoor.

MODBURY   South Devon.

NORFOLK, NORTH   The north of Norfolk.

PENDLE FOREST AND CRAVEN   East Lancashire and the West Riding of Yorkshire.

ROCKWOOD   The West Riding of Yorkshire.

ROSS   South Herefordshire.

RUFFORD FOREST   Nottinghamshire.

SENNOWE PARK   Norfolk.

SOUTH POOL   The Kingsbridge district of Devon.

TAUNTON VALE   Around Taunton, Devon, and in Somerset.

VALE OF LUNE   The border of Lancashire, Westmorland and Yorkshire.

WAVENEY   Suffolk and Norfolk.

WENSLEYDALE   Watershed of River Ure, above Aysgarth.

WESTON AND BANWELL   Somerset.

WINDERMERE   Around Kendal and Windermere, Westmorland.

IRELAND

ANTRIM, EAST   Between Belfast, Antrim and Larne.

ANTRIM, MID   Mid-Antrim and South Derry.

BRAY   Cos. Wicklow and Dublin.

CLARE, COUNTY   Around Ennis.

DERRYGALLON   West Duhallow and North Cork.

DOWN, NORTH   The north part of Co. Down.

DUBLIN, SOUTH COUNTY   South part of Dublin County.

DUNGARVAN   Co. Waterford.

FERMANAGH   Fermanagh, parts of South Donegal, South Tyrone and West Monaghan.

FINGAL   North Co. Dublin and South Co. Meath.

IVEAGH   Co. Down and North Armagh.

KILLEAGH   Co. Cork.

KILLINICK   South Co. Wexford.

KILLULTAGH, OLD ROCK AND CHICHESTER   Co. Antrim.

KILMOGANNY   South Kilkenny and a small part of South Tipperary.

LIMERICK   Co. Limerick.

LITTLE GRANGE   Co. Meath.

LONGFORD, COUNTY   Bordered by counties Cavan, Westmeath, and Roscommon.

NAAS   Co. Kildare.

NEWRY   Cos. Down and Armagh.

ROUTE   North Londonderry and North Antrim.

SLIGO, COUNTY   Whole of Co. Sligo and part of Co. Roscommon.

STONEHALL   Co. Limerick.

TARA   Centre and north of Meath and parts of Cavan.

TYNAN AND ARMAGH   Co. Armagh.

TYRONE, SOUTH   Tyrone, and parts of North Monaghan and South Derry.

DRAGHOUNDS

ENGLAND, WALES AND CHANNEL ISLANDS

CAMBRIDGE UNIVERSITY   Cambridgeshire, East Essex, Newmarket and Thurlow, Fernie, Belvoir, Oakley and Woodland Pytchley country by invitation.

CHESHIRE, NORTH-EAST   North-east Cheshire and north-west Derbyshire.

JERSEY   Jersey, C.I.

MID-SURREY FARMERS'   The Old Surrey, and Burstow, West Kent, Southdown, Eridge, Crawley and Horsham, and Chiddingfold and Surrey Union countries.

OXFORD UNIVERSITY   Oxford and Bicester.

STAFF COLLEGE AND ROYAL MILITARY ACADEMY   From Wokingham and Arborfield to Basingstoke and Aldershot.

Recognized and Registered Foxhound Hunts of Canada and the United States of America

CANADA

BELLE-RIVIERE   Montreal, Quebec.

EGLINGTON AND CALEDON   Terra Cotta, Ontario.

FRASER VALLEY   Surrey, British Columbia.

FRONTENAC   Kingston, Ontario.

HAMILTON   Hamilton, Ontario.

LAKE OF TWO MOUNTAINS, THE   Vaudreuil County, Quebec.

LONDON   London, Ontario.

MONTREAL   Bromont, Quebec.

OTTAWA VALLEY   Stittsville, Ottawa.

TORONTO AND NORTH YORK   Toronto, Ontario.

WELLINGTON–WATERLOO   Hespeler, Ontario.

U.S.A.

AIKEN   Aiken, South Carolina

AMWELL VALLEY   R.D., Ringoes, New Jersey

ANTIETAM   Hagerstown, Maryland

ARAPAHOE   Littleton, Colorado

AUSTIN Lake Cormorant, Mississippi
BATTLE CREEK Augusta, Michigan
BEAUFORT Middletown, Pennsylvania
BEDFORD COUNTY Bedford, Virginia
BELLE MEADE Thomson, Georgia
BLUE RIDGE Clarke County, Virginia
BRADBURY Warwick, Rhode Island
BRANDYWINE West Chester, Pennsylvania
BRIDLESPUR St Charles County, Missouri
BULL RUN Manassas, Virginia
CAMARGO Cincinnati, Ohio
CAMDEN Camden, South Carolina
CASANOVA Casanova, Virginia
CEDAR KNOB Cornersville, Tennessee
CHAGRIN VALLEY Gates Mills, Ohio
CHESTNUT RIDGE New Geneva, Pennsylvania
DEEP RUN Manakin-Sabot, Virginia
DE LA BROOKE Mechanicsville, Maryland
DUTCH FORK West Alexander, Pennsylvania
ELKRIDGE-HARFORD Monkton, Maryland
ESSEX Peapack, New Jersey
FAIRFAX Sunset Hills, Virginia
FAIRFIELD COUNTY Newtown, Connecticut
FARMINGTON Charlottesville, Virginia
FORT LEAVENWORTH Fort Leavenworth, Kansas
FOXCATCHER Elkton, Maryland
FOX RIVER VALLEY Barrington, Illinois
GENESEE VALLEY Geneseo, New York
GLENMORE Staunton, Virginia
GOLDEN'S BRIDGE North Salem, New York
GOSHEN Olney, Maryland
GRASS RIDGE Sonoita, Arizona
GREEN MOUNTAIN Stowe, Vermont
GREEN SPRING VALLEY Glyndon, Maryland
GREENVILLE COUNTY Landrum, South Carolina
HAIGHT JR'S LITCHFIELD COUNTY, MR Litchfield, Connecticut
HARTS RUN Allison Park, Pennsylvania
HICKORY CREEK Dallas, Texas
HILLSBORO Nashville, Tennessee
HOPPER HILLS Honeoye Falls, New York
HOUND AND HORN Schereville, Indiana
HOWARD COUNTY Ellicott City, Maryland

HUBBARD'S KENT COUNTY, MR Chesterton, Maryland
HUNTINGDON VALLEY Philadelphia, Pennsylvania
IROQUOIS Winchester, Kentucky
JEFFORDS' ANDREW BRIDGE, MR Christiana, Pennsylvania
JUAN TOMAS Sandia Park, New Mexico
KESWICK Keswick, Virginia
LAURAY Bath, Ohio
LICKING RIVER Carlisle, Kentucky
LIMEKILN Reading, Pennsylvania
LIMESTONE CREEK Manlius, New York
LONGREEN Collierville, Tennessee
LONG LAKE Long Lake, Minnesota
LONG RUN Louisville, Kentucky
LOS ALTOS Woodside, California
LOST HOUND Edmond, Oklahoma
LOUDON Leesburg, Virginia
MARLBOROUGH Upper Marlboro, Maryland
MECKLENBURG Matthews, North Carolina
MELLS Lynnville, Tennessee
METAMORA Metamora, Michigan
MIAMI VALLEY Dayton, Ohio
MIDDLEBURG Middleburg, Virginia
MIDDLEBURY Middlebury, Connecticut
MIDDLETOWN VALLEY Middletown, Maryland
MIDLAND Columbus, Georgia
MILLBROOK Millbrook, New York
MILL CREEK Wadsworth, Illinois
MISSION VALLEY Shawnee Mission, Kansas
MONMOUTH COUNTY Moorestown, New Jersey
MONTPELIER Montpelier Station, Virginia
MOORE COUNTY Moore County, North Carolina
MOORELAND Huntsville, Alabama
MYOPIA South Hamilton, Massachusetts
NASHOBA VALLEY Pepperell, Massachusetts
NEW BRITTON Indianapolis, Indiana
NEW MARKET New Market, Maryland
NORFOLK Dover, Massachusetts
NORTH HILLS Omaha, Nebraska
OAK BROOK Elk Grove Village, Illinois
OAK GROVE Germantown, Tennessee

OLD CHATHAM   Old Chatham, New York
OLD DOMINION   Warrenton, Virginia
OLD NORTH BRIDGE   Concord, Massachusetts
OLD STONINGTON   Taylorville, Illinois
ORANGE COUNTY   The Plains, Virginia
PICKERING   Phoenixville, Pennsylvania
PIEDMONT   Upperville, Virginia
POTOMAC   Potomac, Maryland
PRINCESS ANNE   Linlier, Virginia
RADNOR   Malvern, Pennsylvania
RAPIDAN   Rapidan, Virginia
RAPPAHANNOCK   Sperryville, Virginia
ROARING FORK   Aspen, Colorado
ROCKBRIDGE   Lexington, Virginia
ROCKY FORK-HEADLEY   Columbus, Ohio
ROLLING ROCK—WESTMORELAND   Ligonier, Pennsylvania
ROMBOUT   Salt Point, New York
ROMWELL   Romney, Indiana
ROSE TREE   York, Pennsylvania
SANTA FE   Rancho Santa Fe, California
SEDGEFIELD   Greensboro, North Carolina
SEWICKLEY   Sewickley, Pennsylvania

SHAKERAG   Atlanta, Georgia
SMITHTOWN   Long Island, New York
SOUTHERN ILLINOIS OPEN   Herrin, Illinois
SPRING VALLEY   Green Village, New Jersey
STEWART'S CHESHIRE, MR   Unionville, Pennsylvania
TRADERS POINT   Zionsville, Indiana
TRIANGLE   Durham, North Carolina
TRI-COUNTY   Milner, Georgia
TRYON   Tryon, North Carolina
TWO RIVERS   Tampa, Florida
VICMEAD   Wilmington, Delaware
WARRENTON   Warrenton, Virginia
WATERLOO   Grass Lake, Michigan
WAYNE-DUPAGE   Wayne, Illinois
WEST HILLS   Los Angeles, California
WICOMICO   Salisbury, Maryland
WINDSOR COUNTY   Woodstock, Vermont
WINDY HOLLOW   Florida, New York
WOLF CREEK   Goreville, Illinois
WOODBROOK   Tacoma, Washington
WOODSIDE   Aiken, South Carolina
WYE RIVER   Easton, Maryland

Hunts in Australia, South Africa and New Zealand

AUSTRALIA

BOWOOD   Tasmania, around Bridport (foxhounds: kangaroo are hunted)
MELBOURNE HUNT   Victoria, centres Cranbourne, Berwick, Pakenham and Beaconsfield
MIDLAND HUNT CLUB   Midland pastoral areas of Tasmania, lower Fingal Valley and east coast (foxhounds: kangaroo, wallaby, deer and hare are hunted)
NORTHERN HUNT CLUB   Tasmania, around Liffey (beagle-foxhound cross: drag hunting)
PINE LODGE   Western Australia, around Forrestdale (foxhounds)
RINGWELL   Tasmania, around Richmond (drag hunting, and live hunting for hare)
WEST AUSTRALIAN HUNT CLUB, THE   Western Australia, north from Perth, around Morley

SOUTH AFRICA

CAPE HUNT AND POLO CLUB   Within 50 miles (80 km) radius of Cape Town (drag hunting, and occasional live hunts for jackal)
CROWTHORNE HUNT   Transvaal, north of Johannesburg to the Magaliesberg (on foot: veld hare is hunted)
HATHERLEY CLUB DRAGHOUNDS   Transvaal, between Johannesburg and Pretoria
RAND HUNT CLUB   Transvaal, north of Johannesburg (drag hunting, and occasional live hunts for jackal

NEW ZEALAND

BIRCHWOOD   Southland, South Island, around Invercargill (drag hunting, sometimes live for hare)

BRACKENFIELD North Canterbury, South Island (harrier-type hounds)

CANTERBURY, SOUTH South Canterbury, South Island (hare is hunted)

CHRISTCHURCH South Canterbury, South Island (harrier-type hounds)

DANNEVIRKE Central and southern Hawke's Bay, North Island (harrier-type hounds)

HAWKE'S BAY HUNT (Inc) The Hawke's Bay, Patangata, Waipawa and Waipururau Counties of Hawke's Bay Province

MANAWATU HUNT (Inc) North Island, centres, Kitwitea, Cheltenham, Waituna West, Feilding, Ohau, Otaki, Waikanae, Shannon, Te Horo and Carnarvon

NORTHLAND HUNT (Inc) North Island, around Whangerei and Kamo (harriers)

OPOTIKI HUNT (Inc) North Island, around Opotiki (hare is hunted)

OTAGO HUNT (Inc) South Island, around Dunedin (drag hunting and live for hare)

PAKURANGA HUNT (Inc) North Island, around Papakura and Auckland, over pastoral country.

POVERTY BAY North Island, centres Whatatutu, Pouawa, Matawhero, Bushmere, Repongaere, Puha, Totangi and Ormond (harrier-type hounds)

RANGITIKEI North Island, in South Rangitikei County (harrier-type hounds)

TARANAKI HUNT CLUB (Inc) Northern part of Taranaki, North Island (hare is hunted)

TAUPO HUNT (Inc) South Auckland, North Island, around Tokoroa and Whakamaru

WAIKATO HUNT (Inc) South Auckland, North Island, around Cambridge (hare is hunted)

WAIRARAPA Southern part of North Island, around Masterton

British Horse Society's List of Horse and Pony Breeding and Administrative Organisations, etc.

The British Horse Society, National Equestrian Centre, Stoneleigh, Warwickshire, has courteously offered to supply the addresses of the societies listed below.

Arab Horse Society
Association of British Riding Schools

British Bloodstock Agency
British Driving Society
British Equine Veterinary Association
British Field Sports Society
British Palomino Society
British Percheron Society
British Show Hack and Cob Association
British Show Jumping Association
British Show Pony Society
British Spotted Horse Society
British Veterinary Association

Cleveland Bay Horse Society
Clydesdale Horse Society
Commons, Open Spaces and Footpaths
  Preservation Society
Connemara Pony Breeders' Society
Connemara Pony Society

Dales Pony Society
Dartmoor Pony Society
Donkey Breed Society
The Donkey Sanctuary

English Connemara Pony Society
Exmoor Pony Society

Fédération Equestre Internationale
Fell Pony Society

Hackney Horse Society
The Haflinger Society
Highland Pony Society
Home of Rest for Horses
Horse and Pony Breeding and Benefit Fund

Hunters' Improvement Society
Hurlingham Polo Association

International League for the Protection of Horses
International Pony Breeders' Association

Jockey Club

London Harness Horse Parade Society

Master of Foxhounds Association

National Master Farriers' and Blacksmiths'
  Association
National Pony Society
New Forest Pony and Cattle Breeding Society

The People's Dispensary for Sick Animals
Ponies of Britain Club

Racehorse Owners' Association
Riding for the Disabled Association
Royal College of Veterinary Surgeons

Shetland Pony Stud Book
Shire Horse Society
Show and Breed Secretaries
The Society of Master Saddlers
Suffolk Horse Society

Thoroughbred Breeders' Association

Weatherbys
Welsh Pony and Cob Society
Western Horseman's Association
The Worshipful Company of Farriers
The Worshipful Company of Loriners
The Worshipful Company of Saddlers

Polo Clubs and Associations

(The following are affiliated to the Hurlingham Polo Association)

Aldershot Polo Club
All Ireland Polo Club
All Jamaica Polo Association
Army Polo Committee
Australian Polo Council
Cambridge University Polo Club
Catterick Garrison Polo Club
Cheshire Polo Club
Cirencester Park Polo Club
Cowdray Park Polo Club
Cyprus Polo Association

Dundee Polo Club
Edinburgh Polo Club
Guards Polo Club
Ham Polo Club
Hertfordshire Polo Club
Hong Kong Polo Association
Indian Polo Association
Kenya Polo Association
Kirtlington Park Polo Club
Malaysian Polo Association
Malta Polo and Saddle Club

Millfield School Polo Club
New Zealand Polo Association
Nigerian Polo Association
Oxford University Polo Club
Pakistan Polo Association
Rhine Army Polo Club
Rhinefield (New Forest) Polo Club
Rhodesian Polo Association

Royal Naval Saddle Club
Rutland Polo Club
Sandhurst Polo Club
South Africa Polo Association
Stourhead Polo Club
Taunton Vale Polo Club
Tidworth Polo Club
Toulston Polo Club

Other Overseas Clubs playing under Hurlingham Polo Association Rules

Accra Polo Club
Aden Polo Club
Assam Polo Club
Barbados Polo Club

Hamburg Polo Club
Royal Jordan Polo Club
County Club de Tangier

Glossary of Foreign Terms

English	French	German	Spanish
Arm	Bras	Oberarm	Brazo
Back	Dos	Rücken	Lomo
Belly	Ventre	Bauch	Vientre
Bridle	Bride	Zäumung	Brida
Bridoon snaffle	Mors de Filet	Trense	Bridón
Brood mare	Poulinière	Mutterstute	Yegua
Buttock	Fesse	Hinterbacke	Nalga
Cannon	Canon	Röhrbein	Caña
Chest	Poitrine	Brust	Pecho
Colt	Poulain	Hengstfohlen	Potrillo macho
Coronet	Couronne	Hufkrone	Corona
Croup	Croupe	Kruppe	Grupa
Curb bit	Mors de Bride	Kandare	Freno
Face	Chanfrein	Nasenrücken	Hocico
Fetlock	Boulet	Fesselkopf	Menudillo
Filly	Pouliche	Stutfohlen	Potranca
Flank	Flanc	Flanke	Flanco
Foal	Foal	Saugfohlen	Potrillo
Forearm	Avant-bras	Unterarm	Antebrazo
Forehead	Front	Stirn	Frente
Fore leg	Membre antérieur	Vorderbein	Pata delantera
Forelock	Toupet	Haarschopf	Copete
Gaskin	Jambe	Unterschenkel	Pierna
Gelding	Hongre	Wallach	Caballo castrado
Girth	Sangle	Gurt	Cincha
Half-bred	Demi-sang	Halbblut	Media sangre
Hind leg	Membre postérieur	Hinterbein	Pata trasera
Hip	Hanche	Hüfte	Cadera
Hock	Jarret	Sprunggelenk	Corvejón
Hoof	Sabot	Huf	Casco
Horse	Cheval	Pferd	Caballo
Jaw	Mâchoire	Kiefer	Maxilar
Knee	Genou	Vorderfusswurzel	Rodilla
Loins	Reins	Lenden	Riñones
Mare	Jument	Stute	Yegua
Martingale	Martingale	Martingal	Martingal
Neck	Encolure	Hals	Pescuezo
Paces	Allures	Gangarten	Aires
Pastern	Paturon	Fessel, Köte	Cuartilla

Poll	Nuque	Genick	Nuca
Pure-bred Arab	pur-sang arabe	Arabisches Vollblut	Purasangre árabe
Reins	Rênes	Zügel	Riendas
Ribs	Côtes	Rippen	Costillas
Saddle	Selle	Sattel	Silla, montura
Shoulder	Epaule	Schulter	Espalda
Stable	Ecurie	Stall	Cuadra, caballeriza
Stallion/entire	Etalon/entier	Zuchthengst/Hengst	Padrillo, semental/entero
Stifle	Grasset	Knie	Gordetillo
Stirrup irons	Etriers	Steigbügel	Estribos
Stud (farm)	Haras, Dépót d'étalons, Jumenterie	Hengstdepot, Gestüt	Caballada, Yeguada
Tail	Queue	Schweif, Schwanz	Cola, rabo
Thigh	Cuisse	Oberschenkel	Muslo
Thoroughbred	pur-sang anglais	Englisches Vollblut	Purasangre inglés
Withers	Garrot	Widerrist	Cruz